HISTORY

OF THE

WAR OF THE INDEPENDENCE

OF THE

UNITED STATES OF AMERICA.

See Pa. 2.

Engraved by A.Daggett, from the original Painting by Colonel Trumbull

WASHINGTON.

HISTORY

OF THE

WAR OF THE INDEPENDENCE

OF THE

UNITED STATES OF AMERICA.

BY CHARLES BOTTA.

TRANSLATED FROM THE ITALIAN,

BY GEORGE ALEXANDER OTIS ESQ.

NINTH EDITION, IN TWO VOLUMES, REVISED AND CORRECTED.

VOL. II.

KENNIKAT PRESS
Port Washington, N. Y./London

KENNIKAT AMERICAN BICENTENNIAL SERIES
Under the General Editorial Supervision of
Dr. Ralph Adams Brown
Professor of History, State University of New York

HISTORY OF THE WAR OF THE INDEPENDENCE
OF THE UNITED STATES OF AMERICA

First published in 1837, 1845
Reissued in 1970 by Kennikat Press
Library of Congress Catalog Card No: 75-120868
ISBN 0-8046-1261-7

Manufactured by Taylor Publishing Company   Dallas, Texas

KENNIKAT AMERICAN BICENTENNIAL SERIES

TABLE OF CONTENTS.

BOOK THIRTEENTH.

BOOK FOURTEENTH.

BOOK FIFTEENTH.

HISTORY

OF

THE AMERICAN WAR.

BOOK NINTH.

1777. By the affairs of Bennington, and that of Fort Schuyler, it appeared that fortune began to smile upon the cause of the Americans. These successes produced the more happy effect upon their minds, the more they were unexpected; for since the fatal stroke which deprived them of Montgomery, they had found this war of Canada but one continued series of disasters. Their late discouragement and timidity were instantly converted into confidence and ardor. The English, on the contrary, could not witness without apprehension, the extinction of those brilliant hopes, which, from their first advantages, they had been led to entertain.

Thus the face of things had experienced a total change; and this army, of late the object of so much terror for the Americans, was now looked upon as a prey that could not escape them. The exploit of Bennington, in particular, had inspired the militia with great confidence in themselves; since they had not only combated, but repulsed and vanquished, the regular troops of the royal army, both English and German.

They began now to forget all distinctions between themselves and troops of the line, and the latter made new exertions and more strenuous efforts to maintain their established reputation for superiority over the militia. Having lost all hope of seizing the magazines at Bennington, general Burgoyne experienced anew the most alarming scarcity of provisions. But on the other hand, the successes of the Americans under the walls of Fort Schuyler, besides having inspirited the militia, produced also this other happy effect, that of enabling them, now liberated from the fear of invasion in the country upon the Mohawk, to unite all their forces on the banks of the Hudson, against the army of Burgoyne. The country people took arms in multitudes, and hastened to the camp. The moment was favorable; the harvests were ended, and the arrival of general Gates to take the command of the army, gave a new spur to their alacrity. This officer enjoyed the entire esteem and confidence of the Americans; his name alone was considered among them as the presage of success. The congress, in their sitting of the fourth of August, had appointed him to the command of the army of the north, while affairs still wore the most lowering aspect; but he had not arrived at Stillwater till the twenty-first.

General Schuyler was promptly apprised that a successor had been given him; but this good citizen had continued until the arrival of Gates to exert all his energies to repair the evil. Already, as we have seen, his efforts had not been fruitless, and victory inclined in his favor. He bitterly complained to Washington, that the course of his fortune was interrupted, and that the fruit of his toils was given to another, who was about to enjoy that victory for which he had prepared the way. But the congress preferred to place at the head of an army, dismayed by its reverses, a general celebrated for his achievements. Moreover, they were not ignorant that if Schuyler was agreeable to the New Yorkers, he was nevertheless in great disrepute with the people of Massachusetts, and the other provinces of New England.

This necessarily counteracted that alacrity with which it was desired that the militia from that quarter should hasten to re-inforce the army of the north, which was then encamped on the islands situated at the confluence of the Mohawk with the Hudson.

Another and very powerful cause contributed to excite the mass of the Americans to rise against the English army, which was the cruelties committed by the savages under St. Leger and Burgoyne, who spared neither age nor sex nor opinions. The friends of the royal cause, as well as its enemies, were equally victims to their indiscriminate rage. The people abhorred and execrated an army which consented to act with such ferocious auxiliaries. Though too true, their deeds of barbarity were aggravated by the writers and orators of the patriot party, which carried the exasperation of minds to its utmost height. They related, among others, an event which drew tears from every eye, and might furnish, if not too horrible, an affecting subject for the dramatic art.

A young lady, by the name of M'Crea, as distinguished for her virtues as for the beauty of her person and the gentleness of her manners, of respectable family, and recently affianced to a British officer, was seized by the savages in her father's house, near Fort

Edward, dragged into the woods, with several other young people of both sexes, and there barbarously scalped and afterwards murdered Thus, this ill fated damsel, instead of being conducted to the hymeneal altar, received an inhuman death at the very hands of the companions in arms of that husband she was about to espouse. The recital of an atrocity so unexampled, struck every breast with horror, as well in Europe as America, and the authors of the Indian war were loaded with the bitterest maledictions.

The Americans represent the fact as it is stated above, other writers relate it differently. According to their account, young Jones, the British officer, fearing that some ill might betide the object of his love, as well in consequence of the obstinate attachment of her father to the royal cause, as because their mutual passion was already publicly talked of, had, by the promise of a large recompense, induced two Indians, of different tribes, to take her under their escort, and conduct her in safety to the camp. The two savages went accordingly, and brought her through the woods; but at the very moment they were about to place her in the hands of her future husband, they fell to quarreling about their recompense, each contending that it belonged entirely to himself; when one of them, transported with brutal fury, raised his club and laid the unhappy maiden dead at his feet. General Burgoyne, on being informed of this horrid act, ordered the assassin to be arrested, that he might suffer the punishment due to his crime. But he soon after pardoned him upon the promise made him by the savages of abstaining for the future from similar barbarities, and of strictly observing the conditions to which they had pledged themselves upon the banks of the river Bouquet. The general believed that this act of clemency would be more advantageous than the example of chastisement. It even appears that he did not think himself sufficiently authorized, by the laws of England, to try and punish with death the murderer of the young lady; as if there existed not other laws besides the English, which bound him to inflict a just chastisement upon the perpetrator of a 'crime so execrable. But if he was warned by prudence to abstain from it, then was he to be pitied for the state of weakness to which he was reduced, and the weight of censure and detestation must fall exclusively upon the counsels of those who had called these barbarians into a civil contest. However the truth was, the condescension of general Burgoyne recoiled upon himself; for the savages, finding they were no longer permitted, as at first, to satiate their passion for pillage and massacre, deserted the camp, and returned to their several homes, ravaging and plundering whatever they found in their way. Thus terminated, almost entirely, this year, the

Indian war; a war impolitic in principle, atrocious in execution, and bootless in result.   The Canadians themselves, and the loyalists who followed the royal army, terrified at the sinister aspect of affairs deserted with one consent; so that Burgoyne, in his greatest need, was left nearly destitute of other force except his English and German regular troops.

Such was his situation, when a party of republicans undertook an enterprise upon the rear of his army, which, if it had succeeded, would have entirely cut off his provisions and retreat towards Canada; and at least demonstrated the danger to which he had exposed himself, in having advanced with so small an army to so great a distance from the strong posts upon the lakes.

General Lincoln, with a strong corps of the militia of New Hampshire and Connecticut, conceived the hope of recovering for the confederation the fortresses of Ticonderoga and Mount Independence, and consequently the command of Lake George.   He knew that these places were guarded only by feeble garrisons.   He advanced from Manchester to Pawlet.   He parted his corps into three divisions; the first, commanded by colonel Brown, was to proceed to the northern extremity of Lake George, and thence to fall by surprise upon Ticonderoga; the second, led by colonel Johnston, was destined to scour the country about Fort Independence, in order to make a diversion, and even an attack, if occasion should favor it; the third, under the orders of colonel Woodbury, had it in view to reduce Skeenesborough, Fort Anne, and even Fort Edward.   Colonel Brown, with equal secrecy and celerity, surprised all the posts upon Lake George and the inlet of Ticonderoga, Mount Hope, Mount Defiance, and the old French lines.   He took possession of two hundred batteaux, an armed brig, and several gun boats; he also made a very considerable number of prisoners.   Colonel Johnston arrived at the same time under the walls of Fort Independence. The two fortresses were summoned to capitulate.   But brigadier Powell, who held the chief command, replied that he was resolved to defend himself.   The Americans continued their cannonade for the space of four days ; but their artillery being of small caliber, and the English opposing a spirited resistance, they were constrained to abandon the enterprise, and to recover their former positions.

Meanwhile, general Burgoyne continued in his camp, on the left bank of the Hudson, where he used the most unremitting industry and perseverance in bringing stores and provisions forward from Fort George.   Having at length, by strenuous efforts, obtained about thirty days' provision, he took a resolution of passing the river with his army, in order to engage the enemy, and force a passage to Albany.

BATTLE OF SARATOGA. Vol. II.—p. 9.

As a swell of the water, occasioned by great rains, had carried away his bridge of rafts, he threw another, of boats, over the river at the same place. Towards the middle of September, he crossed with his army to the right bank of the Hudson, and encamped on the heights and in the plain of Saratoga; Gates being then in the neighborhood of Stillwater, about three miles below. The two armies of course faced each other, and a battle was expected soon to follow.

This measure of passing the Hudson was by many censured with great vehemence; it was considered as the principal cause of the unfortunate issue of this campaign. Some were of the opinion that after the affairs of Bennington and Stanwix, Burgoyne would have acted more wisely, considering the daily increase of the American army, if he had renounced the project of occupying Albany, and made the best of his way back to the lakes. It appears, however, to us but just to remark for his excuse, that at this time he had not yet received any intelligence either of the strength of the army left at New York, or of the movements which sir Henry Clinton was to make, or had made, up the North river towards Albany. He calculated upon a powerful co-operation on the part of that general. Such was the plan of the ministers, and such the tenor of his own peremptory instructions. And to what reproaches would he not have exposed himself, if, by retiring towards Ticonderoga, he had abandoned Clinton to himself, and thus voluntarily relinquished all the advantages that were expected from the junction of the two armies? We may, however, consider as vain the apology which was advanced by Burgoyne himself, when he alledged, that if he had returned to the lakes, Gates might have gone to join Washington, who, falling upon Howe with the combined armies, must have overpowered him, and decided the fate of the whole war. Gates would never have abandoned the shores of the Hudson, so long as the army of Burgoyne was opposed to him, whether in the position of Saratoga, or in that of Ticonderoga. It is, besides, to be observed, that as a great part of the army of Gates consisted in the New England militia, these, at least, would not have followed him, even if he had marched upon the Delaware. But though we think that Burgoyne committed no error in resolving to prosecute his expedition, it nevertheless appears that he ought not to have passed the Hudson. By continuing upon the left bank, he could retire at will towards Ticonderoga, or push forward towards Albany. It was evidently more easy to execute this movement, while having between himself and the now formidable army of Gates, so broad a river as the Hudson. The roads above, from Batten Kill to Fort George, were much easier upon the left than those upon the right bank; and in going down towards Albany, if they were not better, at least they were not worse. The city of Albany, it is true, is situated upon the right bank; but when Burgoyne should have arrived opposite to that city, upon the left, the English from below might have come up with their boats, and transported the troops to the right bank. At any rate, Burgoyne might thus have operated his junction with Clinton. But the former, either confiding too much in his army, which was, in truth, equally brave and flourishing, or not esteeming the Americans enough, notwithstanding the more favorable opinion of them which the actions of Bennington and of Stanwix should have given him resolved to quit the safer ground, and try the fortune of a battle; he considered victory as certain and decisive. In like manner as the British ministers, erroneously estimating the constancy of the colonists, had persuaded themselves that they could reduce them to submission by rigorous laws, the generals, deceiving themselves as strangely with respect to their courage, had no doubt that with their presence, a few threats and a little rattling of their arms, they could put them to flight. From this blind confidence in victory resulted a series of defeats, and the war was irretrievably lost from too sanguine an assurance of triumph.

But let us resume the course of events. The nineteenth of September was reserved by destiny for an obstinate and sanguinary action, in which it was at length to be decided whether the Americans, as some pretended, could only resist the English when protected by the strength of works, or of woods, rivers and mountains, or if they were capable of meeting them upon equal ground, in fair and regular battle. General Burgoyne, having surmounted the obstacles of thick woods and broken bridges, by which his progress was continually interrupted, at length arrived in the front of the enemy, some woods only of no great extent separating the two armies. Without a moment's delay, the English formed themselves in order of battle; their right wing rested upon some high grounds which rise gradually from the river; it was flanked by the grenadiers and light infantry, who occupied the hills. At some distance in front, and upon the side of these, were posted those Indians, Canadians and loyalists who had still remained in the camp. The left wing and artillery, under generals Phillips and Reidesel, kept along the great road and meadows by the river side. The American army drew up in the same order from the Hudson to the hills; Gates had taken the right, and given the left to Arnold. Smart skirmishes immediately ensued between the foremost marksmen of either army. Morgan, with his light horse, and colonel Durbin, with the light infantry, had attacked and routed the Canadians and savages; but the latter having been supported, they were both in their turn compelled to resume their place in the line. Meanwhile, Burgoyne, either intending to turn the left flank of the enemy, or wishing to avoid, by passing higher up, the hollows of the torrents which fall into the Hudson, extended his right wing upon the heights, in order to fall upon Arnold in flank and rear.

But Arnold was, at the same time, endeavoring to execute a similar maneuver upon him, while neither of them was able, on account of the woods, to perceive the movements of his enemy.

The two parties met; general Frazer repulsed the Americans. Finding the right flank of the enemy's right wing so well defended, they left a sufficient guard to defend this passage, made a rapid movement to their right, and vigorously assailed the left flank of the same wing. Arnold exhibited upon this occasion all the impetuosity of his courage; he encouraged his men with voice and example. The action became extremely warm ; the enemy, fearing that Arnold, by cutting their line, would penetrate between their wings, as was manifestly his intention, hastened to re-inforce the points attacked. General Frazer came up with the twenty-fourth regiment, some light infantry and Breyman's riflemen ; he would have drawn more troops from the right flank, but the heights on which it was posted, were of too great importance to be totally evacuated. Meanwhile, such was the valor and impetuosity of the Americans, that the English began to fall into confusion ; but general Phillips soon appeared with fresh men and a part of the artillery ; upon hearing the firing, he had rapidly made his way through a very difficult wood to the scene of danger. He restored the action at the very moment it was about being decided in favor of the enemy.

The Americans, however, renewed their attacks with such persevering energy, that night only parted the combatants. The royalists passed it under arms upon the field of battle ; the republicans retired. They had lost from three to four hundred men in killed and wounded ; among the former were colonels Adams and Coburn. The English had to regret more than five hundred, and among others, captain Jones, of the artillery, an officer of great merit.

Both parties claimed the honor of victory. The English, it is true, kept possession of the field of battle ; yet, as the intention of the Americans was not to advance, but to maintain their position, and that of the English not to maintain theirs, but to gain ground, and as, besides, it was a victory for the republicans not to be vanquished, it is easy to see which had the advantage of the day. On the other hand, the English were now convinced, to the great prejudice of their hopes, and even of their courage, that they would have to grapple with a toe as eager for action, as careless of danger, and as indifferent with respect to ground or cover as themselves.

The day following, general Burgoyne, finding that he must abandon all idea of dislodging the enemy by force, from his intrenched positions, endeavored to console himself with the hope, that time might offer him some occasion, to operate with more effect.

He was, besides, in daily expectation of news from general Clinton, with respect to whose movements he was still entirely in the dark. Resolving, therefore, to pause, he pitched his camp within cannon shot of the American lines. He threw up numerous intrenchments, both upon his right, the part which had been attacked, and upon his left, in order to defend the meadows near the river, where he had established his magazines and hospitals. An English regiment, the Hessians of Hanau, and a detachment of loyalists, were encamped in the same meadows for greater security. General Gates continued to occupy his first position, taking care, however, to fortify himself strongly on the left. With the return of success, his army was continually re-inforced by the accession of fresh bodies of the militia. General Lincoln joined him with two thousand men, well trained and disciplined, from the New England provinces. The English exerted the greatest vigilance to avoid surprise; and the Americans to prevent them from going out of their camp to forage. The skirmishes were animated and frequent.

The British general had for a long time been expecting news from New York; and his impatience was at its height, when, the twentieth of September, he received a letter of the tenth, written in ciphers, by general Clinton, informing him that about the twentieth of the month, he should with two thousand men attack Fort Montgomery, situated on the right bank of the Hudson, and upon the declivity of the highlands. He excused himself upon account of weakness for not doing more; and even declared, that if the enemy made any movement towards the coasts of New York, he should be forced to return thither. Burgoyne immediately dispatched an emissary, two officers in disguise, and some other trusty persons, by different routes, to general Clinton, with a full account of his present situation, urging him to a speedy execution of the diversions he had proposed, and informing him that he was provided with sufficient necessaries, to hold out in his present position till the twelfth of October. Although the assistance promised by Clinton was much less effectual than Burgoyne had kept in view, nevertheless, he still cherished a hope that the attack on fort Montgomery, and the apprehension that the English after its reduction might make their way up the river, would induce Gates either to change the position of his camp, or to send large detachments down the river, to oppose the progress of Clinton, and that in either case, some occasion would be offered him to gain a decisive advantage, and open his passage to Albany. But whoever considers the great superiority, in spirit as well as number, of the army of Gates over that of Burgoyne, and that the former was continually increasing in force, will readily perceive how vain were the expectations of the British general. It appears, therefore, that the mere survey of his own weakness, of that of Clinton, and of the preponderant force of Gates, should have determined him for retreat, if, however, retreat was still in his power. For to cross the river in sight of so formidable an army, would have been too perilous an enterprise; and here it is again perceived how imprudent had been the measure of passing it at first, since from that moment it became alike impossible to advance or recede.

In the beginning of October, general Burgoyne thought it expedient, from the difficulty of his situation and the uncertainty of succor, to lessen the soldiers' rations of provisions; to this measure, from its necessity, they submitted with great cheerfulness. But the twelfth of October was approaching, the term limited for the stay of the army in its present encampment. The seventh was already arrived, and no tidings came of the operations that had been proposed for its relief. In this alarming state of things, the English general resolved to make a movement to the enemy's left, not only to discover whether there were any possible means of forcing a passage, should it be necessary to advance, or of dislodging them for the convenience of retreat, but also to cover a forage of the army. He was impelled by necessity to attempt a decisive stroke. Accordingly he put himself at the head of a detachment of fifteen hundred regular troops, with two twelve pounders, two howitzers, and six six pounders. He was seconded by generals Phillips, Reidesel and Frazer, all officers distinguished for their zeal and ability. The guard of the camp upon the high grounds was committed to the brigadiers general Hamilton and Speight, that of the redoubts and plain near the river, to brigadier Goll.

The force of the enemy immediately in the front of his lines was so much superior, that Burgoyne could not venture to augment his detachment beyond the number we have stated. He had given orders that during this first attack, several companies of loyalists and Indians should be pushed on through by-ways, to appear as a check upon the rear of the enemy's left flank. The column of regulars, having already issued from the camp, were formed within three quarters of a mile of the enemy's left, and manifested an intention to turn it. But general Gates, who observed this movement, instantly penetrated the design of the English, and with exquisite discernment resolved to make a sudden and rapid attack upon the left of this corps, hoping thus to separate it from the remainder of the army, and to cut off its retreat to the camp.   The Americans advanced to the charge with incredible impetuosity, but they were received with equal resolution by major Ackland, at the head of the grenadiers. Gates immediately detached a fresh and powerful re-inforcement to the aid of the first, and the attack was soon extended along the whole front of the Germans, who were posted immediately on the right of Ackland's grenadiers.   Hence the British general found it impracticable to move any part of that body, as he would have desired, for the purpose of forming a second line to support this left flank, where the great weight of the fire still fell.   As yet the right was unengaged, when the British generals perceived that the enemy were marching a strong body round their flank, in order to cut off their retreat.   To oppose this dangerous design of the American general, the light infantry, with a part of the twenty-fourth regiment, which were joined with them at that post, were thrown into a second line, in order to cover the retreat of the troops into camp.   While this movement was yet in process, Arnold came up with three regiments, and fell upon this right wing.   Gates, at the same time, sent a strong re-inforcement to decide the action on the English left, which, being at length totally overpowered, fell into disorder and fled.   The light infantry and the twenty-fourth advanced with all speed to check the victorious Americans, whose riflemen pursued the fugitives with great eagerness ; there ensued an extremely warm affair, and many perished on both sides.

Upon this occasion, brigadier-general Frazer was mortally wounded, an officer whose loss was severely felt by the English, and whose valor and abilities justified their regrets.   Their situation now became exceedingly critical ; even their camp was threatened ; the enemy, emboldened by victory, was advancing to storm it, and if he arrived before the retreating detachment, there could be little hope of defending it.   Phillips and Reidesel were ordered to rally with all expedition those troops which were nearest, or most disengaged, to cover the retreat of the others, while Burgoyne himself, fiercely pursued by Arnold, retired with great precipitation towards the camp. The detachment at length, though with extreme difficulty, regained the intrenchments, having left, however, upon the field of battle, a great number of killed and wounded, particularly of the artillery corps, who had, with equal glory to themselves and prejudice to the enemy, displayed the utmost ability in their profession, along with the most undaunted resolution. Six pieces of cannon also remained in the power of the Americans.

But the business of the day was not yet terminated. The English had scarcely entered the camp, when the Americans, pursuing their success, assaulted it in different parts with uncommon fierceness; rushing to the lines through a severe fire of grape-shot and small arms, with the utmost fury. Arnold especially, who in this day appeared intoxicated with the thirst of battle and carnage, led on the attack against a part of the intrenchments occupied by the light infantry, under lord Balcarres. But the English received him with great vigor and spirit. The action was obstinate and sanguinary. At length, as it grew towards evening, Arnold, having forced all obstacles, entered the works with some of the most fearless of his followers. But in this critical moment of glory and danger, he was grievously wounded in the same leg which had been already shattered at the assault of Quebec. To his great regret, he was constrained to retire. His party still continued the attack, and the English sustained it with obstinacy, till night separated the combatants.

The royalists were not so fortunate in another quarter. A republican detachment, commanded by lieutenant-colonel Brooks, having succeeded by a circuitous movement in turning the right wing of the English, fell, sword in hand, upon the right flank of their intrenchments, and made the most desperate efforts to carry them. This post was defended by lieutenant-colonel Breyman, at the head of the German reserve. The resistance at first was exceedingly vigorous; but Breyman being mortally wounded, his countrymen were damped, and at length routed, with great slaughter. Their tents, artillery, and baggage, fell into the power of the assailants. The Americans established themselves in the intrenchments. General Burgoyne, upon hearing of this disaster, ordered them to be dislodged immediately. But either in consequence of the approach of night, or from the discouragement of his troops, he was not obeyed, and the victors continued to occupy the position they had gained with so much glory. They had now acquired an opening on the right and rear of the British army. The other American division passed the night under arms, at the distance of half a mile from the British camp. The loss in dead and wounded was great on both sides; but especially on the part of the English, of whom no few were also made prisoners. Majors Williams of the artillery, and Ackland of the grenadiers, were among the latter. Many pieces of artillery, all the baggage of the Germans, and many warlike stores, fell into the power of the republicans, who needed them greatly. They were impatient for the return of day, to renew the battle. But deplorable and perilous beyond expression was the situation of the British troops; they bore it, however, with admirable temper and firmness. It was evidently impossible to continue in their present position, without submitting to a certainty of destruction on the ensuing day. The Americans, invigorated and encouraged, would certainly have profited of the access they had already opened to themselves on the right, and of other untenable points, to carry every part of the camp, and completely surround the British army. Burgoyne therefore determined to operate a total change of ground. He executed this movement with admirable order, and without any loss. The artillery, the camp and its appertenances, were all removed before morning to the heights above the hospital. The British army in this position had the river in its rear, and its two wings displayed along the hills upon the right bank. The English expected to be attacked the following day. But Gates, like the experienced general he was, would not expose to the risk of another battle that victory of which he was already certain. He intended that time, famine, and necessity, should complete the work which his arms had so fortunately commenced. There were frequent skirmishes, however, engaged in the course of the day; but of little importance. Towards night, the obsequies of general Frazer were celebrated in the British camp; a ceremony mournful of itself, and rendered even terrible by the sense of recent losses, of future dangers, and of regret for the deceased. The darkness and silence of night aided the effect of the blaze and roar of the American artillery; while at every moment the balls spattered earth upon the face of the officiating chaplain.

General Gates, prior to the battle, had detached a strong division of his army to take post upon the left bank of the Hudson, opposite to Saratoga, in order to guard the passage and prevent the enemy's escape on that side. He now dispatched a second detachment to occupy a passage higher up. He ordered, at the same time, a selected corps of two thousand men to push forward and turn the right flank of the enemy, so as to enclose him on every side. Burgoyne, on intelligence of this motion, determined to retire towards Saratoga, situated six miles up the river, on the same bank. The army accordingly began to move at nine o'clock at night; but such was the badness of the roads, rendered still more difficult by a heavy rain which fell that night, and such was the weakness of the teams for want of forage, that the English did not reach Saratoga till the evening of the ensuing day; the soldiers were harassed with fatigue and hunger. The hospital, with three hundred sick and wounded, and a great number of wheel carriages, were abandoned to the enemy. The English, as they retired, burnt the houses, and destroyed whatever they could use no longer.

The rain having ceased, Gates followed them step by step, and with extreme caution, as they had broken all the bridges, and he was resolved not to give them any opportunity to engage him with advantage.

Fearing that Burgoyne would hasten to detach his light troops, in order to secure the passage of the river near Fort Edward, he rapidly threw several companies of militia into that fort, in order to prevent it. Scarcely had they arrived there, when the English rangers appeared; but finding themselves anticipated, they returned disappointed and dejected. During this time, the main body of the English army, having passed the night of the ninth at Saratoga, left it on the morning of the tenth, and forded Fish Kill Creek, which falls into the Hudson, a little to the northward of that town. The British generals had hoped that they should here be able to cross the river at the principal ford, and escape pursuit upon its left bank. But they found a body of republicans already arrived, and throwing up intrenchments on the heights to the left of Fish Kill Creek. These Americans, however, when they observed the great superiority of the English, retired over the Hudson, and there joined a greater force, which was stationed to prevent the passage of the army. Having lost all hope of passing the river in the vicinity of Saratoga, the British generals had it in mind to push forward upon the right bank, till they arrived in front of Fort Edward, and then to force a passage to the left bank, in defiance of the troops stationed there for its defense. For this purpose, a company of artificers, under the escort of a regiment of the line, with a detachment of marksmen and loyalists, were sent forward to repair the bridges, and open the road to Fort Edward. But they were not long departed from the camp, when the enemy appeared in great force upon the heights on the opposite side of Fish Kill Creek, and seemed preparing to cross it, in order to bring on an immediate engagement.

The regulars and marksmen were immediately recalled. The workmen had only commenced the repair of the first bridge, when they were abandoned by the loyalists, who ran away, and left them to shift for themselves, only upon a very slight attack of an inconsiderable party of the enemy. Hence it became necessary to abandon all hopes of saving the artillery and baggage.

Amidst all these embarrassments, still a new difficulty presented itself; the republicans who lined the further shore of the Hudson, kept up a continual fire upon the batteaux loaded with provisions and necessaries which had attended the motions of the army up the river, since its departure from Stillwater. Many of these boats had been taken, some re-taken, and a number of men lost on both sides. At length, to avoid these inconveniences, the English were forced to land the provisions, and transport them up the hill to the camp; a labor which they accomplished under a heavy fire, with great fatigue and loss. Nothing could now exceed the distress and calamity of the British army; the soldiers as well as the generals were reduced to brood upon the prospect of an ignominious surrender, or total destruction. To attempt the passage of so wide a river, while its shore was guarded with so much vigilance by a formidable body of troops, and in the presence of a powerful enemy, flushed with victory, was an enterprise savoring rather of madness than temerity. On the other hand, the retreat upon the right bank, with the same enemy at the rear, through ways so difficult and impracticable, was a scheme which presented obstacles absolutely insurmountable. Every thing announced therefore an inevitable catastrophe. Nevertheless, in the midst of so much calamity, a ray of hope suddenly gleamed upon the English; and they were near gaining an opportunity of retrieving their affairs all at once. The two armies were only separated by the Fish Kill Creek; report, which magnifies all things, had represented to general Gates the feeble detachment which Burgoyne had sent to escort his pioneers upon the route to Fort Edward as the entire vanguard and center of the British army, already well on their way towards that fort. He concluded, therefore, that only the rear guard remained near the Fish Kill, and instantly conceived the hope of crushing it by an attack with all his forces. He made all his preparations in the morning of the eleventh of October. His scheme was to take advantage of a thick fog, which in those regions, and at this season, usually obscure the atmosphere till a little after sunrise, to pass the Fish Kill very early, to seize a battery which Burgoyne had erected upon the opposite bank, and then to fall immediately upon the enemy. The English general had notice of this plan; he furnished the battery with a strong guard, and posted his troops in ambush behind the thickets which covered the banks of the creek. In this position he waited the enemy's approach, and calculating upon their supposed error, he had little doubt of victory. The brigade of the American general Nixon had already forded the Fish Kill, and that of general Glover was about to follow it. But just as the latter entered the water, he was informed by a British deserter, that not only the rear guard, but the whole royal army, was drawn up in order of battle upon the other bank. Upon this intelligence Glover halted, and sent to apprise Nixon of the danger he was in of being cut in pieces, unless he hastened to recover the left bank.   General Gates was immediately informed of the incident; he revoked all the orders he had given, and directed that the troops should be reconducted to their positions.   General Nixon received the message of Glover in good time; for a quarter of an hour later he would have been lost irrecoverably.   He fe'l back with all expedition; but the fog being dissipated before he was out of sight of the enemy, his rear guard was annoyed by the English artillery, with the loss of a few soldiers.

Frustrated of this hope, general Burgoyne applied his thoughts to devise, if possible, some other way to save the army.   He called a council of war, in which it was resolved to attempt, by a rapid retreat in the night up the Hudson, to gain the fords of that river at or above Fort Edward, and there having forced a passage, to press on to Fort George.   That nothing might retard the march, it was determined to abandon the artillery, baggage, carriages, and all incumbrances.   The soldiers were to carry upon their backs a sufficient quantity of provisions, to support them till they could arrive at Fort George.   All the troops prepared to execute the plan of their general.

But Gates had already, with great foresight, taken all his measures to defeat it.   He had recommended the utmost vigilance to the parties that were stationed to guard the opposite shore of the river; he had posted a strong detachment to guard the fords near Fort Edward, with orders to oppose any attempt of the enemy to pass them, till he should arrive with the army upon his rear.   In addition to this, he had established a camp in force, and provided with artillery, upon the high and strong grounds between Fort Edward and Fort George.   General Burgoyne had sent forward scouts, to examine the route, and especially to ascertain whether it was possible to force the passage opposite to Fort Edward.   They returned with an account that the roads were inconceivably rough and difficult; that the enemy were so numerous and vigilant upon the left bank, that no movement of the army upon the right could escape immediate discovery; and that the passages at the fort were so diligently defended, that it was absolutely impossible to force them without artillery.   They also mentioned the intrenched camp on the hills between the two forts.   Burgoyne had no sooner received this afflicting intelligence, than he was also informed that general Gates, with the main body of his army, was so near, and observed him with such steady attention, that it would be impossible for him to move a step without being instantly followed; he then saw that he must relinquish all hope of saving himself by his own efforts.

In this deplorable extremity, his only refuge from despair was the faint hope of co-operation from the parts down the river; and with the most intense desire he looked for the aid of Clinton.

It exceeds the power of words to describe the pitiable condition to which the British army was now reduced. The troops, worn down by a series of hard toil, incessant effort and stubborn action; abandoned by the Indians and Canadians; the whole army reduced by repeated and heavy losses of many of their best men and most distinguished officers from ten thousand combatants to less than five thousand effective fighting men, of whom little more than three thousand were English. In these circumstances, and in this state of weakness, without a possibility of retreat, they were invested by an army of four times their own number, whose position extended three parts in four of a circle round them; who refused to fight from a knowledge of their own condition; and who, from the nature of the ground, could not be attacked in any part. In this helpless situation, obliged to lie constantly on their arms, while a continued cannonade pervaded all the camp, and even rifle and grape-shot fell in every part of their lines, the troops of Burgoyne retained their ordinary constancy, and while sinking under a hard necessity, they showed themselves worthy of a better fate. Nor could they be reproached with any action or word which betrayed a want of temper, or of fortitude.

At length, no succor appearing, and no rational ground of hope of any kind remaining, an exact account of the provisions was taken on the morning of the thirteenth, when it was found that the whole stock would afford no more than three days' bare subsistence for the army. In such a state, it was alike impossible to advance or to remain as they were; and the longer they delayed to take a definitive resolution, the more desperate became their situation. Burgoyne, therefore, immediately called a council of war, at which not only the generals and field officers, but all the captains of companies were invited to assist. While they deliberated, the bullets of the Americans whistled around them, and frequently pierced even the tent where the council was convened. It was determined unanimously to open a treaty and enter into a convention with the American general.

Gates used his victory with moderation. Only he proposed that the royal troops should lay down their arms in camp; a condition which appeared too hard to the English, and which they peremptorily refused. They all preferred to be led against the enemy, notwithstanding the disadvantage of number, rather than submit to such a disgrace. After several conferences, the articles of capitulation were settled the fifteenth They were to be signed by the two contracting parties on the morning of the seventeenth. In the night, captain Campbell arrived at the British camp, sent express by general Clinton, with the intelligence that he had moved up the Hudson, reduced Fort Montgomery, and penetrated as far as Æsopus. The hope of safety revived in the breasts of some.

The officers were invited to declare, whether in a case of extremity, the soldiers were in a situation to fight, and whether they considered the public faith as pledged by the verbal convention. A great number answered, that the soldiers, debilitated by fatigue and hunger, were unable to make resistance; all were decidedly of the opinion, that the public faith was engaged. Burgoyne alone manifested a contrary opinion. But he was constrained to acquiesce in the general suffrage. Meanwhile, Gates, apprised of these hesitations of his enemy, and the new hopes which occasioned them, formed his troops in order of battle on the morning of the seventeenth, and sent to inform Burgoyne that the stipulated time being arrived, he must either sign the articles, or prepare himself for battle.

The Englishman had taken his resolution; he signed the paper, which had this superscription; *Convention between lieutenant-general Burgoyne and major-general Gates.* The principal articles, exclusive of those which related to the provision and accommodation of the army in its way to Boston, and during its stay at that place, were;

That the army should march out of the camp with all the honors of war, and its camp artillery, to a fixed place, where they were to deposit their arms and leave the artillery; to be allowed a free embarkation and passage to Europe, from Boston, upon condition of their not serving again in America, during the present war; the army not to be separated, particularly the men from the officers; roll calling and other duties of regularity, to be permitted; the officers to be admitted on parole, and to wear their side arms; all private property to be retained, and the public delivered upon honor; no baggage to be searched or molested; all persons, of whatever country, appertaining to, or following the camp, to be fully comprehended in the terms of capitulation, and the Canadians to be returned to their own country, liable to its conditions.

Assuredly, these conditions were very honorable for the British army, considering its ruined state and irretrievable circumstances; but it obtained still more from the magnanimity of general Gates. From tenderness towards the feelings of the vanquished, he ordered his army to retire within their lines, that they might not witness the shame of the English, when they piled their arms.

This conduct demonstrated not only the humanity but the clemency and elevation of character which distinguished the American general; for he was already informed of the horrible ravages recently committed, by general Vaughan, upon the right bank of the Hudson, where, imitating the usages of barbarians, he had laid in ashes, and utterly destroyed the fine village of Æsopus. It is our duty not to pass without mention, that while Gates, in the whole course of this campaign upon the Hudson, displayed all the talents which constitute an able and valiant general, he proved himself not to want any of those qualities which characterize a benevolent and generous heart. Humane towards all whom the fortune of war had thrown into his hands, he was eminently attentive to those who were sick, and suffered them to want for no succor within his power to administer.

The day of the capitulation, the American army amounted to near fifteen thousand men, of whom about ten thousand were regular troops; the English army to five thousand seven hundred and ninety-one, of whom two thousand four hundred and twelve were Germans, and three thousand three hundred and seventy-nine English.

The Americans acquired a fine train of brass artillery, amounting to forty-two pieces of different sorts and sizes, four thousand six hundred muskets, an immense quantity of cartridges, bombs, balls, and other implements of war.

Such was the fate of the British expedition upon the banks of the Hudson. It had been undertaken with singular confidence of success, but the obstacles proved so formidable that those who had expected from it such brilliant results, were themselves its victims; and those it had alarmed at first, derived from it the most important advantages. There can be no doubt, that, if it was planned with ability, as to us it appears to have been, it was conducted with imprudence by those who were intrusted with its execution. For it is to be remarked, that its success depended entirely on the combined efforts of the generals who commanded upon the lakes, and of those who had the management of the war in the state of New York. But far from moving in concert, when one advanced, the other retired. When Carleton had obtained the command of the lakes, Howe, instead of ascending the Hudson, towards Albany, carried his arms into New Jersey, and advanced upon the Delaware. When, afterwards, Burgoyne entered Ticonderoga in triumph, Howe embarked upon the expedition against Philadelphia; and thus the army of Canada was deprived of the assistance it expected from New York.

Perhaps Howe imagined that the reduction of such a city as Philadelphia, would so confound the Americans, and so derange their plans, that they would either immediately submit, or make but a feeble resistance. Perhaps, also, he believed, that by attacking the center, and as it were, the very heart of the confederation, he effected the most useful diversion in favor of the army of the north, thereby depriving the Americans of the ability to oppose it with a sufficient force upon the Hudson.   Finally, it is not impossible, that, listening to his ambition, he had flattered himself that with his own means alone he could acquire the exclusive glory of having put an end to the war.   But whatever might have been the importance of the acquisition of Philadelphia, every one must readily perceive how much greater was that of the junction at Albany, of the two armies of Canada and of New York.   It was very doubtful whether the conquest of a single city could decide the issue of the war; whereas the juncture of the armies, offered almost an assurance of it.   It should also be considered that the Americans, in order to prevent this junction, would have risked a pitched battle, the success of which could scarcely be doubtful, and which could have formed no obstacle to the eventual union.   Besides, when two armies have the same object in view, is it not evident that they can operate with more concert and effect, when they are near to each other, than while remotely separated?   We may therefore consider this expedition as having been wisely calculated in its design, and even in the means of execution, if we except that scourge of the savages, which must be imputed to the British ministers.   Bating this fault, they did not, in our opinion, deserve the reproaches with which they were loaded, as well in parliament as by the writers of the opposite party.   Perhaps also they erred in this, that having too great confidence in the reputation, rank, and military experience of sir William Howe, they neglected to send him more precise instructions.   For it appears from the best information we have found upon this subject, that the orders given to that general in regard to his co-operation with the army of Canada, were rather discretionary than absolute; but all the ruin of the enterprise is clearly attributable to this want of co-operation.   Gates, after the victory, immediately dispatched colonel Wilkinson to carry the happy tidings to congress.   On being introduced into the hall, he said: 'The whole British army has laid down arms at Saratoga; our own, full of vigor and courage, expect your orders; it is for your wisdom to decide where the country may still have need of their services.'   The congress voted thanks to general Gates and his army.   They decreed that he should be presented with a medal of gold, to be struck expressly in commemoration of so glorious a victory.   On one side of it was the bust of the general, with these words around; *Horatio Gates, Duci strenuo*; and in the middle, *Comitia Americana*.   On the reverse, Burgoyne was represented in the attitude of delivering his sword; and in the back ground, on the one side and on the other, were seen the two armies of England and of America. At the top were these words; *Salum regionum septentrion*; and at the foot, *Hoste ad Saratogam in deditione accepto. Die XVII Oct. MDCCLXXVII.* It would be difficult to describe the transports of joy which the news of this event excited among the Americans. They began to flatter themselves with a still more happy future; no one any longer entertained a doubt of independence. All hoped, and not without much reason, that a success of this importance would at length determine France, and the other European powers that waited for her example, to declare themselves in favor of America. *There could no longer be any question respecting the future; all danger had ceased of espousing the cause of a people too feeble to defend themselves.*

While Burgoyne found himself in the most critical situation, Clinton, in the beginning of October, had embarked at New York, with about three thousand men, upon his expedition up the Hudson, for his relief. The Americans, commanded by general Putnam, occupied the steep mountains between which this river flows with rapidity, and which begin to rise in the vicinity of Peek's Kill. In addition to the natural strength of the places in the midst of these mountains, the banks of the Hudson being almost inaccessible, the Americans had secured the passages in divers modes. About six miles above Peek's Kill, upon the western bank, they had two forts, called the one Montgomery, and the other Clinton, separated only by a torrent, which, gushing from the neighboring heights, falls into the river. Their situation, upon heights so precipitous that it was impossible to climb them, entirely commanded the course of the Hudson. There was no other way by which the enemy could approach them, but that of penetrating into the mountains a little below, towards Stony Point and marching through narrow and difficult paths. But such were these defiles that if they had been suitably guarded, it would have been not only dangerous, but absolutely impracticable to thread them. To prevent the enemy from passing above the forts by water, chevaux-de-frize were sunken in the river, and a boom extended from bank to bank. This boom was covered by an immense chain, stretched at some distance in its front. These works were remarkable for their perfection, and had been executed with equal industry and difficulty. They were defended by the artillery of the forts, by a frigate and by several galleys, stationed a little above the boom. Such were the fortifications which the Americans had constructed upon the right bank, and even in the bed of the Hudson, in order to secure these passages, which had been the object of their solicitude from the commencement of hostilities; they being in effect the most defensi-

PUTNAM'S ESCAPE. Vol. II.—p. 25.

ble barriers against a descent of the enemy from Canada. Upon the left bank, on a high point of land, four or five miles below Forts Montgomery and Clinton, they had erected a fort to which they gave the name of *Independence*, and another called *Constitution*, about six miles above the same forts, on an island near the eastern shore. They had also there interrupted the navigation of the river by che · vaux-de-frize and a boom.

General Putnam guarded these different passages with a corps of six hundred regular troops, and some militia, of whom the number was uncertain. An American officer, named Clinton, commanded in the forts.

The British general knew perfectly well that to attack Forts Clinton and Montgomery in front, would have been a vain attempt. He therefore formed the design of marching to the assault upon their rear, by the defiles which commence near Stony Point. But in order to divert the Americans from the thought of re-inforcing the garrisons, he resolved to make such motions upon the left bank, as should alarm them for the safety of Fort Independence. On the fifth of October he landed all his troops at Verplank's Point, a little below Peek's Kill, where general Putnam had established his head quarters. Putnam immediately retired to the strong heights in his rear. The English, having re-embarked the greater part of their troops in the night, landed by break of day upon the right bank, at Stony Point; without loss of time they entered the defiles, and marched towards the forts. In the meantime, the manœuvres of the vessels, and the appearance of the small detachment left at Verplank's Point, persuaded Putnam that the enemy meditated an attack on Fort Independence. The English during this interval were making the best of their way through the mountains. Governor Clinton had not discovered their approach till very late. They appeared before the two forts at nearly the same time, and having without difficulty repulsed the advanced parties which had been sent out to retard them, they furiously began their attack. Their ships of war had also now made their appearance, and supported them with a near fire. The Americans, though surprised, defended themselves with courage for a considerable length of time; but at length, unable to sustain the reiterated efforts of the assailants, and too feeble to man their fortifications sufficiently, after a severe loss in killed and wounded, they retired.

Those who knew the ground, among whom was governor Clinton, escaped. The slaughter was, however, great, the English being irritated by the opposition they met, and by the loss of some favorite officers. The Americans set fire to their frigates and galleys, which, with their stores and ammunition, were all consumed; but the English got possession of the boom and chain.

In a day or two after, Forts Independence and Constitution, upon the approach of the enemy with his land and naval forces, were set on fire and evacuated by their defenders. Tryon was sent on the ninth, at the head of a detachment, to destroy a thriving settlement, called Continental Village, where the republicans had deposited a great quantity of stores.

Thus fell into the power of the English these important passages of the mountains of the Hudson, which the Americans had labored to defend by every mode of fortification. They were justly considered as the keys of the county of Albany. It is therefore evident, that if the royalists had been more numerous, they might have extended an efficacious succor to the army of Burgoyne, and, perhaps, decided in their favor the final issue of the northern war. But they could not take part in it, as well because they were much too weak, as that Putnam, whose army was now increased by the militia of Connecticut, New York, and New Jersey, to six thousand men, menaced them both in front and rear.

Unable to conquer, the English set themselves to sack the country The thirteenth of October, sir James Wallace, with a flying squadron of light frigates, and general Vaughan, with a considerable detachment of troops, made an excursion up the river, carrying slaughter and destruction wherever they went; a barbarity of conduct the more execrable, as it was not justified by the least necessity or utility. They marched to a rich and flourishing village, called Kingston, or Æsopus, upon the western bank of the river; having driven the republicans out of it by a furious cannonade, they set fire to it on every side. All was consumed; not a house was left standing. Extensive magazines of provisions and military stores were also consigned to the flames. In order to justify these atrocities, it was alledged by Vaughan that the Americans had fired through the windows; a fact which they denied with greater probability of truth. For it appears that they evacuated the town as soon as they saw the royal troops were disembarked upon the neighboring shore. The English committed these excesses at the very time that Burgoyne was receiving from general Gates the most honorable conditions for himself and a ruined army.

The American wrote Vaughan a letter full of energy and just indignation; he complained in sharp terms of the burning of Æsopus, and of the horrible devastations committed upon the two banks of the Hudson. He concluded with saying: 'Is it thus that the generals of the king expect to make converts to the royal cause? Their

cruelties operate a contrary effect; independence is founded upon
the universal disgust of the people.   The fortune of war has delivered into my hands older and abler generals than general Vaughan is
reputed to be; their condition may one day become his, and then
no human power can save him from the just vengeance of an offended people.'

But Vaughan and Wallace, having heard that Gates was marching
rapidly upon them, resolved not to wait his approach.   Having dismantled the forts, and carrying off their booty, they retired from
this quarter, and uniting with the remainder of the troops of Clinton,
returned with no ordinary speed to New York.

Upon the whole, the loss which the United States sustained from
this expedition of the English upon the banks of the Hudson, was
extremely severe; for it being universally believed that these elevated
and precipitous places were absolutely inaccessible to the fury of the
enemy, the Americans had deposited there an immense quantity of
arms, ammunition and stores of all sorts.

The artillery lost, including that of the forts, and that of the vessels destroyed or taken, amounted to more than a hundred pieces of
different sizes.   To which must be added, fifteen or twenty thousand pounds of powder, balls in proportion, and all the implements
necessary to the daily service of the artillery.

Meanwhile, the captive army was marched towards Boston.   On
its departure from Saratoga, it passed in the midst of the ranks of
the victorious troops, who were formed in order of battle for this purpose along the road and upon the hills which border the two sides of
it.   The English expected to be scoffed at and insulted.   Not an
American uttered a syllable; a memorable example of moderation
and military discipline!   The prisoners, particularly those incorrigible Germans, ravaged whatever they could lay their hands on during
the march; the inhabitants could judge by what they did, being vanquished, of what they would have done, had they been victors.
They arrived at Boston, and were lodged in the barracks of Cam-
bridge.   The inhabitants held them in abhorrence; they could not
forget the burning of Charlestown, and the late devastations.

Burgoyne, after the capitulation, experienced the most courteous
attentions on the part of the American generals.   Gates invited him
to his table; he appeared silent and dejected.   The conversation
was guarded, and to spare his feelings nothing was said of the late
events; only he was asked how he could find in his heart to burn
the houses of poor people.   He answered that such were his orders,
and that, besides, he was authorized to do it by the laws of war.
Certain individuals in New England, without delicacy as without

reserve, loaded him with insults. But this was confined to the popu-
lace. Well educated men treated him with marked civility. General Schuyler, among others, politely dispatched an aid-de-camp, to
accompany him to Albany. He lodged him in his own house; where
his wife received him in the most flattering manner. Yet Burgoyne;
in the neighborhood of Saratoga, where Schuyler possessed extensive estates, had devoted to the flames his magnificent villa, with its
movables and dependencies, valued at more than thirty-seven thousand dollars. At Boston, Burgoyne was likewise lodged in the habitation of general Heath, who commanded in Massachusetts; he there
wanted for no attention. He walked at his pleasure through the
city, without ever having found occasion to complain of outrage.

But the other officers did not experience the same reception; the
Bostonians would not lodge them in their houses, and therefore it
became necessary to distribute them in the barracks. Burgoyne
complained of it, at first, to general Heath, and afterwards to Gates.
He insisted that a treatment of his officers so little conformable to
their rank, was a violation of the convention of Saratoga. Moreover, fearing that the season, already advanced, might not permit
the transports to arrive soon enough at Boston, where the embarkation was appointed by the capitulation, he requested Washington to
consent that it should take place at Newport, in Rhode Island, or
at some other port of the Sound. Washington, not thinking himself authorized to decide upon this request, submitted it to the determination of congress. That body was much displeased at this
verbal discussion, and especially at the imputation of a breach of
faith; apprehending it might be a pretext which Burgoyne was inclined to use for not keeping his own.

It appeared, besides, to the congress, that the vessels assembled
at Boston for the transport of the troops, were neither sufficient for
so great a number, nor furnished with provisions enough for so long
a voyage. Finally, they observed that the English had not strictly
fulfilled the stipulation in respect to the surrender of arms, as they
had retained their cartridge boxes, and other effects, which, if not
actually arms, are of indispensable use to those who bear them.
Gates undertook to justify the English upon this point, and with
complete success. But the congress had need of a quarrel, and
therefore sought the grounds. They wished to retard the embarkation of the prisoners, under the apprehension that, in defiance of
treaties, they would go to join general Howe, or at least, that arriving
too early in England, the government would be able to fill their
place immediately by an equal number in America. They decreed,
therefore, that general Burgoyne should furnish the rolls of his army,

that a list might be taken of the name and rank of every commissioned officer; with the name, former place of abode, occupation, size, age and description of every non-commissioned officer and private soldier.

Burgoyne considered this demand extraordinary, and therefore resorted to various subterfuges in order to evade compliance. General Howe, on his part, proceeded with much subtilty and illiberality in the exchange of prisoners; and thus the discontents and suspicions were continually increased.

The ambiguous conduct of each of these generals alarmed the congress exceedingly; they decreed, therefore, that the embarkation of Burgoyne and all the captive troops should be suspended, until a distinct and explicit ratification of the convention of Saratoga should be properly notified to congress by the court of Great Britain. At the same time they sent directions to general Heath, to order any vessels which might have arrived, or which should arrive, for the transportation of the army, to quit the port of Boston without delay. An additional force was also provided to guard the British army. Burgoyne then addressed a letter to congress, in which he endeavored to justify his conduct; he protested that he had never thought himself released from the conditions of the convention of Saratoga, and affirmed that all his officers individually were ready to give their written promise to observe all the articles of that capitulation. All was in vain; congress was inflexible; and the prisoners had to make up their minds to remain in America. This decision they took in great dudgeon; and it served as a pretext for the partisans of the ministry to charge the Americans with perfidy. We shall not undertake to decide whether the fears manifested by congress had a real foundation; and we shall abstain as well from blaming the imprudence of Burgoyne, as from praising the wisdom, or condemning the distrust of the congress.

It is but too certain that in these civil dissensions and animosities, appearances become realities, and probabilities demonstration. Accordingly, at that time, the Americans complained bitterly of British perfidy, and the English of American want of faith.

Finding that he could obtain nothing for others, Burgoyne solicited for himself, and easily got permission to return to England. As soon as he was arrived in London, he began to declaim with virulence against those ministers, whose favor a little before he had used every means to captivate, and who had given him, to the prejudice of a general approved by long services, an opportunity to distinguish his name by a glorious enterprise. Burgoyne wanted neither an active genius nor military science and experience; but formed in the wars of Germany, his movements were made with caution, and extreme deliberation, and never till all circumstances united to favor them. He would, upon no consideration, have attacked an enemy, until the minutest precepts of the military art had all been faithfully observed This was totally mistaking the nature of the American war, which required to be carried on with vigor and spirit. In a region like America, broken by so many defiles and fastnesses, against an enemy so able to profit of them, by scouring the country, by preparing ambuscades, by intercepting convoys and retreats, the celerity which might involve a transient peril, was assuredly preferable to the slowness which, under its apparent security, concealed a future and inevitable danger.

This general lost the opportunity to conquer, because he would never run the risk of defeat; and as he would put nothing in the power of fortune, she seemed to have thought him unworthy of her favors. Moreover, the employment of savages in the wars of civilized nations, was never the source of durable success; nor was it ever the practice of prudent generals to provoke the enemy by threats, or to exasperate him by ravages and conflagrations.

While these events were passing in the north, admiral and general Howe were at sea, undecided whether to enter the Delaware, or to take the route of the Chesapeake bay, in order to march against Philadelphia. Washington continued in New Jersey, prepared to defend the passages of the Hudson, if the British army should have taken that direction, or to cover Philadelphia, should it threaten that city. But while waiting for certain information respecting the movements and plans of the British generals, he neglected none of those measures which were proper to place his army in a situation to resist the storm that was about to burst upon it. He collected arms and ammunition, called out the militia of the neighboring provinces, and ordered to join him all the regiments of regular troops that were not necessary for the defense of the Hudson. These different corps were continually exercised in arms and military evolutions; wherein they derived great advantage from the example and instructions of the French officers who had recently entered the service of the United States. Among these, the splendor of rank, added to the fascination of his personal qualities, eminently distinguished the marquis de la Fayette. Animated by the enthusiasm which generous minds are wont to feel for great enterprises, he espoused the cause of the Americans with a partiality common to almost all the men of that time, and particularly to the French. He considered it not only just, but exalted and sacred; the affection he bore it was the more ardent, as independently of the candor of his character, he was of that age, not exceeding nineteen years, in which good appears not only good, but fair, and man not only loves, but is enamored. Inflamed with desire to take part in events which were echoed by all Europe, he had communicated, about the close of 1776, to the American commissioners his intention of repairing to America; they had encouraged him in that resolution. But when they were informed of the reverses of New Jersey, compelled almost to despair of the success of the revolution, they, with honorable sincerity, endeavored to dissuade him from it. They even declared to him that their affairs were so deranged by this unhappy news, that they were not able to charter a vessel for his passage to America. It is said the gallant youth replied, that it was then precisely the moment to serve their cause; that the more people were discouraged, the greater utility would result from his departure, and that if they could not furnish him with a ship, he would freight one at his own expense to convey himself and their dispatches to America. And as he said, he also did. The people were astonished, and much conversation was excited by this determination on the part of so illustrious a personage. The court of France, either to save appearances, and avoid giving umbrage to England, or being really displeased at this departure, forbade La Fayette to embark. It is even asserted, that ships were dispatched with orders to arrest him in the waters of the West Indies. Tearing himself, however, from the arms of his beloved wife, who was in all the bloom of youth, he put to sea, and steering wide of those islands, arrived in Georgetown. The congress omitted none of those demonstrations which could persuade the young Frenchman, and all the American people, in what esteem they held his person, and how much they felt the sacrifices he had made, and the dangers to which he had exposed himself, and was still exposed, for being come to offer his support to the tottering cause of America.

Touched by this flattering reception, he promised to exert himself to the utmost of his knowledge and ability; but requested permission to serve at first only as a volunteer, and at his own expense. This generosity and modesty of the marquis de la Fayette, delighted the Americans the more, as some of the French who had entered their service were never to be satisfied in the articles either of pay, or of rank. It was Silas Deane who had encouraged these exorbitant expectations, by entering in France into such engagements with those officers, as could not be confirmed in America. This conduct had greatly displeased the congress, and was what chiefly determined them to send him, soon after, a successor in the person of John Adams. The congress decreed, that ' whereas the marquis de la Fayette, out of his great zeal to the cause of liberty in which the

United States were engaged, had left his family and connections, and at his own expense come over to offer his services without pension or particular allowance, and was anxious to risk his life in their defense, they accepted his services; and that in consideration of his zeal, illustrious family and connections, he was invested with the rank of major-general in the army of the United States.' The marquis, having repaired to the camp, was received with consideration by general Washington, and soon there was established between them that warm friendship which subsisted until the death of the American general.

The American army was at this time strong in number; it amounted, including, however, the militia, little accustomed to regular battle, to fifteen thousand men. It was full of confidence in its chiefs; and animated by their example and exhortations. The news was then received that the British fleet was in sight of Cape May, at the mouth of the Delaware, steering eastward. Washington immediately conceived some alarm for the banks of the Hudson, which he had always watched with care from the commencement of the war. He ordered the troops that were to come from Peek's Kill to join him in New Jersey, not to move; and those who were already on the march, to halt in their positions.

The seventh of August, the British squadron was perceived anew at the entrance of the Delaware; but it disappeared a little after, and was not heard of again for several days. The commander-in-chief could not penetrate the design of the enemy; still in doubt, he continued stationary, not knowing where the tempest was to strike. But after a certain lapse of time, even the length of delay led him to suspect that the views of Howe were by no means directed towards the Hudson; for the winds having prevailed for a long time from the south, if such had been his intention, he would already have been arrived at the destined spot. Washington was therefore inclined to believe that the English meditated an expedition against some part of the southern provinces. He felt indeed some solicitude for the bay of Chesapeake; but, as it was at no great distance from the mouths of the Delaware, the enemy ought already to have made his appearance there. Upon these considerations, he more feared for the safety of Charleston, South Carolina; but even if so, he was unable to arrive in time to the relief of that city. Besides, that country was naturally unhealthy, and especially at the present season.

There was also danger that Howe might re-embark his troops, and make a sudden push against Philadelphia, which, in the absence of the army, must inevitably fall into his power. It therefore appeared much more prudent to maintain a position which admitted of watching over Pennsylvania, and to leave the Carolinas with their own means only to defend themselves as well as they could against the invasions of the enemy.   But in order to compensate the losses which might perhaps ensue in that quarter, Washington resolved to march with all his troops towards the Hudson, to be ready to turn his arms according to circumstances, either against Burgoyne towards Fort Edward, or against Clinton towards New York, then divested of the greater part of its defenders.

He had scarcely formed this determination, when he was informed that the enemy had appeared with all his forces in the Chesapeake. This intelligence put an end to all his uncertainties, and he then saw distinctly the course he had to pursue.   He dispatched orders to all the detached corps to join him by forced marches in the environs of Philadelphia, for the purpose of proceeding thence, to the head of the Chesapeake.   The militia of Pennsylvania, Maryland, Delaware, and the northern parts of Virginia, were ordered to take arms and repair to the principal army.

While these preparations were making on the part of the Americans, the English fleet entered with full sails into the Chesapeake bay, and profiting of a favorable wind, proceeded as far up as the point called Elk Head.   From the time of its departure from Sandy Hook, this squadron had experienced the most contrary winds, and had been more than a week in doubling the capes of Delaware.   The English generals were there informed that the Americans had so effectually obstructed the navigation of that river, that it would be equally dangerous and fruitless to attempt the passage up to Philadelphia.

Though some persons maintain that they might easily have disembarked at Wilmington, whence there was an excellent road leading directly to that city.   However this was, they preferred to proceed further south, and to sail up the Chesapeake bay as far as that part of Maryland which borders on Pennsylvania, and is at no great distance from Philadelphia.   But in the passage from the Delaware to the Chesapeake, the winds were so constantly unfavorable that they could not enter the bay till towards the last of August.   This delay was excessively prejudicial to the English army ; the troops being crowded into the vessels along with the horses and all the baggage, in the midst of the hottest season of the year.   The health of the soldiers would have suffered still more, if the generals had not taken the precaution to put on board a large stock of fresh provisions and a copious supply of water.   The sea became more propitious in the Chesapeake, and the squadron soon gained the coasts of Maryland.

Thus the two armies advanced, each towards the other, amidst the anxious expectation of the American people.

About this time an expedition was undertaken by general Sullivan, against Staten Island, the commencement of which had created hopes of a more happy termination. He landed without opposition, and took many prisoners, but was afterwards repulsed with heavy loss. He then rapidly retired towards Philadelphia. On the twenty-fifth of August, the British army, eighteen thousand strong, was disembarked not far from the head of the river Elk. It was plentifully furnished with all the equipage of war, excepting the defect of horses, as well for the cavalry as for the baggage. The scarcity of forage had caused many of them to perish the preceding winter, and a considerable number had died also in the late passage.

This was a serious disadvantage for the royal troops; who, in the vast plains of Pennsylvania, might have employed cavalry with singular effect. On the twenty-seventh, the English vanguard arrived at the head of the Elk, and the day following at Gray's Hill. Here it was afterwards joined by the rear guard under general Knyphausen, who had been left upon the coast to cover the debarkation of the stores and artillery.

The whole army took post behind the river Christiana, having Newark upon the right, and Pencada or Atkins on the left. A column commanded by lord Cornwallis, having fallen in with Maxwell's riflemen, routed and pursued them as far as the further side of White Clay Creek, with the loss of some dead and wounded.

The American army, in order to encourage the partisans of independence and overawe the disaffected, marched through the city of Philadelphia; it afterwards advanced towards the enemy, and encamped behind White Clay Creek. A little after, leaving only the riflemen in the camp, Washington retired with the main body of his army behind the Red Clay Creek, occupying with his right wing the town of Newport, situated near the Christiana, and upon the great road to Philadelphia; his left was at Hockesen. But this line was little capable of defense.

The enemy, re-inforced by the rear guard under general Grant, threatened with his right the center of the Americans, extended his left as if with the intention of turning their right flank. Washington saw the danger, and retired with his troops behind the Brandywine; he encamped on the rising grounds which extend from Chadsford, in the direction of northwest to southeast. The riflemen of Maxwell scoured the right bank of the Brandywine, in order to harass and retard the enemy. The militia under the command of general Armstrong, guarded a passage below the principal encampment of Washington, and the right wing lined the banks of the river higher up, where the passages were most difficult. The passage of Chadsford, as the most practicable of all, was defended by the chief force of the army. The troops being thus disposed, the American general waited the approach of the English. Although the Brandywine, being fordable almost every where, could not serve as a sufficient defense against the impetuosity of the enemy, yet Washington had taken post upon its banks, from a conviction that a battle was now inevitable, and that Philadelphia could only be saved by a victory. General Howe displayed the front of his army, but not, however, without great circumspection. Being arrived at Kennen Square, a short distance from the river, he detached his light horse to the right upon Wilmington, to the left upon the Lancaster road, and in front towards Chadsford. The two armies found themselves within seven miles of each other, the Brandywine flowing between them.

Early in the morning of the eleventh of September, the British army marched to the enemy. Howe had formed his army in two columns; the right commanded by general Knyphausen, the left by lord Cornwallis. His plan was, that while the first should make repeated feints to attempt the passage of Chadsford, in order to occupy the attention of the republicans, the second should take a long circuit to the upper part of the river, and cross at a place where it is divided into two shallow streams. The English marksmen fell in with those of Maxwell, and a smart skirmish was immediately engaged. The latter were at first repulsed; but being re-inforced from the camp, they compelled the English to retire in their turn. But at length, they also were re-inforced, and Maxwell was constrained to withdraw his detachment behind the river. Meanwhile, Knyphausen advanced with his column, and commenced a furious cannonade upon the passage of Chadsford, making all his dispositions as if he intended to force it. The Americans defended themselves with gallantry, and even passed several detachments of light troops to the other side, in order to harass the enemy's flanks. But after a course of skirmishes, sometimes advancing, and at others obliged to retire, they were finally, with an eager pursuit, driven over the river. Knyphausen then appeared more than ever determined to pass the ford; he stormed, and kept up an incredible noise. In this manner the attention of the Americans was fully occupied in the neighborhood of Chadsford. Meanwhile, lord Cornwallis, at the head of the second column, took a circuitous march to the left, and gained unperceived the forks of the Brandywine. By this rapid movement, he passed both branches of the river at Trimble's and at Jeffery's Fords, without opposition, about two o'clock in the afternoon, and then turning short down the river, took the road to Dilworth, in order to fall upon the right flank of the American army. The republican general, however, received intelligence of this movement about noon, and, as it usually happens in similar cases, the reports exaggerated its importance exceedingly; it being represented that general Howe commanded this division in person. Washington therefore decided immediately for the most judicious, though boldest measure; this was to pass the river with the center and left wing of his army, and overwhelm Knyphausen by the most furious attack. He justly reflected that the advantage he should obtain upon the enemy's right, would amply compensate the loss that his own might sustain at the same time. Accordingly, he ordered general Sullivan to pass the Brandywine with his division at an upper ford, and attack the left of Knyphausen, while he, in person, should cross lower down, and fall upon the right of that general.

They were both already in motion in order to execute this design, when a second report arrived, which represented what had really taken place as false, or in other words, that the enemy had not crossed the two branches of the river, and that he had not made his appearance upon the right flank of the American troops. Deceived by this false intelligence, Washington desisted; and Greene, who had already passed with the vanguard, was ordered back. In the midst of these uncertainties, the commander-in-chief at length received the positive assurance, not only that the English had appeared upon the left bank, but also that they were about to fall in great force upon the right wing. It was composed of the brigades of generals Stephens, Sterling, and Sullivan; the first was the most advanced, and consequently the nearest to the English; the two others were posted in the order of their rank, that of Sullivan being next to the center. This general was immediately detached from the main body, to support the two former brigades, and, being the senior officer, took the command of the whole wing. Washington himself, followed by general Greene, approached with two strong divisions towards this wing, and posted himself between it and the corps he had left at Chadsford, under general Wayne, to oppose the passage of Knyphausen. These two divisions, under the immediate orders of the commander-in-chief, served as a corps of reserve, ready to march, according to circumstances, to the succor of Sullivan or of Wayne.

But the column of Cornwallis was already in sight of the Americans. Sullivan drew up his troops on the commanding ground above Birmingham meeting-house, with his left extending towards the Brandywine, and both his flanks covered with very thick woods. His artillery was advantageously planted upon the neighboring hills;

but it appears that Sullivan's own brigade, having taken a long circuit, arrived too late upon the field of battle, and had not yet occupied the position assigned it, when the action commenced. The English, having reconnoitered the dispositions of the Americans, immediately formed, and fell upon them with the utmost impetuosity. The engagement became equally fierce on both sides about four o'clock in the afternoon. For some length of time the Americans defended themselves with great valor, and the carnage was terrible. But such was the emulation which invigorated the efforts of the English and Hessians, that neither the advantages of situation, nor a heavy and well supported fire of small arms and artillery, nor the unshaken courage of the Americans, were able to resist their impetuosity. The light infantry, chasseurs, grenadiers, and guards, threw themselves with such fury into the midst of the republican battalions, that they were forced to give way. Their left flank was first thrown into confusion, but the rout soon became general. The vanquished fled into the woods in their rear; the victors pursued, and advanced by the great road towards Dilworth. On the first fire of the artillery, Washington, having no doubt of what was passing, had pushed forward the reserve to the succor of Sullivan. But this corps, on approaching the field of battle, fell in with the flying soldiers of Sullivan, and perceived that no hope remained of retrieving the fortune of the day. General Greene, by a judicious maneuver, opened his ranks to receive the fugitives, and after their passage, having closed them anew, he retired in good order; checking the pursuit of the enemy by a continual fire of the artillery which covered his rear. Having come to a defile, covered on both sides with woods, he drew up his men there, and again faced the enemy. His corps was composed of Virginians and Pennsylvanians; they defended themselves with gallantry; the former, especially, commanded by colonel Stephens, made an heroic stand.

Knyphausen, finding the Americans to be fully engaged on their right, and observing that the corps opposed to him at Chadsford was enfeebled by the troops which had been detached to the succor of Sullivan, began to make dispositions for crossing the river in reality. The passage of Chadsford was defended by an intrenchment and battery. The republicans stood firm at first; but upon intelligence of the defeat of their right, and seeing some of the British troops who had penetrated through the woods, come out upon their flank, they retired in disorder, abandoning their artillery and munitions to the German general. In their retreat, or rather flight, they passed behind the position of general Greene, who still defended himself, and was the last to quit the field of battle. Finally, it being already dark, after a long and obstinate conflict, he also retired. The whole army retreated that night to Chester, and the day following to Philadelphia.

There the fugitives arrived incessantly, having effected their escape through by-ways and circuitous routes. The victors passed the night on the field of battle. If darkness had not arrived seasonably, it is very probable that the whole American army would have been destroyed. The loss of the republicans was computed at about three hundred killed, six hundred wounded, and near four hundred taken prisoners. They also lost ten field pieces and a howitzer. The loss in the royal army was not in proportion, being something under five hundred, of which the slain did not amount to one fifth.

The French officers were of great utility to the Americans, as well in forming the troops, as in rallying them when thrown into confusion. One of them, the baron St. Ovary, was made a prisoner, to the great regret of congress, who bore him a particular esteem. Captain de Flury had a horse killed under him in the hottest of the action. The congress gave him another a few days after. The marquis de la Fayette, while he was endeavoring, by his words and example, to rally the fugitives, was wounded in the leg. He continued, nevertheless, to fulfil his duty both as a soldier in fighting, and as a general, in cheering the troops and re-establishing order. The count Pulaski, a noble Pole, also displayed an undaunted courage, at the head of the light horse. The congress manifested their sense of his merit by giving him, shortly after, the rank of brigadier and the command of the cavalry.

If all the American troops in the action of the Brandywine had fought with the same intrepidity as the Virginians and Pennsylvanians, and especially if Washington had not been led into error by a false report, perhaps, notwithstanding the inferiority of number and the imperfection of arms, he would have gained the victory, or, at least, would have made it more sanguinary to the English. However this might have been, it must be admitted that general Howe's order of battle was excellent; that his movements were executed with as much ability as promptitude ; and that his troops, English as well as German, behaved admirably well.

The day after the battle, towards evening, the English dispatched a detachment of light troops to Wilmington, a place situated at the confluence of the Christiana and the Brandywine. There they took prisoner the governor of the state of Delaware, and seized a considerable quantity of coined money, as well as other property, both public and private, and some papers of importance.

The other towns of lower Pennsylvania followed the fortune of the victorious party; they were all received into the king's obedience.

The congress, far from being discouraged by so heavy a reverse, endeavored, on the contrary, to persuade the people that it was by no means so decisive, but that affairs might soon resume a favorable aspect. They gave out, that though the English had remained in possession of the field of battle, yet their victory was far from being complete, since their loss was not less, and perhaps greater, than that of the Americans. They affirmed, that although their army was in part dispersed, still it was safe; and, in a few days, would be rallied, and in a condition to meet the enemy. Finally, that bold demonstrations might inspire that confidence which, perhaps, words alone would not have produced, the congress appeared to have no idea of quitting Philadelphia. They ordered that fifteen hundred regulars should be marched to that city from Peek's Kill; that the militia of New Jersey, with those of Philadelphia, the brigade of general Smallwood, and a regiment of the line, then at Alexandria, should proceed with all possible dispatch to re-inforce the principal army in Pennsylvania. They empowered general Washington to impress all wagons, horses, provisions, and other articles necessary for the use of the army, on giving certificates to the owners, who were to be satisfied from the continental treasury. The commander-in-chief exerted himself to inspire his troops with fresh courage; he persuaded them that they had not shown themselves at all inferior to their adversaries; and that at another time they might decide in their favor what was left in doubt at the Brandywine. He gave them a day for refreshment, in the environs of Germantown; but took care to send out the lightest and freshest corps upon the right bank of the Schuylkill, as far as Chester, in order to watch the motions of the enemy, to repress his excursions, and at the same time to collect the dispersed and straggling Americans. As to himself, he repaired to Philadelphia, where he had frequent conferences with the congress, in order to concert with them the measures to be pursued for the re-establishment of affairs. But the fifteenth he returned to camp, and repassing, with all his forces, from the left to the right bank of the Schuylkill, proceeded on the Lancaster road as far as the Warren tavern, with the intention of risking another engagement. Conjecturing that the enemy must be much incumbered with their sick and wounded, he ordered Smallwood to hang with his light troops on their flank or rear, as occasion might require, and do them all the harm he could. At the same time, the bridge over the Schuylkill was ordered to be loosened from its moorings, to swing on the Philadelphia side; and general Armstrong, with the Pennsylvania militia, was directed to guard the passes over that river, for the defense of which M. de Portail, chief of engineers, constructed such sudden works as might be of immediate use.

General Howe, having passed the night of the eleventh on the field of battle, sent the following day a strong detachment to Concord, commanded by general Grant, who was joined afterwards by lord Cornwallis. They marched together towards Chester, upon the bank of the Delaware, as if they intended to surprise Philadelphia. Howe, with the main body of his army, advanced to gain the Lancaster road, and had arrived on the sixteenth near Goshen, when he received intelligence that Washington was approaching with all his troops to give him battle, and was already within five miles of Goshen. With great alacrity, both armies immediately prepared for action; the advanced parties had met, when there came up so violent a fall of rain, that the soldiers were forced to cease their fire. The Americans, especially, suffered exceedingly from it in their arms and ammunition. Their gunlocks not being well secured, many of their muskets were rendered unfit for use. Their cartridge-boxes had been so badly constructed as not to protect their powder from the severity of the tempest.

These circumstances compelled Washington to defer the engagement. He therefore recrossed the Schuylkill at Parker's Ferry, and encamped upon the eastern bank of that river, on both sides of Perkyomy Creek. But as this retreat left general Smallwood too much exposed to be surrounded by the enemy, general Wayne, with his division, was detached to the rear of the British, with orders to join him; and carefully concealing himself and his movements, to seize every occasion which their march might offer, of engaging them to advantage.

The extreme severity of the weather entirely stopped the British army, and prevented any pursuit. They made no other movement than merely to unite their columns, and then took post at Tryduffin, whence they detached a party to seize a magazine of flour and other stores, which the republicans had deposited at Valley Forge. Howe discovered by his spies, that general Wayne, with fifteen hundred men, was lying in the woods in the rear, and not far from the left wing of his army. Suspecting some scheme of enterprise, he determined to avert the stroke, by causing Wayne to experience the check he destined for him. Accordingly, in the night of the thirteenth, he detached general Grey, with two regiments and a body of light infantry, to surprise the enemy. That general conducted the enterprise with great prudence and activity. Stealing his way through the woods, he arrived undiscovered, about one in the morning, before the encampment of Wayne. Having forced his pickets without noise, the British detachment, guided by the light of their fires, rushed in upon the enemy, torpid with sleep and chilled with terror. In the midst of this obscurity and confusion, a shocking slaughter was executed with bayonets. The Americans lost many of their men, with their baggage, arms, and stores. The whole corps must have been cut off, if Wayne had not preserved his coolness; he promptly rallied a few regiments, who withstood the shock of the enemy, and covered the retreat of the others. The loss of the English was very inconsiderable. When this attack commenced, general Smallwood, who was coming up to join Wayne, was already within a mile of the field of battle; and, had he commanded troops who were to be relied on, might have given a very different turn to the night. But his militia, who were excessively alarmed, thought only of their own safety; and having fallen in with a party returning from the pursuit of Wayne, they instantly fled in confusion.

Having thus secured his rear, the British general resolved to bring the Americans to action, or to press them so far from Philadelphia as should enable him to push suddenly across the Schuylkill, and turn without danger to his right, in order to take possession of that city. To this end he made such movements upon the western bank, as to give the enemy jealousy that he intended to cross higher up, where the river was more shallow, and after turning his right flank, to seize the extensive magazines of provisions and military stores, which had been established at Reading. In order to oppose so great a mischief, Washington retired with his army up the river, and encamped at Potts Grove. Howe, on intelligence of this change of the enemy's position, immediately crossed the Schuylkill without opposition; a part of his troops being passed at Gordon's Ford, and the rest lower down at Flatland Ford. On the night of the twenty-third, the whole British army encamped upon the left bank; thus finding itself between the army of Washington and the city of Philadelphia.

It was now self-evident that nothing could save that city from the grasp of the English, unless the American general chose to risk a battle for its rescue.

But Washington, more guided by prudence than by the wishes and clamors of the multitude, abstained from resorting to that fatal experiment. He deemed it a measure of blind temerity to commit the fate of America to the uncertain issue of a general engagement. He daily expected the arrival of the remaining troops of Wayne and Smallwood, the continental troops of Peek's Kill and the provincial militia of New Jersey, under the command of general Dickinson. The soldiers were less fatigued than worn down by continual marches, bad roads, want of food, and sufferings of every denomination. A council of war being assembled, and the condition of the army considered, it was unanimously decided to remain on the present ground, until the expected re-inforcements should arrive, and to allow the harassed troops a few days for repose.

Washington resolved to proceed in every point with extreme circumspection, holding himself ready to seize the occasions which Heaven might offer him for the glory of its own cause, and for the good of the republic. Philadelphia was therefore abandoned as a prey which could not escape the enemy.

When it was known in that city that the violent rain which fell on the sixteenth, had prevented the two armies from coming to action, and that Washington had been constrained to retire behind the Schuylkill, congress adjourned itself to the twenty-seventh, at Lancaster. At the same time, the public magazines and archives were evacuated with all diligence; the vessels lying at the wharves were removed up the Delaware. About twenty individuals were taken into custody, the greater part of them Quakers, avowed enemies to the state; having positively refused to give any security in writing, or even verbal attestation, of submission or allegiance to the present government. They were sent off to Staunton, in Virginia, as a place of security.

With unshaken confidence in the virtue of Washington, as a sufficient pledge for the hope of the republic, the congress invested him with the same dictatorial powers that were conceded him after the reverses of New Jersey. At length, the rumor of the approach of the English increasing from hour to hour, they left the city. Lord Cornwallis entered Philadelphia the twenty-sixth of September, at the head of a detachment of British and Hessian grenadiers. The rest of the army remained in the camp of Germantown. Thus the rich and populous capital of the whole confederation fell into the power of the royalists, after a sanguinary battle, and a series of maneuvers, no less masterly than painful, of the two armies. The Quakers, and all the other loyalists who had remained there, welcomed the English with transports of gratulation. Washington, descending along the left bank of the Schuylkill, approached within sixteen miles of Germantown. He encamped at Skippach Creek, purposing to accommodate his measures to the state of things

The loss of Philadelphia did not produce among the Americans a particle of that discouragement which the English had flattered themselves would be the consequence of this event. The latter, on finding themselves masters of that city, erected batteries upon the Delaware, in order to command the whole breadth of the river, prevent any sudden attack by water, and interdict to the republicans all navigation between its upper and lower parts. While they were engaged in these works, the Americans, with the frigate Delaware anchored within five hundred yards of the unfinished batteries, and with some smaller vessels, commenced a very heavy cannonade both upon the batteries and the town. They did not, however, display the judgment which their knowledge of the river might be supposed to afford ; for upon the falling of the tide, the Delaware grounded so effectually that she could not be got off, which being perceived by the English, they brought their cannon to play upon her with so much effect that she was soon obliged to strike her colors. The same fire compelled the other vessels to retire up the river, with the loss of a schooner which was driven ashore.

The Americans, under the apprehension of what afterwards happened, that is, of not being able to preserve Philadelphia, had, with great labor and expense, constructed all manner of works to interrupt the navigation of the river, in order to prevent the British fleet from communicating with the troops that might occupy the city. They knew that the army of Washington, when it should have received its re-inforcements, would soon be in a condition to take the field anew, and to cut off the enemy's supplies on the side of Pennsylvania ; if, therefore, unable to procure them by water, the English must in a short time be compelled to evacuate the city. Pursuant to this reasoning, the Americans had erected works and batteries upon a flat, low, marshy island, or rather a bank of mud and sand which had been accumulated in the Delaware near the junction of the Schuylkill, and which from its nature was called Mud, but from these defenses, Fort Island. On the opposite shore of New Jersey, at a place called Red Bank, they had also constructed a fort or redoubt, well covered with heavy artillery. In the deep navigable channel between or under the cover of these batteries they had sunk several ranges of frames or machines, the construction of which we have already described in a foregoing book. About three miles lower down, they had sunk other ranges of these machines, and were constructing for their protection some considerable and extensive works, which, though not yet finished, were in such forwardness, as to be provided with artillery, and to command their object, at a place on the Jersey side, called Billings Point. These works and machines were further supported by several galleys, mounting heavy cannon, together with two floating batteries, a number of armed vessels, and small craft of various kinds, and some fire-ships.

The English well knew the importance of opening for themselves a free communication with the sea, by means of the Delaware ; since their operations could never be considered secure, so long as the enemy should maintain positions upon the banks of that river ; and accordingly they deliberated upon the means of reducing them. Immediately after the success of the Brandywine, lord Howe, who commanded the whole fleet, had made sail for the mouth of the Delaware, and several light vessels had already arrived in that river, among others the Roebuck, commanded by captain Hammond. That officer represented to general Howe, that if sufficient forces were sent to attack the fort at Billings Point, on the Jersey shore, it might be taken without difficulty ; and that he would then take upon himself to open a passage for the vessels through the chevaux-de-frize. The general approved this project, and detached two regiment under colonel Stirling, to carry it into effect. The detachment, having crossed the river from Chester, the moment they had set foot upon the Jersey shore, marched with all speed to attack the fort in rear.

The Americans, not thinking themselves able to sustain the enemy's assault, immediately spiked their artillery, set fire to the barracks, and abandoned the place with precipitation. The English waited to destroy or to render unserviceable those parts of the works which fronted the river, and this success, with the spirit and perseverance exhibited by the officers and crews of the ships under his command, enabled Hammond, through great difficulties, to carry the principal object of the expedition into effect, by cutting away and weighing up so much of the chevaux-de-frize as opened a narrow passage for the shipping through this lower barrier.

The two regiments of Stirling returned, after their expedition, to Chester, whither another had been sent to meet them, in order that they might all together form a sufficient escort for a large convoy of provisions to the camp.

Washington, who had not left his position at Skippach Creek being informed that three regiments had been thus detached, and knowing that lord Cornwallis lay at Philadelphia with four battalions of grenadiers, perceived that the army of Howe must be sensibly weakened. He determined, therefore, to avail himself of this favorable circumstance, and to fall unexpectedly upon the British army encamped at Germantown.

He took this resolution with the more confidence, as he was now re-inforced by the junction of the troops from Peek's Kill and the Maryland militia.

Germantown is a considerable village, about half a dozen miles from Philadelphia, and which, stretching on both sides of the great road to the northward, forms a continued street of two miles in length. The British line of encampment crossed Germantown at right angles about the center, the left wing extending on the west, from the town to the Schuylkill. That wing was covered in front by the mounted and dismounted German chasseurs, who were stationed a little above towards the American camp; a battalion of light infantry and the Queen's American rangers were in the front of the right. The center, being posted within the town, was guarded by the fortieth regiment, and another battalion of light infantry stationed about three quarters of a mile above the head of the village. Washington resolved to attack the British by surprise, not doubting that, if he succeeded in breaking them, as they were not only distant, but totally separated from the fleet, his victory must be decisive

He so disposed his troops, that the divisions of Sullivan and Wayne, flanked by Conway's brigade, were to march down the main road, and entering the town by the way of Chesnut Hill, to attack the English center, and the right flank of their left wing; the divisions of Greene and Stephens, flanked by Macdougall's brigade, were to take a circuit towards the east, by the Limekiln road, and entering the town at the market-house, to attack the left flank of the right wing. The intention of the American general in seizing the village of Germantown by a double attack, was effectually to separate the right and left wings of the royal army, which must have given him a certain victory. In order that the left flank of the left wing might not contract itself, and support the right flank of the same wing, general Armstrong, with the Pennsylvania militia, was ordered to march down the bridge road upon the banks of the Schuylkill, and endeavor to turn the English, if they should retire from that river. In like manner, to prevent the right flank of the right wing from going to the succor of the left flank, which rested upon Germantown, the militia of Maryland and Jersey, under generals Smallwood and Forman, were to march down the Old York road, and to fall upon the English on that extremity of their wing. The division of lord Sterling, and the brigades of generals Nash and Maxwell, formed the reserve. These dispositions being made, Washington quitted his camp at Skippach Creek, and moved towards the enemy, on the third of October, about seven in the evening. Parties of cavalry silently scoured all the roads, to seize any individual who might have given notice to the British general of the danger that threatened him. Washington in person accompanied the column of Sullivan and Wayne. The march was rapid and silent.

At three o'clock in the morning, the British patroles discovered the approach of the Americans; the troops were soon called to arms; each took his post with the precipitation of surprise. About sunrise the Americans came up. General Conway, having driven in the pickets, fell upon the fortieth regiment and the battalion of light infantry. These corps, after a short resistance, being overpowered by numbers, were pressed and pursued into the village. Fortune appeared already to have declared herself in favor of the Americans; and certainly if they had gained complete possession of Germantown, nothing could have frustrated them of the most signal victory. But in this conjuncture, lieutenant-colonel Musgrave threw himself, with six companies of the fortieth regiment, into a large and strong stone house, situated near the head of the village, from which he poured upon the assailants so terrible a fire of musketry that they could advance no further. The Americans attempted to storm this unexpected covert of the enemy, but those within continued to defend themselves with resolution. They finally brought cannon up to the assault, but such was the intrepidity of the English, and the violence of their fire, that it was found impossible to dislodge them. During this time, general Greene had approached the right wing, and routed, after a slight engagement, the light infantry and Queen's rangers. Afterwards, turning a little to his right, and towards Germantown, he fell upon the left flank of the enemy's right wing, and endeavored to enter the village. Meanwhile, he expected that the Pennsylvania militia, under Armstrong, upon the right, and the militia of Maryland and Jersey, commanded by Smallwood and Forman on the left, would have executed the orders of the commander-in-chief, by attacking and turning, the first the left, and the second the right, flank of the British army. But either because the obstacles they encountered had retarded them, or that they wanted ardor, the former arrived in sight of the German chasseurs, and did not attack them; the latter appeared too late upon the field of battle.

The consequence was, that general Grey, finding his left flank secure, marched, with nearly the whole of the left wing, to the assistance of the center, which, notwithstanding the unexpected resistance of colonel Musgrave, was excessively hard pressed in Germantown, where the Americans gained ground incessantly. The battle was now very warm at that village, the attack and the defense being equally vigorous. The issue appeared for some time dubious. General Agnew was mortally wounded, while charging with great bravery, at the head of the fourth brigade. The American colonel Matthews, of the column of Greene, assailed the English with so much fury that he drove them before him into the town. He had taken a large number of prisoners, and was about entering the village, when he perceived that a thick fog and the unevenness of the ground had caused him to lose sight of the rest of his division. Being soon enveloped by the extremity of the right wing, which fell back upon him when it had discovered that nothing was to be apprehended from the tardy approach of the militia of Maryland and Jersey, he was compelled to surrender with all his party; the English had already rescued their prisoners. This check was the cause that two regiments of the English right wing were enabled to throw themselves into Germantown, and to attack the Americans who had entered it in flank. Unable to sustain the shock, they retired precipitately, leaving a great number of killed and wounded. Lieutenant-colonel Musgrave, to whom belongs the principal honor of this affair, was then relieved from all peril. General Grey, being absolute master of Germantown, flew to the succor of the right wing, which was engaged with the left of the column of Greene. The Americans then took to flight, abandoning to the English, throughout the line, a victory of which, in the commencement of the action, they had felt assured.

The principal causes of the failure of this well concerted enterprise, were the extreme haziness of the weather; which was so thick, that the Americans could neither discover the situation nor movements of the British army, nor yet those of their own; the inequality of the ground, which incessantly broke the ranks of their battalions; an inconvenience more serious and difficult to be repaired for new and inexperienced troops, as were most of the Americans, than for the English veterans; and, finally, the unexpected resistance of Musgrave, who found means, in a critical moment, to transform a mere house into an impregnable fortress.

Thus fortune, who at first had appeared disposed to favor one party, suddenly declared herself on the side of their adversaries. Lord Cornwallis, being at Philadelphia, upon intelligence of the attack upon the camp, flew to its succor with a corps of cavalry and the grenadiers; but when he reached the field of battle, the Americans had already left it. They had two hundred men killed in this action; the number of wounded amounted to six hundred; and about four hundred were made prisoners. One of their most lamented losses was that of general Nash, of North Carolina. The loss of the British was little over five hundred in killed and wounded; among the former were brigadier-general Agnew, an officer of rare merit, and colonel Bird. The American army saved all its artillery, and retreated the same day about twenty miles, to Perkyomy Creek.

The congress expressed in decided terms their approbation, both of the plan of this enterprise and the courage with which it was executed; for which their thanks were given to the general and the army. General Stephens, however, was cashiered for misconduct on the retreat.

A few days after the battle, the royal army removed from Germantown to Philadelphia. The want of provisions would not have permitted Howe to follow the enemy into his fastnesses, and he was desirous of co-operating with the naval force in opening the navigation of the Delaware. Washington, having received a small reinforcement of fifteen hundred militia, and a state regiment from Virginia, again advanced a few miles towards the English, and encamped once more at Skippach Creek. Thus, the British general might have seen that he had to grapple with an adversary, who, far from allowing himself to be discouraged by adverse fortune, seemed, on the contrary, to gain by it more formidable energies ; who, the moment after defeat, was prepared to resume the offensive ; and whose firmness and activity were such, that even the victories obtained by his adversaries only yielded them the effects of defeat. Nor was the taking of Philadelphia attended with those advantages which were expected from it.

The inhabitants of the country were not in the least intimidated by that event ; and the victorious army, surrounded on all sides by enemies, found itself, as it were, immured within the precincts of the city. Washington, posted on the heights of the Schuylkill, maintained a menacing attitude ; he employed his cavalry and light troops in scouring the country between the banks of that river and those of the Delaware. He thus repressed the excursions of the English, prevented them from foraging with safety, and deterred the disaffected or the avaricious among the people of the country from conveying provisions to their camp. Moreover, the congress passed a resolution, subjecting to martial law and to death all those who should furnish the royal troops with provisions, or any other aids whatsoever.

Compelled to relinquish the hope of supporting his army from the adjacent country, the British general now applied himself with diligence to the task of removing the obstructions of the Delaware, and opening a free communication with the fleet. The enterprise presented difficulties and dangers of no ordinary magnitude. To succeed in this operation, it was necessary to seize Mud Island, which was defended by Fort Mifflin, and the point of Red Bank, where the Americans had erected Fort Mercer. After the reduction of these two fortresses, the upper chevaux-de-frize might be destroyed.

General Howe, therefore, resolved to attack them both at the same time, in concert with those ships which had been able to pass the lower barrier. Batteries of heavy artillery had been erected on the Pennsylvania side, in front of Mud Island, to assist in dislodging the enemy from that position. The garrison of Fort Mifflin was commanded by colonel Smith, and that of Fort Mercer by colonel Greene, both officers in great esteem among the Americans.

General Howe had arranged for the attack of Fort Mifflin, that while the batteries on the western shore should open their fire upon its right flank, the Vigilant ship of war, passing up the narrow channel which separates Hog Island from the Pennsylvania shore, should cannonade it in the rear, and the frigates, with the ships Isis and Augusta in front, approaching it by the middle channel, which is considerably wider and deeper. As to Fort Mercer, it was also to be attacked in the rear, on the side of New Jersey, by landing troops on the left bank of the Delaware.

According to these dispositions, the English put themselves in motion on the evening of the twenty-first of October. Colonel Donop, a German officer, who had distinguished himself in the course of this campaign, passed the Delaware from Philadelphia, with a strong detachment of Hessians, at Cooper's Ferry. Then marching down upon the Jersey shore, along the bank of the river, he arrived, at a late hour the following day, in the rear of Red Bank. The fortifications consisted of extensive outer works, within which was a strong palisaded intrenchment, well furnished with artillery. Donop attacked the fort with the utmost gallantry. The Americans, after a slight resistance in the outer intrenchment, finding their number too small to man it sufficiently, withdrew into the body of the redoubt, where they made a vigorous defense.

Their intrepidity and the want of scaling ladders baffled all the efforts of the Hessians. Colonel Donop was mortally wounded and taken prisoner. Several of his best officers were killed or disabled; colonel Mingerode himself, the second in command, received a dangerous wound. The Hessians were then severely repulsed; and lieutenant-colonel Linsing drew them off with precipitation; but even in their retreat they suffered extremely by the fire of the enemy's galleys and floating batteries. The loss of the Hessians was estimated at no less than four or five hundred men. Donop expired of his wounds the next day. The Americans owed much of their success to the Chevalier de Plessis, a French officer, who directed the artillery with great ability and valor. The vanquished returned to Philadelphia.

Meanwhile, the ships had advanced, in order to be in readiness to attack Mud Island. After having made their way with difficulty through the lower barrier, the Augusta man of war, several frigates and other smaller vessels, waited above it for the tide; the moment the flood set in, they proceeded towards their destined stations. But a strong northerly wind prevented the Vigilant from taking the post assigned her between Hog Island and the Pennsylvania shore. Moreover, the obstructions which the Americans had sunk in the bed of the river, had, in some degree, altered its natural channel. By this means, the Augusta and Merlin were grounded so fast, at some distance from the chevaux-de-frize, that there was no possibility of getting them off. The frigates, however, reached their stations, and commenced a cannonade upon Fort Mifflin, while the batteries on shore were also opened upon the garrison. The Americans defended themselves with spirit, and night soon put an end to the engagement. Early next morning the English renewed the attack, not that in the present state of things they expected to reduce the fort, but in the hope that, under cover of their fire, the two ships which were grounded might be got off. Notwithstanding their efforts, the Augusta took fire and blew up; the Merlin, which could not be removed, was hastily evacuated and laid in a train of destruction. The frigates, despairing of success, and fearing the effect of the explosion, retired with the utmost expedition. The congress voted their thanks and a sword to colonels Greene and Smith, for having so gallantly defended the two forts.

The ill success of these two attacks did not, however, discourage the British commanders; and such was the importance of opening the navigation of the Delaware, as well to secure the arrival of stores and supplies, as to obtain a free communication with the fleet, that they resolved to leave no means unessayed for the attainment of this object.

Fort Mifflin was placed at the lower end of Mud Island, having its principal fortifications in front, for the purpose of repelling ships coming up the river. At the opposite extremity, no attack being expected, as the naval means of the British in Philadelphia were too feeble to excite alarm, the fort was surrounded only by a wet ditch. This part, however, was flanked by a blockhouse at each of its angles, one of which had been much damaged in the late attack. A little above Mud Island is another small morassy island called *Province Island*; this the English had occupied in order to be able to batter Fort Mifflin in its rear, and weakest part. They were incessantly employed in conveying thither heavy artillery, provisions, and stores, by a difficult channel, near the west bank of the river, behind Hog Island. They also erected fortifications, in the most suitable places. The Americans perceived distinctly that when the enemy should have completed his works on this island, their position on Mud Island would no longer be tenable.

Washington would have desired, by a sudden expedition, to dislodge the English from Province Island, but as Howe had thrown a bridge over the Schuylkill, he might, while the Americans were attempting this stroke, have fallen upon their rear and cut off their retreat.   If the American general marched with all his army to cover it, he exposed himself to a general battle, which he wished to avoid. It appeared to him imprudent to put so much at hazard, after the late unfortunate actions.   He felt the greater repugnance to embrace adventurous counsels, as he was already apprised of the successes obtained by the northern army; in consequence of which, a great part of the troops employed against Burgoyne, might be drawn to re-inforce his own.   He abstained, therefore, from undertaking the enterprise against Province Island, hoping, however, that the courage of the defenders of Fort Mifflin, and the succors that might be sent them secretly, would suffice to prolong their resistance.

But every thing being prepared on the side of the English, they executed their attack the fifteenth of November.   All the ships, being arrived at their posts, opened a furious cannonade.   The Americans answered it, at first, with no less vigor from the fort, from the batteries of New Jersey, and from the galleys which were stationed near that shore.   But at length, the works being battered down and the ditches filled up with their ruins, their situation became critical.

They perceived the English were taking measures for storming the body of the fortress the following morning, and being sensible that, in the present state of things, it was not defensible, having sent off their stores, they set fire to every thing that was capable of receiving it, and evacuated the place in the night.   They withdrew to Red Bank.   The next day the English took possession of the fort.

It still remained to dislodge the soldiers of congress from Red Bank, before the obstructions of the Delaware could be entirely removed.   This operation was of absolute necessity; for, although some vessels of easy burden, being loaded with provisions from the country about Chester, where the inhabitants were well affected to the royal cause, brought scanty supplies to Philadelphia, yet the scarcity in that city became daily more distressing; and firewood was almost totally wanting.

In consequence of these considerations, general Howe, having covered Philadelphia by intrenchments, extending from the Delaware to the Schuylkill, and having received some re-inforcements from New York, sent Cornwallis with a strong detachment to the Jersey shore, with instructions to collect provisions, and attack Fort Mercer in the rear.   That general, having crossed from Chester to

Billings Point, prepared to execute the orders he had received. He was there joined by a body of forces just arrived from New York. Washington, upon intelligence of this movement, being earnestly desirous to preserve, if practicable, a position so capable of arresting the progress of the enemy, had ordered major-general Greene, an officer he much esteemed for his talents and intrepidity, to pass, also, at the head of a strong detachment, into New Jersey. A hope was entertained that he would be able, not only to protect Fort Mercer, but to obtain some decisive advantage over lord Cornwallis; as the situation of the fort, which the British general could only invest by placing himself between Timber and Manto Creeks, neither of them fordable for a great distance from the Delaware, would expose the assailants to great peril from a respectable force in their rear. General Greene passed the Delaware, and landed at Burlington. He was accompanied by the marquis de la Fayette who was eager to enter the field again, though not yet well cured of his wound.

This division was to be re-inforced by the troops expected from the banks of the Hudson. The march was commenced; but general Greene, being informed that Cornwallis was become greatly superior to him in number, by the junction of the re-inforcement from New York, abandoned the plan of giving him battle. Hence colonel Greene, who commanded the garrison, losing all hope of succor, and apprised of the approach of Cornwallis, evacuated Fort Mercer, and Red Bank, leaving his artillery, with a considerable quantity of cannon ball and stores, in the power of the royalists. The English dismantled the fort, and demolished all the works.

The American shipping having now lost all protection on either side of the river, several galleys and other armed vessels took the advantage of a favorable night to pass the batteries of Philadelphia, and escape to places of security further up. The English, on perceiving this transaction, sent an officer with a party of seamen to man the Delaware frigate, and took such other measures as rendered the escaping of the remainder impracticable. Thus environed, the crews abandoned and set fire to their vessels, which were all consumed, to the amount of seventeen, of different sorts, including two floating batteries, and four fire ships. The English, having secured, as we have seen, the command of the river, labored to clear it of all the impediments with which the Americans had obstructed its channel. But the difficulties they had to surmount were extreme, and the season was far advanced, it being already the last of November. With all these efforts they could only obtain such an opening through the upper barrier as admitted vessels of easy burden. These were accordingly employed for the transport of provisions and stores to Philadelphia. Although the royalists had thus partly succeeded in re-establishing the navigation of the Delaware, the resistance of the republicans had been so strenuous and so long, that general Howe could find no opportunity for attacking the army of Washington before it was re-inforced by the victorious troops of the Hudson. Acting always with prudence, the British general would never expose himself to the hazard of a battle until he was sure of being able to communicate freely with the fleet of the admiral, his brother, as well on account of supplies, as for the security of retreat in case of misfortune. General Greene had remained in New Jersey. He had already been joined by several corps sent by general Gates to the assistance of the army of Pennsylvania ; among them was that of Morgan's riflemen, become celebrated by a multitude of brilliant exploits Washington was not without hopes that Greene would find occasion to gain some advantage that might counterbalance the losses, which it had been impossible to avoid. But Cornwallis had so fortified himself on Gloucester Point, that he was perfectly secure from any enterprise on the part of general Greene. Washington then became apprehensive that the British general, having accomplished all the objects of his expedition into New Jersey, by the reduction of Fort Mercer, the junction with his re-inforcements, and the expediting of a great quantity of provisions to Philadelphia, might suddenly recross the Delaware, and thus enable Howe, with all his forces, to attack the American army while divided. Greene was therefore ordered to repass the river immediately, and join the principal army at Skippach Creek. Similar considerations determined general Howe to direct the detachment of Cornwallis to rejoin him without delay. Before, however, the two parties evacuated New Jersey, Morgan's rifle corps and some detachments of militia, commanded by the marquis de la Fayette, gallantly attacked and routed a body of Hessians and English grenadiers. After this affair, the marquis, who had till then served as a volunteer, was invested by congress with the command of a division of the army.

Washington had at length been re-inforced by the troops which Gates had sent him ; their march had experienced difficulties and frequent delays. Gates himself had shown much repugnance to put them in motion ; and, besides, they had manifested a mutinous spirit towards their chiefs, declaring that they would not march without money and without clothing. Their officers, however, finally succeeded in persuading them to proceed. This aid was composed of four thousand men of approved courage, and flushed with recent victory : but squalid in their appearance, from fatigues and want of necessaries. After the junction of these troops, Washington advanced within fourteen miles of Philadelphia, to a place called White Marsh, where he encamped in a very strong position, with his right to the Wissahickon Creek, and the front partly covered by Sandy Run. At this time the American army consisted of twelve thousand regulars and something over, with about three thousand militia. Howe had with him but little more than twelve thousand fighting men.

He was ardently desirous, however, of giving battle. Hoping that the late re-inforcements would animate his adversary with the same desire, he marched on the fourth of December towards the enemy, fully determined to make another trial of the fortune of arms. He took post on Chesnut Hill, in front of the enemy's right, at only three miles distance. Some skirmishes happened, in which the royalists generally had the advantage. But Howe, finding that the right of the enemy afforded no opening for an attack, changed his ground before day on the seventh, and took a new position opposite to their center and left, not more than a mile from their lines. He continued to extend upon the enemy's left, as if his intention was to turn it, and attack in the rear. Washington did not shun the battle, but chose to receive it in his lines. According to his invariable plan, he thought, first of all, of the preservation of the army, on which depended the fate of all America. At length, the British general, finding that nothing could provoke or entice him into the field, and that his camp was in every part inaccessible, after a variety of fruitless maneuvers, returned to Philadelphia. The British army suffered greatly in these marches and countermarches, from the severity of the weather, both officers and soldiers being totally destitute of tents and field equipage; this, added to the fatigues of war, had reduced them to a deplorable condition. Upon this account, and considering the steadiness of the enemy in declining to fight without every probability of success, general Howe determined to place his troops in winter quarters at Philadelphia; having first, however, sent out a strong detachment of cavalry, under lord Cornwallis, to make a general forage on the western side of the Schuylkill. Washington, in like manner, resolved to give his troops winter lodgings; but he was undecided where to choose them. He was not willing to leave the country exposed to the depredations of the enemy, and yet he wished to avoid extending his quarters too much, lest they should be forced at different points by sudden attacks.

On the west side of the Schuylkill, about twenty miles from Philadelphia, is a deep and rugged hollow, called *Valley Forge*. Upon the mountainous flanks of this valley, and upon a vast plain which overlooks it, as well as all the adjacent country, Washington finally concluded to establish his army for the winter.

His soldiers were too ill clothed to admit of their being exposed to the inclemency of that season under mere tents ; it was therefore decided that a sufficient number of huts should be erected, to be made of logs, and filled in with mortar, in which they would find a more effectual shelter. The whole army began its march towards Valley Forge ; some soldiers were seen to drop dead with cold ; others, without shoes, had their feet cut by the ice, and left their tracks in blood. After the most painful efforts, the troops at length reached their destined quarters. They immediately set about constructing their habitations, which they erected upon the plan of a regular city. All was movement ; some cut down trees, others fashioned them ; in a short time all the barracks were completed, and the soldiers comfortably lodged. After a severe and sanguinary campaign of four months, the two armies appeared thus to enjoy some repose, sufficiently protected from the rigors of the season. The British general had derived no other fruit from all his victories, and from all his maneuvers, than simply that of having procured excellent winter quarters for his army.

1778. In this alternation of good and ill success, passed the year 1777 for the two belligerent parties in America. If the Americans, in the war of Canada and upon the banks of the Hudson, gave brilliant proofs of no common valor ; if, in their campaign of Pennsylvania, they bore their reverses with an heroic firmness, they exhibited in their quarters of Valley Forge such examples of constancy and resignation, as we should not dare to pronounce ever to have been equaled by other nations, in any age or any country. They had not only to endure the extreme inclemency of the season, but the most distressing destitution of things the most necessary to life. These sufferings of the army originated from several causes, such as the pressure of circumstances, the avarice of the contractors or purchasing commissaries, the adverse dispositions of the inhabitants, and, finally, the little experience of congress itself in affairs relating to public administration, especially in the military department.

Scarcely were the troops established in their encampment of Valley Forge, when, Howe having sent a strong detachment to forage on the islands of the Delaware, and the country about Derby, Washington, in order to oppose it, was inclined to march a considerable part of his army towards that point. But on viewing the state of the magazines, it was discovered, with surprise and alarm, that they contained no more than one day's provision.

In such pressing danger of a total famine, and the entire dissolution of the army, it became necessary not only to relinquish the design of marching against the English, but instantly to detach parties different ways to seize, as in an enemy's country, the provision requisite to satisfy the present wants of the army. Washington was authorized to take this measure by the urgency of the conjuncture, and by the decree of congress, which conferred upon him dictatorial powers. The foragers executed their commissions, and by incredible exertions, and not without exciting the greatest discontent among the country people, victualed the camp for a few days; but soon the same distress was felt anew, and the same resource could not the second time afford relief. Whatever efforts were made, little could be gleaned, as well because the adjacent country was already nearly exhausted, as because the inhabitants were careful to conceal in the woods and swamps, their cattle, and other articles, liable to be taken for the use of the army; they acted thus, either from contrariety of opinion, or from love of gain. They preferred to encounter all the perils of carrying their supplies to Philadelphia, where they were paid for them in ready money, to reserving them for the use of their own soldiers, because, in the latter case, they only received certificates to be discharged at some future time. They much doubted whether they would ever be liquidated, so great was their want of confidence in the stability of the government, and they were not ignorant that some of these bills had been refused payment when fully due.

The commander-in-chief had not neglected to write, in the most pressing terms, to the governors of New England, requesting them to send forward subsistence for the army with all possible expedition, and especially supplies of cattle, which abound in those provinces. The purchasing commissaries had repaired thither, and contracted, particularly in Connecticut, for immense quantities of provisions, well knowing the impossibility of subsisting an army, for any length of time, by compulsory requisitions. But these means were slow in operating the desired relief; and a false measure of congress had nearly frustrated the effect which was expected from the contracts. The victories of Howe, and the gloomy aspect of affairs in Pennsylvania, and, perhaps, more than all, the enormous issues of bills of credit, which the congress, controlled by a fatal necessity, were continually making, had occasioned these bills to fall at that epoch to one fourth of their nominal value, so that one hundred dollars in paper would command no more than twenty-five dollars in specie. The price of articles of the first necessity had advanced nearly in proportion, and the commissaries, in order to conclude their bargains, had been obliged to conform to the current rates.

The congress disapproved of their doings, attributing to the avarice of the citizens what was really the effect of the public distress. According.y, they either annulled the contracts or postponed the execution of them. Not satisfied with this, they passed a resolution which could not appear to have been dictated by an indispensable necessity, since, from its very nature, it could never be carried into effect. They invited the different states of the Union to determine and establish by express laws, not only the price of labor, but also that of all articles of common use in human life. The several states complied with the recommendation of congress, and apprized things by law. The result was, that the citizens secreted their effects, and buyers could find nothing they wanted, either in the public markets or elsewhere.

Famine began to prevail in the camp of Valley Forge; already the most alarming consequences were apprehended. Notwithstanding their admirable patience, the soldiers murmured, and a mutiny appeared inevitable. The congress, at length constrained by the force of things, retraced their steps, and recommended to the several state legislatures the repeal of all laws on the subject of prices.

The contracts of the purchasing commissaries were allowed to take effect. But the difficulty of procuring a sufficient number of wheel carriages still delayed the arrival of the convoys. Washington, to prevent the total dissolution of his army, ordered a general forage in the neighborhood of the camp, under the direction of general Greene. Captains Lee and Mac Lane, officers no less sagacious than active, were charged with a similar commission in the states of Maryland and Delaware; and colonel Tilghman in New Jersey. Each of these executed the orders of the commander-in-chief with equal zeal and effect; they penetrated into the most retired places of concealment, where they found grain and cattle in abundance. Captains Mac Lane and Lee, in particular, discovered large droves in the marshy meadows on the Delaware, ready to be expedited for Philadelphia, which they soon caused to take the direction of Valley Forge. Thus the camp found itself again victualed for the present. It may perhaps appear unaccountable, that the American government should not seasonably have employed those means which might have prevented so urgent a peril. It is, however, certain, that soon after the commencement of hostilities, the congress had appointed colonel Trumbull, a man of excellent abilities, and a zealous patriot, to superintend the purchasing of necessaries for the troops. But from his want of experience, and perhaps of sufficient support on the part of the government, as yet not well consolidated, it had resulted, that the army was often on the point of suffering from the deficiency

of supplies ; hence the plans of the commander-in-chief were frequently frustrated, and the movements of his army embarrassed, to
the loss of many fair opportunities for the most important strokes.

When, afterwards, about the middle of the year 1777, the department of colonel Trumbull began to be administered with more regularity, the congress, believing that the more officers of supply they
had under their control, the better the troops would be served, created two commissaries-general, the one of purchases and the other of
issues. They determined that each of these commissaries-general
should have four deputies, to be appointed by congress, not remova-
ble by the head of the department, and accountable to themselves
only.

They afterwards resolved that the quarter-master-general's department should be executed on the following plan :

' First, the military line, to be styled the quarter-master-general's,
is to include the regulating of marches, encampments and order of
battle. Second, the commissary of forage. Third, the commissary
of horses and wagons. Fourth, the agent for the purchase of tents,
intrenching tools, building of barracks, and for all the smaller supplies of the department.' Colonel Trumbull, dissatisfied with this
multiplicity of departments, and still more with this independence of
the deputies with respect to the head of the department, requested
the congress to appoint him a successor. The congress persisted in
their plan. The old order of things being thus annihilated, and the
new not yet organized, there followed those serious inconveniences
which we have mentioned above.

Congress at length perceived the inevitable preponderancy in
times of war, and especially in new states, of military men and affairs
over civil ; they saw there was no possibility of inducing the generals,
who all disapproved it, to execute their plan for the administration of
the army. It was accordingly abandoned, and general Greene, who
enjoyed the entire confidence of the commander-in-chief, was appointed quarter-master-general, and a very suitable person, named
Wadsworth, commissary-general of purchases; both having power
to appoint and remove their assistants. But these measures were
not adopted till very late ; and before the salutary effects of the new
system could be felt, the army was a prey to such mischiefs and
miseries, as brought the republic to the very brink of destruction.
The distresses of the troops were far from being confined to dearth
of sustenance; the greatest scarcity, or rather a total want of all
other necessaries, was also experienced in the camp. It was utterly
unprovided even of clothing, an article so essential to the health, as
well as to the spirits of the soldiers ; tattered and half naked, they

would sooner have been taken for so many mendicants, than defend· ers of a generous country.

Some few had one shirt, but many only the moiety of one, and the greater part none at all. Many, for want of shoes, walked barefoot on the frozen ground. Few, if any, had blankets for the night. Great numbers sickened ; others, unfitted for service by the cold and their nakedness, were excused by their officers from all military duty, and either remained in their barracks, or were lodged in the houses of the neighboring farmers. Near three thousand men were thus rendered incapable of bearing arms. Congress had neglected no care to provide a remedy for so alarming an evil. They had authorized the commander-in-chief, as we have already said, to seize, wherever he might be, and from any person whatever, all articles of necessity for the army ; and nothing could be more essential than to clothe it. But Washington felt great repugnance to using this power ; as, on the one hand, it exasperated the citizens, and, on the other, it accustomed the soldiers to lay hands on the property of others. The congress considered these scruples unseasonable ; they recommended to the legislatures of each state to enact laws, appointing suitable persons to seize and take for the use of the army, all articles proper for the clothing of soldiers, on condition, however, of paying the proprietors for the articles so taken, at a rate to be fixed by the convention of the committees appointed for this purpose by the several states.

They also created a commissary-general of clothing for the troops, to be assisted by a deputy commissary in each state, as well for the purpose of superintending the compulsory requisitions, as in order, if practicable, to procure all that was necessary by way of contracts. But these measures were slow in producing the desired effect. Many detested the thought of wresting from their fellow citizens what they would not sell voluntarily. There prevailed, besides, at this time, in all the states, a scarcity of cloths, linens, leather, and generally of all the articles that were most wanted. Nevertheless, the deputy commissary of the clothing department in Massachusetts, had succeeded in concluding contracts with several merchants for large quantities of merchandise, at the rate of ten to eighteen per cent. above the current price. Their terms appeared exorbitant to some, and even to the congress, and much was said about the avarice of the merchants. It was, however, just to consider, that the bills they received in payment were already fallen to one fourth of their nominal value ; that the merchandise in question was extremely scarce in the country ; that the price of labor was greatly advanced, and that it was become extremely difficult to make remittance to foreign countries.

Whether it was that these murmurs had piqued the merchants, or that cupidity had really more power over them than the promises of the government, several of those who had entered into contracts refused to furnish, unless they were paid in advance. The congress, being informed of this determination, addressed a letter to the state governments, requesting that the goods should be seized from such as refused to fulfill their contracts, at prices to be fixed by commissioners appointed for that purpose under the state authority. These resolutions of congress, and the letters written to the states by Washington, urging them in the most earnest language to come to the succor of his suffering army, at length produced all the effect that was desired ; yet not so promptly, however, but that the greater part of the winter was already elapsed when the first convoys of clothing arrived at the camp.

To all the miseries of the army already enumerated, must still be added the want of straw. The soldiers, overwhelmed with lassitude, enfeebled by hunger, and benumbed with cold in their service by day and by night, had no other bed in their huts except the bare and humid ground. This cause, joined to the others that have been related, propagated diseases ; the hospitals were as rapidly replenished as death evacuated them ; their administration was no less defective in its organization than that of the camp. The unsuitableness of the buildings in which they had been established, the excessive penury of every kind of furniture, and the multitude of sick that crowded them, had generated an insupportable fetor. The hospital fever broke out in them, and daily swept off the most robust as well as the feeble. It was not possible to remedy it by often changing the linen, for of this they were utterly unprovided ; nor by a more salubrious diet, when the coarsest was scarcely attainable ; nor even by medicines, which were either absolutely wanting, or of the worst quality, and adulterated through the cupidity of the contractors ; for such, in general, has been the nature of these furnishers of armies, that they should rather be denominated the *artisans of scarcity*; they have always preferred money to the life of the soldier. Hence it was, that the American hospital resembled more a receptacle for the dying than a refuge for the sick ; far from restoring health to the diseased, it more often proved mortal to the well. This pestilen tial den was the terror of the army. The soldiers preferred perishing with cold in the open air, to being buried alive in the midst of the dead. Whether it was the effect of inevitable necessity, or of the avarice of men, it is but too certain, that an untimely death carried off a multitude of brave soldiers, who, with better attentions, might have deen preserved for the defense of their country in its distress.

All these d'sorders, so pernicious to 'the republic, took their origin in the causes we have related, and partly also in the military organization itself. The chiefs appeared to acknowledge no system, and the subalterns no restraint of obedience. Horses were allowed to perish in the highways, or to escape into the fields, without search. The roads were incumbered with carts belonging to the army, and unfit for service. Hence it happened, that when the incredible exertions of the government and of good citizens had succeeded in collecting provisions for the army, they could not be conveyed to the camp, and, by long delays, they were again dispersed, or wasted. This defect of carriages was equally prejudicial to the transportation of arms and military stores, which were, in consequence, abandoned to the discretion of those who either plundered them, or suffered them to be plundered. An incalculable quantity of public effects was thus dissipated or destroyed. In the camp of Valley Forge, men were constrained to perform, as they really did, with inconceivable patience, the service of beasts of draught, as well in procuring firewood as in drawing the artillery. And certainly, nothing could be imagined to equal the sufferings which the American army had to undergo in the course of this winter, except the almost superhuman firmness with which they bore them. Not but that a certain number, seduced by the royalists, deserted their colors, and slunk off to the British army in Philadelphia; but these were mostly Europeans, who had entered the continental service. The trueborn Americans, supported by their patriotism, as by their love and veneration for the commander-in-chief, manifested an unshaken perseverance; they chose rather to suffer all the extremes of famine and of frost, than to violate, in this perilous hour, the faith they had pledged to their country. They were encouraged, it is true, by the example of their generals, who, with an air of serenity, took part in all their fatigues, and shared in all their privations. But can it be dissembled, that if general Howe had seen fit to seize the opportunity, and had suddenly attacked the camp at Valley Forge, he would inevitably have gained a complete victory? Without military stores and without provisions, how could the Americans have defended their intrenchments? Besides, to enter the field anew, in the midst of so rigorous a season, was become for them an absolute impossibility. On the first of February, four thousand of their men were incapable of any kind of service, for want of clothing. The condition of the rest was very little better. In a word. out of the seventeen thousand men that were in camp, it would have been difficult to muster five thousand fit for service.

We pretend not to decide what were the motives of the British general for not taking advantage of a conjuncture so favorable. It appears to us, at least, that the extreme regard he had to the preservation of his troops, did but lead him on this occasion to reserve them for greater perils; and his circumspection rather deserves the appellation of timidity than of prudence.

Washington was filled with anguish at the calamities of his army. But nothing gave him more pain than to see his soldiers exposed to the most pernicious example;. the officers openly declared the design of resigning their commissions; many of them had already left the army, and returned to their families. This determination was principally owing to the depreciation of paper money; it was become so considerable, and the price of all articles of consumption, as well for this reason as from the difficulties of commerce, was so prodigiously advanced, that the officers, far from being able to live as it became their rank, had not even the means of providing for their subsistence. Some had already exhausted their private resources to maintain a decent appearance, and others, destitute of patrimonial fortune, had been forced to contract debts, or restrict themselves to a parsimony little worthy of the rank with which they were invested. Hence a disinclination for the service became almost universal. Nor should it be supposed that only the less deserving or worthless desired to resign; for the regiments being incomplete, and the number of officers too great, their retreat would not have been an evil; but it was especially the bravest, the most distinguished, the most spirited, who, disdaining more than others the state of degradation to which they were reduced, were fully resolved to quit the army, in order to escape from it. Alarmed at the progress of the evil, Washington endeavored to resist it, by the use of those remedies which he believed the most suitable; he spared neither promises nor encouragements; he wrote the most pressing letters to the congress, that they might seriously consider the subject, and take the proper measures thereon. He exhorted them, especially, to secure half pay to the officers after the war, either for life or for a definite term. He observed that it was easy to talk of patriotism, and to cite a few examples from ancient history of great enterprises carried by this alone to a successful conclusion; but that those who relied solely upon individual sacrifices for the support of a long and sanguinary war, must not expect to enjoy their illusion long; that it was necessary to take the passions of men as they are, and not as it might be wished to find them; that the love of country had indeed operated great things in the commencement of the present revolution; but that to continue and complete it, required also the incentive of interest and the hope of reward. The congress manifested at first very little inclination to adopt the propositions of the commander-in-chief, either because they deemed them too extraordinary, or from reluctance to load the state with so heavy a burden; or, finally, because they thought the grants of lands to the officers and soldiers, of which we have made mention in its place, ought to satisfy the wishes of men possessed of any moderation. But at length, submitting to necessity, they decreed an allowance of half pay for life to the officers of the army, with the reservation, however, to the government, of the power to commute it, if deemed expedient, for the sum of six years' half pay. A short time after they passed another resolution, which restricted the allowance of half pay to seven years, dating from the end of the war. These measures, though salutary, were not taken till too late, and, moreover, were not sufficiently spontaneous on the part of the government. Already more than two hundred officers of real merit had given up their commissions; and it was again exemplified on this occasion, that a benefit long delayed loses much of its value. Nor should the congress have forgotten, that the founders of a new state control not, but are controlled by, soldiers; and that since their support is so indispensable, and it is impossible to resist them, the wiser course is to content them.

In the midst of his anxieties, created by the causes we have mentioned, Washington had the additional chagrin of finding that certain intrigues were in agitation against himself. The impatient, who would have events to succeed each other with the same rapidity as their own desires, and the ambitious, who, to raise themselves, are always ready to impute to others the strokes of fortune, or the effects of necessity, gave out on all occasions, and even published in the gazettes, that the reverses of the two preceding years, in New Jersey and in Pennsylvania, were more owing to the incapacity of the commander-in-chief than to any other cause. They enlarged upon the victories of Gates, whom they placed far above Washington, and were continually extolling the heroic valor of the Americans, which rendered them capable of the most splendid achievements, when they were led to battle by an able commander. Nor was it merely among private persons that these slanders were circulated; discontent caused them to be repeated by men in office, gave them admittance into several of the state legislatures, into the midst of the army, and finally, even into the congress itself. It appeared, that the object of these machinations was to give Washington so many disgusts that he should of himself retire from the head of the army and thus make room for the immediate promotion of Gates to that exalted station. Whether this general himself had any hand in the intrigue, is a matter of uncertainty. If the rectitude and acknowledged generosity of his character be considered, it will appear more probable that he had not. But ambition is a passion of inconceivable subtilty, which insinuates itself under the appearances of virtue, and too often corrupts and sullies the most ingenuous minds. It is certain that Gates was not ignorant of the object of the combination, and that he threw no difficulties in the way. Perhaps he entertained the opinion, and the authors of these machinations with him, that Washington was not able to sustain so great a weight, and intended, by giving him a successor, to save the country. As for us, that respect for truth which ought to be our only guide, compels us to declare that the leaders of this combination, very little concerned for the public good, were immoderately so for their own, and that the aim of all their efforts was, to advance themselves and their friends at the expense of others. Among them, and of the first rank, was general Conway, one of the most wily and restless intriguers, that passed in those times from Europe into America. Declaiming and vociferating, incessantly besieging all the members of congress with his complaints, he pretended that there existed no sort of discipline in the American army, that there was no two regiments which maneuvered alike, and not two officers in any regiment who could execute or command the military exercises; in a word, he had said and done so much, that the congress appointed him inspector and major-general. This appointment excited loud murmurs in the camp, and the brigadier-generals remonstrated. But this man, bent on attaining his purposes, and whose audacity knew no bounds, openly spoke of the commander-in-chief in the most derogatory terms; and, as it always happens in times of adversity, he readily found those who believed him.

The assembly of Pennsylvania was the first to break the ice; on the report that Washington was moving into winter quarters, they addressed a remonstrance to congress, severely censuring this measure of the commander-in-chief, and expressing, in very plain words, their dissatisfaction at the mode in which he had conducted the war. The Pennsylvanians were excessively chagrined at the loss of their capital, forgetful of their own backwardness in strengthening the army, which had twice fought superior numbers in their defense. It was, moreover, believed, at the time, that the members of congress from Massachusetts, and particularly Samuel Adams, had never been able to brook that the supreme command of all the armies should have been conferred upon a Virginian, to the exclusion of the generals of their province, who then enjoyed a reputation not inferior, and perhaps superior to that of Washington. It appeared also that these delegates, being the most zealous partisans of the revolution, were far from approving the moderation of the commander-in-chief. They would have preferred placing at the head of affairs a more ardent and decided republican; and it is asserted that they were on the point of demanding an inquiry into the causes of the unsuccessful issue of the campaigns of the years 1776 and 1777.

This had not effect. But a board of war was created, under the direction of generals Gates and Mifflin, both of whom, if they were not, were thought to be, among the authors of these machinations against Washington. Anonymous letters were circulated, in which he was cruelly lacerated; they made him responsible as well for the disastrous campaigns of Jersey and Pennsylvania, as for the deplorable condition to which the troops were reduced in their winter quarters. One of these letters was addressed to Laurens, the president of congress; it was filled with heavy accusations against the commander-in-chief, Another, similar, was sent to Henry, the governor of Virginia; both transmitted them to Washington. Supported by that elevated spirit, and by that firmness which no reverses of fortune could abate, the serenity he enjoyed was not even for a moment interrupted. He received with the same temper another determination of congress, matured in concert with the new board of war, perhaps to let it be seen that they knew how to act by themselves, or because they had really withdrawn from the commander-in-chief a great part of the confidence they had placed in him in times past. They had projected a new expedition against Canada. It was proposed to place at the head of this enterprise the marquis de la Fayette, whose qualifications, as a Frenchman of illustrious rank, promised peculiar advantages for the conquest of a province recently French. But, perhaps, also, the authors of this scheme had it principally in view, in separating La Fayette from Washington, to deprive the commander-in-chief of the defense he found in so faithful a friend. He was to have been accompanied by the same Conway mentioned above, and by general Starke. Washington, without having been at all consulted upon this expedition, and even without its being communicated to him, received orders to put Hazen's regiment of Canadians on the march for Albany. He obeyed without delay. The marquis, on his arrival at Albany, found nothing prepared for the expedition; neither men, nor arms, nor munitions. He complained of it to congress; the enterprise was relinquished. Washington was authorized to recall the young Frenchman to his camp; as to Conway, he was not invited thither. Soon after, having made himself the object of general animadversion by the arrogance of his manners, and his intrigues against Washington, he requested and obtained leave to resign. He was succeeded in the office of inspector-general by the baron Steuben, a Prussian officer of distinguished reputation, who, perfectly versed in the tactics of Frederick II., undertook to teach them to the soldiers of congress. By his exertions the Americans learned to manœuvre with uniformity, and their discipline was essentially improved.

It would be impossible to express with what indignation the whole army and the best citizens were filled, on hearing of the machinations that were in agitation against the illustrious chief, who possessed their entire affection. An universal outcry arose against the intriguers. Conway no longer durst show himself among the soldiers, who threatened to wreak their vengeance upon him. He repaired to York, in Pennsylvania, where at that time the congress resided. As to Samuel Adams, hurried away by the enthusiasm of his patriotic sentiments, he had probably acted from no other motive but the good of the state; even he thought it prudent, however, to keep aloof from the officers and soldiers, under the apprehension of injury from the effects of their fury. If the congress, yielding to the artifices and importunities of the enemies of Washington, had been induced to take the resolutions we have related, they were nevertheless not ignorant how dangerous, in affairs of state, are changes made without due reflection. They were perfectly aware that France, whose intervention they hoped soon to obtain, would never repose in a man English born, as was Gates, the unbounded confidence she had already placed in the American chief. They could not but perceive that, though there might be a warrior possessed of talents equal to those of Washington, there was none who could rival him in fidelity, in rectitude, in goodness, and still less in the esteem of the people and the affection of the soldiers. Upon these considerations, the congress maintained a firm stand against all intrigues, and manifested no appearance of a disposition to take the supreme command from one who had approved himself so worthy to hold it. Washington was fully apprised of the artifices that were employed to diminish his well earned reputation; far from allowing them to intimidate him, he did not even appear to notice them. He indulged none of that secret discontent which men of weak minds, or whose hearts are devoured by ambition, are too apt, in similar circumstances, to cherish against their country; his zeal for his duty never experienced the smallest remission. This conjuncture certainly enabled him to exhibit his moderation and his constancy in all their splendor; it proved that he could vanquish himself. He was in the midst of an army dejected by repeated defeats, destitute of every accommodation,

and reduced to the verge of famine.   Gates, at the same time, shone
with all the luster of recent victory, and all the renown of his ancient exploits.   As to Washington, lacerated by the public prints,
denounced in anonymous letters, publicly accused by the representation of different provinces, even the congress seemed ready to abandon him to the fury of his enemies.   In the midst of a storm so
formidable, he maintained entire, not only the stability, but even the
calmness of his mind ; all devotion to his country, he seemed to
have forgotten himself.   The twenty-third of January he wrote
from Valley Forge, that neither interest nor ambition had engaged
him in the public service; that he had accepted, and not solicited
the command ; that he had not undertaken it without that distrust
of himself, felt by every man not destitute of all knowledge, from
the apprehension of not being able to perform, worthily, the part
assigned him ; that, as far as his abilities had permitted, he had fulfilled his duty, aiming as invariably at the object proposed, as the
magnetic needle points to the pole ; that as soon as the nation should
no longer desire his services, or another should be found more capable than himself, of satisfying its expectations, he should quit the
helm, and return to a private station, with as much pleasure as ever
the wearied traveler retired to rest ; that he wished from the bottom
of his heart, his successor might experience more propitious gales,
and less numerous obstacles ; that if his exertions had not answered
the expectations of his fellow citizens, no one could lament it more
sincerely than himself ; but that he thought proper to add, a day
would come, when the interests of America would no longer exact
of him an impenetrable mystery ; and that until then he would not
be the first to reveal truths which might prejudice his country, whatever wrongs to himself might result from his silence.   By the concluding words, he alluded to the insidious proceedings of the ambitious, the shameful malversations of the army contractors, and the
peculations or delinquencies of all those by whose fault the army
was reduced to such an extremity of distress and calamity.

May this admirable moderation of Washington teach those in
elevated stations, that popular rewards and public favor should never be measured by the standard of self-love, and that though the
rulers of nations are often ungrateful, men who sincerely love their
country, may still find consolations and glory in knowing how to
control even a just resentment.

Washington, in the midst of so trying a crisis, not only always
kept the mastery of himself, but he often consulted the congress
upon the military operations he meditated, upon the measures to be
taken, in order to fill up the regiments ; and, finally, upon all the

means of placing the army in a condition to commence the ensuing campaign with the necessary resources.

It was known that the British general expected large re-inforcements from Europe; Washington was desirous of resuming hostilities early, in order to attack him before they arrived. This plan was of extreme importance; he was accordingly indefatigable in urging the congress and the governments of the several states, by frequent letters, that the preparations for the campaign might experience no delay. All would equally have wished to comply with the desires of the commander-in-chief; but deliberations are taken of necessity but tardily in popular governments.

What ought to have been ready in the beginning of spring, was but scantily forthcoming in the course of all the summer. Even the organization of the army was not completed until about the last of May. Until then there was observed an extreme disparity, not only between the regiments of different states, but even between those of the same state; a confusion productive of singular detriment to the service. But by a decree of the 27th of May, the infantry, cavalry, artillery, and engineers, were organized upon an uniform system in all parts of the army. These delays might have proved essentially prejudicial to the American arms, if unforeseen events had not prevented the British generals from opening the campaign so soon as they would have desired. They contented themselves with detaching their light troops to scour the country in the neighborhood of Philadelphia and the nearer parts of New Jersey, in order to forage and secure the roads. These excursions produced nothing remarkable, except it be that an English detachment having surprised, in the month of March, a party of Americans at the bridges of Quinton and Hancock, all the soldiers who composed it were barbarously massacred, while crying for quarter. The English, about the same time, undertook an expedition up the Delaware, in order to destroy the magazines of Bordentown, and to take or burn the vessels which the Americans had withdrawn up the river between Philadelphia and Trenton. In both these enterprises they succeeded to their wishes. They attempted also to surprise the marquis de la Fayette, who was encamped at Baron Hill, on the left bank of the Schuylkill, with a considerable body of troops; but he baffled their enterprise by his activity and judicious dispositions, although in the commencement of the action, general Grant had obtained some advantage over him.

While these events were passing on land, hostilities were also prosecuted upon sea, where the Americans daily acquired reputation. They manifested so bold and enterprising a spirit in their maritime expeditions, that the British commerce suffered on their part incredible losses. Since the commencement of the war in 1776, they had already captured upwards of five hundred English vessels, of different sizes, and all with cargoes of great value. Emboldened by their success, even the coasts of Great Britain were not secure from their insults, where they daily took numerous prizes. The royal navy, however, opposed their enterprises, and took many of their ships in the seas of America and of Europe; but the advantage, nevertheless, remained very decidedly with the Americans.

In the meantime, sir Henry Clinton was arrived at Philadelphia, having been appointed commander-in-chief of all the royal forces, in the place of sir William Howe, who returned to England. Dissatisfied with the ministers, who had not sent him all the re-inforcements he considered necessary to the decision of the war, he had offered his resignation, and the ministers had accepted it with promptitude. They did not forgive him for not having more effectually co-operated with Burgoyne, and for not having displayed all the vigor, in the conduct of the war, which they would have desired. And certainly he rather merits the praise of a prudent than of an adventurous commander. If commendation is due him for the vigor and rare ability he actually displayed in certain expeditions, perhaps he will not escape reprehension for not having undertaken any of greater magnitude and of more importance. In the commencement of the war, when the minds in America were most inflamed, and the English had not yet collected their troops, or received their re-inforcements, perhaps this circumspection and this dilatory system of war, was well judged; for never should all be committed to fortune with only a partial exertion of force; and the enemy is attacked at the greatest advantage after his ardor has already cooled. But when a great part of the Americans, exhausted by expenses, wearied by a long war and by the scarcity of every thing, were become more disposed to return to their former condition, and when the English had received all the re-inforcements they could expect, the British general should have placed all his hopes of victory in the rapidity and terror of his arms. This course seems to have been recommended to him by prudence itself, when it is considered, that besides the probability of victory, which a regular battle always offered to the English, the total defeat of the army of congress involved, if not infallibly, at least in all likelihood, the absolute submission of America; while, on the other hand, the rout of the British army would not have rendered the Americans more inflexible than they were, and, moreover, would not in the least have changed the dispositions of the French government, which, since the capitulation of Saratoga, manifestly tended to war. The consequences of a decisive victory were, therefore, more advantageous than those of the most complete discomfiture could have been detrimental. Howe valued himself upon being thought very sparing of the blood of his soldiers, as he could only draw reinforcements from so great a distance; and, perhaps, he feared that if he lost a pitched battle, the inhabitants might rise in fury and utterly exterminate the relics of his routed army. But so sanguinary an overthrow was not to be apprehended with such soldiers and with such officers. Besides, in the worst event, he was sure of a retreat on board the fleet, by rallying the troops in a place accessible to it.

On any hypothesis, things were now got to such a head, that it was essential to strike a decisive blow; for, upon the continuance of a war in which France was about to take part, the independence of America could scarcely appear doubtful. However the truth was, Howe certainly possessed an elevated and generous mind; he had also the desire, though rarely the power, to prevent the atrocities perpetrated by his troops; no curb could restrain the brutal fury of the Germans who followed his standard. Humane towards his soldiers, affable with his officers, a foe to disorder and violence, he was the object of general esteem and affection.

Before his departure, the officers of the army were disposed to give him a brilliant carousal; it consisted in jousts and tournaments, marches, evolutions, triumphal arches and honorary inscriptions. This entertainment, from the variety of ingredients, was called a medley. The evening terminated with a magnificent exhibition of fireworks. Sir William Howe embarked, a few days after, on board the frigate Andromeda. He arrived the second of July at London, where the ministerial party assailed him with torrents of invective, while that in opposition exalted him above the stars.

END OF BOOK NINTH.

BOOK TENTH.

1778. On hearing of the catastrophe which had befallen Burgoyne, and of the almost fruitless victories of Howe, the British nation was seized with sullen affliction and discontent. The dejection was as profound as the hopes conceived had been sanguine, and the promises of ministers magnificent.

The parliament had acquiesced in all their demands, with respect to the prosecution of the war, and they had not failed to transmit to America, with promptitude, whatever was essential to the success of the preceding campaign. The generals invested with command, and the soldiers who had fought under them, were not inferior in reputation to any that England, or even Europe could produce. Hence it was inferred, that there must exist in the very nature of things, some insurmountable obstacle to victory, and the issue of the war began to be despaired of. For better or stronger armies could not be dispatched to America, than those which had already been sent; and if the Americans, in the outset of their revolution, had not only withstood the English troops, but if they had even vanquished and disarmed them, of what might they not be thought capable in future, when, deriving new confidence from their successes, they should have consolidated their state by practice and experience, and availed themselves of the time which had been allowed them, to develope still greater forces against their enemies? Accordingly, so far from there being any prospect of gaining what was not possessed, the danger appeared imminent of losing what was. Great fears were entertained especially for Canada, where the garrisons were extremely feeble, and the victorious army was upon the frontiers. No little apprehension was also felt, lest, in the heat of parties, some commotion might break out within that province, prejudicial to the interests of the king; independence being an enticing lure for every people, and especially for distant nations, and the example of the Americans was likely to influence their neighbors. Nor could it be dissembled, besides, that the Canadians, being French, for the most part, their national aversion would tend to fortify this natural proclivity, and finally, perhaps, produce some formidable convulsion. The British government beheld with grief, that enlistments became every day more difficult in America, where the loyalists appeared intimidated by the recent victories of the republicans; and even in England, where the spirit of opposition showed itself more powerfully than ever, an extreme repugnance was evidenced to bearing arms in a distant and dangerous war, which many pronounced unjust and cruel, and which, even at that epoch, every thing announced, must terminate ingloriously. Nor was the prospect more flattering of obtaining new troops from Germany; for the enormous armies kept on foot by the emperor, and the king of Prussia, exacted such a multitude of recruits, that the agents of England could not hope to procure them in any considerable number. Moreover, the intervention of France and the commissioners of congress with those sovereigns, or that disposition to favor the American cause, which unequivocally manifested itself in all parts of Europe, had already determined several German princes to refuse a passage through their states to those feeble parties of recruits which, with incredible pains and expense, were gleaned by the British agents. But there was one consideration which, more than any other, impeded the success of their negotiations; the moment was manifestly approaching, when France would declare herself in favor of the Americans, no longer by secret intrigues, or the tacit protection afforded to their privateers, but openly, and with arms in hand. Already all her preparations for war, and especially her maritime armaments, were completed. The late victories of the Americans upon the borders of the Hudson, and even the constancy they had exhibited after their reverses upon the banks of the Delaware, were sufficient pledges that their cause might be espoused without any hazard of finding in them a fickle, a faithless, or a feeble ally. The occasion so long and so ardently desired by the French for humbling the British power and arrogance, was at length offered them by propitious fortune. Their wishes were admirably served by the blind obstinacy of the British ministers and generals, who had judged as erroneously of the nature and importance of things, as of the valor and constancy of the Americans. It was not at all doubted in England, that France would avail herself of the means which presented themselves to her grasp, to repair her ancient losses. This inevitable crisis took strong hold of the public attention, and all perceived the necessity either of a long, and in no common degree perilous struggle, or of an accommodation, upon little honorable terms, with that very people whose petitions had always been rejected, and who had been exasperated by so many outrages, before they were assailed by so cruel a war. Though the ministers and their adherents failed not to advance plausible reasons to justify themselves, and to authorize their conduct, yet the general opinion inclined to consider it as the most prudent counsel to listen at length to the demands of the Americans, and to adopt the course of procedure repeatedly proposed by the orators of the opposition, who had recommended that hostilities should be suspended, and a negotiation set on foot, which might lead to an admissible adjustment. Heavy complaints were heard on all parts, that so many favorable occasions for reconciliation had been allowed to escape, as if it was intended to wait the arrival of that fatal moment when it would no longer be possible either to negotiate with honor, or to fight with glory; and when, instead of any hope of subduing or conciliating America, there was too much reason to fear the loss of other inestimable portions of the British empire.

All the attempts made previous to that time, for reducing the Americans to submission by force of arms, having proved completely abortive, it was bitterly regretted that, before undertaking new efforts, the failure of which must secure the triumph of the enemy, there had not been a disposition to listen to the conciliatory propositions submitted to parliament by the earl of Chatham, in the sitting of the thirtieth of May, of the year last elapsed. Foreseeing the calamities which were about to fall upon his country, since the ministers were resolved to prosecute extreme measures, and perceiving distinctly that to the dangers of an intestine struggle would soon be added the perils of a foreign war, this illustrious man, though bowed with age, and laboring under a painful malady, had caused himself to be carried to the house of lords, where, in that strain of admirable eloquence, which always chained attention, he exerted the most magnanimous efforts to appease animosities, to extinguish the flames of war, to procure the repeal of those disastrous laws which had lighted them, and opposed an insuperable bar to the return of concord.

' My lords,' he said, ' this is a flying moment, perhaps but six weeks left to arrest the dangers that surround us. The gathering storm may break; it has already opened, and in part burst. It is difficult for government, after all that has passed, to shake hands with the defiers of the king, defiers of the parliament, defiers of the people. I am a defier of nobody; but if an end is not put to this war, there is an end to this country. I do not trust my judgment in my present state of health; this is the judgment of my better days; the result of forty years' attention to America.

' They are rebels; but what are they rebels for? Surely not for defending their unquestionable rights? What have these rebels done heretofore? I remember when they raised four regiments on their own bottom, and took Louisburgh from the veteran troops of France. But their excesses have been great. I do not mean their panegyric; but must observe in attenuation, the erroneous and infatuated counsels which have prevailed, the door to mercy and justice has been shut against them. But they may still be taken up upon the grounds of their former submission. I state to you the importance of Amer ica; it is a double market; the market of consumption and the market of supply. This double market for millions, with naval stores, you are giving to your hereditary rival. America has carried you through four wars, and will now carry you to your death, if you don't take things in time. In the sportsman's phrase, when you have found yourselves at fault, you must try back. You have ransacked every corner of Lower Saxony; but forty thousand German boors never can subdue ten times the number of British freemen; they may ravage, they cannot conquer.

' But you would conquer, you say! Why, what would you conquer; the map of America? I am ready to meet any general officer on the subject. What will you do out of the protection of your fleet? In the winter, if together, your troops are starved; and if dispersed, they are taken off in detail. I am experienced in spring hopes and vernal promises; I know what ministers throw out; but at last will come your equinoctial disappointment. They tell you—what? That your army will be as strong as last year, when it was not strong enough. You have got nothing in America but stations. You have been three years teaching them the art of war; they are apt scholars; and I will venture to tell your lordships, that the American gentry will make officers enough, fit to command the troops of all the European powers. What you have sent there, are too many to make peace, too few to make war. If you conquer them, what then? You cannot make them respect you; you cannot make them wear your cloth. You will plant an invincible hatred in their breasts against you. You are giving America to France at the expense of twelve millions a year. The intercourse has produced every thing to her; and England, old England, must pay for all. Your trade languishes, your taxes increase, your revenues dwindle; France, at this moment, is securing and drawing to herself that commerce which created your seamen, which fed your islands, which was the principal source of your wealth, prosperity and power. We have tried for unconditional submission; try what can be gained by unconditional redress. We shall thus evince a conciliatory spirit, and open the way to concord.

' The ministers affirm there is no sort of treaty with France. Then there is still a moment left; the point of honor is still safe. The instant a treaty appears you must declare war, though you had only five ships of the line in England; but France will defer a treaty as long as possible, to wait the effect of our self-destroying counsels. You are now at the mercy of every little German chancery; and the pretensions of France will increase daily, so as to become an avowed party in either peace or war. The dignity of the government is objected; but less dignity will be lost in the repeal of oppressive laws, than in submitting to the demands of German chanceries. We are the aggressors. We have invaded the colonists as much as the Spanish armada invaded England. Mercy cannot do harm ; it will seat the king where he ought to be, throned in the hearts of his people ; and millions at home and abroad, now employed in obloquy and revolt, would pray for him. The revocation I propose, and amnesty, may produce a respectable division in America, and unanimity at home. It will give America an option ; she has yet had no option. You have said, " *Lay down your arms,*" and she has given you the Spartan answer, " *Come, take.*" '

Neither the authority of such a man, nor the force of his speech, nor present evils, nor yet the fear of future, were sufficient to procure the adoption of his proposition. Those who opposed it, contended that it would by no means satisfy the Americans, since from the outset they had aimed at independency. They talked of the dignity of the realm, of the weakness of France, of the number of loyalists ready to declare themselves, the moment an occasion should offer itself ; they harangued upon the tyranny of congress, already become insupportable to all the Americans, upon the emptiness of its treasury, and the rapid depreciation of the bills of credit ; finally, they enlarged upon that impatience which was universally manifested for the return of order, and the blessings enjoyed by the rest of the subjects of the British government.

In the midst of these contradictions had been agitated the question of peace and war, while the veil of uncertainty still shaded the future, and experience had not yet ascertained the effect of all the forces sent into America. But now the trial had been made, and the result being on the one hand so calamitous, and so dubious on the other, the obstinacy of ministers was almost universally condemned, while the wisdom and foresight of the earl of Chatham were extolled to the skies. That such opinions should have been entertained by those whose interests and passions were so immediately concerned, is certainly no matter of astonishment ; but it may be advanced with confidence, that the measure proposed by this, in other respects, most sagacious statesman, would have resulted in very doubtful consequences, to use no stronger words.

At this time, the Americans had already declared their independence ; what the proposed concession, seconded by formidable armies, might have operated before this declaration, they could no longer have done after it, especially when by the effect of this very declaration, and of the resistance made to the arms of Howe upon the territory of New Jersey, the Americans confidently expected to obtain the succors of France. Besides, if, at this epoch, the issue of a negotiation was uncertain, it would indubitably have reflected little honor upon the government to have condescended to an arrangement, without having first made a trial of the efficacy of the armies it had collected and sent to America, with so much effort, and at so heavy an expense. Victory, too, as it was reasonable to think, would have produced submission, or at least conditions more favorable to Great Britain.

The ministers therefore being resolved to continue the war, exerted their utmost diligence to repair those evils which the faults of men, or an inauspicious destiny, had drawn upon the state in the course of the preceding year. Their attention was first directed to the means of raising new troops, and of procuring more abundant pecuniary resources than had been granted them by the parliament. They reflected, that although there was a powerful party in the kingdom who condemned the American war, still there existed another who approved it highly, either from conviction or from their devotion to the ministry. To this class they addressed themselves, not doubting their readiness to assist them with zeal in procuring the men and the funds they wanted. Dreading, however, the clamors of the opposition, who might represent this levy of soldiers and money, though voluntary, as a violation of the constitution, they carried this scheme into effect in the recess of parliament, which happened at the beginning of the current year, and which, with the same object in view, they prolonged beyond the accustomed term. They were the more sanguine in their hopes of success, inasmuch as, since the declaration of independence, and the secret alliance with France, of which every day furnished new evidences, the greater part of those who had shown themselves at first the warmest partisans of the Americans, had now deserted them, and gone over to the ministerial party. The ministers accordingly dispatched their agents into the different provinces of the kingdom, and especially those where they had the greatest influence, with instructions to spur the inhabitants to enlist, and to lend their support to the state by voluntary gifts. These emissaries were to expatiate on the ingratitude of the Americans, the enmity of France, the necessities of the country, the glory and splendor of the English name, which must be transmitted unsullied to posterity. Their exertions were attended with success in some cities of the first order, and even in some towns of inferior rank; but none manifested greater zeal than Liverpool and Manchester, each of which raised, at their own expense, a regiment of a thousand men. The Scotch, naturally a warlike people, and much devoted to the cause of government in the present war, exhibited the utmost ardor to engage in the service. Edinburgh levied a thousand men,

Glasgow an equal number.   The Highlanders, a hardy race, descended in hordes from their craggy hills, to follow the royal standard. Equal promptitude was manifested in contributing to the public expense, and free gifts multiplied every day.   The government would have wished that the city of London, on account of its population and wealth, and of its importance as the capital of the kingdom, had placed itself at the head of this contribution.   It was hoped that city would raise and maintain at its own expense five thousand men for three years, or until the end of the war.   This hope proved illusory.   The citizens, being convened, refused peremptorily.   The common council returned an answer equally unfavorable.   The partisans of the ministry were not discouraged.   They vociferated at every corner that it was a shame for the city of London, that, after having voted, but a few days before, considerable sums for the relief of Americans taken with arms in hand leveled against England, it should now refuse to give the slightest succor to the country.   The friends of the ministry assembled, and subscribed twenty thousand pounds sterling.   The same maneuvers took place at Bristol, and with the same success.   This city would not furnish troops ; it consented only to give the same sum as London.   The ministers experienced still more difficulties in the country ; the landholders being grown sulky at the weight of their assessments, and at having been deceived by promises that the American taxes were to be in diminution of their own.   Upon the whole, this project of voluntary levies, and gratuitous contributions, though not absolutely fruitless, was still very far from affording the resources which had been counted upon. It, however, became the subject of violent declamations in parliament ; but with the usual event ; the ministry triumphed.

While such was the procedure of the English government, in order to sustain the struggle in which it was engaged, the congress urged with new fervor the negotiations which they had already, a long time back, set on foot with the court of France.   The American commissioners had left nothing unessayed that could decide it to declare openly in their favor ; but however pressing were their solicitations with the French ministers to induce them to take a definitive resolution, they had not as yet obtained any thing but evasive and dilatory answers.   In this first period of the American revolution, *considering the uncertainty of its issue,* France hesitated to espouse the quarrel of a people whose force appeared insufficient to sustain the pressure of so perilous an enterprise.   She feared lest the colonists might all at once desist, and resume all their ancient relations with England.   Those who directed the counsels of France were not ignorant, that at the very moment in which she should declare herself, the British ministry, by acquiescing in the concessions demanded by the Americans, might instantly disarm them, and that France would then find herself alone saddled with a war, without motive, and without object.

To this consideration was added, that before coming to an open rupture with Great Britain, it was essential to restore order in the finances, and to re-establish the marine, both having suffered excessively from the disorder, disasters and prodigality of the preceding reign. The declaration of independence, it is true, had removed the danger of a sudden reconciliation; *but it was still possible to doubt the success of resistance. Nor should we omit to say, that, though France would rather see America independent, than reconciled with England, she relished the prospect of a long war between them still better than independence. Perhaps, even, she would have liked best of all a conquest by dint of arms, and the consequent subjugation; for, upon this hypothesis, the English colonies, ravaged and ruined, would have ceased to enrich the mother country, by the benefits of their commerce in time of peace; and in time of war, the English would no longer have found in their colonists those powerful auxiliaries, who so often had succored them with so much efficacy.* Should the colonies, though vanquished, preserve their ancient prosperity, then England would be constrained to maintain in them a part of her force, in order to prevent the revolts she would have continually to dread on the part of a people impressed with the recollection of so many outrages and cruelties.

But upon the second hypothesis, or that of independence, it was impossible to dissemble that the example would be pernicious for the colonies of the other European powers, and that the smallest of the probable inconveniences, would be the necessity of granting them, to the great prejudice of the mother country, a full and entire liberty of commerce. These considerations, carefully weighed by the French ministers, so wrought, that repressing their ardor for war, they covered their projects with an impenetrable veil, and drew the negotiation into length. They restricted themselves to expressions of benevolence towards the Americans, and to granting them clandestinely the succors we have spoken of in another place. And even those succors were furnished with more or less mystery, more or less liberality, as fortune showed herself propitious or adverse to the American arms. Such was the rigor with which France adhered, or appeared to adhere, to this wary policy, either with a view of not breaking before the time with England, or in order the more effectually to place the Americans at her discretion, and constrain them to subscribe to all her demands, that when the news arrived at Paris of the capture of Ticonderoga, and of the victorious march of Burgoyne towards Albany, events which seemed to decide in favor of the English, instructions were immediately dispatched to Nantz, and the other ports of the kingdom, that no American privateers should be suffered to enter them, except from indispensable necessity, as to repair their vessels, to obtain provisions, or to escape the perils of the sea. Thus France, pursuing invariably the route prescribed by *reason of state*, which admirably suited her convenience, on the one hand amused the British ministers with protestations of friendship, and on the other encouraged the Americans with secret succors, by the uncertainty and scantiness of them, inflaming their ardor, and confirming their resolution by continual promises of future cooperation. Unshackled in her movements, she thus pledged herself to no party, but tranquilly waited to see what course things would take. The agents of congress did not fail, however, to urge and besiege the cabinet of Versailles to come at length to a final decision. But the French ministers, with many tosses and shrugs, alledged a variety of excuses in support of their system of procrastination, at one time, that the fleet expected from Newfoundland, crowded with excellent seamen, was not yet arrived; at another, that the galleons of Spain were still at sea, and now some other subterfuge was invented. Thus alternately advancing and receding, never allowing their intentions to be fathomed, they kept the Americans in continual uncertainty. Finally, the commissioners, out of all patience, and determined, if practicable, without waiting longer, to extricate themselves from this labyrinth, imagined an expedient for reducing the French ministers themselves to the necessity of dropping the vizor; this was to suggest, that if France did not assist them immediately, the Americans could defer no longer a voluntary or compulsory arrangement with England.

To this effect, they waited upon the ministers about the middle of August, 1777, with a memorial in which they represented, that if France supposed that the war could be continued for any considerable time longer without her interference, she was much mistaken. 'Indeed,' continued the memorial, ' the British government have every thing to lose and nothing to gain, by continuing the war. After the present campaign, they will therefore doubtless make it their great and last effort to recover the dominion of America, and terminate the war. They probably hope that a few victories may, by the chance of war, be obtained; and that these on one hand, and the wants and distresses of the colonists on the other, may induce them to return again to a dependence, more or less limited, on Great Britain They must be sensible, that if ever America is to be conquered by them, it must be within the present year; that if it be impossible to do it in this year of the dispute, it will be madness to expect more success afterwards, when the difficulties of the Americans' former situation are removed; when their new independent governments have acquired stability; and when the people are become, as they soon will be, well armed, disciplined and supplied with all the means of resistance.

'The British ministry must therefore be sensible, that a continuation of hostilities against the colonies, after this year, can only tend to prolong the danger, or invite an additional war in Europe; and they therefore doubtless intend, after having tried the success of this campaign, however it may end, to make peace on the best terms which can be obtained; and if they cannot recover the colonies as subjects, to admit their claim of independency, and secure them by a federal alliance. Therefore no means are left for France to prevent the colonists from being shortly reconciled to Great Britain, either as subjects or allies, but to enter immediately into such engagements with them as will necessarily preclude all others; such as will permanently bind and secure their commerce and friendship, and enable them as well to repel the attacks, as to spurn at the offers of their present enemy.

'France must remember,' it was added, 'that the first resistance of the colonists was not to obtain independency, but a redress of their grievances; and that there are many among them who might even now be satisfied with a limited subjection to the British crown. A majority has indeed put in for the prize of independency; they have done it on a confidence that France, attentive to her most important interests, would soon give them open and effectual support. But when they find themselves disappointed; when they see some of the powers of Europe furnish troops to assist in their subjugation; another power, alluding to Portugal, proscribing their commerce; and the rest looking on as indifferent spectators; it is very probable that, despairing of foreign aid, and severely pressed by their enemies and their own internal wants and distresses, they may be inclined to accept of such terms as it will be the interest of the British government to grant them. Lord George Germain, but a few weeks since declared in the house of commons that his hope of ending the American war this year, was principally founded on the disappointment which the colonists would feel, when they discover that no assistance is likely to be given them from France. The British adherents in America will spare no pains to spread and increase that disappointment, by discouraging representations; they already intimate that France, equally hostile to both parties, foments the present war, only to make them mutually instrumental in each other's destruction.

'Should Great Britain, by these and other means, detach the colonies, and re-unite them to herself, France will irrecoverably lose the most favorable opportunity ever offered to any nation, of humbling a powerful, arrogant, and hereditary enemy.

'But it is not simply the opportunity of reducing Great Britain, which France will lose by her present inactivity; for her own safety, and that of all her American possessions, will be endangered the moment in which a reconciliation takes place between Britain and America. The king and ministry of Great Britain know and feel that France has encouraged and assisted the colonists in their present resistance; and they are as much incensed against her, as they would be, were she openly to declare war. In truth, France has done too much, unless she intends to do more.

'Can any one doubt but that whenever peace with America is obtained by Great Britain, whatever may be the conditions of it, the whole British force now on the continent of America, will be suddenly transported to the West Indies, and employed in subduing the French sugar islands there, to recompense the losses and expenses which Great Britain has suffered and incurred in this war, and to revenge the insult and injury France has done her by the encouragement and assistance which she is supposed to have secretly given the colonists against Great Britain?'

Such was the purport of the memorial presented to the French government, in order to terminate its hesitations; but this also was without success. The ministers were no less ingenious in discovering new evasions; they chose to wait to see the progress of this war. The news of the taking of Ticonderoga, and the fear of still more decisive operations on the part of general Howe, maintained their doubts and indecision. They were loath to have no other part to play than extending the hand to insurgents, when already their wreck appeared inevitable. We venture not to say, that in this occurrence was again verified the vulgar maxim: *the unfortunate have no friends;* but it appeared, at least, that the cabinet of Versailles was determined to procrastinate until the distress of the Americans was arrived at such a point as to become their only law; that it might obtain from them the better conditions for France. Besides, as at this time there was much appearance that the British arms would carry all before them, an accommodation between the mother country and the colonies seemed less probable than ever; and this was what the French government had feared the most. The ministers of England, supposing them victorious in America, would have listened to no conditions short of an absolute submission; and the French appeared to desire this extremity even more than independence, provided only, that it was introduced by a long and desolating war.

Disgusted by so many delays, the American commissioners no longer entertained any doubt as to the secret policy which guided the French in this conjuncture. In their despair, they had well nigh broken off all negotiation with a government that reputed their misfortunes a source of prosperity to itself. Unable, therefore, to accomplish their views with France, and discerning no other prospect of safety, the Americans again addressed themselves to England, proposing to her the recognition of their independence. This point conceded, they would have yielded, in all others, to such conditions as should most tend to save the honor of the mother country. They represented, that if the British ministry knew how to profit of the occasion, it depended on themselves to stipulate an arrangement so conducive to the prosperity of Great Britain, that she would seek in vain to procure herself similar advantages by any other means. But the British government, elated with the first successes of Burgoyne, and persuaded that fortune could not escape him, refused to listen to any overtures for accommodation, and rejected the proposition with disdain. The blindness of the British ministers was incurable; the Americans, in the midst of the most disastrous reverses, and deprived of all hope of foreign succor, strenuously refusing to renounce their independence, insisting even to make it an indispensable condition of their reconciliation, it was manifest that the re-union of the two states was become impossible; and that since the necessity of things and inexorable destiny pronounced that America should no longer be subject, it was better to have her for an ally than for an enemy. But the defeat and capture of Burgoyne, by announcing with such energy the rising greatness of America, had given new ardor to the patriots; new hopes and new fears to the French. Their reciprocal situation became less ambiguous; each began to manifest more positive resolutions. England herself, if her king and his ministers had yielded less to their individual prepossessions, would have prudently paused; and abandoning an enterprise above her strength, would have resorted to the only way of safety that she had left. But pride, obstinacy and intrigue are too often the ruin of states; *and lord Bute was incessantly smoothing that route for king George.* After the victory of Saratoga, the Americans pursued with rare sagacity the policy prescribed by their new circumstances. Their conduct demonstrated as much ability as experience in affairs of state. They reflected, that as their successes had increased their strength, rendered their alliance more desirable, and banished *all doubts* from enlightened minds respecting their independence, nothing could be better calculated on their part, than to give jealousy to France, by pretending a disposition to make alliance with England; and disquietude to England, by the appearance of courting the strictest union with France. They hoped by this conduct to arrive at length to something conclusive. Accordingly, the same express that carried to England the news of the capitulation of Saratoga, was the bearer of dispatches, the drift of which was to insinuate, that the Americans, disgusted by the excessive delays of the French, and indignant at not having received in the midst of their reverses, avowed and more efficacious succors, were eagerly desirous of an accommodation with England, and to conclude with her a treaty of commerce, provided she acknowledged their independence. In order to give more weight to this suggestion, it was added, that the colonists would feel particular gratification in a reconciliation with their ancient country; whereas, in the contrary case, they should be compelled to throw themselves into the arms of the inveterate and implacable enemy of the English name.

General Gates, on whom his recent victory reflected so much luster, wrote, to the same effect, to one of the most distinguished members of parliament. These steps of the chiefs of the American revolution were likewise necessary to satisfy the people, who would not, without extreme repugnance, have seen themselves thrust precipitately into the party of France, before having attempted every probable mode of effecting an adjustment with England. The prejudices they entertained against France were still in all their force; and the persuasion that this power had speculated upon their misfortunes, had greatly exasperated their aversion. These negotiations were no secret to the court of Versailles, as they had been communicated to Franklin, who knew how to make the best use of them; the umbrage they gave the French ministers will be readily conceived. Franklin, about the same time, received instructions to reiterate his expostulations with the government, that it might at length discover itself, since otherwise, it was to be feared that England, convinced by the catastrophe of Burgoyne, and even by the useless victories of Howe, that the reduction of America, by dint of arms, was absolutely impossible, would acknowledge independence. The Americans, he added, finding themselves deserted by the French, will be constrained to listen to the overtures of the English, and to accept of favor wherever they find it; and such an arrangement could not have effect but to the irreparable prejudice of the interests of France. The ministers perceived clearly that the time was come, in which, if they would not lose the fruit of all their policy, it was necessary finally to lay aside the personage of the fox, and to assume the nature of the lion. Judging the British ministers by themselves, they supposed them entirely exempt from all passion, as statesmen ought to be; consequently, fearing the measures which their wisdom might prescribe, they determined to resume, and bring to a conclusion, the negotiations they had opened already, so long since, with the Americans, and which they had so shrewdly prolonged.

This decision appeared to them the more urgent, as they were not ignorant that the great body of the inhabitants of America, their independence once established, would much more willingly have coalesced with the English, a people of the same blood, of the same language, of the same manners, and still not entirely forgetful of former friendship, than with the French, a nation not only foreign and rival, but reputed faithless; whose long hesitations had countenanced the imputation, and against whom, from their tenderest childhood, they had fostered the most unfavorable prepossessions. On the other hand, the Americans had supported three entire years of the most trying distress, without having ever discovered the least disposition to relinquish their enterprise, or the least mark of weariness in their conflict with adverse fortune. Their moderation had not deserted them in success; and the perseverance of their efforts had given to the first victories of the English all the consequences of defeats. These considerations had persuaded the ministers of France, that America had knowledge, power, and will, to keep the faith of treaties.

The resolution of finally taking an active part in this war, by extending an auxiliary hand to the Americans, could not fail, besides, of being highly agreeable to the greater part of the French nation. The motive of it was not merely to be found in the inveterate hatred borne the English, in the remembrance of recent wounds, in the desire of revenge, and in the political opinions, which, at that period, had spread throughout the kingdom, but also in numerous and powerful considerations of commercial advantage. The trade which had been carried on between France and America, since the commencement of disturbances, and especially since the breaking out of hostilities, had yielded the French merchants immense gains. All of these, therefore, eagerly desired that the new order of things might be perpetuated by independence, in order never to see the times revived, in which the prohibitory laws of parliament, and especially the act of navigation, would have deprived them of these benefits. It is true, however, that they had not found this commerce so lucrative as they had anticipated; for several of them, hurried away by the excessive love of gain, and principally those of the maritime cities, had dispatched to America ships loaded with valuable merchandise, a great number of which had been taken on the passage by the British cruisers. But even these losses stimulated their desire to be able to continue the same commerce, and to wit- ness the reduction of that British audacity which pretended to reign alone upon an element common to the whole universe. They hoped that the royal navy in open war would afford protection to the ships of commerce; and that force would thus shield the enterprises of cupidity. The French had, besides, in this conjuncture, the hope, or rather the certainty, that Spain would take part in the quarrel. This was a consideration of weight, in addition to the motives which always influenced them. That kingdom had a formidable marine, and was animated with so strong a desire to make trial of it against England, that the French court, rigidly adhering to its plan of cir- cumspection, had hitherto thought it prudent to check rather than stimulate the cabinet of Madrid. It was not in the least doubted, that all the united forces of the house of Bourbon, already so long prepared, and directed towards the same object, were more than sufficient to take down the intolerable arrogance of the English, to protect rich cargoes from their insults, and even to cause the com- merce of the two Indies to pass almost entirely into the hands of the French and Spaniards.

Thus favored by circumstances, and by the voice of the people, the French government had more need of prudence to restrain it from precipitating its resolutions, than of ardor, to incite it to en- counter the hazards of fortune. Never, assuredly, had any govern- ment to adopt a counsel more recommended by the unanimous and ardent wishes of its subjects, or which promised a more fortunate issue, or more brilliant advantages. Unable, therefore, to resist longer the pressing solicitations of the agents of congress, the minis ters resolved at length to seize the occasion, and to conclude with America the treaty which had been the object of such long negotia- tions. But as, heretofore, the intention of France had been to elude any positive engagement, the articles of the convention, though often and deliberately discussed, were not yet settled. Under the appre- hension, however, that the British government, in case of further delays, might tempt the Americans with conciliatory overtures, the French ministers concluded to signify to the commissioners of con- gress the preliminaries of the treaty of friendship and commerce, to be stipulated between the two states. This communication was made the sixteenth of December, 1777, by M. Gerard, royal syndic of the city of Strasbourg, and secretary of the king's council of state. Its purport was as follows : ' That France would not only acknowledge, but support with all her forces, the independence of the United States, and would conclude with them a treaty of amity and commerce ; that in the stipulations of this treaty she would take no advantage of the present situation of the United States, but that the articles of it should be of the same nature as if the said states had been long established, and were constituted in all the plenitude of their strength ; that his most christian majesty plainly foresaw that in taking this step, he should probably enter upon a war with Great Britain ; but that he desired no indemnification upon that score on the part of the United States ; not pretending to act solely with a view to their particular interest, since, besides the benevolence he bore them, it was manifest, that the power of England would be diminished by the dismemberment of her colonies. The king expected only, with full confidence, from the United States, that whatever was the peace which might be concluded eventually, they would never renounce their independence, and resume the yoke of British domination.' This declaration on the part of France, re-assured the minds of the Americans ; it was followed by very active negotiations during all the month of January. They were immediately communicated to Spain, that she might also, if so inclined, become a party to the convention ; nor was it long before a favorable answer was received from that court.

All difficulties being surmounted, and the conditions acceded to on the one part and on the other, upon the sixth of February was concluded the treaty of amity between his most christian majesty and the United States of America. It was signed on behalf of the king by M. Gerard, and for the United States by Benjamin Franklin, Silas Deane, and Arthur Lee. By this treaty, in which the king of France considered the United States of America as an independent nation, were regulated between the contracting parties, various maritime and commercial interests concerning the duties which merchant vessels were to pay in the ports of the friendly state ; it guarantied the reciprocal protection of vessels in time of war ; the right of fishery, and especially that which the French carried on upon the banks of Newfoundland, by virtue of the treaties of Utrecht and of Paris ; it exempted from the right of *Aubaine*, as well the French in America, as the Americans in France ; it provided for the exercise of commerce, and the admission of privateers with one of the contracting parties, in case the other should be at war with a third power. To this effect, in order to preclude all occasion of dissension, it was determined by an express clause, what articles, in time of war, should be deemed contraband, and what should be considered free, and consequently might be freely transported, and introduced by the subjects of the two powers into enemy ports; those excepted, however, which should be found, at the time, besieged, blockaded or invested. It was also agreed, that the ships and vessels of the contracting parties should not be subject to any visit; it being intended that all visit or search should take place prior to the clearance of the shipping, and that contraband articles should be seized in port, and not upon the voyage, except, however, the cases, where there should exist indications or proofs of fraud. It was stipulated, besides, that in order to facilitate the commerce of the United States with France, his most christian majesty should grant them, as well in Europe as in the islands of America, subject to his dominion, several free ports. Finally, the king pledged himself to employ his good offices and mediation with the emperor of Morocco, and with the regencies of Algiers, Tripoli, Tunis, and other powers of the coast of Barbary, in order that provision should be made in the best possible mode for the accommodation and security of the citizens, ships, and merchandise, 'of the United States of America.' It is to be observed, that this treaty, besides the recognition made in it of American independence, was completely subversive of the principles which the British government had uniformly attempted to establish as well with respect to the commerce of neutrals, in time of war, as with regard to the blockade of the ports of an enemy state by the British squadrons. Consequently, it was easy to foresee that, although France had not contracted to furnish succors of any sort to the United States, Great Britain, nevertheless, on being so wounded to the quick in her pride, and in her most essential interests, would manifest a keen resentment, and would probably declare war against France. Hence it was, that the contracting parties concluded the same day another, eventual, treaty of alliance, offensive and defensive, which was to take its effect so soon as war should break out between France and England. The two parties engaged to assist each other with good offices, with counsel, and with arms. It was stipulated, a thing until then unheard of, on the part of a king, that the essential and express object of the alliance, was to maintain effectually the liberty, sovereignty, and independence of the United States. It was also covenanted, that if the remaining provinces of Great Britain upon the American continent, or the Bermuda islands, came to be conquered, they should become confederates or dependents of the United States; but if any of the islands were taken situated within, or at the entrance of the gulf of Mexico, these should belong to the crown of France. It was agreed, that neither of the two parties could conclude truce or peace with Great Britain without the consent of the other. They reciprocally obligated themselves not to lay down arms, until the independence of the United States should be either formally or tacitly acknowledged in treaties which should terminate the war. They guarantied to each other, that is, the United States to the king of France, his present possessions in America, as well as those he might obtain by the treaty of peace; and the king of France, to the United States, liberty, sovereignty and independence, absolute and unlimited, as well in point of government as of commerce, and likewise those possessions, additions and conquests which the confederation might acquire in the domains of Great Britain in North America. A separate and secret article reserved to the king of Spain the faculty of becoming a party to the treaty of amity and commerce, as well as to that of alliance, at such time as he should think proper.

Thus France, ever bearing in mind the wounds received in the war of Canada, and always jealous of the power of England, at first by wily intrigues and distant suggestions, then by clandestine succors, and if convenient disavowed, had encouraged the English colonies in their resistance; at length, openly taking them by the hand, she saluted them independent. The French government displayed a profound policy, and singular dexterity in the execution of this plan; it may even be affirmed, that in no other affair, however important, and in no other time, has it ever exhibited so much sagacity and stability. Its operations were covert, while it was perilous to come out, and it threw off the mask so soon as the successes of the colonists permitted them to be looked upon as safe allies. It took the field when its armies, and especially its fleets, were in perfect preparation, when all its subjects were favorably disposed, when every thing, in a word, promised victory. It would be difficult to paint the transports of exultation which burst forth in France on the publication of the new treaties. The merchants enjoyed in advance those riches which until then had been confined to the ports of England; the landholders imagined that their taxes would be diminished in proportion to the increased prosperity of commerce; the soldiers, and especially the seamen, hoped to avenge their affronts, and recover their ancient glory; the generous spirits exulted that France declared herself, as she should be, the protectress of the oppressed; the friends of liberal principles applauded her for having undertaken the defense of liberty. All united in blessing the long wished for occasion of repressing the detestable pride of a rival nation. All were persuaded that the losses sustained in the preceding reign were about to be repaired; it was every where exclaimed, that the destinies promised to the crown of France were about to be accomplished. ' Such,' it was said, ' are the happy auspices which usher in the reign of a clement and beloved prince ; too long have we suffered ; let us hail the dawn of a more fortunate future.' Nor was it only in France that this enthusiasm of joy was witnessed ; the same disposition of minds prevailed in almost all the states of Europe. The Europeans lauded, and exalted to the skies, the generosity and the magnanimity of Louis XVI. Such, at that time, was the general abhorrence excited by the conduct of the British government ; or such was the affection borne to the American cause.

Shortly after the subscription of the treaties, and long before they were made public, the British ministry had knowledge of them. It is asserted that some of its members, wishing to embrace this occasion for the re-establishment of concord between the two parties, proposed in the secret councils to acknowledge immediately the independence of the colonies, and to negotiate with them a treaty of commerce and alliance. But the king, either guided by his natural obstinacy, or docile as heretofore to the instigations of lord Bute, refused his consent to this measure. It was therefore resolved to proceed by middle ways, which, if they are the least painful, lead also the most rarely to success. They consisted, on this occasion, not in acknowledging independence, which, at this time, it was easier to deny than to prevent, but in renouncing the right of taxation, in revoking the laws complained of, in granting pardons, in acknowledging for a certain time the American authorities ; and, finally, in negotiating with them. This plan of conduct, which was not less, and perhaps more derogatory to the dignity of the crown than the acknowledgment of independence, offered, besides, less real advantage to England ; it was accordingly blamed by all prudent and intelligent politicians. None could avoid seeing, that if it was questionable, whether these measures would have operated the desired effect before the declaration of independence and the alliance with France, it was indubitable that afterwards they must prove absolutely fruitless. That proclivity which men have by nature towards independence, was likely to prevail in the minds of the Americans over the proposal of resuming their former yoke, whatever were the advantages that could have resulted from it. Another consideration must have acted upon them, and particularly upon their chiefs ; they were not ignorant, that in state matters it is little prudent to confide in the pardon of princes ; neither had they forgotten that these very ministers, who made them such bland proposals, were the same men who had attempted to starve America, had filled it with ferocious soldiers, with devastation and with blood. Besides, if the Americans should have broken the faith which they had just pledged to France, they would have declared themselves guilty of a scandalous perfidy ; abandoned by their new allies, could they have hoped, after such treachery, to find, in their utmost distress, a single power on earth that would deign to succor them ? They would have found themselves exposed, without shield or defense, to the fury and vengeance of Great Britain.

But, perhaps, the British ministers believed, that if the measures proposed were not to bring about an arrangement, they might, at least, divide opinions, give birth to powerful parties, and thus, by intestine dissensions, facilitate the triumph of England. Perhaps, also, and probably they persuaded themselves, that if the Americans rejected the propositions for an adjustment, they would at least have a colorable pretense for continuing the war. But whether the procedure of the ministers at this juncture was free or forced, lord North, in the sitting of the house of commons, of the nineteenth of February, made a very grave speech upon the present state of affairs. He remarked, that sir William Howe had not only been in the late actions, and in the whole course of the campaign, in goodness of troops, and in all manner of supplies, but in numbers, too, much superior to the enemy ; that Burgoyne had been in numbers, until the affair at Bennington, near twice as strong as the army opposed to him ; that sixty thousand men and upwards had been sent to America, a force which even exceeded the demands of the generals ; but fortune had shown herself so unpropitious, that it had been impossible to reap those advantages which were reasonably to have been expected from it. He concluded with saying, that although Great Britain was most able to continue the war, not only from the abundance of men, and the strength of the navy, but from the flourishing condition of the finances, which might be still increased by a loan at low interest, yet out of that desire which every good government ought to have, to put an end to war, the ministry had determined to submit to the deliberations of the house certain conciliatory propositions, from which he expected the most happy results. The general attention was evinced by a profound silence ; no mark of approbation was manifested by any party. Astonishment, dejection and fear overclouded the whole assembly ; so different was the present language of the ministers from what they had ever used before ; it was concluded they had been forced to it by some serious cause. Fox took this opportunity to exclaim, that the treaty of alliance between France and the United States was already signed ; the agitation and tumult became extreme. Lord North moved the resolution, that the parliament could not in future impose any tax or duty in the colonies of North America, except such only as should be deemed beneficial to commerce, and the product even of those to be collected under the authority of the respective colonies, and to be employed for their use and advantage. He proposed, besides, that five commissioners should be appointed, empowered to adjust with any assembly or individual whatsoever, the differences existing between Great Britain and her colonies, it being understood, however, that the compacts were not to take effect till ratified by the parliament.

The commissioners were, also, to be authorized to proclaim armistices wherever they should think proper, to suspend prohibitory laws, and generally all laws promulgated since the tenth of February, one thousand seven hundred and sixty-three; and to pardon whoever, and as many as they pleased. Finally, they were to have authority to appoint governors and commanders-in-chief in the reconciled provinces.

Thus the British ministers, now urged by necessity, all at once conceded what they had refused during fifteen years, and what they had been contending for in a sanguinary and cruel war, already of three years standing. Whether it was the fault of fortune, or their own, they appeared in this conjuncture, as in all others, inflexible when they should have yielded, and pliant when too late. Incapable of controlling events, they were dragged along by them. The bills proposed passed almost without opposition in parliament; but without, they excited universal discontent. ' Such concessions,' it was vociferated, ' are too unworthy of the British name and power ; they would only be admissible in an extremity, such as, Heaven be thanked, England is still far from being reduced to ; they are calculated to sow discouragement among us, to enervate our armies, to embolden our enemies, and to detach our allies. Since the right of taxation is renounced, which was the first motive and cause of the war, why not go farther, and acknowledge independency ? ' In a word, the ministers were charged with having done too much, or too little ; the common fate of those, who from timidity betake themselves to half measures ; whose prudence and vigor prove equally vain. Nor were the ministers only exposed to the animadversions of the opposite party ; the most moderate citizens expressed a no less decided disapprobation. Nevertheless, the king appointed, not long after, for commissioners, the earl of Carlisle, lord Howe, William Eden, George Johnstone, and the commander-in-chief of the English army in America ; individuals highly distinguished, either by their rank, or by the celebrity of their achievements, or by their intelligence and experience in American affair ; the earl of Carlisle, Eden and Johnstone, sailed from St. Helen's the twenty-first of April on board the ship *Trident*.

In the midst of this complication of novel events, and of novel measures, and while the entire British nation was anxiously looking towards the future, the marquis de Noailles, ambassador of his most christian majesty, at the court of England, in pursuance of instructions from his sovereign, delivered, on the thirteenth of March, to lord Weymouth, secretary of state for foreign affairs, the following declaration :

'The United States of America, which are in full possession of the independence declared by their act of the fourth of July, one thousand seven hundred and seventy-six, having made a proposal to the king to consolidate, by a formal convention, the connections that have begun to be established between the two nations, the respective plenipotentiaries have signed a treaty of amity and commerce, intended to serve as a basis for mutual good correspondence.

' His majesty, being resolved to cultivate the good understanding subsisting between France and Great Britain, by all the means compatible with his dignity, and with the good of his subjects, thinks that he ought to impart this step to the court of London, and declare to it, at the same time, that the contracting parties have had attention not to stipulate any exclusive advantage in favor of the French nation, and that the United States have preserved the liberty of treating with all nations whatsoever on the same foot of equality and reciprocity.

' In making this communication to the court of London, the king is firmly persuaded, that it will find in it fresh proofs of his majesty's constant and sincere dispositions for peace ; and that his Britannic majesty, animated by the same sentiments, will equally avoid every thing that may interrupt good harmony ; and that he will take, in particular, effectual measures to hinder the commerce of his majesty's subjects with the United States of America from being disturbed, and cause to be observed, in this respect, the usages received between trading nations, and the rules that may be considered as subsisting between the crowns of France and Great Britain.

' In this just confidence, the underwritten ambassador might think it superfluous to apprise the British ministry, that the king his master, being determined effectually to protect the lawful freedom of the commerce of his subjects, and to sustain the honor of his flag, his majesty has taken, in consequence, eventual measures, in concert with the United States of North America.'

This declaration, so full of matter in itself, and presented with very little ceremony by the French ambassador, stung British pride to the quick.   If it was one of those shrewd turns which are not unusual among princes in their reciprocal intercourse, it was also one of those which they are not accustomed to forgive. France had foreseen its consequences, and far from dreading them, they were the very object of her wishes and hopes. Lord North communicated, the seventeenth of March, the note of the French minister to the house of commons, with a message from the king, purporting that his majesty had thought proper, in consequence of this offensive declaration on the part of the government of France, to recall his ambassador from that court; that he had been sincerely desirous to preserve the tranquillity of Europe ; and that he trusted he should not stand responsible for its interruption, if he resented so unprovoked, and so unjust an aggression on the honor of his crown, and the essential interests of his kingdoms, contrary to the most solemn assurances, subversive of the law of nations, and injurious to the rights of every sovereign power in Europe. He concluded with saying, that relying with the firmest confidence on the zeal of his people, he hoped to be in a condition to repel every insult and attack, and to maintain and uphold the power and reputation of his crown.

This resolution surprised no one ; it was already the subject of conversation in all companies. Lord North moved the usual address of thanks to the king, with assurance of the support of parliament. A member named Baker proposed that the king should be entreated to remove from his counsels those persons in whom his people could no longer repose any sort of confidence. This amendment was supported with great spirit. It was then that governor Pownall, a man of weight, and particularly conversant in American affairs, rose and spoke in much the following terms :

' I do not deem it consistent with the business of this solemn day, which is about to decide upon the immediate re-establishment, or irreparable ruin of our country, to go into the inquiry whether the present ministers are longer to be trusted with the conduct of the battered ship of the state, in the midst of tempests, or whether we are to commit the helm to other hands. Considerations of far higher importance, if I am not mistaken, demand all your attention. For whatever these ministers may be, against whom I hear such bitter murmurs, if we have the wisdom to take this day a suitable resolution, I have not the least doubt that even they will be capable of executing it with success. If, on the contrary, persisting in the measures which have brought us into this critical position, we add a new blunder to all our past errors, neither these nor any other ministers can save us from perdition.

' Besides, those who are desirous of investigating the causes of our disasters, and who impute them to the present servants of the crown, will have an early opportunity for sifting that subject to their wish, in the regular examination of their conduct, which is to occupy this house in a few days. But what is the business before us, and what is the subject of our immediate deliberations? Faithless and haughty France rises against us; she threatens us with war, if we presume to resent, nay, if we do not accept the insulting conditions she dictates. Where is the citizen who loves his country, where is the Briton who is not fired with indignation, who is not impatient to avenge the outrages of this implacable rival? I also have British blood in my veins; I feel it in the transports which animate me, I approve high ard magnanimous resolutions. But what I condemn, and so long as I have life will always condemn, is the impolicy of hurrying to encounter two wars instead of one, and of choosing rather to add a new enemy to the old, than to be reconciled with the latter, in order to operate in concert against the former. To vanquish France and America together, is an enterprise to be reckoned among impossible events; to triumph over the first after having disarmed the second, is not only possible, but easy. But in order to attain this object, it is necessary to acknowledge, what we can no longer prevent, I mean American independence. And what are the obstacles which oppose so salutary a resolution? or by what reasons can it be combated? Perhaps the desire of glory, or the honor of the crown? But honor resides in victory; shame in defeat; and in affairs of state, the useful is always honorable.

'We should consider also, that in acknowledging the independence of the United States, we acknowledge not only what is, but also what we have already recognized, if not in form, at least in fact. In those very acts of conciliation which we have so lately passed, we acknowledge, if we would speak ingenuously, that we have renounced all sort of supremacy. If our intention is to maintain it, we have already gone too far; but if our desire of peace be sincere, we have not gone far enough; and every step we shall take to put the Americans back from independency, will convince them the more of the necessity of going forward. Inveterate inclinations are not so easily changed, and resolutions taken after long and mature deliberations, are not so lightly diverted.

'If we look well into the great acts of their proceedings, we shall soon be satisfied that they were not suddenly taken up as an ebullition of enthusiasm, or in the bitterness of passion or revenge, but rather as coming on of course, by a train of events, linked together by a system of policy. Their march was slow, but in measured steps; feeling their ground before they set their foot on it; yet when once set, there fixed forever. They made their declaration of rights in 1774, itself but little compatible with British supremacy. They afterwards confirmed it by a manifesto, in which they proclaimed their reasons for taking up arms; and finally they declared their independence, which is but the pinnacle and accomplishment of that work which they had long since commenced, which they were assisted in perfecting by the very nature of things, and which they have so valiantly defended in three successive campaigns.

' If these people, when they viewed their cause abandoned, as to all assistance which they looked to in Europe; when sinking, as to all appearance of what the utmost exertions of their own resources had done; when clouded with despair; would not give up the ground of independence, on which they were determined to stand; what hopes can there be, and from what quarter, that they will now, when every event of fate and fortune is reversed to us, and turned in their favor; when they feel their own power able to resist, to counteract, and in one deplorable instance superior to, and victorious over ours; when they see their cause taken up in Europe; when they find the nations among which they have taken their equal station, acknowledging their independency, and concluding treaties with them as such; when France has actually and avowedly done it; when it is known that Spain must follow, and that Holland will; what hopes can there be, and from what quarter, that they will, all at once, pull down their own new governments, to receive our provincial ones? that they will dissolve their confederation? that they will disavow all their reasons for taking up arms; and give up all those rights which they have declared, claimed and insisted upon, in order to receive such others at our hands, as supremacy on one hand will, and dependency on the other can admit them to? And how can we hope to conquer, when surrounded by his allies, the enemy, who, single, has repulsed your attacks? France abounds in hardy and gallant warriors; she will inundate with them the plains of America; and then, whether we shall be able, I say not to conquer, but to resist, let each be his own judge.

' We are in sight of the coasts of France; we see them lined with formidable maritime preparations; and though we may not fear, we ought at least to guard against, an attack upon this very territory, where we are meditating the destruction of America, who combats us, and of France, who seconds her. It follows that those soldiers who might have been sent to America, must remain in Great Britain to defend our hallowed laws, our sacred altars, our country itself, against the fury of the French. Already the numerous fleet of Brest is perfectly prepared to put to sea; already the coasts of Normandy swarm with troops that seem to menace a descent upon our natal land. And what are we doing in the mean time? We are here deliberating whether it is better to have divers enemies, than one only; whether it is more expedient to encounter at once America and Europe in league for our destruction, than to make head against Europe with the arms of America to back us? But am I alone in maintaining that the safety of England is attached to the measure I propose? All prudent men profess the same opinion; the unanimous voice of the people repeats it; the pompous but vain declamations of the ministers they have learned to interpret as the denunciations of irreparable calamities to the country. Of this the too certain proof is found in the fall of the public funds; which took place the moment there was any mention of this new ministerial frenzy, of this obstinacy more Scotch than English. Tell us then, ministers, sometimes so weakly credulous, at all times so obstinate in your resolutions, if you have easily effected the late loan, and what is the rate of interest you have paid? But you are silent. Will not this then suffice to convince you of the perversity of your measures?

'I know there are some who are careful to give out that the acknowledgment of independence, besides being a measure little to our honor, would offer no certain advantage, since we have no assurance that it would satisfy the Americans. But how can we believe that the Americans will prefer the alliance of France to ours? Are not these the same French who formerly attempted to subjugate them? Are not these the same French whose wishes would have led them to extinguish the name and language of the English? How can it be supposed that the Americans have not yet reflected that England, their bulwark, once prostrated, they will be abandoned, without defense, to the power of France, who will dispose of them as she sees fit? How should they not perceive this artifice of the French, not new, but now prepared and rendered more dangerous by our own imprudence, which consists in laboring to dissolve our union in order to crush us separately? The Americans will undoubtedly prefer the friendship and alliance of France to dependency; but believe me, when I assure you, that they will like infinitely better the alliance of Great Britain, conjointly with independence. Besides, it is a secret to nobody that the Americans are incensed against France for having in this very negotiation profited of their distress, to try to drive a hard and inequitable bargain with them; thus setting a price upon their independence. Let us avail ourselves, if we are wise, of the effects of French avarice, and we may thus make friends of those whom we can no longer have for subjects. Independent of the reasons I have urged, the interest of reciprocal commerce alone, if every other part of the ground be taken equal, would determine the Americans to prefer our friendship to that of France. But why should I multiply arguments to convince you of that which I can in an instant demonstrate beyond all doubt? I have seen, and read with my own eyes, a letter written by Benjamin Franklin, a man, as you all know, of irrefragable authority with his countrymen. In this letter, transmitted to London since the conclusion of the treaty of alliance between France and America, he affirms that if Great Britain would renounce her supremacy, and treat with the Americans as an independent nation, peace might be re-established immediately. These are not the news and silly reports with which our good ministers allow themselves to be amused by refugees. But if we may count upon the friendship and alliance of independent America, it is equally clear, that instead of being weakened by the separation, we should become but the more capable of attack, and the more vigorous for defense. For a part of these troops, which are now employed to no effect in our colonies, might then be taken with advantage to form such garrisons in Canada and Nova Scotia, as would put those provinces out of all insult and danger. The rest of the forces there might be employed to protect our islands, and to attack those of France, which, thus taken by surprise, would inevitably fall into our hands. As to the fleet, we could so dispose it as to cover and defend at once all our possessions and our commerce in the two hemispheres. Thus delivered from all disquietude on the part of America, we should be enabled to bend all our thoughts and all our forces against France; and make her pay the forfeit of her insolence and audacity.

' On these considerations, I think that, abandoning half measures, we should extend the powers of the commissioners to the enabling them to treat, consult, and finally to agree and acknowledge the Americans as independent; on condition, and in the moment, that they will, as such, form a federal treaty, offensive and defensive and commercial with us. If I am not greatly mistaken, we should reap more advantage from this single resolution, than from several victories, in a war become hopeless.

' But if, on the contrary, we persist in our infatuation, we shall learn, to our irreparable prejudice, how costly it is to trust more to appearances than reality, and how dangerous to listen to the pernicious counsels of fury and pride. Be assured, if the commissioners are not empowered to acknowledge independence, they had better never go: their going will be a mockery, and end in disgrace.'

These considerations, weighty in themselves, and the emphatic manner of the orator, made a deep impression upon the minds of his auditors; it was perceived that several members of the ministerial party began to waver. But the minister of war, Jenkinson, a personage of no little authority, immediately answered by the following speech :

' Nations, no less than individuals, ought to pursue that which is just and honest; and if this be their duty, it is equally also their interest, since it generally conducts them to glory and to greatness. On the other hand, what can be more fatal to the felicity of states, than the uncertainty and instability of counsels ?

' Resolutions always fluctuating betray, in those who govern, either weakness of mind, or timidity of spirit ; and prevent them from ever attaining the end proposed. This axiom admitted, I hope to have little difficulty in persuading the house that in the present question, where we see prejudiced men hurried away by vain chimeras, it is as rigorously required by justice and our dignity as by the most essential interests of the state, that we should not depart from the counsels we pursue. However fortune may turn her wheel, the war we wage is just. Such the wisdom of parliament has decreed it ; such the voice of the people has proclaimed it ; such the very nature of things confirms it. Why it has not been more successful, I will not now take upon me to say. Whatever may have been the causes, the want of success has at last brought upon us the insults and meditated attacks of the French. Is there any one here, who, in such a situation, would have Great Britain despond, would have her stoop to unworthy resolutions, and, through fear of the French, acknowledge herself vanquished by her ancient subjects ? But what do I say ? There are men who would have us tremble for ourselves ; and who imagine they already see the French banners floating at the gates of London. But disregarding the vain terrors of these, I know not whether to say ambitious or timorous men, I pledge myself to demonstrate, that the course we have hitherto pursued is not only that of justice and honor, but that it is capable of conducting us to the object of our desires.

' I shall begin with asking these bosom friends of rebels, if they are certain that it is all America, or only a seditious handful, whose craft and audacity have raised them to the head of affairs, who claim independency ? For my own part, I confess that this independence appears to me rather a vision that floats in certain brains, inflamed by the rage of innovation, on that side of the Atlantic as well as on this, than any general wish of the people. This is what all men of sense declare, who have resided in the midst of that misguided multitude ; this is attested by the thousands of royalists who have flocked to the royal standard in New York, and who have fought for the king in the plains of Saratoga, and on the banks of the Brandywine. This, finally, is proclaimed by the very prisons, crowded with inhabitants, who have chosen rather to part with their liberty, than to renounce their allegiance ; and have preferred an imminent peril of death, to a participation in rebellion. If their co-operation has not proved of that utility, which, from their number and force, was to have been expected, this must be imputed not to their indifference, but rather to the inconsiderate zeal which caused them to break out prematurely. There is every reason to think that to such subjects as remained faithful until England set up the pretension of taxation, many others will join themselves now that she has renounced it ; for already all are convinced how much better it is to live under the mild sway of an equitable prince, than under the tyranny of new and ambitious men. And why should I here omit the ties of consanguinity, the common language, the mutual interests, the conformity of manners, and the recollection of ancient union ? I appeal even to the testimony of my adversary, with regard to the avarice and revolting behavior of France, during the negotiation of alliance ; and can it be doubtful that to this new, insatiable, arrogant and faithless friend, the Americans will prefer their old, tried, benefi- cent and affectionate fellow-citizens ? Nor should I omit to mention a well known fact ; the finances of congress are exhausted ; their soldiers are naked and famishing ; they can satisfy none of the wants of the state ; creditors are without remedy against their debtors ; hence arise scandals without end, private hatreds, and unanimous maledictions against the government.

' There is not an individual among the Americans, but sees that, in accepting the terms offered by Great Britain, the public credit will be re-established, private property secured, and abundance in all parts of the social body restored. They will concur, with the more ardor, in establishing this prosperity, when they shall see powerful England resolved on continuing the war with redoubled energy. Certainly they will not believe that any succors they can receive from haughty France will compel us very speedily to accept of ignominious con- ditions. Yes, methinks I already see, or I am strangely mistaken, the people of America flocking to the royal standard ; every thing invites them to it ; fidelity towards the sovereign, the love of the English name, the hope of a happier future, their aversion to their new and unaccustomed allies, and, finally, the hatred they bear to the tyranny of congress.

' It is then that we shall have cause to applaud our constancy, then shall we acknowledge that the most honorable counsels, as the most worthy of so great a realm, are also the most useful and safe. So far from thinking the new war against France ought to dismay as, I see in it only grounds of better hopes. If, up to the present time, we have had but little success against the Americans, whatever may have been the cause of it, where is the Englishman who does not hope, nay, who does not firmly believe, that the French are about to furnish us with occasions for the most brilliant triumphs? As for myself, I find the pledge of it in the recollection of our past achievements, in the love of our ancient glory, in the present ardor of our troops, and especially in the strength of our navy. The advantages we shall gain over the French by land and sea, will recompense the losses we have sustained in America. The Americans, finding their hopes frustrated, which they had so confidently placed on the efficacy of the succors of their new allies, will be struck with terror; they will prefer the certain peace of an accommodation to future independence, rendered daily more uncertain by new defeats of their allies. Besides, who will presume to affirm that fortune will not become more propitious to us even upon the territory of America? Is it going too far to believe, that when our armies shall direct their march towards the open and fertile provinces inhabited by the loyalists, they will be more successful than they could be in mountainous, steril, savage regions, swarming with rebels? For myself, I have not a particle of doubt that we shall find in Georgia and the Carolinas, the most ample indemnification for the unlucky campaigns of New Jersey and of Pennsylvania. But I admit, which God forbid, fresh disasters; I will nevertheless maintain that we ought to prosecute what we have commenced. If we lose our colonies, we shall not lose honor. I would rather American independence, if ever it must exist, should be the offspring of inexorable destiny, than of a base condescension on our part.

'Shall France then find us so tame, as, at the bare shadow of her enmity, to abandon our possessions, and tamely yield up to her all our glory; we, who have the time still green in memory, when, after having by victories on victories trampled upon her pride and prostrated her power, we triumphantly scoured all seas, and the continent of America?

'Of what country then are the authors of such timid counsels? English perhaps. As for myself, I cannot believe it. Who are these pusillanimous spirits, who paint our affairs as if they were desperate? Are they women or affrighted children? I should incline to believe the latter, if I did not see them often holding forth within these walls their sinister predictions, indulging their favorite whim of reviling their country, expatiating with apparent delight upon its weakness, and magnifying the power of its ambitious enemy. And what is then this France, at the gathering of whose frowns we are to shudder?

Where are her seamen trained to naval maneuvers? Where are her
soldiers formed in battles? I will tell those who do not know it, or
who affect not to know it, that she is at this very moment attacked
with an internal malady that will paralyze her strength at the very
moment she may wish to move. Who of you is ignorant that she
labors under an annual deficiency of thirty millions? Who knows
not that she is destitute of the resources of loans? her rich capital
ists being as distrustful as they are rare.

'But it is not in the sinking of credit only that France is distress-
ed; the spirit of free inquiry, and the effects of an extended commerce, have introduced opinions among the French people, that are
wholly incompatible with their government. Contrary to all prece-
dent, contrary to all ideas of that government, a reasoning has propagated, and even entered into some of the lines of business, that the
twentieth is a *free gift*, and that every individual has a right to judge
of its necessity, and oversee its employment.

'Besides this, one bad effect of the zeal with which they pretended to take up the American cause, and which they now learn
in earnest to have an affection for, has tainted their principles with
the spirit of republicanism. These principles of liberty always diminish the force of government; and if they take root and grow up
in France, we shall see that government as distracted and unsettled
as any other.

'I hear talk of the difficulty of borrowing among ourselves, and
of the depression of the public funds; but the lenders have already
come forward; and I understand the first payment is already made.
The interest they have demanded is not only not usurious, but it is
even much more moderate than our enemies would have wished, or
than our croaking orators predicted. As to the fall of the funds, it
has been very inconsiderable, and they have even risen to-day. But
how shall I treat the grand bugbear of French invasion? We have
a formidable fleet, thirty thousand regular troops; and at a moment's
warning, could muster such a body of militia as would make France
desist from, or bitterly rue her projects. It is no such easy task to
vanquish Britons; their country falls not a prey so lightly to whom-
soever. We are told also that the Americans are ready to contract
alliance with us, and that they have manifested such a wish; and
we have already seen men credulous enough to catch at the lure.
Do we not know that those who agitate these intrigues, if indeed
any credit is due to such rumors, are the very same persons who
violate the capitulation of Saratoga, the same who imprison, who
torture, who massacre the loyal subjects of the king? For my part,
I fear the gift and its bearer; I fear American wiles; I fear the

French school; I fear they wish to degrade us by the refusal, after having mocked us by their offers. Hitherto I have been considering exclusively what policy demands of you; I will now briefly remind you of the claims of justice, gratitude and humanity. Think of those who, in the midst of the rage of rebellion, have preserved their fidelity to the king, to yourselves, to the country. Have compassion for those who have placed all their hopes in your constancy.

'Take pity on the wives, on the widows, on the children of those, who, now exposed without defense to the fury of the insurgents, offer up their prayers to Heaven for the prosperity of your arms, and see no glimpse of any period to their torments but in your victory. Will you abandon all these? Will you allow them to become the victims of the confidence they placed in you? Will the English show less perseverance in their own cause, than the loyalists have manifested on their behalf? Ah! such abominable counsels were never yet embraced by this generous kingdom. Already, methinks, I see your noble bosoms pant with indignation; already I hear your voices cry vengeance on outrages so unexampled, while your hands grasp the arms which are about to inflict it. On, then, ye fathers of the state! accomplish the high destiny that awaits you. Save the honor of the kingdom, succor the unfortunate, protect the faithful, defend the country. Let Europe acknowledge, and France prove to her cost, that it is pure British blood which still flows in your veins. To condense therefore in a few words what I feel and what I think, I move, that the proposition of my adversary being rejected, the king be assured that his faithful commons are ready to furnish him with the means that shall be necessary to maintain the honor of his people, and the dignity of his crown.'

As soon as Jenkinson had finished speaking, there followed an incredible agitation in the house. At length the votes were taken, and it was carried almost unanimously, that an address of thanks should be presented to the king, that war should be continued against the colonies, and declared against France.

But in the sitting of the house of lords of the seventh of April, after the duke of Richmond had concluded a very solid and very eloquent speech, proving that it was time to give another direction to the affairs of the kingdom, that house became the scene of a melancholy event. The earl of Chatham, though sinking under a mortal infirmity, had dragged himself to his place in parliament. Shocked at the new measures that were thrown out there, and determined not to consent to the separation of America, he pronounced these words, which were the last of his life: 'I have made an effort, almost beyond the powers of my constitution, to come down to the house on this day to express the indignation I feel at an idea, which, I understand, has been proposed to you, of yielding up the sovereignty of America!

' My lords, I rejoice that the grave has not closed upon me; that I am still alive to lift up my voice against the dismemberment of this ancient and most noble monarchy! Pressed down, as I am, by the hand of infirmity, I am little able to assist my country in this most perilous conjuncture ; but, my lords, while I have sense and memory, I will never consent to deprive the royal offspring of the house of Brunswick, the heirs of the princess Sophia, *of their fairest inheritance.*

' Where is the man that will dare to advise such a measure? His majesty succeeded to an empire as great in extent as its reputation was unsullied. Shall we tarnish the lustre of this nation by an ignominious surrender of its rights and fairest possessions? Shall this great kingdom, that has survived, whole and entire, the Danish depredations, the Scottish inroads, and the Norman conquest; that has stood the threatened invasion of the Spanish armada, now fall prostrate before the house of Bourbon? Surely, my lords, this nation is no longer what it was! Shall a people that, seventeen years ago, was the terror of the world, now stoop so low as to tell its ancient inveterate enemy, Take all we have, only give us peace! It is impossible. In God's name, if it is absolutely necessary to declare either for peace or war, and the former cannot be preserved with honor, why is not the latter commenced without hesitation? I am not, I confess, well informed of the resources of this kingdom; but I trust it has sufficient to maintain its just rights. But, my lords, any state is better than despair. Let us at least make one effort; and if we must fall, let us fall like men!

Here the earl of Chatham ended his speech. The duke of Richmond rose, and endeavored to prove that the conquest of America by force of arms was become impracticable ; that consequently it was wiser to secure her friendship by a treaty of alliance, than to throw her into the arms of France. The earl of Chatham wished to reply, but after two or three unsuccessful attempts to stand, he fell down in a swoon on his seat. He was immediately assisted by the duke of Cumberland, and several other principal members of the house. They removed him into an adjacent apartment, called the Prince's chamber. The confusion and disorder became extreme. The duke of Richmond proposed, that in consideration of this public calamity, the house should adjourn to the following day ; and it was accordingly done. The next day the debate was resumed upon the motion of the duke of Richmond; but it was finally ejected by a large majority.

The eleventh of May was the last day of William Pitt, earl of Chatham; he was in his seventieth year. His obsequies were celebrated the eighth of June, with extraordinary pomp, in Westminster Abbey; where a monument was erected to him a short time after. This man, whether for his genius, his virtues, or the great things he did for his country, is rather to be paralleled with the ancients, than preferred to the moderns. He governed for a considerable time the opulent kingdom of Great Britain; he raised it to such a pitch of splendor, as the English at no other period had ever known, or even presumed to hope for; and he died, if not in poverty, at least with so narrow a fortune, that it would not have been sufficient to maintain his family honorably; a thing at that time sufficiently remarkable, and which in the present age might pass for a prodigy! But his grateful country recompensed in the children the virtue of the father. The parliament granted a perpetual annuity of four thousand pounds sterling to the family of Chatham, besides paying twenty thousand pounds of debts which the late earl had been compelled to contract, in order to support his rank and his numerous household. No individual until that time, except the duke of Marlborough, had received in England such high and liberal rewards. The earl of Chatham was no less distinguished as a great orator, than as a profound statesman, and immaculate citizen. He defended with admirable eloquence, before parliament, those resolutions which he had maturely discussed and firmly adopted in the consultations of the cabinet. Some, it is true, blamed in his speeches the too frequent use of figures, and a certain pomp of style much savoring of the taste of those times. But this great minister surpassed all the rulers of nations of his age, in the art of exciting, even to enthusiasm, the zeal of the servants of the state, civil as well as military; a talent which Heaven confers but rarely, and only upon privileged individuals. In a word, he was a man whose name will never be pronounced without encomiums, and the resplendent glory of whose virtues will eternally recommend them to imitation.

We now resume the thread of events. The British ministers, seeing that war with France was become inevitable, took all the measures they judged necessary to sustain it. They exerted themselves therein with the more ardor, as they could not but perceive that if England showed herself with disadvantage in this contest against France and America, Spain, and perhaps even Holland, would not long remain neuter; whereas, on the other hand, a prompt and brilliant victory might intimidate the two latter powers from declaring themselves. Their attention was occupied especially in pressing their maritime preparations, as therein consisted the principal defense of the kingdom, and the pledge of success. But on a strict examination into the state of the navy, it was found to be neither so numerous, nor so well provided, as had been supposed, and as the urgency of circumstances required. This afflicting discovery excited a general clamor. In the two houses of parliament, the duke of Bolton and Fox inveighed with great asperity against the earl of Sandwich, who was first lord of the admiralty. No diligence, however, was omitted to remedy all deficiencies. To cheer the public mind in so trying a conjuncture, and especially to inspirit the seamen, by giving them a chief possessed of their full confidence, the ministers appointed to the command of the fleet lying at Portsmouth, admiral Keppel, an officer of distinguished ability, and highly celebrated for his brilliant achievements in the preceding wars. Lords Hawke and Anson, those two bright luminaries of the British marine, had honored him with their esteem and closest friendship ; in a word, no choice could have been so agreeable to the British nation at large as that of admiral Keppel. He refused not the appointment, notwithstanding that he was already arrived at an age in which man prefers repose to action, and that he could aspire to no greater glory than what he had acquired ; he must even have felt a sort of repugnance to commit it anew to the hazard of battles. To these considerations was added another untoward particular, which was, that, as a whig, the ministers eyed him with jealousy ; a circumstance which, in the course of events, might occasion him many disgusts. But more thoughtful for the good of his country, which claimed his services, than of his private convenience, he hesitated not to accept the charge, to which he was invited by the public voice. The vice-admirals, Harland and Palliser, both officers of high reputation, were appointed to second him in command. On his arrival at Portsmouth, Keppel, instead of a great fleet ready to proceed to sea, found, to his extreme surprise, only six sail of the line prepared for immediate service, crews incomplete, provisions insufficient, and naval munitions wanting. The ministers alledged that the other ships had been detached on different services, but that they were to return shortly. However it was, the admiral exerted an activity so astonishing, that by the middle of June he found himself in condition to put to sea with twenty ships of the line, and not without expectation of prompt re-inforcements. He sailed from St. Helens on the thirteenth, accompanied by the fervent prayers of all England. The posture of affairs was inexpressibly critical and alarming. It was known that France had a numerous fleet at Brest, completely manned and equipped for sea ; the ships which conveyed the riches of India were expected from day to day, and might become the prey of the French. This disaster, so great in itself, by the loss of such treasures, must have involved another of still greater consequence, that of an immense number of sailors, who were counted upon to man the ships of war. To this momentous consideration were joined the defense of the vast extent of the British coasts, the safety of the capital itself, the preservation of the arsenals, the repositories of all the elements of the greatness of England, and the basis of all her hopes ; and all these objects, rather of vital than of great importance, were confided to the protection of twenty ships !

Meanwhile the land preparations were pushed with no less ardor than the maritime. The recruiting service was prosecuted with success ; the militia were assembled, and formed into regiments upon the model of regular troops. Encampments were established in such places as were thought most exposed to the attempts of the enemy. Thus the English made their dispositions to meet the impending war. The government had already ordered, by way of reprisal, the detention of all the French vessels that were found in the ports

But France, who for a long time had purposed to turn her arms against England, was better provided with all the implements of war. Her fleet was numerous, and all her arsenals were in full activity. The court of Versailles, on intelligence of the hostile manner with which king George had answered the declaration of the marquis de Noailles, immediately dispatched orders to the different ports, prohibiting the departure of all English vessels. This measure, taken reciprocally by the two powers, produced but little effect ; the masters of merchant vessels, foreseeing a rupture, had hastened to recover their own shores. France, henceforth, laying aside all hesitations, felt it due to herself to assume the attitude which becomes a great and powerful nation. She was disposed to perfect the work commenced by her declaration, and to re-assure the minds of her new allies by a step from which it was impossible to fall back without shame. She therefore resolved to receive, and formally acknowledge, the American commissioners, as ambassadors of a free and independent nation. How England must have been stung by this affront it is not difficult to imagine.

On the twenty-first of March, the three commissioners were introduced by the count de Vergennes before the throne, whereon was seated the king, Louis XVI., in the midst of the grandees of his court. In this ceremony, none of those formalities were omitted which it was usual to observe, whenever the kings of France gave audience to the ambassadors of sovereign and independent nations ;

a truly remarkable event, and such as history, perhaps, affords no
example of! The Americans herein experienced better fortune
than other nations that have acquired independence; as, for example,
the Switzers and Dutch, who were not without difficulty, nor till after a long time, acknowledged independent by those very powers that
had assisted them to break the yoke of their masters.

France, having thus dropped the mask, could not but perceive that
in the present war she must depend more upon her fleets than upon
her armies. She was not unmindful, that an essential part of maritime war consists in capturing, as well the armed ships of the enemy, to diminish his power, as those of commerce, to exhaust his resources; an object always of primary importance, but most especially such in a war with England. The court of Versailles accordingly determined to employ an incentive that should stimulate the ardor
of both officers and crews. It had been usual in France, in order
to encourage the armaments on cruise, to grant certain recompenses
to the captors of ships of war; and to those of merchant vessels, one
third of the produce of their sale. The king, by a decree of the twenty-eighth of March, ordained that the enemy ships of war and cruisers,
which should be taken by his own, should belong in full and entire
property to the commanders, officers and crews, who should have
captured them; and that, in like manner, two thirds of the value
of merchant ships and of their cargoes, should become the property
of the captors; the other third, being reserved, to be deposited in
the fund destined for the relief of invalid seamen. This decree, signed by the king, and countersigned by the duke de Penthievre, grand-
admiral of France, was to have been put in execution the fourth of
the following May; nevertheless, whether Louis XVI., as some think,
swayed by the natural benignity of his character, was reluctant to
give the signal for the effusion of blood, or that policy disposed him
to wait till the English should have committed the first hostilities,
the edict was not published and executed until the beginning of July.

With a view to prevent the English government, fearing for itself,
from being able to send re-inforcements to America, regiments were
ordered to march from all parts of France upon the coasts that look
towards England. Already a formidable army was found assembled,
and ready, in all appearance, to be embarked on board the grand armament at Brest, for a descent upon the opposite shore. All the
labors of that port were pushed with unexampled activity; more than
thirty ships of the line were already completely equipped there, besides a great number of frigates; the latter were particularly intended for cruising against the British commerce. Another considerable
fleet was about to put to sea from the port of **Toulon**.

This sudden resurrection of the French marine was the subject of extreme surprise to all nations, and particularly to England, who, accustomed to domineer upon the ocean, scarcely knew how to believe that there should thus all at once have risen up a power in condition to contend with her for the scepter of the seas. In truth, the state of debility into which France had fallen at the epoch of the death of Louis XIV. not only rendered it impossible to remedy the weakness in which the French navy was left at the conclusion of the war of the Spanish succession, but it even occasioned those ships which remained to perish in the docks for want of repairs. The wars of Italy, of Flanders, and of Germany, which took place under the reign of Louis XV., by drawing all the efforts and all the resources of the state to the land service, produced a fatal coldness towards the marine department. France contented herself with arming a few ships, rather to protect her own commerce, than to disturb that of the enemy; hence disastrous defeats, and losses without number. To all these causes was joined the opinion, natural to the inhabitants of France, satisfied with the fertility of their lands, and the multitude of their manufactures, that they have little need of a strong navy and of maritime traffic. But finally, the increase of the products of their colonies, and the immense gain they derived from the sale of them in foreign markets, drew the attention of the French to the importance of external commerce.

They perceived, at the same time, that without a military marine to protect the mercantile, maritime commerce must always be uncertain, and consequently sickly and unprofitable; and that war may destroy, in a few days, the fruits of a long peace. On these considerations, the court of France devoted its cares to the creation and maintenance of a fleet sufficiently formidable to command respect during peace, or to make war with success, and protect commerce from the insults of enemy vessels.

The present American war, which opened so brilliant a perspective to the French, furnished also a powerful incentive to these new designs. In order not to want skillful officers to manage the ships, the seamen of the merchant shipping, in imitation of the example of the English and Dutch, were called into the service of the royal navy. Besides this, in pursuance of a well conceived plan, there were sent out in the year 1772, 1775, and 1776, three fleets, commanded by three excellent seamen, the counts d'Orvilliers, De Guichen, and Duchaffault. These excursions served as schools of practice, in which the officers and crews formed themselves to evolutions and manœuvres. In brief, the efforts of the French government were so unremitting, and it was so seconded by the general ardor, that at the commencement of the present war, its navy equaled, if it did not surpass, that of England ; speaking, however, of the fleets which the latter had then fitted for immediate service, or in such forwardness that they could put to sea within a short space of time.   Nor was France disposed to keep this navy idle in her ports.   The cabinet of Versailles meditated two expeditions equally important ; the one was to be executed by the armament at Brest, the other by the fleet of Toulon.   The latter, putting to sea as soon as possible, was to repair with all celerity to America, and suddenly to make its appearance in the waters of the Delaware.

Hence two events were likely to result, equally pernicious to Great Britain ; namely, that the squadron of lord Howe, which had gone up that river, and which was greatly inferior in force to that of France, would, without any doubt, have been destroyed, or must have fallen into the power of the French.   That squadron annihilated or taken, the army under general Clinton, pressed in front by Washington, and in rear by the French fleet thus possessed of the Delaware, would also have been constrained to surrender, or, certainly, would have had an extremely perilous retreat.   So decisive a blow must have put an end to the whole American war.   This plan of campaign had been debated and agreed upon at Paris, between the commissioners of congress and the ministry.   Nor was the execution of it delayed ; on the thirteenth of April, the French fleet sailed from Toulon.   It was composed of twelve sail of the line, and four large frigates, and commanded by the count d'Estaing, a man of great valor, and of an active genius.   It took out a considerable corps of troops to serve on shore.   Silas Deane, one of the American commissioners, who was recalled, and M. Gerard, whom the king had appointed his minister to the United States, were on board.   Fortune showed herself favorable to these first essays.   The wind seconded the voyage of the fleet ; and, though the British ministry had been promptly advised of its departure, their ignorance of the route taken by the count d'Estaing, and the strong west winds which prevailed for some days, so retarded the decisions of the admiralty, that it was not till the first of June they ordered admiral Byron to make sail with twelve ships for America ; he was to replace lord Howe, who had requested leave to return to England.   As for the fleet of Brest, more considerable, and commanded by the count d'Orvilliers, who was impatient to realize the hopes which had been placed in his talents, it was destined to scour the seas of Europe, in order to keep alive upon the coasts of Great Britain the fear of an invasion.   He relied especially upon his frigates, which were very numerous, to intercept the merchant fleets laden with rich cargoes, which the English then expected from the two Indies. Thus things were rapidly verging to an open rupture between the two states, and immediate hostilities were expected, though war was not yet declared on either part, according to the established usages of Europe. Universal attention was roused by the contest going to commence between France and England ; events of moment were expected from the collision of two such powerful nations. Nor was fortune slow to light the first fires of this conflagration, which soon involved the four quarters of the world in its flames. Scarcely had admiral Keppel got out to sea, the thirteenth of June, from St. Helens, and shaped his course for the bay of Biscay, when he discovered, at no great distance, two ships of considerable size, with two other smaller vessels, which appeared to be watching the motions of his fleet. These were the two French frigates called the *Licorne* and the *Belle Poule*. The admiral found himself in a very delicate situation. On the one hand he desired much to make himself master of the ships, in order to procure information respecting the state and position of the Brest fleet ; on the other, war was not yet declared between the two nations, and the causing it to break out might be imputed to his temerity. Nor did he find any thing in the instructions of the ministers which could remove his perplexity ; as they were exceedingly loose, and left every thing almost entirely to his discretion. It should be added, that Keppel being of a party in opposition to that of the ministers, his conduct, in case he commenced hostilities, was liable to be interpreted unfavorably, since his adversaries might attribute to political motives what appeared to be the inevitable result of circumstances. In this painful embarrassment, Keppel, like the good citizen he was, chose rather to serve his country at his own peril, than to hazard its interest by his indecision. Accordingly, the seventeenth of June, he ordered his ships to give chase to the French. Between five and six in the afternoon, the English frigate Milford came up with the Licorne, and her captain, in very civil terms, summoned the French commander to repair under the stern of admiral Keppel. The Frenchman at first refused ; but seeing the Hector ship of the line come up, which saluted with ball, he submitted to his destiny, and following that vessel, took station in the British fleet.

During this time, captain Marshall, with his frigate Arethusa, of twenty-eight six pounders, in company with the Alert cutter, was in pursuit of the Belle Poule, which carried twenty-six twelve pounders, and was accompanied by a corvette of ten guns.

The Arethusa, being the better sailer, arrived about six in the evening within musket shot of the Belle Poule. Marshall informed the French captain, M. de la Clocheterie, of his orders to bring him under the stern of the admiral. To this, de la Clocheterie returned a spirited refusal. The Arethusa then fired a shot across the Belle Poule, which she returned with a discharge of her broadside. A fierce engagement between the two frigates ensued ; animated by an equal emulation, and bent on carrying the victory, in this first action, the most extraordinary efforts of resolution were displayed on both sides. The conflict continued for more than two hours, with severe damage to both parties, as the sea was calm, and the vessels extremely near. The French were superior in the weight of metal, the number of their crew, and the proximity of their coasts; while the English were benefited by the number of guns, and especially by the presence of two ships of the line, the Valiant and the Monarch ; which, though prevented by the calm from coming up to take part in the action, nevertheless greatly disquieted the French captain, and exceedingly circumscribed his movements. Finally, after an obstinate contest, the English frigate, finding herself too close upon the coasts of France, despairing of being able to overpower her adversary, and having sustained much injury in her masts, spars and rigging, profited of a light breeze, which sprung up at that moment, to withdraw. She was afterwards towed off to the fleet by the Valiant and Monarch. During her retreat, the French saluted her with fifty balls ; but she returned them not one. The Belle Poule would even have pursued her, but for the damage she had received herself, besides the proximity of the two men of war, and even of the whole English armament.

La Clocheterie, thinking it more prudent to consult his safety, went to cast anchor for the night in the midst of the shoals, near Plouascat. The next morning, the two English ships came to reconnoiter his position, and ascertain whether it was possible to approach the frigate near enough to take her. But finding the obstacles of the rocks insuperable, they abandoned the enterprise, and returned to join the fleet. For the same causes, and at the same time, the English cutter and the French corvette joined battle with equal fury, but with different success. After an hour of the most vigorous resistance, the corvette surrendered. The Arethusa, in this action, had eight men killed and thirty-six wounded. The loss of the Belle Poule was forty killed, and fifty-seven wounded. Among the first was M. de St. Marsault, lieutenant of the frigate ; among the second, M. de la Roche de Kerandraon, ensign ; Bouvet, an auxiliary officer, and M. de la Clocheterie himself, who received two contusions.

In the morning of the eighteenth, the frigate Licorne, which had been stationed in the middle of the English fleet, having made a movement which gave the English some suspicion, they fired a shot across her way, as a signal to keep in company with the other ships. Immediately, to the great astonishment of the admiral, and of the whole English fleet, she discharged a broadside and a volley of musketry into the America, of sixty-four guns, commanded by lord Longford, which lay the nearest to her. This done, she struck her colors, as if, tired of this middle state between peace and war in which she was kept, she had preferred, though a prisoner, to constitute herself in open war. Keppel sent her to Plymouth. In the mean time, another French frigate, named the Pallas, fell in with the English fleet; the admiral detained her, changing her officers and crew. Such was his conduct with regard to French vessels of war. As to merchant ships, though a great number of them fell within his reach, he permitted them to continue their voyage without interruption, not thinking himself authorized to stop them.

The action of the Belle Poule excited no little enthusiasm in France, where the remembrance of so many defeats was still recent; and it is unquestionable that the officers and all the crew of that frigate had signalized as much valor as nautical ability. Their conduct occasioned a sincere joy, and it was diligently extolled, in order to animate the public mind by these brilliant beginnings. The king showed himself lavish of favors towards those who had fought; he appointed M. de la Clocheterie captain of ship; Bouvet, lieutenant of frigate; and gave the cross of Saint Louis to Roche Kerandraon. Pensions were granted to the sister of Saint Marsault, to the widows, and to the children of those who had fallen in the action. The English were not so generous towards captains Marshall, and Fairfax, commander of the cutter; but they received the encomiums of the admiralty and of their fellow-citizens.

But the king of France, considering the affair of the Belle Poule, and the seizure of other frigates, as a sufficient motive for executing his projects, ordered reprisals against the vessels of Great Britain. He immediately caused to be published his decree concerning prizes, as if the sending of the count d'Estaing to America, with such orders as he was the bearer of, was not yet to be reputed a commencement of war. The English went through the same formalities, thus authorizing by words what they had already done, at least with regard to ships of war. Until this time, the two parties had endeavored to harm each other by all possible means, without resorting to the accustomed declarations.

The papers found aboard the French frigates, and the questions put to the prisoners, furnished admiral Keppel with important intelligence. He learned that in the port of Brest were thirty-two ships of the line, with ten or twelve frigates, all in complete readiness to put to sea ; whereas all his own forces consisted in twenty sai. of the line and three frigates. He found himself already in sight of the Isle of Ouessant, and consequently near the coasts of France. His position was truly embarrassing. The proximity and superiority of the enemy rendered his present station imminently perilous. To encounter the hazards of a battle which might expose the safety of the kingdom, was rather an act of temerity, than a courageous resolution. On the other nand, to retire from the coasts of an enemy he had braved a moment since, appeared to him a step too unworthy of his own reputation, and of the English name. But finally, consulting utility more than appearances, and his duty rather than the point of honor, he tacked about for England, and entered Portsmouth the twenty-seventh of June.

Immediately, some, from the spirit of party, and in order to exculpate the ministers, others to appease the national pride, pulled him to pieces without mercy. It might have seemed that his retreat had sullied the glory of England ; and some were so transported by their fury as to compare Keppel to Byng. The admiral supported with admirable constancy the outrages of the multitude, and the invectives of the party who excited them. He busied himself only with the means of re-inforcing his fleet, and of putting it in condition to scour the seas anew ; the admiralty powerfully seconded his zeal, and the success corresponded to his exertions. The first divisions of the East and West India fleets arrived about that time, and furnished a great number of excellent seamen to the naval armament. Thus re-inforced, it weighed anchor and put to sea the ninth of July. It was composed of twenty-four ships of the line, which were afterwards joined by six more of the same class. It comprehended a ship of one hundred guns, named the Victory, which bore the admiral's flag, six of ninety, one of eighty, and fifteen of seventy-four ; the rest were of sixty-four.

They were all well manned and equipped, and commanded by excellent officers. The frigates were insufficient in number ; there were only five or six, with two fire-ships. The fleet was divided into three squadrons ; the van was commanded by sir Robert Harland, vice-admiral of the Red ; the center by admiral Keppel, assisted by admiral Campbell, a consummate seaman, who, on the score of ancient friendship, had chosen to accompany him as the first captain of the Victory. The rear was conducted by sir Hugh Palliser, vice-admiral of the Blue, and one of the members of the board of admiralty. Finding themselves so strong, and no longer doubting of victory, the English made their appearance upon the coasts of France.

They sought the French fleet with all diligence, impatient to give it battle, in order to preserve their commerce, to efface the dishonor of having a few days before yielded the sea to the enemy ; finally, to sustain their ancient renown, and to cause fortune to incline in their favor from the very commencement of hostilities. Meanwhile, the French fleet had also come out of port the eighth of July. It was in like manner formed in three divisions ; the first commanded by the count Duchaffault, the center by the count d'Orvilliers, captain-general, and the third by the duke de Chartres, prince of the blood, who was seconded and guided by admiral de la Motte Piquet. These three divisions comprised thirty-two sail of the line, among which were the admiral's ship, la Bretagne, of one hundred and ten guns, la Ville de Paris, of ninety, which carried the count de Guichen ; two of eighty, twelve of seventy-four, one of seventy, two of sixty-four, one of sixty, and two of fifty, besides a great number of frigates. It was the intention of the count d'Orvilliers not to come to an engagement except with great probabilities of success ; and this by no means for want of an intrepid valor, and of a perfect knowledge of naval tactics ; but he chose first to exercise his crews thoroughly. He hoped, also, without exposing himself to the hazards of an action, to give England some severe blows, by employing his light vessels to capture the convoys which she daily expected from the two Indies. He shaped his course for the Isle of Ouessant, in the full persuasion that the British fleet, which he supposed to consist but of twenty sail of the line, would not presume to venture out of port, or, if it showed itself, that he should certainly defeat or disperse it, and that, in all events, he should acquire the dominion of the sea. Fortune appeared to favor these first efforts ; scarcely had he quitted the road of Brest, when he discovered the English frigate, the Lively, which admiral Keppel had detached upon discovery ; he ordered her to be chased, and she was soon taken. The entire world was attentive to what might ensue, on seeing the two most potent nations of Europe marshaled the one against the other, on the ocean. To this object, and not in vain, had the government of France aimed all its calculations for several years back. Its ships were completely equipped, its seamen well trained, its captains excellent. It remained only that fortune should smile upon such magnanimous designs. The two fleets came in sight of each other in the evening of the twenty-third of July, the Isle of Ouessant being thirty leagues distant, and the wind at west. The count d'Orvilliers, believing the enemy weaker than he was in reality, desired impatiently to bring him to action. But on approaching the British fleet, and finding it nearly as strong as his own, he avoided an engagement no less cautiously than he had eagerly sought it at first. As he had the advantage of the wind, it was impossible for the English to force him to it, against his will. During the night, two French ships were driven by the force of the wind to the leeward of the British fleet. Admiral Keppel, having perceived it in the morning, made signal to give chase and cut them off from the main body of their fleet. He hoped that in order to save them, the French admiral would give him battle, or at least that these ships would be taken, or so forced out of their course that it would be impossible for them to rejoin their fleet. The count d'Orvilliers preferred not to make any movement to succor them; and thus the two vessels, though they had the good fortune to escape the English, were chased so far, that they could take no part in the events which followed.

During the four following days the two fleets remained in sight; the British admiral endeavoring all the time to get the wind, or to beat up so near the French fleet as to force it to action. But to arrive at this object, it was impossible to maintain the disposition entire; and therefore Keppel had commanded that the ships should take rank according to their swiftness, as they gained to the windward, with attention, however, to keep their distances as much as possible. This movement was also necessary, in order not to lose sight of the enemy. But it was not without danger, since it might offer the French an occasion to fall suddenly with superior force upon some one of the English ships. It was also the cause, that on the twenty-seventh, the day of battle, the French fleet was formed in better order than that of England, which appeared deranged. On the morning of that day, the wind continuing from the west, and favoring the French, the two fleets were separated, one from the other, a distance of only three leagues, in such a manner, however, that the English rear found itself a little more to the leeward than the center and van. Keppel therefore ordered Palliser, who commanded it, to press up to the windward, in order to form in a line with the two other divisions of the fleet. Palliser executed the orders of the admiral. This movement induced the count d'Orvilliers to believe, and perhaps not without reason, as Palliser continued to crowd more and more to the windward, that it was the intention of the enemy to attack the French rear, and to gain on the opposite tack the weathergage of that division. To defeat this maneuver, he directly put his ships about, and reversing his order of battle, his rear became van. This very movement, together with some variations in the wind, of which the English dexterously availed themselves, brought the two fleets so near each other, that the action commenced immediately, the wind blowing from the west, and the French running from north to south, the English from south to north. This manner of combating, by which a close and stationary action was avoided, the ships firing only as they passed each other in opposite directions, was the result of the maneuver just made by the French fleet.

It suited the count d'Orvilliers so much the better, as, since he had not been able to decline the engagement, it assured him, at least, that it could not be decisive. For it was a necessary consequence of this order of battle, that the two fleets must break their line during the action, and that the party who should have sustained the least damage, could not immediately pursue their advantages, whether against any particular ship of the enemy, or against his entire fleet. The two fleets thus standing on opposite tacks, and but a slight distance apart, the first ships of the English van, and those of the French rear, which, as we have said, was become the van, began to exchange broadsides, and the battle was joined successively, as the whole English line passed close alongside of the whole French line; so that the rear, commanded by sir Hugh Palliser, and the van by the count Duchaffault, were the last to attack each other. The effects of this collision were very destructive on both sides; but as the French, according to their custom, had fired at the tackling, and the English, as they usually do, at the body of the ships, the hulls of the French vessels were more severely damaged than those of their enemies; whereas the English were much greater sufferers in their masts, yards, and rigging. The French, profiting of this advantage of their sails, soon tacked, and formed their line anew. The British van and center also in a short time recovered their stations, though the admiral's ship had suffered extremely. But the ships of Palliser and several others, not only had not yet tacked, but being in a disabled condition, they obeyed the wind, and fell rapidly to leeward. In this state of things, whether the count d'Orvilliers intended, as the English pretend, to cut their line, and separate these ships from the rest of the fleet, or, as the French affirm, wishing to place himself under the wind, in order, as he expected a second battle, to deprive the English of the advantage he would thus gain for himself, of using the lower batteries with effect, he made signals for all his fleet to advance by a successive movement, and penetrate between the ships of Keppel and those of Palliser.

The English admiral, perceiving the design of his adversary, immediately put his ships about, and stood athwart the enemy's foremost division, directing at the same time sir Robert Harland to form his division in a line astern, in order to face the enemy, till sir Hugh Palliser could bring up his ships. It is not clear, whether this movement of Keppel frustrated the project of the count d'Orvilliers for intercepting Palliser's division, or whether it was merely the intention of that admiral to get under the wind; but certain it is, that in consequence of this evolution the English remained to the windward. It was therefore in their power to renew the battle, provided, however, that all their ships had been in condition to take part in the action; and this would have been the wish of Keppel. But the squadron of Palliser, since the admiral and Harland had thrown themselves between him and the French, to whom they were now very near, found itself to the windward of the other divisions, and, of course, remote from the French fleet, and little within reach to be of any assistance in case of a new engagement. On this consideration, Keppel made a signal for all the ships to the windward to resume their respective posts in the order of battle. Here a mistake happened, which prevented the execution of his orders. Palliser's ship, the Formidable, not having repeated the signal, the captains of the other ships understood that of Keppel as an order to rally in the wake of the commander of their own division, which they did accordingly.

Meanwhile, the French continued drawn up, to leeward, in order of battle. Keppel renewed the same signal, but with no better success. Afterwards, about five in the evening, [Palliser says at seven,] he commanded the captain of the frigate Fox to convey to Palliser a verbal message of the same import as the order he had already intimated by signals. It was still in vain; neither the Formidable nor the other ships obeyed. On seeing this, and the day far spent, Keppel made the signal to each of the ships of Palliser to resume their stations in the line; excepting, however, the Formidable, apparently from a certain regard to the rank and particular functions of the vice-admiral. This time, his orders were executed; but night came, and put an end to all possibility of further operations against the enemy.

Such were the causes which prevented admiral Keppel from renewing the battle; whether the disobedience of Palliser proceeded from the impossibility of managing his ships, disabled in the engagement, as seems probable, and as the court martial decided, in the solemn trial which followed, or that it was owing to any personal pique of that officer, who, being of the ministerial party, was politically at variance with Keppel. Be this as it may, the French thence took occasion to say, that from noon till night they offered battle to Keppel, who would not accept it. The fact in itself is incontestable; but as to the intentions of the British admiral, it is certain that he was well disposed to recommence the action, but was prevented by the obstacles we have just related

Satisfied with their conduct in this combat, and with its issue, which might be represented as a victory, a thing so important at this first epoch of the war, or finding the condition of their fleet too shattered to warrant their exposing themselves to the hazards of a second battle, the French profited in the night of a fair wind to recover their own coasts; and entered the next day with full sails into the port of Brest. They had, however, left in the place of battle, three ships with lights at the mast heads, to deceive the English into the belief that all their fleet was still there. At break of day, the French fleet was already at such a distance that it was only discernible from the mast heads of the largest ships in the British fleet; nothing remained in sight but the three vessels above mentioned. Keppel ordered the Prince George, the Robust, and another ship, to give them chase, but as they were good sailers, and the English had suffered extremely in their sails and rigging, this pursuit was fruitless. Admiral Keppel made the best of his way to Plymouth, where he purposed to repair the damages of his fleet; he left, however, some ships that had suffered the least, to protect the British trade, and especially the fleets which were expected.

The English, in this action, had one hundred and forty killed, and about four hundred wounded. The loss of the French is uncertain; but it is probable that it exceeded that of the English. Some private authorities lead to this belief, as also the throng of sailors and marines with which they are accustomed to fill their vessels.

The two fleets proceeded again to sea the next month. But whether they mutually sought to meet each other, as they gave out, or that each endeavored to avoid the other, as it was reciprocally asserted, it is certain that they did not meet again. It is equally indisputable that the trade of England was effectually protected; while, on the other hand, an immense number of French vessels, with rich and valuable cargoes, fell into the power of the enemy. These losses excited the complaints of the cities of Bordeaux, Nantz, Saint Malo, and Havre de Grace.

Such was the issue of the battle of Ouessant, which commenced the European war. The English observed in it, to their great surprise, that the French not only fought with their accustomed valor but that they displayed also no ordinary dexterity in profiting of the advantage of wind, in the management of their ships, and in their naval evolutions. Hence they could not but infer, that if they obtained successes in the present war, they would have to pay dearer for them than in the last.

Public rejoicings were made in France, to animate the people, and inspire them with better hopes. The impression was quite different in England; some complained of Keppel, others of Palliser, according to the various humors of the parties; all of fortune. After certain warm discussions, the admiral and vice-admiral were both put upon trial; but both were acquitted; the first, to the universal exultation of the people; the second, to the particular gratification of the friends of the ministry.

END OF BOOK TENTH.

BOOK ELEVENTH.

1778. THE unfortunate issue of the war of Canada, and the in-
utility of the advantages obtained in the campaign of Pennsylvania,
had at length shaken the obstinacy of the British ministers. They
began to believe that it was impossible to reduce the Americans by
force of arms; and every day confirmed them in this persuasion,
since France, so powerful by land and by sea, had united her forces
to those of the congress   It was too manifest to be doubted, that if
the Americans had been able to withstand, in the preceding campaign, the utmost efforts of England, it would be infinitely more easy
for them to resist in future; their union being more consolidated by
time, their hopes secured by propitious fortune, and their arms
seconded by those of a formidable potentate. Besides, it was no
longer to be hoped that as many troops could be sent to America in
future years as had been sent thither in the past. For, without ref-
erence to the almost absolute impossibility of procuring more German troops, and the extreme slowness of recruiting in England, there
was to be feared an invasion of the French, in the very heart of the
kingdom, and moreover, it was necessary to throw strong garrisons
into the West India islands, to shelter them from the assaults of the
French, who were known to have a respectable force in their vicinity. It was no mystery in the British cabinet, that the principal object which the French were aiming at in the present war, after the
separation of America from Great Britain, was the conquest of the
rich colonies of England in the West Indies; and that in anticipation
of events they had assembled numerous troops in their own possessions. The English islands of the West Indies thus found themselves
exposed, almost without defense, to the attempts of the enemy.
Whether the ministers had believed that war with France was not
likely to break out immediately, or that they had relied upon their
sanguine hopes of a complete triumph in the preceding campaign,
they had flattered themselves that, in any event, their victories upon
the American continent would enable them to pass into their islands,
in good time, all the succors that could be necessary. *Jealousy* was
also entertained of Canada, not only on the part of the Americans,
but also, and much more, on that of the French; for the Canadians
were more French than English, and the memory of their origin
appeared to be still dear to them. It was therefore necessary to leave
in that province such garrisons as could answer for it. These various considerations not only rendered it impracticable to re-inforce

the armies which acted against the United States, but even imposed the necessity of weakening them by detachments for the different exigencies of the service.   But, on the other hand, the courage of the ministers did not desert them.   They hoped that offers of accommodation, a new mode of conducting the war, and, perhaps, victories over France, would enable them to compass that which by arms alone they had hitherto failed to obtain.   They persuaded themselves that the Americans, tired of a long war, and finding their resources exhausted, would readily consent to an arrangement; or that, even if the congress refused, the greater part of the nation, at least, would manifest an eagerness to listen to their proposals; and already they beheld intestine dissensions opening the way to the re-establishment of ancient relations, if not an absolute subjugation.

To provide for this consummation, the clause had been added to the act of conciliation, which empowered the commissioners to treat, not only with any public authority, but even with every description of private citizens whatsoever.   After having encountered an obstinate resistance in the inhabitants of the northern provinces, they had been assured by the refugees, in whom they put all their trust, that they would find far more pliable matter in those of the south. They determined accordingly to make these the seat of the war, in the hope, that as they abounded more in subjects devoted to the crown, they would manifest greater repugnance to combating the troops of the king, and more inclination to listen to his negotiators. Besides, the fertile lands and exuberant pasturage of these provinces rendered them extremely accommodate for the subsistence of armies, at the same time that the inhabitants would have a motive in this very abundance the more to dread the devastations inseparable from war.   But whatever was the foundation of these hopes, the ministers were resolved to resume hostilities as soon as the negotiations should cease to promise any result, in order to avoid the appearance of yielding to the threats of France.   Without allowing themselves to be intimidated by the consequences which might attend the war with America, they considered themselves bound by that regard which every state owes to its own honor and dignity, to try yet for a time the fortune of arms.   If it proved necessary at last to acknowledge the independence of America, which was become the principal point in contest, they thought it could never be too late for that, and they reputed it better to submit honorably to adverse fortune and the decision of the sword, than to bow ignominiously, and without combat, to the menaces of an arrogant enemy.   Such were the motives which influenced the British ministers in the present period of the war, and which were afterwards the basis of all their res-

olutions. But perfectly sensible that if England made no new overtures, the congress would not fail to ratify the treaty contracted with
France, and that it would become then much more difficult for that
body to retract its resolutions, the British ministers hastened to
transmit to America the bill of conciliation, even before it had yet
been approved in parliament. They flattered themselves that the
Americans thus finding that England renounced what had been the
first and capital cause of the differences, that is, the right of taxation, all other difficulties would be promptly smoothed, and the ratification of the treaty readily prevented. This first point gained, the
commissioners would only have had, as it were, to appear, in order
to affix the seal to a definitive arrangement. Accordingly, copies
of the bill were received at New York about the middle of the month
of April. Governor Tryon, a shrewd and active man, as we have
seen, after having caused it to be published in the city, found means
to circulate it among the Americans, much extolling the good dispositions of the government towards America. He wrote at the same
time to general Washington, and to Trumbull, the governor of New
Jersey, requesting them, a thing really without example, to bring this
project of an act of parliament to the knowledge of soldiers and of
inhabitants. Washington referred the whole to the congress, that
they might take the proper measures. Trumbull replied to Tryon
in a very energetic style, that he was not a little surprised at this
strange mode of negotiation between two nations; that in similar
cases, demands and propositions are addressed, not to the multitude,
but to those who govern; that there had been a time, indeed, when
such a proposal of the mother country might have been received
with alacrity and gratitude, but that such time was irrevocably elapsed.
He reminded of petitions rejected, hostilities commenced and prosecuted with so much barbarity on the part of the English, their insolence in good fortune, the cruelties exercised against prisoners,
injuries which had interposed an insuperable obstacle to reconciliation. 'Peace,' he added, ' cannot subsist but with our independence.
The English will then find the Americans as sincere friends as they
are now determined and dangerous enemies. If they would have
peace, let them abandon all insidious procedures, and demand it
openly of those who can grant it.' Meanwhile, the congress, on receipt of their general's dispatches, deliberated upon the step they
had to take.

Considering themselves as already sure of the assistance of France,
and indignant of these new machinations of the English, they decreed
that any men, or body of men whatsoever, who should presume to
make any separate or partial convention or agreement with commis-

sioners under the crown of Great Britain, should be reputed and treated as enemies of the United States; that these states could not enter into any conference or treaty with the agents of Great Britain, except they should, as a preliminary thereto, either withdraw their fleets and armies, or else in positive and express terms acknowledge the independence of the United States. Finally, it being the design of the enemy to full the inhabitants of America, by this soothing sound of peace, into a neglect of warlike preparations, it was earnestly recommended to the different states to use the most strenuous exertions to have their respective quotas of continental troops in the field as soon as possible; and that all the militia of the said states might be held in readiness to act as occasion might require. The congress then, in order to show of how little importance they esteemed the bills of parliament, and the intrigues of Tryon to diffuse them, embraced the generous counsel of causing them to be published in the public prints, together with the resolutions they had just passed.

But on the other hand, under the apprehension that many of those who had hitherto attached themselves to the English party, in despair of finding pardon in their country, might not only persist in their obstinacy, but profiting of the amnesty offered by the British government, might also employ their influence to draw over to its interest even such as had remained faithful to the common cause, they passed a resolution, recommending to the several states, to grant a full remission of all guilt and penalties, except the restrictions they might deem necessary, to all those who had borne arms against the United States, or assisted the enemy in any way whatsoever. Each individual was assured of pardon for the offenses he might have committed up to that time, and the citizens were invited to a mutual forgiveness and oblivion of past wrongs and injuries.

But the English soldiers in America, strangers to the political considerations by which states are guided, and bitterly irritated at the obstinate resistance of the Americans, were inconceivably shocked at hearing of the unexpected resolutions of the ministers. They were for absolute conquest, and submission without reserve. They could not endure this shameful condescension; they asked why this ignominious retraction, why this solicitude to offer what at first was refused with so much pertinacity? They expected, upon the faith of promises, a re-inforcement of twenty thousand of their fellow-soldiers, and they received in their stead acts of concession. The discontent was so extreme in the camp, as to manifest itself in seditious words, and acts of violence; the soldiers in their fury presumed even to rend their colors; others, and principally the Scotch, tore in pieces the acts of parliament. If such was the indignation of the

British troops, it is easy to conceive what was the despair of the American refugees   They saw blasted in a moment their confident hopes of returning victorious to their habitations; and perhaps some of them gnashed at finding themselves frustrated of intended vengeance.

With so much industry and so little fruit did the agents of England labor in America to conciliate minds towards the mother country; and with so much energy and success did th- congress endeavor to baffle all their efforts!

The second of May was the day destined to carry to its utmost height the exultation of the Americans, and to put the seal to the dismemberment of the vast and powerful British empire.   On this day arrived at Casco Bay, the French frigate *La Sensible*, commanded by M. de Marigny.   She had been selected as an excellent sailer, to bear to the congress the treaties concluded with France; she had departed from Brest the eighth of March, having on board Simon Deane, brother of Silas.   She brought, besides, happy news of all the European continent, and of an unanimity still more sincere than ever, of the people and of the princes in favor of America. The congress was immediately convened: we shall not attempt to describe their satisfaction and alacrity at the sight of the treaties. They were ratified as soon as read.   Unable to control the flush occasioned by so great an event, they forgot the rules of prudence.   New states too frequently err in this; allowing themselves to be hurried away by an inconsiderate ardor, and impatient to communicate it to the people they govern, they are betrayed into impolitic steps.   In this respect, widely different from ancient states; these, always circumspect and wrapped up in mystery, are reluctant to break silence even when every thing appears to exact it.   The congress at once made public the dispatches they had just received; this disclosure was disagreeable to several powers, and especially to Spain, who would have chosen not to declare herself before the appointed time. The proclamation issued to that effect, spoke not only of the treaty of commerce concluded with France, but even of the treaty of alliance, it announced, without any reserve, that the emperor of Germany, the kings of Spain and Prussia, were determined to support them; that the king of Prussia, in particular, would not permit that the troops levied in Hesse and Hanau should pass through his territories in order to embark in the English vessels, and that he would be the second potentate in Europe who would acknowledge the independence of America; that fifty thousand French were marched upon the coasts of Normandy and of Brittany; and, finally, that the navies of France and Spain (as if the intervention of this power was already secured) amounted to two hundred ships, ready to sail for the succor of America. The congress afterwards drew up and published a solemn address to the people of America; this piece was wrought with much care, though a little strange from its tumid style, and the religious sentences with which it was interspersed. It was recommended to all ministers of the gospel, of whatever denomination, to read this address to their congregations, immediately after divine service. It represented in the most vivid colors the vicissitudes of the state in the course of the late years; the virtue, the courage, the patience of the Americans; the perfidy, the injustice, the cruelty, the tyranny of the English; the assistance of God visibly afforded to the just cause; and the ancient weakness of the colonies succeeded by their present security. 'The haughty prince,' continued the address, 'who spurned us from his feet with contumely and disdain, and the parliament which proscribed us, now descend to offer terms of accommodation.

'While in the full career of victory, they pulled off the mask, and avowed their intended despotism. But having lavished in vain the blood and treasure of their subjects in pursuit of this execrable purpose, they now endeavor to ensnare us with the insidious offers of reconciliation. They intend to lull you with fallacious hopes of peace, until they can assemble new armies to prosecute their nefarious designs. If this is not the case, why do they strain every nerve to levy men throughout their islands? Why do they meanly court every little tyrant of Europe to sell them his unhappy slaves? Why do they continue to imbitter the minds of the savages against you? Surely, this is not the way to conciliate the affections of America. Be not, therefore, deceived. You have still to expect one severe conflict. Your foreign alliances, though they secure your independence, cannot secure your country from desolation, your habitations from plunder, your wives from insult or violation, nor your children from butchery. Foiled in their principal design, you must expect to feel the rage of disappointed ambition. Arise then! to your tents! and gird you for battle! It is time to turn the headlong current of vengeance upon the head of the destroyer. They have filled up the measure of their abominations, and like ripe fruit must soon drop from the tree. Although much is done, yet much remains to do. Expect not peace, while any corner of America is in possession of your foes. You must drive them away from this land of promise, a land flowing indeed with milk and honey. Your brethren, at the extremities of the continent, already implore your friendship and protection. It is your duty to grant their request. They hunger and thirst after liberty. Be it yours to dispense to them the heavenly gift, " since a kind Providence has placed it in your power." '

The congress also published those articles of the treaty of amity and commerce which related to the reciprocal intercourse between the two nations, to the end that the inhabitants of the United States might govern themselves conformably to the same. They exhorted them to consider the French as their brethren, and to behave towards them with the friendship and attention due to the subjects of a great prince, who with the highest magnanimity and wisdom had treated with the United States on terms of perfect equality and mutual advantage, thereby rendering himself the protector of the rights of mankind.

Great were the rejoicings in all parts of the United States ; the name of Louis XVI. was in all mouths. Every where he was proclaimed the protector of liberty, the defender of America, the savior of the country. These joyful tidings were announced with great solemnity to the army, which still occupied the camp of Valley Forge ; the soldiers were under arms, and all the corps formed in order of battle.

Meanwhile, the three pacificatory commissioners, Carlisle, Eden, and Johnstone, had arrived in the waters of the Delaware at the beginning of June ; they repaired to Philadelphia the ninth. General Clinton notified their arrival to Washington, praying him to send a passport to doctor Ferguson, secretary of the commissioners, that he might, without danger, deliver their dispatches to the congress. Washington refused the passport, and his refusal obtained the special approbation of the government. The commissioners then decided to forward their letters by the ordinary post. The congress received them in their sitting of the thirteenth, with an express from Washington. They were read to certain words in the letter directed ' to his excellency Henry Laurens, the president and others, the members of congress.' No sooner were they heard, than a violent clamor arose ; many members exclaimed that the reading ought to be interrupted on account of the offensive language against his most christian majesty.

The words were these : ' We cannot but remark the insidious interposition of a power, which has from the first settlement of the colonies been actuated with enmity to us both ; and notwithstanding the pretended date or present form of the French offers to North America, it is notorious that they have only been made, because it was believed that Great Britain had conceived the design of an amicable arrangement, and with a view to prevent reconciliation, and prolong this destructive war.' After animated debates, the further consideration of the subject was adjourned to the next sitting. The question was agitated with equal vehemence the following days. Finally, the congress, having demonstrated, by the warmth of this discussion, the respect they bore to their august ally, reflected, on the other hand, that it was more prudent to answer than to keep silence. It was easy to lay before the people such motives as were likely to dissuade them from accepting the proposals of England, whereas a refusal to notice them might occasion discontents prejudicial to the state. They determined, accordingly, to read the dispatches of the commissioners. They consisted in the letter addressed to the president of congress, a copy of their commission, and three acts of parliament. The commissioners offered in their letter more than would have been required, in the origin of the quarrel, to appease the minds of the colonists and re-establish tranquillity; but less than was necessary at present to obtain peace. They endeavored to persuade the Americans that the conditions of the arrangement were not only favorable, but also perfectly sure, and of such a nature that the two parties would know, for the future, upon what footing they were to live together; that their friendship would thus be established upon solid bases, as it should be, in order to be durable. They declared themselves ready to consent to an immediate cessation of hostilities by sea and land; to restore a free intercourse, and to renew the common benefits of naturalization throughout the several parts of the empire; to extend every freedom to trade that the respective interests of both parties could require; to agree that no military force should be kept up in the different states of North America, without the consent of the general congress, or of the particular assemblies; to concur in such measures as would be requisite to discharge the debts of America, and to raise the credit and the value of the paper circulation; to perpetuate the common union by a reciprocal deputation of agents from the different states, who should have the privilege of a seat and voice in the parliament of Great Britain; or if sent from Britain, in that case, to have a seat and voice in the assembly of the different states to which they might be deputed respectively; in order to attend to the several interests of those by whom they were deputed; to establish the right and power of the respective legislatures in each particular state, of settling its revenue and its civil and military establishment, and of exercising a perfect freedom of legislation and internal government, so that the British states throughout North America, acting with those of Europe in peace and war, under one common sovereign, might have the irrevocable enjoyment of every privilege that was short of a total separation of interest, or consistent with that union of force on which the security of British religion and liberty depended.

Finally, the commissioners expressed their desire to open conferences with congress, or with some of its members, either at New York, at Philadelphia, or at Yorktown, or in such other place as it might please the congress to appoint.

Thus, to terminate a war, already pushed to a great length, those who in its origin would hear of nothing short of the absolute reduction of America, abated all the rigor of their conditions.

Meanwhile, the congress took into serious consideration the state of affairs. The debates that ensued upon this subject, were drawn into length; not that any individual thought of renouncing independence, but all took an interest in the form of the answer to be given to the commissioners. The discussion was continued until the seventeenth of June. On that day, the congress answered with as much conciseness as dignity; they already felt how greatly their position was meliorated by the success of their arms and the alliance of France. Their reply purported, that the acts of the British parliament, the very commission of the agents, and their letters to congress, supposed the people of the United States to be subjects of the crown of Great Britain, and were founded on the idea of dependence, which was utterly inadmissible; that, nevertheless, the Americans were inclined to peace, notwithstanding the unjust claims from which the war had originated, and the savage manner in which it had been conducted. That congress would therefore be ready to enter upon the consideration of a treaty of peace and commerce, not inconsistent with treaties already subsisting, when the king of Great Britain should demonstrate a sincere disposition for that purpose; of which no other proof could be admitted but that of an explicit acknowledgment of the independence of the United States, or the withdrawing of his fleets and armies.

Thus, the Americans, steady in their resolutions, chose rather to trust to their own fortune, which they had already proved, and to the hope they placed in that of France, than to link themselves anew to the tottering destiny of England; abandoning all idea of peace, war became the sole object of their solicitude. Such was the issue of the attempts to effect an accommodation; and thus were extinguished the hopes which the negotiation had given birth to in England. But not consenting to concessions until the time for them was passed, the English justified the refusal of the Americans. It can not be affirmed that these overtures on the part of the first, were only an artifice to divide the second among themselves, to detach them from France, and to have them afterwards at their discretion, but it is certain · that after so many rancorous animosities, so many sanguinary battles, after the innumerable excesses of rapine, cruelty and lust, the Americans could not be blamed for suspecting the British ministers of a design to insnare them.

The wound was incurable, and friendship could not be restored. This was a truth of universal evidence; the seeming inclined to believe the contrary, was sufficient to inspire apprehensions of treachery, and the extreme of distrust in all flattering promises. Whoever shall reflect attentively upon the long series of events which we have related up to this time, will perceive that the Americans were alway, constant in their resolution, the English always versatile, uncertain, and wavering. Hence it is not at all surprising that those found new friends, and that these not only lost theirs, but also made enemies of them at the very moment when they could do them the least harm, and might receive the most from them. Vigorous resolutions prevent danger; half measures invite and aggravate it.

But the chiefs of the American revolution were not without apprehension that the insidious caresses, the new concessions of England, and the secret intrigues of the commissioners, might act powerfully upon the minds of such citizens as were weak or impatient for repose. The congress, however, was not disposed to give any other answer except that which has been recounted above. They excited therefore several writers to justify their resolutions and to defend the cause of America. This course appeared to them the more proper, inasmuch as the English commissioners, having lost all hope of succeeding with the congress, had resorted to the expedient of disseminating in the country a multitude of writings, by which they endeavored to persuade the people that the obstinacy of congress would hurry America into an abyss, by alienating her from her old friends, and giving her up a prey to an inveterate enemy. This step of the commissioners furnished the patriots with a new argument to put the people on their guard against the artifices and intrigues of the agents of England. Among the writers of this epoch, deserving of particular mention, is Drayton, one of the deputies of South Carolina, and a man of no common erudition. He endeavored to demonstrate in the public papers, that the United States having already treated with France, as free states, and in order to maintain their independence, they could not now negotiate with the British commissioners upon the basis of submission, without renouncing that faith and ingenuousness which ought to preside over all their transactions, without exposing the American people to be accounted faithless and infamous, and consequently to lose for ever all hope of foreign succors; while on the other hand they would find themselves placed without resource in the power of those who had given them heretofore such fatal proofs of their perfidy and cruelty. ' Besides,' he added, ' the conventions that we might make with the commissioners would not be definitive; they would need the ratification of the king, of the ministers, and of the parliament; and what assurance have we that they would have it? But let it be supposed, can we be assured that a future parliament will not annul all these treaties? Let us not forget, that we have to do with an enemy as faithless and fraudulent as barbarous. How is it possible not to suspect a snare, when we hear the commissioners offer us propositions which exceed their powers, and contradict even the acts of parliament?' Thus the patriots repulsed the offers, the promises, and the arguments of the British commissioners. Finding no accessible point, the latter were at length convinced that all hope of conciliation must be relinquished. If they could still have remained under any illusion upon this point, it must soon have been dissipated by the evacuation which their generals made, at the same instant, of the city of Philadelphia, the acquisition of which had been the fruit of so much blood, and of two arduous campaigns. The ministers feared, what actually happened, that a French fleet might suddenly enter the Delaware, and place the British army, which occupied Philadelphia, in extreme jeopardy. Their design was, besides, to carry the war into the southern provinces, and to send a part of the troops to defend their islands of the West Indies against the attacks of the new enemy. The diminution that must result from it in the army of the continent, induced them to send orders to Clinton, by the commissioner Eden, to evacuate Philadelphia without delay, and to fall back upon New York. This measure, dictated by prudence, and even by necessity, was interpreted by the Americans as a symptom of terror; and it consequently must have had the most prejudicial influence upon the success of the negotiations. What need have we, they said, to enter into an accommodation with the English, when their retreat is a virtual avowal of the inferiority of their arms?

Be this as it may, Clinton prepared to execute the orders of his government. But in order to repair by land to New York, it was necessary to traverse New Jersey, a province, in which, for reasons already stated, he must expect to meet only with enemies. It was, besides, exhausted by long war. Foreseeing, therefore, that he might want provisions, the English general, before evacuating Philadelphia, had collected them in considerable quantity, and loaded them upon a great number of carriages. It is true, that as the fleet of lord Howe still remained in the waters of the Delaware, the army might have been transported to New York by sea; the Americans themselves expected it, and Washington apprehended it much. But the difficulties and delays of the embarkation, and perhaps also the fear of encountering the French fleet in superior force, deterred the English from taking this route. Clinton and Howe having made the necessary dispositions, the whole army passed the Delaware very early on the twenty-second of June; and, descending the river a little, landed at Gloucester Point, upon the territory of New Jersey. It immediately proceeded, with all its baggage, towards Haddonfield, where it arrived the same day.

Washington was soon apprised in his camp at Valley Forge, that the British army was in motion; without loss of time he sent general Dickinson to assemble the militia of New Jersey under arms. At the same time, in order to support them by a respectable corps of continental troops, he ordered general Maxwell to march into New Jersey. Their mutual efforts were to embarrass, by all possible impediments, the retreat of the British army; to break up the roads, to cut the bridges, to fell trees, and to plant them in abattis. It was recommended to them at the same time to avoid hazardous movements and unexpected actions. Such were the first steps taken by Washington in order to retard the enemy, until he could advance himself with the main body of his army into New Jersey, and observe in person what there was to be done. In the meantime, he assembled his council of war at Valley Forge, and submitted to their deliberation whether it was proper, by harassing the enemy's rear, to do him all the harm possible, without, however, coming to a general engagement; or whether it was more advisable to attack him in front, and try the fortune of a decisive battle. The opinions differed, and were for some time in balance. General Lee, who a little before had been exchanged for Prescott, considering the equality of the forces of the two armies, and the posture of affairs, become too favorable to be exposed without necessity to the hazard of battles, perhaps also having little confidence in the discipline of the American troops, was of the opinion that they should not be put to the test anew, and that an action should be avoided. He was for being content with following the enemy, observing his motions, and preventing him from ravaging the country. This counsel was adopted by the greater part of the generals. The others, among whom was Washington himself, thought differently, and were inclined, in case a favorable occasion should present itself, to engage a general affair. They could not bring their minds to endure that the enemy should retire with impunity during so long a march, and they persuaded themselves that they had every thing to expect from soldiers whose constancy, the rigor of the seasons, and the scarcity of things the most necessary to life, had not been able to subdue. They reflected, besides, that the English army was embarrassed with the most cumbersome baggage, and they doubted not but that, in the numerous defiles it would have to thread, some favorable occasion must offer itself to attack with advantage. Nevertheless, the opinion of the majority prevailed, not without evident dissatisfaction on the part of Washington, who, according to his character of personal pertinacity, remained steadfast in his way of thinking.

The same day in which the English abandoned Philadelphia, he moved from his camp of Valley Forge, and crossing the Delaware at Coryells Ferry, because Clinton was marching up the river, he went to take post at Hopewell. He was in great uncertainty respecting the designs of the enemy. Their slow march, which was the effect of the immoderate quantity of their baggage, and not a stratagem, induced him to suspect that their aim was to draw him beyond the Rariton, into the open plains of New Jersey, and then, rapidly, turning his right, to lock him against the river, and constrain him to join battle with disadvantage. He proceeded, therefore, with extreme circumspection, and did not allow himself to be enticed to venture across the Rariton.

Meanwhile, the English had already reached Allentown. Washington detached Morgan with his light horse, to harass their right flank, while Maxwell and Dickinson infested them on the left, and general Cadwallader in rear. But when Clinton found himself in Allentown, he reflected upon the way he had to take in order to arrive at New York. By turning towards the Rariton, he might proceed to Brunswick, pass the river there, push for Staten Island, and thence to New York. Another route presented itself on the right, by passing through Monmouth and gaining with rapidity the heights of Middletown, whence it was easy to pass to Sandy Hook; from that point, the fleet of Howe, which awaited the army, could transport it to New York. General Clinton conceived it an extremely hazardous enterprise to attempt the passage of the Rariton, with an army encumbered by such immense convoys, and in the presence of that of Washington, which he knew was soon to be re-inforced by the northern troops, under the command of general Gates. He concluded therefore to pursue the road of Monmouth, and immediately commenced the march. Washington, who till then had remained in doubt, because the road from Allentown leads alike to New Brunswick and to Monmouth, as soon as he got this intelligence, detached general Wayne with a thousand regular troops to reinforce the corps of Cadwallader, in order to enable him with more effect to harass, and retard the enemy. The simultaneous action of the detachments of Wayne, Cadwallader, Dickinson and Morgan, being of extreme importance, the commander-in-chief put them all under the command of major-general La Fayette. But the danger increasing at every instant, as the American van had already come up with the English rear, Washington judged it necessary to support it by other corps of regular troops. He directed general Lee to press forward with two brigades. As the senior, Lee took the command of the whole vanguard, leaving to the marquis de la Fayette only that of the militia and light horse. General Lee occupied Englishtown. Washington followed a little distance from the main body of the army, and encamped at Cranberry. Morgan continued to infest the right flank of the English, and Dickinson their left. Things were fast verging to a decisive event. The British army was encamped upon the heights of Freehold; descending thence towards Monmouth, a deep valley is entered, three miles in length and one in breadth; it is broken with hillocks, woods, and morasses. General Clinton, seeing the enemy so near, and the battle inevitable, withdrew all the baggage from the rear, and passed it into the charge of the van, commanded by general Knyphausen, that while himself with the rear guard kept the enemy in check, it might be conducted without molestation to a place of safety upon the hills of Middletown. The rear guard, which he retained during the night of the twenty-seventh in his encampment at Freehold, consisted of several battalions of English infantry, both heavy and light, the Hessian grenadiers, and a regiment of cavalry.

The next morning at daybreak, Knyphausen descended into the valley with the vanguard and his convoy, on his way towards Middletown, and was soon at a good distance from the camp. Clinton, with the selected corps he had kept with him, still maintained his position, as well to retard the enemy, as to give time for the baggage to gain the heights. Washington, promptly informed of all that passed, and apprehensive that the English would effect their design of posting themselves in the mountains of Middletown, the distance being only a few miles, in which case it became impossible to interrupt their retreat to New York, resolved to give them battle without further delay.

He ordered general Lee to attack the enemy in front, while Morgan and Dickinson should descend into the valley upon his flanks, the first to the right, the second to the left, in order to attempt the column of Knyphausen, encumbered with its long train of carriages and packhorses. Each put himself in motion to obey. General Clinton, having resumed his march, was already descended from the

heights of Freehold, when he perceived that the Americans were
also descending with impetuosity in order to attack him. He was
informed at the same instant, that Knyphausen was exposed to the
greatest peril, his convoy being engaged in defiles, that continued
several miles. Clinton, finding himself under the necessity of fighting, instantly took the only resolution that could extricate him from
the embarrassments of his position. He determined to turn upon
the Americans who menaced his rear, and to charge them with the
utmost vigor. He persuaded himself that, thrown into disorder by
this unexpected attack, they would hasten to recall to their succor
the corps they had detached to int rcept the baggage. Thus the
English rear guard, commanded by Cornwallis and Clinton himself,
and the American vanguard, conducted by general Lee, and the
marquis de la Fayette, advanced the one against the other with a
firm resolution to engage.

The artillery began to play, and the Queen's dragoons charged
and routed the light horse of La Fayette. Lee, surprised at the unexpected determination of Clinton to face about upon the Americans,
and the rapidity with which he had carried it into execution, was
constrained to form his troops upon ground by no means favorable.
He had behind him a ravine which rendered his retreat almost impracticable in case of check. Perhaps also he was piqued at being
forced to join battle after having supported the contrary opinion.
At the first charge of the English he fell back, not without disorder, probably occasioned by the difficulty of the ground. The
enemy pursued him across the ravine, and pressed him hard before
he had time to rally. In this critical moment, Washington arrived
with his corps. Having kept himself ready to move at any instant,
he had pushed forward at the first sound of the firing, having ordered
his soldiers to leave behind them whatever could impede their march,
even to the knapsacks, which they usually carried upon all occasions.
On seeing the retreat or rather flight of the troops of Lee, he was
not master of his anger: he addressed some very harsh words to that
general, and applied himself with equal prudence and courage to
restore the fortune of the day. It was necessary, first of all, to arrest for a few moments the impetuosity of the English, in order to
give time for all the corps of the rear guard to come up. Accordingly, the commander-in-chief ordered the battalions of colonels
Stewart and Ramsay to occupy an important post on the left, behind
a tuft of wood, and there to sustain the first efforts of the enemy.
Stung by the reproaches of his general, and stimulated by the point
of honor, even Lee made extreme exertions to rally his troops. He
disposed them on more advantageous ground, where they defended

themselves valiantly. The English were constrained to renew their
attacks in order to dislodge them. But at length, Lee, as well as
Stewart and Ramsay, overpowered by numbers, were forced to fall
back; they withdrew, however, without any confusion. Lee retired
to rally anew behind Englishtown; but in the meantime the American rear guard had arrived upon the field of battle. Washington
disposed these fresh troops, partly in a neighboring wood, and partly
upon a hill situated on the left, from which some pieces of cannon,
which lord Sterling had planted there, severely annoyed the enemy.
The infantry were drawn up in the center, at the foot of the hill in
front of the enemy. At the same time, general Greene, who, on this
day, commanded the right wing, and who had advanced considerably,
on being apprised of the retreat of the vanguard, very prudently
concluded also to fall back.

As soon as he was arrived upon the field of battle, he took a very
strong position on the right of lord Sterling. He likewise posted
his artillery upon a lofty eminence, whence it cruelly infested the
left wing of the enemy. The English, being thus arrested, and find
ing so harsh a reception in front, attempted to turn the left flank of
the Americans; but they were repulsed by the light infantry which
Washington had sent there for this purpose. They then directed
their efforts against his right, which they endeavored to surround.
But overwhelmed by the artillery of Greene, they were soon forced
to retreat. As soon as Washington saw them give way, he caused
them to be charged vigorously by the infantry under general Wayne.

The English turned the back, and recrossing the ravine, went to
form anew upon the same ground where general Lee had made his
first halt. Victory was no longer doubtful; but the new position of
the English was still formidable. Their flanks were covered by
woods and deep morasses, and their front, being protected by the
same ravine which had deranged the troops of Lee in the beginning
of the action, could only be reached through a narrow pass.

Washington, nevertheless, made his dispositions for renewing the
engagement, having ordered general Poor to charge them upon the
right with his own brigade and a corps of Carolinian militia, and
general Woodfort to attack them upon the left, while the artillery
should play on them in front. Both exerted themselves with alacrity
to execute their orders, and to surmount the obstacles which defended
the flanks of the British army. But the ground was so broken
and difficult that night came on before they had been able to obtain
any advantage. The action soon ceased throughout the line. Washington would have desired to re-commence it the next morning, with
the day; he therefore kept all his troops under arms during the night.

He was vigilant that every thing should be ready; sparing neither cares nor fatigue. But the thoughts of Clinton were very differently occupied. His vanguard and his baggage were already arrived in safety near Middletown. His calculation had not deceived him, for he had no sooner attacked the corps of Lee, than that general hastened to recall the light troops which had been detached to fall upon the baggage and the soldiers that guarded it, as they filed through the valley. During the action, they had continued to march upon Middletown, and they had arrived the same evening at secure positions on the hills. Clinton, besides, had not to blush for this day, since with his rear guard he had repulsed the American van, and had finally arrested the whole army of the enemy. His troops were greatly inferior in number to those of Washington; but it would have been an imprudence, even for an army of equal force, to risk a new engagement, when so great a part of it was at such a distance, and in a country whose inhabitants and whose surface presented little else but opposition and obstacles. The loss of the battle would have been followed by the total ruin of the army. On all these considerations, he decided for retreat. He took advantage of the obscurity of night in order not to be followed, and to avoid the intolerable sultriness of the climate during the day. About ten at night, the Americans say at midnight, he put his columns in motion for Middletown, with so profound a silence, that the enemy, though extremely near, and attentive to observe him, perceived not his retreat. Clinton wrote, that his march was favored by moonlight. This circumstance afforded the Americans an abundance of merriment; it being observed that the moon was then at its fourth day, and that it was set a little before eleven at night. Washington, on his part, had to take into consideration the excessive heat of the season, the weariness of his troops, the nature of the country, very sandy, and without water; finally, the distance which the enemy had already gained upon him during the night. He consequently relinquished the thought of pursuing them, and allowed his army to repose in the camp of Englishtown until the first of July. He took this step with the less reluctance, as he considered it now impracticable to prevent or disturb the embarkation of the English at Sandy Hook.

Such was the issue of the battle of Freehold, or of Monmouth, as it is called by the Americans. If they had the worse in its commencement, it terminated in their favor. And it appears very probable, that if the division under Lee had made a firm stand, they would have gained the most decisive victory. The English, in this engagement, had three hundred killed, and an equal number wounded; about one hundred were made prisoners. Many of them also deserted, especially of the Hessians. Few were slain on the side of the Americans. On the one part and on the other many soldiers died, not of wounds, but of the intense heat of the weather, added to the fatigue of the day. Washington greatly commended his troops for the valor they had signalized, and particularly general Wayne. The congress voted thanks to the army, and especially to the officers and commander-in-chief. But general Lee, a man of an irascible character, could not brook the indignity he believed to have been offered him by Washington, in the presence of his soldiers. He therefore wrote two letters to the commander-in-chief, in which his resentment caused him to forget all bounds of respect. They occasioned the revival of an affair which the usual prudence and moderation of Washington would have inclined him to pass by. Lee was arrested and brought before a court martial, to make answer to the three following charges; for disobedience, in not attacking the enemy on the twenty-eighth of June, agreeably to his instructions; for having made an unnecessary, disorderly, and shameful retreat; and for disrespect to the commander-in-chief in his two letters. He defended himself with great ingenuity, and with a sort of eloquence, so that impartial and military men remained in doubt whether he was really culpable or not. Nevertheless, the court martial found him guilty of all the charges, bating the epithet of shameful, which was expunged, and sentenced him to be suspended for one year; a judgment certainly either too mild, if Lee was guilty, or too severe, if innocent. This affair occasioned much conversation, some approving, others blaming the sentence. The congress, though with some hesitation, confirmed it.

On the first of July, Washington directed the march of his army towards the Hudson, in order to secure the passages of the mountains, now the English were in force at New York. He left, however, some detachments of light troops, and particularly Morgan's dragoons, in the lower parts of New Jersey, to take up deserters, and to repress the incursions of the enemy.

While such were the operations of Washington and of Clinton in New Jersey, general Gates, with a part of the northern army, had descended along the banks of the Hudson, in order to disquiet the English in New York. By this judicious movement, the garrison of that city, under apprehensions for itself, was prevented from marching to the support of those who were engaged with the enemy in New Jersey.

Meanwhile, the British army was arrived, the thirtieth of June, at Middletown, not far from Sandy Hook. The fleet under lord Howe was already at anchor there, though it had been detained a long time in the Delaware by calms. Sandy Hook had been in time past a peninsula, which, forming a point, extended in the mouth of the bay of New York; but in the preceding winter it had been disjoined from the main land by a violent storm and inundation, and converted into an island. The timely arrival of the fleet delivered the army from the imminent peril to which it would have been exposed, had it been unable to pass this new strait. But a bridge of boats was constructed with incredible expedition; and the whole army passed over the channel into Sandy Hook island, whence it was soon after conveyed by the fleet to New York; ignorant of the extreme danger it had so narrowly escaped.

The count d'Estaing, with his powerful armament, was at length arrived in the seas of America. After having made his appearance upon the coasts of Virginia, he had entered the mouth of the Delaware, in the night of the eighth of July. If he could have gained that position a few days sooner, and before the fleet of Howe had got out of the river, or even if he had fallen in with it on its passage from the Delaware to Sandy Hook, it is beyond doubt that he would have entirely destroyed that squadron, which only consisted of two ships of the line, a few frigates, and a certain number of transports. The British army would then have been inclosed by the Americans at land, and by the French at sea. Hemmed in by mountains and an impassable tract of country, it would have found it impossible to force its way to New York. Destitute of provisions, and cut off from all communication, it must have been compelled at last to surrender, and at Middletown would have been renewed the capitulation of Saratoga. This event might therefore have decided the fate of the whole war. But after having commenced with favorable winds, the voyage of the French admiral was so protracted by frequent calms, or by rough weather, that he not only did not arrive in time to surprise the squadron of Howe in the Delaware, and the army of Clinton at Philadelphia, as had been the scope of his plan, but also that he did not enter the waters of that river until the one was withdrawn to the anchorage of Sandy Hook, and the other behind the walls of New York.

But though the land troops might think themselves in safety within that city, the fleet was exposed to manifest peril in the road of Sandy Hook. As soon as the count d'Estaing was informed of the movements of the enemy, he promptly took his resolution. He put to sea anew, and suddenly made his appearance, the eleventh of July, in sight of the British squadron anchored at Sandy Hook. His own consisted of twelve ships of the line, perfectly equipped, among which were two of eighty guns, and six of seventy-four; he had, besides, three or four large frigates. On the other hand, the British squadron was composed of only six ships of sixty-four guns, three of fifty, and two of forty, with some frigates and sloops. They were not in good condition, having been long absent from England, and their crews were very deficient in number. It is also to be observed, that when the French fleet appeared so unexpectedly, that of Howe was not in the order of battle suitable to receive it. If, therefore, the count l'Estaing, immediately upon his arrival, had pushed forward and attempted to force the entrance of the harbor, there must have ensued, considering the valor and ability of the two parties, a most obstinate and sanguinary engagement; an engagement, however, which the superiority of the French would in all probability have decided in their favor.

The count d'Estaing appeared disposed to enter; the English prepared to receive him. But such is the nature of the mouth of the bay of New York, that, though sufficiently broad, it is obstructed by a bar, which runs from Long Island towards Sandy Hook, so that between the latter and the extremity of the bar, there is left but a very narrow ship channel. Nevertheless, the bar being at a certain depth under water, light vessels may pass it with facility, especially at flood tide; but it was doubtful whether large ships, like those of the French, could surmount this obstacle. The count d'Estaing took counsel of the American pilots, sent him by the congress; he feared that his ships, and especially the Languedoc and Tonnant, which drew more water than the others, would not be able to pass. He therefore relinquished the enterprise, and withdrew to anchor upon the coast of New Jersey, about four miles from Sandy Hook, and not far from the town of Shrewsbury. There, having recruited his water and provisions, he concerted with the American generals respecting the expedition of Rhode Island, which he meditated, since he had missed that of the Delaware.

The English imagined that the French admiral was only waiting in this anchorage for the high tides at the end of July. Under the apprehension of an approaching attack, they accordingly prepared themselves for a vigorous defense. The ardor manifested on this occasion by their troops, both in the land and sea service, cannot be too highly commended. Meanwhile, several English vessels that were bound to New York, far from supposing that the French were become masters of the sea, fell daily into their power, under the very eyes of their own people of the squadron, whose indignation was vehement; but they had no means of remedy.

Finally, on the twenty-second of July, the whole French fleet appeared at the entrance of Sandy Hook. The wind favored it, and the tide was very high. The English expected an action which must necessarily issue either in a victory without example, or in the total destruction of their fleet ; but after some uncertain movements, the count d'Estaing all at once stood off towards the south, and relieved his enemy from all fear. His departure could not have been better timed for the English ; for from the twenty-second to the thirtieth of July, several ships of admiral Byron's squadron, which had been dispersed and shattered by storms and a tedious passage, arrived successively at Sandy Hook. If the count d'Estaing had remained a few days longer on that station, not one of them could have escaped him. Of this number were the Renown and the Centurion of fifty guns, the Reasonable of sixty-four, and the Cornwall of seventy-four.

Admiral Howe, thus finding himself, with infinite gratification, in condition to resume the open sea, sailed in search of the count d'Estaing, whom he afterwards found at Newport in Rhode Island.

But previous to relating what passed between the two admirals, the order of history requires that we should recount what happened between the British commissioners and the congress. The former had not entirely abandoned their enterprise, and they still continued upon the American continent.

Johnstone, one of their number, had formerly resided a long time upon the shores of America, where he had formed an acquaintance with many of the principal inhabitants of the country. He had likewise been governor of one of the colonies, where his active and cultivated genius, with his insinuating manners, had procured him an extensive influence. Being, besides, a member of parliament, he had there always warmly defended the cause of America, and had shown himself one of the most resolute antagonists of the ministry. These motives, to which, perhaps, it was owing that he had been selected for a commissioner, persuaded him that he might succeed in effecting in America, by his suggestions and a private correspondence, what his colleagues, perchance, could not have obtained by open negotiations, always subject to the restraints of circumspection and distrust. He believed, at least, that by enticing the principal republicans with brilliant prospects of honors and wealth, he should smooth the difficulties which impeded the operations of the commissioners. It is not known whether he pursued this course of his own motion, or with the privity, or even by the command of the government. Nevertheless, the tenor of the letters he wrote upon this head, would lead to the belief that the ministers were no strangers to his designs. In fact, contrary to the uniform practice of those who exercise a delegated power, he praised the resistance which the Amer-

icans had made, up to that time, against the unjust and arrogant
laws of England ; a frankness he would scarcely have ventured, if
he had not been guided by the instructions of the ministers. The
style in which he wrote to the most considerable citizens, and even
to the members of congress, would sooner have caused him to be
taken for an agent of that body, than for an envoy of the British
government. He professed a desire to be admitted into the interior
of the country, and to discourse face to face with men, whose virtues he admired above those of the Greeks and Romans, in order to
be able to describe them to his children. He affirmed that they had
worthily wielded the pen and the sword in vindicating the rights of
their country, and of the human race ; he overwhelmed them with
protestations of his love and veneration. The congress had some
suspicions, and at last positive knowledge of these intrigues. They
recommended to the different states, and directed the commander-
in-chief, and other officers, to hold a strict hand to the effect that all
correspondence with the enemy should cease. By a subsequent resolution, it was ordained that all letters of a public nature received
by any members of congress, from the agents or subjects of the king
of Great Britain, should be laid before that assembly.

Thus became public those letters addressed by Johnstone to three
members of congress, one to Francis Dana, another to general
Reed, and a third to Robert Morris. In the first, he assured that
doctor Franklin had approved the conditions of the arrangement that
was proposed ; that France had been induced to conclude the treaty
of alliance, not from any regard for the interests of America, but
from the dread of reconciliation ; that Spain was dissatisfied, and
disapproved the conduct of the court of Versailles. In the second,
after lavishing praises on general Reed, he continued with saying,
that the man who could be instrumental in restoring harmony between the two states, would deserve more from the king and people,
than ever was yet bestowed on human kind. In the third, which he
had also filled with compliments, he admitted ·that he believed the
men who had conducted the affairs of America incapable of being
influenced by improper motives, and added the following words :
' but in all such transactions there is risk ; and I think that whoever
ventures, should be secured, at the same time, that honor and emolu-
ment should naturally follow the fortunes of those who have st.ered
the vessel in the storm, and brought her safely into port. I think
Washington and the president have a right to every favor that grateful nations can bestow, if they could once more unite our interests,
and spare the miseries and devastations of war.' Such were the
baits with which, as the Americans said, George Johnstone attempted

the fidelity of the first authorities of the United States; such were the words of blandishment he caused to resound in their ears, in order to seduce them to betray their country. But that which gave the congress most offense, and which they profited of with the greatest address to render the British cause and propositions alike odious to the inhabitants of America, was the following transaction general Reed stated that a lady had sought him, on the part of John stone, and had earnestly exhorted him to promote the re-union of the two countries, promising, in case of success, a reward of ten thousand pounds sterling, and any office in the colonies in the king's gift. The general replied, as he affirmed, *that he was not worth purchasing; but that such as he was, the king of Great Britain was not rich enough to do it.* The congress, in their indignation, declared that these being direct attempts to corrupt and bribe the congress of the United States of America, it was incompatible with their honor to hold any manner of correspondence or intercourse with George Johnstone ; especially to negotiate with him upon affairs in which the cause of liberty and virtue was interested.

This declaration, which was sent by a flag to the commissioners, produced a very severe answer from Johnstone, which, if he had clothed in more moderate language, would have gained him more credit with his readers. He affected to consider the declaration of congress as an honor, and not as a matter of offense ; he observed that while that assembly only contended for the essential privileges necessary to the preservation of their liberty and the redress of their grievances, their censure would have filled his soul with bitterness and with grief ; but since the congress, deaf to the piteous cries of so many citizens overwhelmed by the calamities of war, had sullied by motives of personal ambition the principles of their first resistance ; since he saw them bend the knee before the ambassador of France, and form alliance with the ancient enemy of the two countries, with the manifest intention of reducing the power of the mother country, he was quite unconcerned what might be the opinions of such men with regard to him. As to the accusations drawn from his letters, he neither denied nor confessed. He simply affirmed, that the present resolution of congress was no better founded than that they had taken concerning the cartridge-boxes of Burgoyne's army. He reserved, however, the liberty of justifying his conduct, before his departure from America; and added, that in the mean time, he should abstain from acting in the character of a commissioner.

His colleagues, Carlisle, Clinton, and Eden, issued a counter declaration, wherein they disclaimed all participation and knowledge of the matters specified by the congress in their resolutions. They

expressed, at the same time, the highest opinion of the abilities of
Johnstone, of the uprightness of his intentions, and of the equity
and generosity of those sentiments and principles upon which he was
desirous of founding a reconciliation between the disunited parts of
the British empire.

But the design of the commissioners in this declaration was not
so much to exculpate themselves, as to counteract the impression
produced by the treaties with France, and to demonstrate to the
people at large that congress had no right to ratify them.   They
had placed great hopes in this step.   They were not ignorant that
many Americans had abated their ardor, and even conceived a secret
discontent, since the much magnified succor of the count d'Estaing
had proved of so little, or rather of no utility.   The commissioners
were also, as usual, stimulated by the refugees, who reminded them
continually of the multitude and power of the loyalists.   They expatiated, therefore, upon the perfidy of France, upon the ambition of
congress, and they exerted themselves, especially, to prove that the
latter, in a case of this importance, where the salvation or the ruin of
all America was at stake, had not, even by their own constitution,
the power to ratify the treaties with France, without consulting their
constituents; at a time, too, when such offers of accommodation
were expected on the part of Great Britain, as not only far exceeded
the demands, but even the hopes of the inhabitants of America.
They concluded with observing, that the faith of the nation was not
pledged by the ratification of congress.

The opposite party wanted not writers who endeavored to defeat
the effect of these insinuations.   The most conspicuous among them
were Drayton, already mentioned, and Thomas Paine, author of the
work entitled Common Sense.   Whatever were the merits of this
controversy, it is certain that the publications of the commissioners
were absolutely fruitless.   Not a proselyte was made.

The British agents, being now persuaded that all hopes of reconciliation were illusory, determined, before their departure, to publish
a manifesto, in which they threatened the Americans with the extremes of the most desolating war that man could conceive.   They
hoped that terror would produce those effects which their conciliatory
offers had failed of attaining.   This plan of hostilities had long been
advocated in England, by the friends of coercion, as the readiest and
most effectual.   It would bring, they believed, such distress on the
colonies as would not fail to compel them to submit.   They represented the vast continent of America as peculiarly open to incursions
and ravages ; its coasts were of so immense an extent, that they could
not possibly be guarded against an enemy that was master at sea ;

there were innumerable bays, creeks and inlets, where descents might be made unobstructed. The rivers were such as afforded a navigation for ships of force far into the interior of the country ; thus it would be easy to penetrate to most of the towns and settlements, and to spread destruction into the heart of every province on the continent.

The commissioners, inclining to adopt these views, commenced their manifesto with a retrospect of the transactions and conduct of the congress ; charging them with an obstinate rejection of the proffers of accommodation on the part of Great Britain, and representing them as unauthorized to exercise the powers they had assumed. On the other hand, they magnified their own endeavors to bring about a restoration of peace and happiness to America. They gave notice, that it was their intention to return shortly to England, as their stay in a country where their commission had been treated with so little notice and respect, was inconsistent with the dignity of the power they represented. They professed, however, the same readiness as ever to promote the objects of their mission, and to continue the conciliatory offers that were its principal motive. Finally, they solemnly warned the people of the alteration that would be made in the future method of carrying on the war, should the colonies persist in their resistance to Great Britain, and in their unnatural connection with France.

' The policy, as well as the benevolence of Great Britain,' said they, ' has hitherto checked the extremes of war, when they tended to distress a people, still considered as fellow-subjects, and to desolate a country shortly to become again a source of mutual advantage ; but when that country not only estranges herself from England, but mortgages herself and her resources to her enemy, the whole contest is changed ; and the question is, how far Great Britain may, by every means in her power, destroy or render useless a connection contrived for her ruin, and for the aggrandizement of France ? Under such circumstances, the laws of self-preservation must direct the conduct of Great Britain ; and if the British colonies are to become an accession of power to France, will direct her to render that accession of as little avail as possible to her enemy.'

This manifesto, which was the object of the severest animadversion, and which was even condemned by several orators of parliament, and particularly by Fox, as cruel and barbarous, produced no greater effect upon the minds of the Americans than had been operated by the offers of peace.

The congress immediately issued a proclamation, warning all the inhabitants who lived in places exposed to the descents and ravages of a ferocious enemy, to remove, on the appearance of danger, to the distance of at least thirty miles, together with their families, their cattle, and all their movable property. But if the measures adopted by the British commissioners were justly censured, those taken by the congress are at least by no means to be commended. They rec ommended, that whenever the enemy proceeded to burn or destroy any town, the people should, in the same manner, ravage, burn and destroy the houses and properties of all tories and enemies to the independence of America, and secure their persons ; without treating them, however, or their families, with any cruelty ; since the Americans should abhor to imitate their adversaries, or the allies they had subsidized, whether Germans, blacks, or savages.

Such are the excesses to which even the most civilized men are liable to be transported, when under the pestilent influence of party spirit. The British threatened to do what they had already done, and the Americans, the very thing they so justly condemned in their enemies. But impassioned man is more prone to imitate evil in others, than dispassionate man to imitate good.

Some time after, lest the extreme rigor of the English declarations should give birth to new thoughts among the people, the congress published a manifesto, in which they premised, that since they had not been able to prevent, they had endeavored, at least, to alleviate the calamities of war. But they asserted that the conduct of their enemies had been the very reverse. ' They,' said the manifesto, ' have laid waste the open country, burned the defenseless villages, and butchered the citizens of America. Their prisons have been the slaughter-houses of her soldiers, their ships of her seamen ; and the severest injuries have been aggravated by the grossest insults. Foiled in their vain attempts to subjugate the unconquerable spirit of freedom, they have meanly assailed the representatives of America with bribes, with deceit, and the servility of adulation. They have made a mock of religion by impious appeals to God, while in the violation of his sacred command. They have made a mock even of reason itself, by endeavoring to prove that the liberty and happiness of America could safely be intrusted to those who have sold their own, unawed by the sense of virtue or of shame. Treated with the contempt which such conduct deserved, they have applied to individuals. They have solicited them to break the bonds of allegiance and imbue their souls with the blackest crimes. But fearing that none could be found through these United States equal to the wickedness of their purpose, to influence weak minds, they have threatened more wide devastation.

' While the shadow of hope remained that our enemies could be taught by our example to respect those laws which are held sacred among civilized nations, and to comply with the dictates of a religion which they pretend, in common with us, to believe and revere, they have been left to the influence of that religion and that example. But since their incorrigible dispositions cannot be touched by kindness and compassion, it becomes our duty by other means to vindicate the rights of humanity.

' We, therefore, the congress of the United States of America, do solemnly declare and proclaim, that if our enemies presume to execute their threats, or persist in their present career of barbarity, we will take such exemplary vengeance as shall deter others from a like conduct. We appeal to that God who searcheth the hearts of men, for the rectitude of our intentions ; and in his noly presence declare, that as we are not moved by any light and hasty suggestions of anger or revenge, so, through every possible change of fortune, we will adhere to this our determination.'

At the same epoch, the marquis de la Fayette, indignant at the manner in which the British commissioners had spoken of France in their letter of the twenty-sixth of August, in attributing her interference in the present quarrel to ambition, and to the desire of seeing the two parties consume each other in a long war, wrote to the earl of Carlisle, demanding reparation for the insult offered to his country, and challenging him to single combat.

The earl declined this meeting, saying, that as he had acted on that occasion in the character of a commissioner, his language and conduct had been official, and consequently he was accountable for them to no one except to his king and country. He concluded his answer with observing, that in regard to national disputes, they would be better adjusted when admiral Byron and the count d'Estaing should have met upon the ocean.

A short time after, the commissioners, unable to effect any of the objects of their mission, embarked for England. All hope from negotiation being now vanished, every thought was devoted with new ardor to the way of arms. Meanwhile, the congress had returned to Philadelphia, a few days after the English evacuated that city. On the sixth of August they received publicly, and with all the ceremonies usual on similar occasions, M. Gerard, minister plenipotentiary of the king of France. This envoy delivered at first his letters of credence, which were signed by Louis XVI., and directed *to his very dear great friends and allies, the president and members of the general Congress of the United States of America.* He made a very apposite speech in which he set forth the benevolent intentions of France towards the United States, and the reciprocal obligation of the two contracting parties to execute the engagements stipulated in the eventual treaty, in order to defeat the hostile measures and designs of the common enemy. He announced, that on his part, his most christian majesty had already sent to their assistance a numerous and powerful fleet. He closed, with expressing a hope that the principles which might be adopted by the respective governments would tend to strengthen those bonds of union, which had originated in the mutual interest of the two nations.

The president, Henry Laurens, answered with much ease and dignity ; that the present treaties sufficed to demonstrate the wisdom and magnanimity of the most christian king ; that the virtuous citizens of America could never cease to acknowledge the hand of a gracious Providence, in raising them up so powerful and illustrious a friend. That the congress had no doubt, but that the confidence his majesty reposed in the firmness of the United States would receive additional strength from every day's experience. That since England, from her insatiable lust of domination, was resolved to prolong the war, and with it the miseries of mankind, they were determined to fulfill all the conditions of the eventual treaty, although they had no more ardent wish than to spare human blood, by laying down at once their resentments and their arms ; that they hoped the assistance of so wise and generous an ally, would at length open the eyes of Great Britain, and bring her to a sense of justice and moderation. The authorities of Pennsylvania, many strangers of note, the officers of the army, and a great number of distinguished citizens, were present at this audience. The public joy was now at its height. All hearts were filled, not only with the hope of independence, for that was considered as no longer doubtful, but also with brilliant anticipations of future prosperity ; the American empire, with the interference of France, appeared already established for ever.

Thus a king extended an auxiliary hand to a republic against another king ! Thus the French nation came to the succor of one English people against another English people ; thus the European powers, who until then had acknowledged no other independent nations in America, except the savages and barbarians, looking upon all the others as subjects, began to recognize as independent and sovereign a civilized nation, and to form alliance with it, as such, by authentic treaties. An event assuredly worthy to arrest our particular attention ; since the discovery of America by Columbus, none of equal or of similar importance had passed before the eyes of men. Such, in America, were the fruits either of the love of liberty or the desire of independence. Such were the consequences, in Europe, of a blind obstinacy, 'or of a pride perhaps necessary on the one part; of jealousy of power and a thirst of vengeance on the other!

The fourteenth of September, the congress appointed doctor Benjamin Franklin minister plenipotentiary of the United States at the court of France.

We have already related how, and by what causes, the expedition of the Delaware, by which the allies had hoped to destroy the British fleet and army at a single blow, had failed to have effect. Desirous, therefore, of achieving some other enterprise of importance, which might both honor their arms, and procure them an essential advantage, they resolved to direct their operations against Rhode Island. This expedition offered them greater facilities than any other; the situation of places being such that the land troops of the Americans, and the naval forces of the French, could lend each other mutual assistance, and bring their joint energies to bear upon the same point. This design had been concerted between the generals of congress and d'Estaing, while he lay at anchor off Sandy Hook. General Sullivan had already been sent into that part, in order to take the command of the troops destined for the expedition, and in the meantime to assemble the militia of New England. General Greene had likewise been directed to proceed to Rhode Island; born in that province, he possessed great credit and influence among its inhabitants. The general of the British army, having penetrated the design of the allies, had sent from New York considerable re-inforcements to major-general Pigot, who commanded in Rhode Island, which carried his garrison to six thousand men. General Sullivan had established his camp near Providence; it was composed of about ten thousand men, including militia. The plan which had been agreed upon was, that while Sullivan should make a descent upon the island from the northward, d'Estaing was to force the harbor of Newport from the south, destroy the British shipping at anchor there, and assault the town with vigor. The British garrison, thus pressed between two fires, it was thought, would soon, of necessity, be compelled to surrender.

The state of Rhode Island is principally composed of several adjacent islands, the largest of which gives its name to the whole province. Between the eastern coast of this island and the main land, is an arm of the sea, which, extending considerably towards the north, expands into the bay of Mount Hope. This arm is denominated Seaconnet, or the eastern passage. Between Rhode Island and the island of Conanicut is another very narrow passage, named the Main Channel. Finally, between the western coast of Conanicut island and the main land is found a third arm of the sea, known by the

name of the western, or Narraganset passage. The town of Newport is situated upon the western shore of Rhode Island Proper, opposite to the island of Conanicut. At a short distance from the
town, to the northeast, rise a chain of hills which stretch almost across
the island from the eastern passage to the Main Channel. The
English had fortified these heights with much care, in order to cover
the town against an attack from the Americans, who were likely to
approach by the north part of the island.

General Pigot prepared himself for an able and vigorous defense.
He very prudently recalled the garrison of Conanicut island, and
concentrated his forces about Newport. He also withdrew into the
town the artillery and the cattle.   The posts that were dispersed in
different parts of the island, and especially the soldiers who occupied
the northern point, were ordered to fall back upon the town as soon
as they should discover the enemy's approach.   The part of the town
which looked towards the sea was fortified with extreme diligence;
vessels of transport were sunk in such places as might obstruct the
approaches by water to the most important batteries ; the rest were
burned.   The frigates were removed higher up for safer moorings.
But to provide for the worst, they were stripped of their artillery and
stores.   The seamen belonging to the vessels sunk or destroyed, were
employed to serve the artillery of the ramparts ; a service they well
understood, and greatly coveted.

Meanwhile the count d'Estaing, on his departure from Sandy
Hook, after standing to the southward as far as the mouth of the
Delaware, changed his course and bore to the northeast upon Rhode
Island.   He arrived the twenty-ninth of July at Point Judith, and
anchored with the most of his ships just without Brenton's Ledge,
about five miles from Newport. Two of his vessels went up the
Narraganset passage, and cast anchor to the north of Conanicut.
Several frigates entered the Seaconnet passage ; the English on their
approach set fire to a corvette and two armed galleys which had been
stationed there.   During several days the French admiral made no
attempt to penetrate the Main Channel, in order to attack the town
of Newport, as it had been concerted with the Americans. This
delay was occasioned by that of the re-inforcements of militia which
general Sullivan expected, and which were deemed essential to the
security of the enterprise. Finally, the eighth of August, all the
preparations being completed, and the wind favorable, the French
squadron entered the harbor of Newport, and coasting the town, discharged their broadsides into it, and received the fire of the batteries
on shore ; but little execution was done on either side. They anchored a little above the town, between Goats Island and Conanicut, but

nearest to the latter, which was already occupied by the Americans. The English in the meantime, finding they could not save several frigates and other vessels of less force, concluded to burn them.

The next day, general Sullivan, who had moved from Providence down to that part of the main land which bears from the east upon Rhode Island, crossed the Seaconnet passage at Howland's Ferry, and landed with all his troops upon the north end of the island. It appears that this movement was highly offensive to the count d'Estaing, who expected to have been the first to set foot on shore in the island. General Sullivan hoped that the attack would now be delayed no longer, when the same day, the ninth of August, signals announced the whole squadron of lord Howe, who, on receiving intelligence that Rhode Island was menaced by the French, had hastened to the succor of general Pigot. Notwithstanding the re-inforcement he had lately received, he was still inferior to his enemy, considering the size of his ships, and their weight of metal. His squadron, though more numerous, consisted of only one ship of seventy-four, seven of sixty-four, and five of fifty guns, with several frigates. He hoped, however, that fortune would offer him an occasion to join battle with the advantage of wind, or of some other circumstances. And certainly if, from the time he had taken the resolution of moving to the relief of Rhode Island, the winds had not retarded his progress, he would have arrived at the very moment when the French squadron was dispersed in the different channels formed by the adjacent islands; in which case he would have had all the chances of victory in his favor. But his passage was so difficult, that he was unable to arrive till the day after that in which the count d'Estaing had put himself in safety, with all his fleet, in the Main Channel.

Having carefully examined, as well the nature of the places, as the position of the French ships, and having also communicated to the same end with general Pigot, the British admiral concluded that there was no hope left him of succoring the town, especially as the winds continued contrary. The harbor was so situated, the entrance so narrow, the apparatus of defense on the island of Conanicut so formidable, that the enterprise could not have been attempted, not only by an inferior squadron, as was that of Howe, but even by a greatly superior force, without temerity. For the same cause, if the French admiral, agreeably to the plan concerted with Sullivan, had been disposed to persist, and not to quit his station until he had afforded that general all the co-operation in his power, there is good reason to believe that the town of Newport would have fallen into the hands of the allies.

But the count d'Estaing, like a true Frenchman, full of ardor and impatience, upon a change of wind to the northeast, in the morning of the tenth, was seized with an impulse that he could not master, to profit of this circumstance to sail out of the harbor, in order to attack the enemy. He accordingly stood out to sea, in search of the British fleet. Admiral Howe, on seeing so formidable an armament advance to engage him, and being under the wind, which gave the French the weathergage, declined coming to action, and maneuvered with great ability in order to gain that advantage for himself. A contest ensued for it, which lasted the whole day ; the French admiral striving to retain it with equal eagerness. The wind still continuing on the eleventh unfavorable to the British, Howe resolved, notwithstanding, to meet the enemy. He therefore formed his squadron so that it could be joined by three fire-ships, which were towed by the frigates. The French also disposed their ships in order of battle, and the moment already approached that was to decide which of the two powerful adversaries should remain master of the American seas. But at the same instant, a strong gale commenced, which, soon after increasing, became a violent storm. The tempest, which lasted forty-eight hours, not only separated and dispersed the two fleets, but did them so much damage, that they were both rendered unfit for action, and compelled to put into port to repair. The French squadron suffered even more than the English, especially in their masts and rigging. The Languedoc, of ninety guns, the admiral's ship, lost her rudder and all her masts. Floating in this condition, at the mercy of the currents, she was met by the English ship Renown, of fifty guns, commanded by captain Dawson, who attacked her with so much vigor and dexterity, that had not darkness interposed, together with the gale, which had not yet sufficiently abated, she must inevitably have struck ; as she could only use seven or eight of her guns. Some French ships appeared with the return of day. They bore down upon captain Dawson, and gave chase, though without being able to come up with him. But they at least delivered their admiral from the imminent peril to which they found him exposed.

The same day, the English ship Preston, of fifty guns, fell in with the Tonnant, of eighty, with only her mainmast standing. He attacked her ; but was compelled, by the coming on of night, to discontinue the engagement till next morning, when the appearance of several French ships constrained ·him to withdraw. The British squadron returned to Sandy Hook and New York, for the purpose of refitting ; the repairs were pushed with the greatest diligence. The French recovered the harbor of Newport.

In the mean time, general Sullivan, though impeded by bad weather, and other difficulties which had retarded the arrival of his stores and artillery, had advanced very near to Newport. He already had occupied Honeymans Hill, and was engaged with great activity in constructing batteries. The besieged were not wanting to themselves ; they erected new fortifications and new batteries, to answer those of the Americans. But notwithstanding their efforts, if the count d'Estaing, on returning from his more prejudicial than useful enterprise upon the sea, had chosen to co-operate with the Americans, it is certain, that the position of general Pigot would have been excessively critical.

Assailed on the one side by the Americans, the English could not have hoped to defend themselves, if the French, on the other, in addition to the fire of their ships, had landed, as they easily might have done, a strong detachment on the southern point of the island, in order to assault the left flank of the town, which was known to be the weakest. But the count d'Estaing had very different intentions. He dispatched a letter to Sullivan, informing him that, in pursuance of orders from his sovereign, and of the advice of all his officers, he had taken the resolution to carry the fleet to Boston. His instructions were, it is true, to sail for that port if his fleet should meet with any disaster, or if a superior British fleet should appear on the coast.

The injuries sustained by the storm, and the information which had been received that Byron had arrived at Halifax, were considered as producing the state of things contemplated by the instructions of the ministry. The Americans, convinced that the departure of the count d'Estaing would be the ruin of the expedition, added entreaties to remonstrances, in order to dissuade him from so fatal a measure.

Generals Greene and La Fayette besought him that he would not, by persisting in his resolution, abandon the interests of the common cause ; they represented to him the importance, to France, as well as America, of the enterprise commenced ; that it was already so well advanced as to leave no doubt of success ; that it could not be relinquished in its present stage without shaming and disgusting the Americans, who, confiding in the promised co-operation of the French fleet, had undertaken it with alacrity, and made incredible exertions to provide the requisite stores ; that to be deserted at so critical a moment would furnish a triumph. to the disaffected, who would not fail to exclaim, that such was French faith, and the fruit of the alliance ; that the successive miscarriages of the Delaware, of Sandy Hook, and finally this of Newport, could not but carry to its height the exasperation of minds. They added, that with a fleet in so shattered a condition, it would be very difficult to pass the shoals of Nantucket; that it could be repaired more conveniently at Newport than at Boston; and finally, that its present station afforded advantages over Boston for distressing the enemy, while in the event of the arrival of a superior fleet, it would be no more secure at Boston than at Newport. All was fruitless. The count d'Estaing got under sail the twenty-second of August, and three days after came to anchor in the harbor of Boston.

Whatever is to be thought of this resolution of d'Estaing, which, it appears, was not only approved, but even strenuously recommended by his council, it is certain that it made a violent impression upon the minds of the republicans, and excited loud clamors throughout America. The militia, who with so much zeal had hastened to join Sullivan in Rhode Island, finding themselves thus deserted by their allies, immediately disbanded, so that the besiegers were reduced, in a short time, from about ten thousand men to not more than half that number, while the force of the enemy consisted of six thousand veterans.

In so abrupt a reverse of fortune, and seeing the allied fleet retire, while that of the enemy approached, the American general soon hetermined to fall back upon the main land, and evacuate the island entirely. He began the twenty-sixth of August to pass his heavy artillery and baggage towards the northern point of the island, and on the twenty-ninth he put himself in motion, with all the army. Though warmly pursued by the English and Hessians, he rejoined his van without loss. But the enemy coming up in more force, there ensued a very hot affair in the environs of Quaker Hill, in which many soldiers fell on both sides. At length, the Americans repulsed the English with admirable resolution. In the night of the thirtieth, the corps of Sullivan recovered the main land by the passages of Bristol and Howland's Ferry. Such was the issue of an expedition, undertaken, not only with the fairest prospect of success, but which had been carried to the very threshold of a brilliant termination. The American general made his retreat in time; for the next day general Clinton arrived with four thousand men and a light squadron, to the relief of Newport. If the winds had favored him more, or if general Sullivan had been less prompt to retreat, assailed on the island by an enemy whose force was double his own, and his way to the continent intercepted by the English vessels, his position would have been little less than desperate. His prudence received merited acknowledgments on the part of congress.

Admiral Howe, having refitted his ships with astonishing dispatch, stood out to sea, and sailed towards Boston. He hoped to arrive there before his adversary, and consequently to intercept his retreat thither, or at least to attack him in the outer harbor. He arrived, indeed, on the thirtieth of August, in the bay of Boston. But he was unable to accomplish either the one or the other of his designs; the count d'Estaing was already in port; and the batteries erected by the Americans upon the most commanding points of the coast rendered all attack impracticable. The British admiral, therefore, returned to New York, where he found a re-inforcement of several ships, which rendered his fleet superior to that of the French. He availed himself of this circumstance, and of the permission he had received some time before, to resign the command to admiral Gambier, until the arrival of admiral Byron upon that station, which took place the sixteenth of September. Lord Howe soon after returned to England. This illustrious seaman rendered important services to his country, in the campaigns of Pennsylvania, New York, and Rhode Island, services which would have had more brilliant results, if the ability of the commanders on shore had equaled his own. Even to say nothing of the activity he displayed in transporting to a distant country so numerous an army as that of his brother sir William, the talent and firmness with which he surmounted the obstacles that opposed his entrance into the Delaware, deserve the highest commendation. When the count d'Estaing made his appearance with a formidable fleet, and much superior to his own, he nevertheless prepared to receive him at Sandy Hook; afterwards by offering him battle, he baffled his designs against Newport; and then the French admiral, disabled by the tempest, forced to seek refuge in the port of Boston, issued no more, except to make the best of his way to the West Indies; thus totally abandoning the execution of the plan concerted by the allies for the campaign of this year upon the coasts of America. Finding Newport secure, general Clinton returned to New York. He afterwards detached general Grey, who was at New London, upon an expedition of much importance towards the east. Buzzards Bay, and the adjacent rivers, served as a retreat for a multitude of privateers, the number and boldness of which occasioned infinite prejudice to the British commerce of New York, Long Island, and Rhode Island. Clinton resolved to chastise an enemy that seemed to defy him, and to put an end to his maritime excursions. This task was committed to the charge of general Grey. He arrived with some transports, effected his landing in the bay, and destroyed about sixty large vessels, besides a number of small craft. Proceeding then to New Bedford and Fair Haven, upon the banks of the river Acushnet, and conducting himself more like a pirate than a real soldier, he destroyed or burned warehouses of immense value, full of sugar, rum, molasses, tobacco, drugs and other merchandise. Not content with these ravages, he passed into the neighboring island, called Martha's Vineyard, the soil of which is very fertile, and which served as a refuge for the most daring cruisers. He levied on the inhabitants a contribution of live stock to the great refreshment of the garrisons of New York. He carried off, besides, a considerable quantity of arms and ammunition.

Returned to New York, he soon undertook another expedition, against the village of Old Tappan, where he surprised a regiment of American light horse. His conduct on this occasion was not exempt from the reproach of cruelty. A few days after, the English made an incursion against Little Egg Harbor, upon the coast of New Jersey, where they destroyed much shipping, and brought off a considerable booty. They afterwards attacked by surprise the legion of Pulaski, and made great slaughter of it. The carnage would have been still greater, if Pulaski had not come up, with his usual bravery, at the head of his cavalry. The English re-embarked, and returned to New York.

It was at this epoch that the French and American generals meditated a new expedition against Canada. Besides the possession of so important a province, there appeared a possibility of ruining the British fisheries upon the banks of Newfoundland, and, by reducing the cities of Quebec and Halifax, of putting an end to the maritime power of England upon those shores. The French were the principal movers of this enterprise; their minister, and d'Estaing, perhaps, with covert views; the marquis de la Fayette, whose youth answered for his ignorance of these political wiles, with frankness, and from the love of glory. He was to have been employed in the expedition as one of the first generals. The count d'Estaing published a manifesto, addressed to the Canadians in the name of his king, in which, after reminding them of their French origin, their ancient exploits, and happiness they had enjoyed under the paternal scepter of the Bourbons, he declared that all the ancient subjects of the king in North America, who should cease to acknowledge the English domination, should find safety and protection. But Washington showed himself opposed to this project, and he developed his motives to the congress; his opinion prevailed.

The congress alleged that their finances, their arsenals, their magazines, their armies, were not in a state to warrant the undertaking of so vast an enterprise; and that they should experience too pungent regrets to find themselves in the event unable to fulfill their engagements towards their allies. Such was their public language; but the truth is, they apprehended a snare, and that the conquest of Canada would have been made for France, and not for America.

The retreat of the count d'Estaing, at the moment when Newport was about to fall into the power of the combined armies, had greatly irritated the minds of the Americans, particularly in the northern provinces. Many began to entertain a loathing towards allies who seemed to forget all interests except their own. To this motive of aversion was added the remembrance, still recent, especially with the lowei classes, of ancient quarrels and national jealousies, which the new alliance, and the need of French succors, had not sufficed to obliterate. Washington and other leading Americans endeavored to appease these discontents, which, they foresaw, might lead to serious mischief. The count d'Estaing, on his part, was no less careful, during his stay in the port of Boston, not only to avoid all occasion of misunderstanding, but also to conciliate by every means in his power the affection of his new allies. The conduct of the French officers, and even of the common sailors, was truly exemplary. This extreme circumspection, however, did not prevent the occurrence, on the thirteenth of September, of a violent affray between some Bostonians and the French. The latter were overpowered by number, and the chevalier de Saint Sauveur lost his life in it. The selectmen of the town, to allay the resentment of the French, showed themselves very solicitous to punish the offenders. They published a reward to whoever should make known the authors of the tumult. They declared, at the same time, that the citizens had not been in fault, but English sailors made prisoners by the cruisers, and deserters from the army of Burgoyne, who had enlisted in the Boston privateers. Tranquillity was restored. The count d'Estaing, whether he was satisfied, or that from prudence he chose to appear so, made no further inquiry into this affair. No offender was discovered. The government of Massachusetts decreed a monument to be erected to Saint Sauveur.

The night of the sixth of the same month of September had witnessed a scene far more serious, at Charleston, South Carolina, between the French and American sailors. It terminated in a formal battle. The Americans were the first to provoke their allies by the most reproachful language; the latter resented it. From words it came to blows; the French were soon driven out of the city, and forced to take refuge on board their ships. Thence they fired with artillery and musketry against the town; the Americans, on their part, fired upon the French vessels from the adjoining wharves and shore. Many lives were lost on both sides. A reward of a thousand pounds sterling was promised, but in vain, to whoever should discover the authors of this broil. The commander-in-chief of the province exhorted the inhabitants, in a proclamation, to consider the French as good and faithful allies and friends. There was even a law passed, about this time, to prevent the recurrence of a similar licentiousness, whether of words or actions. Thus ended the riots of Boston and of Charleston, which were attributed, if not with truth, at least with prudence, to British artifice and instigation. For the chiefs of the American government were not without apprehension that these animosities might deprive them of their new allies, whose resolutions, they knew, were not irrevocable.

The savages took a more active part than ever in the campaign of this year. Though they had been intimidated by the success of general Gates, and had sent him congratulations for himself and the United States, the intrigues and presents of the British agents had not lost their power over them. Moreover, the emigrant colonists, who had retired among these barbarians, excited them continually by instigations, which, together with their natural thirst for blood and pillage, determined them without scruple to make incursions upon the northern frontiers, where they spread terror and desolation. The most ruthless chiefs that guided them in these sanguinary expeditions, were colonel Butler, who had already signalized himself in this war, and a certain Brandt, born of mixed blood, the most ferocious being ever produced by human nature, often too prodigal of similar monsters. They spared neither age, nor sex, nor condition, nor even their own kindred; every where indiscriminately they carried devastation and death. The knowledge which the refugees had of the country, the insulated position of the habitations, scattered here and there in the wilderness, the distance from the seat of government, and the necessity of employing the national force in other remote parts, offered the Indians every facility for executing their enterprises, and retiring with impunity. No means had hitherto been found of repressing the inroads of so cruel an enemy.

But in the midst of this general devastation, there happened an event which, perhaps, would be found without example in the history of inhuman men. Inhabitants of Connecticut had planted on the eastern branch of the Susquehanna, towards the extremity of Pennsylvania, and upon the road of Oswego, the settlement of Wyoming. Populous and flourishing, its prosperity was the subject of admiration. It consisted of eight townships, each containing a square of five miles, beautifully situated on both sides of the river. The mildness of the climate answered to the fertility of the soil. The inhabitants were strangers alike to excessive wealth, which elates and depraves, and to poverty, which discourages and degrades. All lived in a happy mediocrity, frugal of their own, and coveting nothing from others. Incessantly occupied in rural toils, they avoided idleness, and all the vices of which it is the source. In a word, this little country presented in reality the image of those fabulous times which the poets have described under the name of the *Golden Age*. But their domestic felicity was no counterpoise to the zeal with which they were animated for the common cause; they took up arms and flew to succor their country. It is said they had furnished to the army no less than a thousand soldiers, a number truly prodigious for so feeble a population, and so happy in their homes. Yet, notwithstanding the drain of all this vigorous youth, the abundance of harvests sustained no diminution. Their crowded granaries, and pastures replenished with fat cattle, offered an exhaustless resource to the American army.

But neither so many advantages, nor even the retired situation of these unfortunate colonists, could exempt them from the baneful influence of party spirit. Although the tories, as they called them, were not so numerous as the partisans of liberty, yet they challenged attention by the arrogance of their character and the extent of their pretensions. Hence, not only families were seen armed against families, but even sons sided against their fathers, brothers against brothers, and, at last, wives against husbands. So true it is, that no virtue is proof against the fanaticism of opinion, and no happiness against political divisions. The tories were, besides, exasperated at their losses in the incursions they had made in company with the savages in the preceding campaign; but that which envenomed them the most was, that several individuals of the same party, who, having quitted their habitations, were come to claim hospitality, then so much in honor among the Americans, and particularly at Wyoming, had been arrested as suspected persons, and sent to take their trial in Connecticut. Others had been expelled from the colony. Thus hatreds became continually more and more rancorous. The tories swore revenge; they coalesced with the Indians. The time was favorable, as the youth of Wyoming were at the army. In order the better to secure success, and to surprise their enemies befcre they should think of standing upon their defense, they resorted to artifice. They pretended the most friendly dispositions, while they meditated only war and vengeance.

A few weeks before they purposed to execute their horrible enterprise, they sent several messengers, charged with protestations of their earnest desire to cultivate peace. These perfidies lulled the inhabitants of Wyoming into a deceitful security, while they procured the tories and savages the means of concerting with their partisans, and of observing the immediate state of the colony. Notwithstanding the solemn assurances of the Indians, the colonists, as it often happens when great calamities are about to fall on a people, seemed to have a sort of presentiment of their approaching fate. They wrote to Washington, praying him to send them immediate assistance. Their dispatches did not reach him; they were intercepted by the Pennsylvanian loyalists; and they would, besides, have arrived too late. The savages had already made their appearance upon the frontiers of the colony; the plunder they had made there was of little importance, but the cruelties they had perpetrated were affrightful; the mournful prelude of those more terrible scenes which were shortly to follow!

About the commencement of the month of July, the Indians suddenly appeared in force upon the banks of the Susquehanna. They were headed by the John Butler and Brandt already named, with other chiefs of their nation, distinguished by their extreme ferocity in the preceding expeditions. This troop amounted in all to sixteen hundred men, of whom less than a fourth were Indians, and the rest tories, disguised and painted to resemble them. The officers, however, wore the uniforms of their rank, and had the appearance of regulars. The colonists of Wyoming, finding their friends so remote, and their enemies so near, had constructed for their security four forts, in which, and upon different points of the frontier, they had distributed about five hundred men. The whole colony was placed under the command of Zebulon Butler, cousin of John, a man, who with some courage was totally devoid of capacity. He was even accused of treachery; but this imputation is not proved. It is at least certain that one of the forts which stood nearest to the frontiers, was intrusted to soldiers infected with the opinions of the tories, and who gave it up, without resistance, at the first approach of the enemy. The second, on being vigorously assaulted, surrendered at discretion. The savages spared, it is true, the women and children, but butchered all the rest without exception. Zebulon then withdrew, with all his people, into the principal fort, called Kingston. The old men, the women, the children, the sick, in a word, all that were unable to bear arms, repaired thither in throngs, and uttering lamentable cries, as to the last refuge where any hope of safety remained. The position was susceptible of defense; and if Zebulon had held firm, he might have hoped to withstand the enemy until the arrival of succors. But John Butler was lavish of promises, in order to draw him out, in which he succeeded, by persuading him that if he would consent to a parley in the open field, the siege would soon be raised and every thing accommodated. John retired, in fact, with all his corps; Zebulon afterwards marched out to the place appointed for the conference, at a considerable distance from the fort; from motives of caution, he took with him four hundred men well armed, being nearly the whole strength of his garrison. If this step was not dictated by treachery, it must, at least, be attributed to a very strange simplicity. Having come to the spot agreed on, Zebulon found no living being there. Reluctant to return without an interview, he advanced towards the foot of a mountain, at a still greater distance from the fort, hoping he might there find some person to confer with. The farther he proceeded in this dismal solitude, the more he had occasion to remark that no token appeared of the presence or vicinity of human creatures. But far from halting, as if impelled by an irresistible destiny, he continued his march. The country, meanwhile, began to be overshaded by thick forests; at length, in a winding path, he perceived a flag, which seemed to wave him on. The individual who bore it, as if afraid of treachery from his side, retired as he advanced, still making the same signals. But already the Indians, who knew the country, profiting of the obscurity of the woods, had completely surrounded him. The unfortunate American, without suspicion of the peril he was in, continued to press forward in order to assure the traitors that he would not betray them. He was awakened but too soon from this dream of security; in an instant the savages sprung from their ambush, and fell upon him with hideous yells.

He formed his little troop into a compact column, and showed more presence of mind in danger than he had manifested in the negotiation. Though surprised, the Americans exhibited such vigor and resolution that the advantage was rather on their side, when a soldier, either through treachery or cowardice, cried out aloud, *'The colonel has ordered a retreat.'* The Americans immediately break, the savages leap in among the ranks, and a horrible carnage ensues. The fugitives fall by missiles, the resisting by clubs and tomahawks. The wounded overturn those that are not, the dead and the dying are heaped together promiscuously. Happy those who expire the soonest! The savages reserve the living for tortures! and the infuriate tories, if other arms fail them, mangle the prisoners with their nails! Never was rout so deplorable; never was massacre accompanied with so many horrors. Nearly all the Americans perished; about sixty escaped from the butchery, and with Zebulon, made their way good to a redoubt upon the other bank of the Susquehanna.

The conquerors invested Kingston anew, and to dismay the relics of the garrison by the most execrable spectacle, they hurled into the place above two hundred scalps, still reeking with the blood of their slaughtered brethren. Colonel Dennison, who commanded the fort, seeing the impossibility of defense, sent out a flag to inquire of Butler what terms would be allowed the garrison, on surrendering the fort? He answered, with all the fellness of his inhuman character, and in a single word—the *hatchet*. Reduced to this dreadful extremity, the colonel still made what resistance he could. At length, having lost almost all his soldiers, he surrendered at discretion. The savages entered the fort, and began to drag out the vanquished, who, knowing the hands they were in, expected no mercy. But impatient of the tedious process of murder in detail, the barbarians afterwards bethought themselves of enclosing the men, women, and children promiscuously in the houses and barracks, to which they set fire and consumed all within, listening, delighted, to the moans and shrieks of the expiring multitude.

The fort of Wilkesbarre still remained in the power of the colonists of Wyoming. The victors presented themselves before it; those within, hoping to find mercy, surrendered at discretion, and without resistance. But if opposition exasperated these ferocious men, or rather these tigers, insatiable of human blood, submission did not soften them. Their rage was principally exercised upon the soldiers of the garrison; all of whom they put to death, with a barbarity ingenious in tortures. As for the rest, men, women, and children, who appeared to them not to merit any special attention, they burned them as before, in the houses and barracks. The forts being fallen into their hands, the barbarians proceeded, without obstacle, to the devastation of the country. They employed at once, fire, sword, and all instruments of destruction. The crops of every description were consigned to the flames. The habitations, granaries, and other constructions, the fruit of years of human industry, sunk in ruin under the destructive strokes of these cannibals. But who will believe that their fury, not yet satiated upon human creatures, was also wreaked upon the very beasts? That they cut out the tongues of the horses and cattle, and left them to wander in the midst of those fields lately so luxuriant, and now in desolation, seeming to enjoy the torments of their lingering death?

We have long hesitated whether we ought to relate particular instances of this demoniac cruelty; the bare remembrance of them makes us shudder. But on reflecting that these examples may deter good princes from war, and citizens from civil discord, we have deemed it useful to record them. Captain Bedlock having been stripped naked, the savages stuck sharp pine splinters into all parts of his body; and then a heap of knots of the same wood being piled round him, the whole was set on fire, and his two companions, the captains Ranson and Durgee, thrown alive into the flames. *The tories appeared to vie with, and even to surpass, the savages in barbarity.* One of them, whose mother had married a second husband, butchered her with his own hand, and afterwards massacred his father-in-law, his own sisters, and their infants in the cradle. Another killed his own father, and exterminated all his family. A third imbrued his hands in the blood of his brothers, his sisters, his brother-in-law, and his father-in-law.

These were a part only of the horrors perpetrated by the loyalists and Indians, at the excision of Wyoming. Other atrocities, if possible, still more abominable, we leave in silence.

Those who had survived the massacres were no less worthy of commiseration; they were women and children, who had escaped to the woods at the time their husbands and fathers expired under the blows of the barbarians. Dispersed and wandering in the forests, as chance and fear directed their steps, without clothes, without food, without guide, these defenseless fugitives suffered every degree of distress. Several of the women were delivered alone in the woods, at a great distance from every possibility of relief. The most robust and resolute alone escaped; the others perished; their bodies and those of their hapless infants became the prey of wild beasts. Thus the most flourishing colony then existing in America was totally erased.

The destruction of Wyoming, and the cruelties which accompanied it, filled all the inhabitants of America with horror, with compassion, and with indignant fury. They fully purposed, on a future day, to exact a condign vengeance; but in the present state of the war, it was not in their power to execute their intent immediately. They undertook, however, this year, some expeditions against the Indians. Without being of decisive importance, they deserve to be remarked for the courage and ability with which they were executed. Colonel Clarke, at the head of a strong detachment, marched from Virginia against the settlements established by the Canadians on the upper Mississippi, in the country of the Illinois.

He purposed, also, to chastise, even in their most sequestered receptacles, this ruthless race. Having descended the Ohio, he directed his march northward, towards Kaskaskias, the principal village of the Canadian establishments. The republicans came upon the inhabitants in sleep, and met with very little resistance. They afterwards scoured the adjacent country, and seized other places of

the settlement. Filled with dismay, the inhabitants hastened to
swear allegiance to the United States. Thence, colonel Clarke
marched against the barbarian tribes ; he penetrated into their
inmost retreats and most secret recesses, and put all to sword
and fire.

The savages experienced in their own huts and families those
calamities which they had so frequently carried home to others.
This castigation rendered them, for a while, more timid in their
excursions, and encouraged the Americans · to defend themselves.

A similar expedition was undertaken, some time after, by another
colonel Butler, against the tories and Indians of the banks of the
Susquehanna; the same who had been the authors of the ruin of
Wyoming. He ravaged and burned several villages; the houses,
barns, harvests, mills, every thing was laid in ashes and desolation.
The inhabitants had been apprised in season, and had made their
escape, else they would doubtless have paid dearly for Wyoming.
The Americans, having accomplished their object, retired within their
limits, but not without having encountered excessive fatigues and no
little peril. Thus terminated the Indian war of this year. The
republicans had not only to combat the English in front, and to repel
the savages and refugees who assailed them in rear ; they were also
not a little infested by the disaffected within the country. Of this
class none were more animated than the Quakers. At first, they
had embraced, or at least appeared to embrace, the principles of the
revolution, and even still there existed among them several of the
most distinguished patriots, such as generals Greene and Mifflin.
Nevertheless, the greater number inclined for England, whether
because they were weary of the length of the war, or that they had
merely desired the reformation of the laws, and not independence.
Perhaps, too, they had persuaded themselves, that after the conquest
of Philadelphia, all America would be reduced, without difficulty,
and that therefore it was useful to their interests to appease the
victor by a prompt submission, in order to obtain favors from the
British government, which would be refused to the more obstinate.
They at least showed themselves forward to serve the English, as
guides and as spies. Several of them, as we have related, had been
sent out of the state, or imprisoned. Some had even suffered at
Philadelphia the penalties denounced against those who conspired
against liberty, and held correspondence with the enemy. The
republicans hoped, by these examples, to cure the restless spirit of
the opposite party. The efforts of the discontented were not, however, greatly to be feared ; the open assurance and consent of the

friends of the revolution easily triumphed over the secret artifices of their adversaries.

In the meantime, the marquis de la Fayette, desiring to serve his king in the war, which he doubted not was about to break out in Europe, and hoping also to promote by his representations the cause of the United States with the French government, requested of congress permission to repass the Atlantic.

Washington, who bore him a sincere affection, and who considered, besides, the importance of his name, was desirous that only a temporary leave might be granted him, without the discontinuance of his appointments. He wrote to congress, accordingly, and they readily acceded to his views ; they, moreover, addressed a letter to the marquis, returning him their thanks for the disinterested zeal which led him to America, and for the services he had rendered to the United States, by the exertion of his courage and abilities on so many signal occasions. They also directed doctor Franklin to present him with a sword decorated with devices commemorative of his achievements. Finally, they recommended him strongly to the most christian king. The marquis de la Fayette took leave of congress, and sailed for Europe, with the intention of returning as soon as possible. On his arrival in France, he was received equally well by the king and by the people. Franklin delivered him the sword, engraved with the emblems of his brilliant exploits. He was represented wounding the British lion, and receiving a branch of laurel from the hands of America, released from her chains. America herself was figured by a crescent, with these words ; *Crescam, ut prosim.* On the other side was inscribed, *Cur non ?* the motto which M. de la Fayette had chosen at his departure from France. This masterpiece of art appeared a recompense worthy of the valiant defender of America.

The count d'Estaing still lay at anchor in the harbor of Boston, where he was occupied in victualing his fleet. This operation would have been of very difficult accomplishment, from the scarcity of wheat experienced by the northern colonies, since the interruption of their commerce with those of the south, if the privateers of New England had not made so considerable a number of prizes, that not only the fleet, but also the inhabitants of Massachusetts and Connecticut, were thereby abundantly supplied. Admiral Byron was no sooner arrived at New York, than he applied himself with the utmost diligence to refitting his ships, in order to resume the sea. The moment he was prepared for it, he got under sail, and stood for Boston, for the purpose of observing the motions of the French squadron. But the adverse fortune which attended him from Europe to America, seemed still to pursue him on these shores. A furious tempest having driven him off the coast, his ships were again so damaged and shattered, that he was constrained to take shelter in Rhode Island. The count d'Estaing embraced this opportunity of quitting the harbor of Boston unmolested, and sailed the third of November for the West Indies; where he was called by the orders of his sovereign, and the events of the war. The English well knowing his designs, and the weakness of the garrisons in the islands of their dependency, commodore Hotham departed the same day from Sandy Hook, and also shaped his course for the West Indies, with six ships of war. They had on board five thousand land troops, commanded by major-general Grant. Admiral Byron followed him the fourteenth of December, with all his fleet.

About the same time colonel Campbell embarked at New York, with a strong corps of English and Germans, upon an expedition against Georgia. He was convoyed by commodore Hyde Parker, with a squadron of a few ships. Thus the theater of the war, after several campaigns in the provinces of the north and of the center, was all at once transported into the islands and states of the south.

END OF BOOK ELEVENTH.

BOOK TWELFTH.

1778. D' ESTAING and Hotham were not yet arrived in the West Indies, when commodore Evans had made a descent upon the two islands of St. Pierre and Miquelon, both very favorably situated for the fishery of Newfoundland. Being almost without defense, he occupied them easily; and, as if he had wished to efface every vestige of the French domination, he imitated the conduct of barbarians, and utterly destroyed the habitations, storehouses, and scaffoldings which had been constructed for the use of the fishery. He afterwards embarked all the inhabitants, who, with the garrisons, amounted to two thousand souls, and sent them to Europe.

The French made themselves ample amends for this loss, by seizing, as they did soon after, the island of Dominica; which, being situated between Guadaloupe and Martinico, was of the last consequence to the future operations in that part. Of this the British government was not ignorant, and therefore had fortified it with diligence, and furnished it with a formidable artillery. But neither the garrison nor the munitions corresponded to the importance of its local position; the public magazines were nearly empty, and all the soldiers in the island scarcely amounted to five hundred; the greater part militia. For a long time, the members of the opposition in parliament, and the merchants of London, had complained aloud that the islands of the West Indies were left without sufficient garrisons, and, as it were, abandoned to the discretion of the enemy. But all these remonstrances had been vain; whether the war of America had absorbed all the cares of the ministers, or that it had deprived them of the means of sending troops into those islands. The French, on the contrary, were in such force in their colonies, as to be in a condition not only to defend themselves, but also to attack their neighbors. Moreover, they had been the first to receive the news of the declaration of war in Europe. The English frigates dispatched to announce it, had fallen into the power of the French, upon the coasts of St. Domingo; so that admiral Barrington, who was stationed at Barbadoes with two ships of the line and two frigates, was first informed of the state of affairs from the manifesto published at Martinico, by the marquis de Bouille, governor of that island. The capture of the frigates had likewise apprised him that war was not only declared but commenced. This admiral showed himself very undecided with respect to the course he had to pursue; not having new instructions, he felt bound to adhere to the old, which required him to continue in the station of Barbadoes.

The marquis de Bouille, an active man, and prompt in taking his resolutions, willing to avail himself of the uncertainty and weakness of the English, determined to commence his operations with an enterprise of importance. Having embarked with two thousand land troops in eighteen transports, under convoy of the frigates Tourterelle, Diligente, and Amphitrite, he arrived at the island of Dominica, the seventh of September, about daybreak. He immediately put all his forces on shore. M. de Fonteneau, protected by the fire of the Diligente, pushed forward to fort Cachac, and seized it without resistance. The English cannonaded briskly from fort Roseau, and the battery of Lubieres. Nevertheless, M. de la Chaise, at the head of the rangers of the Auxerrese regiment, advanced impetuously up to the battery ; the French soldiers entered by the embrasures, and grappling the mouths of the cannon, made themselves masters of them. During this time, the viscount de Damas had gained the heights which commanded fort Roseau, and the marquis de Bouille, with the main body of his troops, had entered the suburbs. The frigate Tourterelle also battered the fort on her part ; the English, however, defended themselves with vigor. But at length, governor Stuart, seeing his forces so inferior, and the French about to scale for the assault, demanded to capitulate. The marquis de Bouille, whether with intent to engage by his moderation the governors of other English islands to surrender more easily, or because he feared the arrival of Barrington, who was very near, or, as it should be presumed, merely consulting the generosity of his own character, granted the most honorable conditions to the enemy. The garrison were treated with all the honors of war, and the inhabitants secured in the possession of all their property ; no change was to be made in the laws or the administration of justice. If, at the termination of the war, the island should be ceded to France, they were to have the option of retaining their present system of government, or of conforming to that established in the French islands. They were also to be at liberty, in such case, to retire with all their property, wherever they might see fit ; those who should remain, were not to be bound to any duty to the king of France, more than what they had owed to their natural sovereign.

The French found on the fortifications and in the magazines an hundred and sixty-four pieces of excellent cannon, and twenty-four mortars, besides a certain quantity of military stores. The privateers that were found in the ports of the island, were either destroyed or carried away. The capitulation was observed with the strictest fidelity; no kind of plunder or irregularity was permitted. As a recompense for their services upon this occasion, the general distributed among his soldiers a pecuniary gratification. He remained but a short time at Dominica, and having left the marquis Duchilleau for governor, with a garrison of fifteen hundred men, he returned to Martinico. But if the moderation and generosity of the marquis de Bouille were deserving of the highest encomium, the conduct of Duchilleau was no less memorable for its violence and inhumanity. He countenanced the unbridled licentiousness of his troops, and thus abandoned, as it were, the vanquished to the discretion of the victors. Such are the deplorable effects of national hatred! The inhabitants of Dominica were not delivered from the rigorous domination of Duchilleau until peace was re-established between the two states.

As soon as he was informed of the attack upon Dominica, admiral Barrington, deeming the importance of the occurrence as paramount to his instructions, sailed with all possible speed to its assistance, in order, if not too late, to frustrate the attempt of the enemy. But he did not arrive until the marquis de Bouille was already in safety under the cannon of Martinico. His presence, however, contributed much to re-assure the inhabitants of the neighboring English islands, whom the fate of Dominica and their own defenseless condition had filled with consternation.

But this expedition was only the prelude to more important events, which succeeded soon after. The count d'Estaing and commodore Hotham had taken their departure for the West Indies, as we have related, on the same day; the first for Martinico, the second for Barbadoes. The two fleets sailed in a parallel direction during great part of the voyage, and very near each other, but without knowing any thing of their proximity; the English, however, suspecting the danger, were extremely careful to keep their squadron as close and collected as possible. If it consisted of smaller vessels than those of the French, it was also much more numerous. The count d'Estaing, if he had been at all aware of the real state of things, might have profited of his great superiority to overwhelm the British fleet, and especially its numerous vessels of transport, which carried out the land forces, wherein consisted the only means of preserving to the British crown its rich possessions in those seas. A violent storm, however, having dispersed the two fleets, three English vessels fell in with those of the French, and were taken. This incident apprised d'Estaing of what had fallen out; but from the dispersion of his squadron he was unable to give chase. He determined, nevertheless, to change his course; and, instead of continuing to stand for Martinico, he steered in the direction of Antigua, under the persuasion that the

British were bound for that island, and not to Barbadoes. He hoped to be able to arrive there before they were landed, or even anchored in the ports, and consequently to prostrate at a single blow their whole force by sea and land. This stroke would have been almost without remedy for England ; so complete a victory would have enabled the count d'Estaing to annihilate her domination in the West Indies. But fortune had decided otherwise. The English shaped their course directly for Barbadoes, and reached it safely the tenth of December. Hotham there made his junction with Barrington, who was already returned.

The French admiral, having arrived very promptly in the waters of Antigua, remained cruising there for several days ; but at length, not seeing the enemy appear, and concluding that they had taken another direction, he changed his own, and stood for Martinico.

The English generals, having no suspicion of the vicinity of so formidable an enemy, determined without delay to attack St. Lucia. Its position in the front of Martinico, its natural strength, and its works, rendered this post of extreme importance for the operations of the war. Admiral Barrington, having taken on board his squadron a corps of four thousand selected troops, sailed for St. Lucia, and arrived there the thirteenth of December. General Meadows landed at the head of a strong detachment, and advanced with celerity to gain the heights which command the north shore of the bay of *Grand Cul de Sac*. They were occupied by the chevalier de Micou, the commandant of the island, with some few regulars, and the militia of the country. He made the most of a few pieces of artillery to annoy the debarkation of the English, and their march towards the hills. But unable with so small a force to prolong the valiant resistance he opposed at first, he fell back upon the capital, called Morne Fortune. The English took possession of the heights. At the same time, general Prescott had landed with five regiments, and had occupied all the positions contiguous to the bay. The next morning, Meadows forming the van and Prescott the rear, the English marched against the town of Morne Fortune. Overpowered by number, the chevalier Micou was forced to abandon it to the enemy. He retired into the more rough and difficult parts of the island, where he was also protected by his artillery. As fast as he fell back, Prescott took care to occupy the posts with troops and artillery. But general Meadows thought it essential to make himself master of Careenage harbor, situated three miles to the north of Grand Cul de Sac bay ; the French might, in fact, have landed succors there, and attacked the British in flank. In defiance of the difficulty of the places, and the heat of a burning sun, he pressed forward to seize

the height called de la Vierge, which rises on the north side of Careenage harbor, and completely commands its entrance. Another
detachment occupied the south point of the harbor, and erected a
battery upon it. General Calder, with the rest of the troops, took
position on the south side of Grand Cul de Sac bay, so that from
this point to the northern shore of the Careenage, all the posts fell
into the power of the English. The squadron of Barrington lay at
anchor in Grand Cul de Sac bay, his vessels of war at the entrance,
and those of transport within. The chevalier de Micou continued
still to occupy a very strong fort upon the crest of the mountains.
The English might already consider themselves as sure of success,
and the French had no hope left but in the immediate succor of the
count d'Estaing, when this admiral all at once appeared in view of
the island, with his original squadron of twelve sail of the line, accompanied by a numerous fleet of frigates, privateers, and transports,
which brought a land force of nine thousand men. He had received
early intelligence of the attack on St. Lucia; an event which he
considered as the most fortunate that could have happened, it seeming to afford the means of destroying at a single blow, and from his
great superiority almost without risk, the British power in the West
Indies. Accordingly, he had not delayed a moment to embark, in
order to pounce upon an enemy that did not expect him. And in
truth, if he had arrived twenty-four hours sooner, his hopes must
have been realized. But the English were already in possession of
the principal posts, and had fortified themselves therein ; moreover,
the day was far advanced, when the French armament appeared ;
it was necessary to defer the attack until the ensuing morning. Admiral Barrington profited of the night, to make his dispositions for
sustaining it. He caused the transports to be removed into the bottom of the Grand Cul de Sac, to be as remote from danger as possible ; the ships of war he placed in their respective stations, so as to
form a line across its entrance, and repel the efforts of the enemy to
the most advantage. His force consisted only of his own ship, the
Prince of Wales, of seventy-four guns, the Boyne, of seventy, St.
Albans and Nonesuch, of sixty-four, the Centurion and Isis, of fifty
each, and three frigates.

The count d'Estaing, not mistrusting that Careenage harbor was
already occupied by the enemy, stood in for it with his whole fleet,
on the morning of the fifteenth. His purpose was to take land there,
and hasten to attack the right flank of the English, who, as he had
observed himself, occupied the Grand Cul de Sac. But no sooner
had he presented himself before the entrance of the Careenage than
the English batteries erected upon the two points, opened a heavy

fire, which damaged several of his vessels, and particularly his own ship, the Languedoc. Convinced of the impossibility of operating a descent in this part, he bore down, with ten sail of the line, on the British admiral, with intent to force the passage, and penetrate into the bay, which must have proved the utter ruin of the English. A warm engagement ensued; but, supported by the batteries from the shore, the British valiantly sustained the attack of an enemy so superior. D'Estaing drew off a little; but, towards evening, he renewed the battle with twelve ships. His efforts were still more impetuous ; he directed the fire of his artillery principally against the left of the British line. But neither the re-inforcement he had received, nor the singular firmness and gallantry displayed by all his people, were capable of rendering this attack more successful than the former. The English made so vigorous and so well supported a defense, that d'Estaing was again compelled to retire, with his ships severely damaged, and in no little confusion. Admiral Barrington acquired imperishable glory; he secured to his country the possession of an island which, only twenty-four hours after its conquest, had been upon the point of falling anew under the dominion of its ancient masters. But d'Estaing, finding that fortune was disposed to frown on his maritime attacks, resorted to his land forces, which were very considerable. Accordingly, in the night of the sixteenth and the following morning, he landed his troops in Choc bay, which lies between Gros islet and the Careenage. His intention was to attack general Meadows, who, with a corps of thirteen hundred men, was encamped in the little peninsula de la Vierge, situated between the Careenage and the above named Choc bay. He had great hopes of being able to surprise and cut him off entirely, as well by reason of the difficulty of the places which separated this corps from all the others, as from the diversions which he proposed to make by threatening several points at once. In pursuance of this plan, he advanced from Choc bay towards the peninsula, with five thousand of his best troops, in order to attack the lines of Meadows, which were drawn across the isthmus that joins it to the main land. He had formed three columns ; the right was commanded by himself, the center by the count de Loewendal, and the left by the marquis de Bouille. The French moved at first with admirable order; but as they approached, their position became extremely critical. They found themselves severely enfiladed by the artillery of Morne Fortune, which the chevalier de Micou, on evacuating that fort, had neglected to spike. But notwithstanding this impediment, they rushed on to the charge with incredible impetuosity. The English expected their approach with equal coolness; they suffered them to advance to the intrenchments without opposition; when, after firing once, they received them on the bayonet. That fire had, of course, a dreadful effect; but the French, notwithstanding, supported the conflict with undaunted resolution. Already seventy of them had leapt within the intrenchment, where they acquitted themselves strenuously; but the English enveloped them, and soon they were all victims of their temerity. Nevertheless, the assailants recovered their breath, and returned to the charge with no less eagerness and fury than at first. The English encountered them with the same intrepidity, and a second time compelled them to withdraw. But d'Estaing, in the transport of his ardor, unable to endure that so feeble a detachment should baffle the efforts of his numerous veterans, ordered a third attack. He was promptly obeyed. But the soldiers, being much exhausted by their exertions in the first two, no longer displayed the same vigor. They were totally broken, and obliged to retreat, leaving their dead and wounded in the power of the victors. It was, however, agreed soon after, that the French should be permitted to bury the one, and to carry off the other; d'Estaing having rendered himself accountable for the wounded as prisoners of war. General Meadows manifested, in this affair, equal ability and valor; though wounded in the very commencement of the action, no persuasions could induce him to quit the field until it was decided. The loss of the French was serious. Four hundred were killed on the spot; five hundred were so severely wounded as to be rendered incapable of service; five hundred others were wounded slightly. The loss of the English, in consequence of the advantage of their position, was inconsiderable. The count d'Estaing left his troops on shore still, for several days after the battle; during this time he continued standing off and on with his fleet, in sight of the island, hoping that some occasion might present itself of operating more effectively. But at length he embarked his troops, in the night of the twenty-eighth, and sailed to Martinico the following day, having abandoned the enterprise of St. Vincent and Grenada, which islands he had purposed to attack. The day after his departure, the chevalier de Micou capitulated; his garrison consisted of only an hundred men. He obtained the most favorable conditions. He marched out with all the honors of war; his soldiers retained their baggage, but not their arms. The inhabitants, and especially the curates, were protected in their persons, property, and religion. They were to pay to the king of Great Britain the same taxes only, that they were accustomed to pay to the king of France; finally, they were not to be compelled to bear arms against their late sovereign.

The English found in the forts fifty-nine pieces of cannon, a great number of muskets, and an immense quantity of military stores. Thus fell into the power of the English the island of St. Lucia ; it was an acquisition of extreme importance to them. They made of it a place of arms for all their forces in the West Indies, and the repository of all their munitions. From its proximity to Martinico, they were enabled, without risk, to watch all the movements of the French in the bay of Fort Royal, and to intercept the re-inforcements and convoys that might approach it by the channel of St. Lucia. They strengthened it with many new works, and constantly maintained in it a numerous garrison, notwithstanding the great loss of men it cost them from the insalubrity of the climate.

A few days after the retreat of the count d'Estaing, admiral Byron arrived in that part with nine sail of the line, and came to anchor at St. Lucia.

There resulted from it a sort of tacit truce between the two parties ; the English having too decided a superiority of naval, and the French of land forces. This armistice, which lasted five months, was not interrupted until the squadron of commodore Rawley had joined the fleet of Byron, and the count d'Estaing had been re-inforced by that of the chevalier de la Motte Piquet, and of the count de Grasse. These several re-inforcements were dispatched from Europe to the West Indies about the close of the year ; the two governments having reflected at the same time how important it was to have formidable maritime forces in the midst of these rich islands, situated at little distance one from the other, and intermingled, as it were, with those of the enemy.

It is time to return upon the American continent. The British ministers and generals had taken the determination to direct their greatest efforts towards the southern parts of the confederation. Under the persuasion that the inhabitants of these provinces supported with repugnance the yoke of the republicans, they hoped to find in the loyalists an efficacious co-operation for the re-establishment of the royal authority. Other, and no less powerful motives, conduced to decide them for this expedition. The provinces of the south, and especially Georgia and Carolina, abound in fertile lands, which produce copious crops of wheat, and particularly of rice, than which nothing could be more essential to the support of a fleet and army, at so great a distance from their principal sources of supply. The parts of the American territory which had hitherto fallen into the power of the English, had offered them but a feeble resource, and they were obliged to draw the greatest part of their provisions from Europe, through all the perils of the sea, and the swarms of

American privateers which continually preyed on their convoys. It is, besides, to be observed, that the rice of Georgia and South Carolina served to nourish the French fleets, and the troops that formed the garrisons of their islands in the West Indies.

The quiet and security which these provinces had hitherto enjoyed, admitted so vigorous a cultivation, that the products of it not only furnished an inexhaustible resource to the allies of the Americans, but, being exported to the markets of Europe, constituted the material of a commerce, by which they received those supplies which were necessary, as well to the support of the war, as to the conducting of the common business and affairs of life. The English also reflected that, as Georgia borders upon East Florida, the latter was exposed to constant alarms and incursions on the part of the republicans ; and they were convinced that there existed no effectual means of securing the quiet of that province, short of compelling the troops of congress to evacuate Georgia and the Carolinas. The conquest of the first of these provinces, they had little doubt, would insure them that of the two others ; and they promised themselves with full assurance the possession of Charleston, a rich and populous city, and of extreme importance, both for its situation and port. Such were the advantages the English expected to derive from their expedition against the southern provinces.

To these considerations was added another ; the severity of the season no longer admitted operations in the mountainous provinces of the north. Accordingly, general Clinton, as we have related in the preceding book, had embarked for Georgia, under convoy of commodore Hyde Parker, a detachment of twenty-five hundred men, consisting of English, Hessians and refugees. He hoped by the assistance of these last, and their partisans, to find easy admission into that province. This corps was under the command of colonel Campbell, an officer of distinguished valor and capacity. Clinton, at the same time, had ordered general Prevost, who commanded in the Floridas, to collect all the troops that could be spared from the defense of those provinces, and to march also against Georgia, in order that it might be attacked at once in front, on the part of the sea, by Campbell, and in flank, on the banks of the Savannah river, by Prevost. The plan of this expedition thus arranged, commodore Hyde Parker and colonel Campbell arrived, towards the close of December, at the isle of Tybee, situated near the mouth of the Savannah. The transports had little difficulty in passing the bar and entering into that river. They were followed, a few days after, by the ships of war, so that all the fleet lay together at anchor in its waters on the twenty-seventh of December, ready to execute the orders of the commanders for the invasion of the province. The latter, not knowing what were the forces, the measures of defense, and the intentions of the republicans, detached some light infantry to scour the adjacent banks. They took two Georgians, from whom it was understood that no intimation had been received in the province of the project of the royalists ; that consequently no preparations for defense had been made ; that the batteries which protected the entrance of the rivers were out of condition, and that the armed galleys were so placed that they might easily be surprised. It was also learned that the garrison of Savannah, the capital of the province, was very feeble, but that it was soon to be re-inforced. Upon this intelligence, the British commander no longer delayed to commence his operations.

The whole country on the two banks of the Savannah, from its mouth to a considerable distance above, being a continued tract of deep marsh, intersected by the extensive creeks of St. Augustine and Tybee, it offers no point capable of serving as a place of debarkation. The English were therefore under the necessity of moving higher up, in order to reach the usual landing place, at which commences a very narrow causeway that leads to the city. This post, extremely difficult of itself, might have been vigorously defended by the Americans. But, surprised by an unexpected attack, or destitute of sufficient force, they made no opposition to the descent of the English, who landed at first their light troops. The causeway leads through a rice swamp, and is flanked on each side by a deep ditch. Six hundred yards above the landing place, and at the head of the causeway, rises an abrupt eminence, upon which was situated the house of a certain *Gerridoe.* It was occupied by a detachment of republicans. As soon as the light infantry, the greater part Scotch Highlanders, had landed under the command of captain Cameron, they formed, and pushed forward along the dike to attack the post of the Americans. The latter received them with a smart fire of musketry ; Cameron was mortally wounded. Incensed at the loss of their captain, the Highlanders advanced with such rapidity, that the Americans had no time for charging again, and instantly fled. The English seized the height ; colonel Campbell, having ascended it, in order to view the country, discovered the army of the enemy drawn up about half a mile east of the town of Savannah. It was commanded by major-general Robert Howe, and appeared disposed to make a firm stand, to cover the capital of the province. It consisted in a strong corps of continental troops, and the militia of the country. It was so disposed that its two wings extended on the two sides of the great road leading to Savannah. The right, under the command of colonel Eugee, and composed of Carolinians, was to the south, having its flank towards the country protected by a wooded swamp and by the houses of Tatnal. The left, having the road on its right flank, was covered on the left by rice swamps. It consisted for the most part of Georgians, under the orders of colonel Elbert. One piece of cannon was planted at each extremity of the American line, and two pieces occupied the traverse, across the great road in the center. About one hundred yards in front of this traverse, at a critical point between two swamps, a trench was cut across the road, and about one hundred yards in front of the trench, ran a marshy rivulet, the bridge over which had been destroyed. Lastly, the Americans had on their rear the town of Savannah itself, which was surrounded by a moat.

The British commander, having left a detachment to guard the landing-place, and another to secure a neighboring cross road to cover his rear, advanced directly towards the enemy. He endeavored to devise the most expedient mode of attacking them in the strong position they occupied. By the movements of the Americans, he was not long in perceiving that they expected and even desired that he should engage their left wing; he accordingly omitted no means in use on similar occasions, with experienced commanders, that could serve to cherish that opinion and continue its delusion. He drew off a part of his forces to form on his right, where he also displayed his light infantry. His intention, however, was to attack the right wing of the Americans. While making his dispositions, chance threw into his hands a negro, by whom he was informed of a private path through the wooded swamp on the enemy's right, which led to their rear. The negro offered to show the way, and promised infallible success. Colonel Campbell resolved to profit of the occasion which fortune seemed to have provided him. He accordingly directed sir James Baird to pursue with his light infantry the indicated path, turn the right of the Americans, and fall in by surprise upon their rear. The New York volunteers under colonel Trumbull were ordered to support the light infantry. While Baird and Trumbull, guided by the negro, proceeded to execute this movement, Campbell posted his artillery in a field on the left of the road, concealed from the enemy by a swell of ground in the front. It was destined to bear upon the Carolinians, and to cannonade any body of troops in flank, which they might detach into the wood to retard the progress of Baird's light infantry. Meanwhile, the republicans continued to ply their artillery with great animation; the royalists were motionless; a circumstance which doubtless would have excited alarm if their enemies had been either more experienced, or less sanguine. At length, when Campbell conceived that Baird had reached his position, he suddenly unmasked his artillery, and marched briskly on to the enemy, who were still totally blind to their danger.

The charge of the English and Hessians was so impetuous, that the Americans, unable to withstand its shock, immediately fell into confusion and dispersed. The victors pursued them. During this time, the light infantry of Baird had gained the rear of the American right. They fell in with a body of Georgian militia, who were stationed to guard the great road from Ogeeche, and routed them at the first onset. As they were in pursuit of the fugitives, on their way to fall upon the main body of the Americans, the latter, already discomfited, came running across the plain full in their front. The disorder and dismay that now ensued, were past all remedy: the victory of the English was complete. Thirty-eight commissioned officers, upwards of four hundred non-commissioned and privates, forty-eight pieces of cannon, twenty-three mortars, the fort with its ammunition and stores, the shipping in the river, a large quantity of provisions, with the capital of Georgia, were all in the hands of the conquerors before dark. The loss of the Americans, owing to their prompt flight, was very small. Only about fourscore fell in the action and pursuit, and about thirty more perished in their attempts to escape through the swamp. The English lost perhaps not twenty men in dead and wounded. This singular good fortune was the fruit of the excellent dispositions of colonel Campbell. He distinguished himself no less by a humanity the more deserving of praise, as he could not have forgotten the harsh treatment he had received in the prisons of Boston. Not only was the town of Savannah preserved from pillage, but such was the excellent discipline observed, that though the English entered it with the fugitives, as into a city taken by storm, not a single person suffered who had not arms in his hand, and who was not, besides, in the act either of flight or resistance. A strong circumstantial testimony, that those enormities so frequently committed in time of war, should with more justice be charged to the negligence or immediate participation of the chiefs, than to the ungovernable license of the soldiers.

1779. Having thus made themselves masters of the capital, the British troops soon overran the whole province of Georgia. Their commander issued a proclamation, by which he offered pardon to deserters, and exhorted the friends of the English name to repair to the royal standard, promising them assistance and protection; this step was not altogether fruitless. A considerable number presented themselves; they were formed into a regiment of light dragoons.

But the more determined republicans, preferring exile to submission, withdrew into South Carolina.

The English also employed all their address to induce the republican soldiers they had made prisoners to enlist in the service of the king; but their efforts were nearly fruitless. They were, therefore, crowded on board vessels, where, from the heat of the weather in the following summer, and the bad air concomitant with their mode of confinement, the greater part perished. The officers were sent on parole to Sunbury, the only town in the province which still held for the congress; but Moses Allen, the chaplain of the Georgians, was retained, and thrust, a prisoner on board the vessels, among the common soldiers. This minister of religion had not contented himself with exciting the people to assert their independence, in his discourses from the pulpit; he appeared also, with arms in hand, on the field of battle, exhibiting in his own person an admirable example of valor, and devotion to the cause of country.

Weary of the protracted rigors of his captivity, he one day threw himself into the river, hoping to escape, by swimming, to a neighboring island; but he was drowned, to the great regret of all his fellow-citizens, who venerated his virtues, and justly appreciated his intrepidity. The Americans, too much enfeebled to keep the field, passed the Savannah at Zubly, and retreated into South Carolina. The English, on the contrary, now masters of the greater part of Georgia, frequently scoured the banks of the river, in order to disquiet the enemy, who was still in possession of the countries situated on the left bank.

In the meantime, general Prevost had put himself on the march from East Florida, to execute the orders of general Clinton. He had to struggle with the most formidable impediments, as well from the difficulty of the places as from the want of provisions. At length, after excessive fatigues and hardships, being arrived in Georgia, he attacked the fort of Sunbury. The garrison, consisting of about two hundred men, made some show of defense; and gave him the trouble of opening trenches. But, although they were supported by some a med vessels and galleys, yet all hope of relief being now totally cut off by the reduction of the rest of the province, they found it necessary to surrender at discretion. They were treated humanely. This happened just at the time when colonel Campbell had already set out on an expedition for the reduction of Sunbury. The two English corps made their junction with reciprocal felicitations. General Prevost repaired to Savannah, where he took the command of all the British troops that, coming from New York and from St. Augustine, had conquered to the king the entire province of Georgia.

After such brilliant success, the British commanders deliberated upon what they had to do next. They were perfectly aware that their forces were not sufficient to act in a decisive manner against Carolina, a powerful province, animated with the same spirit, especially in the maritime parts, and governed by men endowed with the best talents, and exercising a great influence over the multitude. The reduction of Georgia was, in truth, the only object which general Clinton had as yet proposed to himself. He had purposed to defer the invasion of Carolina until the arrival of the re-inforcements which admiral Arbuthnot was to bring him from England. Nevertheless, considering the importance to the success of future operations of continuing offensive war, rather than halting upon the defensive, it was determined to make several excursions into Carolina, in order to keep alive in that province the terror of the royal arms, and to re-animate the hopes of the loyalists. Major-general Gardner was accordingly detached with a numerous corps, to take possession of Port Royal. But this expedition had the most disastrous issue; the Carolinians fell vigorously upon the English, and expelled them from the island with severe loss, both in officers and soldiers.

On the failure of this project, the British generals endeavored to excite a movement among the adversaries of congress. They inhabited, as we have related, in very considerable number, the back parts of Georgia and the two Carolinas. The hope placed in them was one of the principal causes that had occasioned the invasion of the southern provinces to be undertaken. Of these loyalists there were several sorts; some, more violent and rancorous, had not only abandoned their country, but had attached themselves to the Indians, in order to inflict all possible mischief on their fellow-citizens, in the incursions on the frontiers. Others lived solitary and wandering upon the extreme confines of the Carolinas, watching with the most eager attention for any favorable occasion that might offer itself, for the recovery of their settlements. Others, finally, either less bitter or more politic, continued to reside in the midst of the republicans, feigning an acquiescence in the will of the majority. Though they had quitted arms for the labors of agriculture, they were still always ready to resume them, whenever the possibility of a new change should become perceptible. In the meantime, they had recourse to artifice, and exerted their utmost diligence to keep their outlawed friends advised of all that passed within the country, and especially of all the movements of the republicans; of this, the generals of the king were not ignorant.

In order, therefore, to encourage and support the loyalists, they moved up the Savannah as far as Augusta. As soon as they were in possession of that post, they left no means unattempted that could re-animate their partisans, and excite them to assemble in arms. They sent among them numerous emissaries, who exaggerated to them the might of the royal forces. They assured them that if they would but unite, they would become incomparably superior to their enemies; they were prodigal of promises and presents; they exasperated minds already imbittered by flaming pictures of the cruelties committed by the republicans. Such were the opinions propagated by the British generals among the friends of the king. Their instigations produced the intended effect; the loyalists took arms, and putting themselves under the command of colonel Boyd, one of their chiefs, they descended along the western frontiers of Carolina, in order to join the royal army. More properly robbers than soldiers, they continually deviated from their route, in order to indulge their passion for pillage. What they could neither consume nor carry off, they consigned to the flames. They had already passed the Savannah, and were near the British posts, when they were encountered by colonel Pickens, who headed a strong detachment of Carolinians, levied in the district of Ninety-six. Instantly, the action was engaged with all the fury excited by civil rancor, and all the desperation inspired by the fear of those evils which the vanquished would have to suffer at the hands of the victors. The battle lasted for a full hour. At length the loyalists were broken and completely routed. Boyd remained dead upon the field; all were dispersed; many fell into the power of the republicans. Seventy were condemned to death; only five, however, were executed. This success made a deep impression throughout Georgia, where the disaffected were already on the point of arming against the congress. The incursions of the loyalists were repressed, and the republicans could proceed with greater security in their preparations for defense against the royal arms. Another consequence of it was, that the English evacuated Augusta, and, retiring lower down, concentered their force in the environs of Savannah.

This measure was the more prudent on their part, as general Lincoln, to whom congress had intrusted the command of all the troops in the southern provinces, was already arrived, and had encamped at Black Swamp, on the left bank of the Savannah, at no great distance from Augusta. This general, born in Massachusetts, having distinguished himself in the campaigns of the north, had been proposed to the congress by the Carolinians themselves, on their first receiving intelligence of the projects of the enemy against the southern provinces. The congress had yielded the more readily to their recommendation, as they had themselves a high opinion of the talents of general Lincoln, and were not ignorant how essential it is to the suc-

cess of operations, that soldiers should have perfect confidence in
their chiefs. The president, Lowndes, employed all the means in
his power to inflame the ardor of the inhabitants of South Carolina,
and to excite them to take arms in defense of country. In private,
as well as in public, he addressed them the most stimulating exhortations; he directed that all the cattle of the islands and towns situated upon the coast, should be withdrawn into the interior of the country. The militia assembled and joined the continental troops. The
same zeal for the public cause broke forth at the approach of danger
in North Carolina; in a few days, two thousand of its militia were
imbodied under the generals Ashe and Rutherford. If this corps could
have been furnished with arms as promptly as the conjuncture required,
it would have made its junction in time with that of general Howe,
and perhaps might have decided in his favor the fortune of the day
of Savannah. The enthusiasm of the Carolinian patriots was then
at its height; every day added to the strength of their army. They
had indeed great efforts to make. Washington was far from them,
and before succors could arrive, they were exposed to the most fatal
reverses. Moreover, the commander-in-chief was himself much occupied with the guard of the passes of the mountains, and his forces
were continually mined by a pest which was still but imperfectly remedied; the shortness of engagements. It was not to be expected,
then, that he should strip himself in order to re-inforce the army of
the south; yet more, the same intestine disease which enfeebled the
army of Washington, was also the cause that little reliance could be
placed in that of Lincoln, although it was already combined with the
relics of the corps of Robert Howe. With the exception of six hundred continental troops, the rest were militia, little accustomed to
war, and bound only to a few months of service. General Lincoln,
however, not in the least discouraged, found resources even in his
own ardor. In order at first to show himself to the enemy, he had
repaired to Black Swamp, on the north side of the Savannah. This
movement, together with the recent discomfiture of the loyalists, had
induced the British general to retire down the river, leaving, however, an advanced post at Hudson's Ferry. But Lincoln extended his
views farther; he purposed to restrict the enemy still more, and to
press him close upon the coast, in order to deprive him of the resources he would find in those fertile countries, and to put an end
to the intercourse, whether open or secret, which he kept up with
the loyalists of the upper parts. He accordingly ordered general
Ashe to leave his baggage behind, and, passing the Savannah, to take
post on a little river called *Briar Creek* This order was executed
with diligence, and the camg seated in a very strong position. It

was covered in front by the creek, which for several miles above was too deep to be forded; on the left by the Savannah and a deep morass; the right was secured by a corps of cavalry. General Ashe had with him about two thousand men.

Notwithstanding the strength of his encampment, the English resolved to attack him. Colonel Prevost, who was posted at Hudson's Ferry, set out on this expedition. Having divided his force in two columns, he advanced the right, with two pieces of cannon, towards Briar Creek, with an apparent view of intending to pass it, in order to take up the attention of the republicans. The left, consisting of nine hundred men, among which were grenadiers, light infantry, and horse, he led himself a circuitous march of about fifty miles, in order to cross Briar Creek, and thereby, turning the right, to fall unexpectedly upon the rear of the enemy. At the same time, general Prevost made such dispositions and movements on the borders of the river, between Savannah and Ebenezer, as were likely to divert general Lincoln from thinking of Ashe. This general, who, in such a proximity of the enemy, should have redoubled his watchfulness, instead of having the country scoured by his cavalry, had detached it upon some distant and unprofitable expedition. The English, therefore, arrived so unexpectedly, though in open daylight, that the Americans received the first notice of danger from the havoc which the assailants made in their camp. The militia were panic struck, and fled without firing a shot. But many of them encountered in flight that death which they might have avoided by a gallant resistance. Their cowardice did not shield them; the deep marsh and the river which should have afforded security became now the instruments of their destruction. Blinded by their flight and terror, they were swallowed up in the one, or drowned in the other. The regular troops of Georgia and the Carolinas, commanded and animated by general Elbert, made a brave resistance; but, abandoned by the militia, and overwhelmed by number, they were also compelled to retreat. This rout of Briar Creek took place the third of March. The Americans lost seven pieces of cannon, all their arms and ammunition, with not a few killed and prisoners. The number of the drowned and wounded is not known; but it appears that more perished in the water than by wounds. Of all the corps of general Ashe, scarcely four hundred soldiers rejoined general Lincoln, who, in consequence of this disaster, found his forces diminished more than a fourth part. This victory rendered the royal troops again masters of all Georgia. It opened them communications with the loyalists in the back parts of this province and the two Carolinas. Those who were not yet recovered of the terror inspired by their recent defeat, took fresh courage ; there was nothing now to prevent their going to re-inforce the royal army.

The Carolinians, though deeply affected at so severe a check, were not, however, disheartened ; and, in order to prevent the victorious enemy from overrunning their fertile territory, they made every exertion to assemble their militia, and to re-animate their ardor. Rigorous penalties were decreed against those who should refuse to march when called out, or to obey their commanders ; high bounties were promised ; regiments of horse were organized ; the officers were chosen among the most leading men of the country. John Rutledge, a man of extensive influence, was elected governor of the province, and empowered to do whatever he should judge necessary to the public welfare. Animated by the love of country, and stimulated by the prospect of those evils which would be their portion if the English should gain possession of the province, the republicans displayed so much zeal and activity in their preparations for defense, that by the middle of April, general Lincoln found himself at the head of more than five thousand fighting men.

While these preparations were in process in the Carolinas, general Prevost busied himself in Georgia in re-organizing all those parts of the service which had suffered by the war. He established an internal administration in the province, and strenuously urged the loyalists to rally around him. He did not immediately attempt to cross the Savannah, because it was extremely swoln by the rains ; and, besides, he had not a sufficient force to attack lower Carolina, where there were none but patriots ; and general Lincoln, notwithstanding the rout of Briar Creek, still maintained his position on the left bank, ready to oppose him, if he inclined to pass. Not, however, that the American general was in a condition to act offensively before he was re-inforced ; he might even have deemed himself extremely fortunate in not being attacked. But as soon as he found his force augmented, as we have just seen, he made a movement which provoked another of extreme importance, on the part of his adversary. He marched, about the beginning of May, towards Augusta, whether to protect an assembly of the deputies of the province, which was to convene in that town, or for the purpose of taking a strong position in upper Georgia, in order to watch over the interests of the confederation in that part, and to interrupt the transmission of provisions and recruits which the loyalists furnished to the British. He was already arrived in Georgia, and all his measures were taken for the execution of his design. He had left general Moultrie, with fifteen hundred men, in front of general Prevost, in order to dispute his passage across the Savannah. He considered this corps the more sufficient for the defense of the left bank and the approaches of Charleston, the capital of South Carolina, inasmuch as the breadth of the river, the marshes which border it on the north side, and the numerous creeks which intersect that province, appeared to him obstacles capable by themselves of arresting the enemy.

But general Prevost saw his position in a different light. His army was increased by the junction of the loyalists. He hoped that his presence in Carolina would excite some movements there; he wanted provisions, which he was sure of finding in abundance in that province; and lastly, he calculated that the effect of his invasion would be to recall Lincoln from Georgia, and perhaps to afford an opportunity of engaging him with advantage. Determined by these considerations, he put himself at the head of a corps of three thousand men, among English, loyalists, and Indians, and passed the Savannah with its adjacent marshes, though not without excessive difficulties. The militia under Moultrie, surprised and dismayed at such intrepidity, gave way, and after a feeble resistance fell back upon Charleston. Moultrie, with the handful he had left, and the light horse of Pulaski, exerted his utmost efforts to retard the enemy; but he was soon compelled to yield to force. Astonished himself at the facility with which he had triumphed over the natural impediments of the country, and the resistance of the republicans, Prevost extended his views to objects of greater moment. The drift of his expedition was at first merely to forage; he was disposed to give it a nobler aim, and ventured to meditate an attack upon the important city of Charleston. He promised himself that it would soon fall into his power, when he should have acquired the control of the open country.

The loyalists, in the eagerness of their hopes and wishes, which they too frequently substituted for realities, failed not to improve this disposition, which was so favorable to them. They assured Prevost that they had correspondence with the principal inhabitants of the city, and that the moment the royal standard should be descried from its battlements, their adherents would rise and throw open its gates. Moreover, they offered to serve as guides to the army, and to furnish all the information that could be desired respecting the nature of the country. Another consideration came to the support of their representations; though general Lincoln could not but know the British had crossed the Savannah, and menaced the capital, yet he manifested no intention of moving to its relief; so fully was he persuaded that the royalists designed nothing more than to pillage the country. General Prevost, therefore, pursued his march towards Charleston in great security, hoping, in the consternation at his sudden appearance, to enter it without opposition. Meanwhile, when Lincoln was convinced, by the continual approaches of the enemy, of the reality of his designs, he immediately detached a body of infantry, mounted on horseback, for the greater expedition, to the defense of the capital, and collecting the militia of the upper country, returned with his whole force to act as circumstances might offer for its relief. The English had arrived at Ashley river, which bathes the walls of Charleston on the south; they passed it immediately, and took post within little more than cannon shot of that city, between the river Ashley and another called the Cooper, which flows a little to the north of it. The Carolinians had made all the preparations for defense which the shortness of time admitted. They had burnt the suburbs, and cut a trench in the rear of the city from one river to the other. The fortifications had been repaired, and batteries erected upon all the chain of works which formed the cincture of the town. Governor Rutledge had arrived there two days before, with five hundred militia, as well as colonel Harris, who had brought the succor sent by general Lincoln, after a forced march of more than forty miles at every stage. The count Pulaski was also come to re-inforce the garrison with the dragoons of his legion, which was called the *American Legion.* The presence of all these troops re-assured the inhabitants; they would have thought themselves fortunate in obtaining an honorable capitulation if this succor had not reached them, or if the English, instead of suspending their march, as they did, had made their appearance two days sooner. The garrison passed the whole night under arms; the houses, and the entire circuit of the walls, were illuminated. On the following morning, the British general summoned the town, offering very favorable conditions. The Americans sent out their commissioners to negotiate, and the conference was opened. But they neglected nothing that could draw it into length, as soon as they discovered that the besiegers were not in force sufficient to carry the place, before, in all probability, general Lincoln would arrive to its deliverance. Accordingly, they proposed that their province should remain neuter during the war; and that, at the conclusion of peace, it should be decided whether Charleston was to belong to the United States or to Great Britain.

The English answered that their generals had not come there with legislative powers, and that since the garrison were armed, they must surrender prisoners of war. Other proposals were made on both sides, which were not accepted, and the English lost the whole day in this negotiation, which was not broken off till in the evening. The inhabitants, expecting to be attacked during the night, made every preparation for a vigorous defense. Finding himself totally disappointed in every hope that had been held out to him relative to Charleston, general Prevost began to reflect that the ramparts were furnished with a formidable artillery, and flanked by a flotilla of armed shipping and galleys; that the garrison was even more numerous than his own army; that he had neither battering artillery, nor a naval force to co-operate with his land forces; that the vanguard of the army of Lincoln had already appeared, and that himself was fast approaching; and lastly, that if he were repulsed with any considerable loss, which was much to be apprehended, his situation, involved as he was in a labyrinth of rivers and creeks, surrounded on all sides by a superior enemy, seemed scarcely to admit of a hope that any part of his army could have been preserved. Under these considerations, he profited of the obscurity of night, and directed his retreat towards Georgia. But instead of taking the way of the land, which was too dangerous, he passed his troops into the islands of St. James and St. John, which lie to the southward of Charleston, and whose cultivation and fertility offered abundant resources. As from Charleston to Savannah there extends along the coast a continued succession of little contiguous islands, so separated from the continent as to afford both navigable channels and excellent harbors, Prevost could be at no loss about the means of repairing to the latter city.

His immediate design was to establish his camp on the island of Port Royal, situated near the mouth of the Savannah, and no less remarkable for its salubrity than fruitfulness. These quarters were the more desirable, as the sickly and almost pestilential season already approached in the Carolinas and Georgia, and the British troops, not yet accustomed to the climate, were peculiarly exposed to its mortal influence.

While Prevost was engaged in passing his troops from one island to another, general Lincoln, who by the main land had followed the movements of the enemy, thought it a proper opportunity to attack colonel Maitland, who, with a corps of English, Hessians and Carolinian loyalists, was encamped at the pass of Stono Ferry, on the inlet between the continent and the island of St. John; this post, besides its natural advantages, was well covered with redoubts, an abattis, and artillery. The Americans attacked with vigor, but they found a no less obstinate resistance. At length, overwhelmed by the enemy's artillery, and unable with their field pieces to make any impression on his fortifications, they retired at the approach of a re-inforcement which came to the support of Maitland. The English, after establishing posts upon the most important points, proceeded to occupy their cantonments on the island of Port Royal. The

Americans returned, for the most part, into theirs ; and the unhealthiness of the season put a stop to all further operations of either party. The English thus remained in peaceable possession of the whole province of Georgia ; and the Americans found some consolation in having raised the siege of Charleston, though the vicinity of the enemy still left them in apprehension of a new invasion in South Carolina.   The incursion of which this rich and flourishing province had just been the theater, so far from serving the interests of the king, was highly prejudicial to his cause.   If it enriched his officers and soldiers, it caused the ruin of a great number of inhabitants. The royal troops were not satisfied with pillaging ; they spared neither women, nor children, nor sick.   Herein they had the negroes for spies and companions, who, being very numerous in all the places they traversed, flocked upon their route in the hope of obtaining liberty.   To recommend themselves to the English, they put every thing to sack, and if their masters had concealed any valuable effects, they hastened to discover them to their insatiable spoilers.   Such was the rapacity of these robbers, that not content with stripping houses of their richest furniture, and individuals of their most precious ornaments, they violated even the sanctuary of the dead, and, gasping for gold, went rummaging among the tombs.

Whatever they could not carry off, they destroyed.   How many delightful gardens were ravaged !   What magnificent habitations were devoted to the flames !   Every where ruins and ashes.   The very cattle, whatever was their utility, found no quarter with these barbarians.   Vain would be the attempt to paint the brutal fury of this lawless soldiery, and especially of those exasperated and ferocious Africans.   But the heaviest loss which the planters of Carolina had to sustain, was that of these very slaves.   Upwards of four thousand were taken from them : some were carried to the English islands ; others perished of hunger in the woods, or by a pestilential disease which broke out among them soon after.

And here should be recollected the barbarous manifesto published by the British commissioners on quitting America, after the failure of their negotiations ; their abominable threats were but too faithfully executed in Carolina.   A cry of horror arose throughout the civilized world, against the ferocity of the British armies.   Such, also, was the disordered state of things to which Georgia, by various progressive steps, was at length reduced.

About the same time, general Clinton meditated, in his camp at New York, a project whose execution appeared to him to correspond with the views of the ministry. or, at least, proper to second the expedition of Carolina.   He expected to insure its success by keeping Virginia in continual alarm by cruel but useless devastations upon the coast of that opulent province. Having assembled a suitable number of ships, under the command of commodore Collier, he embarked a corps of two thousand men, conducted by general Matthews. They proceeded to the Chesapeake, and leaving a sufficient force in Hampton Road to block up that port and the entrance of the river James, went to take land on the banks of Elizabeth river. The British immediately pushed forward against the town of Portsmouth, and entered it without resistance. Fort Nelson was also abandoned to them at the first rumor of their approach. They found it equally easy to occupy the town, or rather the ruins of the town of Norfolk, on the opposite side of the river. Pursuing their march with the same celerity, they made themselves masters of Suffolk, on the right bank of the Nansemond river. In all these places, as well as at Kempers Landing, Shepherds, Gosport, Tanners Creek, in a word, throughout the extent of territory into which they penetrated, their passage was marked by cruelty and devastation. They demolished the magazines, brought off or destroyed the provisions, and burned or took away an immense quantity of shipping. Several thousand barrels of salted provisions, which had been prepared for Washington's army, and a great quantity of stores, also fell into their power. Their booty in tobacco even surpassed their hope ; in brief, this rich and fertile country was converted in a few days into one vast scene of smoking ruins. In their indignation the Virginians sent to ask the English *what sort of war this was ?* They answered, *that they were commanded to visit the same treatment upon all those who refused to obey the king.* Listening to the insinuations of the refugees, who incessantly affirmed that Virginia contained a host of loyalists, that were only waiting for a rallying point to raise the province in revolt, the British commanders were much inclined to prolong their stay in it ; and thought of fortifying themselves in Portsmouth, in order to make it their place of arms. They wrote, accordingly, to general Clinton, demanding his orders. But Clinton, weary of this piratical war, and less eager than commodore Collier to swallow the brilliant delusions of the refugees, did not approve the plan proposed. On the contrary, he directed the chiefs of the expedition, after securing their prizes, to rejoin him at New York. He needed this force himself, for an enterprise of no little importance, which he was upon the point of undertaking, up the Hudson. Virginia, therefore, ceased for that time to be the theater of these barbarous depredations.

The Americans had constructed, at great labor and expense, very strong works at the posts of Verplanks Neck and Stony Point, situated on nearly opposite points of land, the first on the east, and the other on the west side of the Hudson. They defended the much frequented pass called Kings Ferry, which could not fall into the power of the English without compelling the Americans to take a circuit of ninety miles up the river, in order to communicate between the northern and southern provinces. General Clinton had therefore resolved to seize these two positions. Washington, who lay with his army at Middlebrook, was at too great a distance to interrupt the execution of the design.

The English, accordingly, set out upon this expedition about the last of May. Commodore Collier conducted the squadron that ascended the river, general Vaughan the column of the right, which landed on the eastern bank, a little below Verplanks, and Clinton in person, the column of the left, with which he disembarked on the western bank, below Stony Point. The Americans, finding the enemy so near, and not being prepared to receive him, evacuated Stony Point, where they were soon replaced by the royal troops. But at Verplanks there was more resistance ; the republicans had erected on this point a small but strong and complete work, which they called Fort la Fayette; this was defended by artillery and a small garrison. It was unfortunately commanded by the heights of Stony Point, upon which the English, by their exertions during the night, had planted a battery of heavy cannon, and another of mortars. Early on the following morning, they opened a tempest of fire upon Fort la Fayette. The attack was supported in front by commodore Collier, who advanced with his galleys and gunboats within reach of the fort; and general Vaughan, having made a circuit through the hills, was at length arrived, and had closely invested it on the land side. The garrison, seeing that all possibility of relief was now cut off, and that their fire was totally overpowered and lost in the magnitude of that which they received, surrendered at discretion the following morning. They were treated humanely. General Clinton gave direction for completing the works of Stony Point; and with a view to the ulterior operations of the campaign, encamped his army at Philipsburgh, about half way between Verplanks and the city of New York. But neither Clinton nor Washington was disposed to run the hazard of a battle ; they both expected re-inforcements, the one from England, the other from the allies of the United States. Such was the cause of the inaction of the belligerent parties, during this campaign in the middle provinces.

In defect of conquests, the British generals were disposed, at least, to rid themselves of the privateers that tormented them, and to resume the war of devastation.

The coasts of Connecticut which border the sound, afforded shel-

ter to a multitude of extremely enterprising privateersmen, who intercepted whatever made its appearance in their waters, to the utter
destruction of the commerce of New York by the sound, and consequently to the infinite prejudice of the British fleet and army, which
had been accustomed to draw the greater part of their provisions
from that part. With a view of curing the evil, Clinton ordered
governor Tryon to embark for Connecticut with a strong detachment.
He accordingly proceeded to make a descent at New Haven, where
he dislodged the militia, after some irregular resistance, and destroyed
whatever he found in the port. Thence he advanced to Fairfield,
which he devoted to the flames. Norwalk and Greenfield were in like
manner laid in ashes. The loss of the Americans was prodigious ; besides that of their houses and effects, a considerable number of ships,
either finished or on the stocks, with a still greater of whale boats and
small craft, with stores and merchandise to an immense amount, were
all destroyed. Tryon, far from blushing at such shameful excesses,
even boasted of them, insisting that he had thereby rendered important services to the king. Could he have thought that in a war against
an entire people, it was rather his duty to desolate than to conquer?
And what other name can be given to ravages and conflagrations
which conduce to no decisive result, but that of gratuitous enormities?
But, if this mental obliquity, if this cruel frenzy in an individual, who
was not a stranger to civilization, have but too many examples in the
history of men, still, is it not astonishing, that he should have persuaded himself that by such means he could induce the Americans to
replace themselves under the royal standard ? It is worthy of remark,
in effect, that in the midst of ravage and combustion, he issued a
proclamation, by which he exhorted the inhabitants to return to their
ancient duty and allegiance. But whether this mode of operation
was displeasing to Clinton, who perhaps had only desired the destruction of the shipping, and not that of houses and temples, or from whatever other more real motive, he ordered Tryon to cease hostilities, and
to rejoin him immediately, at New York. But the melancholy ves-
tiges of the rage of the English were not effaced by his retreat, and
these piratical invasions redoubled the abhorrence attached to their
name.

While the coasts of Connecticut were thus desolated by the
British arms, the Americans undertook an expedition which afforded
a brilliant demonstration that, so far from wanting courage, they
could vie in boldness with the most celebrated nations of Europe.
The English had labored with such industry in finishing the works
at Stony Point, that they had already reduced that rock to the condition of a real fortress. They had furnished it with a numerous and

selected garrison. The stores were abundant, the defensive preparations formidable. These considerations could not, however, discourage Washington, who, on hearing of the capture of Stony Point and Verplanks, had advanced and taken post on the brow of the mountains of the Hudson, from forming the design to surprise and attempt both these forts by assault. He charged general Wayne with the attack of Stony Point, and general Howe with that of Verplanks. He provided the first with a strong detachment of the most enterprising and veteran infantry in all his army.

These troops set out on their expedition the fifteenth of July, and having accomplished their march over high mountains, through deep morasses, difficult defiles, and roads exceedingly bad and narrow, arrived about eight o'clock in the evening within a mile of Stony Point. General Wayne then halted to reconnoiter the works, and to observe the situation of the garrison. The English, however, did not perceive him. He formed his corps in two columns, and put himself at the head of the right. It was preceded by a vanguard of a hundred and fifty picked men, commanded by that brave and adventurous Frenchman, lieutenant-colonel Fleury. This vanguard was itself guided by a forlorn hope of about twenty, led by lieutenant Gibbon. The column on the left, conducted by major Stewart, had a similar vanguard, also preceded by a forlorn hope under lieutenant Knox. These forlorn hopes, among other offices, were particularly intended to remove the abattis and other obstructions, which lay in the way of the succeeding troops. General Wayne directed both columns to march in order and silence, with unloaded muskets and fixed bayonets. At midnight they arrived under the walls of the fort. The two columns attacked upon the flanks, while major Murfee engaged the attention of the garrison by a feint in their front. An unexpected obstacle presented itself; the deep morass which covered the works was at this time overflowed by the tide. The English opened a most tremendous fire of musketry, and of cannon loaded with grape-shot; but neither the inundated morass, nor a double palisade, nor the bastioned ramparts, nor the storm of fire that was poured from them, could arrest the impetuosity of the Americans; they opened their way with the bayonet, prostrated whatever opposed them, scaled the fort, and the two columns met in the centre of the works. General Wayne received a contusion in the head, by a musket ball, as he passed the last abattis; colonel Fleury struck with his own hand the royal standard that waved upon the walls. Of the forlorn hope of Gibbon, seventeen out of the twenty perished in the attack. The English lost upwards of six hundred men in killed and prisoners. The conquerors abstained from pillage and from all disorder; a conduct the more worthy to be commended, as they had still present in mind the ravages and butcheries which their enemies had so recently committed in Carolina, in Connecticut, and in Virginia. Humanity imparted new effulgence to the victory which valor had obtained.

The attack meditated against Verplanks had not the same success; general Howe encountered insurmountable obstacles. Meanwhile, Clinton had received intelligence of the capture of Stony Point; and, being resolved not to suffer the enemy to establish themselves in that position, he instantly detached a corps of cavalry and light infantry to dislodge them. But Washington had attained his object; he had originally intended nothing more than to make himself master of the artillery and stores of the fort, to destroy the works, and to bring off the garrison. It was absolutely inconsistent with his views to risk a general action, in order to favor a partial operation; he therefore ordered general Wayne to retire; which he did successfully, after having dismantled the fortifications. This expedition, so glorious for the American arms, was celebrated with rapture in all parts of the confederation. The congress decreed their acknowledgments to Washington, and to Wayne, to Fleury, Stewart, Gibbon, and Knox. They presented general Wayne with a medal of gold, which represented this brilliant achievement. Fleury and Stewart received a similar medal of silver. Not willing to leave the bravery of their soldiers without its retribution, they ordered an estimate of the military stores taken at Stony Point, and the value thereof to be shared among them.

Rendered more daring and adventurous by the success of this enterprise, the republicans frequently harassed the outposts of the royal army. The continual skirmishes that followed were alternately advantageous or disastrous to the two parties. One of the most considerable was engaged at Paulus Hook, on the right bank of the Hudson, opposite to New York; the Americans were treated rather roughly in it.

An expedition of much more importance took place on the river Penobscot, near the eastern confines of New England, on the side of Nova Scotia. Colonel Maclean had embarked from Halifax with a strong division of regulars, with a view of establishing a post, at the mouth of that river, in the county of Lincoln. On his arrival in the Penobscot, he took possession of an advantageous situation, and proceeded to fortify himself. From that position he purposed to annoy the eastern frontiers of the confederation; and by this diversion in Massachusetts, he hoped to prevent the inhabitants of that province from sending re-inforcements to the army of Washington.

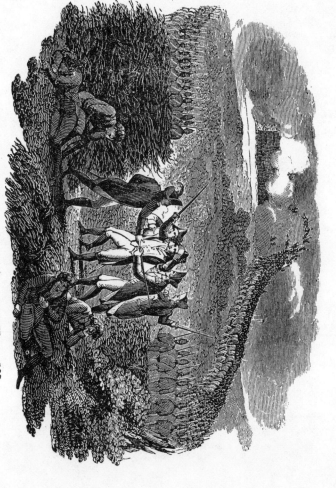

STORMING OF STONEY POINT. Vol. II.—p. 192.

This movement occasioned an unusual alarm at Boston, and it was determined to make all possible efforts to dislodge the enemy from a post which smoothed his way to more considerable enterprises. An armament was fitted out with extraordinary dispatch; and in order to secure vessels of transport as well as sailors, an embargo of forty days was laid on all their shipping. The crews and the troops were assembled with equal promptitude, and all the preparations for the expedition were soon completed. The squadron was under the conduct of commodore Saltonstall, and the land troops were commanded by general Lovell. They sailed for the mouth of the Penobscot.

Colonel Maclean had received at first rumors, and afterwards undoubted intelligence, of the preparations that were making at Boston. He employed all the means which the shortness of notice left at his disposal, to secure his defense. The republicans appeared; their first attempts to land were rendered vain by the intrepid resistance of the royal troops; they redoubled their efforts, and at length succeeded in effecting that object. General Lovell, instead of attacking immediately, which would have ensured him victory, set about intrenching himself. The English resumed courage. There was a continual firing of artillery for fifteen days. Finally, the works which covered the position of the English being partly ruined, the Americans resolved to proceed to the assault. Colonel Maclean was informed of their design, and prepared himself to receive them.

In the morning he was under arms; but a profound silence prevailed in the camp of the besiegers; their stillness and immobility appeared inexplicable. The colonel sent to reconnoiter, and he soon learns, to his extreme surprise, that the enemy's lines are totally evacuated, that he has not left even a guard, and that he has re-embarked his troops, arms and stores. The cause of so abrupt a resolution was not long in disclosing itself. Commodore Collier had suddenly made his appearance at the mouth of the Penobscot. He had been apprised of the critical situation of Maclean, and had immediately departed from Sandy Hook, with a sufficient squadron. His maneuvers now indicated the design to attack the flotilla of Massachusetts; the republicans fell into confusion, and the royalists completed their discomfiture without difficulty. The vessels of war and of transport were all taken or blown up, to the incalculable detriment of the Bostonians, who had taken on themselves the whole burthen of this expedition. The soldiers and sailors, to escape the conqueror, were forced to penetrate the most dismal solitudes and pathless forests, where the extremes of hardship attended their retreat.   Saltonstall and Lovell, but especially the first, became the objects of public execration.   They were every where loaded with the reproaches of stupidity and cowardice.   The fatal issue of the enterprise of Penobscot, was calculated to teach the inhabitants of Massachusetts a truth, which it cost them much to learn, namely, that in confederate states, nothing is more imprudent than to operate partially.   For it appears that their leaders in this affair, far from concerting with the generals of congress, did not even acquaint them with their designs.   Thus, with the exception of the conquest of Georgia, the operations of this campaign were conducted with a sort of languor, and produced no results of any considerable impor tance.   The month of July was, however, sufficiently remarkable for the terrible reprisals which the Americans, under the conduct of general Sullivan, exercised against the Indians.   The expeditions undertaken against them the preceding year, by the colonels Butler and Clarke, had not completely satisfied the congress; they were still animated with desire to exact an exemplary vengeance for the enormities of Wyoming.   Moreover, they deemed it indispensably necessary to repress the incursions of these savages, who, rendered more daring by impunity, and excited by the presents of British emissaries, incessantly desolated the frontiers of the confederation. But by far the most formidable of all the Indian nations, were the Six Tribes, who derived a degree of power from the league contracted between them, from a scheme of polity more resembling that of civilized states, and, especially, from the great number of European adventurers who had established themselves among them, and had taught them to wield their arms, and to make war with more dexterity.   Interlinked with these, were other savage tribes of inferior note.   The Oneidas, however, should be excepted, who observed a perfect neutrality towards the congress.   The American government, therefore, resolved a decisive stroke, to deliver itself forever from this cruel scourge, and at the same time to visit upon the heads of these barbarians the innocent blood of Wyoming.   Circumstances appeared to favor the execution of this design, since the war, as we have already seen, was become strangely torpid in the maritime parts.   Agreeably to the plan of the expedition, general Sullivan, who was charged with its execution, proceeded up the Susquehanna, with a corps of about three thousand men, as far as Wyoming, where he waited the arrival of general James Clinton, who joined him from the banks of the Mohawk, at the head of sixteen hundred soldiers.   He was followed by a great number of pioneers, sumpter-men, carters, and other species of workmen, to open the roads, transport provisions, and ravage the country.   The

stock of provisions was considerable, but not so abundant as general
Sullivan could have wished   The army had to traverse an immense
tract of country, where no supplies were to be expected.   The
horses were sufficient in number, and the artillery consisted of six
field pieces with two howitzers.   The two generals made their junction at Wyoming, the twenty-first of August.   They immediately
set out for the upper parts of the Susquehanna.   Upon the rumor of
their destination, the Indians had made all the preparations in their
power, to avert from their country the impending perdition.   Under
the conduct of the same Johnson, Butler, and Brandt, who have
been mentioned in the preceding book, they had assembled in great
number, and had been joined by two hundred and fifty loyalists.
Full of confidence in their strength, they had advanced as far as
Newtown, a village which lay upon the route of Sullivan.   Here,
while waiting his approach, they threw up a very extensive intrenchment, which they strengthened with a palisade, and some imperfect
redoubts after the European manner.   As soon as Sullivan arrived,
he ordered the attack.   The Indians defended themselves with great
vigor for more than two hours, though they had no artillery.   To
dislodge them more easily from their lines, the American command
er ordered general Poor to draw off to the right, and turn their
position.   At sight of this movement, which had not slackened the
attack in front, the Indians lost their courage, and fled in disorder.
Few were killed, however, and none fell into the power of the
victors.   The Americans took possession of Newtown.   The terror-
struck savages made no other stand.   Sullivan had, therefore, no
further obstacle to contend with in overruning their country, except
the excessive difficulty of the ways, and the embarrassment of subsistence.   His patience and dexterity triumphed over both.   He
guided his troops into the very heart of the settlements, whose inhabitants, men, women, and children, had already escaped to the
deserts, and buried themselves in the most inaccessible forests.   The
habitations were burned, the crops were ravaged, the fruit trees cut
down.   The officers charged with the execution of these devastations, were themselves ashamed of them ; some even ventured to
remonstrate that they were not accustomed to exercise the vocation
of banditti.   But Sullivan, being himself controled by superior
orders, was inexorable.   His soldiers served him with ardor ; the
remembrance of Wyoming was fuel to their rage.   They burned an
immense quantity of grain.*   They utterly destroyed forty villages.
and left no single trace of vegetation upon the surface of the ground.

* One hundred and sixty thousand bushels of corn were destroyed

All the cattle which had not been removed by the Indians, were brought off, or killed upon the spot.   None of the bounties of nature, none of the products of human industry, escaped the fury of the Americans.

This expedition was not only remarkable for the rigor with which it was executed, but also for the light it threw upon the condition of these savage tribes.   They were found more advanced in civilization than was believed, or even than could have been reasonably supposed.   Their houses were placed in the most pleasant and healthy situations; they were roomy, neat, and not without a sort of elegance, so that little more could have been wished.   Their fields, covered with luxuriant harvests, attested that the art of culture was not unknown to them.   The antiquity and marvellous beauty of their fruit trees, with the number of their orchards, were incontestable indications that it was no little time since they were arrived at this degree of civil improvement.   The sowing of grain and planting of trees being an incontrovertible proof that man looks forward to the future, it is manifest how erroneous was the opinion, which had hitherto been maintained, that the savages were totally devoid of forecast.   Their progress is to be attributed to the increase of their population, to their intercourse with Europeans, and particularly to the efforts of missionaries, who, in times past, and even perhaps at this epoch, had lived, or were living among them.   The catastrophe of which they were now the victims, so filled them with consternation, that they never after made any considerable movement.   General Sullivan, having accomplished his mission, returned to Easton, in Pennsylvania.   His officers and soldiers addressed him letters of thanks and felicitation, which were also made public by means of the press; whether they did this of their own motion, or in compliance with the insinuations of Sullivan, who was rather a light man, and exceedingly vain withal.   A short time after, alledging the derangement of health, he requested leave to resign, and obtained it easily; the members of congress were weary of his continual ostentation, no less than of the habitual asperity of his language with respect to themselves.

Having related the events, which took place upon the American continent, between the royalists and republicans, and between the latter and the savages, the order of this history requires that we should pass to the recital of the operations of the English and French in the West Indies, after the first had been re-inforced by the squadron of commodore Rawley, and the second by that of the count de Grasse.   By the addition of these new forces, the strength of the hostile fleets was rendered nearly equal.   The English were strongly desirous of a naval battle; but the count d'Estaing, being much

superior in land forces to admiral Byron, had principally in view the
conquest of the neighboring English islands.   He declined a general
engagement, which, if unsuccessful, would render his superiority by
land of no avail.   He therefore lay quietly at anchor in Fort Royal
of Martinico, waiting a favorable occasion to attempt some enterprise of moment for the service of his sovereign.   Fortune delayed
not long to offer it; admiral Byron had sailed the sixth of June from
St. Lucia, for the island of St. Christophers, where the West India
fleet of merchantmen had assembled, to wait for convoy.   His intention was to escort them with his whole squadron, for some considerable part of their voyage to Europe.   He. reflected that he
could not leave a part of it in any of the ports of those islands, without
exposing it to the attacks of an enemy greatly superior in force; he
knew, besides, that M. de la Motte Piquet was then on his way from
France with a strong re-inforcement to d'Estaing; and it was plain,
that no ordinary convoy would have been sufficient for the protection
of the British merchant fleet, in case of its falling in with that squadron.   No sooner was Byron departed from St. Lucia, than the
French hastened to profit of his absence.   D'Estaing detached the
chevalier de St. Rumain, with five ships and four hundred land
troops, between regulars and militia, to attack the island of St. Vincents.   This officer fully answered the confidence of the admiral;
notwithstanding the currents which drifted him out of his course, and
the loss of one ship, he at length effected his landing.   He immediately occupied, sword in hand, the heights which command Kingston,
the capital of the island.   The Caribbs, or aborigines, an intrepid
and warlike race, came in multitude to join the assailants.   Governor
Morris, though he had more troops to defend himself than de Rumain
had to attack him, perhaps through fear of the Caribbs, whom the
avarice and cruelty of the English had greatly exasperated, surrendered upon terms.   The capitulation was honorable, and similar to
that which the governor of Dominica had obtained, when that island
fell into the power of the French.

In the meantime, the count d'Estaing was re-inforced by the
arrival of the squadron commanded by M. de la Motte Piquet.   His
fleet now consisted of twenty-five sail of the line, among which were
two of eighty guns and eleven of seventy-four.

This increase of force rendered him superior to Byron, who had
only nineteen sail of the line, of which one of ninety guns, and eleven
of seventy-four; the others of inferior rate.   La Motte Piquet had
also brought a re-inforcement of regular troops, with a copious supply
of naval and military stores and provisions.   The count d'Estaing,

with such means at his disposal, was encouraged to extend the scale of his projects.

The conquest of Grenada was the immediate object of his enterprise. The natural strength of that island presented great difficulties; but its situation and products rendered it highly important. He had long thought of this expedition, but had chosen to defer its execution until he should become possessed of a superiority by sea. The junction of la Motte Piquet having therefore decided him, he sailed the thirtieth of June from Martinico, and the second of July came to anchor in the harbor of Molinier. He immediately landed twenty-three hundred men, for the most part Irish, in the service of France, under the conduct of colonel Dillon. They rapidly occupied the adjacent posts. The governor of the island was lord Macartney, and its garrison consisted of two hundred regulars, with six hundred militia. They were posted upon a height called *Morne de l'Hopital,* which, besides being naturally very steep, the English had rendered still more difficult of access by rude walls of stone, erected from distance to distance up the ascent. They had also fortified its declivity with a strong palisade, and, above it, with three intrenchments, towering in gradation. This hill commands the town of St. George, the fortress, and harbor. D'Estaing sent to summon Macartney. He answered, in truth he did not know the force of the French, but that he well knew his own, and was determined to defend himself. The French commander was not ignorant that the principal hope of success lay in the celerity of his operations. He was fully persuaded that, if he delayed his attack, he should be interrupted by the arrival of Byron, to the relief of the island. He, therefore, gave orders for the assault, without hesitation. The following night the French approached the hill, and by two o'clock in the morning they had invested it on every side. To divide the attention of the enemy, they were formed in three columns, the right commanded by the viscount de Noailles, the left by Dillon, and that of the center by the count d'Estaing in person, who had intrepidly put himself at the head of the grenadiers. The artillery, not having cannon to serve, requested and were permitted to form the van. The action was commenced by a false attack at the foot of the hill, on the part of the river St. John. At this signal, the three columns, with great order and greater resolution, pressed up the hill to the assault. The besieged sustained their onset with much firmness, and for an instant the success appeared doubtful. The English even pretend to have repulsed the assailants. But animated by their chiefs, they returned to the charge with irresistible impetuosity. The soldiers supported and impelled one another. Neither the palisades, nor the steepness of the acclivity, nor the parapets, nor the most violent fire could arrest the French; their victory was complete. D'Estaing, with his grenadiers, sprung the first into the English intrenchments. The others followed. In a moment all the works were inundated with enemies. The English demanded quarter; the French granted it. The darkness of the night had increased the horror of the combat, and even the glory of the victors. They seized eleven cannon, of different sizes, and six mortars. At break of day they turned this artillery against the fort, which was still in the power of the English. At the first discharge, Macartney sent a flag, with an offer to capitulate. D'Estaing granted him an hour and a half for framing his proposals; those, which at the end of this time he presented, were rejected. The French general then framed some terms himself, with which he required immediate compliance, without the smallest deviation on either side, or relaxation on his. But these were so unexampled and extraordinary, that Macartney and the inhabitants thought it better to abandon themselves, without any condition, to the discretion of the conquerors, than to accept them; and accordingly did so. If the French in this assault displayed a valor deserving of eternal memory, the moderation and humanity which they manifested after the victory, merit no inferior encomium. The capital was preserved from pillage, to which it was liable by the ordinary rules of war. The inhabitants were protected in their persons and properties. Dillon, in particular, distinguished himself by the generosity of his behavior. The French found in the fort an hundred pieces of cannon and sixteen mortars; they made seven hundred prisoners. They also seized thirty merchant vessels, with rich cargoes, that lay in the harbor. Their loss, in killed and wounded, amounted to little more than a hundred men.

The count d'Estaing had soon occasion to felicitate himself upon the promptitude with which he had prosecuted his enterprise of Grenada. For, on the sixth of July, Byron, with all his fleet, appeared in view of St. George's harbor. It was accompanied by a great number of transports, filled with troops, drawn from St. Lucia. This admiral, after accompanying the homeward bound West India fleet till out of danger, and appointing them a convoy to see them safe home, had returned with eighteen ships of the line and one frigate to St. Lucia. On being apprised of the reduction of St. Vincent, he sailed immediately with a body of troops under general Grant for its recovery. They had not proceeded far, when they were informed that the count d'Estaing had attacked Grenada. On this intelligence they directly changed their course, and made the best of their way for its relief. The French admiral had been apprised, by the frigates he had sent out upon discovery, of the approach of the British fleet. He immediately ordered the captains of his ships to get under sail, and form their line well off the coast. Some had already obeyed, and the others were preparing to follow them, when the British armament came up, all sail out, and offered battle to the count d'Estaing. The winds blew from the east and east northeast, and were consequently favorable to a squadron coming from St. Lucia towards Grenada.

Upon sight of the British fleet, the French admiral ordered those ships which had not yet hoisted their anchors, to slip their cables, and proceed to take their stations with the others in order of battle. But as the British approached with rapidity, these vessels placed themselves in the line wherever they could the soonest, without having regard to their ordinary posts. The English had the advantage of the wind, and were standing for Grenada, under the persuasion that Macartney still held out. Their transports were far astern of their rear. The French were under the wind, and standing upon the opposite tack. The British admiral was eager to come to close action, from a confidence that he could thus put the French fleet to rout, and recover the island. On the other hand, the count d'Estaing, who, by the reduction of Grenada, had attained his principal object, was in no disposition to hazard anew a point already decided. His intention was, therefore, to avoid a decisive engagement, and to confine himself to the preservation of his new acquisition. With these different views, the two admirals advanced to the encounter. Only fifteen of the French ships were able at first to take part in the action, the others having been forced to leeward by the violence of the currents. Vice-admiral Barrington, who commanded the British rear, advanced with three ships, the Prince of Wales, the Boyne, and the Sultan, and closed with the van of the enemy. A warm engagement ensued, but the three English ships, not being supported in time by the rest of their division, and having to contend with a much superior force, were extremely damaged, especially in their sails and rigging.

Such is the ordinary effect of the manner of firing of the French in naval battles; and in this, they leveled from a good distance and under the wind, which also contributed to raise their shot higher. Barrington was wounded. Meanwhile, the rest of the British squadron joined him; and on his part, d'Estaing had rallied those of his ships which had not been able at first to form in a line with the fifteen that commenced the action. The English still continued to push their way towards Grenada, while their transports kept on their left towards the open sea, their line of battle covering them from the

French fleet. The two armaments being thus drawn out on opposite tacks, the battle continued till they were entirely passed each other. But the English ships having arrived in chase, and consequently rather in disorder, whereas the French, as later from port, and in better condition, had more command of their movements, and had kept their distances better, it followed that some of the first had to endure the whole weight of fire from many or from all of the second. Among those that suffered the most were the Grafton, the Cornwall, and the Lion. The last was so shattered as to be very near going to the bottom; and the Monmouth, having ventured singly to arrest the progress of the French van, in order to bring on a close action, had been left little better than a wreck. Meanwhile, the head of the British van, continuing its course, was arrived at the mouth of St. George's harbor. But the French colors that waved on the fort, and the fire of the batteries, no longer permitted admiral Byron to doubt of the capture of the island. Convinced, that in the present state of his fleet he could not hope for success against so great a superiority of force, he directed captain Barker, who had charge of the transports, to alter his course and make the best of his way to Antigua or St. Christophers. In order to protect him from the pursuit of the enemy, he stood with his fleet to the northward. But the three ships, the Grafton, Cornwall and Lion, from their disabled condition, not only remained far astern, but fell so fast to the leeward that it was to be feared they would be cut off by the French. The count d'Estaing, having observed their situation, had in effect put his ships about and steered to the south, in order to effect what Byron apprehended, that is, to intercept them. But, to defeat this design, the British admiral instantly changed his tack, and steered again to the southward. While the hostile fleets thus maneuvered in sight of each other, the Lion bore away, with what sail she had left, to the west, and in a few days arrived at Jamaica. D'Estaing might easily have seized her; but he chose not to disperse his fleet, for fear of falling to leeward of Grenada, whither it was his intent to return for moorings. The Grafton and Cornwall found means to rejoin their admiral before the French could reach them. The Monmouth, no longer able to keep the sea, was sent with all dispatch to Antigua. The two fleets continued in sight the one of the other, till night, the English still plying to windward, in order to cover the retreat of the transports. The inferiority of their force, and the condition of their ships, deterred them from renewing the engagement. The French remained to leeward, without attempting to disquiet them, whether by reason of this position, or because their admiral thought it imprudent to run new risks. He might claim a victory for what he had already achieved, and he had probably motives for avoiding decisive actions. The following morning he came to anchor in the road of St. George's, amidst the acclamations of the soldiers and of the French inhabitants, who had been spectators of the action. The British transports, one only excepted, which fell into the hands of the enemy, all arrived in safety at St. Christophers. Admiral Byron, after remaining a few days longer at sea, repaired to the same island, for the purpose of refitting his ships, which were grievously damaged.

The British lost in this engagement one hundred and eighty-three killed, and three hundred and forty-six wounded. The loss of the French was more considerable, owing as well to the mode of firing of the English, as to the great number both of sailors and land forces with which their ships were crowded. Besides many officers of note, they had about two hundred men killed, and the number of their wounded amounted to nearly eight hundred.

The news of the battle of Grenada was welcomed in France with great demonstrations of joy. According to the usage observed on occasion of important victories, the king wrote to the archbishop of Paris, directing that a *Te Deum* should be sung in the metropolitan church. The count d'Estaing pretended, in effect, to have been victorious; he alledged in his favor that he had kept his lights burning during all the night subsequent to the engagement; that Byron had for several hours refused to renew it, though all the while he had the advantage of the wind; that the British had made no movement to preserve the Lion, when retiring with difficulty towards the west; that the French fleet had captured one of the enemy's ships, conquered Grenada, and baffled the project of Byron for its recovery; and, finally, that it had secured the empire of the sea in the West Indies. It is indeed true, that the British admiral, in consequence of the disabled condition of his fleet, had found it necessary to take shelter at St. Christophers, where he was decided to remain until the enemy should become weaker or himself stronger. His retreat spread consternation among the inhabitants of all the British islands, who had not for a long time, nor perhaps ever before, seen the French masters at sea. A short time after the action, d'Estaing, having repaired his ships, set sail afresh, and paraded with his whole force, in sight of St. Christophers. Byron lay safely moored in the harbor of Basse Terre; the French admiral sought in vain to draw him out to combat. Finding him obstinate in his immobility, he shaped his course for St. Domingo, where he assembled the merchantmen of the different islands, and dispatched them for Europe, under convoy of three ships of the line and three frigates.

In this state of things, there being much of the season for operations still unexpired, the count d'Estaing deliberated upon the course to be pursued, with most advantage to the interests of his sovereign. But in the meantime, he received letters from America, advising him of the extreme dissatisfaction with which the republicans observed that the alliance with France had hitherto produced nothing, upon the American continent, that corresponded either to the greatness of their ally, or to the general expectation of the Americans. It was represented to the French admiral that the enormous expenses incurred in the expedition of Rhode Island, had been worse than fruitless; that the zeal with which the French fleet had been equipped and victualed by the Bostonians, had produced no better effect than its immediate desertion of their coasts upon distant expeditions; that the benefits of the alliance were a nullity for the Americans, since the loss of Savannah and all Georgia, which had resulted from the retirement of the French, was not compensated by the recovery of Philadelphia, even throwing that event into the scale, as an indirect consequence of their co-operation, and supposing that the American arms would not otherwise have compelled the British to abandon that capital; that the occupation of Georgia by the enemy was fraught with consequences still more alarming, since it opened him an easy entrance into the Carolinas; that he was already established in the heart of America, and drew his sustenance thence; that meanwhile, the French commanders were cruising the West Indian seas, enriching themselves with the conquest of British possessions, and leaving the Americans to sustain by themselves the whole burden of this desperate war; that it ought not, therefore, to be wondered at, if the number of the discontented increased every day in proportion to the rapid diminution of the partisans of France. These complaints were concluded with the most earnest instances and obsecrations that he would not abandon a faithful ally in the midst of surrounding perils.

The count d'Estaing could not but listen to these representations, although he had received instructions from his court, to return immediately to Europe with the twelve ships of the line and four frigates, which composed the fleet of Toulon. He was directed, by the same instructions, to detach three sail of the line and two frigates, under the conduct of La Motte Piquet, for the station of St. Domingo, and to leave eight other ships of the line to winter at Martinico, under the command of the count de Grasse, who was to co-operate with the marquis de Bouille, for the reduction of other English islands. Such were then the intentions of the French ministers; their negotiations with the court of Spain were in full activity, and they wished the Americans to feel all their distress, in order to obtain in the treaty they were about forming with his catholic majesty, more favorable stipulations for each member of the family compact. But d'Estaing thought it better to obey the generous impulses of his heart, than the orders of the ministry. To deprive the Americans of all pretext for doubting the sincerity of his good dispositions towards them, he set sail with twenty-two sail of the line and eight frigates. He had two objects in contemplation, both of the highest importance; but he could come to no decision until he had first advised with the generals of congress. The first was the destruction of the force under general Prevost, and thus freeing the province of Georgia from the presence of the English, and South Carolina from the danger of their vicinity. The second was more decisive, and likely to be attended with more difficulties; and that was, to attack, conjointly with Washington, the British force at New York, by sea and land at the same time. The success of these two enterprises would have sufficed to put an end to the war upon the American continent.

It was on the first of September that the count d'Estaing made his appearance upon the coasts of Georgia, with twenty ships of the line. He had detached two to Charleston of South Carolina, to give notice of his arrival in those waters. It was totally unexpected to the English; their ship, the Experiment, of fifty guns, commanded by captain Wallace, was obliged, after a stubborn resistance, to surrender to the French. Three British frigates shared the like fate, as well as five transports loaded with provisions. This prize was highly acceptable to the victors, who were much in want of supplies. General Prevost was then at Savannah, with only a part of his troops; the remainder were still in their cantonments, on the island of Port Royal, near the coast of Carolina. At sight of so pressing a danger, he sent orders by express to colonel Maitland, who commanded on that island, to rejoin him with all possible celerity. He likewise recalled the detachment that occupied Sunbury. The vessels at anchor in the Savannah were removed higher up, to secure them from the fire of the enemy, or sunk to obstruct his passage. Other impediments for the same purpose were planted in the river. The British also destroyed the batteries they had erected on the island of Tybee, and compelled the blacks to work without intermission at the fortifications. The seamen, who had been put ashore, joined the land troops, and were especially employed for the service of the artillery.

The news of d'Estaing's arrival excited transports of exultation at Charleston. General Lincoln immediately commenced his march for Savannah at the head of a strong detachment. A great number of small craft were dispatched to the French admiral, to facilitate the debarkation of troops upon the coast, which large vessels cannot approach very near. With the assistance of these light vessels, d'Estaing, who had anchored off the bar which lies at the mouth of the Savannah, was enabled to land his troops at Beaulieu, about thirteen miles from the town of Savannah. At the same time his frigates were occupied in taking possession of the lower river, and of the different inlets; approaching as near to the town and lines as the circumstances of water and defense would admit. On the fifteenth of September, the French appeared under the walls of Savannah. They were accompanied by Pulaski's legion, who had made a forced march to join them. After some slight skirmishes, general Prevost contracted all his posts within the cover of the artillery on the works. Colonel Maitland not being yet arrived, the garrison, far from being sufficient for acting offensively, were scarcely competent to the defense of the works.

D'Estaing imperiously summoned Prevost to surrender the place; he announced in high language, that he commanded the same troops, a detachment of whom had recently taken the Hospital Hill, in Grenada, by storm; that he owed it to his humanity to remind him of it, after which, it could not be imputed to him, if he should not be able to restrain the fury of his soldiers, in the event of a fruitless resistance. The Americans observed with extreme displeasure and jealousy, that the summons was made exclusively in the name of the king of France.

General Prevost, reflecting that his re-inforcements had not yet joined him, and that his lines were still in a very imperfect state of defense, thought it prudent to gain all the time that was possible, by pretending a willingness to negotiate a capitulation. He accordingly answered the French admiral, that he neither could nor should surrender without being first made acquainted with the conditions, and that he begged him to be more explicit on that head. Messages passed backwards and forwards; and at length, so shrewd was Prevost, and so simple or so confident was d'Estaing, that a truce of twenty-four hours was agreed upon, to afford time for deliberation. During this interval, colonel Maitland arrived with the troops from Port Royal, after having surmounted a variety of obstructions, and made his way through almost impassable swamps and morasses. On the junction of this re-inforcement, upon which depended, in truth, the principal hope of defense, Prevost gave the French admiral to understand, that he should hold out to the last. Two days before, however, general Lincoln had joined the camp of the besiegers with about three thousand men, among regular troops and militia. The French amounted to between four and five thousand. The garrison, including sailors and loyalists, consisted of about three thousand men; the French established their quarters to the right, and the Americans to the left of the place. After the refusal of the British commander to surrender upon the first summons, the allies could not expect that a mere assault should triumph over a formidable garrison, intrenched behind works which they strengthened every day. It was, therefore, resolved to commence a regular siege. The trenches were opened immediately, and were carried on with so much vigor, that by the twenty-fourth of September, a sap had been pushed to within three hundred yards of the abattis, on the left flank of the town. The besieged were active in their endeavors to interrupt the works; but their efforts were ineffectual. Finally, the trenches being completed, and the batteries armed, the bombardment commenced in the night of the third of October; the fire became still more violent at daybreak on the morning of the fourth, when thirty-seven pieces of cannon and nine mortars were unmasked; while sixteen other pieces of cannon enfiladed the works from the shipping. To increase the terror, the besiegers launched carcasses into the town, which burned several houses. Five entire days of this tempestuous fire caused infinite mischief to the town, but made little impression upon the fortifications, which the besieged repaired with diligence, wherever they were at all damaged. It even seemed, that amidst the storm of balls and bombs, they daily acquired new strength and solidity. The garrison, and such of the inhabitants as joined the troops in defending the ramparts, received little injury. But the fate of the women, children, and unarmed multitude, was indeed worthy of pity. Their lives were continually threatened by the fall of their burning roofs. Many perished, others, more unfortunate, were miserably crippled. Touched by their distress, general Prevost wrote to d'Estaing, requesting permission that they should be sent aboard ships down the river, and placed under the protection of a French ship of war, in which state they were to continue until the business of the siege should be decided. At the same time acquainting him, that his own wife and family should be among the first to profit of the indulgence. The anticipation of such a request was more to have been expected from a generous enemy than its refusal; since the reduction of the place depended on force, and not on famine. But the French admiral, whether he acted of himself or at the instigation of general Lincoln, who, like all the inhabitants of Massachusetts, carried the spirit of party to the extreme, after a delay of three hours, returned a haughty answer to this demand. He objected that Prevost had deceived him by the truce, and that his present proposition very probably concealed a new artifice. He suspected him of intending by this stratagem to cover the rich spoils of Carolina. He assured him, finally, that he sincerely lamented the unhappy condition of the individuals for whom he petitioned, but that general Prevost must impute it wholly to himself, and those illusions which had darkened his understanding.

Whatever was the ability of the British engineers, and especially that of captain Moncrieffe, who rendered eminent services in this siege; whatever was the valor with which the garrison defended the breaches, incessantly repaired by their exertions, the British general could have had little hope of holding out long, and still less of a successful defence, if the enemy had persevered in his gradual approaches. But d'Estaing experienced great difficulties. Far from expecting to encounter so obstinate a resistance under the walls of Savannah, he had calculated with such confidence on a prompt surrender, that he had come to anchor with his fleet of heavy capital ships, upon an inhospitable coast, and in a most critical season of the year. He had even signified to the Americans, that he could not remain on shore more than eight or ten days. Twenty had already elapsed since the siege had commenced, and still there appeared no immediate prospect of its termination. The season was growing worse every day, and the naval officers were continually representing to their admiral the perils to which he would expose the ships and troops of the king, if he persisted any longer in the prosecution of this expedition. It might also happen, that a British fleet would arrive with every advantage united, and force the French squadron to engage, at a moment when a part of its crews and artillery were thus employed in the siege of Savannah. Under these considerations, although the trenches were not yet carried to the requisite perfection, and though no considerable breach had been opened, the count d'Estaing resolved to attempt the assault. Necessity now urged him to this extreme counsel, after having delayed to embrace it, when, at his landing, he had found the works not yet completed, and the garrison not yet re-inforced by colonel Maitland.

He consulted with general Lincoln upon the plan of attack; it was determined to direct it against the right flank of the place. On this side, a swampy hollow way might bring the besiegers under cover to within fifty yards of some of the principal works, and, at some points still nearer.

The ninth of October, before day, the count d'Estaing and general Lincoln, having formed the flower of both armies in three columns, advanced by the hollow way to reconnoiter the point of attack. But through the darkness, they took a greater circuit to the left, and got deeper in the bog than they needed or intended to have done; a circumstance which, besides the loss of time, could scarcely fail of producing some disorder in the columns. They, however, soon formed anew, approached the foot of the walls, and mounted to the assault with incredible spirit and audacity. It is said, that the English had notice of it the preceding evening, and that they were, consequently, prepared. It is certain, at least, that they defended themselves with a vigor not inferior to that which assailed them. A redoubt on the Ebenezer road became the scene of the most terrible conflict. But every where the same courage was displayed, and no where could it be conjectured which of the parties victory was disposed to crown. D'Estaing and Lincoln were at the head of their columns, exposed to the most violent fire. Prevost, Maitland and Moncrieffe, displayed an equal ardor; they continually stimulated their soldiers to repulse from their walls, to exterminate these rebels to the king, and those inveterate enemies of the British name. The combat was supported for above an hour with the same fury. But little by little the assailants became exhausted by their efforts. They were excessively galled by the artillery, which Moncrieffe had disposed with extreme dexterity, and which assailed them in almost every direction with a deluge of balls and grape-shot. The violence of the attack abated, and the besieged hailed the moment in which they saw their safety in their own hands. They made a vigorous sally; a corps of grenadiers and marines was at the head of the column which, in a few instants, swept the ramparts and ditches. Not content with this first success, and hurried on by their impetuosity, the English pursued their enemies, and drove them in the greatest confusion through the abattis into the hollow we have mentioned. This movement was executed with such rapidity, that the re-inforcements which Prevost had pushed forward could not arrive in time to take part in it. Nor should it be omitted, that in the height of the assault, the count Pulaski, at the head of two hundred light horse, charging at full speed, attempted to penetrate into the town, in order to assail the British in rear. But he received a mortal wound; his troops, on seeing him fall, were discouraged, and fell back.

When the fog and smoke were dissipated, which had darkened the air during the combat, horrible was the spectacle that discovered itself. Heaps of dead and dying covered the ground, and particularly near the Ebenezer redoubts; streams of blood rilled from the wrecks; lamentable cries arose on every side. The allies requested a truce, with leave to bury the dead, and carry off the wounded; the first was granted, but a restriction laid in point of distance as to the rest. The assault of Savannah cost the allies a great sacrifice of men. The loss of the French in killed and wounded amounted to upwards of seven hundred ; more than forty of whom were officers. Among the wounded were d'Estaing himself, the viscounts de Fontange and de Bethizy, and the baron de Steding. The Americans lost in slain and wounded about four hundred. The loss on the British side, as they fought secure, was inconsiderable. Great civilities now passed between the French camp and the British lines, and many apologies were made for the answer returned general Prevost with respect to the women and children. They were now pressed to place themselves in the situation which they had then requested ; the Chimera, commanded by the chevalier de St. Rumain, was named for the reception of the general's wife, her children and company. Prevost answered with a certain bluntness, that what had been once refused, and that in terms of insult, could not in any circumstance be deemed worth the acceptance.

A few days after died the count Pulaski, a Pole of illustrious birth. Finding no opportunity in his own country to employ his sword in the defense of liberty, of which he was one of the most zealous partisans, he took the generous resolution to repair to the succor of the cause he adored in America. If he lost his life there, he also left a name revered by all the brave. It is related, that when his death was announced to the king of Poland, he exclaimed, ' Pulaski ! always valiant, but always foe to kings.' It cannot be denied that king Stanislaus had good reason to complain of him. The congress decreed him a monument.

The eighteenth of October, the allied army raised the siege of Savannah ; its retreat was effected so precipitately, that it was impossible for the English to pursue it. General Lincoln passed his regular troops to the left bank of the Savannah, the militia disbanded The French re-embarked with all their troops, artillery and stores The count d'Estaing immediately set sail to clear the coasts of America. His intention was to return to Europe with a part of his fleet, and to send the remainder to the West Indies ; but a violent storm dispersed his ships, and he had great difficulty in getting them together again.

Such was the issue of the count d'Estaing's campaign upon the coasts of North America, of that campaign in which the allies had placed such sanguine hopes. After missing the expedition of the Delaware, he twice abandoned that of Newport at the moment for its accomplishment. Finally, under the walls of Savannah, he showed himself at first too circumspect ; he delayed the attack, and afterwards precipitated an assault which resulted in discomfiture.

He conquered, it is true, two important islands in the West Indies, and fought with no little glory a veteran British fleet, commanded by the most able seamen. D'Estaing was no less precipitate in counsel than impetuous in execution. If fortune, as the friend of the adventurous, had shown herself more propitious to his efforts, or to the excellent plans which had been framed for him by the French ministry, he would indubitably have given paralyzing strokes to the naval power of England ; he would have afforded America all that assistance on which she had founded her hopes of promptly terminating the war.

It must be admitted, however, that if the co-operation of the French admiral was not so advantageous to the Americans as they might reasonably have expected, it was, nevertheless, far from being without its utility. His presence was a check upon the English, and prevented them from moving so soon as they purposed to have done against the southern provinces. Moreover, the British ministers, fearing not only for Rhode Island, but even for New York, if their troops continued dispersedly to occupy both these provinces, besides other positions, ordered general Clinton to evacuate the first. He accordingly did so, the twenty-fifth of October, and withdrew the garrison to New York. Thus Rhode Island, which had fallen without resistance into the hands of the royalists, returned peaceably into the power of the republicans. As the fleet of the count d'Estaing was then upon the coasts of Georgia, the British generals, under the apprehension of its coming suddenly upon Rhode Island, made their retreat from Newport with so much precipitation, that they left behind them all their heavy artillery, and a considerable quantity of stores. The Americans took possession of them immediately. They kept the British colors floating on the ramparts for several days ; this stratagem decoyed into their power many of the king's vessels, which came to surrender themselves at Newport.

Having related the military operations of this campaign, as well on the American continent as in the West Indies, it is not without interest to cast a glance upon the affairs of the interior, and to examine what was, at this epoch, the state of the finances, what were the opinions and the intrigues of the different parties which agitated a people embarked in the tumultuous career of revolution. If the union of the arms of France with those of the congress had procured real advantages to the Americans, and if it authorized them to hope well of the future, it cannot be denied, on the other hand, that it had a prejudicial effect upon their public spirit. This powerful protection itself, with the hopes which were its immediate and necessary result, easily persuaded the colonists that their quarrel approached its decision, that England would soon have to yield, and that in the meantime they might take their ease till the moment of deliverance should arrive. This same cause, which should have excited their emulation towards their great ally, and stimulated them to concur with fresh ardor to the common aim, seemed, on the contrary, to have abated their courage. They were impatient to enjoy that repose during the continuance of danger which they ought not to have desired until they had fully attained their intent. Amidst the brilliant images of approaching felicity with which their glowing imaginations continually regaled them, they forgot to reflect that success might still elude them while in the act of grasping it. France, on seeing their torpor, might have changed her counsels; had she not in their indolence a plausible pretext and a new motive for a policy which never hesitates to serve itself at the sacrifice of its allies? Was it not possible even that Spain, whose accession was ardently desired as the pledge of victory, might refuse to combat for a cause so frigidly supported by its own defenders? The Americans seemed not to recollect, that, if formidable armies hasten the final decision of wars, they only also can render the conditions of peace honorable. All these considerations were in a manner slighted by the bulk of the nation. Content with what they had hitherto done, and placing great reliance in the efficacy of French succors, they seemed inclined to leave to their allies the care of settling their quarrel. The indifference which had infected all classes, was as profound as the enthusiasm of former years had been intense. There could not have existed a more sinister augury; experience demonstrates that though it be but too easy to inflame a people the first time, nothing is more difficult than to re-kindle its ardor when once extinct. The leading Americans, and Washington in particular, were too enlightened not to take alarm at this state of things; they saw the evil in all its extent, and spared no exertions in applying such remedies as they could. They had recourse to exhortations, to the remembrance of past exploits; they represented the necessity of not forfeiting the respect of the allies; the perils that still impended; the power and the intrigues of England; all was in vain. Imbosomed in apathy, these reckless spirits abandoned to chance the decision of their dearest interests; nothing could rouse them. The recruiting of the army progressed with the most tedious slowness. The soldiers that were under Washington, some because they had completed their engagements, others because they were tired of serving, deserted their colors, and retired to their homes. And by what means were they to be replaced? Scarcely a few individuals were found who would engage, according to the regulations of congress, for three years or till the end

of the war. Engagements for a shorter term cou d be of no utility
to the service, and the backwardness of the people warranted no calculation even upon that resource. To draw them by lot, and constrain them to march, was thought, and was, in fact, too dangerous
a measure to be adopted in the present temper of minds. The same
lethargy seemed to have overspread the army itself. It was well for
it, that the English were so little enterprising.

Such was the real origin of the languor that characterized all the
operations of this year's campaign. Washington, besides, adhering
to his uniform purpose of never coming to action, except with every
probability of success, would not commit to the hazard of battles the
fate of a cause, *which he considered as already gained*. Far from
challenging the enemy, he deemed himself extremely fortunate in
not being attacked. If events had taken the direction they should
have done, he would doubtless have found some opportunity to strike
an important blow for the service and glory of his country. Perhaps
the English would not have passed the year so quietly as they did
in New York ; and perhaps Rhode Island would have fallen less
tardily under the domination of America.

The royal troops, in effect, had been much weakened in the first
months of the year, by the detachments they were obliged to make
to the West Indies and Georgia. But it almost always happens that
the most propitious occasions are lost amidst the tumult of popular
revolutions ; wherein the government, as being new, shows itself the
more feeble, as the opinions of individuals manifest themselves with
less restraint, and greater violence ; and public opinion, which can
only originate from the settled order of things, as yet, has no basis.
If sometimes success attend the enterprise, it must more frequently
be imputed to chance than to calculation. Such was, at this epoch,
the condition of the people of America. If in Georgia and Carolina
some efforts were made to repel the enemy, it was principally the
work of the militia of these two provinces, whose interest was then
immediately at stake. The others folded their arms, or contented
themselves with the adoption of spiritless measures. As if they considered themselves released from the ties of the confederation, they
made not their own cause of the danger that menaced the neighboring provinces. Nor were the Americans chargeable only with luke-
warmness, and this strange indifference to the fate of country ; there
also began to prevail among them a shameless thirst of gain, an
unbridled desire of riches, no matter by what means acquired. The
most illicit, the most disgraceful ways, were no obstacle to this
devouring passion. As it happens but too often in political revolutions, there had sprung up a race of men who sought to make them

private advantage of the public distress. Dependence or independence, liberty or no liberty, were all one to them, provided they could fatten on the substance of the state. While good citizens were wasting themselves in camps, or in the discharge of the most arduous functions ; while they were devoting to their country, their time, their estates, their very existence, these insatiable robbers were plundering, and sharing out, without a blush, the public fortune, and private fortunes. All private contracts became the object of their usurious interference and nefarious gains ; all army supplies enriched them with peculations; and the state often paid dearly for what it never obtained. Nor let any imagine that the most sincere and virtuous friends of their country ever made so pompous a parade of their zeal ! To hear these vile beings, they only were animated with a genuine and glowing patriotism. Every citizen of eminent rank, or invested with any public authority whatever, who refused to connive at their rapines, was immediately denounced as lukewarm, tory, royalist, sold to England ; it would seem that the first duty of those who governed the republic in times of such distress, was to fill the coffers of these flaming patriots. That their own praises should always have hung upon their lips is not to be wondered at ; for there nas never existed a robber, who had not been first a cheat ; but what seems really strange, and almost staggers belief, is that they could have found partisans and dupes. This public pest spread wider every day; it had already gangrened the very heart of the state. The good were silenced, the corrupt plumed themselves upon their effrontery ; every thing presaged an approaching ruin ; it was the hope of England. Shall we attempt to penetrate the causes of so great a change, in a nation once so distinguished for the purity of its manners ?

It will be found, that besides the general relaxation, which war too generally produces in the morals of the people, new governments, destitute of money, are constrained to procure it, and all their resources at the hands of usurers. The example is contagious ; it rapidly obtains throughout the community. These same governments find themselves compelled by the force of circumstances to give the preference and yield much to individuals who adhere, or pretend to adhere to their party. They accept for security in the most important transactions, a zeal for the public good, whether real or feigned. If it is necessary that they should welcome such sort of beings when they present themselves, they must, for the same reason, be tender in punishing when they detect them in delinquency Briefly, in such an order of things, the man of worth must, of ne cessity, make room for the man of naught. Not only unpunished, but tolerated, but employed, but encouraged, the species rapidly multiplies. Like pestilential bodies, whose bare contact infects those that are sound, vice soon poisons honesty in the hearts it can steal upon.

But one of the first and most operative causes of so deplorable a change in American morality, unquestionably lay in the depreciation of paper money. It was such at the commencement of this year, that eight dollars in bills could only command one in specie. The fall of this paper was daily accelerated, as well from the continual emissions by the congress, as by the little efficacy of the French succors, and the disasters of Georgia. In the month of December, a dollar in specie could hardly be obtained with forty of paper.* Nor is there any thing surprising in this, when it is considered that, independent of the dubious stability of the state, there was, in the month of September, the sum of one hundred and fifty-nine millions, nine hundred and forty-eight thousand, eight hundred and eighty-two dollars of the paper of congress in the thirteen United States. If to this mass be added the bills emitted by the particular provinces, it will readily be seen how immeasurably the aggregate amount of this sort of debt surpassed the resources of the new republic. The rapid declension of this currency is further accounted for by the extreme activity with which the loyalists and English employed themselves in counterfeiting it. There often arrived from England entire chests of those spurious bills, and so perfectly imitated that they were scarcely to be distinguished from the genuine. The British generals, and especially Clinton, though in reluctant obedience to the orders of the ministry, spared no pains in disseminating them throughout the continent. It cannot be doubted, but that the cabinet of St. James considered this falsification of the bills of credit, as a most efficacious mean for the recovery of its colonies. The British ministers were perfectly aware that it was the only pecuniary resource at the disposal of congress for the support of the war, and they calculated by draining it to disarm the Americans. Unquestionably it was neither the first time nor the last that this mode of making war has been resorted to ; but it will always, nevertheless, be held in abhorrence by all good men. For public faith should always be respected, even between enemies ; and of all perfidies is there one more frightful, and especially more vile than the counterfeiting of money ? In addition to all this, the commerce which the Americans had been wont to carry on, by means of their products, with England and other nations, was totally interrupted ; and as their soil and industry fur-

---

* The cost of a simple repast, or a pair of shoes, was from forty to fifty dollars of this depreciated paper.

nished them with but a small part of the articles essential to war, they were under the necessity of procuring them from abroad, and with gold and silver. Hence it resulted that specie, which even before the war had become distressingly scarce, diminished progressively, and daily advanced in price, in the ratio of its rarity. The bills proportionably lost their value in public estimation. From their alarming depreciation it followed not only that all purses were closed, and that the markets, scantily, and with extreme difficulty supplied, became the object of the continual murmurs of the people, but even that the faith of contracts was violated, and that individual probity was every where relaxed. With little, debtors acquitted themselves of much towards their creditors. Very few, at first, resorted to this unworthy expedient; but as evil propagates itself more rapidly than good, a multitude of citizens stained themselves with the same reproach, and the contagion became general. Herein the faithless and avaricious debtor was no respecter of persons ; Washington himself experienced this odious return from persons he had generously succored in their necessities.

The distress of the times had likewise given birth to another race of men, who devoted themselves to the business of speculating upon the depreciation of bills, dexterously profiting of a temporary rise or fall; and these variations of current price depended much less on the more or less favorable posture of public affairs, than upon news invented and circulated by those jobbers, or their intrigues and monopolies. Useful arts, and the labors of a fair commerce, were abandoned for the more alluring chances of paper negotiations. The basest of men enriched themselves; the most estimable sunk into indigence. The finances of the state, the fortunes of individuals, experienced the same confusion. Nor was avarice the extent of the evil; the contagion of that pestiferous passion attacked the very source of every virtue. Private interest every where carried it against the interests of the public. A greater number than it is easy to believe, looked upon the love of country as a mere illusion, which held out no better prospect than ruin and desolation. Nobody would enlist without exorbitant bounty ; nobody would contract to furnish the public supplies, none would supply the contractors, without enormous profits first lodged in their hands; none would accept of an office or magistracy without perfect assurance of a scandalous salary and illicit perquisites. The disorder, the depravation, were pushed to such a point, that perhaps never was the ancient adage more deplorably confirmed, that *there is no halting-place on the road of corruption.*

To the insatiable thirst of gold was joined the rage of party spirit ;

even the members of congress could not escape its vortex. Hence they too often disputed among themselves about their personal affairs, instead of discussing the grave and important interests of the state. When a feeble nation places itself under the patronage of one that is powerful, and looks up to it for protection, that nation must expect to find its bosom agitated by the tumults of party and the fury of faction. Some citizens, more occupied with their country's interests, or their own ambition, than the necessity of maintaining a good understanding with the more powerful nation, depart from the route which policy would have prescribed. Unguarded in their language and actions, they are continually liable to give umbrage to the agents of their great ally. Others, guided by the love of their country, or by their private interest, show themselves more feeble; they yield without resistance, they flatter and caress. Each of these parties is equally in error. The first, pluming themselves in vain upon the *name* of independents, cannot in all respects assume the manners it implies, when they have an indispensable need of a tutelary support. The second omit to reflect that their excessive condescension does but embolden their ally to crave without measure as without end. To observe a just medium between these extremes, requires a consummate prudence. The latter class are, of course, by far the most agreeable to the agents of the guardian power; they find them docile instruments, and if, as too often happens, assailable on the side of avarice, or ambition, prompt to serve as spies, as informers, as tools, whose base devotion no longer knows a check. The contrast and rivalship of these two factions soon degenerate into open war. The one reproaches the other with sacrificing the state to their cupidity, with betraying it, selling it to their protectors; with no longer having a country save that of their new masters; they load them with contempt and execration. These answer their adversaries that an ill-timed arrogance may deprive the state of an indispensable prop; that it will be time enough to put on airs of independence when it is actually achieved; that in all their discussions, wise men, and especially statesmen, describe a curve, when a right line leads to a precipice; that affairs of state should not be swayed by the self love of individuals; that in policy the most useful is always the most honorable; and, finally, that no one ought to blush when he attains the object of his aim. Such was the language of the more moderate among those called dependents. But others, hurried away by the spirit of party, or wishing to disguise their baseness, exclaimed aloud that the Independents were the enemies of France; that they were friends of England; with her they kept up a trai-

torous correspondence; to her they betrayed the secrets of the
state; that they would fain violate the faith of treaties, and dissolve
the alliance solemnly concluded with the French, in order to listen
to the proposals of England, and throw themselves into her arms.
It is to be observed, in effect, that at this very time, the British
ministers were laboring incessantly to seduce the chiefs of the American government with new offers of peace, even at the acknowledgment of independence. The scope of this conduct might have
been to excite the jealousy of France, or to foment factions in America, or perhaps really to obtain peace and alliance with the United
States.

However it was, these overtures had in part the effect which the
British cabinet probably had expected; they were but too well
seconded by a species of men who find their proper element in confusion; and intestine dissensions agitated every part of the American
continent. Not private citizens only, but the very members of the
government, applied themselves with infinitely more ardor to pull
each other to pieces, than to the discharge of their duties. These
seeds of discord had long been germinating; they developed themselves with still greater rapidity, when Silas Deane returned to the
United States aboard the squadron of the count d'Estaing. At first
commercial agent of America in Europe, he had been one of the
three commissioners who had signed the treaty of alliance at Paris
Secretly irritated at having been recalled, in haste to turn accuser
before being accused himself, and careful to make his court to the
French, he declared every where, and afterwards printed, that the
congress would not hear the report of his mission to Paris; that
they refused to adjust his accounts; that Arthur Lee, one of the three
commissioners, William Lee, American consul in Europe, and their
two brothers, members of congress, kept up a secret correspondence
with England; that they, and all their adherents, endeavored in various ways to disgust the court of France, and especially in opposing
the reimbursement to particular Frenchmen of sums which they
had expended at the commencement of the war in the purchase of
arms and military stores for account of America. That they were
now intriguing to displace Franklin, as they had before attempted to
pull down Washington; that, in a word, they had conspired to
change men and things, and to give another direction to the policy of
the state. The writing which Deane published and distributed with
profusion, in the month of December, 1778, produced a vehement
stir; the spirit of party eagerly seized this new subject of discord
and hatred. The brothers Lee answered with moderation; but
Thomas Paine and William Drayton stepped forward to avenge them

roundly. They retorted upon Deane, that the congress not only consented to hear him, but that they had already heard him, and had notified him that they were ready to give him audience anew; that if they had not passed his accounts, it was for want of verifications; Deane having himself, either through forgetfulness or design, left them behind in France; that if Arthur Lee kept up a correspondence with England, he was sufficiently authorized in it by his character of ambassador; that during his residence at Paris, he had addressed the congress letters incomparably more able, luminous, and fraught with intelligence, than those of his calumniator, who had never written a word of any solidity; that the friendship of a power so generous as France could be better preserved by an erect and noble deportment, than by a servile adulation towards its agents; that if the reimbursement of those Frenchmen who had furnished arms and munitions had not been yet effected, it was because that Deane himself, in concert with the other commissioners of congress, had written that no payment was to be made for these supplies, which were to be considered as the voluntary gifts of zealous friends of America; that no thought had ever been entertained of recalling Franklin, because it was perfectly well known how much the advices furnished by that estimable man, as well as the contracts he had made in France, differed from every thing in the correspondence and operations of Silas Deane; that neither was it forgotten what difference of manners and pretensions existed between those Frenchmen who had treated with Franklin for an engagement in the American service, and those whom Deane had sent out to America; that no one could better judge than himself whether the facts recapitulated were likely to redound to his honor; that, as for the rest, it little became Deane to call up the intrigues, real or supposed, of which Washington had been the object, since himself, when he resided at Paris as agent for the congress, had suggested for serious deliberation, whether it would not be advantageous to confide the supreme command of the American troops to one of the most distinguished generals of Europe, as for example, to prince Ferdinand, or Mareschal de Broglie; that it was right and proper to keep the faith pledged to France, but that it was right and proper also, agreeably to the usage of all states, to hear the propositions, and to receive the overtures, which promised to promote the welfare of the country, from whatever quarter they might come.

The tenor of the paragraphs published by Paine and Drayton was far from being agreeable to Gerard, the minister of France; he noticed with pain the avowal of negotiations kept up with England, and the declaration of a refusal to liquidate the disbursements made by his countrymen. He addressed very energetic complaints to the congress; in order to appease him, that assembly declared that they disapproved the contents of the published memorials, and that they were convinced that the supplies furnished by certain French individuals could not be considered as a gift. The congress had, in truth, been made debtor for them in the accounts presented, whether the intention of those who furnished them had never been to offer them as a mere donative, or that Deane had made them the object of a sordid speculation. Opinions were then much divided on that point. The congress, moreover, renewed the declaration that the United States would never conclude either peace or truce with Great Britain, without the formal and previous consent of their august ally. Thomas Paine requested and obtained leave to resign the office he filled, of secretary of congress for the foreign department. The government either was, or pretended to be dissatisfied with him, for the disclosure he had made, in this discussion, of facts which it would rather have kept still under the veil.

So many elements of discord would perhaps have sufficed to kindle civil war in America, if its inhabitants had been less familiarized with liberty. Their attention was, besides, taken up by two important objects; one was the imminent peril to which the two Carolinas were exposed a short time after, in consequence of the siege of Charleston by sir Henry Clinton; the other, the negotiations opened with Spain, and soon afterwards, the active part she took in the war. The court of Madrid, as we have already seen, glowed with a desire to interfere in the grand quarrel which had just broken out. Besides the mutual hatred which animated the English and Spanish nations, Spain had also in view to humble the odious British arrogance, to recover Gibraltar and Jamaica, and to conquer the *two Floridas, which appeared to her essential to the entire command of the gulf of Mexico.* She was now also stimulated by France, who, not content with representing to her the common interest she had in this war, pressed her and summoned her every day to fulfill the stipulations of the family compact. Meanwhile, particular considerations pointed her to a more circumspect procedure. American independence could scarcely seem to smile upon her entirely, when she reflected on the contagion of example, and her own colonies. Her backwardness to declare herself was also perhaps concerted with France, in order to obtain better conditions from the Americans. The court of Versailles had regretted to find itself constrained to take a decisive step, after the unexpected victory of general Gates, which had started the apprehension that England would consent, for the sake of reconciliation with her colonies, to acknowledge their independence. France would much rather have persisted in her original plan, and stood aloof still for a long time, waiting for the Americans to be reduced to the last extremity, in order to wring from them more advantageous conditions for herself, than those of 'he two treaties of commerce and alliance. But the success of the Americans having baffled her designs, she still had in reserve the chance of making them pay a round price for the accession of Spain. With this drift, she magnified excessively the advantages they might expect from it, in order to extort from their impatience, what precipitation had defeated her of at the time of her own declaration. The ultimate object of all these maneuvers, was to secure to the subjects of France, in the future treaty of peace, the fisheries of Newfoundland, to the exclusion of the citizens of the United States ; and to Spain, the possession of the two Floridas, the exclusive navigation of the Mississippi, with the sovereignty of the regions situated on the left bank of that river, and behind the frontiers of the confederate provinces. Accordingly, to prove to the Americans how strong an interest he took in their cause, and to Europe, according to usage, his ardent desire to preserve peace, the king of Spain offered his mediation. He considered it, moreover, as a justificative measure of the war he was about to undertake, for he was by no means ignorant that England would not accept it. The court of London knew too well that Spain, united to France by the strictest ties, could not be an impartial mediatrix ; it knew also, that mediators of this description always finish with becoming declared enemies. The court of Madrid intending also to establish, as the basis of the negotiation for peace, that Great Britain should treat her colonies as independent, it was not presumable that she would accept a condition which was precisely the principal point in contest. Nevertheless, the marquis d'Almadovar, his catholic majesty's ambassador, presented to the court of London a plan of accommodation, which contained, besides the article above, those which follow. That, in order the more easily to extinguish the flames of war, the crowns of France and of Great Britain should lay down arms and consent to a general truce ; that their respective plenipotentiaries should convene at a place agreed upon, for the purpose of adjusting their differences; that Great Britain should grant a like truce to the American colonies ; that a line of boundary should be drawn, which neither of the belligerent parties might transcend during the armistice ; that both his Britannic majesty and the colonies should send one or more commissioners to the city of Madrid, in order to consent to the preceding conditions, and all such others as might tend to conciliation. To this offer of mediation the British ministers made only evasive and dilatory answers. If they were not disposed to accept it, since it involved the acknowledgment of independence, they avoided also to reject it too ostensibly, as well not to excite the discontent of their nation, as to gain time to open negotiations with the courts of Europe. Their intention was to offer advantageous conditions to France, in order to detach her from America, and to America, in order to detach her from France. And, in case, as they presumed, these negotiations should fail of success, they purposed to use strenuous endeavors with the other powers, in order to excite some movement in Europe against France. They hoped thus to find her so much employment on shore, that she would be obliged to neglect her marine, and that it would of course become an easy task to vanquish it. They conceived also, that when America should see her ally engaged in a new struggle, she would show herself more disposed to enter into an arrangement with England. Such was then the policy of the powers at war, and of those that were inclined to take part therein.

Meanwhile, France and Spain, with a view of obtaining from America the conditions which, since her separation with England, were the main scope of their counsels, notified to the congress, through M. Gerard, the French minister at Philadelphia, the offer of mediation made to the court of London by that of Madrid. He was directed to observe, that the object of all mediation being peace, it was natural to presume that conferences were about to be opened for its negotiation and conclusion. He invited the congress to appoint plenipotentiaries to take part in these negotiations, whether with England or with Spain; he also urged the expediency of their making known the basis on which they were disposed to treat. He added, that he felt it his duty to intimate that circumstances did not permit the United States to carry their pretensions higher than their fortune; that, consequently, it was desirable that they should be moderate in their demands, in order not to furnish England with a pretext for standing out, and that Spain might be enabled to prosecute her mediation to a successful conclusion. ' As to the acknowledgment of American independence,' continued the French minister, ' it is to be expected that Great Britain, out of that pride which sovereigns have, and which it becomes them to have, will manifest an extreme repugnance to making it in form. This case has been provided for in the treaty of alliance, where it is stipulated that its object is to obtain for the United States independence, whether express or implied. France knows, by her own experience, what it costs monarchs to proclaim in formal terms the independence of those they have once governed as subjects Spain, in preceding ages, did but tacitly acknowledge the independence of Holland, aftei a war of thirty years, and not formally till after a resistance of seventy. Up to this very time, the republic of Geneva and the thirteen Swiss Cantons have not as yet been able to obtain from the states of which they made part, an express acknowledgment of their independence and sovereignty. As for the rest, since you enjoy the object of your wishes, you ought to attach very little importance to mere words.' It is to be remarked, that the French minister affected to be much in earnest in his efforts to bring over the Americans to this way of thinking, because he was convinced that they would not adopt it ; and that therefore to induce France and Spain to exact on their behalf an express acknowledgment of independence, they would acquiesce in whatever demands those powers might choose to make.

In order to confirm them the more in the refusal of what he demanded, he took care to remind them that the United States appeared to him, from their situation and the vigor of their resistance, to have higher claims than ever Holland, Geneva, and Switzerland could have made any pretensions to. Fearing, however, the insufficiency of these means to decide the Americans to yield the desired concessions, he proceeded to suggest, that not only was it necessary to enable the mediator by the moderation of their demands to inspire England with pacific dispositions, but that it was moreover expedient to offer the mediator such advantages as might determine him to make common cause with France and America, in case Great Britain should refuse peace. He extolled the power of the triple alliance that was meditated, and represented it as the guaranty of certain triumph. He set forth that though the arms of France and America were indeed capable of resisting those of the enemy, the junction of the forces of Spain could alone render them preponderant, and prevent the catastrophe which might result from a single sinister event; that hitherto the balance had been equal between the two parties, but that a new weight was necessary to make it turn in favor of the Americans. The French minister closed this declaration with a disclosure of the pretensions of his court with respect to the fishery of Newfoundland, and those of Spain relative to the two Floridas, the Mississippi, and the western territory, which now forms the state of Kentucky. The congress deliberated upon these communications. They considered, on the one hand, that the intervention of Spain was very desirable for America; but on the other, that she held it at too high a rate. They consequently felt the utmost repugnance to subscribe to all the concessions which the courts of Versailles and Madrid appeared disposed to wrest from them. Very warm debates ensued upon these different points. All the members consented to guaranty to Spain the possession of the two Floridas, but also refused to grant her the exclusive navigation of the Mississippi; the relinquishment of the western territory was objected to by many, and that of the Newfoundland fishery almost universally, especially on the part of the New England deputies. Beside this extreme diversity of opinions, a powerful motive prevented the Americans from taking any definitive resolution; they had penetrated, that such was the eagerness of the Spaniards to come to blows with the English, that in any event, it could not be long before a rupture must take place between the two nations. In effect the congress consumed so much time in answering, in appointing plenipotentiaries, and in preparing their instructions, that hostilities were already commenced between these powers, not only in Europe, but also in America.

By the beginning of August, don Bernard Galvez, governor of Louisiana, for the king of Spain, had undertaken with success an expedition against the British possessions upon the Mississippi. This news, and still much more, the certain intelligence that the same don Galvez had solemnly proclaimed the independence of the United States at New Orleans, caused the Americans to drop at once all further thought of concession. Notwithstanding the hostilities now commenced between Spain and England, the French minister persisted in maintaining that England manifested pacific dispositions, and that the cabinets of Versailles and Madrid were more than ever animated by the same sentiments. But enlightened by what passed before their eyes, the Americans instructed their plenipotentiary at the court of France, as also the one destined to treat with that of London, to keep steadily in view that the first object of the defensive war waged by the allies, was to establish the independence of the United States; that consequently the preliminary basis of all negotiation with Great Britain must be the acknowledgment of the freedom, independence and sovereignty of the said states, which acknowledgment must be secured and guarantied according to the form and stipulations of the treaty of alliance with his most christian majesty. As to the right of fishery upon the banks of Newfoundland, the Americans insisted that it should be preserved to them, with the clause that if they were disquieted by England in its exercise, France should consider it as case of alliance. They further enjoined their plenipotentiaries to use all possible exertions to obtain from England the cession of Canada and Nova Scotia, in favor of the United States, observing, however, that the rejection of this proposition should not be an obstacle to the re-establishment of peace The idea of this last demand had been suggested by the deputies of Massachusetts, and other provinces of New England. The plenipotentiaries were authorized to agree to a suspension of arms during the continuance of the negotiations, with the reservation, however, that the ally of the United States should likewise consent to it, and that the troops of the enemy should entirely evacuate their territory. Such was the substance of the instructions given to the American plenipotentiaries; as to the rest, they were to be guided by their own wisdom, the laws of the confederation, and the counsels of the court of France.

The war being already actually commenced between Spain and England, the chevalier de la Luzerne, who succeeded M. Gerard at Philadelphia, could no longer urge with the congress the advantages and necessity of the co-operation of the Spanish force, as a motive for their yielding the above mentioned concessions. But he did not omit to place in the strongest light all the benefits which would result to the United States from connecting themselves with the court of Madrid by treaties of commerce and alliance, which should regulate their common and respective interests, whether present or future.

'It is evident,' he said, 'that Spain will display more vigorous efforts against England, when she knows the advantage that is to accrue to herself from a war undertaken chiefly for the utility and interests of the United States. On the other hand, it is no less manifest, how extremely it interests the honor and consolidation of the republic to have its independence formally acknowledged by so great and powerful a monarch as his catholic majesty, and to be united to him by treaties of amity and alliance. An alliance,' he added, 'than which nothing could more gratify his most christian majesty, who, united to the king of Spain by the most sacred ties, and to America by the bonds of the tenderest friendship, could not but desire with ardor to see the most complete and durable harmony established between them.' The French minister expatiated largely upon this subject, adding still other arguments drawn from public law.

All his efforts were vain. The congress saw too clearly that if Spain took part in the war, it was neither out of regard for the interests, nor for the independence of America, which in the present state of things was no longer a matter of doubt, but for her own sake, and particularly to reduce the maritime power of England. Accordingly, they showed themselves little disposed to make new sacrifices. Wishing, however, to testify their desire to form alliance with the king of Spain, they appointed John Jay their minister plenipotentiary to the court of Madrid. His instructions were to endeavor to dispose that court to be satisfied with a mere treaty of amity and commerce with the United States. He was, moreover, directed to declare, that if his catholic majesty entered into the league against Great Britain, the United States would consent that ne should secure for himself the possession of the Floridas; and even, if England gave her consent to it in the treaty of peace, the United States would guaranty him this new acquisition with the condition that they should continue to enjoy the navigation of the Mississippi to the sea.   As to the territory situated on the eastern bank of the river, they declared that it could not be renounced.   The minister of congress was likewise to solicit the king of France, as the chief of the alliance, to employ his mediation in order to accelerate the conclusion of the treaties with Spain.   He was charged with some other demands at the court of Madrid.   But piqued at the refusal of congress to consent to the stipulations which she had most at heart, Spain not only demonstrated on her part a disposition equally unyielding, but after having declared war against Great Britain, she would neither acknowledge the independence of the United States, nor receive nor send ambassadors.   At the same time in which Jay was appointed plenipotentiary to the court of Madrid, John Adams was elected minister plenipotentiary to negotiate a treaty of peace and commerce with England.

Such was, then, the situation of affairs in America.   In Europe they took the direction which had been foreseen by all prudent men, and which was desired even by those who pretended a wish to attain an opposite object.   Spain had completed her maritime armaments; she was arrived at the point where she had purposed to throw off the mask.   She wanted to take an open part in the war; and joining her forces with those of France, to aim such rapid blows at the excessive naval power of England, as should transfer to the Bourbons the scepter of the sea.   She would fain have a plausible pretext to justify her conduct.   She accordingly resolved to renew her offers of mediation at the court of London, and to urge the British government in such a manner, that it should at length be constrained to declare itself the first.   The marquis d'Almodovar, the Spanish minister at London, made, in the month of June, the most pressing instances to the British ministry, in order to extort a definitive answer.   The moment seemed the better chosen, as it was already known that the count d'Orvilliers had sailed from Brest with the whole French armament, and was standing to the south in order to join, near the isle of Cizarga, with the Spanish fleet, which lay, in excellent condition, expecting him in those waters.   The two allied courts felt yet more confirmed in their resolution, when they saw the English marine in no situation to balance their united forces.   Whether from absolute necessity, or from negligence on the part of ministers, it is certain that the armaments of England at this period were very far inferior to her dangers.

She answered, nevertheless, that she could not admit the condition
of independence, even with the modifications proposed by Spain.
The Spanish minister then departed from London, after having delivered a declaration to lord Weymouth, secretary of state. This
rescript recapitulated, beside the rejection of the mediation, several
other motives of war, such as insults offered at sea to the Spanish
flag, hostile incursions upon the lands of the king, instigations to the
savages to infest the Spanish subjects of Louisiana, the violation of
the rights of his catholic majesty in the bay of Honduras, and other
like grievances. The court of London answered by a counter declaration, in which it endeavored, as usual, to destroy all the assertions of that of Madrid. The king of England recalled lord Grant-
ham, his ambassador in Spain. He afterwards issued a proclamation of reprisals on that power, and another regulating the distribu-
tion of prizes. At the same time, France, as the preponderant and
leading part of the alliance, published a manifesto, in which she laid
before the eyes of Europe the motives which had constrained the
two allied courts to take up arms.

These motives, detailed at great length, may be reduced to the
following points ; the necessity of avenging injuries received, and
the desire, certainly sincere, to put down the tyrannical empire which
England had usurped, and pretended to maintain upon the ocean.
The king of Spain likewise published different official papers. Two
royal cedulas demonstrated to the nation the necessity and justice
of the war. They were followed by a very prolix manifesto, which
advanced a hundred causes of rupture with Great Britain ; the
greater part had been already announced in the declaration of the
marquis d'Almodovar. It was added in this, and represented as a
direct outrage, that at the very time when the British ministers rejected the propositions openly made by Spain, as mediatrix, they
had employed secret agents to make the most alluring offers to the
court of France, if she would abandon the colonies and conclude a
separate peace with England. ' At the same epoch,' said the manifesto, ' the British cabinet had clandestinely dispatched another agent
to doctor Franklin at Paris. Divers propositions were made to that
minister, in order to detach the Americans from France, and bring
them to an arrangement with Great Britain. The British government offers them conditions not only similar to those it has disdained
and rejected when they proceeded from the part of his catholic majesty, but much more favorable still.' The first wrongs specified,
that is, the insults on the Spanish flag, the hostile incursions upon
the king's territory, and the unjust decrees of courts of admiralty,
might have obtained a sufficient reparation, if the two parties had

been at that time less animated with enmity towards each other. As to the reproach of duplicity imputed to the British ministers with respect to their conduct during the discussions of the mediation, if the historian cannot positively applaud them, he will find at least that it is difficult to blame them for it, and still more so to discover in it a sufficient ground of war. In effect, these political wiles, far from being new or extraordinary, are but too frequent; all statesmen, and especially those who employ them, consider such means, if not honorable, at least allowable for attaining their ends. But, as we have already observed, the primary and capital motive, to which all the others did little more than serve as a veil, was the wish to destroy the maritime superiority of England. The king of Spain even made the avowal of it, herein also imitating the candor of the king of France. He formally declared in his manifesto, that in order to obtain a durable peace, it was necessary to set bounds to the immoderate power of England by sea, and to demonstrate the falsity of those principles upon which she founded her usurpation. He concluded with observing, that the other maritime powers, and all the nations of the universe, were interested in the triumph of so equitable a cause. This argument was no doubt as just as it was noble; but it would have been more honorable still, if the tyrannical domination of England, about which so much noise was then made, had not been, not only peaceably tolerated for a long series of years, but even formally acknowledged. The king of Great Britain replied with another manifesto, wherein no little address was displayed in refuting the assertions of the two kings, his enemies. It closed with the most energetic, but the most ordinary protestations of his regard for humanity. Since these pompous declamations have been brought into use between the governments of civilized nations, is it found that wars are become less frequent, or less destructive?

While the two belligerent parties were endeavoring to justify their conduct in the sight of the universe, while each of the kings was protesting that he had not been the first disturber of peace, the fleets of France and Spain presented themselves with formidable parade upon the coasts of Great Britain. They consisted of sixty-six ships of the line, comprehending a Spaniard of one hundred and fourteen guns, the San Trinidad, two Frenchmen of one hundred and ten, and one hundred and four, the *Bretagne* and the *Ville de Paris*, eight others of eighty, and fifteen of seventy-four; the rest of less force. This immense armada was followed by a cloud of frigates, corvettes, cutters, and fire ships. It was commanded in chief by the count d'Orvilliers, who mounted the Bretagne; the vanguard was under the conduct of the count de Guichen, and the rear

under the conduct of don Gaston. The vanguard was itself preceded by a light squadron commanded by M. de la Touche Tre-
ville, and composed of five swift sailing ships, and all the frigates
which were not attached to the first divisions. The object of this squadron was to discover and announce whatever should appear at sea.
Finally, the armament was followed by another squadron of observa-
tion, composed of sixteen ships of the line, at the orders of don Lewis
de Cordova. The design of the allies was, according to appearances, to make a descent upon that part of the coasts of Great
Britain which they should find the most conveniently accessible.
Every thing seemed to conspire in their favor; even the importance
of the enterprise, the immensity of their forces, the defenseless condition of Ireland, the inferiority of the British marine, the weakness
of the regular troops that remained for the defense of England, since
the greater part had been sent to America and the West Indies.
Beside this fleet, one of the most tremendous which the ocean had
ever borne, three hundred transports were prepared at Havre de
Grace, St. Malo, and other ports on that coast. All was in movement in the northern provinces of France. Upwards of forty thousand men lined the coasts of Normandy and Britanny; many other
regiments were on the march to join them from other parts of the
kingdom. The king appointed the generals who were to conduct
the expedition. The troops, who were already assembled upon the
coasts that looked towards England, daily exercised themselves in
the various maneuvers of embarkation and debarkation. Each
soldier manifested the most eager desire to set foot on the opposite
shore, in order to combat and prostrate an ancient rival. An artillery as numerous as well served, was attached to this army; five
thousand grenadiers, the flower of the French troops, had been
drawn from all the regiments, to form the vanguard, and strike the
first blows.

England was seasonably apprised of the preparations of France,
and the invasion with which she was menaced. The ministers had
promptly directed all the measures of defense, which the shortness
of time and the present state of the kingdom admitted; they had
assembled thirty-eight ships of the line, under the command of admiral sir Charles Hardy, and had sent him to cruise in the Bay of Biscay, in order, if still possible, to prevent the junction of the two
hostile fleets. It is difficult to comprehend, that armaments which
occupied so vast an extent of sea, and whose light squadrons were
reciprocally on the look out, should not have encountered, or come
to any knowledge the one of the other. The king of England issued
a proclamation, informing his subjects that the enemy threatened to

invade the kingdom.   The officers in command upon the coasts were
ordered to stand on the alert, and at the first appearance of danger to
remove the cattle and provisions to a proper distance.   The militia
exercised continually in arms, and held themselves in readiness to
march to the places of debarkation.   The royal guards themselves
expected every moment the order to march.   All minds were
strongly excited at the danger of the country ; but amidst the sentiments of fear and hope which agitated them, the resolution to resist
valiantly was general.

Meanwhile, the combined fleet, which had been detained a long
time by calms at the entrance of the channel, all at once made its
appearance there, the fifteenth of August ; it presented itself before
Plymouth with dread display.   The alarm was immediately spread
among the inhabitants of the coasts ; the militia flew to their post ;
the guards were doubled at the arsenals of Plymouth and Portsmouth.
The bank in the latter town was closed ; all commerce was suspended.   From all parts of the coast of Cornwall, whole families were
seen flying towards the inland countries with their most valuable
effects.   A new incident added to the universal panic.   The Ardent
ship of the line, of sixty-four guns, which had sailed from Portsmouth, in order to join the fleet of Admiral Hardy, fell into the hands
of the French in view of Plymouth.   During this time the British
admiral was standing off and on near the mouth of the channel ; his
inferiority, and the position of the enemy, not permitting him to
bring succor to his country, amidst the perils that menaced it.   But
what men could not do, was operated by chance.   At the moment
when the success of this great enterprise was going to be decided,
all at once there sprung up a violent gale from the northeast, which
forced the combined fleet to quit the channel for the open sea.   The
gale having abated, it displayed itself anew from the Lands End and
the Scilly islands to the chops of the channel, with intent to intercept admiral Hardy, and to prevent his retreat into the ports of England.   Nevertheless, he profited with so much ability of a favorable
wind, that on the thirty-first of August he made good his entrance
into the channel in full view of the allies, who could not hinder him.
His design was, to entice them up to the narrowest part of the strait,
where the superiority of numbers would avail them little, and the
advantage of position would thus compensate the inequality of forces.
The allies followed him as far as Plymouth.   Each of the hostile
fleets preserved the best order ; the British, to avoid being approached till after having arrived at the desirable point, and to be always
prepared to fall upon such of the enemy's vessels as should chase
them too near ; the French and Spaniards, to keep together, and to

gain Plymouth before the enemy. But admiral Hardy having eluded
all the projects of his adversary, the count d'Orvilliers decided to
retire from the coasts of England, and return to Brest. His retreat
was attributed at the time to several causes, such as the continued
prevalence of east winds, the want of provisions, the proximity of
the equinox, and the great sickness and mortality among his crews,
by which some of the ships were totally disabled.

Such was the issue of an expedition which seemed to portend the
downfall of a most powerful empire. If there never had been so
great a naval force assembled on the seas, so never were effects less
answerable to appearances. Enfeebled by the loss of more than
five thousand sailors, victims of the epidemic, the combined fleet
could attempt no enterprise during the rest of the campaign. It
followed that the weaker gathered those fruits which the stronger
might reasonably have expected. Not only the numerous fleets
of British merchantmen, loaded with the riches of the two Indies,
arrived happily in the ports of Great Britain, but the squadron of
Hardy put to sea again, and captured a multitude of French and
Spanish vessels. Europe was astonished; she had not expected
that so many preparations and such mighty efforts were to end in this
wise. The glory of the British marine thus acquired a new luster.
The allies had, assuredly, shown no want either of ability or of
valor; but the greater part of men judge of merit by success, and
the arms of the enemies of England lost much of their splendor.
But whatever might be the causes which prevented the great nava.
armaments of the belligerent powers from coming to a decisive action, a few days after their retreat several partial combats were engaged, in which the French, the English, and the Americans seemed
to vie for the palm of deep and desperate valor. The count d'Orvilliers had sent out from Brest, to observe the movements of the
British fleet, the frigate Surveillante, commanded by the chevalier
du Couedic, and the cutter Expedition, at the orders of the viscount
de Roquefeuil. These two vessels fell in, near the isle of Ouessant,
with the British frigate Quebec, captain Farmer, accompanied also
by a sloop called the Rambler. The two parties immediately engaged with fury. The forces, skill, and bravery being equal on botn
sides, the action lasted three hours and a half. The frigates fought
so close that several times their yards got entangled. Their artillery
had already made a frightful ravage; the decks were covered with
dead and wounded, their masts shivered and shot away; they could
no longer be steered. Nor one nor other, however, seemed disposed
to retire or surrender. The French captain received a wound in
the head, and fainted; but on recovering sense, he immediately re-

sumed the command. Two fresh wounds in the belly could not
constrain him to give over ; on the contrary he gave orders for boarding. Captain Farmer displayed, on his part, an invincible courage.
To smooth the way for boarding, the French threw a great quantity
of grenades aboard the Quebec. Her sails took fire ; the flames
spread, and soon caught other parts of the ship. The English exerted themselves to extinguish them, and obstinately refused to strike.
The chevalier du Couedic, to avoid the combustion, was forced to
think of retiring, which he with difficulty accomplished. His bowsprit got embarrassed with the rigging of the enemy. At length
the fire took the magazine of the British frigate, and she blew up,
with her colors waving to the last.

The French captain, with an example of humanity that cannot be
honored enough, devoted all his cares to saving the greatest possible
number of his enemies, who, to escape the flames, threw themselves
headlong into the sea. Only forty-three of them could be rescued
from the waves, the sole survivors of three hundred men who composed the company of the Quebec. Captain Farmer was swallowed
up with the wreck of his ship. The French frigate was unable to
move ; the cutter Expedition disengaged herself from the Rambler,
which she had combated with advantage, in order to succor the
Surveillante. She took her in tow, and brought her the following
day into the port of Brest. The French government, faithful to
its own examples, and those of civilized nations, sent free to England the forty-three Englishmen, not willing to retain those prisoners, who, in the same day, had escaped the fury of men, cannon,
fire and water. The French had forty killed and a hundred wounded. The king promoted the chevalier du Couedic to the rank of
captain of a ship. But he could not long enjoy the glorious reputation which his valor and humanity had acquired him ; his wounds
proved mortal three days after the engagement. He was deeply
regretted in France ; his name was pronounced with distinction
throughout Europe, but no where with warmer eulogium than in
England.

A few days before, the coasts of Great Britain had witnessed a
combat no less sanguinary, and no less honorable for the two parties.
Paul Jones, a Scotchman by birth, but engaged in the service of the
United States, had established his cruise at first in the seas of Ireland, and afterwards in those of Scotland, where he was waiting for
an opportunity to make some prize, or, according to his practice, to
land upon some point of the coast in order to sack the country.
His flotilla was composed of the *Bonhomme Richard*, of forty guns,
the Alliance, of thirty-six, both American ships ; the Pallas, a French

frigate of thirty-two, in the pay of congress, with two other smaller vessels. He fell in with a British merchant fleet, on its return from the Baltic, convoyed by captain Pearson, with the frigate Serapis, of forty-four guns, and the Countess of Scarborough, of twenty.

Pearson had no sooner perceived Jones, than he bore down to engage him, while the merchantmen endeavored to gain the coast. The American flotilla formed to receive him. The two enemies joined battle at about seven in the evening, with great resolution, and the conflict was supported on both sides with equal valor. The Serapis had the advantage of metal and maneuver; to obviate which, Jones took the resolution to fight her closer. He advanced till the two frigates were engaged yard to yard, and their sides so near that the muzzles of their guns came in contact. In this position they continued to fight from eight in the evening till ten, with an audacity bordering on frenzy. But the artillery of the Americans was no longer capable of producing much effect. The Richard, having received several heavy shot between wind and water, could now make no use whatever of her lower batteries, and two or three of her upper guns had burst, to the destruction of those who served them. Jones, at length, had only three left that could be worked, and he employed them against the masts of the hostile frigate. Seeing the little impression made by chain shot, he resorted to another mode of attack. He threw a vast quantity of grenades and fire works on board the British frigate. But his own now admitted the water on all sides, and threatened every moment to go to the bottom. Some of his officers, having perceived it, asked him if he would surrender? ' No,' he answered them in a tremendous tone, and continued to push the grenades. The Serapis was already on fire in several places; the English could with difficulty extinguish the flames. Finally, they caught a cartridge, which, in an instant, fired all the others with a horrible explosion. All who stood near the helm were killed, and all the cannon of that part were dismounted. Meanwhile, Pearson was not disheartened; he ordered his people to board. Paul Jones prepared himself to repulse them. The English, in jumping on board him, found the Americans ready to receive them on the point of their pikes; they made the best of their way back to their own vessel. But during this interval, the fire had communicated itself from the Serapis to the Bonhomme Richard, and both were a prey to the flames. No peril could shake these desperate men. The night was dark, the combatants could no longer see each other but by the blaze of the conflagration, and through dense volumes of smoke, while the sea was illuminated afar. At this moment, the American frigate Alliance came up. Amidst the confusion

she discharged her broadside into the Richard, and killed a part of
her remaining defenders. As soon as she discovered her mistake,
she fell with augmented fury upon the Serapis. Then the valiant
Englishman, seeing a great part of his crew either killed or disabled,
his artillery dismounted, his vessel dismasted, and quite enveloped
in flames, surrendered. All joined to extinguish the fire, and at
length it was accomplished. The efforts made to stop the numerous leaks of the Richard proved less fortunate; she sunk the next
morning. Out of three hundred and seventy-five men that were
aboard that vessel, three hundred were killed or wounded. The
English had but forty-nine killed, and their wounded amounted to
no more than sixty-eight. History, perhaps, offers no example of
an action more fierce, obstinate and sanguinary. During this time
the Pallas had attacked the Countess of Scarborough, and had captured
her, not, however, without a stubborn resistance. After a victory so
hard earned, so deplorable, Jones wandered with his shattered vessels for some days, at the mercy of the winds in the North sea. He
finally made his way good, on the sixth of October, into the waters
of the Texel.

The events which we have just related are all that claim notice in
the latter months of 1779, after the accession of Spain to the alliance formed against England. But at the commencement of the
following year, other powers manifested dispositions which menaced
that state with new enemies, or at least with exceedingly dubious
friends.

1780. Ever since the commencement of the war, the Dutch had
carried on privately a very lucrative commerce; they conveyed into
the ports of France ship timber, as well as all sorts of military, and
especially naval, stores. The English were apprised of it, and the
British government had often complained of it, in strong terms, to the
States-General, not only as contrary to the rules which England was
accustomed to observe in time of war, with respect to the commerce
of neutrals, and which themselves either tacitly or expressly acknowledged, but also as a violation of the treaties of commerce and alliance existing between the two nations. The same government had
also remonstrated against the protection granted in Holland to French
and American privateers. The States-General answered only by
disavowal, or evasive explanations. But about the beginning of January, intelligence was received in England, that a numerous convoy of
Dutch vessels, laden with naval stores for account of France, was
already at sea, and that, in order to escape the vigilance of the British cruisers, this fleet had placed itself under the protection of the

count de Byland, who, with a squadron of ships of the line and frigates, convoyed another merchant fleet bound for the Mediterranean.
The British admiralty dispatched captain Fielding, with a sufficient
number of ships, to examine the convoy, and to seize any vessels
containing contraband articles. The British squadron having met
that of Holland, captain Fielding requested permission to visit the
merchant ships. It was refused him. This notwithstanding, he
dispatched his boats for that purpose, which were fired at, and prevented from executing their orders by the Dutch. Upon this, the
Englishman fired a shot ahead of the Dutch admiral; it was answered by a broadside; and count Byland, having received Fielding's in
return, and being in no condition of force to pursue the contest further, then struck his colors. Most of the Dutch vessels that were
in the predicament which occasioned the contest, had already, by
pushing close to the shore, escaped the danger, and proceeded without interruption to the French ports. The others were seized. The
Englishman then informed the Dutch admiral that he was at liberty
to hoist his colors and prosecute his voyage. He hoisted his colors
indeed; but he refused to separate from any part of his convoy; and
he accordingly, with the whole of the fleet, which was seized, accompanied the British squadron to Spithead. The ships and their cargoes were confiscated as contraband. This intelligence excited a
violent clamor in Holland. The Dutch were at this time divided in
two parties, one of which held for France, and the other for England.
All those who belonged to the first were exceedingly indignant; they
exclaimed that no consideration should induce them to endure
patiently so daring an outrage. Even the partisans of the English
could not venture to justify their conduct. It was easy to foresee
that this incident was about to produce a rupture. Far from fearing, the British government wished it; it preferred an open war to
the clandestine assistance which Holland was lending to France.
It had, besides, already fixed a hankering eye upon the Dutch riches,
which, in the security of peace, were spread over the seas, or were
amassed, without defense, in distant islands. Moreover, the States-
General had made no preparation for war, and it was to be supposed
that they could not very suddenly enter the field.

This event, the instigations of France, the disposition to profit of
the critical situation of Great Britain, at that time assailed by so many
powerful enemies, and especially the desire to liberate the commerce
of neutrals from British vexations, gave origin to that league of the
states of the north, known by the name of the *Armed Neutrality*.
It had, if not for author, at least for chief, the empress of Russia, Cath-

arine II., who was immediately joined by the kings of Sweden and Denmark. The bases of this confederacy were, that neutral vessels might freely navigate from one port to another, even upon the coasts of belligerent powers; that all effects appertaining to one of these powers, become free so soon as they are on board a neutral vessel, except such articles as by a prior treaty should have been declared contraband; that to determine what articles were to be considered contraband, the empress of Russia referred to the tenth and eleventh articles of her treaty with Great Britain, the obligations of which were to be extended to all the other belligerent powers; that to specify what ports were to be deemed blockaded, it was agreed that those only should be accounted as such, before which there should be stationed a sufficient number of enemy ships to render their entrance perilous; finally, that the preceding principles should serve as rules in judicial proceedings, and in sentences to be pronounced respecting the legality of prizes. To command respect for this confederation, the three allied courts agreed, that each of them should keep a part of its naval force equipped, and stationed so as to form an uninterrupted chain of ships prepared to protect their common trade, and to afford each other mutual support and succor. They also agreed, that when any vessel whatever should have shown by its papers that it was not carrier of any contraband article, it might place itself under the escort of ships of war, which should prevent its being stopped, or diverted from its destination. This article, which ascribed to the state interested, or to its allies, the right of judging of the nature of cargoes with respect to contraband, appeared to exclude the right of visit, so strenuously claimed by England; against whom, notwithstanding the general terms that were employed, it was manifest that all this display of maritime force was directed. The allies accompanied the foregoing stipulations with professions of the most generous sentiments; they declared that they were armed for the defense of the rights of nature and of nations; for the liberty of the human race, and for the prosperity of Europe in particular. In effect, the European nations, with the exception of the English, manifested an extreme satisfaction with this new plan of the northern powers; the wisdom and magnanimity of Catharine II. became the object of universal encomium; so universal was the hatred which the maritime vexations of England had excited against that power! The articles of the armed neutrality were communicated to all the European states, especially to France, Spain, Holland, England, and Portugal, with invitation to accede to them. The courts of Versailles and Madrid, eager to profit of the circumstance to sow the seeds of division be-

tween Great Britain and neutrals, hastened to address their felicitations to the empress of Russia, and to answer that they were ready
not only to join the confederacy, but that they had long before given
their admirals and sea officers such instructions that the principles of
the armed neutrality were already in force as to them.   They added,
that equity had directed them to those very measures which were now
proclaimed by the confederate powers of the north.   The court of
Lisbon, accustomed to an excessive condescension towards England, declined the alliance.   The States-General of Holland deliberated upon the course they had to pursue.   The British ministers,
either hoping or fearing what was to happen, or in order to constrain
them to declare themselves, had already required them to furnish to
England the subsidies stipulated by the treaty of alliance.   The
Dutch alledged the inevitable tardiness of their deliberations; the
truth was, they were determined to give nothing.   The cabinet of St.
James then took a resolution calculated to compel them to a decision, and to prevent their joining the northern confederacy.   It gave
them to understand, that notwithstanding the number and power of
its enemies, it was resolved to proceed to the last extremities with
the Dutch nation, unless it adhered to the ancient system of neutrality.   Accordingly the king of Great Britain issued a proclamation,
purporting that the non-performance of the States-General with respect to the succors stipulated by the treaty of alliance, was to be
considered as a violation of that treaty ; that they had thereby fallen
from those privileges which they derived only from the alliance ; and
that the subjects of the United Provinces were, therefore, hencefor-
ward to be considered upon the same footing with those of other
neutral states not allied.   By this step the British king, even before
his demand had been expressly rejected, freed himself from the obligations of the treaty of alliance.   He hoped, by this vigorous proce
dure, so to intimidate the Dutch, that they would decline entering into
the almost universal combination of Europe against the maritime pretensions of England.   His expectations were much disappointed.
The French party possessed a decided preponderance in the republic, particularly in the most influential provinces, such as Holland and
West Friesland.   The impression also produced by the insult offered
Byland, was too recent; hence, after long and frequent debates, it
was voted, with unanimity of provinces, that the subsidies to England
should not be paid ; moreover, that the escort of ships of war should
be given to the merchantmen of the republic, with the exception
only of those which, according to the stipulations of former treaties,
might be deemed contraband.   It was further decreed, that the in-

vitation of the empress of Russia should be accepted with gratitude, and that a negotiation for that purpose should be opened with prince Gallitzin, her majesty's envoy extraordinary to the States-General.

Already surrounded with enemies, and seeing Russia waver, whose power and alliance demanded a serious attention, England, without consenting to admit the principles of the armed neutrality, answered by vague generalities, which manifested, at least, a desire to preserve peace. Meanwhile, amidst the open or covert perils against which she had to defend herself, she not only betrayed no symptoms of discouragement, but even discovered a determination to prosecute the war with vigor upon the American continent. The only change which took place in her plans, as we have already seen, was to leave merely sufficient garrisons in New York, and to direct all her efforts against the southern provinces. Accordingly, to enable Clinton to attack the Carolinas, admiral Arbuthnot had set sail for America, in the month of May, with a fleet of ships of war and upwards of four hundred transports. But soon after his departure from the coasts of England, he received intelligence that the French, under the conduct of the prince of Nassau, had attacked the isle of Jersey, situated near the coasts of Normandy. Thinking it better to conform to the empire of circumstances, than to his instructions, he sent back his convoy into Torbay, and repaired with his squadron to the relief of Jersey. The attempt of the French miscarried. The admiral resumed his original route. But such were the obstacles that ensued this retardment, that he lost much time in getting out of the channel, and gaining sea room to shape his course for America; so that it was late in August before he arrived at New York. The English, at first, however, made no movement, because they were inhibited by the count d'Estaing, at that time engaged in the siege of Savannah. Finally, on intelligence of the issue of that enterprise, and the departure of the French admiral from the coasts of America, Clinton had embarked with seven thousand men, under convoy of Arbuthnot, upon the expedition of South Carolina.

England intended not only to carry on the war with energy upon the American continent, and to defend her possession in the West Indies, but she even projected conquests in this quarter, if the occasion should present itself. The ministers accordingly resolved to send to those islands a considerable re-inforcement, both of ships and troops, under the conduct of admiral Rodney, a man in whom the government, and even the whole British nation, had reposed extreme confidence. It appeared the more essential to dispatch these succors to the West Indies, as the French were preparing on their part to pass thither a formidable re-inforcement under the count de Guichen. But before admiral Rodney had put to sea, it was deemed expedient to employ him in a more important expedition. Spain had commenced hostilities by laying close siege and blockade to the fortress of Gibraltar. The blockade was confided to admiral don Barcelo, a seaman of great vigilance. He exerted his utmost diligence to prevent any sort of supplies from finding their way into the place. The garrison already began to suffer severely from scarcity. They could not even hope to receive provision from the neighboring coasts, by means of light boats which might have eluded the watchfulness of the Spaniards; for the inhabitants of the Barbary shores, and especially the emperor of Morocco, had declared themselves for Spain, as soon as they ascertained the inferiority of the English in the Mediterranean. There remained, therefore, no other way of re-victualing the place but from England itself, and the convoy destined for this purpose required a formidable escort. Rodney was charged with this enterprise. He departed from the British coasts in the first days of the year, with a fleet of twenty-one sail of the line, and a considerable number of provision vessels. Fortune favored his first efforts. He had only been a few days at sea, when he fell in with a convoy of fifteen Spanish merchantmen, bound from St. Sebastian to Cadiz, under the guard of the Guipuscoa, a new ship of sixty-four guns, of four frigates from thirty-two to twenty-six, and of two smaller vessels. Rodney gave chase, and took the whole fleet. The capture was the more fortunate, as the greater part of the vessels were loaded with wheat, flour, and other sorts of provision; and the remainder with bale goods and naval stores. The former he conveyed to Gibraltar, and the latter he sent back to England, where the naval stores were much wanted. But this was only the prelude to greater and more brilliant success. On the sixteenth of January, admiral Rodney fell in, off cape St. Vincent, with a Spanish squadron of eleven ships of the line, under the command of don Juan Langara. The Spanish admiral, if he had chosen, might have avoided the encounter of a force so prodigously superior to his own. But the moment he descried the enemy's sails from his mast head, instead of sending out his frigates to reconnoiter, and falling back upon a port, he immediately formed his ships in order of battle. When, on the near approach of the English, he became certain of their superiority, he endeavored to withdraw, but it was already too late. Admiral Rodney had given the signal for a general chase, with orders to engage as the ships came up in rotation; taking at the same time the lee gage, to prevent the enemy's retreat into their own ports. The English ships so much outsailed the Spanish, that by four in the evening the headmost had come up with them, and began to engage ; their fire was returned with great spirit and resolution by the Spaniards. The night was dark, tempestuous and dismal; the proximity of the shoals of St. Lucar rendered the scene more terrible. Early in the action the Spanish ship San Domingo, of seventy guns and six hundred men, blew up, and all on board perished. The action and pursuit continued until two in the morning. The Spanish admiral's ship, the Phœnix, of eighty guns, with three others of seventy, were taken and carried safely into Gibraltar. The San Eugenio and San Julian had also surrendered to the English, who had shifted their officers, and put a certain number of British seamen on board each of them. But the sea being rough, the night tempestuous, and the breakers very near, the English officers, having no pilots that knew the Spanish coast, placed themselves at the discretion of their prisoners, who, from vanquished becoming victors, carried the two ships into the port of Cadiz. Two other ships of the line and two frigates, all greatly damaged, escaped into the same port. The following day the English had great difficulty in extricating their fleet from the shoals, and getting back into deep water. Don Juan de Langara had been wounded severely.

Admiral Rodney hastened to profit of his victory ; he entered Gibraltar. In a short time he deposited there all the supplies he had brought ; provision became so abundant that the fortress found itself in a situation to endure a long siege without further recruit. After having accomplished, with equal utility to his country and glory to himself, the orders of his court, Rodney proceeded, about the middle of February, with a part of his force, for the West Indies. He left the rest of his fleet with the Spanish prizes on their way to England, under the conduct of rear-admiral Digby. Fortune, who had shown herself so propitious to the English, seemed disposed to serve them still on their return. They perceived at a great distance a squadron consisting of several French ships of different sizes. It was a convoy bound to the Isle of France, under the protection of the Proteus and Ajax, both of sixty-four guns, and of the frigate la Charmante. The viscount du Chilleau commanded the whole. As soon as he discovered the English, he made a signal to the Ajax and the bulk of the convoy to make their escape by the rear. As to himself, he rallied about the Proteus, the frigate, and some smaller vessels, in order to take up the attention of the enemy. His stratagem succeeded. Rear-admiral Digby gave no heed to the Ajax, and the

greater part of the convoy which retired under her escort; he was
fully occupied in pursuit of the Proteus, which sailed with such
celerity that she had little to fear ; but unluckily, she carried away
some of her spars, which so retarded her progress that she fell into
the hands of the English, together with three transports. Such was
the success of Rodney's expedition to Gibraltar. It was celebrated
in England by unusual rejoicings, as well on account of its real importance, as because it was the first good news which had arrived
for so long a time. The parliament voted public thanks to George
Rodney.

Thus England, while she defended herself, on the one hand,
against her enemies in Europe, prepared herself, on the other, to
attack at once the republicans upon the American continent, and the
French and Spaniards in the West Indies. Her resolution in the
midst of so many perils, and such powerful foes, became the object
of universal admiration. Her constancy was compared to that of
Louis XIV., who nobly faced the coalition of all Europe against him.
She was declared to imitate the still more recent example of Frederic the Great, who had withstood all the efforts of the most formidable confederacy. Even those who had the most openly blamed the
conduct of the British government towards its colonies, were now
the very men who most extolled her present magnanimity. But
thinking men better appreciated the truth ; if they commended the
firmness of the British monarch, they neither compared him to Louis
XIV. nor yet to Frederic the Great. They reflected that England,
being an island, cannot, without extreme difficulty, be attacked in its
interior parts, and in the very elements of its force ; and that naval
battles are never so decisive as those of land. It cannot be denied,
however, that the ardor and intrepidity of the British nation seemed
to increase with all the dangers of its position. The most formidable
antagonists of the ministry suspended their attacks, in order to devote
themselves exclusively to the necessities of the state. ' Let us first
triumph abroad,' they exclaimed ; ' we will then settle this controversy between ourselves.' In the country, as in the most opulent
cities, a multitude of private individuals engaged to advance large
sums in order to levy and organize troops. Not private subjects
only, but political and commercial bodies vied in promptness to offer
the state their voluntary contributions. The East India Company
presented the government with three ships of seventy-four guns, and
a sum sufficient to raise and maintain six thousand seamen. Extraordinary bounties were given to those who presented themselves to
serve the king by sea or land. This lure, together with the love

of country and hatred for the French and Spaniards, drew sailors to the ships in multitudes; upon the whole surface of the kingdom the militia were seen forming themselves to the exercise of arms In a word, all Great Britain was in motion to combat the Bourbons. The people of Europe, who had thought at first that she would find it difficult to resist the formidable forces which that house had marshaled for her destruction, began to believe that so much courage and firmness might be crowned with victory, or at least render the struggle still for a long time dubious, and consistent with her safety.

END OF BOOK TWELFTH.

BOOK THIRTEENTH.

1780. I HAVE now to describe an obstinate war, remarkable for its numerous encounters and variety of success, and one which, perhaps, more than any other, has demonstrated how uncertain is the fate of arms, how inconstant the favor of fortune, and with what pertinacity the human mind can arm itself in pursuit of that whereon it has fixed its desires. Victory often produced the effects of defeat, and defeat those of victory ; the victors frequently became the vanquished, the vanquished the victors. In little actions was exhibited great valor ; and the prosperous or unfortunate efforts of a handful of combatants had sometimes more important consequences than in Europe attend those terrible battles, where valiant and powerful nations rush to the shock of arms. The Carolinas saw no cessation of this fierce conflict, till by numberless reverses the cause of Great Britain began to be considered altogether hopeless upon the American continent.

Sir Henry Clinton, as we have related in the preceding book, had departed from the state of New York for the expedition of the Carolinas ; the first object of it was the conquest of Charleston, the reduction of which, it was calculated, would involve that of the entire province. He took with him seven to eight thousand men, English, Hessians and loyalists. Among them was found a corps of excellent cavalry, a species of force very essential to the success of operations in open and flat countries. Clinton had likewise taken care to fill his transports with an immense quantity of military stores and provision. The English moved towards their object, animated with extreme ardor and confidence of victory. The winds and sea were at first highly favorable ; but there afterwards arose a most violent tempest, which dispersed the whole fleet, and greatly damaged the most of the vessels. Some arrived about the last of January at Tybee, in Georgia ; others were intercepted by the Americans. One transport foundered, with all its lading ; the horses, both artillery and troop, that were on board, nearly all perished. These losses, distressing at any time, were grievous and next to irreparable, under the present circumstances. They, moreover, so retarded the enterprise of Charleston, that the Americans had time to put that place in a state of defense.

All the dispersed corps at length re-assembled in Georgia. The victorious troops of Savannah received those of Clinton with a high flush of spirits ; all exerted themselves with emulation to remedy the disasters sustained in the passage. When all their preparations were completed, that is, on the tenth of February, they set sail in the transports, under convoy of some ships of war. Favored by the winds, they soon reached the mouth of North Edisto, a river which empties itself into the sea at a short distance from the Isle of St. John upon the coast of South Carolina. After having reconnoitered the places and passed the bar, the British army landed, and took possession first of the above mentioned island, and next, that of James, which stretches to the south of Charleston harbor. It afterwards, by throwing a bridge over Wappoo Cut, extended its posts on the main land to the banks of Ashley river, which washes the walls of Charleston. From Wappoo Cut it was intended to pass the troops in galleys and flat boats to the left bank of the Ashley, upon which Charleston stands. But the delays occasioned by the events of the passage having given the Americans time to erect new fortifications, and to re-inforce the garrison, Clinton determined not to undertake the siege till after having drawn a re-inforcement from general Prevost, stationed at Savannah, whom he accordingly directed to send him twelve hundred men, including the greatest number of cavalry possible. He had likewise written to Knyphausen, who, after his departure, commanded in the state of New York, to forward him, with all expedition, re-inforcements and munitions. A few days after, general Patterson joined him with the troops from Georgia, after having endured excessive fatigues, and surmounted the numerous obstacles thrown in his way, not only by swoln rivers and miry roads, but also by the enemy, whose light detachments nad hung on his left flank from Savannah to far within the frontiers of Carolina. Meanwhile, Clinton intrenched himself upon the banks of the Ashley and of the adjacent arms of the sea, in order to se cure his communications with the fleet. During this interval colonel Tarleton, of whom there will be frequent mention in the course of this history, an officer of cavalry, as skillful as enterprising, had repaired to the fertile island of Port Royal, where, employing money with the disaffected and force with the patriots, he spared no exertions for the acquisition of horses to replace those lost in the passage. If he could not collect as many as the exigencies of the service demanded, yet the success much surpassed his expectations. Thus, about the last of March, every thing was in preparation for commencing the siege of Charleston ; the British army was separated from the place only by the waters of the river Ashley.

On the other hand, the Americans had omitted none of those preparations, whether civil or military, which they deemed the most suitable for a vigorous defense ; although, in truth, it had not been in their power to effect all that was requisite to meet the danger of the emergency. The paper currency was so out of credit with the inhabitants of South Carolina, that it was excessively difficult to purchase with it the necessaries of war. The want of soldiers was felt with equal severity. The militia, impatient to enjoy repose after the painful operations of Georgia, during the preceding winter, had disbanded and retired to their habitations.

Another motive also discouraged them from marching to the succor of Charleston; and that was, the fear of the small-pox, which it was known prevailed in that city. Moreover, the six regiments of the line, belonging to the provinces, were so enfeebled by desertions, diseases, battle, and the expiration of engagements, that all together did not amount to a thousand soldiers. It should be added, that many of the Carolinians were induced to profit of the amnesty offered by general Prevost, at Savannah, some through loyalty towards the king, others to preserve their effects from pillage. In effect, the English put to sack and devastation, without lenity, the property of all those who continued to serve under the banners of congress; and, besides, the victory of Savannah had penetrated minds with a great terror of the British arms. The major part were reluctant to immure themselves within a city which they believed little capable of resisting the assaults of so audacious an enemy.

Such was the penury of means to which South Carolina was reduced; the congress displayed not much more energy. They had been seasonably apprised of the designs of the English, and would fain have averted the storm they saw going to burst upon South Carolina. But on the one hand, the weakness of the army of Washington, which a great number of his soldiers had abandoned at the termination of their engagement; on the other, the force of the garrisons which Clinton had left in the state of New York, rendered it unadvisable to detach any effective succor to Charleston. Nevertheless, to support by words those whom they were unable to assist by deeds, or under the persuasion that the people, re-animated at the peril which menaced South Carolina, would voluntarily fly to arms, the congress wrote to the chiefs of that province, to arm themselves with constancy, for it was intended to send them a re-inforcement of nine thousand men. But the fact proved that they could only send fifteen hundred, of the regular troops of North Carolina and Virginia. The congress dispatched, besides, two frigates, a corvette, and some smaller vessels, to maintain, if possible, a communication by sea with the besieged city. The Carolinians were also exhorted to arm their slaves; a scheme, however, which was not put in execution, whether because of the universal repugnance that was felt to such a measure, or because there was not at hand a sufficiency of arms for the purpose. Notwithstanding this coldness of the citizens, the magistrates of Charleston, encouraged by the presence and words of general Lincoln, who directed all that concerned the military part, held a general council, in which it was resolved to defend the city to the last extremity. Yet more, knowing how important in the operations of war, and especially in all cases of emergency, is the unity of measures and power, they conferred a sort of dictature on John Rutledge, their governor, giving him authority to do whatever he should think necessary to the safety of the republic. They withheld, however, the power over the life of citizens; as he could punish none with death without a legal trial. Vested with such an authority, Rutledge called out the militia; but few displayed their colors. He then issued a proclamation, summoning all persons inscribed on the military rolls, or having property in the city, to muster and join the garrison; their disobedience forfeited their estates. At so rigorous an order, some made their appearance; but still the number of those who took arms was far from answering the wishes of the governor. The inhabitants of the country seemed plunged in a kind of stupor; they wished, before they took their side, to see what would be the fate of events; in brief, the garrison of so considerable a city scarcely amounted to five thousand men, inclusive of regulars, militia, and seamen. The first, who were principally relied on for the defense of the place, were to the number of about two thousand. Meanwhile, the fortifications were pushed with indefatigable industry. They consisted, on the land side, in a chain of redoubts, lines and batteries, extending from one river to the other, and covered with an artillery of eighty cannon and mortars. In the front of either flank, the works were covered by swamps, originating from the opposite rivers, and tending towards the center; through which they were connected by a canal passing from one to the other. Between these outward impediments and the works were two strong rows of abattis, the trees being buried slanting in the earth, so that their heads, facing outwards, formed a kind of fraise work against the assailants; and these were further secured by a ditch double picketed. In the center, where the natural defenses were unequal to those on the flanks, the Americans had constructed a horn work of masonry, as well to remedy that defect, as to cover the principal gate. Such were the fortifications which, stretching across the neck behind the city, and from the Ashley river to Cooper's river, defended it on the part of the land. But on the two sides where it is washed by these rivers, the Americans had contented themselves with erecting numerous batteries, constructed, the better to resist shot, of earth mingled with palmetto wood. All parts of the shore, where it was possible to land, had been secured by strong palisades. To support the defenses on shore, the Americans had a considerable marine force in the harbor, consisting in eight of their own frigates, with one French frigate, besides several smaller vessels, principally galleys. These were judiciously moored at a narrow pass, between Sullivan's island and the middle ground ; and if they had continued in this position, they might have severely annoyed the British squadron, on its approach to Fort Moultrie, situated on Sullivan's island, so much celebrated for the obstinate and successful defense which it made against the attack of the English in 1776. But when admiral Arbuthnot advanced with his ships to Charleston bar, the American flotilla, abandoning its station, and leaving Fort Moultrie to its own fortune, retired to Charleston ; where most of the ships, with a number of merchant vessels, being fitted with chevaux-de-frize on their decks, were sunk to obstruct the channel of Cooper's river, where it flows between the left part of the town and a low sand bank called Shute's Folly. Thus, with the exception of Fort Moultrie, there remained nothing to prevent the British fleet from entering the harbor, to co-operate with the land forces. In this manner the inhabitants prepared to defend themselves valiantly against the attack of the enemy ; but they still founded their hope on the succors of their neighbors of North Carolina and Virginia.

Lincoln and Rutledge exhibited a rivalship of zeal and talent in their efforts to impart fresh confidence to the besieged, and new strength to the works. They were admirably seconded by two French engineers, de Laumoy and de Cambray. The troops of the line were charged with the defense of the intrenchments, as the post of peril, and the militia had the guard of the banks of the river.

As soon as Clinton had completed all his preparations, the twenty-ninth of March, having left a detachment to guard his magazines at Wappoo Cut, he passed the Ashley river without opposition, twelve miles above Charleston. Immediately after his debarkation he sent a body of infantry and cavalry to occupy the great road and scour the country to within cannon-shot from the place. The army then followed, and took post across the isthmus behind the city, at the distance of a mile and a half. From this moment, the garrison lost all communication with the land ; the enemy being masters of both sides of the Ashley, there remained no way open for succors of men and provision but across the Cooper on their left. The royalists had soon transported to their camp, through the assistance to captain Elphinstone with his boats and armed galleys, all the heavy artillery, stores, and baggage. On the night of the first of April, they broke ground within eight hundred yards of the American works ; and in a week their guns were mounted in battery.

In the meantime, admiral Arbuthnot had made his dispositions for passing the bar in order to gain the entrance of Charleston harbor. The frigates, as drawing less water, passed without any difficulty ; but the ships of the line could not be got over till after having been lightened of their artillery, munitions, and even their water ; the whole squadron passed on the twentieth of March. Arbuthnot came to anchor at Five Fathom Hole ; he had still, however, to surmount, before he could take an active part in the siege of Charleston, the obstacle of Fort Moultrie, occupied by colonel Pinckney with a respectable force. The English admiral, profiting of a south wind and flood tide, weighed anchor on the ninth of April, and passing it under a press of sail, took his station within cannon-shot from the city near James island. Colonel Pinckney had opened all his artillery upon the British vessels, at the moment of their passage ; but such was the rapidity of their way, that it did them little damage. The dead and wounded were less than thirty ; a solitary transport was abandoned and burned.

In this state of things, the batteries ready to be opened, and the place already invested by sea and land, Clinton and Arbuthnot sent a joint summons to general Lincoln, holding out the fatal consequences of a cannonade and storm, and stating the present as the only favorable opportunity for preserving the lives and property of the inhabitants. The American answered spiritedly, that he was determined to defend himself. The English immediately commenced their fire ; the place answered it briskly. But the besiegers had the advantage of a more numerous artillery, particularly in mortars, which made great ravages. The pioneers and miners, under the direction of the same Moncrieffe who had gained so much honor in the defense of Savannah, pushed forward the works with extreme rapidity. The second parallel was already completed and furnished with its batteries ; every thing promised the English an approaching victory ; but the Americans had assembled a corps on the upper part of Cooper river, at a place called Monk's Corner. They were under the conduct of general Huger ; and from that position they could invest the besiegers on their rear, revictual Charleston, and in case of extremity, enable the garrison to evacuate the place, and retreat with safety into the country.

Besides, however feeble was this corps, it might serve as an incentive and rallying point for continual accessions. North Carolina had already dispatched to their camp a great quantity of arms, stores and baggage. Under these considerations, general Clinton detached fourteen hundred men, under lieutenant-colonel Webster, to strike at this body of republicans before it should become more considerable, to break in upon the remaining communications of the besieged, and to seize the principal passes of the country. Colonel Webster was accompanied by Tarleton and Ferguson, both partisans of distinguished gallantry. The Americans had established their principal cantonments on the left side of the Cooper, and being masters of Biggins Bridge, on that river, they had passed all their cavalry to the right bank. This position was strong, the bridge being accessible only by a causeway through an impracticable morass; but they were off their guard, having neglected to post videttes, and to reconnoiter the environs. Moreover, their dispositions were defective , they had placed the cavalry in front, and the infantry in rear. The English arrived, unexpectedly, at three in the morning; their attack was impetuous; it routed the Americans in a few instants; all perished save those who sought safety by flight. General Huger, and the colonels Washington and Jamieson, threw themselves into the morass, and were fortunate enough to escape by favor of the darkness. Four hundred horses, a prize of high value, fell into the hands of the victors, with many carriages loaded with arms, clothing and stores. The royalists took possession of the bridge, and, soon after, secured another passage lower down, and overrun the country on the left side of the river, particularly the district of St. Thomas. In this manner the besieged were deprived also of the Cooper river, and Charleston found itself completely enclosed. The garrison was not judged sufficiently strong to warrant any opposition to this enterprise. The Americans attempted only to fortify a point on the left bank, called Point Lamprey; but Webster's corps being considerably re-inforced, and lord Cornwallis having taken the command on that side of the river, they found themselves constrained to abandon this last post. The British foraged without obstacle, prevented the assembling of the militia, and cut off every species of succor. A few days after, Tarleton, having advanced with incredible celerity upon the banks of the Santee river, attacked and routed another body of republican cavalry, commanded by colonel Buford ; arms, horses, munitions, every thing fell into the power of the victor. Adverse fortune continued to pursue the republicans. Admiral Arbuthnot landed on Sullivan's island a body of seamen and marines, men of approved hardihood. He began to enclose Fort Moultrie ; having procured a full knowledge of the state of the garrison and defenses of the place, he prepared to storm it on the part of the west and

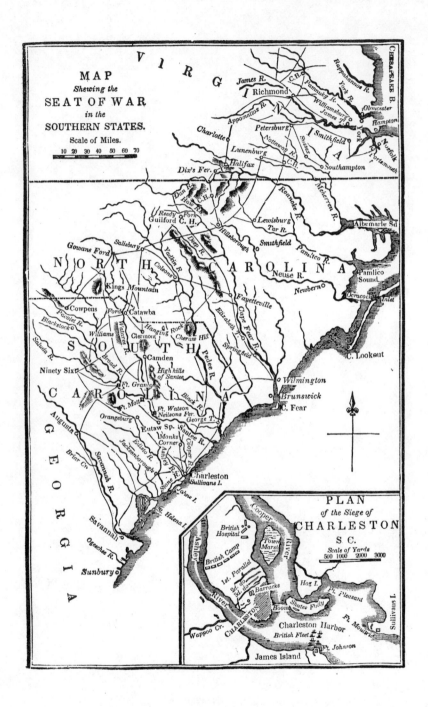

MAP
Shewing the
SEAT OF WAR
in the
SOUTHERN STATES.

Scale of Miles.

10 20 30 40 50 60 70

PLAN
of the Siege of
CHARLESTON
S.C.

Scale of Yards
500 1000 2000 3000

northwest, where the works were the weakest. The garrison, sensible of the impossibility of relief, the English being masters of the sea, and seeing the means of attack incomparably superior to those of resistance, surrendered, the seventh of May. Thus Fort Moultrie, which four years before had repulsed all the forces of admiral Hyde Parker, fell, without firing a shot, into the power of the royalists.

In the meantime, the besiegers had completed their third parallel, which they carried close to the canal we have already described; and by a sap pushed to the dam which supplied it with water on the right, they had drained it in several parts to the bottom. They hastened to arm this parallel with its batteries, and to complete the traverses and other mines of communication. The place being thus environed, and the bombardment about to commence, Clinton summoned Lincoln anew. A negotiation was opened, but the American commander required not only that the citizens and militia should be free with respect to their persons, but that they should also be permitted to sell their property, and retire with the proceeds wherever they might see fit; the English general refused to grant these conditions. He insisted that the whole garrison should surrender at discretion; and, as to property, he would agree to nothing further than that it should not be given up to pillage. The conferences were broken off, and hostilities recommenced. The fortifications were battered with violence by the heavy artillery; bombs and carcasses overwhelmed the town, and lighted frequent conflagrations; the Hessian marksmen felled all that showed themselves at the embrasures, or on the ramparts. Neither shelter nor retreat remained to the besieged; every thing indicated that the moment of surrender must soon arrive. The fire of the place was already become languid; its artillery was in part dismounted, and its best cannoniers either killed or out of service; and the English had pushed on their works till they issued in the ditch of the place. The city was menaced with an assault; discord began to break out within; the timid and those attached to the royal party murmured aloud; they conjured Lincoln not to expose to inevitable destruction, so rich, so important a city. They represented that the stock of provision was nearly exhausted; that the engineers considered it impossible to sustain a storm; in a word, that there was not the least way of safety left open.

In so terrible an extremity, Lincoln divested himself of his natural inflexibility; and, on the twelfth of May, the capitulation was signed. The garrison were allowed some of the honors of war; but they were not to uncase their colors, nor their drums to beat a Brit-

ısn march.   The continental troops and seamen were to keep their
baggage, and to remain prisoners of war until they were exchanged.
The militia were to be permitted to return to their respective homes,
as prisoners on parole ; and while they adhered to their parole, were
not to be molested by the British troops in person or property.   The
citizens of all sorts to be considered as prisoners on parole, and to
hold their property on the same terms with the militia.   The officers
of the army and navy to retain their servants, swords, pistols, and
their baggage unsearched.   As to general Lincoln, he was to have
liberty to send a ship to Philadelphia with his dispatches.

Thus, after a siege of forty days, the capital of South Carolina
fell into the hands of the royalists.   Seven general officers, ten continental regiments, much thinned, it is true, and three battalions of
artillery, prisoners of the English, gave signal importance to their
victory ; the whole number of men in arms who were taken, was
estimated at six thousand.   Four hundred pieces of artillery, of
every sort, were the prey of the victors, with no small quantity of
powder, balls and bombs ; three stout American frigates, one French,
and a polacre of the same nation, augmented the value of the conquest.   The loss of men was not great on either side, and was not
very unequally shared.

The Carolinians complained greatly of their not being properly
assisted by their neighbors, particularly the Virginians, in this long
and arduous struggle.   The conduct of general Lincoln was unanimously blamed, though very differently judged.   Some reproached
him for having allowed himself to be cooped up in so extensive and
indefensible a town, instead of continuing the war in the open field.
They said that if he had taken this course, he might have preserved
to the Union a considerable army, and the most fertile part of the
province ; that it would have been much better to harass and fatigue
the enemy by marches, retreats, ambuscades, and well concerted attacks ; that Washington had acted very differently, and with greater
utility to his country, when, to the loss of his army, he preferred that
of the island of New York, and even of the city of Philadelphia
itself.   It was not Lincoln alone, however, who should have been
made responsible for events, but the congress and the neighboring
provincial states ; since they promised, at the approach of danger,
re-inforcements which they did not furnish.

Other censors of the general's conduct condemned him for not
having evacuated the town, when all the roads were still open on the
left side of the Cooper river.   But if he followed an opposite counsel, it should be attributed, at first, to this same hope of promised
succor ; and then, after the rout of Monk's Corner, and the English

had occupied the country between the Cooper and the Santee, to the fear he justly entertained of encountering an infinite superiority of force, particularly in cavalry, and to the repugnance he felt to leave Charleston at discretion in the hands of the enemy.

As soon as general Clinton had taken possession of that capital, he hastened to take all those measures, civil as well as military, which were judged proper for the re-establishment of order; he then made his dispositions for recovering the rest of the province, where every thing promised to anticipate the will of the victor. Determined to follow up his success, before his own people should have time to cool, or the enemy to take breath, he planned three expeditions; one towards the river Savannah, in Georgia, another upon Ninety-Six, beyond the Saluda, both with a view to raise the loyalists, very numerous in those parts; the third was destined to scour the country between the Cooper and Santee, in order to disperse a body of republicans, who, under the conduct of colonel Buford, were retiring by forced marches towards North Carolina. All three were completely successful; the inhabitants flocked from all parts to meet the royal troops, declaring their desire to resume their ancient allegiance, and offering to defend the royal cause with arms in hand. Many even of the inhabitants of Charleston, excited by the proclamations of the British general, manifested a like zeal to combat under his banners. Lord Cornwallis, after having swept the two banks of the Cooper and passed the Santee, made himself master of Georgetown. Such was the devotion, either real or feigned, of the inhabitants towards the king; such was their terror, or their desire to ingratiate themselves with the victor, that not content with coming in from every quarter to offer their services, in support of the royal government, they dragged in their train, as prisoners, those friends of liberty, whom they had lately obeyed with such parade of zeal, and whom they now denominated their oppressors. Meanwhile, colonel Buford continued his retreat with celerity, and it appeared next to impossible that he should be overtaken. Tarleton, nevertheless, offered to attempt the enterprise, promising to reach him. Cornwallis put under his command, for this object, a strong corps of cavalry, with about a hundred light infantry mounted on horseback. His march was so rapid, that on the twenty-eighth of May he had gained Camden, where he learned that Buford had departed the preceding day from Rugeleys Mills, and that he was pushing on with extreme speed, in order to join another body of republicans that was on the march from Salisbury to Charlotte, in North Carolina. Tarleton saw the importance of preventing the junction of these two corps; accordingly, notwithstanding the fatigue of men and horses, many of these having already dropped dead with exhaustion, notwithstanding the heat of the season, he redoubled his pace, and at length presented himself, after a march of one hundred and five miles in fifty-four hours, at a place called Wacsaw, before the object of his pursuit. The English summoned the Americans to throw down their arms ; the latter answered with spirit, that they were prepared to defend themselves. The colonel drew up his troops in order of battle; they consisted of four hundred Virginia regulars with a detachment of horse. He formed but one line, and ordered his artillery and baggage to continue their march in his rear, without halting ; his soldiers were directed to reserve their fire till the British cavalry were approached within twenty yards. Tarleton ost no time in preparation, but charged immediately. The Americans gave way after a faint resistance; the English pursued them with vigor, and the carnage was dreadful. Their victory was complete ; all, in a manner, that were not killed on the spot, were wounded and taken. Such was the rage of the victors, that they massacred many of those who offered to surrender. The Americans emembered it with horror. From that time it became with them a proverbial mode of expressing the cruelties of a barbarous enemy, to call them *Tarleton's quarter*. Artillery, baggage, munitions, colors, every thing, fell into the power of the English. It appears that colonel Buford committed two faults, the most serious of which was the having awaited on open ground an enemy much superior in cavalry. If, instead of sending his carriages behind him, as soon as he perceived the royal troops, he had formed them into a cincture for his corps, the English would not have attempted to force it, or would have exposed themselves to a sanguinary repulse. The second was that of forbidding his men to fire at the enemy, till he was within twenty paces; it ensued that Tarleton's cavalry was enabled to charge with more order and efficacy. That officer immediately returned, followed by the trophies of his victory, to Camden, where he rejoined lord Cornwallis. The American division, which had advanced to Charlotte, changed its plan, on hearing of the discomfiture of Wacsaw, and fell back with precipitation on Salisbury.

This reverse destroyed the last hopes of the Carolinians, and was soon followed by their submission. General Clinton wrote to London, that South Carolina was become English again, and that there were few men in the province who were not prisoners to, or in arms with the British forces. But he was perfectly aware that the conquest he owed to his arms could not be preserved but by the entire re-establishment of the civil administration. To this end, he deemed it essential to put minds at rest by the assurance of amnesty, and to oblige the inhabitants to contribute to the defense of the country, and to the restoration of the royal authority. Accordingly, in concert with admiral Arbuthnot, he published a full and absolute pardon in favor of those who should immediately return to their duty, promising that no offenses and transgressions heretofore committed in consequence of political troubles, should be subject to any investigation whatever. He excepted only those who, under a mockery of the forms of justice, had imbrued their hands in the blood of their fellow-citizens, who had shown themselves adverse to revolt and usurpation. He had then to reflect that a great number of the Carolinians were prisoners of war on parole, and that while they were considered as such, they could not equitably be constrained to take arms in favor of the king. But, in the pride of victory, Clinton thought he might sport with the public faith, and got over this difficulty by declaring, in a proclamation issued on the third of June, that the prisoners of war were free, and released from their parole, with the exception of the regular troops taken in Charleston and Fort Moultrie; he added, that they were re-established in all the rights and all the duties of British subjects. But that no doubt might remain with regard to his intentions, and to prevent all conjecture, he gave notice that every man must take an active part in support of the royal government, and in the suppression of that anarchy which had prevailed already but too long. For the attainment of this object, he required all persons to be in readiness with their arms at a moment's warning; those who had families, to form a militia for home defense; but those who had none, to serve with the royal forces for any six months of the ensuing twelve, in which they might be called upon to assist, as he said, ' in driving their rebel oppressors, and all the miseries of war, far from the province.' They were not to be employed, however, out of the two Carolinas and Georgia. Thus citizens were armed against citizens, brothers against brothers; thus the same individuals who had been acknowledged as soldiers of the congress, since they had been comprehended in the capitulation as prisoners of war, were constrained to take arms for the king of England; a violence, if not unprecedented, at least odious, and which rebounded, as we shall see by the sequel, on the heads of those who were guilty of it. General Clinton, seeing the province in tranquillity, and the ardor, which appeared universal, of the inhabitants to join the royal standard, distributed his army in the most important garrisons; when, leaving lord Cornwallis in command of all the forces stationed in South Carolina and Georgia, he departed from Charleston for his government of New York.

That city, during his absence, had been exposed to a danger as unexpected as alarming. A winter, unequaled in that climate for its length and severity, had deprived New York and the adjoining islands of all the defensive benefits of their insular situation ; the Hudson river, with the straits and channels by which they are divided and surrounded, were every where clothed with ice of such a strength and thickness, as would have admitted the passage of armies, with their heaviest carriages and artillery. This change, so suddenly wrought in the nature of their situation, caused the British commanders extreme disquietude ; they feared the more for the safety of New York, as its garrison was then very feeble, and the army of Washington not far off. Accordingly, they neglected none of those prudential measures which are usual in similar cases ; all orders of men in New York were embodied, armed and officered. The officers and crews of the frigates undertook the charge of a redoubt ; and those of the transports, victualers and merchantmen, were armed with pikes, for the defense of the wharves and shipping. But Washington was in no condition to profit of this unlooked for event. The small army which remained with him hutted at Morristown, was inferior in strength even to the British regular force at New York, exclusive of the armed inhabitants and militia. He sent lord Sterling, it is true, to make an attempt upon Staten Island, and to reconnoiter the ground ; but that general, observing no movement in his favor on the part of the city, returned to his first position. Thus the scourge of short engagements, and the torpor which prevailed at that time among the Americans, caused them to lose the most propitious occasion that could have been desired, to strike a blow that would have sensibly affected the British power. If their weakness constrained them to inaction in the vicinity of New York, the English did not imitate their example. As soon as the return of spring had freed them from the danger they had apprehended during the season of ice, they renewed their predatory exploits in New Jersey. Their object in these excursions of devastation and plunder, was to favor the operations in Carolina, in order that the enemy, feeling insecure at various points, might carry succor to none.

About the beginning of June, and a few days previous to the return of general Clinton, the generals Knyphausen, Robertson, and Tryon, who, during his absence, commanded the troops cantoned at New York, had entered New Jersey with a corps of five thousand men, and had occupied Elizabethtown ; they conducted themselves there with generosity, and abstained from all pillage. They afterwards advanced and took possession of Connecticut Farms, a new and flourishing village. Irritated at the resistance they had experienced in their march having been harassed incessantly by the country militia, who had risen against them from all the neighboring parts, they set fire to this place; only two houses escaped; even the church was a prey to the flames. This disaster was signalized by a deplorable event, which contributed not a little to redouble the indignation of the republicans against the royalists. Among the inhabitants of Connecticut Farms was a young gentlewoman, as celebrated for her virtues as for the singular beauty of her person. Her husband, James Cadwell, was one of the most ardent and influential patriots in that province. He urged her, and resorted to the entreaties of friends to persuade her to withdraw from the danger; but trusting to her own innocence for protection, she awaited the invaders. She was surrounded by her little children, and near her a nursery maid held in her arms the youngest of her offspring. A furious soldier appeared at the window, a Hessian, as it is said; he took aim at this unfortunate mother, and pierced her breast with an instantly mortal shot; her blood gushed upon all her tender orphans. Other soldiers rushed into the house, and set it on fire, after having hastened to bury their victim. Thus, at least, the republicans relate this horrible adventure. The English pretended that the shot had been fired at random, and even that it was discharged by the Americans, since it came from the part by which they retired. However the truth may be, the melancholy fate of this gentlewoman fired the breasts of the patriots with such rage, that they flew from every quarter to take vengeance upon the authors of so black a deed. The royal troops had put themselves on the march to seize a neighboring town called Springfield. They had nearly reached it, when they were informed that general Maxwell awaited them there, with a regiment of New Jersey regulars and a strong body of militia, impatient for combat. The English halted, and passed the night in that position. The next morning they fell back with precipitation upon Elizabethtown, whether their commanders thought it imprudent to attack an enemy who bore so menacing a countenance, or that they had received intelligence, as they published, that Washington had detached from Morristown a strong re-inforcement to Maxwell. The Americans pursued them with warmth, but to little purpose, from the valor and regularity displayed in their retreat.

At this conjuncture, general Clinton arrived at New York, and immediately adopted a plan from which he promised himself the most decisive success. His purpose was to dislodge Washington from the strong position he occupied in the mountainous and difficult country of Morrisonia, which, forming a natural barrier, had furnished the American captain-general with an impregnable shelter against the attacks of the English, even when his force was the most reduced. Accordingly, Clinton, having embarked a considerable body of troops at New York, executed such movements as made it appear that his design was to ascend the Hudson river, in order to seize the passes in the mountains towards the lakes. He had persuaded himself that Washington, as soon as he should be informed of this demonstration, would instantly put himself in motion, and, in the fear of losing these passes, would advance with the whole or the greater part of his force, in order to defend them. The British general intended to seize this occasion to push rapidly with the troops he had at Elizabethtown, against the heights of Morrisonia, and thus to occupy the positions which constituted the security of Washington. And, even on the supposition that their distance should render it unadvisable to maintain them, the destruction of the extensive magazines which the republicans had established there, offered a powerful attraction. Washington, in effect, who watched all the movements of Clinton, penetrated his designs. Fearing for West Point, and the important defiles of that part, he retained with him only the force indispensably requisite to defend the heights of Morrisonia, and detached the rest upon the banks of the Hudson, under general Greene. The royalists then marched with rapidity from Elizabethtown towards Springfield. This place is situated at the foot of the heights of Morrisonia, on the right bank of a stream that descends from them, and covers it in front. Colonel Angel guarded the bridge with a small detachment, but composed of picked men. Behind him the regiment of colonel Shrieve formed a second line, and ascending towards the heights near Shorts Hill, were posted the corps of Greene, Maxwell, and Stark. There were few continental troops, but the militia were numerous and full of ardor.

On arriving at the bridge, the royalists attacked colonel Angel with great impetuosity. He defended himself bravely, killing many of the enemy, and losing few of his own. At length, yielding to number, he fell back in perfect order upon the second line. The English passed the bridge, and endeavored to pursue their advantage. Shrieve resisted their efforts for a while; but too inferior in men, and especially in artillery, he withdrew behind the corps of Greene. The English, then examining the situation of places, and the strength of the American intrenchments, abandoned the design of assaulting them. Perhaps the approach of night, the impracticable nature of the country, the obstinate defense of the bridge, the sight of the militia rushing towards the camp from all parts, and the danger of losing all communication with Elizabethtown, contributed to this abrupt change in the resolutions of the British generals. Exasperated at these unexpected obstacles, they devoted to pillage and flames the flourishing village of Springfield; they afterwards return-ed upon Elizabethtown. Enraged at seeing this conflagration, the republicans pursued the British troops with so much violence, that only their discipline and the ability of their commanders could have saved them from total destruction. They profited of the cover of night to abandon the shores of New Jersey, and passed into Staten Island. Thus the design of Clinton was baffled by a resistance for which he was little prepared. The English gained by this expedi-tion only the shame of repulse, and eternal detestation on the part of their enemies. Washington, in official reports, greatly commend-ed the valor of his troops.

But it is time to resume our narrative of the affairs of Carolina. The English administration, which, after the conquest of that prov-ince, had been established by the royal troops, deliberated upon the means of repairing the evils caused by the war and by civil dissen-sions, in order to confirm the return of monarchical authority. Since that of the congress had ceased to exist in the country, the paper currency had fallen into such discredit, that it was not possible to circulate it at any rate whatever. Many individuals had been forced to receive, as re-imbursement for credits of long standing, those depre-ciated bills; others had balances still due them upon contracts stip-ulated according to the nominal value of the paper. It was resolved, therefore, to compel the debtors of the first to account with them by a new payment in specie, for the difference that existed between the real and the nominal value of the bills; and to establish a scale of proportion, according to which, those who owed arrearages should satisfy their creditors in coined money. To this end, thirteen com missioners were appointed. They were to inform themselves with accuracy of the different degrees of the depreciation of the paper, and afterwards to draw up a table of reduction, to serve as a legal regulation in the payment of the debts above specified. The com-missioners proceeded in the execution of this difficult task with equal justice and discernment; they compared the price of the products of the country, during the circulation of the bills, with that they had borne a year before the war. Examining then the different rates of exchange of the bills for specie, they formed, not only year by year, but also month by month, a table, the first column of which contain-ed the dates, the second the ratio of the value of the bills to that of specie, the third the ratio of the value of bills to the price of produce, and the fourth the proportional medium of depreciation. This ex-tinction of the value of bills of credit, occasioned by the presence of the English in Georgia and Carolina, induced those inhabitants who still held them, to carry or send them into otner provinces, where they continued to have some circulation. But this influx itself, added to the loss of Carolina, and the sinister aspect which the situation of the affairs of congress presented at this epoch, accelerated the fall of paper money in all the states of the confederation. Too well convinced that there was no remedy capable of arresting the progress of this appalling evil, the congress determined to yield to the storm. They decreed that in future their bills should pass, no longer at their nominal, but only at their conventional value; and they also drew up a scale of depreciation for the regulation of payments. This resolution, which, though assuredly a violation of the public faith, was, with the exception of dishonest debtors, both agreeable and advantageous to all classes. Can there, in fact, exist, for a nation, a greater calamity than to have a currency as the representative of money, when that currency is fixed by law, and variable in opinion? It is also to be considered that the bills of credit were then in the hands, not of the first, but of the last possessors, who had acquired them at their depreciated value. It was only to be regretted that the congress had made so many solemn protestations of their intention to maintain the nominal value of their paper. Even the tenor of the bills, the terms of the law of their creation, all the public acts which related to them, were so many engagements that a dollar in paper should always be given and received for a dollar in silver. Scarcely were a few months elapsed since the congress, in a circular letter, had spoken of the same resolution they had now taken, as a measure of the most flagrant injustice. In that letter they affirm, that even the supposition of a similar breach of faith, ought to excite universal abhorrence. But such is the nature of new governments, especially in times of revolution, where affairs of state are so much under the control of chance, that they frequently promise what they cannot perform; the empire of circumstances seems to them a fair plea for not keeping faith. Their precarious positions should render them at least less prodigal of promises and oaths; but, as inexperienced as presumptuous, and vainly believing their object attained, when they have found means to push on for a day, they seem the more bold in contracting engagements, the less it is in their power to fulfill them.

The proclamation by which the British commanders had absolved the prisoners of war from their parole, and restored them to the condition of British subjects, in order to compel them to join the royal troops, had created a deep discontent among the Carolinians. The greater part desired, since they had lost liberty, to remain at least in tranquillity at their homes, thus conforming themselves to the time, and submitting to necessity. If this repose had been granted them, they would not have exerted themselves to obtain a change ; they would have supported less impatiently the unhappy situation of the republic ; little by little they would have accustomed themselves to the new order of things, and would have forgotten the past. But this proclamation rekindled their rage. They cried with one voice, ' If we must resume arms, let us rather fight for America and our friends, than for England and strangers ! ' Many did as they said. Released from their parole, considering themselves at liberty to take arms anew, and determined to venture all to serve their cause, they repaired by circuitous and unfrequented ways into North Carolina, which was still occupied by the troops of congress. Others continued to remain in the country, and in the condition of prisoners of war, deferring to take their resolution till the British officers should actually summon them to enter the field. The greater part, submitting to circumstances, could not resolve to abandon their property, and withdraw into distant provinces, as some of their fellow-citizens had done. In dread of the persecutions of the English, and even of their own countrymen, and desirous to win favor with their new masters, they had recourse to dissimulation. They preferred to change their condition, and from prisoners of war to become British subjects. This resolution appeared to them the more expedient, as a report was then in circulation, perhaps purposely forged, that the congress were come to the determination no longer to dispute with the English the possession of the southern provinces. This rumor was directly opposite to the truth ; for in the sitting of the twenty-fifth of June, the congress had declared with much solemnity that they purposed to make every possible exertion for their recovery. But the prisoners of Carolina knew nothing of what passed without, and from day to day they became more confirmed in the idea that their country would remain under British domination. Thus, between choice and compulsion, the multitude resumed the bonds of submission. But the English could have wished to have all under their yoke ; they saw with pain that within as well as without the province, there remained some individuals devoted to the party of congress. Their resentment dictated the most extraordinary measures against the property and families of those who had emigrated, and of those who had remained prisoners of war. The possessions of the first were sequestrated and ravaged ; their families were jealously watched, and subjected, as rebels, to a thousand vexations. The second were often separated from their hearths, and confined in remote and unhealthy places. These rigors constrained some to retract, and bend the neck under the new slavery ;

others to offer themselves as good and loyal subjects of the king. Among them were found individuals who had manifested the most ardor for the cause of liberty, and who had even filled the first offices, under the popular government. They generally colored their conversion with saying, that they had never aspired to independence, and that they abhorred the alliance of France. Thus men will rather stain themselves with falsehood and perjury, than live in misfortune and poverty! Such was the conduct of the inhabitants of the country ; but those of the city, having, by the terms of capitulation, the right to remain in their habitations, were not comprehended in the proclamation of the third of June. It was requisite, therefore, to employ other means to induce them to stoop to allegiance. The English and more zealous loyalists maneuvered in such a manner, that more than two hundred citizens of Charleston subscribed and presented to the British generals an address, by which they congratulated them upon their victories. This step had been concerted. It was answered them, that they should enjoy the protection of the state and all the privileges of British subjects, if they would sign a declaration of their allegiance and readiness to support the royal government. They obeyed ; and their example had many imitators. Hence arose a distinction between subjects and prisoners. The first were protected, honored and encouraged ; the second were regarded with contempt, persecuted and harassed in their persons and property. Their estates in the country were loaded with taxes, and even ravaged. Within the city they were refused access to the tribunals, if they had occasion to bring suits against their debtors ; while, on the other hand, they were abandoned to all the prosecutions of their creditors. Thus forced to pay, they were not permitted to receive. They were not suffered to go out of the city without a pass, which was often refused them without motive, and they were even threatened with imprisonment unless they took the oath of allegiance. Their effects were given up to the pillage of the soldiery ; their negroes were taken from them ; they had no means of redress, but in yielding to what was exacted of them ; while the claims of subjects were admitted without question. The artisans were allowed to labor, but not to enforce payment for their work, if their customers chose to refuse it. The Jews had been permitted to purchase many valuable goods of the British traders who had followed the army ; but unless they became subjects, they were not allowed to sell them. In brief, threats, fraud, and force, were industriously exercised to urge the inhabitants to violate their plighted faith, and resume their ancient chains. The greater part had recourse to dissimulation, and, by becoming subjects, were made partakers of British protection; others, more firm, or more virtuous, refused to bend. But they soon saw an unbridled soldiery sharing out their spoils; some were thrown into pestilential dungeons; others, less unfortunate or more prudent, condemned themselves to a voluntary exile.

Amidst the general desolation, the women of Carolina exhibited an example of more than masculine fortitude. They displayed so ardent, so rare a love of country, that scarcely could there be found in ancient or modern history an instance more worthy to excite surprise and admiration. Far from being offended at the name of rebel ladies, they esteemed it a title of distinction and glory. Instead of showing themselves in assemblies, the seat of joy and brilliant pleasures, they repaired on board ships, they descended into dungeons, where their husbands, children and friends were in confinement; they carried them consolations and encouragements. 'Summon your magnanimity,' they said; ' yield not to the fury of tyrants; hesitate not to prefer prisons to infamy, death to servitude. America has fixed her eyes on her beloved defenders; you will reap, doubt it not, the fruit of your sufferings; they will produce liberty, that parent of all blessings; they will shelter her forever from the assaults of British banditti. You are the martyrs of a cause the most grateful to Heaven and sacred for men.' By such words these generous women mitigated the miseries of the unhappy prisoners. They would never appear at the balls or routs that were given by the victors; those who consented to attend them were instantly despised, and dropped by all the others. The moment an American officer arrived at Charleston as a prisoner of war, they sought him out, and loaded him with attention and civilities. They often assembled in the most retired parts of their houses, to deplore without restraint the misfortunes of their country. Many of them imparted their noble spirit to their hesitating and wavering husbands; they determined them to prefer a rigorous exile to their interests and to the sweets of life. Exasperated at their constancy, the English condemned the most zealous to banishment and confiscation. In bidding a last farewell to their fathers, their children, their brothers, their husbands, these heroines, far from betraying the least mark of weakness, which in men might have been excused, exhorted them to arm themselves with intrepidity. They conjured them not to allow fortune to vanquish them, nor to suffer the love they bore their families to render them unmindful of all they owed their country. When comprehended, soon after, in the general decree of banishment issued against the partisans of liberty, they abandoned with the same firmness their natal soil. A supernatural alacrity seemed to animate them when they accompanied their husbands into distant countries, and even when immured with them in the fetid ships, into which they were inhumanly crowded. Reduced to the most frightful indigence, they were seen to beg bread for themselves and families. Among those who were nurtured in the lap of opulence, many passed suddenly from the most delicate and the most elegant style of living, to the rudest toils and to the humblest services. But humiliation could not triumph over their resolution and cheerfulness; their example was a support to their companions in misfortune. To this heroism of the women of Carolina, it is principally to be imputed, that the love, and even the name of liberty, were not totally extinguished in the southern provinces. The English hence began to be sensible, that their triumph was still far from secure. For, in every affair of public interest, the general opinion never manifests itself with more energy than when women take part in it with all the life of their imagination. Less powerful as well as less stable than that of men when calm, it is far more vehement and pertinacious when roused and inflamed.

Such was the spectacle presented at that time in South Carolina; on the one hand, an open resistance to the will of the conqueror, or a feigned submission; on the other, measures that continually operated an effect directly contrary to that which their authors expected from them. Meanwhile, the heat of the season, the dubious state of the province itself, and the necessity of deferring the campaign until the harvest was over, occasioned an almost general suspension of arms. It was not possible for the English to think of the conquest of North Carolina before the last of August or the beginning of September. Lord Cornwallis resolved to canton his troops in such a manner, that they should be in readiness to support the loyalists, to repress the discontented, and to undertake the invasion of that province as soon as the proper season should arrive. He was particularly careful to collect provision and munitions of war. His principal magazines were established at Camden, a large village situated on the banks of the river Wateree, and upon the road which leads into North Carolina.

He feared lest the loyalists of that province, stimulated by excess of zeal, should break out before the time, which might lead to their destruction. His emissaries continually exhorted them to await the time of harvest in tranquillity, and to content themselves with preparing subsistence for the royal troops, who would advance to their succor towards the month of September. These prudent counsels had not the effect to prevent the loyalists of Tryon county from rising at the instigation of colonel Moore. But instantly crushed by a corps of republicans, under the command of general Rutherford they paid dearly for the contempt with which they had presumed to treat admonitions dictated by foresight. Eight hundred loyalists, however, under the conduct of colonel Bryan, made good their junction with the royal troops. But while the British generals were making their dispositions to profit of the favorable season to attack North Carolina, in order to open themselves a passage into the heart of Virginia, the congress exerted all diligence to put themselves in a situation to recover South Carolina. Their efforts, as we shall see, were not without success. Thus the flames of war, for the moment almost extinguished, were on the point of being rekindled with more violence than ever.

Before entering upon the recital of the events of the bloody campaign that ensued, it is necessary to describe what passed in the West Indies between two powerful and equally spirited rivals. Already a very obstinate action had taken place between the chevalier de la Motte Piquet and commodore Cornwallis, in the waters of La Grange, to the east of Cape Francois. The first had four ships, two of which of seventy-four guns, the Annibal and the Diademe. The other had only three, the heaviest of which was the Lion, of sixty-four guns. But this engagement was merely a prelude to the battles that followed shortly after. About the last of March, the count de Guichen had arrived in the West Indies with such considerable re-inforcements, that the French fleet there amounted to twenty-five sail of the line. Resolved to profit of their superiority by sea as well as by land, the French embarked a strong body of troops, under the conduct of the marquis de Bouille, and presented themselves with twenty-two ships of the line before the island of St. Lucia. Their intention was to carry it by assault. But general Vaughan, who commanded on shore, had neglected no measure of defense; and admiral Hyde Parker, who had repaired thither from the coasts of America, had so advantageously posted sixteen sail of the line at Gros Islet, that the French commanders abandoned the project, and returned to Martinico. A few days after, admiral Rodney arrived at St. Lucia with re-inforcements from Europe; his junction with Parker placed at his command twenty-two sail of the line. Full of confidence in his strength, the English admiral sailed immediately for Fort Royal bay in Martinico, in order to challenge his enemy to battle. But the count de Guichen, who was not disposed to engage a decisive action, except when he should think it expedient, did not go out of the port. Rodney, having left some swift sailing frigates to watch the motions of the French, and to give notice, in case they should sail, returned with the remainder of his fleet to St. Lucia. The count de Guichen did not remain long inactive. He put to sea, in the night of the thirteenth of April, with twenty-two sail of the line, and four thousand land troops, prepared to undertake any operation that should offer some hope of success. Rodney was soon advised of it, and sailed in quest of him; his fleet consisted of twenty ships of the line, and the Centurion of fifty guns. He commanded the center himself, rear-admiral Hyde Parker the van, and rear-admiral Rowley the rear division. The French were standing through the channel of Dominica, intending afterwards to stretch off to windward of Martinico. Their van was under the conduct of the chevalier de Sade, the main body was led by the commander-in-chief, the count de Guichen, and the rear by the count de Grasse. The two armaments came in sight of each other towards evening, on the sixteenth of April. The French, whose ships were encumbered with soldiers, and who found themselves under the wind, endeavored to avoid an engagement. But the English bore down upon them. The count de Guichen profited of the night to maneuver so as not to be obliged to join battle; Rodney, on the contrary, in order to render it inevitable. On the succeeding morning, the two fleets executed various evolutions with admirable skill; and, a little before one o'clock, the French rear was brought to action by the British van. For it is to be observed, that in tacking to take an inverse order of battle, the French van was become rear. Meanwhile, Rodney arrived with his division upon the French center; his own ship, the Sandwich, of ninety guns, was encountered by M. de Guichen, in the Couronne, of eighty, and by his two seconds, the Fendant and Triumphant. But in crowding sail before the action, the French fleet had not been able to keep its distances perfectly. Its rear, moreover, which had become head of the line, being composed of more heavy sailing ships than those of the two other divisions, there had resulted thence a considerable chasm between that squadron and the center. This separation was still increased by the drift of the Actionnaire, which, instead of standing, as the last vessel of the center, the first of the rear, had suffered herself to fall to leeward of the line. Rodney resolved to seize the opportunity, and moved in order to cut off this rear guard from the rest of the fleet. But the Destin, commanded by M. Dumaitz de Goimpy, being at the head of that division, threw herself across his way, and engaged the Sandwich with so much vigor as to arrest his passage. The French ship would have been crushed, however, by a force so greatly superior, if the count de Guichen, perceiving the design of his adversary, had not made a signal to the ships of his center to put about, and push wind aft, all together, in order to rejoin and extricate the rear. This movement, executed with extreme celerity, completely baffled the plan of the British admiral, and, consequently, saved the French fleet from a total defeat. Rodney, now finding himself exposed to have the blow he had meditated against his adversary retorted upon himself, recoiled instantly, and pressed to regain his place in the line with his other ships. Soon after he made his dispositions for renewing the action; but seeing the crippled condition of several of his ships, and the particularly dangerous state of the Sandwich, which was with difficulty kept above water, he thought it more prudent to desist. The count de Guichen drew off to refit; he afterwards touched at Guadaloupe, in order to put ashore his sick and wounded. Rodney continued to maneuver in the open sea for some days, and then returned to cruise off Fort Royal bay, hoping to intercept the French fleet, which he believed was on its way for that anchorage. But at length, the enemy not appearing, and finding it necessary to disembark the sick and wounded, and to refit and water his fleet, he put into Choc bay, in St. Lucia. The loss of the British, in this action, amounted to one hundred and twenty killed, and to three hundred and fifty-three wounded. Of the French, two hundred and twenty-one died, and five hundred and forty were wounded. Rodney, in the report of the battle which he sent to England, passed high encomiums on the talents and gallantry of the French admiral; and added, that he had been admirably seconded by his officers. This was an indirect reproach to his own; of whom, generally, he felt that he had much reason to complain. The two parties alike claimed the honor of victory, as it is usual in every combat, the issue of which is not decisive. After having repaired his ships, and taken aboard the troops under the command of the marquis de Bouille, M. de Guichen again put to sea. His design was to ascend to windward of the islands by the north of Guadaloupe, and then to disembark his land forces at Gros Islet, in St. Lucia. Apprised of this movement, Rodney immediately set sail in search of the French fleet. He issued from the channel of St. Lucia, as it was standing off the extremity of Martinico, towards Point de Salines. At sight of the British armament, the French admiral became sensible that he must abandon the attack of St. Lucia. His prudence is to be applauded in abstaining from coming to battle, although his position to windward of the enemy had placed it in his power; but he inclined first to secure the advantages which were offered him by the nature of those seas, and the direction of the wind. He maneuvered to retain the weather-gage, and, at the same time, to draw the English to windward of Martinico. In case of a check, he had in that island a certain refuge, and if victor, he left none for his enemy. The British admiral labored on his part to gain the wind, and continued to approach more and more. The hostile fleets had received each a re-inforcement of one ship of the line; the French, the Dauphin Royal; the English, the Triumph. These evolutions, in which the two admirals displayed no ordinary degree of skill and judgment in seamanship, were prolonged for several days, and still Rodney had not been able to attain the object of his efforts. The French, whose ships were superior in point of sailing, to entice the English, as has been said, more to windward of Martinico, suffered themselves to be approached from time to time, and then suddenly spreading all sail, departed out of reach: this sport succeeded with them at first perfectly; but at length the French were nearly entangled into a general engagement, in a situation which presented more than one sort of peril; for their intention being to avoid it, they found themselves in no suitable order for battle. The wind had gradually veered to the south. Vigilant to profit of this change, Rodney put his ships about, and pushed on the other tack to gain the wind upon the French. He would have effected his purpose, if the wind had not, in this critical moment, suddenly shifted to the southeast. The count de Guichen could then also put himself on the other tack, which movement presented such a front to the English as no longer permitted them to gain the wind of him. He afterwards continued to retire in order to avoid an action. But in consequence of the last maneuvers, the two fleets being brought within cannon-shot of each other, the English pressed forward their van upon the French rear. It was already towards night fall, on the fifteenth of May. The headmost of the British ships, and particularly the Albion, found themselves exposed unsupported to the fire of the whole French division, and were excessively damaged. The others rejoined them; but the French, being better sailers, then retired. Such was the second rencounter between admiral Rodney and the count de Guichen. The French preserved the advantage of the wind. The two armaments continued in sight of each other during the three ensuing days, both maneuvering according to the plan of operations adopted by their respective admirals. Finally, in the morning of the nineteenth of May, the English being advanced to the windward of Martinico about forty leagues, and distant between four and five, to the southeast, from the French, the count de Guichen determined to accept battle, and accordingly took in sail. But as soon as the British van was within reach, he made a signal for his own to bear down upon it, and the action was engaged with great spirit on both sides. The other divisions formed successively in order of battle, the French retaining the weathergage. The conflict became general, the two fleets combating, the one with its starboard, the other with its larboard guns. But the ships of the French van and center having shortened sail in order to come to closer action with the enemy, it was to be feared lest the English should tack all at once in order to charge the rear, which was then at a considerable distance astern. To prevent the fatal consequences that might have ensued from such a movement on the part of the enemy, M. de Guichen put about himself, and proceeded to form again in a line with his rear. No maneuver could have been more suitable to the conjuncture; if it had not been executed in season, the French admiral would have found himself in the most perilous predicament. A few moments after, nine British ships, having tacked, advanced with a press of sail upon the French rear; but when they saw that the main body and van had rejoined it, and that the three divisions presented themselves in the best order, they resumed their station in their own line. Rodney rallied such ships as were dispersed, and again drew up his fleet in order of battle. The two armaments thus remained in presence until night, and even till the succeeding morning, but without renewing the engagement; they probably found that they had suffered too much in this and in the preceding action. Rodney sent the Conqueror, the Cornwall, and the Boyne, which were the most damaged, to be repaired at St. Lucia, and set sail with the rest of his fleet for Carlisle bay, in the island of Barbadoes. The Cornwall went to the bottom near the entrance of Careenage harbor. The count de Guichen returned with his fleet to Fort Royal bay, in Martinico. The loss of the English in these two last actions was sixty-eight killed, and three hundred wounded. The French lost one hundred and fifty-eight killed, and upwards of eight hundred wounded. Among the former were numbered many officers of distinction, and even the son of count de Guichen. The English also had to regret several officers of much reputation. Such was the result of the three battles fought between the French and English in the West Indies; their forces were nearly equal; their valor and skill were entirely so.

Here it may be observed, of what importance are the talents and experience of commanders to the event of combats, and to preserve nations from the most terrible reverses. For it is evident, that if either of the two hostile admirals, in the course of the three days we have been describing, or during all those which they passed in observing each other, had committed a single fault, the defeat and ruin of his fleet must have been its inevitable consequence.

If hitherto the forces of France and of England had been pretty equally balanced in the West Indies, it was not long before the first acquired a decided superiority, by the junction of a Spanish squadron which arrived in those seas. Spain had conceived an ardent desire to acquire Jamaica; and the French as eagerly coveted the possession of the other islands which were still in the power of the enemy. If these objects had been attained, the English would have witnessed the total extinction of their domination in the West Indies. With such views don Joseph Solano had departed from Cadiz, about the middle of April, with twelve sail of the line and some frigates. This squadron escorted upwards of eighty transports, containing eleven thousand Spanish infantry, with a prodigious quantity of artillery and munitions of war; an armament as formidable as flourishing, and suited, without question, to justify the hopes with which the allied courts had flattered themselves, particularly that of Madrid. Already don Solano was well on his way across the Atlantic, shaping his course for Fort Royal, in Martinico. It was there he purposed to make his junction with all the French forces. Rodney continued at anchor in Carlisle bay, attending to the health of his crews, recruiting his provisions and water, and refitting his ships. He had no mistrust of the storm that was about to burst upon him. But captain Mann, who was cruising at large with the frigate Cerberus, fell in with the Spanish convoy; aware of all the importance of the discovery, and feeling assured that his admiral would receive it well, he took upon himself to quit his cruise and return to the West Indies, in order to give the alarm. Upon this intelligence, Rodney put to sea with the least possible delay, for the purpose of meeting the Spanish squadron; confident of victory, if he could fall upon it before its union with the French fleet. Conjecturing with reason, that it was bound to Martinico, he awaited it upon the route usually taken by vessels destined for that island. His dispositions were very judicious; but the prudence and precautions of the Spanish admiral rendered them fruitless. Without any intimation of the design of the English, and of the danger that menaced him, don Solano, as if directed by a secret presentiment, instead of steering directly towards Fort Royal, of Martinico, shaped his course more to the north on his right, and stood for the islands of Dominica and Guadaloupe. As soon as he was arrived in their vicinity, he detached a very swift sailing frigate to the count de Guichen, to request him to come out and join him. The French admiral issued with eighteen ships; and being informed that the English were cruising to windward of the Antilles, in order to avoid encountering them, he sailed under the lee of those islands. This voyage was so well conducted, that the two armaments came together between Dominica and Guadaloupe Assuredly if all these forces, which greatly surpassed those of Rodney, could have been preserved entire, or if the allies had acted more in concert, they must have attained their object, namely, the absolute annihilation of the British power in the West Indies. But these forces, in appearance so formidable, bore within themselves the elements of their own destruction. The length of the passage, the want of fresh provision, the change of climate, and the defect of cleanliness, had generated among the Spanish soldiers a contagious fever, which had spread with incredible rapidity, and made horrible ravages. Besides the deaths in the passage, the squadron had put ashore twelve hundred sick at Dominica, and at least an equal number at Guadaloupe and Martinico. The salubrity of the air, and that of the new diet on which they were put in those islands, did not, however, abate the fury of the pestilence; it swept off every day the most valiant soldiers; it soon attacked also the French, though with less violence than the Spaniards. This unexpected scourge not only diminished the ardor of the allies, but also deprived them of great part of the means essential to the success of their enterprises; they were, moreover, thwarted by the clash of opinions. The Spaniards wanted to undertake in the first place the expedition of Jamaica, the French that of St. Lucia and the neighboring islands. It followed, that all these projects miscarried alike. Compelled to relinquish the brilliant hopes with which they had flattered themselves, the allies re-embarked their troops, scarcely yet well recovered, and made sail in company towards the leeward islands. The count de Guichen escorted the Spaniards into the waters of St. Domingo, and then, leaving them to pursue their voyage, came to anchor at Cape Francois. Here he made his junction with the squadron of M. de la Motte Piquet, who had been stationed in that part for the protection of commerce. The Spaniards proceeded to the Havanna. At the news of the juncture of the allied fleets, Rodney repaired to Gros Islet bay, in St. Lucia. But as soon as he was advised that they had sailed from Martinico, he profited of a re-inforcement of ships and troops that was arrived to him from England, under the conduct of commodore Walsingham, to put Jamaica in a respectable state of defense against the attacks of the allies. He kept the rest of his force at St. Lucia, to watch the motions of the enemy and cover the neighboring islands. Thus vanished the high hopes which had been conceived in France as well as in Spain, from the formidable warlike apparatus directed against the British West Indies. This failure was less the fault of fortune than of that diversity of interests which too frequently produces a want of harmony between allies; they will not march together towards the same object, and disunited they cannot attain it.

The events we have been relating were succeeded, in the West
Indies, by a sort of general truce between the two parties. But
though the fury of men was suspended for a while, that of the elements broke out in a manner much more tremendous. It was now
the month of October, and the inhabitants of the islands were in the
enjoyment of that unexpected tranquillity which resulted from the
cessation of arms, when their shores, and the seas that washed them,
were assailed by so dreadful a tempest, that scarcely would there be
found a similar example in the whole series of maritime records,
however replete with shocking disasters and pitiable shipwrecks. If
this fearful scourge fell with more or less violence upon all the islands
of the West Indies, it no where raged with more destructive energy
than in the flourishing island of Barbadoes. It was on the morning
of the tenth that the tornado set in, and it hardly began to abate
forty-eight hours after. The vessels that were moored in the port,
where they considered themselves in safety, were wrenched from
their anchors, launched into the open sea, and abandoned to the
mercy of the tempest. Nor was the condition of the inhabitants on
shore less worthy of compassion. In the following night, the vehemence of the hurricane became yet more extreme; houses were
demolished, trees uprooted, men and animals tossed hither and
thither, or overwhelmed by the ruins. The capital of the island
was well nigh rased to a level with the ground. The mansion of
the governor, the walls of which were three feet in thickness, was
shaken to its foundations, and every moment threatened to crumble
in ruins. Those within had hastened to barricade the doors and
windows to resist the whirlwinds; all their efforts were of no avail.
The doors were rent from their hinges, the bars and fastenings forced; and chasms started in the very walls. The governor with his
family sought refuge in the subterraneous vaults; but they were soon
driven from that shelter by the torrents of water that poured like a
new deluge from the sky. They issued then into the open country,
and with extreme difficulty and continual perils repaired under the
covert of a mound, upon which the flagstaff was erected; but that
mass being itself rocked by the excessive fury of the wind, the apprehension of being buried under the stones that were detached from
it, compelled them again to remove, and to retire from all habitation.
Happily for them they held together; for, without the mutual aid they
lent each other, they must all inevitably have perished. After a
long and toilsome march in the midst of ruins, they succeeded in
gaining a battery, where they stretched themselves face downward
on the ground, behind the carriages of the heaviest cannon, still a
wretched and doubtful asylum, since those very carriages were con-

tinually put in motion by the impetuosity of tne storm. The other houses in the city, being less solid, had been prostrated before that of the governor, and their unhappy inhabitants wandered as chance directed during that merciless night, without shelter and without succor. Many perished under the ruins of their dwellings; others were the victims of the sudden inundation; several were suffocated in the mire. The thickness of the darkness, and the lurid fire of the lightning, the continual peal of the thunder, the horrible whistling of the winds and rain, the doleful cries of the dying, the despondent moans of those who were unable to succor them, the shrieks and wailings of women and children, all seemed to announce the destruction of the world. But the return of day presented to the view of the survivors a spectacle which the imagination scarcely dares to depict. This island, lately so rich, so flourishing, so covered with enchanting landscapes, appeared all of a sudden transformed into one of those polar regions where an eternal winter reigns. Not an edifice left standing; wrecks and ruins every where; every tree subverted; not an animal alive; the earth strown with their remains, intermingled with those of human beings; the very surface of the soil appeared no longer the same. Not merely the crops that were in prospect, and those already gathered, had been devoured by the hurricane; tne gardens, the fields, those sources of the delight and opulence of the colonists, had ceased to exist. In their place were found deep sand or steril clay; the enclosures had disappeared; the ditches were filled up, the roads cut with deep ravines. The dead amounted to some thousands; thus much is known, though the precise number is not ascertained. In effect, besides those whose fallen houses became their tombs, how many were swept away by the waves of the swoln sea and by the torrents, resembling rivers, which gushed from the hills? The wind blew with a violence so unheard of, that if credit be given to the most solemn documents, a piece of cannon, which threw twelve-pound balls, was transported from one battery to another at more than three hundred yards distance. Much of what escaped the fury of the tempest fell a prey to the frantic violence of men. As soon as the gates of the prisons were burst, the criminals sallied forth, and joining the negroes, always prepared for nefarious deeds, they seemed to brave the wrath of Heaven, and put every thing to sack and plunder. And perhaps the whites would have been all massacred, and the whole island consigned to perdition, if general Vaughan, who happened to be there at the time, had not watched over the public safety at the head of a body of regular troops. His cares were successful in saving a considerable quantity of provision, but for which resource the inhabitants would only have escaped the ravages of the hurricane, to be victims of the no less horrible scourge of famine. Nor should it be passed over in silence by a sincere friend of truth and honorable deeds, that the Spanish prisoners of war, at this time considerably numerous in Barbadoes, under the conduct of don Pedro San Jago, did every thing that could be expected of brave and generous soldiers. Far from profiting of this calamitous conjuncture to abuse their liberty, they voluntarily encountered perils of every kind to succor the unfortunate islanders, who warmly acknowledged their services. The other islands, French as well as English, were not much less devastated than Barbadoes. At Jamaica, a violent earthquake added its horrors to the rage of the tornado; the sea rose and overflowed its bounds with such impetuosity, that the inundation extended far into the interior of the island.

In consequence of the direction of the wind, the effects of the sea-flood were the most destructive in the districts of Hanover and Westmoreland. While the inhabitants of Savanna la Mer, a considerable village of Westmoreland, stood observing with dismay the extraordinary swell of the sea, the accumulated surge broke over them, and in an instant, men, animals, habitations, every thing, was carried with it into the abyss. Not a vestige remained of that unhappy town. More than three hundred persons were thus swallowed up by the waves. The most fertile fields were left overspread with a deep stratum of steril sand. The most opulent families were reduced in a moment to the extreme of indigence. If the fate of those on shore was deplorable beyond all expression, the condition of those who were upon the water was not less to be pitied. Some of the vessels were dashed upon shoals and breakers, others foundered in the open ocean, a few made their way good into port, but grievously battered and damaged. The tempest was not only fatal to ships under sail; it spared not even those that were at anchor in the securest havens Some bilged in port, and many were drifted out to sea by the resist less fury of the billows. Among the first was the Thunderer, of seventy-four guns, which sunk with all on board. Several frigates were so shattered that they were not thought worth repairing. The English had to regret, in all, one ship of seventy-four, two of sixty-four, and one of fifty guns, besides seven or eight frigates.

Amidst so many disasters, they found, at least, some succor in the humanity of the marquis de Bouille. A number of English sailors, the wretched relics of the crews of the Laurel and Andromeda, wrecked upon the coasts of Martinico, fell into the power of that general. He sent them free to St. Lucia, saying, that he would not treat as prisoners men who had escaped the rage of the elements. He expressed a hope that the English would exercise the same generosity towards those Frenchmen whom a similar destiny might have delivered into their power. He testified his regrets that he had only been able to save so few of the English seamen, and that among them there was not a single officer. He concluded with observing that, as the calamity had been common and general, humanity should be extended alike towards all its victims. The merchants of Kingston, the capital of Jamaica, animated by the most honorable social sentiments, immediately made a subscription of ten thousand pounds sterling for the relief of the sufferers. The parliament, as soon as it was apprised of this catastrophe, voted, notwithstanding the pressure of the expenses of the war, a donation of eighty thousand pounds sterling to the inhabitants of Barbadoes, and another of forty thousand to those of Jamaica. Nor was public munificence the only source of their succors ; a great number of private citizens likewise contributed largely to alleviate the distresses of these unfortunate West Indians.

The fleet of the count de Guichen, and that of admiral Rodney, were not exposed to the hurricane. The first was already departed for Europe, in the month of August, escorting, with fourteen sail of the line, a rich and numerous fleet of merchantmen. In consequence of his departure, and in ignorance of his designs, Rodney, to whom, moreover, the Spanish troops landed at the Havana gave no little disquietude, detached a part of his force to cover Jamaica, and made sail with the rest for New York. But before he reached the American continent, and even before he departed from the West Indies, there had happened a surprising revolution in public affairs, of which we shall give an account in due time. While men were engaged in so fierce a war upon the continent, and in the islands of America, while they had to combat there the fury of the elements, the belligerent powers were far from remaining inactive in Europe. Greater unity was observable in the counsels of England ; but, however excellent her marine, it was inferior in force to that of the allied courts. These, on the other hand, had more ships and more soldiers ; but often directed towards very different objects, by opposite interests, they did not obtain the success to which they might have aspired. Thus, for example, the Spaniards, always principally aiming at the conquest of Gibraltar, assembled their forces, and lavished their treasure, at the foot of that fortress. From the same motive they kept their ships in the port of Cadiz, instead of joining them with those of France, and attempting in concert to strike a decisive blow at the British power. It followed that France was obliged to send her squadrons into that same port; and, meanwhile, the British fleets were blockading her Atlantic ports, intercepting her commerce, capturing her convoys, and the frigates that escorted them.

Admiral Geary, who, on the death of sir Charles Hardy, had been appointed to the command of the channel fleet, had put to sea with about thirty sail of the line. He fell in, the third of July, with a fleet of French merchantmen, loaded with cochineal, sugar, coffee, and cotton, under the guard of the ship of war Le Fier, of fifty guns. The English gave chase, and captured twelve sail, and probably would have swept the whole convoy, but for a thick fog and the great proximity of the coasts of France; the rest made their ports in safety. Several other French ships, and even some frigates, fell, a short time after, into the power of the English, but not without a gallant resistance. As we cannot go into a narrative of all the encounters that took place, we will not, however, omit the name at least of the chevalier de Kergarion, captain of the Belle Poule, who with that frigate, of only thirty-two guns, defended himself a long time against the Nonesuch man of war, of sixty-four, commanded by James Wallace. Nor was it till after the death of the intrepid Kergarion, that his successor, M. de la Motte Tabouret, yielded to the necessity of striking his colors; his frigate was completely dismasted; the greater part of the crew had perished.

The allies made themselves ample amends for these losses on the ninth of August. Towards the latter end of July, a numerous fleet of king's ships and merchantmen had set sail from the ports of England for the two Indies. Five of the first, besides much of munitions of war, arms and artillery, were loaded with an immense quantity of rigging for the use of the British fleet, stationed in those distant seas. Eighteen others were either victualing ships or transports, carrying military stores and recruits, to re-inforce the army of America. The others were vessels of commerce, whose cargoes were extremely valuable. This fleet was escorted by the Romulus ship of the line, and three frigates. It was pursuing its voyage, having in sight, at a great distance, the coasts of Spain, when, in the night of the eighth of August, it fell into the midst of a squadron of the combined fleet, which was cruising upon the accustomed route of ships destined for the East or West Indies. The hostile squadron was commanded by admiral don Lewis de Cordova. The English mistook his lanterns at mast head for those of their own commander, and steered accordingly. At break of day, they found themselves intermingled with the Spanish fleet. Don Cordova enveloped them, and shifted the crews of sixty vessels; the ships of war escaped him. His return to Cadiz was a real triumph. The people flocked to behold the prisoners, and this rich booty; a spectacle the more grateful for being uncommon, and little expected. Near three thousand prisoners were put ashore, of every condition, and of every age. Of this number were sixteen hundred sailors, a heavy loss for England, and passengers not a few. The English even regretted much less the cargoes of commercial articles than the munitions of war, of which their armies and fleets in both Indies experienced the most pressing need. . So brilliant a success was received by the Spanish nation with infinite exultation. The news of it spread, on the contrary, a sort of consternation in Great Britain. The ministers found themselves the objects of the bitterest reproaches; the public voice accused them of temerity. 'They knew,' it was exclaimed, 'that the allies had a formidable force at Cadiz; why did they not direct the convoy to avoid the coasts of Spain?'

The events of maritime war did not divert attention from the siege of Gibraltar. Spain, as we have already seen, attached an extreme importance to the conquest of this place. She appeared to make it the capital object of the war, and the aim of all her efforts. It must be admitted, in effect, that, apart from all political considerations, so powerful a monarch could not have seen, without indignation, a fortress upon his own territory possessed by foreigners, who, from its summit, appeared to set him at defiance. Gibraltar revived the history of Calais, which had also long appertained to England, but which the French at length recovered; the Spaniards promised themselves the like good fortune. Accordingly, after that place had been revictualed by Rodney, the Spanish admiral, don Barcelo, exerted all his vigilance to prevent its receiving any fresh succors. On the other hand, general Mendoza, who commanded the troops on shore, endeavored to press the fortress on the land side. He daily added new works to his camp of St. Roch, and pushed his approaches with all possible diligence. But whatever was the assiduity and ability of the Spanish commanders, they were so thwarted by the instability of the winds and sea, and the British officers displayed so much talent and activity, that, from time to time, victualing transports found their way into the place. The garrison forgot their sufferings, and resumed courage, while the Spaniards could but gnash with rage at seeing the resistance protracted so long beyond their confident expectations.

The efforts of the garrison were powerfully seconded by some ships of war which admiral Rodney had left in the port; one of this number was the Panther, of seventy-four guns. To remove so troublesome an obstacle, the Spaniards formed a design to burn this squadron with the transport vessels at anchor behind it. They hoped even to involve in the conflagration the immense magazines of munitions which had been constructed upon the shore. They prepared for this purpose seven fire-ships, which were to be accompanied by an immense number of armed galleys and boats. Don Barcelo advanced his fleet, and formed it in line of battle across the mouth of the harbor, as well to direct and second the attack, as to intercept any vessel that should attempt to escape. On the side of the land, don Mendoza held himself in readiness to menace the garrison upon all points; he was to commence the most vigorous bombardment as soon as the fire should break out on board the British squadron. The night of the sixth of June was chosen for the enterprise. The darkness, the wind, and the tide, were alike propitious. The English manifested a perfect security. The fire-ships advanced, and every thing promised success, when the Spaniards, either through impatience, or from the extreme obscurity of the night, misjudging their distance, or else not wishing to approach nearer, applied the fire with too much precipitation. This unexpected sight apprised the English of their danger. Immediately, without terror, and without confusion, officers and soldiers throw themselves into boats, intrepidly approach the fire-ships, make fast to them, and tow them off to places where they can do no mischief. The Spaniards, after this fruitless attempt, withdrew.

Meanwhile, don Mendoza busied himself with unremitting ardor in urging the labors of his lines. General Elliot, to whom the king of England had confided the defense of the place, suffered his adversary to go on; but when he saw his works well nigh completed, he opened upon them so violent a cannonade, that in a short time he demolished and ruined them entirely. He also made frequent sallies, in which he filled up the trenches, and spiked the artillery of the besiegers. The English became daily more confident; the Spaniards, on the contrary, seemed less animated and sanguine. Chagrined that a handful of men—since the garrison of Gibraltar, including officers, did not exceed six thousand combatants,—should not only presume to resist them, but even to attack them with success, they had recourse to an expedient, which at length rendered the defense of the place exceedingly difficult and perilous, and finally operated the total destruction of the city; and that was, to construct an immense number of craft which they called gun-boats. Their burthen was from thirty to forty tons, and their crew from forty to fifty men; they were armed at the prow with a twenty-six pounder; others mounted mortars. Besides a large sail, they had fifteen oars on each side. As they were easily worked, it was intended to employ them to overwhelm the town and forts with bombs and balls during the nights, and even, if the opportunity should present itself, to attack the frigates. It was believed that two of these gun-boats might engage a frigate with advantage, because of their little elevation above the water, and the diminutive scope they afforded to the balls of the enemy. The governor of Gibraltar not having a similar flotilla at his disposal, it became almost impossible for him to avoid its effects. The Spaniards were sensible of it, and this consideration revived their ardor, and reanimated their hopes.

While the arms of England prevailed upon the American continent; while those of the two ancient rivals balanced each other in the West Indies, and the war was carried on in Europe with such variety of success that it was singularly difficult to conjecture what would be the issue of the mighty struggle, the situation of affairs in the United Provinces, which had hitherto offered only doubt and incertitude, began to assume a less ambiguous aspect. It seemed to have been decreed by destiny, that the quarrel of America should shake the whole globe. The coalition of the arms of Holland with those of the Bourbons and of the congress, seemed to consummate the formidable league that was to level the last stroke at the British power. From the very commencement of the troubles of America, her cause had found many more partisans in Holland than that of England. Many motives concurred to this disposition of minds; the political opinions which obtained generally in Europe; the persuasion that prevailed among the Hollanders that the interests of protestantism were inseparable from this discussion; the apprehension entertained by the dissenters of the usurpations, real or supposed, of the church of England; and, finally, the similarity of the present condition of the Americans to that in which the United Provinces found themselves in the time of their wars against Spain. It is, therefore, not to be wondered at, if the French party in Holland gained every day upon the English party. It is also to be observed, that even those most attached to the latter party by the remembrance of ancient friendship, by the community of commercial predilections, and by the apprehension of the evil that France might do them in future, were among the most forward to condemn the policy pursued by the British government towards its colonies. They censured it the more sincerely, as they foresaw that one of its inevitable consequences would be to interrupt the good understanding they wished to preserve, and to confirm the ascendency of French politics in Holland.

To these considerations should be added, the jealousy that existed
of the power of the stadtholder, allied by consanguinity to the king
of England ; it was feared lest that monarch might lend him support
to accomplish the usurpations he meditated, or was suspected of
meditating.   The republicans, therefore, were not without anxious
apprehensions respecting the intentions of the British government.
They dreaded the dark reach of its policy ; they shuddered in thinking that it might one day subject them by the hand of the stadtholder
to that same destiny which it was now striving to entail on America.
Every day these sinister images were presented to all eyes ; they
had a powerful influence on public opinion.   Of the seven United
Provinces, that which inclined the most decidedly for France was
by far the most wealthy and powerful—Holland.   The first of the
cities of the republic, Amsterdam, manifested the same sentiments.
To foment these dispositions, and to draw other provinces and
other cities into the same way of thinking, the French government
had recourse to the agency of that love of gain, whose empire is particularly so despotic with those who apply themselves to commerce.
It declared that it would cause to be seized upon sea every Dutch
vessel found employed in any sort of trade with Great Britain, those
only excepted which belonged to the cities of Amsterdam and Har-
lem.   The effect of this measure was, that several important cities,
among others Rotterdam and Dordrecht, had gone over to France,
in order to participate in the privileges she granted.

It was already two years since from this complication of different
interests, there had resulted a standing negotiation, at Aix la Chapelle, between John Neuville, acting in the name of the pensioner
Van Berkel, a declared partisan of France, and William Lee, commissioner on the part of congress.   Van Berkel, as chief of the government of the city of Amsterdam, succeeded, after many and
protracted discussions, in bringing about a treaty of amity and commerce between that city and the United States of America.   This
treaty, it was said, was merely eventual, since it was not to take
effect until the independence of the colonies should have been acknowledged by England.   But was it not a recognition of that independence as already absolute, to negotiate and treat with the United
States ?   The treaty, it is true, had only been concluded with the
single city of Amsterdam ; but it was hoped that the preponderance
of that capital in the province of Holland would easily draw after it
the rest of that province, and that the example of Holland would
guide the other six.

These negotiations were conducted with so much secrecy, that no whisper of them had reached England. But the congress, ardently desirous that the result of these mysterious stipulations should be as public as possible, appointed to this effect their president, Laurens, minister plenipotentiary to the States-General. This resolution was the more readily adopted, since it was not doubted in America, and the correctness of the opinion was demonstrated by the event, that the Dutch were exasperated to the last degree by the insulting shackles which England attempted to impose on their commerce with France, and especially by that intolerable seizure of the convoy of the count de Byland. Far from attempting to palliate these outrages, and to appease discontents, M. York, ambassador of the king of England at the Hague, had just delivered the States-General a memorial, framed in so arrogant a style, that it was universally considered as offensive to the dignity of a free and independent nation.

But fortune, who seems to make her sport of the best concerted projects, willed that those of the Hollanders should come to the knowledge of the British ministers before they could receive their accomplishment. No sooner was Laurens departed from the American shores, than he was encountered and captured off Newfoundland, by the British frigate Vestal. At sight of the enemy, he had thrown all his papers overboard ; but by the celerity and dexterity of a British sailor, they were rescued from the water before they were materially injured. Laurens was carried to London, and shut up in the tower as a state prisoner. Among his papers, the British ministers found the treaty above mentioned, and some letters relative to the negotiations at Aix la Chapelle. Forthwith, M. York made a great stir at the Hague. He required the States-General, in the name of his master, not only to disavow the doings of the pensioner Van Berkel, but also to make instant reparation to his Britannic majesty, by the exemplary punishment of that magistrate and his accomplices, as perturbators of the public peace, and violators of the laws of nations. The States-General withholding their answer, the British envoy renewed his instances with excessive fervor ; but the Dutch government, either from its reluctance to drop the mask at present, or merely from the accustomed tardiness of its deliberations, signified to York that the affair should be taken under serious consideration. The States-General were inclined to gain time to recall into their ports the rich cargoes they had afloat upon the ocean, as well as those which, in the security of a long peace, had been deposited in their islands.

On tne other hand, the British ministers, goaded by impatience to lay hand upon those riches, and little disposed to allow the Dutch sufficient leisure to make the necessary war preparations, pretended not to be at all satisfied with the answer of the States-General. They recalled the ambassador at the Hague immediately. A little after, there followed on both sides the usual declarations. Thus were dissolved all those relations of good understanding, which had so long existed between two nations connected by reciprocal congenialities, and by many and important common interests. This new enemy was the more to be apprehended for England, as his dexterity in maritime war was rendered more formidable by his proximity. But on the one hand, pride, perhaps necessary to a powerful state, and the thirst of conquest, always blamable and never satisfied; on the other, intestine dissensions, and the debility of land force, which inspired more dread of continental neighbors than could well comport with independence, precipitated Great Britain and Holland into a war decidedly and openly condemned by all sound statesmen.

It is time to remand our attention upon the American continent. After the capture of Charleston and invasion of South Carolina, a great and astonishing change was wrought in the minds of the colonists. Their salvation resulted from those very causes which seemed to prognosticate an impending perdition. So true it is that the spur of adversity forces men to exert, for their own interests, efforts to which the sweets of prosperity cannot induce them! Never was this truth better exemplified than in the present conjuncture; the reverses of Carolina, far from having dejected the Americans, developed in them, on the contrary, a courage more active, and a constancy more pertinacious. They could no longer be reproached with that torpor which they had manifested in the preceding years, with that apathy which had been the source of so much pain to their chiefs, as of such heavy disasters to the republic. A new ardor inflamed every heart to fly to the succor of country; there seemed a rivalry for the glory of immolating all to the republic; things looked as if the first days of the revolution were come back, when the same spirit and the same zeal broke out on all parts against England. Every where private interests were postponed to the public weal; every where it was exclaimed, ' Let us drive this cruel enemy from the most fertile provinces of the Union; let us fly to the succor of their inhabitants; let us crush the satellites of England that have somehow escaped American steel, and terminate at a single blow a war protracted too long.' Thus ill fortune had again tempered the souls of this people, at the very moment when they were supposed the victims of dejection and despair.   Their rury was still quickened by the devastations which the royal troops had recently committed in Carolina and New Jersey.   Their hope became confidence, on observing that the consequences of the reduction of Charleston had been to divide the enemy's forces, and to distribute them at so great distances, that they might be attacked at every point with assurance of success.   And how were these hopes multiplied by the authentic advice of the approaching arrival of French succors !   Already a great number of Americans counted the conquest of New York as a compensation of the occupation of Charleston.

The marquis de la Fayette was in effect just returned from France, whence he had brought the most cheering intelligence.   He announced that the troops were already embarked, and the ships that bore them on the point of getting under sail for America.   This report might be depended on.   The marquis de la Fayette had ascertained it with his own eyes, after having exerted himself with much zeal to accelerate the preparatives of the expedition.   He was warmly thanked for it by Washington and the congress.   His presence was grateful to the American people ; it redoubled, especially, the ardor of the soldiers, who mutually incited one another, to show themselves not unworthy of the allies they expected.   They declared aloud that an eternal reproach would be their portion, if, through a base apathy, they should lose the glorious occasion about to be offered them in this powerful co-operation of France.   They reminded each other that the eyes of all Europe were upon them, and that on the issue of the present campaign depended the liberty, the glory, the future destiny of the American republic.   The congress, all the established authorities, and even private citizens of weight with the multitude, dexterously profited of this new enthusiasm; they neglected no means that could cherish and propagate it.   The congress addressed circular letters to all the states, earnestly exhorting them to complete the regiments, and dispatch to the army the contingent that each of them was bound to furnish.   These instances were strongly seconded by generals Washington, Reed, and other influential chiefs.

Their efforts had all the success desirable.   The militia had recovered their spirits, and they rejoined their colors from all quarters. The authority of congress revived on every side, and acquired new vigor.   Sensible to the wants of the state, the capitalists subscribed with promptitude considerable sums to the relief of the public treasure, the exhaustion of which was then extreme.   The city of Philadelphia first gave the example of these sacrifices ; it was not unfruitful. It was soon followed by all Pennsylvania and the other provinces. The ladies of Philadelphia, animated by the most ardent patriotism, formed a society, and placed at their head mistress Washington, a wife worthy of such a husband. After having subscribed for the use of the state to the extent of their means, they went from house to house to stimulate the liberality of the citizens in favor of the republic. Their zeal was not steril; they collected large sums, which they lodged in the public chest, to be used in bounties to such soldiers as should merit them, and in augmentation of pay to all. They were imitated with enthusiasm by the ladies of the other states. But among all the institutions that signalized this epoch, none is more worthy of attention than the establishment of a public bank. The funds lodged in it by the stockholders, by lenders, and by congress, might be employed to defray the army. The congress found herein not only a great facility on the part of the most wealthy commercial houses of Philadelphia, but even received from them the most generous offers. The subscribers obligated themselves to furnish a capital of three hundred thousand pounds Pennsylvania currency, which rates the Spanish dollar at seven shillings and sixpence. It was to have two directors, with authority to borrow money upon the credit of the bank for six months, or any shorter time, and to give the lenders bills bearing an interest of six per cent. The bank was to receive the deposits of congress; that is, the public revenue accruing from taxes or other sources; but when these deposits and the funds borrowed should not suffice, the stockholders were bound to furnish such proportion as should be deemed necessary, of the sums for which they might have subscribed. The sums obtained in the different ways above mentioned, were not to be employed for any other purpose but that of procuring supplies for the troops. The stockholders were to appoint an agent, whose office it should be to make purchases, and to transmit the articles bought, such as meat, flour, rum, etc., to the commander-in-chief, or to the minister of war; this agent should have authority to draw upon the directors for his payments. The said agent was also to keep open a store well stocked with rum, sugar, coffee, salt, and other articles of general consumption, with obligation to sell them by retail at the same price he should have bought them for in quantity of those with whom he should have contracted for the supplies of the army, with a view of being more promptly and better served by those contractors. Although, out of the bank, few lenders presented themselves, because the greater part, before advancing their money, would have wished more stability in the state, yet subscribers were soon found for a capital of three hundred and fifteen thousand pounds of Pennsylvania. Each of them gave their written obligation to furnish the directors a definite sum in gold or silver coin. Thus, private citizens, prompted by the most laudable zeal for the country, stepped forward to support the public credit with their personal responsibility ; a conduct the more worthy of encomium, as the situation of affairs still offered but too many motives of doubt and distrust.

Could it have been imagined, however, that at the very moment when a victorious enemy still threatened the existence of their infant republic, the Americans did not rest content with offering their blood and their treasure for its defense? Amidst the din of arms, they were studious to accelerate the advancement of philosophy, science and the arts. They reflected that, without the succor of these lights, war tends directly to barbarism, and even peace is deprived of its most precious sweets. In devoting themselves to these noble cares, they regarded not merely the advantages that were to redound thence for the greater civilization of their country ; they had also in view to demonstrate at home and abroad, by this profound security, in the midst of so many agitations, what was their contempt for the danger, and their confidence in the success of their enterprise. Such were the considerations under which the state of Massachusetts founded at Boston a society, or academy of arts and sciences. Its statutes corresponded to the importance of the institution. Its labors were principally directed to facilitate and encourage a knowledge of the antiquities and natural history of America ; to ascertain the uses to which its native productions might be applied ; to promote medical discoveries, mathematical inquiries, physical researches and experiments, astronomical, meteorological and geographical observations ; improvements in the processes of agriculture, arts, manufactures and commerce ; the academy was, in brief, to cultivate every art and science that could tend to advance, according to its own language, the ' interests, the honor, the dignity, and the happiness of a free, independent and virtuous people.' On the fourth of July, after having celebrated with the greatest solemnity the anniversary of independence, the president of congress, the governor of the state of Pennsylvania, and the other authorities, both of the city and province, as also the chevalier de la Luzerne, the minister of France, repaired with no ordinary pomp to the university, to attend the collation of degrees. The director of the studies delivered an address well suited to the occasion. The generous spirit of the students was fired with new ardor for their country ; all the audience shared their enthusiasm, and drew from it the must felicitous presages. It was amidst this general display of zeal and efforts to proceed with honor in the chosen career, that the succors sent by France to the support of her allies, made their appearance at Rhode Island. At this sight, transports of exultation burst forth throughout the American continent. They consisted of a squadron of seven sail of the line, among which was the Duc de Bourgogne, of eighty-four guns, with five frigates and two corvettes, under the conduct of M. de Ternay. This force convoyed a great number of transports, which brought six thousand soldiers, at the orders of the count de Rochambeau, lieutenant-general of the armies of the king. According to an agreement made between the court of Versailles and the congress, Washington, as captain-general, was to command in chief all the troops, as well French as American. The king of France had created him, to this intent, lieutenant-general of his armies, and vice-admiral of his fleets. The inhabitants of Newport celebrated the arrival of the French by a general illumination. General Heath received them with every mark of welcome and courtesy.

It being rumored at that time that Clinton meditated an attack upon Rhode Island, the French troops were put in possession of all the forts. They fortified themselves therein with so much diligence, that in a short time they were in a situation to defy the efforts of any enemy whatsoever.

The general assembly of the state of Rhode Island sent a deputation to compliment the general of his most christian majesty. They said many things of the profound acknowledgment of America towards that generous monarch. They promised on their part every sort of aid and succor. The count de Rochambeau answered them that the corps he had brought was merely the vanguard of the army which the king his master was about to send to their assistance. That his majesty sincerely wished the liberty and happiness of America, and that his troops should observe an exemplary discipline among those whom they were to regard in the light of kindred. He concluded with saying, that, as brothers, he himself, his officers, and all his people, had voluntarily devoted their lives to the service of the Americans.

The presence and promises of the French general inspired all hearts with courage and with hope ; but the partisans that England had preserved in the country, were forced to disguise their rage. Washington, the more to cement the union of the two nations, ordered that in the banners of his army, the ground of black. which is the color of America, should be surrounded with white, the distinctive color of France.

At this epoch, admiral Arbuthnot, who still occupied the New York station, had with him only four ships of the line ; and, far from contemplating an attack, was himself in dread of being attacked. A few days after, however, admiral Graves arrived from England, with six other sail of the line. This superiority of force decided the English to undertake an expedition against Rhode Island. Admiral Graves repaired thither first with his squadron, to see if any mean would offer itself to destroy that of the enemy in the very harbor of Newport ; but the French had made such imposing preparations of defense, that, without temerity, nothing could be attempted against them. The British squadron made the best of its way back to New York. Meanwhile, general Clinton, being resolutely determined not to suffer the French to establish themselves on a permanent footing in that part, formed a design to attack Rhode Island with a picked corps of six thousand men, that should disembark at some point the most favorable to the enterprise. The admiral gave into the plan, although, to his private judgment, it presented little probability of success. The British squadron got under sail, and already it had proceeded as far as Huntingdon bay, in Long Island, when Washington, who watched all the movements of his adversary, began to stir. Seeing general Clinton advance with so considerable a corps, and finding himself, thanks to fresh re-inforcements, at the head of twelve thousand men, he descended by forced marches along the banks of the Hudson. Arrived at Kings Bridge, he menaced to carry even the city of New York, then disgarnished, and exposed almost without defense to a coup de main. On the other hand, the militia of New England had run to arms, panting to give the French, in the outset, a high notion of their force and of their zeal. Already ten thousand men were on the march towards Providence, and a still greater number were preparing to follow them. The British generals were not long in being apprised of all these movements, and found themselves still more divided in opinion than before. These motives, combined, determined Clinton to relinquish his projects ; he returned without delay to New York, with all his forces. The timidity manifested by the English in this occurrence, was a fresh spur to the ardor of the Americans. They already considered the garrison of New York as vanquished, and within their grasp. They had, moreover, a particular subject of encouragement. The French that were arrived in Rhode Island, had brought an immense quantity of the coined money of their country. According to the custom of the military of their nation, they never lost any occasion of spending it to the last crown. It followed that in a short time French specie became so common in the

United States, as to restore some vigor to the body politic, which, from the exhaustion of its finances, was become languid to a point even almost threatening an absolute dissolution. The bills of credit, it is true, experienced an increase of depression ; but this evil excited no alarm. For a long time, this paper had lost all confidence, and the state soon after relieved itself of it altogether, as will be seen in the sequel of this history.

The various causes we have noticed had generally infused new life into the Americans of the different states ; but it is to be observed that they operated with more efficacy on the inhabitants of the southern provinces. These were more immediately exposed to danger, and they had, besides, peculiar motives for detesting the insolence of the English. Accordingly, as soon as the occasion was offered them, they assembled upon different points of North Carolina, and upon the extreme frontier of South Carolina. These assemblages, commanded by daring chiefs, gave no little annoyance to the royal troops. They insulted their posts, and sometimes even carried them. But among all the officers who distinguished themselves at the head of these desultory parties, none appeared with more splendor than colonel Sumpter. Born himself in South Carolina, his personal importance, military talents and prowess, had rendered him there an object of general consideration. The greater part of those Carolinians whom their aversion to British domination had induced to fly from their homes, had hastened to place themselves under the standard of their intrepid fellow-citizens. They were already sufficiently numerous to keep the field, and to menace the enemy upon all points. They had no pay, no uniforms, nor even any certain means of subsistence ; they lived upon what chance, or their own courage, provided them. They experienced even a want of arms and munitions of war ; but they made themselves rude weapons from the implements of husbandry ; instead of balls of lead, they cast them of pewter, with the dishes which the patriots cheerfully gave them for that purpose. These resources, however, were very far from sufficing them. They were seen, several times, to encounter the enemy with only three charges of ammunition to a man. While the combat was engaged, some of those who were destitute of arms or ammunition, kept themselves aside, waiting till the death or wounds of their companions should permit them to take their place. The most precious fruit, to their eyes, of the advantages they gained over the English, was that of being enabled to acquire muskets and cartridges at the expense of the vanquished. At length, colonel Sumpter, finding himself at the head of a numerous corps, attacked one of the most important positions of the enemy, at Rocky Mount. He was repulsed, but not discouraged. Never giving repose either to himself or to his adversaries, he fell, a short time after, upon another British post, at Hanging Rock, and put to the edge of the sword all that defended it, regulars and loyalists. He subjected to a similar fate colonel Bryan, who was come from North Carolina with a body of loyalists of that province. Infesting the enemy upon all points at once, he eluded all their efforts to quell him. His invincible courage and perfect knowledge of the country offered him continually new resources. As rapid in his attacks as industrious in his retreats, victor or vanquished, he escaped all the snares of his foes. Colonel Williams served no less usefully the same cause, at the head of a light detachment of Carolinians of the district of Ninety-Six. In one of his frequent excursions he surprised and cut in pieces a body of loyalists on the banks of the river Ennoree. This partisan war had the double advantage of restoring confidence to the Americans, of continually mining the forces of the English, and of supporting the party of congress in these provinces. These smart skirmishes were only, however, the prelude of the bloody battles that were about to ensue between the principal armies.

As soon as Washington was first apprised of the siege of Charleston, he had put on the march towards South Carolina a re-inforcement of fourteen hundred continental troops of Maryland and of Delaware, under the conduct of the baron de Kalb. That officer displayed great activity in the execution of his orders, and, if it had been possible for him to gain the point of his destination, it is probable that things would have taken another direction. But the defect of provision, the difficulty of places, and the excessive heat of the season, opposed him with such and so many impediments, that he could only progress step by step. It is related, that this detachment had no other subsistence for many days than the cattle that were found astray in the woods. Sometimes, finding themselves totally destitute of flesh and flour, the soldiers were constrained to sustain life with the grain of unripe wheat and such fish as they could procure; they supported such hardships and distress with an heroic constancy. In passing through Virginia, they were re-inforced by the militia of that province; and, on their arrival at the banks of Deep river, they made their junction with the troops of North Carolina, commanded by general Caswell. These detachments, combined, formed a corps of six thousand effective men; a force so considerable with respect to the United States, as to induce the congress to employ it without delay for the expulsion of the English from the two Carolinas. Wishing to confide this operation to a man whose name should exercise a happy influence, they made choice of general Gates. The baron de Kalb was recalled ; as a stranger, unacquainted with the country, and ignorant of the proper mode of governing undisciplined militia, he could not retain the command.

General Gates arrived at the camp on Deep river the twenty-fifth of July. He immediately reviewed the troops, to ascertain their number and quality. He afterwards advanced upon the Pedee river, which, in the lower parts, separates the northern from the southern Carolina. The name and fortune of Gates produced so favorable and so rapid an effect, that not only the militia flocked to his standard, but also that munitions and provision abounded in his camp. The general impulse was given. Already the inhabitants of that tract of country which extends between the Pedee and Black rivers, were in arms against the royal troops. Colonel Sumpter, with a corps of infantry and light horse, incessantly harassed the left of the English, in the hope of intercepting their communication with Charleston ; his parties scoured all the environs.

As soon as general Gates was arrived upon the confines of South Carolina, he issued a proclamation, by which he invited the inhabitants to join him in vindicating the rights of America. He promised an entire amnesty, and remission of all penalty in favor of those from whom the victors should have extorted oaths, excepting only such individuals as should have exercised acts of barbarity or depredation against the persons and property of their fellow-citizens. This proclamation was not unfruitful; not only the people ran to arms in multitude to support the cause of congress, but even the companies levied in the province for the service of the king either revolted or deserted. Strengthened by these accessions, colonel Sumpter became every day a more formidable enemy for the English. While Cornwallis was occupied at Charleston with the administration of Carolina, lord Rawdon had taken the command of the troops cantoned at Camden and the adjacent country. He had directed upon Georgetown a convoy of sick soldiers, under the escort of a detachment of Carolinians, commanded by colonel Mills. About the middle of the route, these militia mutined, and having seized their officers, conducted them with the sick English to the camp of general Gates. Colonel Lisle, one of those who had taken oath to the king, gained over a battalion of militia that had been levied in the name of Cornwallis, and led it entire to colonel Sumpter. The latter, who incessantly scoured the western bank of the Wateree, had captured considerable convoys of munitions of war, rum and provision that had been sent from Charleston upon Camden. There had also fallen into his power, at the same time, a great number of sick, with the soldiers that formed their escort. Already the route from Camden to Ninety-Six was invested by the republicans; and they began to show themselves in force upon that from Camden to Charleston. Thus the affairs of the king in the Carolinas began to assume an unfavorable aspect. Lord Rawdon, seeing so lowering a tempest about to burst upon him, and destitute of sufficient means to avert its effects, concentered what troops he had in the vicinity of Camden, and distributed his cantonments upon the right bank of Lynches Creek. He hastened to give notice of his critical position to lord Cornwallis. In the meantime, Gates appeared with all his forces upon the other bank, and encamped in the front of the enemy. There ensued very warm and frequent skirmishes, with balanced success. The American general would have desired a decisive action, and to profit of his superiority to attack lord Rawdon even in his quarters. But on examination, finding the enemy's position too strong, he dropped the design. His conduct appeared dictated by wisdom; but at the same time, he let slip an opportunity for gaining a signal advantage. If he had ascended by forced marches to the source of the Lynche, he turned without difficulty the left wing of lord Rawdon, and might even seize Camden on the rear of the British army; this stroke would have decided the fate of the campaign; but either Gates did not see it, or was afraid to undertake it. A short time after, the British general, seeing his right menaced by a movement of the Americans, and fearing for his magazines and hospital, abandoned the banks of the Lynche, and fell back upon Camden with all his troops. His retreat was in no shape molested by the enemy. At that very time lord Cornwallis arrived in camp. Having surveyed the state of things, and finding to what a degree the forces and audacity of the republicans were augmented, he detached numerous parties on discovery, filled up the companies with the more vigorous convalescents, ordered distributions of arms, and the remounting of Tarleton's legion, which needed horses. Notwithstanding all his efforts, he had not, however, been able to assemble above two thousand men, of whom about fifteen hundred were veteran troops, the rest loyalists and refugees. To attack, with means so feeble, an enemy so superior, appeared little less than temerity. Cornwallis might indeed have made his retreat to Charleston; but in that case he must have left about eight hundred sick, with a vast quantity of valuable stores, to fall into the hands of the enemy. He likewise foresaw, that excepting Charleston and Savannah, a retreat would be attended with the loss of the two whole provinces of South Carolina and Georgia. On the other hand, he observed, that the major part of his army was composed of soldiers as perfectly equipped as inured to war, and commanded by officers of approved valor and ability. He saw in victory the entire reduction of the two Carolinas, whereas even discomfiture could scarcely have worse consequences than retreat.

Under these considerations, he determined not only to face the enemy, but even to hazard a general action. Camden, the center of the British line, not being a fortified place, and the boldest resolutions being often also the most fortunate, Cornwallis would not await the Americans in his cantonments. He formed a design to attack the position of Rugeleys Mills, which the enemy occupied, with a view of forcing him to an engagement. On the fifteenth of August, all the royal troops were ordered to hold themselves in readiness to march. About ten o'clock in the evening, the columns put themselves in motion for Rugeleys. The first, commanded by colonel Webster, consisted in light infantry and dragoons. The second, under the conduct of lord Rawdon, was composed of Irish volunteers and loyalists. Two English battalions formed the reserve. In the rear was the baggage and a detachment of grenadiers. The English marched, amid the obscurity of the night, in the most profound silence. The columns passed the little stream of Saunder, and had already left Camden ten miles behind them. But while the English were advancing upon Rugeleys Mills, the Americans themselves had quitted that place, at ten o'clock, with intent to surprise them. Gates and Cornwallis had both at once formed the same design, the one against the other. The American van consisted in the legion of cavalry of colonel Armand, flanked on the right by the light infantry of colonel Porterfield, and on the left by the light infantry of major Armstrong. Next, marched the brigades of Maryland regulars, with the militia of North Carolina and Virginia. The baggage followed the rear guard, formed of a numerous corps of volunteers, with light horse at the two flanks. General Gates had commanded his troops to march compactly and in silence, and not to fire without order. He had sent to Wacsaw, on his rear, the sick, the unnecessary baggage, in a word, whatever might tend to impede his march. So many precautions, on both sides, indicated that the two generals had mutually penetrated one the other. It was yet only two in the morning, when the advanced guard of the British army encountered the head of the first American column. It was briskly repulsed by colonel Porterfield; but that officer received a serious wound. The English, supported by two regiments of infantry, charged the Americans in their turn. The action was engaged with spirit, and the loss considerable on both sides; but, all of a sudden, equally fearing to hazard a nocturnal conflict, the two generals suspended the fire, and again the most profound silence reigned in the midst of darkness; the day was impatiently awaited.

Meanwhile, Cornwallis ascertained by the people of the country, that the ground was as propitious to him as it was unfavorable to the enemy. Gates, in effect, could not advance to the attack but through a narrow way, bordered on either side by deep swamps. This circumstance, by depriving the Americans of the advantage of superior number, re-established an equality of forces. The British general formed his plan of battle accordingly. By daylight he disposed the front of his army in two divisions; that of the right, commanded by colonel Webster, had its right flank covered by a morass, and its left supported upon the great road; the other division, under the conduct of lord Rawdon, had in like manner a morass on its left, while its right was re-united by the highway to the corps of Webster. The artillery was placed between the two divisions. A battalion, drawn up behind each, served them as a sort of rear guard. Tarleton's legion was posted upon the right of the road, in readiness to attack the enemy or receive him, according to the occasion. The Americans, on their part, made all the dispositions that appeared to them the most suitable. Gates divided his vanguard in three columns. That of the right, commanded by general Gist, having the morass on its right, connected by its left upon the great road with the column of the center, composed of the North Carolina militia, led by general Caswell. The column of the left comprised the militia of Virginia, at the orders of general Stevens. Behind the Virginians were posted the light infantry of Porterfield and Armstrong. Colonel Armand had placed his cavalry behind the left, to face the legion of Tarleton. The continental troops of Maryland and Delaware formed the reserve. They were inured to war, and upon their valor rested the chief hope of success. They were commanded by general Smallwood. The artillery was placed in part upon the right of the continental troops, and in part upon the highway.

Such was the order of battle of the two armies; when, just as the action was about to commence, Gates, not satisfied with the position of the divisions of Caswell and Stevens, very imprudently ordered them to change it for another which appeared to him better. Cornwallis, at sight of this movement, resolved to profit of it instantly. Accordingly, he ordered colonel Webster to advance and make a vigorous attack upon Stevens, whose troops were still undulating, from their not having yet been able to reform their ranks. Colonel Webster obeyed with celerity. The battle thus commenced between the right of the English and the left of the Americans ; it soon became general. The morning being still and hazy, the smoke hung over and involved both armies in such a cloud that it was difficult to see the state of destruction on either side. The British troops, however, intermingling a quick and heavy fire with sharp charges at the point of the bayonet, evidently gained ground upon the Americans. At length the Virginians, pressed by colonel Webster, and already half broken by the unadvised movement directed by Gates, after a feeble resistance, shamefully betook themselves to flight. The Carolinian militia, finding themselves uncovered, soon began to give way, and at last turned the back with a similar baseness. Their officers attempted in vain to rally them ; they were themselves involved in the rout. The left wing of the Americans was totally broken ; Gates and Caswell made some efforts to reform it ; but Tarleton adroitly seized the decisive moment, and, with a furious charge, carried to its height the confusion and consternation of that wing ; all the troops that composed it threw themselves into the neighboring woods. Their flight exposed the left flank of a Carolinian regiment, and of the regulars of Maryland and Delaware, who were already attacked in front. The right wing of the English, now completely victorious, turned furiously upon the American center. This division defended themselves with the utmost gallantry ; if it was not in their power to restore the fortune of the day, they saved at least the honor of the republican standard.

Opposing the enemy with a terrible fire, or the push of their bayonets, they withstood all his efforts. The baron de Kalb led them several times to the charge ; and they even recovered lost ground. But at length, surrounded on all sides, overwhelmed by number, and penetrated by cavalry, they were constrained to abandon the field of battle, but without having left a bloodless victory to their foes. Pierced with eleven wounds, the baron de Kalb fell dying into the power of the victors. The rout was general ; each provided for his own safety. General Gist could rally no more than a hundred infantry, and the dragoons of Armand. The British cavalry pursued the vanquished with vehemence for the space of twenty-three miles, and without halting, till exhaustion imposed the necessity of repose.

The loss of the Americans in this action was very considerable. The number of the dead, wounded and prisoners, was estimated at upwards of two thousand. Among the first was general Gregory, and among the prisoners, the baron de Kalb, and general Rutherford, of Carolina. Eight pieces of brass cannon, two thousand stand of arms, several colors, with all the baggage and stores, fell into the hands of the conqueror. The loss of the British, in killed and wounded, amounted, including officers, only to three hundred and twenty-four.

Three days after the battle, the baron de Kalb, perceiving the approach of death, requested his aid-de-camp, the chevalier Dubuisson, to express, in his name, to generals Gist and Smallwood, his high sense of the valor displayed in the battle of Camden by the regular troops of Maryland and Delaware. He spent his last breath in declaring the satisfaction which he then felt in having fallen in the defense of a cause so noble, and, to him, so dear. The congress ordered that a monument should be erected to him at the city of Annapolis, the capital of Maryland.

General Gates was reproached with several grave errors. The least excusable was doubtless that of having undertaken to change his order of battle in presence of the enemy. Perhaps he was also in fault to march in the night unwarlike militia, who knew not even how to keep their ranks. He retreated to Hillsborough, in North Carolina. Generals Gist and Smallwood fell back upon Charlotte-town, and afterwards upon Salisbury, where they endeavored to rally the fugitives and to reorganize their divisions; but the cause of England triumphed throughout the province of South Carolina; the banners of the republic no longer waved in any part of it. Colonel Sumpter alone continued to show himself upon the banks of the Wateree, with a corps of about a thousand men, and two field pieces. But on the news of the late discomfiture of Gates, he retired promptly towards the fords of Catawba, in the upper parts of North Carolina. Lord Cornwallis, a man of great activity, reflecting that his advantages were insecure till he should have destroyed this last body of republicans, detached colonel Tarleton in pursuit of it. The latter, moving with his accustomed celerity, fell unexpectedly upon the position of Sumpter, who had thought he might take some repose on the banks of Fishing creek. Tarleton surprised him so completely, that his men, lying totally careless and at ease, were mostly cut off from their arms. Their only resource was in a prompt flight; but a great number fell into the hands of the enemy, who slaughtered them after they had surrendered. Tarleton alledged that he could not grant them life, because his whole party was not equal in number to one third of Sumpter's. At length the carnage ceased, when the English and loyalists that were detained prisoners in the rear of Sumpter's position had been liberated. The cannon, stores and baggage, were the prey of the victors. Colonel Sumpter, with a few of his followers, made good their escape. The disaster of his corps could not be imputed to him; he had not omitted to send out scouts upon the direction of the enemy, but that service was acquitted with an unpardonable negligence. Tarleton returned to Camden the third day, with his prisoners, booty, and the loyalists he had retaken.

After the battle of Camden, Cornwallis, in order not to lose by his tardiness the fruits of victory, could have wished to advance immediately into North Carolina, a feeble province, and very ill disposed towards the congress. Thence he could march to the conquest of Virginia. Unquestionably, the presence of the victorious army in that part would have dispersed the relics of the vanquished, prevented their rallying anew, and encouraged the friends of the royal cause to show themselves, and even to act. But the British general encountered divers obstacles that opposed the execution of this plan. The heat of the season was excessive, the climate unhealthy, and the hospitals were encumbered with wounded and sick. The necessaries for encampment were almost entirely wanting; there was not a single magazine upon the frontiers of the Carolinas; and North Carolina could furnish but very little provision. Yielding to these considerations, Cornwallis relinquished all ulterior operation, distributed his troops in cantonments, and returned to Charleston. He thought himself sure at least of the submission of all South Carolina, and of the not distant conquest of North, as soon as the season and the state of his magazines should favor the enterprise. In the meantime, he wrote frequently to the friends of royalty in North Carolina, exhorting them to take arms, to assemble in force, and to make themselves masters of the most ardent republicans, with their munitions and magazines. He counseled them even to seize the fugitives and stragglers of the rebel army. He promised them, that it should not be long before he marched to their assistance. And to inspire them with confidence in his words, even before he could move with his whole army, he detached major Ferguson, an able and enterprising partisan, upon the western frontiers of North Carolina. He had under his command a thousand loyalists and a corps of cavalry. His mission was to encourage by his presence the enemies of the revolution, and especially to open a correspondence with the inhabitants

of Tryon county, who, more than the others, showed themselves at
tached to the name of England.

Unable to operate in the field, Cornwallis turned his attention towards the internal administration, in order to consolidate the acquisition of South Carolina. Resolved to have recourse to extreme
remedies for terminating the crisis in which that province found itself,
he purposed to spread terror among the republicans by the rigor of
punishment, and deprive them of the means to do harm, by depriving them of the means to subsist. Accordingly, he addressed orders
to all the British commanders, that without any delay they should
cause to be hung all those individuals, who, after having served in
the militia levied by the king, had gone over to the rebels; that they
should punish with imprisonment and confiscation those, who, having
submitted at first, had taken part in the last rebellion, to the end that
their effects might be applied to indemnify those subjects whom they
should have oppressed or despoiled. It cannot be denied, that if it
was possible to excuse such severity towards those who had exchanged
the condition of prisoners of war for that of British subjects, it was
worthy of an eternal blame in respect to those who had wished to
remain in the first of these conditions. In effect, had they not been
released from their parole by the authentic proclamation of Cornwallis himself, under date of the third of June? But victors, too often,
by vain subtilties, or even without deigning to have recourse to them,
especially in political convulsions, makes port of violating their faith,
as if it were a necessity for them to add to the evils inseparable from
war, all the vexations of perfidy! However this might be, and however rigorous were the orders of Cornwallis, they were every where
punctually executed. Carolina was become a theater of proscriptions. Several British officers openly testified their abhorrence of
this reign of blood; but the greater part, and Tarleton more than any
other, commended it without shame, as useful and necessary to the
success of the royal cause. Already Tarleton had complained bitterly of the clemency, as he called it, exercised by Cornwallis prior
to the battle of Camden; this clemency, he said, was not only good
for nothing, but also prejudicial in every thing, since it rendered
friends less hearty, and enemies more audacious. This reproach
would certainly have been founded, if it were true that in war utility
alone deserves regard, and that nothing is due to humanity, good
faith and justice. Nobody denies, for example, that to poison springs,
massacre all the prisoners that can be taken, bring off into slavery all
the inhabitants of a country, without distinction of age or sex, and
without regard for the law of nations, might sometimes have a use-

ful tendency. We see, nevertheless, that in all time, civilized nations, and conquerors not entirely barbarous, have abstained from these horrible extremities. But in the present occurrence, the English showed themselves without pity for the most respectable men of the country. The inhabitants of Camden, of Ninety-Six, of Augusta and other places, saw inhumanly gibbeted men whose only crime was that of having been too faithful to a cause which they considered as that of their country and of justice.

All minds were penetrated with horror ; all hearts were inflamed with an implacable and never-dying hatred against such ferocious victors. A cry of vengeance resounded amidst this exasperated people ; all detested a king who had devoted them to the oppression of these brutal executors of his will. His standard became an object of execration. The British generals learned by cruel experience, that executions and despair are frail securities for the submission of a people planted in distant regions, actuated by a common opinion, and embarked with passion in a generous enterprise. Nor were these the only rigors which Cornwallis thought it expedient to exercise, in order to confirm the possession of the provinces conquered by his arms. To complete the reduction of the patriots, he employed arrests and sequestrations. He feared that the presence in Charleston of the leading men, who, persevering in their character of prisoners of war, had refused to accept that of subjects, might tend to keep alive a spirit of resistance. He likewise learned, as the British writers affirm, that these prisoners had maintained a secret correspondence with the enemies of the English name, the proofs of which had been found in the baggage of the American generals captured at the battle of Camden. These motives appeared to him sufficient to justify the seizure and imprisonment at St. Augustine, in East Florida, of more than thirty of the most influential chiefs of the American party. They were all of the number of those who had taken the most active part in the organization of the republican government, and who had shown themselves the most ardent partisans of the present war. Then, desirous to prevent those who were, or whom he believed, opposed to Great Britain, from assisting the congress with their pecuniary means, or with a hope to constrain them to submission, he issued a proclamation, purporting the sequestration of the possessions of whoever should hold correspondence with the congress, act in its name, join the enemies of England, or excite the people to revolt by word or deed. He constituted, at the same time, a commissioner over sequestrated estates, with obligation to account to the families of the forfeited for a part of their net revenue ; a fourth to those consisting of a wife and children, and a sixth to wives without children. A clause required, however, that these families should reside in the province. These different measures, combined with a rigorous watchfulness over the movements of the suspected, appeared to the English a sure guaranty for the return of tranquillity and obedience in the province of South Carolina. *And as to North Carolina*, it could no longer hope to resist them when the weather became temperate, and the harvests were over. We shall see, in the course of this history, how far these hopes were confirmed by the event.

While the season had caused the suspension of hostilities in the two Carolinas, and while, in the state of New York, the superiority of the Americans by land, and that of the English by sea, had occasioned a similar cessation of arms, an unexpected event arrested the general attention. During some time, a design had been maturing in the shades of mystery, whose execution, had it succeeded to the wish of its authors, would have involved the total ruin of the army of Washington, and, perhaps, the entire subjugation of America. A single instant more, and the work of so many years, cemented at such a cost of gold and blood, might have been demolished to its foundations by a cause altogether unthought of. The English had well nigh arrived, by means of treason, at that object which with five years of intrigues and of combats they had not been able to attain; and it was even at the hands of the man they least suspected, that the Americans were to have received the most fatal blow. They had but too manifest a proof, that no confidence can be placed in courage when disunited from virtue. They learned that men who displayed the most enthusiasm for a cause, are often also those who become the soonest unfaithful; and that an insatiable thirst of pelf, coupled with mad prodigalities, easily conduct the ambitious spendthrift to barter basely for gold even the safety of his country. Private virtues are incontestably the original and only basis of public integrity; and it should never be forgotten, that the man without morals, who arrives at the first offices of the republic, has no other object but to satiate his ambition or his cupidity at the expense of his fellow-citizens. If he encounter obstacles, he is ripe for deeds of violence within, and treason without. The name of general Arnold was deservedly dear to all the Americans; they considered him as one of their most intrepid defenders. Numerous wounds, and especially that which had almost deprived him of the use of one leg had forced him to take repose at his seat in the country.

The congress, with the concurrence of Washington, in recompense for his services appointed him commandant of Philadelphia, immediately after that city was evacuated by the English, and return-ed under American domination. Here Arnold lived at an enormous expense, and showed himself extremely grasping in order to support it. He had established himself in the house of Penn, and had fur-nished it in the most sumptuo''s manner. His play, his table, his balls, his concerts, his banquets, would have exhausted the most im-mense fortune. His own, and the emoluments of his employment, being far from sufficient to defray such extravagance, he had betaken himself to commerce and privateering. His speculations proved unfortunate ; his debts accumulated, his creditors tormented him. His boundless arrogance revolted at so many embarrassments ; yet he would diminish nothing of this princely state. Under these cir-cumstances, he conceived the shameful idea of re-imbursing himself from the public treasure for all he had squandered in riotous living. Accordingly, he presented accounts more worthy of a shameless usurer than of a general. The government, astonished and indig-nant, appointed commissioners to investigate them. They refused not merely to approve them ; they reduced the claims of Arnold to half. Enraged at their decision, he loaded them with reproaches and insults, and appealed from it to the congress. Several of its members were charged to examine these accounts anew, and to make report. They declared that the commissioners had allowed Arnold more than he had any right to demand. His wrath no longer observed measure ; the congress itself became the object of the most indecent invectives that ever fell from a man in high station. This conduct, far from restoring tranquillity, produced a quite contrary effect. That spirit of order for which the Americans are distinguished, did not permit them to quit thus an affair already in progress. Arnold was accused of peculation by the state of Pennsylvania, and brought before a court martial to take his trial. Among the charges laid against him, he was accused of having converted to his own use the British merchan-dise he had found and confiscated at Philadelphia, in 1778 ; as also of having employed the public carriages for the service of different private individuals, and especially for his own and that of his associ-ates in the commerce of New Jersey. The court sentenced him to be reprimanded by Washington. This sentence neither satisfied the accused nor the accusers. The latter exclaimed that more regard had been shown to the past services of Arnold than for justice ; the former broke into bitter complaints of the iniquity of his judges and ingratitude of his country. His pride could not brook so public a disgrace ; he had seen himself the idol of his fellow-citizens, and he was now become the object of their contempt, if not hatred In the blindness of his vengeance, and in the hope that he might still glut his passions with British gold, since he no longer could with American, he resolved to add perfidy to avidity, and treason to pillage. Determined that his country should resume the yoke of England, he developed his projects in a letter which he addressed to colonel Robinson. General Clinton was immediately made acquainted with its contents. He committed this secret negotiation to major Andre, his aid-de-camp, a young man as distinguished for the suavity of his manners and the gentleness of his temper, as for the singular comeliness of his person. Arnold and Andre corresponded together, under the assumed names of Gustavus and Anderson. The American general was promised a corresponding rank in the British army, and considerable sums of gold. He, on his part, engaged to render the king some signal service. The consequence of this understanding was a demand that West Point should be given up to the royal troops. That fortress, situated upon the western bank of the Hudson, is of extreme importance, in that it defends the passage of the mountains in the upper part of the river. Accordingly, the Americans had been at such pains and expense to render it impregnable, that it was called with reason *the Gibraltar of America.* Into this all-important citadel, Arnold formally pledged himself to introduce the English. Hence, pretending to have taken an aversion to the residence of Philadelphia, and that he wished to resume an active service in the army, he requested and obtained the command of West Point, and of all the American troops cantoned in that quarter. But his plan embraced more than the mere delivery of the fortress ; he purposed so to scatter his forces in the environs, that Clinton might easily fall upon them by surprise, and cut them off at the same stroke. Masters of West Point, and having no more enemies before them, the English would then have marched rapidly against Washington, who had distributed his troops upon the two banks of the Hudson ; their destruction must have been total and inevitable. Thus, therefore, besides West Point, and those passes which had been so often disputed, and for which the British government had undertaken the fatal expedition of Burgoyne, the Americans would have lost their whole army, their artillery, their munitions of war, and their best officers. May it not even be conjectured, that if the English should have profited of the confusion and consternation which could not fail to have resulted from so sudden a catastrophe, the United States would have found themselves necessitated to receive the law of the conqueror?

About the middle of September, Washington had been called to Hartford, in Connecticut, upon some affairs which required his presence. The conspirators considered the occasion propitious for the accomplishment of their designs. It was agreed that, in order to concert more particularly the last measures, major Andre should repair secretly to the presence of Arnold. Accordingly, in the night of the twenty-first of September, he landed from the Vulture sloop of war, which already long since Clinton had stationed up the river not far from West Point, to facilitate the correspondence between the two parties. Arnold and Andre passed the whole night in conference. The day having dawned before all their dispositions were concluded, the British aid-de-camp was concealed in a secure place. The following night, he wished to regain the Vulture; but the boatmen would not convey him thither, because the excess of his precautions had inspired them with some distrust. He was obliged to take the way of the land. Arnold gave him a horse and a passport under the name of Anderson. Until then he had worn the British uniform under a riding coat; he threw it off, and took a common dress, though, it is said, much against his will, and at the earnest importunity of Arnold. He had already safely passed the American guards and outposts, and might reasonably hope to arrive without obstacle at New York; but fate had reserved a different issue for the infamous perfidy of Arnold, and the generous devotion of major Andre towards his country.

As he was going through Tarrytown, a village situated in the vicinity of the first British posts, three soldiers of the militia, who happened to be there, threw themselves across his passage. He showed them his passport; they suffered him to continue his route. All of a sudden, one of these three men, more distrustful than his comrades, thought he had observed something particular in the person of the traveller; he called him back. Andre asked them where they were from. 'From down below,' they replied, intending to say from New York. The young man, too frank to suspect a snare, immediately answered, 'And so am I.' They arrest him. He then declared himself, for what he was, a British officer. He offered all the gold he had with him, a valuable watch, rewards and rank in the British army as the price of his release; all his efforts were vain. John Paulding, David Williams, and Isaac Van Wert,—such were the names of the three soldiers,—were found incorruptible; a disinterestedness the more worthy of eulogium, as they were poor and obscure. Thus, in the very moment when one of the most distinguished chiefs of the American army, a man celebrated throughout the world for his brilliant exploits, betrayed, out of a base vengeance, the country he had served, and sold it for a purse of gold, three common soldiers

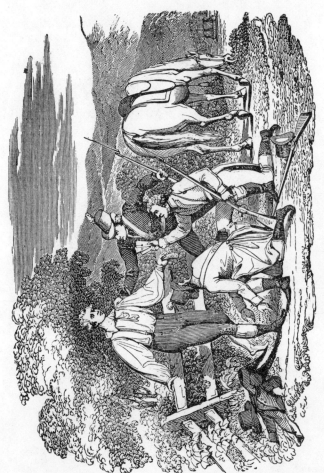

CAPTURE OF ANDRE Vol. II.—p. 300

preferred the honest to the useful, and fidelity to fortune. They diligently searched their prisoner, and found in his boots several papers written by the hand of Arnold himself, containing the most detailed information with respect to the positions of the Americans, their munitions, the garrison of West Point, and the most suitable mode of directing an attack against that fortress. Major Andre was conducted before the officer who commanded the advanced posts. Afraid of hurting Arnold by an immediate disclosure of his true character, and braving the danger of being instantly put to death as a spy, if it should be discovered that he had concealed his real name, he persisted in affirming that he was Anderson, as indicated by his passport. The American officer was at a loss what to decide; he could not persuade himself that his general, after having so often shed his blood for the country, was now resolved to betray it. These hesitations, the negations of Andre, the distance at which Washington, and even Arnold, found themselves, gave the latter time to escape. As soon as he heard that Andre was arrested, he threw himself into a boat and hastened on board the Vulture. The news of this event excited universal amazement. The people could scarcely credit the treachery of a man in whom they had so long placed the utmost confidence. The peril they had run filled them with consternation; the happy chance which had rescued them from it, appeared a prodigy. ' God,' they said, ' has not permitted that men of honor should be victims of perfidy; it is his almighty hand that has saved us; he approves and protects the cause of America.' Maledictions were heaped upon Arnold, praises upon those who had arrested Andre.

Meanwhile, Washington returned from Connecticut to his camp. Suspecting, first of all, that the plot might have more extensive ramifications, and not knowing on what individuals to fix his eye, he busied himself in taking the most prompt and efficacious measures to baffle their pernicious designs. He feared also lest the contagion of example might incite even those who were strangers to the conspiracy to entertain rash desires for a new order of things. He knew that the way once cleared by some audacious individuals, the multitude are but too apt to hurry blindly after them. These apprehensions offered themselves the more naturally to his mind, as the pay of his troops was considerably in arrear, and as they were in want of many of the necessaries not only of war, but even of life. The precautions of the commander-in-chief were fortunately superfluous. Nobody stirred; nothing led to the presumption of Arnold's having had accomplices.

When major Andre, from the time elapsed, could infer that Arnold must be in safety, he revealed nis name and rank. He appeared less solicitous about his safety, than to prove that he was neither an impostor nor a spy. He endeavored to refute the appearances which seemed to depose against him. He affirmed that his intention had been merely to come and confer, upon neutral ground, with a person designated by his general; but that thence he had been trepanned and drawn within the American lines. From that moment, he added, none of his steps could be imputed to his default, since he then found himself in the power of others. Washington, meanwhile, created a court martial; among its members, besides many of the most distinguished American officers, were the marquis de la Fayette and the baron de Steuben. Major Andre appeared before his judges; they were specially charged to investigate and define the nature of the offense, and the punishment it involved, according to the laws of war. The demeanor of the young Englishman was equally remote from arrogance and from meanness. His blooming years, the ingenuous cast of his features, the mild elegance of his manners, had conciliated him an interest in every heart.

In the meantime, Arnold, being safely arrived on board the Vulture, immediately wrote a letter to Washington. He impudently declared in it that it was the same patriotism of which he had never ceased to give proofs since the origin of the contest, which had now prescribed him his present step, whatever men might think of it, always so ill judges of the actions of others. He added, that he asked nothing for himself, having already but too much experience of the ingratitude of his country, but that he prayed and conjured the commander-in-chief to have the goodness to preserve his wife from the insults of an irritated people, by sending her to Philadelphia among her friends, or by permitting her to come and rejoin him at New York. This letter was followed by a dispatch from colonel Robinson, likewise dated on board the Vulture. He earnestly demanded that major Andre should be released, urging, in his defense, that he had gone ashore on public business and under the protection of a flag, as well by the invitation of Arnold as by the command of his own general; that he was the bearer of a regular passport for his return to New York; that all his doings during the time he had passed with the Americans, and especially the change of his dress and name, had been dictated by the will of Arnold. The colonel concluded with alledging that the major could no longer be detained without a violation of the sanctity of flags and a contempt for all the laws of war as they are acknowledged and practiced by all nations.   General Clinton wrote in much the same style in favor of Andre.   In the letter of that general was enclosed a second from Arnold; its language could not pretend to the merit of reserve. He insisted that in his character of American general, he was invested with the right to grant Andre the usual privilege of flags, that he might approach in safety to confer with him; and that in sending him back, he was competent to choose any way he thought the most proper.   But major Andre betrayed less anxiety respecting his fate than was manifested in his behalf by his countrymen and friends. Naturally averse from all falsehood, from all subterfuge, desirous, if he must part with life, to preserve it at least pure and spotless to his last hour, he confessed ingenuously that he had by no means come under the protection of a flag; adding, that if he had come so accompanied, he should certainly have returned under the same escort.   His language manifested an extreme attention to avoid imputing fault to any; abjuring, on the contrary, all dissimulation in regard to what concerned him personally, he often avowed more than was questioned him; so much generosity and constancy were universally admired.   The fate of this unfortunate young man wrung tears of compassion even from his judges.   All would have wished to save him, but the fact was too notorious.   The court martial, on the ground of his own confession, pronounced that he was, and ought to be considered as a spy, and as such to be punished with death. Washington notified this sentence to Clinton, in the answer to his letter.   He recapitulated all the circumstances of the offense, inviting him to observe, that although they were of a nature to justify towards major Andre the summary proceedings usual in the case of spies, still he had preferred to act in respect of him with more deliberation and scruple; that it was therefore not without a perfect knowledge of the cause that the court martial had passed the judgment of which he apprised him.   But Clinton, half delirious with anguish at the destiny of Andre, whom he loved with the utmost tenderness, did not restrict himself to the efforts he had already made to preserve him.   He again wrote to Washington, praying him to consent to a conference between several delegates of the two parties, in order to throw all the light possible upon so dubious an affair.   Washington complied with the proposal; he sent general Greene to Dobb's Ferry, where he was met by general Robertson on the part of the English.   The latter exerted himself with extreme earnestness to prove that Andre could not be considered as a spy. He repeated the arguments already advanced of the privilege of flags, and of the necessity that controlled the actions of Andre while he was in the power of Arnold. But perceiving that his reasoning pro- duced no effect, he endeavored to persuade by the voice of humani ty; he alledged the essential importance of mitigating by generous counsels the rigors of war; he extolled the clemency of general Clin- ton, who had never put to death any of those persons who had violat- ed the laws of war; he reminded, that major Andre was particularly dear to the general-in-chief, and that if he might be permitted to re- conduct him to New York, any American, of whatever crime ac- cused, and now in the power of the English, should be immediately set at liberty. He made still another proposition; and that was, to suspend the execution of the judgment, and to refer the affair to the decision of two officers familiar alike with the laws of war and of nations, such as the generals Knyphausen and Rochambeau. Finally, general Robertson presented a letter from Arnold, directed to Wash- ington, by which he endeavored to exculpate the British prisoner, and to take all the blame of his conduct upon himself. He did not re- tire till after having threatened the most terrible retaliations, if the sentence of the court martial was executed; he declared in particu- lar, that the rebels of Carolina, whose life general Clinton had hith- erto generously spared, should be immediately punished with death. The interposition of Arnold could not but tend to the prejudice of Andre; and even if the Americans had been inclined to clemency, his letter would have sufficed to divert them from it. The conference had no effect.

Meanwhile, the young Englishman prepared himself for death. He manifested, at its approach, not that contempt which is often no other than dissimulation, or brutishness; nor yet that weakness which is peculiar to effeminate, or guilty men; but that firmness which is the noble characteristic of the virtuous and brave. He re- gretted life, but he sighed still deeper at the manner of losing it. He could have wished to die as a soldier, that is, to be shot; but he was doomed to the punishment of spies and malefactors, to the infamous death of the halter. This idea struck him with horror; he painted it with force to the court martial. It made him no answer, not will- ing to grant his request, and esteeming it a cruelty to refuse it ex- pressly. Two other causes of despair increased the anguish of the unhappy youth. One was the fear that his death would reduce to indigence and wretchedness a mother and three sisters, whom he tenderly loved, and whom he supported with his pay; the second, lest the public voice should accuse Clinton of having precipitated him, by his orders, into his present dreadful situation. He could not think, without the most bitter regrets, that his death might be laid to the charge of that man, whom he loved and respected the most. He obtained permission to write to him; he used it but to recommend to his protection his unhappy mother and sisters, and to bear testimony that it was not only against his intentions, but even against his positive orders, that he had introduced himself into the camp of the Americans, and had assumed a disguise. The second day of October was destined to be the last of his existence. Brought to the foot of the gibbet, he said; And must I die thus? He was answered, that it could not be otherwise. He did not dissemble his profound grief. At length, after having passed a few moments in prayer, he pronounced these words, which were his last; ' Bear witness that I die as a brave man should die.' Such was the just but melancholy end of a young man deserving in so many respects of a better destiny. It cast a damp of sadness over enemies as well as friends. Arnold gnashed with rage, if, however, that polluted soul was still capable of remorse. The English themselves eyed him with abhorrence, both as traitor, and as original cause of the death of the hapless Andre. In policy, nevertheless, any instrument being thought good, provided it serves the end proposed, Arnold was created brigadier-general in the British armies. Clinton hoped that the name and influence of this renegade would induce a great number of the Americans to join the royal standard. Arnold at least was well aware, that since he had abandoned them, he could not show too much fervor for the cause of England. And such being the irresistible ascendant of virtue, that even the most depraved are forced to assume its semblance, he thought fit to publish a memorial, by which he hoped to mask his infamy. He alledged that in the commencement of the troubles, he had taken arms because he believed the rights of his country were infringed; that he had given into the declaration of independence, although he had thought it ill timed; but that when Great Britain, like a relenting and tender mother, had extended her arms to embrace them, offering them the most just and the most honorable conditions, the refusal of the insurgents, and especially their alliance with France, had entirely changed the nature of the quarrel, and transformed a glorious cause into a criminal revolt; that ever since that epoch he had been desirous to resume the relations of ancient allegiance towards England. He declaimed with violence against the congress; he painted in the most odious colors its tyranny and avarice; he railed against the union with France, affecting a profound grief that the dearest interests of the country had thus been sacrificed to an arrogant, inveterate and pertidious enemy. He represented France as too feeble to establish independence, as the bitterest foe of the protestant faith, as deceitfully pretending a zeal for the liberty of the human race, while she held her own children in vassalage and servitude. Arnold finished with declaring, that he had so long delayed the disclosure of his sentiments, from a wish, by some important service, to effect the deliverance of his country, and at the same time to avoid as much as possible the effusion of blood. He addressed this memorial to his countrymen in general. A few days after, he published another, directed to the officers and soldiers of the American army. He exhorted them to come and place themselves under the banners of the king, where they would find promotion and increase of pay. He vaunted of wishing to conduct the flower of the American nation to peace, liberty and safety; to rescue the country from the hands of France, and of those who had brought it to the brink of perdition. He affirmed that America was become a prey to avarice, an object of scorn for her enemies, and of pity for her friends; that she had exchanged her liberty for oppression. He represented the citizens thrust into dungeons, despoiled of their property; the youth dragged to war, blood streaming in torrents. 'What,' he exclaimed, 'is America now, but a land of widows, orphans and beggars? If England were to cease her efforts for her deliverance, how could she hope to enjoy the exercise of that religion for which our fathers once braved ocean, climate and deserts? Has not the abject and profligate congress been seen of late to attend mass, and to participate in the ceremonies of an anti-christian church, against the corruptions of which our pious ancestors would have borne testimony at the price of their blood?' These declamations of a traitor proved the more fruitless the more they were insolent and exaggerated. America, moreover, had writers who stepped forward to refute them, in a style as animated as the reasoning was triumphant. They observed, among other things, that none more than Arnold, even subsequent to the rejection of accommodation with England, had been the devoted and obsequious courtier of France, none more than him had danced attendance upon her generals and agents; that on the first arrival of the minister Gerard at Philadelphia, he had pressed him to inhabit his house; that he had lavished, in his honor, the most sumptuous banquets, the most splendid balls, the most gorgeous galas; that he had been the supple flatterer of Silas Deane, the most servile tool of France; in a word, that on all occasions he had given the French grounds to believe that they had not in all the United States a more sincere friend than himself. 'But such,' it was said, 'is the ordinary conduct of the ambitious; alternately cringing and super-cilious, they are not ashamed to tax others with their own vices.' Thus Arnold found retorted against himself those arguments from which he had anticipated the most success.

As to the congress, they deemed it beneath their dignity to appear to take the least notice of the perfidy or the pamphlets of Arnold. Only to testify their high sense of the noble conduct of the three soldiers who had arrested major Andre, they passed a resolution creating in favor of each of them a life annuity of two hundred dollars, free of all deductions. They also decreed that they should be presented with a silver medal, struck express, bearing upon one face the word *Fidelity*, and upon the other the following motto; *Vincit amor patriæ*. The executive council of Pennsylvania issued a proc-lamation, summoning Benedict Arnold, in company with some other vile men, to appear before the tribunals to make answer for their defection, and declaring them, otherwise, subject to all the pains and penalties usually inflicted on criminals convicted of high treason. This was the only act in which any public authority deigned to make mention of Arnold.

The details of the conspiracy of New York have necessarily diverted our attention for some time from the theater of war. We proceed now to recount the various success of the British arms in the Carolinas. The month of September approached its close, when the British generals, who had re-inforced their troops and recruited their necessary stores and provision, resolved to re-enter the field and complete those operations which they had commenced, and which were to be the most important fruit of the victory of Camden. They flattered themselves that the rumor alone of their march upon North Carolina would suffice to determine the American army to evacuate it immediately. They already beheld in no distant per-spective not only the conquest of that province, but also that of Vir-ginia. They calculated that when to the possession of the two Carolinas, of Georgia and New York, they should have added this, Virginia, so fertile and so powerful, the Americans, crushed by the burthen of the war, must of necessity submit to the laws of Great Britain. The decline and humiliation of their enemies appeared to them inevitable. Lord Cornwallis and general Clinton were to co-operate simultaneously to bring about this grand result; the first, by advancing from South into North Carolina; the second, by sending a part of his army from New York into the lower parts of Virginia, where, after having passed the Roanoke, it was to operate its junc-tion with the army of Cornwallis upon the confines of North Carolina. In pursuance of this plan, Clinton had detached upon the Chesapeake bay a corps of three thousand men, under the command of general Leslie. He landed his troops as well at Portsmouth as upon the adjacent points of that coast, ravaging and burning all the magazines, and especially those of tobacco, of which an immense quantity was destroyed. Many merchant vessels fell into the hands of the English. In this quarter, they were to wait for news of the approach of Cornwallis, then to push rapidly forward to the banks of the Roanoke, where the junction was to be effected. But the distance being great, and as unforeseen accidents might impede the contemplated union of the two corps, Clinton had directed Leslie to obey the orders of Cornwallis. His intention was, that if the junction by land was found subject to insurmountable obstacles, Cornwallis might cause a part of that corps to come round to him in the Carolinas, by way of the sea. That general, on his part, had put himself on the march from Camden upon Charlottetown, a village situated in North Carolina. Nevertheless, to hold South Carolina in check, and to preserve the way open to retreat thither, if it was necessary, he had not contented himself with leaving a strong garrison in Charleston. Several detachments were distributed upon different points of the frontier ; colonel Brown was posted at Augusta, colonel Cruger at Ninety-Six, and colonel Trumbull with a stronger corps at Camden. Lord Cornwallis had then advanced, with the main body of the army and some cavalry, by the way of Hanging Rock, toward Catawba, while Tarleton with the rest of the cavalry passed the Wateree and ascended along its eastern bank. The two corps were to rendezvous, and re-unite at Charlottetown. They arrived there in effect about the last of September. But the English were not slow in perceiving that they had undertaken a far more arduous enterprise than they had contemplated. The country in the environs of Charlottetown was steril, and broken by narrow and intricate defiles. The inhabitants were not only hostile, but also most vigilant and audacious in attacking detached parties, in cutting off couriers and convoys while on the way from Camden to Charlottetown. Hence the royalists could not sally into the open country, whether to forage, or gain intelligence, except in strong detachments. Moreover, colonel Sumpter, always enterprising, and prompt to seize any occasion for infesting the British, seemed to be every where at once, upon the frontiers of the two Carolinas. Another partisan corps, of similar audacity, had just been formed under the conduct of colonel Marion. Finally, the alarming intelligence was announced, that colonel Clarke had assembled a numerous body of mountaineers from the upper parts of the Carolinas, a most hardy and warlike race of men. Though the valiant defense of colonel Brown had defeated a coup de main which they had attempted against Augusta, yet they still kept the field. Their chief had led them into the mountainous part, in order to unite with colonel Sumpter, or, at least, if the corps of Ferguson prevented that, to await new re-inforcements of the inhabitants of those regions, whose ardor he well knew

The royalists thus found themselves surrounded by clouds of republicans. Placed in the midst of a country where every thing combined against them, they more resembled a besieged army than troops marching upon an expedition. An unexpected accident came to aggravate yet more the distress of their position. Colonel Ferguson, as we have already seen, had been detached by lord Cornwallis upon the frontiers of North Carolina, to encourage the loyalists to take arms. A considerable number had repaired to his standard, but the greater part were of the most profligate and of the most ferocious description of men. Believing any thing admissible with the sanction of their chief, they put every thing on their passage to fire and sword. Excesses so atrocious must have inflamed the coldest hearts with the desire of vengeance ; they transported the mountaineers with fury. They descended into the plain by torrents, arming themselves with whatever chance threw within their reach. They foamed at the name of Ferguson ; they conjured the chiefs they had given themselves, to lead them upon the track of this monster, that they might make him expiate the ravages and blood with which he had stained himself. Each of them carried, besides his arms, a wallet and a blanket. They slept on the naked earth, in the open air ; the water of the rivulet slaked their thirst ; they fed on the cattle they drew after them, or on the game they killed in the forests. They were conducted by the colonels Campbell, Cleveland, Selby, Seveer, Williams, Brandy and Lacy. Every where they demanded Ferguson with loud cries. At every step they swore to exterminate him. At length they found him. But Ferguson was not a man that any danger whatever could intimidate. He was posted on a woody eminence which commands all the adjacent plain, and has a circular base. It is called Kings Mountain. An advanced guard defended its approach by the direct road. The mountaineers soon forced them to fall back ; then, forming in several columns, they endeavored to make their way good to the summit. The attack and the defense were equally obstinate ; some from behind trees others under the cover of rocks, maintained an extremely brisk fire At length those commanded by Cleveland arrived upon the brow of the hill. The English repulsed them with the bayonet. But the column of Selby came up at the same instant, and it was necessary to dispute the ground with it immediately. It began to give way, when colonel Campbell took part in the combat. Ferguson received him with gallantry; but what could avail his efforts against assaults incessantly renewed, and always with more fury! He was surrounded; and he did all that a man of skill and courage could do to extricate himself. But already the crown of the mount was inundated with Americans. They summoned Ferguson in vain to surrender; he perished sword in hand. His successor immediately demanded and obtained quarter. The carnage had been dreadful; the royalists had to regret above eleven hundred men in killed, wounded and prisoners, a loss extremely serious in the present circumstances. All the arms and munitions fell into the power of the conquerors. They observed the laws of war towards the English; but they displayed an excessive rigor against the loyalists. They hung several without listening to their remonstrances. They alledged, that this execution was only a just reprisal for that of the republicans put to death by the loyalists at Camden, at Ninety-Six, and at Augusta. They even insisted that the persons whose lives they had taken, had forfeited them by their crimes according to the laws of the country. Thus was added to the inevitable rigors of war all the ferocity of civil dissensions.

The mountaineers, after this victory, returned to their homes. The check of Kings Mountain was a heavy blow to the British interests in the Carolinas. The position of Cornwallis became critical. The loyalists no longer manifested the same zeal to join him; and he found himself with a feeble army in the midst of a hostile and steril country. He clearly foresaw that a movement forward would but increase the embarrassments under which he already labored. Compelled, therefore, to relinquish for the present the invasion of North Carolina, where the public mind was decidedly in favor of the republicans, he resolved, at least, to maintain himself in South Carolina until he should have received re-inforcements. He accordingly abandoned Charlottetown, repassed the Catawba, and took post at Winnsborough. From that point, he was at hand to correspond with Camden and Ninety-Six; and the fertility of the adjacent country secured him better quarters. At the same time, he sent orders to general Leslie, who was still in Virginia, to embark his troops forthwith, and after having touched at Wilmington, to repair with all expedition to Charleston.

The retreat of the English from Charlottetown to Winnsborough, and their defeat at Kings Mountain, animated the republicans with uncommon alacrity. They hastened in multitude to place themselves under the standards of their most daring chiefs, among whom the more prominent were the colonels Sumpter and Marion.   The latter scoured the lower, the former the upper parts of the province. Sometimes Camden, sometimes Ninety-Six were menaced.   The royal troops could scarcely quit their camp for provision, wood or forage, without running the greatest hazard of being surprised   To put an end to these continual alarms, Tarleton made a movement which menaced colonel Marion ; but the American, who intended only to harass his enemy, and not to engage him in the open field, retired precipitately.   The Englishman pursued him ; but he received, at the same instant, orders from lord Cornwallis, enjoining him to turn upon colonel Sumpter.   That partisan was on the march towards Ninety-Six; he had already surprised major Wemis upon Broad river, and captured many prisoners, both horse and foot. Tarleton, exerting a scarcely credible diligence, appeared unexpectedly in the presence of Sumpter, who was encamped upon the right bank of the river Tiger, at a place called Blackstocks.   The position of the Americans was formidably strong ; it was covered in front by the river, log houses and palisades ; and upon the two flanks by inaccessible mountains, or narrow and difficult defiles.   Tarleton, hurried on by his ardor, and fearing lest Sumpter should pass the Tiger and escape him, left his light infantry, and even a part of his legion, behind, and pushed forward upon the enemy with a body of grenadiers and the rest of his cavalry.   The action was engaged with reciprocal desperation.   A British regiment was so roughly treated that it was compelled to fall back in the greatest disorder. Tarleton, to restore the battle, headed an impetuous charge upon the center of the Americans ; they received it without giving way.   The Englishman then found himself constrained to retreat, leaving upon the field of battle a great number of dead and wounded, among whom were found several officers of note.   But night being come, colonel Sumpter, who was dangerously wounded in the shoulder, did not judge it prudent to await the British troops that Tarleton had left behind him, and he accordingly repassed the river.   His wound not permitting him to retain the command, he was carried by faithful soldiers into the secure regions of the mountains.   The greater part of his corps then disbanded.   Tarleton, afte▪ having scoured, for a few days, the country on the left bank of the Tiger, returned by easy marches to resume his position upon Broad river, in South Carolina.

This petty war, these frequent rencounters, more and more invigorated the warlike spirit of the troops of the two parties.

Meanwhile, general Gates had succeeded in assembling some few
troops, the greater part cavalry, and in order to support the partisans
of congress, as well as to afford them a rallying point, he recrossed
the river Yadkin, and took post at Charlottetown, with intent to
winter there. He thought that hostilities could not be continued
during the bad season which was then about to set in. While he
applied himself with zeal to these preparatory dispositions, and fortune seemed inclined to smile upon him anew, general Greene arrived
at camp. His military reputation and his tried devotion to the cause
of the republic, had decided the congress and Washington to intrust
him with the command in the southern provinces, in the room of
Gates. The latter evinced, in this conjuncture, that country was
dearer to him than power and glory. He supported so unpleasant
an incident with such constancy, that he did not betray a single mark
of discontent. When he passed through Richmond, in returning to
his own province, the assembly of Virginia sent a deputation to compliment him. It gave him assurance that the remembrance of his
glorious achievements could not be effaced by any misfortune, praying him to be persuaded that the Virginians in particular would never
neglect any occasion to manifest the gratitude they bore him, as
members of the American Union. General Greene brought with
him no re-inforcement from the northern army ; he expected to find
sufficient forces in the southern quarter. He was accompanied only
by colonel Morgan with some riflemen, who had acquired the highest
reputation. His army was consequently extremely feeble ; but the
woods, the swamps, the rivers, with which the country was every
where broken, were means of defense sufficient to re-assure him.
As his intention was merely to infest the enemy, by avoiding general actions, he hoped to be able to harass, and little by little to reduce him. It was about the same time that general Leslie arrived
from Virginia at Charleston, with a re-inforcement of more than two
thousand regular troops. He found fresh orders in that city, in pursuance of which, he put himself immediately on the march with fifteen hundred men, to rejoin lord Cornwallis at Winnsborough.

1781. This addition of force renewed with the British general
the desire to reduce North Carolina, and to proceed thence into
Virginia. But the better to secure the success of this enterprise, a
council of war decided that it should not be confided to the army of
Cornwallis alone ; and that it was proper that it should be supported
by another expedition simultaneously directed on the part of Virginia

itself; not that the troops which could be employed in that part were in a situation to achieve the conquest of the province without the assistance of lord Cornwallis, but they might at least be able to discourage the Virginians from passing re-inforcements to general Greene.   Agreeably to this plan, Arnold had been detached to the Chesapeake bay, where he was to disembark his troops at whatever point he might judge the most favorable to a mischievous impression.   The English also flattered themselves, that his name and example would influence a great number of the Americans to desert from the colors of the republic to those of the king.   Arnold received this commission with ecstasy; he departed to execute it with fifty transports and sixteen hundred men.   The moment he had landed, he commenced the most shocking ravages.   Richmond and Smithfield experienced all his fury.   But the country was alarmed on all parts; the inhabitants flew to arms; he was obliged to fall back upon Portsmouth, where he labored to intrench himself.   He would not abandon that coast, because he was sensible how much his presence disquieted the Americans.   On the other hand, however, he could not, with forces so insufficient, keep the field in the midst of a province whose numerous population was animated by the most violent hatred against England.

This piratical expedition, therefore, produced but very imperfectly the effect which the British generals had hoped from it.   It delayed, it is true, those succors which the Virginians destined for the Carolinas; but not one of them joined Arnold.   Devastations, plunder, conflagrations, had no such fascination as could gain him partisans. The campaign had already opened in South Carolina.   The two hostile generals maneuvered each according to the plan he had framed.   Lord Cornwallis had set out from Winnsborough, and was marching between the Broad and Catawba rivers, on the upper route, towards North Carolina.   He had already arrived at Turkey Creek. To arrest his progress, general Greene resolved to demonstrate an intention to attack Ninety-Six, while colonel Morgan, with five hundred Virginian regulars, some companies of militia, and the light horse of colonel Washington, was detached to guard the passages of the river Pacolet.   As to Greene himself, he went to encamp at the confluence of Hicks Creek with the Pedee, opposite to Cheraw Hill. He was blamed, by many military critics, for having thus divided his forces.   In effect, if the English had pushed rapidly forward, they might have thrown themselves between the corps of Greene and Morgan, and crushed them both without difficulty.   But perhaps the American general had calculated that the royalists were embarrassed by too many obstacles to act with such celerity; perhaps, also, he had not yet heard of the junction of Leslie and Cornwallis. The latter general immediately detached Tarleton with his legion of cavalry and a body of infantry to cover Ninety-Six. On arriving in that part, Tarleton found every thing quiet; the enemy had retired after some light skirmishes. He then determined to march against Morgan, confident of being able either to rout him by surprise, or at least to drive him beyond the Broad river, which would have left the ways clear to the royal army. He consulted lord Cornwallis by letter, who not only approved his design, but resolved also to concur to its execution, by ascending the left bank of the Broad, in order to menace the rear of Morgan. Every thing went well for them at first. Tarleton, after having passed with equal celerity and good fortune the rivers Ennoree and Tiger, presented himself upon the banks of the Pacolet. Morgan retreated thence forthwith, and Tarleton set himself to pursue him. He pressed him hard. Morgan felt how full of danger was become the passage of Broad river, in the presence of so enterprising an enemy as now hung upon his rear. He therefore thought it better to make a stand. He formed his troops in two divisions; the first, composed of militia, under the conduct of colonel Pickens, occupied the front of a wood, in view of the enemy; the second, commanded by colonel Howard, was concealed in the wood itself, and consisted of his marksmen and old continental troops. Colonel Washington, with his cavalry, was posted behind the second division, as a reserve. Tarleton soon came up, and formed in two lines; his infantry in the centre of each, and his horse on the flanks. Every thing seemed to promise him victory. He was superior in cavalry, and his troops, both officers and soldiers, manifested an extreme ardor. The English attacked the first American line; after a single discharge, with little harm to the enemy, it fled in confusion. They then fell upon the second; but here they found a more obstinate resistance. The action was engaged and supported with equal advantage. Tarleton, to decide it in his favor, pushed forward a battalion of his second line, and at the same time directed a charge of cavalry upon the right flank of the Americans. He was afraid to attack their left, supported by colonel Washington, who had already vigorously repulsed an assault of the British light horse. The maneuver of Tarleton had the expected effect; the American regulars gave way, and were thrown into disorder. The English rushed on, persuaded that the day was now their own. Already Tarleton, with his cavalry, was in full pursuit of the routed, when colonel Washington, whose troop was still entire, fell upon the enemy with such impetuosity, that in a few moments he had restored the battle. During this interval, colonel Howard had rallied his continental troops, and led them back upon the English. Colonel Pickens had also, by prodigious efforts, re-assembled the militia, and again brought them to the fire. Morgan was visible every where; his presence and words re-animated the spirits of his soldiers. He profited of that moment of enthusiasm to precipitate them in one general charge upon the enemy. The shock was so tremendous, that the English at first paused, then recoiled, and soon fled in confusion. The Americans pursued them with inexpressible eagerness. It was in vain that the British officers employed exhortations, prayers, and threats, to stay the fugitives; the discomfiture was total. Tarleton lost, in dead, wounded, and prisoners, more than eight hundred men, two pieces of cannon, the colors of the seventh regiment, all his carriages and baggage. He regretted especially the horses killed or taken in this engagement. The nature of the country, which is flat and open, renders cavalry of the utmost importance to a campaign in that quarter.

Such was the issue of the battle of Cowpens, the effects of which were heavily felt by the English during the whole course of the war of the Carolinas and Virginia; it was, in a word, decisive of the fate of those provinces. The destruction of the British cavalry, the total defeat of Tarleton, who had been, until that epoch, the terror of the inhabitants, animated them with fresh spirits. Dejection and despondency were exchanged for confidence and enthusiasm. The congress voted public thanks to colonel Morgan, and presented him with a medal of gold. Colonels Washington and Howard received medals of silver, and colonel Pickens a sword.

The news of the sanguinary check of Cowpens was extremely afflictive to lord Cornwallis. He had lost in it the best part of his light troops, and they were to have been the principal instrument of his ulterior operations. But far from allowing himself to be discouraged by this blow, he resolved to prosecute his designs with the corps he had left. He hoped to obtain from it the same service as from light troops, by destroying his heavy baggage, and all the carriages that were not of absolute necessity. Two entire days were employed in the destruction of superfluous incumbrances. A few wagons only were kept, for the accommodation of the sick and wounded, and the transportation of salt and ammunition. The soldier witnessed the annihilation of his most valuable effects; the casks containing wine and rum were all staved, and the troops set forward with no other provision than a small quantity of flour. The royal army submitted to all these inconveniences with admirable temper and patience, and manifested the utmost eagerness to accomplish the wishes of its general. He had two objects in view at that time. One was, to fall immediately upon Morgan, worst him, retake the prisoners he had made, and prevent his junction with general Greene, who still continued upon Hicks Creek. The second, and by far the most important, was to push forward by forced marches upon Salisbury, and towards the sources of the Yadkin, before Greene should have crossed that river. If he effected this design, it followed of necessity, that the American general would be cut off from the succors he expected from Virginia, and constrained either to retreat precipitate ly, with the loss of his artillery and baggage, or to accept a battle under every disadvantage. Lord Cornwallis set out upon the first of these projects. He directed his march with celerity upon the Catawba, in the hope of surprising and crushing Morgan before he could pass that river. But the Americans were upon their guard. After his victory of Cowpens, Morgan, who knew very well that Cornwallis was not far off, had sent his prisoners upon his rear, under the guard of an experienced officer, and soon after set forward himself with all his troops towards the Catawba. Such was the diligence of his march, that on the twenty-ninth of January he had crossed the river, with all his artillery, stores, baggage and prisoners. The Americans were no sooner upon the left bank than the British appeared on the right ; the chagrin of Cornwallis is readily conceived. Morgan, still keeping his prisoners on the march towards Virginia, neglected no measures that might tend, if not to arrest, at least to retard the progress of the royal troops. But they soon had even the elements to contend with. There had fallen the preceding night such an abundant rain in the neighboring mountains, that the ford of Catawba became immediately impassable. If this swell of the waters had taken place a few hours sooner, Morgan would have found himself in a critical position.

In this state of things, general Greene arrived at the camp of Morgan, and took the command upon himself. Penetrating the designs of Cornwallis, he had left orders with the troops stationed at Hicks Creek, to make the best of their way, without baggage or incumbrance of any sort, towards the mountainous part, in order to approach the sources of the rivers, where they become more fordable. Their point of rendezvous was indicated at Guildford Court House, in North Carolina. While Greene rejoined the corps of Morgan, upon the left bank of the Catawba, general Huger executed his orders with as much zeal as intelligence. The rains were such as to be thought extraordinary even at this season ; the bridges were broken, the streams excessively swoln, the roads deep and heavy, or stony and knobbed by frost.   The soldiers were destitute of shoes, of clothing, and often of bread.   They seemed to vie with the English in constancy, and supported all their sufferings without a murmur.   Not one of them deserted, and in this respect they had more merit than their adversaries.   The Americans, in disbanding, repaired to their homes and repose; whereas the English deserter must have wandered in a country where every thing opposed him. During the march of this division upon Guildford, the waters of the Catawba diminished, and the royal troops prepared themselves to cross it.   But the republicans seemed determined to dispute their passage.   Besides the intrepid phalanx of Morgan, all the militia of the counties of Rohan and Mecklenburgh, where the British name was loathed, had assembled upon that point.   Notwithstanding these obstacles, Cornwallis took a resolution to attempt the enterprise.

He was excited to this movement by the hope of giving the enemy a decisive blow, either by reaching the corps of Huger before its arrival at Guildford, or by throwing himself between it and Virginia.   He accordingly marched and counter-marched along the right bank of the Catawba, holding out an intent to pass in different places, in order to elude the attention of the Americans.   But his real design was to cross at Gowan's Ford.   In effect, on the morning of the first of February, the English entered the water; the river was broad, deep, and full of large stones.   The republicans were drawn up on the left bank, and commanded by general Davidson.   But this corps was composed entirely of militia; Morgan with his veterans guarded another passage.   The English, however, had to encounter a very brisk and well-directed fire ; but they supported it with intrepidity, successfully traversed the bed of the river, and gained the opposite bank.   The Americans were formed to receive them, and the action commenced.   General Davidson was killed at the first discharge; his militia betook themselves to flight, and the detachments posted at other points ran off in the same manner. The whole royal army arrived without obstacle upon the left bank. A single corps of militia, amidst the general rout, made a stand at the post of Tarrant; colonel Tarleton charged them vigorously, and routed them with severe execution.   But colonel Morgan retired untouched, and with celerity, towards Salisbury.   He hoped to arrive there in season to cross the Yadkin at that place, and thus to put a large river between him and the royal army.   The English followed him with great ardor, panting to take their revenge for the defeat of Cowpens.   But the American displayed so much activity, and threw so many impediments in the way of his pursuers, that he

passed the Yadkin with all his troops, and without any loss, in the
first days of February; partly by the ford, and partly in batteaux.
He drew all the boats he could find to the left bank. The English
at length arrived, under the conduct of general O'Hara. They perceived the enemy drawn up on the opposite side, prepared to oppose
their passage. They would, nevertheless, have attempted it but for
the sudden swell of the Yadkin, through the rains that fell that very
day. The pious inhabitants of America considered this sudden
increment of the rivers as a manifest token of the protection which
Heaven granted to the justice of their cause. They observed, that if
the waters of the Catawba, and afterwards those of the Yadkin, had
swelled a few hours sooner, their army, unable to cross, must have
been cut in pieces by the furious enemy that pursued it. If, on the
contrary, these rivers had not increased all of a sudden, a few hours
later, the British would have passed as easily as the Americans, and
would have intercepted their retreat. These two consecutive events,
and the critical moment at which they took place, were esteemed
alike providential. Seeing the impossibility of crossing the Yadkin
at the ford of Salisbury, which is the most commodious, and the
most frequented, Cornwallis resolved to march up the river, hoping
to find it fordable at the place where it branches; this he effected;
but the delay occasioned by the circuit, afforded the Americans time
enough to reach Guildford without being disquieted. It was there,
that, on the seventh of February, the two divisions of the American
army operated their junction; that of general Huger, which, notwithstanding all his diligence, was the last to arrive, and that of colonel
Morgan. Greene felt the more joy at this union, as it was highly
honorable to his ability. Thus, by the prudence of the American
commanders, and by the fortitude and celerity of their soldiers,
together with a happy coincidence of fortuitous causes, was defeated
the double plan of lord Cornwallis. He could neither exterminate
Morgan, nor prevent his re-union with Huger. There remained now
but one operation which could indemnify him for so many losses;
and that was to cut Greene off from Virginia. The two armies
were already upon the confines of that province. It is separated
from North Carolina by the Roanoke, which in its upper part is
called the Dan. The British general, conceiving that river not fordable in the lower parts, calculated that if he could gain the high
country, he should be at liberty to move as he might see fit. For
supposing that Greene could not pass the Dan, he would then be
surrounded on all sides; on the north by Cornwallis himself, on the
west by great rivers, on the south by lord Rawdon, who remained

at Camden with a respectable force, and on the east by the sea. Moreover, notwithstanding the juncture of the American troops, they were still so inferior to those of the English, that the latter considered themselves perfectly assured of a complete victory. The two parties were equally aware that success must depend on the rapidity of marches; they accordingly both bent their course, with all possible velocity, upon the formidable parts of the Dan. The English, desirous to repair the time lost in their preceding passages, exerted prodigious efforts, and occupied the fords the first. The position of Greene was now truly critical. He turned rapidly towards a lower ford, called Boyds Ferry, uncertain of the safety or destruction of his army, since he was ignorant if that ford was practicable. The royal troops pursued him with vehemence; they looked upon their approaching victory as a positive certainty. Greene, in so pressing an emergency, summoned all the faculties of his soul, and did all that could have been expected of a consummate general.

He formed a strong corps of his best light troops, consisting in the regiments of cavalry of Lee, of Bland, and of Washington, in companies of light infantry, drawn from regiments of the line, and in some riflemen. He charged the commander of this corps to sustain the efforts of the enemy, and to bear in mind that the salvation of the army was in his hands. As to himself, with the rest of his troops and the heavy baggage, he proceeded with all expedition towards Boyds Ferry. The royalists pushed forward with eagerness from Salem to the sources of the Haw, from that point to Reedy Fork, from there to Troublesome Creek, and thence towards the Dan. But the detached corps which has just been mentioned, by continual skirmishes, and the breaking up of roads and bridges, materially retarded their march. Greene had already reached the margin of the river; he found it fordable; some boats at hand accelerated the passage; he gained the Virginian shore; all the baggage was passed over with equal success. Even the gallant rear guard, which had preserved the army, arrived a little after, and crossed with the same happy auspices, to the safe side of the river.

It was not long before the English, full of earnestness, made their appearance upon the right of the Dan; they perceived upon the opposite bank the American army formed in menacing array. All their hopes were vanished; the fruit of all their efforts, of all their sufferings, was lost irrecoverably. The retreat of general Greene and the pursuit of lord Cornwallis, are worthy to be placed among the most remarkable events of the American war; they would have done honor to the most celebrated captains of that, or any former epoch

Compelled so unexpectedly to relinquish the object of his sanguine hope, lord Cornwallis meditated upon the course he had now to pursue. The attack of Virginia, with forces so enfeebled as were his own, appeared to him the more perilous, as the American army preserved the most imposing attitude. Under this consideration, he determined to remain in North Carolina, of which he was master, and set himself to levy troops in the name of the king. With this intent he quitted the banks of the Dan, and repaired by easy marches to Hillsborough ; where, having erected the royal standard, he invited the inhabitants, by an energetic proclamation, to form themselves into regular companies. But these efforts were not attended with the success he had hoped ; a great number of the country people came to his head quarters, but the greater part to satisfy their curiosity, to gain intelligence, and to make their profit of it. All manifested an extreme repugnance to arming against the congress. Lord Cornwallis complained publicly of their coldness. He saw that he could place no dependence upon the assistance of the people of this province, formerly so celebrated for their attachment to the name of the king. The long domination of the republicans, and the horrible enormities committed by the royal troops in different parts of the American continent, had given birth to sentiments of quite another cast. Insensibly detached from the cause of the king, the inhabitants, besides, could not forget the vicinity of the republican army, which at any moment might again penetrate into their province. About this time, a British squadron, and a body of troops detached from Charleston, took possession of Wilmington, a city of North Carolina, situated not far from the mouth of Cape Fear river. They fortified themselves there, seized munitions of war, and even some vessels, both French and American. This expedition had been ordered by Cornwallis prior to his departure from Winnsborough, in pursuit of Morgan. Its principal object was that of opening a communication between the country about Hillsborough and the sea, by the way of Cape Fear river ; an object of the utmost importance, as it afforded a sure mode of passing supplies to the army.

The retreat of Greene into Virginia, although it had not produced upon the minds of those Carolinians who remained faithful to the king, all that effect which Cornwallis had expected from it, had, nevertheless, excited, in some, fresh hopes and desires of a new order of things. The British general redoubled his efforts and instances to induce them to take arms. The district situated between the Haw and the Deep river, was represented as particularly abounding in loyalists ; Cornwallis sent them Tarleton, to animate and

imbody them.   His exhortations were not in vain.   The family of
Pill, one of the most considerable of the country, was also the most
ardent to set the example.   Already a colonel of that family had
assembled a considerable body of his most audacious partisans, and
was on his way to join Tarleton.   But general Greene, who was fully
sensible how prejudicial it would prove to the arms of congress if he
suffered its cause to succumb entirely in North Carolina, and fearing
lest the loyalists might operate a revolution in that province, had
detached anew, upon the right bank of the Dan, a body of cavalry
under the conduct of colonel Lee, with a view of intimidating the
partisans of England, re-assuring those of the congress, and disquiet-
ing the movements of the enemy in the interior of the country.   He
intended also himself, as soon as he should have received his re-inforcements, which were already on the march, to repass the river,
and show himself again upon the territory of the Carolinas.   The
recovery of those provinces was the fixed aim of all his thoughts.

   Meanwhile, colonel Lee was by no means tardy in acting according to the instructions of his general.   The troop assembled by
colonel Pill was the first that fell in his way.   These loyalists, totally
unacquainted with the profession of arms, knew so little how to clear
their march, that thinking they were going to meet Tarleton, they
threw themselves headlong into the corps of Lee.   The Americans
enveloped and charged them with rapid vigor.   The loyalists, still
supposing their affair was with Tarleton, and that he mistook them
for republicans, were eager to make themselves known by reiterated
cries of ' Long live the king.'   The fury of the assailants did but
rage the fiercer, and in a few instants all that survived were obliged
to surrender.   Thus, this inexpert troop were led to slaughter by a
presumptuous chief, who had imagined that the spirit of party could
fill the place of knowledge and talents !   At the news of this event,
which was rather an execution than a combat, Tarleton, who was
not far off, put himself in motion, with intent to encounter Lee ; but
an order of Cornwallis checked him, and drew him back to Hillsborough.   The cause of this sudden resolution of the British general,
was, that Greene, though even yet he had received only a small part
of his re-inforcements, had boldly re-passed the Dan, and menaced
again to overrun Carolina.   Not, however, that his real intention
was to give his adversary battle before having assembled his whole
force ; but he wished to show Cornwallis and the patriots of the province that he was in being, and able to keep the field.   He chose a
position upon the left of the Dan, and very high up, towards the
sources of the Haw, in order to avoid the necessity of fighting.

Cornwallis, on hearing that the American banners had re-appeared in Carolina, quitted Hillsborough forthwith, and crossing the Haw at a lower ford, proceeded to encamp near Allemance creek, detaching Tarleton with his cavalry to scour the country as far as Deep river. Thus the two armies found themselves so near each other, as to be separated only by the river Haw. Hence frequent skirmishes ensued. In one of these rencounters, Tarleton did great mischief to the corps of Lee, which was joined by the mountaineers and militia, under the command of captain Preston. The two generals maneuvered a long time with uncommon ability; the American to avoid battle, the Englishman to force him to it. Greene had the good fortune, or the skill, to continue master of his movements. But towards the middle of March, ne received re-inforcements, which consisted principally of continental troops. He was joined, at the same time, by militia from Virginia, under the conduct of general Lawson, as also by some Carolinian militia, led by the generals Butler and Eaton. Having acquired more confidence in his strength, Greene took a resolution no longer to decline a decisive action, but, on the contrary, to march directly to the enemy. He accordingly pushed forward with all his troops, and took post at Guildford Court House. He had reflected that being superior in number, and principally in cavalry, he could not experience a total and irreparable defeat. The worst consequence that could follow a loss of battle, was that of placing him under the necessity of retiring into Virginia, where he would have found the utmost facility in re-establishing his army. He had also to consider that the numerous militia assembled in his camp would soon disband, unless he availed himself immediately of their first ardor. On the other hand, if the English were beaten, far from their ships, entangled in a country where they were detested, and without means of retreat, how could their army escape a total destruction? They had therefore much more at risk than the Americans, in refering the decision of their fate to the chance of arms.

Lord Cornwallis saw distinctly, on his part, that it would be an inexcusable imprudence to remain longer in the midst of a population which every thing taught him to distrust, while a formidable enemy menaced him in front. But retreat, in all respects so prejudicial to the interests of the king, was accompanied with so many dangers, that it became next to impracticable. In turning his eyes upon his camp, the British general beheld all soldiers nurtured in the toils of war, and trained to victory in a host of combats. Banishing then all hesitation, he embraced, if not the least perilous, assuredly the most honorable course, and gave orders to advance upon

Guildford. This resolution was undertaken irrevocably to put an end to uncertainties by striking a decisive blow. To relieve his march, and facilitate his retreat in case of a check, lord Cornwallis sent his carriages and baggage under strong escort to Bells Mills, a place situated upon the Deep river. Greene in like manner passed his wagons to Iron Works, ten miles in the rear of his position. The reconnoitering parties of the two armies went out in all directions for intelligence. The legion of Lee and that of Tarleton fell in with each other in one of these excursions, and a fierce conflict ensued. Lee at first had the advantage; but he was obliged to give way in his turn, when Tarleton had been re-inforced. These skirmishes were but the prelude of the battle for which both parties were preparing themselves.

The Americans, on their side, numbered about six thousand men, the greater part militia of Virginia and North Carolina ; the remainder consisted in regular troops from Virginia, Maryland and Delaware. The English, including the Hessians, amounted to upwards of twenty-four hundred soldiers. All the adjacent country was clothed with thick wood, interspersed, here and there, with spots of cultivation. A gentle and woody declivity traversed and extended far on both sides of the great road which leads from Salisbury to Guildford. This road itself runs through the center of the forest. In front, and before coming to the foot of the hill, there was a field six hundred yards in breadth. Behind the forest, between its lower edge and the houses of Guildford, lay another field still more open, and adapted to military evolutions. General Greene had thrown troops into the wood that covered the slope, and had likewise occupied the contiguous plain. In this position he purposed to receive the enemy. His order of battle consisted in three divisions; the first, composed of the militia of North Carolina, and commanded by the generals Butler and Eaton, was posted towards the foot of the hill, upon the fore edge of the forest; its front was covered by a thick hedge; two pieces of cannon defended the great road. The second division comprised the militia of Virginia, under the conduct of the generals Stevens and Lawson; it was formed in the wood parallel to the first, and about eight hundred yards behind it. The regular troops, under general Huger and colonel Williams, filled the plain which extends from the forest to Guildford; this ground permitted them to maneuver, and to signalize their valor. Two other pieces of cannon, planted upon an eminence which covered their flank, commanded also the highway.

Colonel Washington, with his dragoons and Linch's riflemen, flanked the right wing, and colonel Lee, with a detachment of light infantry and the dragoons of Campbell, the left. The British general drew up on his part. General Leslie, with an English regiment and the Hessian regiment of Bose, occupied the right of the first line; and colonel Webster, with two English regiments, the left. A battalion of guards formed a sort of reserve to the first, and another under general O'Hara to the second. The artillery and grenadiers marched in close column upon the great road. Tarleton was posted there likewise with his legion; but his orders were not to move, except upon emergency, until the infantry, after having carried the forest, should have advanced into the plain behind it, where cavalry could operate with facility. The action was commenced on both sides by a brisk cannonade. The English, afterwards, leaving their artillery behind, rushed forward through the fire of the enemy into the intermediate plain. The Carolinian militia suffered them to approach without flinching, then began to fire. Tne English made but one discharge, and immediately ran forward to charge with bayonets. The Carolinians showed no firmness. Without awaiting the shock of the enemy, notwithstanding the strength of their position, they recoiled, and took shamefully to flight. Their officers vainly endeavored to dissipate their terror, and to rally them. Thus the first line of the American army was totally routed. General Stevens, seeing the panic of the Carolinian militia, hastened to re-assure those he commanded, by giving out that the other had orders to fall back, after the first discharges. He opened his ranks to let the fugitives pass, and reclosed them immediately. The English, still advancing, attacked the militia of Virginia. These bravely withstood their shock, and disputed the ground with them for some time. At length, obliged to give way, they also fell back, not without some disorder, upon the continental troops. Meanwhile, as well by the effect of the combat, as from the inequality of the ground, and thickness of the wood, the line of the British was likewise broken, and open in several places. Their commanders, to fill up these vacant spaces, pushed forward the two reserves. Then, all this division, having passed the forest, formed in the plain that was behind it, and fell upon the continental troops; but all the impetuosity of this attack was of no avail against the intrepidity of that division. Their resistance was so obstinate that victory for a while appeared uncertain. General Leslie, finding he could make no impression upon the left of the Americans, and having suffered excessively in the attempt, was constrained to retire behind a ravine, in order to await the news of what might have passed in other parts. The action was supported in the center with inexpressible fierceness. Colonel Stewart, with the second battalion of guards and a company of grenadiers, had fallen so vigorously upon the troops of Delaware, that he had broken them, and taken from them two pieces of cannon; but the Marylanders came promptly to their assistance, and not only restored the battle, but even forced the English to recoil in disorder. At this moment colonel Washington came up with his cavalry, charging the royalists with impetuosity; he put them to flight, cut most of them down, and recovered the two pieces of cannon.

Colonel Stewart himself perished in the carnage. At this instant the fate of the day hung by a single thread. If the Americans had done all that was in their power, the whole British army was crushed. After the defeat of the British guards and the death of Stewart, if the republicans had occupied the hill which rises on the side of the great road upon the hinder border of the wood, and furnished it with artillery, it cannot be doubted that victory would have declared for them. For then the English would not have had power to advance fresh troops into that part; their left wing would have been separated from the center and right; and the battalions of guards would not have been able to recover from the confusion into which they had been thrown. But the Americans, content with the advantage they had already obtained, instead of taking possession of the height, repaired to the posts they occupied before the engagement. At sight of this error, lieutenant-colonel Macleod hastened to take advantage of it; he advanced the artillery, placed it upon the aforesaid eminence, and opened a destructive fire against the front of the continental troops. The grenadiers and another English regiment reappeared at the same instant upon the right of the plain, and made a vigorous charge upon their flank. Another English regiment fell at the same time upon their left, and Tarleton came up at full speed with his legion. General O'Hara, though dangerously wounded, had succeeded in rallying the British guards. All these succors arrived so opportunely that the disorder of the center and first line was promptly repaired.

The American regulars, who had to sustain unsupported the whole weight of the action, finding themselves assailed on so many parts, began to think of their retreat. They made it step by step, without breaking their ranks; and invariably preserving a menacing attitude. They were constrained, however, to abandon upon the field of battle, not only the two field pieces which they had retaken, but two others besides. Colonel Webster, then rejoining the center with his left wing, made a brisk charge upon the extremity of the right of Greene, and forced it to give way. Cornwallis abstained from sending the cavalry of Tarleton's legion in pursuit of the Americans; he had need of them in another part. His right was still engaged with the left of Greene. The Hessian regiment of Bose, commanded by colonel de Buy, who in this day displayed an undaunted valor, and the other British troops, exerted the most desperate efforts to break the enemy, who defended himself with equal gallantry. The ground was rough, and incumbered with trees and bushes ; the Americans availed themselves of it to combat as marksmen with their accustomed dexterity. If broken, they reformed, if forced to retire, they returned, if dispersed, they rallied, and charged anew. In the height of this engagement, or rather of this multitude of partial rencounters, Tarleton, who had defiled behind the right wing of the royalists, and who was covered by the smoke of their arms, as they and purposely fired altogether to this end, fell briskly upon the enemy, and in a moment swept them from the ground they occupied. The militia threw themselves into the wood, and the Hessians at last found themselves entirely disengaged from this long and obstinate conflict.

Thus terminated the stubborn and much varied battle of Guildford, which was fought on the fifteenth of March. The American loss in killed, wounded, prisoners, and missing, amounted to upwards of thirteen hundred men. The prisoners were few. Almost all the wounded belonged to the continental troops, and the fugitives dispersed, or returned to their homes, to the militia. The generals Huger and Stevens were among the wounded. The loss of the British was, in proportion to their number, much more considerable. Their dead and wounded exceeded six hundred. Besides colonel Stewart, they had to lament colonel Webster. The generals Howard and O'Hara, the first in the army after lord Cornwallis, and colonel Tarleton, received very severe wounds.

After the action, Greene withdrew behind the Reedy Fork, where he remained some time to collect the fugitives and stragglers. Afterwards, continuing his retreat, he went to encamp at Iron Works, upon Troublesome Creek. Cornwallis remained master of the field of battle. But he was not merely unable to reap any of the ordinary fruits of victory, he was even constrained to embrace those counsels, which are the usual resource of the vanquished. The fatigue of his soldiers, the multitude of his wounded, the strength of the new position which the American general had taken, and the superiority of the enemy in light troops, and particularly in cavalry, prevented him from pursuing his success. Moreover, the number and spirit of the partisans of congress seemed to increase with the coldness of the loyalists. Far from rearing the crest after the battle of Guildford, they showed themselves quite deaf to the invocations of Cornwallis, who urged them to take arms and assemble under his banners. To crown his embarrassments, the scarcity of provision became continually more and more sensible. These motives united, determined the British general to fall back as far as Bells Mills, upon the Deep river; leaving at New Garden those of his wounded that were least in condition to move. They fell into the power of the republicans.

After having given his troops a few days' repose at Bells Mills, and collected some provision, he marched towards Cross Creek, upon the road to Wilmington. Greene followed him briskly, and with a cloud of light infantry and horse, continually infested his rear. He did not cease the pursuit till Cornwallis had arrived at Ramsays Mills. The British had destroyed the bridge at that place over the Deep river, and the country, being excessively steril, afforded no means of sustenance. Swayed, however, by his daring and enterprising character, the American general resolved to profit of the present condition of the royalists. He took the determination to march boldly upon South Carolina, which was then almost entirely stripped of troops. He accordingly defiled by forced marches towards Camden. Though worsted at Guildford, Greene thus showed himself in the field, with forces more formidable than ever. It was the victors who fled before the vanquished; the latter seemed to have gained new alacrity and new ardor by their reverses.

After a painful march, lord Cornwallis reached Wilmington, on the seventh of April. Here he held a council upon two operations, both of extreme importance. One was to repair forthwith to the relief of South Carolina; the other to march into Virginia, in order to make his junction with the troops of Arnold and with those which had lately been sent thither under the conduct of general Philips. The British generals were much divided in opinion respecting the course to be adopted in a conjuncture which might decide the fate of the whole war. Some were inclined that the army should march immediately into Virginia. They alledged ' that all the country between the Cape Fear river and Camden was poor, exhausted, and interrupted by frequent rivers and creeks; that the passage of the Pedee, in the presence of so formidable an enemy, was a rash enterprise; that the road by Georgetown presented the same difficulties; that the transportation of the troops to Charleston by sea, was an undertaking that would require too much time and toil; that there was nothing to fear for the latter city; that by attacking Virginia with an imposing force, Greene would be forced to abandon the Carolinas; that it would be impossible to arrive in time to the relief of lord Rawdon, who was then at Camden; and that if he was beaten before the arrival of re-inforcements, these succors themselves would be exposed to the almost inevitable peril of being cut in pieces by an enemy incomparably superior in force.'

The partisans of the contrary opinion maintained, ' that the roads of Virginia were not less, and perhaps more difficult, than those of the Carolinas ; that the tediousness of embarkations proceeded always from cavalry, and that this might easily make its way good by land ; the cavalry officers had asserted it, and especially Tarleton, who had offered to execute it; that consequently, with fair wind, nothing was easier than to arrive in season to the succor of the Carolinas ; that since it had not been possible to conquer Virginia, it was essential at least to retain those provinces ; that the invasion of Virginia involved the certain sacrifice of two provinces, already in possession, if not of three, from the dubious prospect of gaining one only ; that the people of the Carolinas, imboldened by the approach of Greene, and by the distance of the royal army, were already openly tending to a new order of things ; that the colonels Sumpter and Marion showed themselves audaciously in the open field ; that if there was nothing to fear for Charleston, there was assuredly equal reason for security with respect to Camden, defended by a numerous garrison, and a general as skilful as valiant; that so long as the places of Charleston and Camden should remain in the power of his majesty, the Carolinas could not be wrested from his authority, without being immediately and easily replaced under the yoke ; that it was deeply to be regretted that the march upon Camden had not been undertaken at the very moment when, the army being still upon Cross Creek, it was ascertained that thence to Wilmington the Cape Fear river no longer afforded an open and safe navigation ; that whatever uncertainty might have been thrown upon the success of this operation by the delays which had already taken place, it was nevertheless still possible, and that, consequently, it ought to be undertaken.'

The first opinion obtained. After having made some stay at Wilmington, for the refreshment of his troops and the collection of provision, Cornwallis directed his march upon Virginia. This resolution of the commander of the British forces had the most remarkable consequences; it led to an event which may be considered as the principal cause of the prompt termination of this war, and the consequent acknowledgment of American independence.

END OF BOOK THIRTEENTH.

BOOK FOURTEENTH.

1781   AFTER having pursued each other alternately, for a considerable length of time, Greene and Cornwallis diverged, as we have
seen, the first upon South Carolina, the second upon Virginia.   But
while they were thus contending for American provinces, England
and Holland were preparing for war, and had even already commenced reciprocal hostilities.   The former, who appeared to have
anticipated this war for some time back, and who, being already completely armed, could seize the occasion for making it with advantage,
hoped, by a sudden and impetuous attack, to level a decisive blow
at the power and wealth of her enemy.   Such was the motive
which had induced her to hasten her declaration of war.   It was not
doubted in England but that the success which would be gained
over Holland, would afford ample compensation for the losses which
had been sustained on the part of the French and Americans.   The
British cabinet expected thus to bring into the negotiations for peace,
whenever they should take place, such an aggregate of advantages,
as would be sufficient to procure it the most favorable conditions.
The Hollanders, on the other hand, persuaded themselves that they
saw in the simultaneous display of those formidable forces to which
they were about to join their own, the sure means of resuscitating
their ancient maritime glory.   They were especially elated with the
prospect of recovering the rich possessions which had been wrested
from them in preceding wars, and of rescuing their commerce from
the outrageous vexations of England.   The ardor which animated all
minds, manifested itself in the preparations that were made in the
ports of the republic.   The States-General ordered the equipment
of ninety-four ships of war, of which, eleven of the line, fifteen of
fifty guns, two of forty, and the rest of less force.   Eighteen thousand seamen formed the crews of this fleet.   Fast-sailing vessels
were dispatched to the different Dutch possessions, to apprise the
governors of the commencement of hostilities, and to recommend
to them the greatest vigilance.   The king of France ordained that in
all the ports of his dominions, any Dutch vessels found therein should
receive prompt notice of the new danger they had to fear at sea, on
the part of an alert and enterprising enemy.   In taking this care of
the interests of her new ally, France wished to manifest her gratitude for the warmth with which Holland had espoused her cause.
But unfortunately all these precautions could not operate the beneficial effects which were expected from them   The English. who.

long before the rupture, had meditated the design of attacking Holland, profited with success of all the means which they had prepared for her annoyance, before she had time to put herself in a state of defense. Some ships of war and several merchant vessels with valuable cargoes fell into their power. In the number of the first was the Rotterdam, of fifty guns, which was taken by the Warwick ship of the line. But these losses were trivial, in comparison with those which the Dutch sustained in the East Indies. The British commanders in that part had received early instructions to make themselves masters of the possessions of the republic, whether insular or continental. The security of a long peace had occasioned in them a desuetude of all defensive precaution ; and thus the riches therein amassed might easily become the prey of the first enemy who should present himself.

Admiral Rodney, who towards the close of the preceding year had returned from New York to St. Lucia, and general Vaughan, concerted their operations forthwith. Herein they moved with the more alacrity, as the king, by a late order, had granted to his land and sea officers a considerable part of the booty that should be gained upon the Dutch. After a vain attempt to re-capture the island of St. Vincent, and having, in order to mask the real design, alarmed the inhabitants of Martinico by a sudden appearance upon their coasts, Rodney and Vaughan presented themselves unexpectedly, the third of February, before the island of St. Eustatius, belonging to the Dutch. Their forces consisted of seventeen ships, and four thousand land forces. This island was as defenseless as the wealth it contained was prodigious. Although it is rough and mountainous, and affords one only landing place, and that easily defensible, yet the governor, with a handful of men for all garrison, could have no hope of being able to repulse an attack. The population itself comprised but a very small number of Dutch ; the remainder was composed of men of divers countries and sentiments ; French, Spaniards, Americans, English, all persons occupied exclusively with their commerce, and strangers to military service. The governor himself, almost without soldiers and without arms, would sooner have believed any thing else, than that he was menaced with an approaching attack.

The island of St. Eustatius is by nature arid and steril. It produces not above six or seven hundred hogsheads of sugar a year. But it was become at this epoch the most frequented and richest emporium of the West Indies. Being a free port, it attracted a vast conflux of merchants from all parts of the world, assured of finding in it protection, facility of exchanges, and money in abundance. Its neutrality in the midst of belligerent powers, had brought it to this flourishing condition, and rendered it the mart of nations.   Thither went the Spaniards and French to dispose of their commodities, and to procure the manufactures of England.   Thither repaired the English to sell these merchandises, and to buy those of France and Spain.

But no people derived more profit than the Americans from the fortunate neutrality of St. Eustatius.   They carried thither the produce of their soil, and to the incalculable utility of the cause they defended, they obtained, in return, arms and military stores, with which the French, Spaniards, Dutch, and even the English themselves, kept that market well supplied.   Hence, an orator of the House of Commons, hurried away by a blamable resentment, did not scruple to say, 'that if St. Eustatius had been sunk to the bottom of the ocean, American independence would have been crushed in an instant.'   The facts which followed were but too much in consonance with this inhuman language.   All Europe resounded with complaints against British avarice.

Rodney and Vaughan sent a peremptory summons to the governor to surrender the island and its dependencies within an hour ; accompanied with a declaration or threat, that if any resistance was made, he must abide by the consequences.   M. de Graaf, totally ignorant of the rupture, could scarcely believe the officer who delivered the summons to be serious.   He, however, returned for answer, that, being utterly incapable of making any defense against the force which invested the island, he must, of necessity, surrender it ; only recommending the town and inhabitants to the clemency and mercy of the British commanders.   We are about to relate what were the effects of this recommendation.   The wealth found in the place was so immense, as to excite the astonishment even of the conquerors, notwithstanding even their intimate previous knowledge of its nature and circumstances.   All the storehouses were not only filled with the most precious merchandises, but the very streets and beach were covered with hogsheads of tobacco and sugar.   The value of the commodities was estimated at a loose, but supposed moderate calculation, as being considerably above three millions sterling.   All, without distinction, were seized, inventoried and confiscated.

The loss of the Dutch was severe ; it fell principally upon their West India company, with the magistracy and citizens of Amsterdam, to whom a considerable part of the property belonged.   The English observed it with no little gratification ; they were irritated against that city more than against any other part of the United Provinces, on account of the warmth it had manifested in favor of France.   The greatest weight of the calamity, however, appears to have fallen upon the British merchants, who, confiding in the neutrality of the place, and in some acts of parliament, made to encourage the bringing of their property from the islands lately taken by the French, had accumulated a great quantity of West India produce, as well as of European goods, in this place.   Nor was the loss of the Dutch confined to the seizure of the merchandise on shore; above two hundred and fifty vessels of all denominations, and many of them richly loaded, were taken in the bay; exclusive of a Dutch frigate of war, of thirty-eight guns, and five armed vessels of less force.   But fortune showed herself still more adverse to the Hollanders.   Rodney having information that a fleet of about thirty large ships, richly laden with sugar and other West India commodities, had, just before his arrival, sailed from St. Eustatius for Holland, under convoy of a flag-ship of sixty guns, he, with his ordinary activity, immediately dispatched two ships of the line, the Monarch and Panther, with the Sybil frigate, in pursuit of them.   These soon overtook the convoy.   The Dutch admiral, Krull, notwithstanding the great inferiority of his force, resolved to brave all the dangers of combat, rather than to surrender dishonorably.   With his ship, the Mars, he engaged the Monarch, of seventy-four guns; but he was killed soon after the commencement of the action, and his successor immediately struck.   The Panther and Sybil having in the mean time restrained the flight and separation of the merchantmen, the whole convoy was taken.

The Dutch colors were kept up for some time in the fort of St. Eustatius; this stratagem was fatal to a considerable number of French, Dutch, and American vessels, which were thus decoyed into the hands of their enemies.   The violation of the property of private men, though enemies, a violation not sanctioned by the usages of civilized nations, excited energetic remonstrances on the part of the inhabitants of the British West India islands, and of Great Britain itself, so far as they were interested.   They alledged, that their connections with St. Eustatius, and the property they had lodged in it, were all in pursuance to, and under the sanction of repeated acts of the British parliament; that in every age, all conquerors who have not chosen to be classed with barbarians, have respected not only the private property of their fellow-citizens, but even that of their enemies; and that this example might have the most pernicious consequences.   'In effect,' said they, 'if, through the incalculable chances of war, our islands should fall into the power of the enemy, would he not be authorized, by the right of reprisal, to violate the property of private Englishmen, and even to ruin them totally?   Did the French give an example of this barbarous conduct when they became masters of Grenada?   Did they lay hands upon the property of a single private individual, though they had taken the island by assault, and without any capitulation? If the count d'Estaing went so far as to sequester, until peace, the estates of absentees, the court of Versailles was not slow to condemn this resolution of its admiral, by ordering the removal of the sequestrations. St. Eustatius was a free port, and as such recognized by all the maritime powers of Europe, not excepting England herself. Our laws had not only permitted, but even encouraged a commerce with that island. The officers of the British customs delivered clearances for those very goods destined for St. Eustatius, which are now subjected to confiscation. Has not this trade furnished the means of subsistence to the islands of Antigua, and St. Christophers, whose inhabitants, but for this resource, must have perished by famine, or thrown themselves into the arms of the enemy? The colonists of St. Eustatius are indebted in large sums to British merchants; how will they be able to clear these balances if their effects remain confiscated?

'In a word, it is to be presumed that the conquest of the Dutch islands by the arms of the king, has been undertaken with nobler views than that of pillaging and ruining their inhabitants.'

All these representations were of no avail. Rodney had acted in strict conformity to the instructions of his government. He answered the complainers, that he could not recover from his astonishment that British merchants, instead of sending their goods into the windward islands belonging to England, had sent them to a leeward island, whither they could only have been transported with intent to supply the wants of the enemies of their king and country. But it is to be observed, that if these British merchants were in fault, the commanders of the king's vessels were still more blamable for having brought in and sold at this same port of St. Eustatius the prizes they had captured at sea; some laden with provisions, others with arms and military stores; which thus found their way to the enemies of Great Britain, and served to recruit their resources for continuing the war. Rodney added, that the island of St. Eustatius was Dutch, every thing in it was Dutch, was under the protection of the Dutch flag, and as Dutch it should be treated. The rigor of these principles was applied likewise to the neighboring small islands of St. Martin and Saba, which fell at the same time into the power of the English. But the British commanders, not content with pillaging property, proceeded to wreak their cruelty on persons. All individuals not English were not only banished from the island, but subjected to the most odious vexations. The Jews, who were numerous and wealthy, were the first to experience the brutality of the conqueror. They were all crowded into the custom house; searched from head to foot; then the skirts of their coats were docked to the waist. Their trunks and portmanteaus were forced open and ransacked. Stripped of their money and effects, they were, in that state of nakedness and wretchedness, transported as outlaws, and landed on the island of St. Christophers. A sea captain named Santon was the superintendent and chief executioner of the barbarity of his chiefs. The Americans soon shared the fate of the Jews. After having undergone a total spoliation, these unhappy people were sent to St. Christophers, as a race devoted to misery and death. Among them, however, were many of those loyalists, who had been obliged to fly their native country through the part which they had taken in support of the British cause and government.

Thus expelled by their fellow-citizens as friends to the English, and expelled by the English as friends to the Americans, these ill-fated refugees were punished as severely for having preserved their fidelity towards the king, as if they had violated it. The assembly of St. Christophers manifested the most honorable compassion for these victims at once of rapine and of cruelty; they passed an immediate act for their relief and future provision, until they should have time to recover from their calamitous situation. The French and Dutch merchants were banished the last from St. Eustatius. This decree was executed with particular rigor towards those of Amsterdam. In the meantime, public sales were advertised, invitation given, and protection offered, to purchasers of all nations and sorts; and the island of St. Eustatius became one of the greatest auctions that ever was opened in the universe. It was attended by an immense concourse of the merchants of friendly or neutral nations; they bought as well for their own account as on commission for the French and Spaniards, to whom their vicinity and the war rendered those goods more valuable. Thus, after having so cruelly treated the inhabitants of St. Eustatius, under the pretence that they had supplied the enemies of England, in the ordinary way of commerce, the British commanders undertook themselves to supply those enemies by opening a public market, and bidding buyers by proclamation. Never perhaps was a more considerable sale; the gains of Rodney and Vaughan were immense; but it was fated that they should not long enjoy them; Heaven, as we shall soon see, had in reserve an exemplary chastisement for their avarice.

The loss of St. Eustatius was not the only misfortune which befell the Dutch in the West Indies. It seemed as if the English, in their zeal to reduce their new enemy, had forgotten that they had any other to encounter. Holland possessed on the continent of South America, in that vast country anciently called Guiana, the important colony of Surinam. The governor had made no preparations for defense; he was even ignorant of the declaration of war. But all of a sudden he was visited by a squadron of British privateers, mostly belonging to Bristol. In contempt of all danger, they entered the rivers of Demerary and Issequibo, and brought out from under the guns of the Dutch forts and batteries, almost all the vessels of any value in either river. The colonists of that part, seized with consternation at the approach of these audacious cruisers, sent to make a tender of their submission to the governor of Barbadoes; requiring no other terms but a participation of those which had been granted to St. Eustatius, without knowing, however, what they were. The governor readily consented to their wishes. When shortly after they were apprised of the fate of St. Eustatius, they began to tremble for their own. But Rodney showed himself more humane towards the colonists of Demerary, Issequibo, and Berbice, who had voluntarily put themselves under the British dominion, than he had been towards those of St. Eustatius. He guarantied the safety of persons and property, and made no change in their existing laws and authorities.

Thus fortune every where smiled upon the English, in their first attempts against the Dutch possessions in the West Indies. They were less successful against the Spaniards, who had recently invaded, in considerable force, the confines of West Florida. Don Galvez, the governor of Louisiana, and admiral don Solano, after having been battered by a horrible tempest, had arrived before, and laid siege to Pensacola, the capital of that province. The place was strong; and general Campbell, the commandant, defended himself for a long time with great valor. But a bomb having fallen upon the powder magazine, it exploded, and demolished the principal redoubt. The Spaniards occupied it immediately, and made their dispositions for assaulting the body of the place. Campbell then thought it best to capitulate; he obtained the most honorable conditions. Thus all West Florida, which had been for the English one of the most precious fruits of the war of Canada, returned after a few years under the dominion of the Spaniards.

The order of history requires that we should now turn our attention from fields of battle, upon the cabinets which directed the operations we have witnessed; and that we should endeavor to describe what was, at this period, the policy of the belligerent powers.

The Americans conceived they had grounds to complain bitterly of the French, their allies. They alledged that, saving some vain demonstrations from without, France had afforded them no efficacious assistance whatever; and that she left them to struggle by themselves against a powerful enemy. They affirmed, that ' the

French troops disembarked at Rhode Island, had not been able to render them any service, through defect of a sufficient naval force : that they must continue equally useless, so long as they were not supported by a respectable squadron ; that no success could be hoped for, in that part, without being masters at sea ; that, meanwhile, the English continued to possess Georgia, the greatest part of South Carolina, all New York, and, moreover, they had now invaded Virginia ; that not a French battalion had been seen to move for the defense or recovery of any of these provinces ; that while awaiting the co-operation of their allies, the United States were oppressed by the weight of an enterprise so much above their strength, that the war consumed their population, paralyzed all industry, suspended al culture, and, consequently, drained the sources of public revenue ; and that to crown so many calamities, there appeared no prospect of their termination.

While the Americans thus vented their discontent, no little astonishment was excited in Europe, that so formidable a coalition should have proved so feeble in effect against the common enemy. Far from bending, the English seemed, on the contrary, to have acquired more elastic forces, and a more daring spirit. They pressed the Americans with vigor, while they held the mastery of the West Indian seas, possessed themselves of the Dutch colonies, made conquests in the East Indies, and kept fortune in equilibrium in Europe. This state of things seemed to cloud the glory of the French and Spanish names. The court of Versailles, as the soul and principal mover of all this mass of forces, was itself the object of the heavy complaints of the catholic king, who reproached it for not having promoted the execution of his favorite projects, the conquest of Jamaica, and the reduction of Gibraltar ; the siege of which he had already commenced. The Hollanders, on their part, who already felt the anguish of so considerable losses, exclaimed that they were abandoned, without any appearance of sympathy, to perils which they should not have involved themselves in but for the counsels and instigations of France. Their complaints were the more dolorous, as they had just been informed that a formidable expedition was fitting out, in the ports of Great Britain, against the Cape of Good Hope, an establishment so vital for the preservation of their East India commerce. They saw themselves menaced, in the oriental hemisphere, with blows no less cruel than those which had so lately stunned them in the New World. They perceived but too clearly that before it would be possible for them to complete their preparations of defense, and to dispatch succors into those remote regions, the English would have time to accomplish their long meditated designs.

Yielding to these various considerations and to the voice of his own interest, the king of France determined to exert twofold vigor and activity in the present campaign, in order to repair the time lost in the preceding year. Accordingly the labors of the arsenal at Brest were pushed with new ardor, while upon the different points of the kingdom, the land forces held themselves in readiness to act. Three principal objects were contemplated by the ministry. The first was, to send such a fleet to the West Indies, as, when united to the squadron already in the ports of Martinico, should secure to France a maritime superiority in those seas. This fleet, the command of which was intrusted to the count de Grasse, was to carry out a strong body of land troops. By means of this re-inforcement, the marquis de Bouille would find himself in a situation to undertake some important expedition against the British islands. After the accomplishment whereof, and before the season of hostilities should have elapsed, the count de Grasse was to repair to the coasts of America, in order to co-operate with the count de Rochambeau and general Washington. The second, was to send a squadron into the African seas, in order to shield the Cape of Good Hope from the danger that menaced it. After having provided for the security of that colony, the squadron was to proceed to the East Indies, where admiral Hughs had given a temporary superiority to the British flag. Finally, the ministers meditated a brilliant stroke, in the seas of Europe, in favor of the allied courts, and principally of Spain. An expedition against Minorca was decided with unanimity. The English had penetrated, in great part, the plans of their enemies; and were preparing to oppose them with all those obstacles which they deemed the most likely to render them abortive. They exerted an extraordinary activity in equipping a fleet, which was to carry lord Cornwallis a re-inforcement of several English regiments and three thousand Hessians. It was hoped that this addition of force would enable that general not only to maintain the conquests he had made, but also to extend still further the progress of his arms. The victories of Camden and Guildford had inspired the British nation with new confidence; all promised themselves a speedy conclusion of the war, and the subjugation of America. The British ministers even flattered themselves that the fleet they sent to the West Indies, though it was not considerable, would nevertheless prove sufficient, by its junction with the naval force already stationed there, to uphold the present preponderance of England in those seas. The public attention was particularly attracted by an armament which consisted of one ship of seventy-four guns, one of fifty-four, three of fifty, with some frigates, cutters, fire-ships and other light vessels. This squadron was to serve as escort to a great number of transports loaded with an immense quantity of arms and military stores. General Meadows embarked in it with a body of three thousand picked soldiers. The fleet was under the orders of commodore Johnstone Manifold were the conjectures in public circulation respecting the object of this expedition, which the government studied to cover with impenetrable secrecy. It was generally presumed to be destined for the East Indies, in order to reduce all the French possessions in that part. This supposition, so far as appeared from the events which followed, was not destitute of foundation. But it would seem also that the war which broke out against Holland, constrained the British ministry to change the destination of this armament, or at least to restrict it to the attack of the Cape of Good Hope, and the re-inforcement of the troops which guarded the establishments in the hither peninsula of India. It was deemed essential to provide for their safety, even though it were not permitted by circumstances to think of conquering those of the enemy. But of all the cares which occupied the British cabinet at this epoch, it assuredly had none more urgent than that of re-victualing Gibraltar. Herein, besides the importance of the place, the honor of the British nation was deeply interested. The Spaniards and English seemed to have set each other at defiance at the foot of this rock. The first, relying upon the fleet which they had at Cadiz, expected to be able to intercept whatever succors should approach for the relief of the garrison. It already began to suffer excessively from the scarcity of provisions; the supplies which admiral Rodney had introduced the preceding year, were almost entirely consumed, and what remained were so marred as to be scarcely edible. Already general Elliot had been constrained to lessen a fourth of his soldiers' ration. In order to give them the example of privations, the officers ceased to dress their hair with powder. But the inhabitants of the city suffered still more from the absolute want of the necessaries of life. Such was the vigilance, and such the industry of the Spaniards in their endeavors to cut off all relief by sea, that since the supplies of Rodney, scarcely a few vessels from the African shore and Minorca had been able to make good their entrance into the port of Gibraltar. But how far were these feeble succors from being in proportion to the exigency! Besides, the prices which the masters of these vessels demanded for their commodities were so exorbitant, as to exceed the faculties of the greater part of the inhabitants. The miserable remains of the old provisions, spoilt as they were, commanded extravagant rates.*

* Old sea biscuit, quite moldy, brought a shilling sterling the pound; and difficult to be found   Sour flour, and damaged peas, were worth one shilling and four pence the

The garrison supported all their sufferings with a heroic firmness; but without prompt succors it was impossible to prevent that formidable place, the key of the Mediterranean, from soon returning under the domination of its ancient masters. The general attention, in England, was directed towards this important point.

In Holland, meanwhile, the greatest industry was exerted in equipping a fleet that should be capable of maintaining the dignity of the republic, and of resuscitating its ancient glory. It was particu.arly intended to protect the commerce of the Baltic against the rapacity of England. These laudable intentions, however, were not attended with all that effect which was to have been wished. The government overruled the conflicting parties, but it could not prevent their fermenting covertly. Besides, a long peace had enervated minds, and caused the neglect of naval preparations.

Such were, about that time, the projects and dispositions of the powers engaged in this memorable contest. The preparatives of war were immense; the universe was in expectation of the most important events. The English were the first to put to sea. Their intent was to succor Gibraltar. On the thirteenth of March, a fleet of twenty-eight ships of the line set sail from Portsmouth. It was obliged to cruise some days upon the coasts of Ireland, to wait for the victualing ships and merchantmen which were assembled, in very great number, in the road of Cork. The convoys bound to the two Indies departed under the protection of the fleet. When conducted out of danger from the hostile fleets, they were to continue their voyage. The squadron of commodore Johnstone sailed in company with the great fleet; being destined upon the expedition against the Cape of Good Hope, it was to escort the East India convoy up to that point. The armament was commanded by the admirals Darby, Digby, and Lockhart Ross, each heading one of the three divisions of which it was composed. The necessity of revictualing Gibraltar was notoriously evident, and the preparations made by Great Britain for its accomplishment, could no longer be concealed. The English themselves openly professed their intentions on that head. The Spaniards were consequently too well advised, not to have taken all the precautions in their power to confound the efforts of their enemies. They had armed, in the port of

pound. Black salt, the sweepings of warehouses, eight pence per pound; butter, three shillings per pound; a turkey, when to be had, thirty shillings; a sucking pig, forty shillings; a duck, ten shillings and six pence; a lean fowl, nine shillings; a loin of veal, at least a guinea; and the head of an ox was sold at a still greater price. Firewood was so scarce, that cold water was used for washing linen, and the flatiron was dispensed with; a thing which proved very prejudicial to the health of the troops, during the cold, humid season, which prevailed in the course of that winter.

Cadiz, a fleet of thirty sail of the line. The court had placed it under the conduct of don Lewis de Cordova, a seaman of high reputation. This was without doubt an imposing force, and the Spaniards had exaggerated it greatly beyond the truth, in order to deter the English, if possible, from executing their intended enterprise. Wishing to corroborate also, by his audacity, any discouraging apprehensions which the enemy might have entertained, don Lewis often issued from the port of Cadiz, to parade along the coast of Portugal, and even upon the route which the English must keep in sailing towards Gibraltar. The Spaniards, moreover, gave out that they were about to be joined by strong divisions of the French squadrons then at anchor as well in the Atlantic ports as in that of Toulon. There was, in effect, in the single port of Brest, so formidable a fleet, that it would have sufficed alone to make a stand against the whole British armament, and even to engage it with good hope of victory. No less than twenty-six sail of the line were in that port in readiness to put to sea. If this fleet should have made its junction with that of Spain, the allies would have acquired such a preponderance in those seas, as to have rendered the re-victualing of Gibraltar an extremely difficult enterprise for the English. The Spaniards confidently depended upon the co-operation of the French. But the latter had it too much at heart to prosecute their designs in the West Indies, and upon the American continent, as likewise to re-establish their affairs in the east, to be willing to direct all their efforts singly towards an object which had no real and direct utility but for Spain alone. Accordingly, the count de Grasse put to sea, the twenty-second of March, from the port of Brest, shaping his course towards the West Indies. M. de Suffren sailed in company with him, having under his orders a squadron consisting of five ships of the line, several frigates, and a strong body of land forces. He had instructions to separate from the great fleet off Madeira, and to steer to the south, towards the point of Africa; to preserve the Cape of Good Hope, and afterwards proceed to the East Indies. Thus all these naval forces, charged by their respective governments with the most important operations, got under sail almost at the same time. Without the delay which detained the English upon the coasts of Ireland, it is altogether probable that the French would have fallen in with them, and that they would have settled, by a decisive battle in the seas of Europe, that quarrel for which they were going to fight in the two Indies.

Admiral Darby, sped by a favorable wind, stood for Cape St. Vincent, which having made, he proceeded with the greatest circumspection, on account of the proximity of the Spanish armament.

But don Lewis de Cordova, who for several days had been cruising in the bay of Cadiz, was no sooner apprised of the approach of the English, than he lost all confidence in his own force. Forgetting the importance of the post he had to defend, instead of awaiting the enemy, he returned with precipitation to Cadiz, leaving him the ways free to Gibraltar.

Admiral Darby reconnoitered Cadiz, and finding the Spaniards were in no disposition to come forth, he immediately pushed forward his convoy, consisting of about a hundred sail, under the guard of a certain number of ships of war. A part of this squadron was to take post in the bay of Gibraltar itself, to cover the transports against the attempts of the Spanish gunboats; the rest was destined to cruise at the entrance of the strait, towards the Mediterranean, in order to oppose any hostile force that might present itself on that side. The admiral himself remained before Cadiz to observe the motions of the Spaniards with due diligence. The event justified his dispositions. The gunboats, it is true, made frequent attacks upon the transports, and that with the more audacity, as their inconsiderable size screened them in a manner from the effects of the enemy's artillery. The annoyance of this musquito fleet put the English out of all patience; but still it had no result of any importance. They succeeded in getting ashore all their munitions of war, and all their provisions; their exultation equaled the consternation of the Spaniards; all Europe was in astonishment. The king of Spain, who had set his heart upon the conquest of Gibraltar, and who had already expended so much treasure in the prosecution of this enterprise, persuaded himself that he was on the point of reaping the fruit of his efforts.— When apprised of the event which still retarded the attainment of his hopes, he flattered himself that his land troops would prove, perhaps, more fortunate than his naval forces. His ardor was also stimulated by an eager desire to wipe off the stain which he was apprehensive would attach to his arms from the relief of Gibraltar. The labors of the camp of St. Rock were resumed with increase of activity; the trenches and works which beset the fortress, were furnished with an immense quantity of artillery. The batteries mounted no less than one hundred and sixty pieces of heavy cannon, with eighty mortars of the largest caliber. On the twelfth of April, the British fleet being still at anchor in the port of Gibraltar, the whole or this train began to shower upon the place its tremendous volleys of balls and bombs. The narrow extent of the spot upon which they fell left no other refuge to the besieged but the casemates and vaulted places. General Elliot, the governor, did not remain a peaceable spectator of this tempest; he answered it bolt for bolt, thunder for thunder

The whole mountain, enveloped in flame and smoke from its base to its summit, resembled a volcano in the height of the most terrible eruption. The two neighboring shores of Europe and Africa were lined with people, who had thronged thither to contemplate this dreadful spectacle. But the inhabitants of the unhappy town were more exposed even than the soldiers themselves. Their terror was great, but their dangers were still greater. The limbs of the dead and dying were scattered upon the ground; women, with children in their arms, ran distractedly, imploring a shelter which could not be offered them. Some were seen crushed at the same time with their precious burthen, and torn in a thousand pieces by the bursting bombs. Others, with trembling hands, let themselves down precipices, in order to retire the farthest possible from the seat of danger; many threw themselves into the casemates, where, breathing an infected air, and deprived of repose by the dismal cries of the wounded who expired around them, they thought themselves happy in having escaped an inevitable death. The town, situated upon the declivity of the rock, and next the sea towards the west, was demolished to its foundations. The Spanish gunboats contributed especially to this disaster. Under cover of night, they slipped between the British vessels, and after having effected their purpose, profited of a wind, which commonly springs up in the morning, to return to the port of Algesiras. Their destructive fire often reached those unhappy persons who had sought, upon the flank of the mountain, a refuge against the artillery of the Spanish lines. It continued to batter the place for upwards of three weeks, with hardly any intermission, and was answered with equal vigor. The firing was then relaxed on both sides; the besiegers became sensible that their efforts resulted in little more than a vain noise, and the besieged thought it imprudent to expend their ammunition without necessity. Scarcely a few shot, discharged by intervals from the fortress, attested that the garrison were upon the alert; the greater part of the time, general Elliot observed, in apparent tranquillity, the fruitless toils of his enemy. It was calculated that in this short space of time, the Spaniards consumed fifty tons of gunpowder; they had fired seventy-five thousand volleys of cannon balls, and twenty-five thousand of bombs. Notwithstanding the narrowness of the place in which the English were immured, they had lost but few men by the fire of this immense artillery; their wounded did not exceed two hundred and fifty. As to the inhabitants, seeing their houses destroyed, and in continual dread of new disasters, they demanded permission to retire. General Elliot acquiesced in their desires, after having furnished them with all the assistance in his power. The greater part embarked in the fleet which had victualed the place, and repaired to England.

Before it had arrived there, fortune, propitious to the French, inflicted a heavy stroke upon their enemies; which was considered as a just chastisement for the robberies committed at St. Eustatius. Intelligence had been received in France, that a numerous convoy of ships laden with the rich spoils of that island, had left it about the last of March, and were on their way for the ports of Great Britain. It was also known, that this convoy was to be followed by another not less valuable, which was freighted with the produce of Jamaica. The first was guarded by four ships of war under admiral Hotham. The moment could not have been more favorable to the French, since the great English fleet was employed in succoring Gibraltar The court of Versailles knew very well how to profit of so fair an occasion ; it had equipped with great celerity, in the port of Brest, a squadron destined to intercept the expected convoys. The chevalier de la Motte Piquet put to sea the fifteenth of April, at the head of eight ships of the line, all excellent sailers. He struck into the middle of tle convoy of St. Eustatius, and dispersed it entirely. Twenty-two ships fell into his power, two others were taken by privateers. Some few, with the ships of war that had escorted them, made their way good into the ports of Ireland. The British merchants who had insured the captured ships, lost by this stroke upwards of seven hundred thousand pounds sterling. Admiral Darby, during his homeward passage, was very early informed of the disaster. He instantly made his dispositions for cutting off the retreat of la Motte Piquet. But the French admiral, attentive to all the movements of the enemy, and content with the brilliant advantages which he had just obtained, left the convoy of Jamaica to pursue its voyage in tranquillity, and returned without accident to Brest. So rich a capture created no little festivity in France.

Those who had projected this expedition, and those who had executed it, were loaded with just praises. The fleet of admiral Darby recovered the ports of England. In the meantime, the two fleets of Johnstone and Suffren had put to sea for the Cape of Good Hope. These two admirals had the most exact information respecting each other's departure, intended route, and ulterior destination. But the Englishman was obliged to touch at the bay of Praya in St. Jago, the most considerable of the Cape de Verd islands. He was occupied in recruiting his water and provision for the long voyage he was about to undertake, and a great part of his crews were on shore. M. de Suffren was soon apprised of it, and immediately shaped his course with press of sail for the bay of Praya, where he hoped to surprise the enemy He kept so close along under a tongue of land which covers the port towards the east, that he was already on the point of entering it without being discovered. But the British ship Isis, which lay near the mouth of the bay, perceived beyond the eastern point the tops of several masts. Afterwards, by the mode of maneuvering, it was known that they were French, and the signal of enemy sails was given immediately. The commodore recalled his crews from the shore, and made all his dispositions for battle Meanwhile the French squadron doubled the point, and appeared all at once at the entrance of the bay. The attack commenced forthwith. The English had one ship of seventy-four guns, four others of inferior force, three frigates, with several East India Company ships, armed for war. The French had two ships of seventy-four, and three of sixty-four guns. After having cannonaded the Isis, which presented herself the first, they forced the entrance of the harbor, passing into the midst of the British squadron, and firing double broadsides, M. de Tremignon, with his ship the Hannibal, which was ahead of the rest, advanced as far as possible, and with admirable intrepidity cast anchor in the midst of the British line, which assailed him from right and left. He was followed by M. de Suffren, in the Hero, and afterwards the chevalier de Cardaillac joined them with the Artesien. The two other ships could not approach near enough to support them, and having fallen to leeward after having discharged a few broadsides, they stood out to sea. Two British ships, the Isis and the Romney, were unable to take any considerable part in the action; the first having suffered severely from the fire of the French, at the time of their entrance into the bay, the second finding herself advanced too far within it. The engagement was therefore reduced to that of three ships of the line on either side; the French fired both starboard and larboard guns, as they had placed themselves in the centre of the English. But at length, the British frigates, with the armed ships of the India Company, having rallied, came up to the support of the commodore. After the action had lasted an hour and a half, the Artesien, having lost her captain, and being no longer able to sustain so fierce a fire, cut her cables and drew off. M. de Suffren, finding himself deprived of his rear guard, and exposed to be cannonaded at once on both sides as well as in front and rear, took a similar resolution to withdraw from the harbor. The retreat of the Hero and Artesien left the Hannibal alone to sustain the whole weight of the enemy's fire, and of course she suffered excessively; she lost first her mizzenmast, then her mainmast, and at last her rudder. Nevertheless, by incredible exertions she made her way good to the mouth of the bay, where she was taken in tow by the ship Sphynx. Her masts being refitted as well as it was possible, she rejoined the rest of the squadron. The English would fain have followed the French, in order to re-commence the engagement; but the wind, the currents, the approach of night, and the disabled state of the Isis, prevented them from doing it. Such was the combat of Praya, which gave occasion to several observations upon the conduct of the two admirals. The British commander was censured for having anchored so imprudently in an open and defenseless bay, when he must have known that the enemy could not be far off. Vainly would he have alledged, that he believed himself protected by the neutrality of the place, the island of St. Jago belonging to the crown of Portugal; for he affirmed himself, that when the French see an opportunity for seizing their advantage, they are not wont to respect these neutralities; an accusation which, though it were founded, appears not the less extraordinary from the mouth of an Englishman. Commodore Johnstone committed, besides, great errors, in landing so great a part of his crews, in placing his weakest ships at the entrance of the bay, and in letting the Hannibal escape notwithstanding her crippled condition. M. de Suffren, it was said on the other hand, ought not to have attempted to combat at anchor. Every probability assured him a complete victory, if, instead of losing time in coming to anchor, he had immediately resorted to boarding, or even if he had fought under sail an enemy that was in a good degree surprised and unprepared for action.

As soon as the British squadron was refitted, it put to sea in pursuit of the French; but finding them drawn up in order of battle, it avoided a second engagement; night, which soon came on, separated the two squadrons. Commodore Johnstone returned to the bay of Praya. M. de Suffren, continuing his voyage to the south, and towing the Hannibal, repaired to *False Bay* at the Cape of Good Hope. He was rejoined there by his convoy, which, during his attack of Praya, he had left at sea, under the escort of the corvette la Fortune. Thus was frustrated the design which the English had meditated against the Cape. Constrained to relinquish all hope of conquest, they directed their force against the commerce of their enemies. Commodore Johnstone was advised by his light vessels, that several ships of the Dutch East India Company, very richly laden, lay at anchor in the bay of Saldana, not far from the Cape itself. Upon making the coasts of Africa, acting himself as pilot to his squadron in the midst of shoals and reefs, crowding all sail by night, concealing himself by day, he maneuvered with such dexterity, that he arrived unexpectedly before the bay. He captured five of the

most valuable ships ; the others were burnt. After having obtained
this advantage, which preserved him at least from the reproach of
having undertaken an expedition without utility, he detached a part
of his force to India, under general Meadows, and returned himself
with the Romney, his frigates, and rich prizes, to England. M. de
Suffren, having thrown a strong garrison into the Cape of Good Hope,
continued his voyage for the East Indies. Thus the war which
raged already in Europe, America, and Africa, was about to redouble
its violence upon the distant banks of the Ganges.

Meanwhile, Gibraltar continued to hold out ; to the furious attack
given that place, had succeeded an almost total calm. The gunboats, alone, profited of the obscurity of night, to keep the garrison in continual alarms. In order to restrain them, the governor
caused his advanced batteries to be armed with guns and mortar
pieces, peculiarly calculated to throw their shot to a great distance.
As they could now reach the camp of St. Roch, every time the gunboats made their attacks, the Spanish lines were assailed by the most
violent fire. Don Mendoza, having perceived that general Elliot did
thus by way of reprisal for the assaults of the gunboats, ordered the
commanders of the flotilla to desist from all further insult against the
place, and to keep their station quietly in the port of Algesiras. He
enjoined them, however, to exert the greatest vigilance to prevent
the entrance of supplies into the place. The Spaniards were indefatigable in pushing forward their trenches. They had now brought
them quite to the foot of the rock, so that the circumvallation extended from right to left across the whole breadth of the isthmus by
which the rock itself connects with the main land. They had excavated upon their left the mine of communication between their outer
circumvallation and the parallels. General Elliot, full of security
upon the summit of the rock he defended, unwilling to lavish his
ammunition, without utility, had not disturbed the workmen. But
when he saw that their works were completed, he resolved to destroy them by the most unexpected and vigorous sally. The twenty-
seventh of November, towards midnight, he issued from the place at
the head of three brigades of infantry, commanded by general Ross.
These troops were followed by a great number of pioneers, miners,
and engineers. The sally was conducted with suitable order and
silence. The English appeared all of a sudden before the advanced
guards, and routed them in a few instants ; they found themselves
masters of the first parallel, and proceeded to destroy it. The engineers, furnished with combustible materials, set fire to every thing
that was capable of receiving it. The carriages of the cannon were
rendered unserviceable, and the pieces, including the mortars, were

spiked with admirable promptitude.   The workmen tore up the platforms and traverses, and leveled the breastworks with the ground. All the magazines were successively consigned to the flames. A single half hour witnessed the destruction of those works which had been erected at so vast an expense of toil and treasure. The Spaniards, whether from the stupor of consternation, or supposing the enemy to be much stronger than he was in reality, were afraid to go out of their camp to repulse him. They contented themselves with keeping up an incessant, though harmless fire, with balls and grape-shot. The English, after having accomplished their purpose, returned sound and safe into the fortress.

In the meantime, a project was conceived in Europe, the execution of which could not fail to give a severe shock to the British power in the Mediterranean. The Spaniards remained very ill satisfied with France; they believed themselves authorized to reproach her with having hitherto consulted exclusively her own interests, to the prejudice of her allies. They complained with peculiar bitterness, that she had in no shape promoted the expeditions of Jamaica and Gibraltar, as if she were loth to see the prosperity of the Spanish arms in the seas of America and upon the European continent. The revictualing of Gibraltar, on the part of the English, by dint of force, without a single movement of any sort being made by the French to prevent it, and the despair experienced by the Spaniards at having consumed themselves in vain efforts for the reduction of that place, had prodigiously increased their ill humor, and caused it to degenerate into an open discontent. The Spanish people murmured in bold language; the court was become the object of the most vehement animadversion. It was accused of having undertaken this expedition merely in subservience to the ambitious views of France, and not at all for the interests of the Spanish nation; the Spaniards called it *a court war, a family war.* Stimulated by the vivacity of these complaints, and reflecting, moreover, that the reduction, in whatever mode, of the British power, was the augmentation of her own, France took the resolution to give into some enterprise whose immediate fruit should be gathered by Spain. An expedition against Jamaica necessarily involving long delays, and a fresh attack upon Gibraltar promising no better than dubious results, it was determined to attempt an operation, the success of which appeared the more probable, as the English were far from expecting it; and that was, the conquest of the island of Minorca. If France had motives for wishing it with eagerness, it must have been still more desirable for the Spaniards. Minorca is so favorably situated for cruising, that it was become the habitual resort of an immense number of privateers. Their audacity

was not confined to infesting the seas, and disturbing the navigation
and commerce of the Spaniards and French; they even intercepted
neutral vessels employed in trafficking with these two nations; this
island also served as a place of arms for the English. They deposited
in it the munitions of war and provisions, which they drew from the
neighboring coasts of Africa, whether for the use of their shipping or
for the consumption of Gibraltar. The facility of the enterprise was
another persuasive invitation to attempt it. In effect, however imposing was fort St. Philip, from its position and works, the garrison
which guarded it was far from corresponding to the strength and
importance of the place; it consisted of only four regiments, two of
them British and two Hanoverians, who altogether did not exceed
two thousand men. Notwithstanding the salubrity of the air, and the
abundance of fresh provisions, these troops were infected with the
scurvy. They were commanded by the generals Murray and Draper.

In pursuance of the plan concerted between the courts of Versailles
and Madrid, the count de Guichen departed from Brest, towards
the last of June, with eighteen sail of the line, and repaired to the
port of Cadiz, in order to join the Spanish fleet which awaited him
there. He had under him two general officers of great reputation,
M. de la Motte Piquet, and M. de Beausset. The Spanish fleet,
commanded by don Lewis de Cordova, and by the two vice-admirals, don Gaston and don Vincent Droz, was composed of thirty
ships of the line. A corps of ten thousand selected troops was
embarked without any delay on board of this armament. It set sail
the twenty-second of July, and after having been much thwarted by
the winds, appeared in sight of Minorca the twentieth of August.
The debarkation was effected in Musquito Bay. The whole island
was occupied without obstacle, including the city of Mahon, its
capital. The garrison, too feeble to defend all these posts, had
evacuated them and thrown itself into fort St. Philip. A little
after, four French regiments arrived from Toulon, under the conduct
of the baron de Falkenhayn. The two courts had confided the
general command of all the forces employed upon this expedition to
the duke de Crillon, distinguished as well for his military knowledge,
as for his courage and thirst of glory. He had entered into the
service of Spain, and, as a Frenchman of illustrious birth, he was
thought the most suitable personage to head the common enterprise.

But the siege of fort St. Philip presented difficulties of no ordinary magnitude. The works are cut in the solid rock, and mined in
all their parts. The glacis, and covered way, likewise cut in the
rock, are mined, countermined, palisaded, and furnished with batteries
which defend their approaches. Around the fosse, which is twenty

feet in depth, runs a covered and looped gallery, which affords a
secure shelter to the garrison. Subterraneous communications are
excavated between the outer works and the body of the place. In
the latter, which forms a sort of labyrinth, are sunk deep wells withdrawn covers, and barbacans pierce the walls in all directions. The
castle itself, also surrounded by a countermined covered way, is
defended not only by counterscarps and half moons, but also by a
wall sixty feet high, and a fosse thirty-six feet deep. Finally, the
nucleus, which is a square tower flanked by four bastions, presents
walls eighty feet high, and a ditch forty feet deep, and cut in the
rock. This ditch has also its corridor and lodges. In the center of
all is an esplanade for marshaling the garrison. Around it are constructed the soldiers' barracks, and magazines for the munitions, both
bomb proof, and all wrought in the hard rock. To add to their safety,
the English had totally rased the neighboring city of St. Philip.

The allies approached the citadel with circumspection ; its lofty
position overlooking all the adjacent country, it was not by scooping
trenches, but by transporting and heaping earth, that they formed
their parallels. They raised a wall of about two hundred feet in
length, five in height, and six in thickness. This laborious construction was finished, without the besiegers having experienced any loss,
as Murray did not attempt a single sally, whether in consequence of
the weakness of the garrison, or from excess of confidence in the
strength of the place. He contented himself with keeping up a fire
of cannon and mortars, which produced no effect. The parallels
being completed, the duke de Crillon unmasked his batteries, and
fulminated the fortress with one hundred and eleven twenty-four
pounders, and thirty-three mortar pieces opening thirteen inches of
diameter.

During the siege of fort St. Philip, the combined fleets of France
and Spain, amounting to near fifty sail of the line, under the count
de Guichen, bent their course towards the coasts of England. The
intention of the French admiral was to throw himself in the way
of the British fleet, and to attack it. The great inferiority of the
British rendered their defeat almost inevitable. The count de Guichen also designed, by this movement, to prevent the enemy from
passing succors from England to Minorca. He even hoped to cut
off and capture the convoys that were then on their passage from the
two Indies, bound for the ports of Great Britain. His views were
likewise directed upon another convoy, which was assembled at the
port of Cork, in Ireland, in order to watch its opportunity to make
sail for the East and West Indies. Perhaps the French admiral was
not without hopes that the sudden appearance of so formidable an

armament upon the coasts of the British islands, might afford him an occasion to reach them with a stroke of the last importance. He hastened therefore to occupy the entrance of the channel in all its breadth, by extending his line from the isle of Ushant to those of Scilly. Admiral Darby was then at sea with twenty-one ships of the line, and on the way to meet his convoy. He had the good fortune to fall in with a neutral vessel, which apprised him of the approach of the combined squadrons. But for this intelligence, he must inevitably have fallen headlong into the midst of forces so superior to his own, that he could hardly have retained the smallest hope of safety. He instantly retired with all sails upon Torbay. He was there soon re-inforced by several ships of the first rank, which carried his fleet to thirty sail of the line. He disposed his order of battle in the form of a crescent within the bay itself, although it is open, and little susceptible of defense. These dispositions, however, appeared to him sufficient to repulse the enemy, in case they should present themselves. But the peril was really extreme ; they menaced at once the fleet and the maritime cities. None was more exposed than Cork, an unfortified place, and containing immense magazines of every denomination. All England was thrown into a state of the most anxious alarm. The allied armament at length appeared in sight of Torbay. The count de Guichen immediately held a council of war, to deliberate upon the course to be pursued in the present conjuncture. His own opinion was in favor of attacking the British fleet in the position it now occupied. He alledged, that it might be considered as if caught in a net, and that a more auspicious occasion could never present itself for wresting from Great Britain the dominion of the sea. He represented what disgrace, what eternal regrets, would be incurred by allowing it to escape them. He maintained that the enemy, cramped in his movement within a bay, from which there was no outlet, must inevitably become the prey of the innumerable fire-ships with which the combined fleets might support their attack. Finally, he declared that the honor of the arms of the two allied sovereigns was staked upon the issue of this expedition. Don Vincent Droz not only concurred in the opinion of the admiral, but even offered to lead the attempt at the head of the vanguard. But M. de Beausset, the second in command, a seaman of high reputation, manifested a contrary opinion. He contended that the situation of the English squadron would enable it to fight them at their great disadvantage ; they could not attack it in a body, but must form their line ahead, and fall down singly upon the enemy. This would expose every ship to the collected fire of the whole British fleet, lying fast at anchor, and drawn up in such a manner as to point all its guns at any object within

its reach. He concluded with observing, that since an attack under
such circumstances could by no means be justified, it became expedient to bend their attention exclusively upon an expedition, which,
though less brilliant, was certainly of great moment, the capture of
the West India convoy, probably at that instant not very far from the
shores of Europe. Don Lewis de Cordova, and all the other Spanish
officers, with the exception of don Vincent Droz, adopted the sentiment of M. de Beausset. The project of attacking the British fleet
was therefore rejected by a majority of votes. But if the allies would
not, or knew not how to profit of the occasion which fortune had
provided them, she seemed to take her revenge in baffling the designs
to which they had given the preference. Contagious maladies began
to rage on board their fleet, and especially on board the Spanish ships
The weather became shortly after so tempestuous, that the two admirals were obliged to think of their safety. The count de Guichen
returned to Brest, and don Lewis de Cordova to Cadiz. The British convoys reached their ports without obstacles. Thus this second
appearance of the allies upon the coasts of England proved as vain
as the first. Its only fruit was that of having impeded the succors
destined for Minorca. But if this campaign between France, Spain
and England passed, in the seas of Europe, without any great effusion of blood, and almost entirely in demonstrations of little avail, it
was at least remarkable for the reciprocal animosity manifested between the English and Dutch. It brought to mind those fierce and
sanguinary battles which had procured so much celebrity for these
two nations in the seventeenth century. The Dutch carried on a
very lucrative commerce with the produce of their colonies in the
Baltic sea. Having become, as it were, the general factors of the
nations of the north and of the south of Europe, their gains were
immense. They were drawn, besides, towards the countries of the
north, by the necessity of procuring from that part all the articles
employed in the construction of shipping. This intercourse was
become still more essential to them since their rupture with Great
Britain, in order to be able to put their navy in a condition to defend
the possessions and commerce of the republic, and to maintain the
honor of its flag. Their arsenals, however, were far from being
supplied with all the stores and materials requisite to the present
emergency. The English perceived of what importance it was for
them to impede the supplies of their enemies. With this intent, so
early as the month of June, they had put to sea four ships of the
line and one of fifty guns, under the command of admiral Hyde
Parker, a very expert seaman, and father of him who served at that
time upon the coasts of America. His instructions were, to scour

the northern seas, and do all the harm possible to the Dutch trade, and, at his return, to take under his protection a rich convoy which was assembled in the port of Elsineur.

Admiral Hyde Parker accomplished his mission with diligence; and already, being returned from the Baltic, he was conducting the convoy through the German ocean on his way home. Since his departure from Portsmouth, he had been joined by other ships, among which one of seventy-four guns, called the Berwick, one of forty-four, named the Dolphin, and several smaller vessels; so that his squadron was composed of six sail of the line, exclusive of the rest. The Dutch, during this time, had not neglected their preparatives. They had succeeded in fitting out a squadron of seven ships of the line, with several frigates or corvettes. They had given the command of it to admiral Zoutman. He set sail, towards the middle of July, with a convoy of merchantmen, which he purposed to escort into the Baltic. The Dutch squadron was joined soon after by a stout American frigate called the Charlestown; and, on the fifth of August, it fell in with admiral Hyde Parker upon the Dogger Bank. The British squadron was to windward; at sight of the imposing force of the enemy, it sent its convoy homeward, under the guard of frigates, and bore down upon the Dutch. The latter, as soon as they discovered the English, likewise dispatched their convoy towards their own ports, and prepared themselves for battle. They appeared to desire it with no less ardor than their adversaries. The English formed their line with seven ships, of which one of eighty guns, but old and in bad condition, two of seventy-four, excellent, one of sixty-four, one of sixty, one of fifty, and lastly, a frigate of forty-four. The line of the Dutch was formed in like manner with seven ships, one of seventy-six, two of sixty-eight, three of fifty-four, and one frigate of forty-four. The light vessels kept themselves aside of the line, ready to carry succor wherever it might be required. The English came down upon the Dutch with full sails, and before the wind; the latter awaited them, firm at their posts. A profound silence, the ordinary sign of pertinacious resolution, reigned on board of both squadrons. No other sound was heard but that of the creaking of pulleys, the whistling of the wind, and the dashing of waves. The soldiers were formed upon the deck, the cannoniers stood by their pieces, awaiting the signal to commence the fire. It was not given until the squadrons were within half musket shot distance of each other. The two admiral ships, namely, the Fortitude, which carried Parker, and the admiral de Ruyter, mounting Zoutman, attacked each other close alongside with extreme impetuosity. The other ships imitated them, and soon the action became general. The Dutch had the superiority in weight of metal, and in the aid of frigates, particularly in that of the Charlestown. The rapidity of their evolutions enabled them to act against the whole line, assailing the ships of the enemy in flank. The English, on the other hand, were advantaged by the agility of maneuvers and a better supported fire. During near four hours, the action was kept up with an equal spirit, and a balanced success. The Dutch stood firm upon every point of their line, and the English redoubled efforts to carry a victory which they deemed it beneath them to relinquish. But the rage of men was constrained to yield to the force of elements. The ships, on the one part as well as on the other, were so terribly shattered that they were no longer manageable. They floated upon the water, like wrecks, at the discretion of the wind, and their relative distance became at length so great, that it was impossible to renew the engagement. The English received incalculable damage in their masts and rigging.

After some hasty repairs, Hyde Parker endeavored to re-form his line, in order to recommence the battle, provided Zoutman did not decline it. He attempted to follow him, on seeing him stand for the Texel. But all his efforts were vain. The Dutch ships, however, were in no better condition. During the passage they had now before them, their masts fell one after another; the leaks were so considerable, that the work of pumps became fruitless. All the captains successively made their admiral signals of distress. The Holland, of sixty-eight guns, went to the bottom, within thirty leagues of the Texel; the crew had but just time to save themselves, leaving, in their precipitation, the unhappy wounded to a certain death. The frigates were obliged to take the other ships in tow to enable them to gain the port.

The loss of the English in killed and wounded amounted to four hundred and fifty, among whom were several distinguished officers. In the number of the slain was captain Macartney, who commanded the Princess Amelia, of eighty guns. The valor he signalized in the combat honored his last moments; but it was still less astonishing than the intrepidity of his young son. This child, yet but seven years old, remained constantly at the side of his father in the very height of the action; the unfortunate but heroic witness of the stroke which snatched him from his fond affection. Lord Sandwich, first lord of the admiralty, knowing that captain Macartney had left a numerous family, and little fortune, adopted this courageous infant. In England, unanimous praises were lavished upon all those who had combated at the Dogger Bank. King George himself, as soon as he knew that admiral Hyde Parker was arrived at the Nore, went to pay him a visit on board of his ship, and expressed to him, as well as to all his officers, the high sense he entertained of their valiant conduct in this bloody rencounter. But the old seaman, irritated against the board of admiralty, who, in giving him so inadequate a force, had frustrated him of an occasion for signalizing himself by a great victory, told the king, with the blunt freedom of his profession, that he wished him younger officers and better ships ; that for his own part, he was become too old to serve any longer. In defiance of the solicitations of the sovereign, of the courtiers, and of the ministers, he persisted in his resolution, and immediately tendered his resignation.

The government and public were no less forward, in Holland, to acknowledge the services of the officers and men who, in the action of the fifth of August, had sustained the ancient renown of the flag of the United Provinces. The stadtholder, in the name of the States-General, addressed public thanks to rear-admiral Zoutman, apprising him, at the same time, of his promotion to the rank of vice-admiral. The captains Dedel, Van Braam, and Kindsburghen, were created rear-admirals. The same honor, and particular regrets, were conferred upon the count de Bentinck, who was put ashore mortally wounded. He had displayed equal skill and gallantry in the command of the Batavia. The loss of the Dutch in killed and wounded was greater than that of the English. Such was the issue of the naval battle of Dogger Bank, the best conducted, and the best fought of all this war. It would be impossible to decide who came off with the advantage ; but it is certain that the Dutch, having been constrained to regain their ports for the purpose of refitting, found themselves under the necessity of abandoning their design, which had been to repair to the Baltic. This disappointment, however, did not prevent the nation from cherishing new hopes ; the glorious recollection of past times revived in every breast.

As soon as the count de Guichen had re-entered the port of Brest, the French government began to frame new designs. It was not ignorant that the count de Grasse, who commanded the West India fleet, must soon stand in need of supplies and re-inforcements, both of ships and troops. Naval stores are extremely scarce in that quarter, and the nature of the climate and of the waters is singularly prejudicial to ships, which get out of condition there with an incredible rapidity. The forces which had been sent thither in this and the preceding campaign, might appear sufficient to execute the plans which had been formed in favor of the United States, and against the more feeble of the British islands. But in order to attempt the expedition of Jamaica, to which Spain was continually stimulating

her ally, it was requisite to have recourse to more formidable armaments, as well by land as by sea.   The court of Versailles was also
aware that the state of affairs in the East Indies required that fresh
forces should be sent thither, and moreover that the want of arms
and munitions of war began to be felt with urgency.   Orders were
therefore given for the immediate equipment, at Brest, of a convoy
laden with all the necessary articles.   Re-inforcements of troops
were prepared for embarkation, and the armament was pushed with
extraordinary activity.   As soon as it was in readiness, the count de
Guichen put to sea at the head of the great fleet, and the marquis de
Vaudreuil with a particular squadron.   The convoys destined for the
two Indies sailed under their protection.   After having escorted
them till they were out of danger from the fleets upon the watch in
the ports of England, the count de Guichen was to stand to the south,
in order to join the Spanish squadron in the port of Cadiz.   The
object of their combined action was to intercept the succors which
the English might attempt to send to Minorca.   As to the marquis
de Vaudreuil, his destination was to conduct the re-inforcements of
troops to the West Indies, and to unite with the count de Grasse,
who was making dispositions in concert with the Spaniards for the
attack of Jamaica.

For a long time there had not issued from the ports of France
convoys so numerous and so richly laden with stores of every denomination.   The news of these immense preparations soon found its
way to England ; but, strange as it must seem, the ministers were not
informed of the force of the formidable squadrons that were to escort
the transports.   They consequently directed admiral Kempenfeldt
to put to sea, with twelve ships of the line, one of fifty guns, and four
frigates, in order to cut off the French convoys.   But the count de
Guichen had nineteen sail of the line ; and Kempenfeldt, instead of
taking, ran great risk of being taken.

In defiance of all probabilities, chance did that which human prudence could not have brought to pass.   The twelfth of December,
the weather being stormy, and the sea rough, the British admiral fell
in with a French convoy.   He had the good fortune to be to windward
of the fleet of escort, which for that reason could not act.   The
Englishman profited with great dexterity of so favorable an occasion :
he captured twenty vessels, sunk several, and dispersed the rest.
He would have taken more of them if the weather had been less
thick, the sea more tranquil, and the number of his frigates greater.
Night came on ; the two admirals had rallied their ships.   Kempenfeldt sailed in company during the whole night, with intent to engage
the enemy at break of day.   He knew not, however, what was his

force. When the morning came, he discovered it to leeward, and finding it so superior to his own, he changed his plan. Not willing to lose by imprudence what he had acquired by ability, or a benign glance of fortune, he made the best of his way towards the ports of England, where he arrived in safety with all his prizes. The number of his prisoners amounted to eleven hundred regular troops, and six or seven hundred seamen. The transports were laden with a considerable quantity of artillery, arms, and military stores. The provisions, such as wine, oil, brandy, flour, biscuit, salt meats, &c. were not in less abundance. But this loss was still but the commencement of the disasters of the French fleet. It was assailed, the following day, by a furious tempest accompanied with continual thunder and lightning, and a most impetuous wind from the southwest. The greater part of the ships were obliged to recover the port of Brest, in the most deplorable condition. Only two ships of the line, the Triumphant and the Brave, with five or six transports, were able to continue their voyage. This event had the most afflicting consequences for France ; she had not only to regret armaments and munitions of immense value, but also the precious time consumed in the reparation of the ships of war. Six whole weeks elapsed before it was possible for them to make sail anew for the West Indies. This delay, as we shall see, was extremely prejudicial to the French arms in that part.

While the war was thus prosecuted in Europe with varied success, the count de Grasse sailed prosperously towards Martinico. To accelerate his voyage, he had caused his ships of war to tow the transports. Such was his diligence that he appeared in sight of that island with an hundred and fifty sail, thirty days only after his departure from Brest. Admiral Rodney was promptly informed of the approach of the French admiral. He saw very clearly the importance of preventing the junction of this new fleet with the squadrons already existing in the ports of Martinico and of St. Domingo. The count de Grasse brought with him twenty ships of the line, with one of fifty guns, and seven or eight others awaited him in the ports above mentioned. Rodney had only twenty-one ships of the line. It is true, that Hyde Parker had four others at Jamaica. But besides their being thought necessary to the defense of the island, they were to leeward of the principal fleet, and consequently it would have been next to impracticable for them to join it. Under these considerations Rodney sent the two admirals Hood and Drake with seventeen ships to cruise before the entrance of Fort Royal harbor, in Martinico whither he knew the count de Grasse had bent the course of his voyage.

It is quite difficult to explain the motives which induced the British admiral to establish this cruise under Fort Royal; his fleet was there liable to fall to leeward, and thus to be compelled to leave between itself and the land a free passage for the French fleet into the port. A station more to windward, off the point of Salines, seemed proper to obviate these inconveniences. It was written, that Hood, who was a man of great skill in naval affairs, had made remonstrances on the subject of these dispositions; but that Rodney, whose character was headstrong, had dismissed him with an order to obey punctually. The event soon demonstrated that the station of the point of Salines would have been more suitable than that of Fort Royal. The twenty-eighth of April, at evening, the count de Grasse appeared off that point, with a most magnificent display of force. Admiral Hood was immediately apprised by his frigates of the appearance of the French. He instantly formed his line of battle, and bore down upon the ene-my. His intention was to press to windward, in order afterwards to approach so near the coasts of Martinico as to prevent the French from passing between his ships and the land. Night came on during this maneuver. At daybreak the English discovered the fleet of the count de Grassé, standing along the coast in the best order. His convoy of transports defiled behind the line of battle which he pre-sented to the enemy. All his efforts were exerted to double the Diamond Rock, which once past, nothing could prevent his entrance into the port. The English, being to leeward, were not able to pre-vent the four ships of the line, with that of fifty guns, in Fort Royal harbor, from coming out to join the great fleet. This junction carried the forces of the count de Grasse to twenty-six sail of the line; and gave him a decided superiority over Hood, although that admiral was joined, at the same time, by a ship of seventy-four guns, which came from St. Lucia. The English, however, persuading themselves that a part of the French ships were merely armed in flute, took confi-dence, and again bore down upon their adversaries. The French admiral, mindful to save his convoy, and reposing on his force, neither sought nor shunned an engagement. As soon as the English were within long shot of the French, the fire commenced on both sides. It was supported thus, at a great distance, for about three hours, with heavy damage to the first, and very little to the second. During the action the convoy entered the bay of Fort Royal. Disengaged from this care, the French advanced in order to engage the enemy in close fight. The English, on the contrary, began to retire, but in good order. Their ships, being coppered, had such a superiority in point of sailing, that it became impossible for the count de Grasse to come up with them. Besides, the French rear guard not having crowded alı sail, there had resulted such an opening between it and the remainder of the fleet, that admiral Hood was near profiting of it to cut the line. The count de Grasse perceived it in time, and filled up so dangerous a void. He continued to pursue the English for two days, and afterwards came to anchor in Fort Royal. Admiral Hood had gained Antigua; his ships, the Centaur, the Russell, the Torbay and the Intrepid, were excessively damaged in this engagement. Admiral Rodney was still at St. Eustatius, much occupied with the sale of the immense booty he had made, when he learned that the count de Grasse, after having obtained an advantage over sir Samuel Hood, was safely moored at Fort Royal. He perceived that it was time to think of something besides his mercantile interests, and that the exertion of all his force was required of him if he wished to maintain himself in the West Indies. He accordingly directed the promptest dispositions, and hastened with three ships and a body of troops to rejoin admiral Hood at Antigua. His plan was, to put to sea again immediately, in order to oppose the designs of the enemy, who, not content with his first successes, appeared to meditate others, and more considerable. The French, in effect, lost no time; they were disposed to profit of the advantages which they had now secured themselves.

After having attempted, though without effect, to surprise St. Lucia, they proceeded with all expedition to attack the island of Tobago. M. de Blanchelande debarked the first, at the head of sixteen hundred men. He seized Scarborough and the fort which defended it; general Ferguson, the governor, had little over four hundred regular troops; but they were supported by a great number of militia, well trained, and much attached to England. These sentiments were common to all the inhabitants of Tobago. The governor, finding himself too weak to defend the coasts, with drew into the interior of the island, to a post called Concordia. From this lofty situation, the sea is discovered on the right and on the left; an important advantage for being promptly apprised of the approach of succors. The marquis de Bouille disembarked soon after, with a re-inforcement of three thousand men. He made his junction with M. de Blanchelande under the walls of Concordia, which was then closely invested. At the same time, the count de Grasse appeared in sight of the island with twenty-four ships of the line, to prevent its being relieved. Governor Ferguson, as soon as he found himself attacked, had dispatched a swift-sailing vessel to Rodney with the intelligence, and a request for prompt assistance. Rodney had already passed from Antigua to Barbadoes. Whether he believed the assailants more feeble, and the besieged more strong, than they really were, or that he was not apprised of the sailing of the French admiral with all his fleet for Tobago, instead of repairing with all his own to the relief of that island, he contented himself with sending admiral Drake thither with six sail of the line, some frigates, and a body of about six hundred troops. Drake approached Tobago; but seeing the enemy in such force, he relinquished the enterprise, and hastened to regain Barbadoes. The count de Grasse pursued him, but could not prevent his reaching that island in safety, and advising admiral Rodney of the critical state of affairs. Meanwhile, the governor of Tobago was hard pressed. The French having taken possession of different heights which overlooked Concordia, he determined to retreat to a post on the Main Ridge, where a few huts had been built, and some provisions and ammunition previously lodged for the purpose. The garrison was already arrived at Caledonia, and thus occupied the road or path which leads to the post which they had in view. This road is so narrow and difficult that a few men might defend it against a whole army. The marquis de Bouille had reflected, that time and the nature of his enterprise did not admit of the lingering process of a regular siege. It was evident, however, that if the British governor should entrench himself in those inaccessible positions, the reduction of the island would acquire a series of operations as protracted as perilous. It would moreover prove an obstacle to the execution of ulterior designs. Finally, it was to be presumed that Rodney could not long delay to appear. Under these considerations, the marquis de Bouille thought proper to resort to more expeditious means than are usually employed in war. Departing from the accustomed lenity of his character, perhaps through irritation at the obstinacy of the islanders, and perhaps, also, from resentment for the late transactions at St. Eustatius, he sent to apprise the governor that he should begin with burning two habitations and two sugar plantations. His menaces were immediately accomplished. They were followed by that of consigning twice as many to the same fate, at the commencement of every four hours, until the island was laid waste or that a surrender should be made.

The inhabitants, convinced that perseverance was total ruin, were in no disposition to wait the slow approach of succors which the precipitate retreat of Drake rendered hourly more uncertain. They began to murmur; and very soon, to negotiate for conditions with the French general. Governor Ferguson at length perceived the impossibility of controlling events. He observed a manifest discouragement in his regular troops themselves, and felt that the moment of capitulation was come. He obtained honorable terms, and similar to those which the marquis de Bouille, naturally gene-rous towards his vanquished enemies, had granted to the inhabitants of Dominica. These transactions took place in the early part of June. Admiral Rodney appeared shortly after in view of the island with all his armament. But, on intelligence of its surrender, and at sight of the imposing force of the count de Grasse, he avoided an engagement, and returned to Barbadoes. In this manner, the French, availing themselves with equal sagacity and promptitude of their naval superiority in the West Indies, both galled their enemies at sea, and deprived them of a rich and well fortified island.

These operations, however, were still but a part of the plan formed by the French government, and committed to the care of the count de Grasse. The instructions of that admiral enjoined him, after having attempted all those enterprises which the season should admit of in the West Indies, to repair with all his force to the coasts of America, and there to co-operate with the French troops and those of congress, to the entire extirpation of the British power in those regions. Washington and Rochambeau awaited his arrival, in order to commence the work. Already, by means of swift-sailing vessels, they had concerted the plan of their combined action, after their junction should have taken place. It was hoped by the republicans, that besides his fleet, the French admiral would furnish five or six thousand land troops, munitions of war and provisions, and especially money, of which the Americans, and the French themselves, expe-rienced the greatest penury. Finally, they pressed him to show himself promptly, as well to support their efforts as to prevent the arrival of British re-inforcements. The count de Grasse was per-sonally stimulated by these important considerations. His imagina-tion offered him a vivid perspective of the glory to be acquired by achieving what the count d'Estaing had attempted in vain, namely, the finishing of the American war by a decisive stroke. He accord-ingly made sail from Martinico for Cape Francois, in the island of St. Domingo. He was constrained to tarry there some time, to take on board the troops and military stores destined for the continent. But he exerted himself in vain to procure the needed funds. He was joined, in that anchorage, by five ships of the line. All his prep-arations being completed, he sailed the fifth of August, and com-menced with escorting his numerous convoy till out of danger. Afterwards, having touched at the Havanna for money, which the Spaniards readily furnished him, he directed his course with a favor-able wind for the Chesapeake. His fleet, composed of twenty-eight sail of the line and several frigates, carried three thousand regular troops, with every kind of succor; and might be considered as the great hinge upon which the fortune of the war, at least in America, was to turn.

On the other hand, admiral Rodney, who followed with an attentive eye the movements of the count de Grasse, saw the importance of taking a decisive resolution. He instantly detached admiral Hood to the coast of America with fourteen sail of the line to join admiral Graves, and counteract the designs of the enemy. Being nimself in feeble health, he set sail for England with some ships much out of condition, and a large convoy. Rodney was censured with extreme asperity for the counsels taken by him about that time; and some even made him responsible for the sinister events which ensued shortly after. His adversaries contended, that if he had sailed with all his force, and without delay, in quest of the French admiral, had touched at Jamaica, in order to make his junction with the squadron of Hyde Parker, and then had proceeded to the coasts of North America, the count de Grasse would at least have found himself compelled to relinquish his projects, if not exposed to a defeat. 'Instead of adopting this measure,' said they, 'the only one that suited the occasion, Rodney, by returning to England with a part of the heaviest ships of his fleet, has reduced it to an alarming state of weakness, and abandoned the field of battle to the enemy.

'It is a capital error thus to have divided the armament into several little squadrons, as leaving some ships at the leeward islands, where the French have not left one, and detaching three others to Jamaica, which nobody thought of attacking, and, finally, sending sir Samuel Hood with an unequal and insufficient force to America. Is it possible to be too much astonished that our admiral has chosen to fritter away his force into small parts, at the very moment when the French assembled all theirs upon a single point? The world may see what are the effects of this fatal resolution; it has already cost but too many of England's tears.' Rodney nevertheless found defenders. 'The admiral's return to Europe,' they answered, 'was rather constrained by the state of his health, than decided by his choice. The ships he has brought with him are in such a worn out state, that they could not have been repaired in the West Indies. The French admiral having under his protection a rich and numerous convoy, it was fairly to be presumed that he would not have left it to pursue its homeward voyage without a respectable escort. It was even to be supposed that he would have sent the greater part of his fleet along with the merchantmen to France, and that he would only have retained those ships which were in condition to undergo the American service. But independent of that circumstance, the force sent to America under sir Samuel Hood, when combined with that of admiral Graves, would have been perfectly adequate to sustain the brunt of the whole French fleet. But what has Graves done? Instead of keeping his squadron entire and together in the port of New York, he preferred to fatigue himself in a fruitless cruise before Boston, until the bad weather which he met had disabled the greater part of his ships. Hence it followed of necessity that even after the arrival of admiral Hood at New York, our force was still inferior to that of the French. It indeed now appears that no timely notice had been received by admiral Graves either of the count de Grasse's motions, or of Hood's destination to the coasts of America. But if the expresses which sir George Rodney had dispatched for that purpose were taken by the enemy, or otherwise detained, it is no fault on his side; it is a misfortune to be regretted; but which could neither have been absolutely foreseen, nor prevented if it could. Finally, the commander-in-chief cannot be reproached for having detached sir Samuel Hood to America, instead of repairing thither himself; for what naval officer is more worthy of all our confidence than Hood?'

Without undertaking to decide between these opposite opinions, we shall content ourselves with remarking, that though, in military facts, it is not allowable to judge by the event, it is nevertheless just to consider the causes which have produced it; and nothing is more certain than that the conduct of admiral Rodney, in the present conjuncture, had an influence upon the chances of the continental struggle, upon the fortune of America herself, and even upon the issue of all this war.

Having sketched the events which signalized the present year, as well in Europe as in the West Indies, we are now to record those which occupied the scene upon the continent of America. It was the theater of the principal efforts of the two parties that contended, arms in hand, for its possession. Every where else the contest had in view the success of the campaign, and to obtain a better peace; there, its object was existence itself. But before undertaking the portraiture of military operations, it is necessary to apply the attention to objects which, though less brilliant and glorious, are, however, the first source, and the firmest foundation of warlike exploits. Such, doubtless, is the internal administration of the state. The situation of the United States at the commencement of the year 1781, presented, in general, only objects of affliction and disquietude. The efforts which the Americans had made the preceding year, and the events which had passed in the Carolinas, had revived public spirit and produced happy effects. But these effects being founded only upon the fugitive ardor of particular men, and not upon a settled and permanent order of things, it followed that discouragement and distress re-appeared with more alarming symptoms than ever. The public treasury was empty, or only filled with bills of credit, no longer of any worth. The army supplies totally failed, or were only procured by compulsion, accompanied with certificates of receipt, which had lost all sort of credit. The inhabitants became disgusted, and concealed their commodities. If by dint of effort some scanty recruit of provision was at length collected, it could not be transported to the place of its destination, for want of money to pay the wagoners. In some districts, where it was attempted to impress them, there arose violent murmurs ; which even degenerated into more strenuous collisions. No where had it been possible to form magazines ; scarcely did there exist here and there some repositories, which often contained neither food nor clothing of any denomination ; even the arsenals were without arms. The soldiers, covered with tatters, or half naked, destitute of all comforts, implored in vain the compassion of the country they defended. The veterans deserted ; the recruits refused to join the army. The congress had decreed that by the first of January, there should be thirty-seven thousand men under arms ; it would have been difficult to have mustered the eighth part of that number in the month of May. In a word, it seemed as if America, at the very crisis of her fate, was about to prove wanting to herself, and that after having gained the better part of her career, she was more than half inclined to retrace her steps. Far from the Americans being thought capable of waging an offensive war, it was scarcely believed that they could defend their firesides. Already, it began to be feared that instead of assisting the French to drive out the soldiers of king George, they would prove unable to prevent the latter from expelling the troops of Lewis XVI. So disastrous was the change of fortune occasioned by the exhaustion of the finances, and, still more, by the want of a system of administration proper to re-establish them. This state of things was not overlooked by the American government, and it exerted every utmost effort to apply a remedy. But its power was far from corresponding to its intentions. The only means that congress had for administering to the wants of the state, consisted in a new emission of bills of credit, or an increase of taxes. But the paper money had lost all sort of value. The congress itself had been constrained to request the different states to repeal the laws by which they had made the bills of credit a tender in all payments. It had even ordained that in all future contracts for the supplies of the army, the prices should be stipulated in specie. This was the same as declaring formally that the state itself would no longer acknowledge its own bills for current money, and that this paper not only no longer had, but no longer could have, the least value. As to taxes, the congress had not the right to impose them; it belonged exclusively to the provincial assemblies. But these exercised it with more backwardness than could comport with the public interests. This coldness proceeded from several causes. The rulers of the particular states were, for the most part, men who owed their places to popular favor. They apprehended losing it, if they subjected to contributions of any importance, the inhabitants of a country where, from the happy, shall I call it, or baleful facility of issuing paper money, to answer the public exigencies, they were accustomed to pay no taxes, or next to none. Moreover, although the bills of congress were entirely discredited, the particular states still had theirs, which, though much depreciated, were still current at a certain rate; and the provincial legislatures apprehended, and not without reason, that taxes, *payable in specie*, would cause them to fall still lower. Nor should it be passed over in silence, that no general regulation having established the quota of contribution to be paid by each province according to its particular faculties, all, through mutual jealousy, were reluctant to vote taxes, for fear of loading themselves more than their neighbors. Such was the spirit of distrust and selfishness which made its appearance every where, whenever it was necessary to require of the citizens the smallest pecuniary sacrifice. While they were looking at one another with a jealous eye, and none would give the example, the finances of the state were entirely exhausted, and the republic itself was menaced with a total dissolution. It could not be hoped, on the other hand, that the particular states would consent to invest the congress with authority to impose taxes, as well because men with authority in hand are little disposed to part with it, as because the opinions then entertained by the Americans on the subject of liberty, led them to view with disquietude any increase of the power of congress. Finally, it should be observed, that at this epoch, the Americans cherished an extreme confidence in the pecuniary succors of friendly powers, and especially of France. They were persuaded that no more was necessary than that a minister of congress should present his requisition to any European court, in order to obtain immediately whatever sums of money it might please him to specify. As if foreigners were bound to have more at heart than the Americans themselves, the interests and prosperity of America. In a word, the resource of paper money was no more, and that of taxes was yet to be created. Nor could it be dissembled, that even upon the hypothesis of a system of taxation in full operation, and as productive as possible, the produce would still fall infinitely short of supplying the gulf of war, and, by consequence, that the revenue would continue enormously below the expense. Indeed, so ruinous were the charges of this war, that they amounted to no less than twenty millions of dollars a year; and not more than eight could have been counted upon, from the heaviest taxes which, under these circumstances, the United States would have been able to bear. A better administration of the public treasure might doubtless have diminished the exorbitant expenses of the military department; but it is nevertheless clear that they would always have greatly exceeded the revenue. Actuated by these different reflections, the congress had hastened to instruct doctor Franklin to use the most pressing instances with the count de Vergennes, who at that time had the principal direction of affairs relating to America, in order to obtain from France a loan of some millions of livres, towards defraying the expense of the war. Franklin was also directed to solicit permission of the court of Versailles to open another loan for account of the United States, with the French capitalists that were inclined to favor the cause of America. The same instructions were sent, with a view of effecting similar loans, to John Adams, and John Jay; the first, minister plenipotentiary of the United States, near the republic of Holland; the second, at the court of Madrid. The latter was to insinuate to Spain, so great was the discouragement which prevailed at that time in America, that the United States would renounce the navigation of the Mississippi, and even the possession of a port upon that river; the other was to persuade the Dutch that important commercial advantages would be granted them. Franklin, especially, was to represent to France, that without money the affairs of America were desperate. It was recommended to these different envoys to set forth all the resources which America offered as guarantee of her fidelity in fulfilling her engagements. The congress attached so much importance to the success of these negotiations, that not content with having sent these new instructions to their ministers, they also dispatched colonel Laurens to France, with orders to support by the most urgent solicitations the instances of Franklin at the court of Versailles.

The court of Madrid was inflexible, because Jay would not agree to the renunciation above mentioned. Holland showed herself no better disposed, because she doubted the responsibility of the new state. France alone, who judiciously considered that aiding the victory of the United States, and preserving their existence, was of more worth to her than the money they demanded, granted six millions of livres, not as a loan, but as a gift. She seized this occasion to express her dissatisfaction at the coldness with which the Americans themselves contemplated the distress of their country. She exhorted them to reflect, that when it is desired to accomplish honorable enterprises, it is requisite not to be avaricious in the means of success. The court of Versailles did not omit to make the most of its munificence, by setting forth all the weight of its own burdens. But the sum it gave being too far short of the wants, it consented to become security, in Holland, for a loan of ten millions of livres, to be negotiated there by the United States. Notwithstanding this guarantee, the loan progressing but slowly, the king of France consented to make an advance of the sum total, which he drew from his own treasury. He would not, however, authorize the loan proposed to be opened with his subjects. The Americans had thus succeeded in procuring from the court of France a subsidy of sixteen millions of livres. A part of this sum, however, was already absorbed by the payment of preceding drafts of the congress upon Franklin, for particular exigencies of the state. The remainder was embarked for America in specie, or employed by colonel Laurens in purchases of clothing, arms, and munitions of war. The intention of the giver of the six millions was, that this sum, being specially destined for the use of the American army, should be kept in reserve, at the disposal of general Washington, or placed in his hands, to the end that it might not fall into those of other authorities, who might perhaps apply it to other branches of the public service. This condition was far from being agreeable to the congress; on the contrary, it displeased that body particularly, under the impression that its soldiers would thus become, as it were, stipendiaries of France; and it feared lest they might abate much of their dependence on itself. It therefore decreed, that the articles bought with the money given by France, should be consigned, on their arrival in America, to the department of war; but that all the ready money should be placed in the hands of the treasurer, to remain under his charge, and to be expended agreeably to the orders of congress, and for the service of the state. This succor on the part of France was of great utility to the United States; it increased exceedingly their obligations towards Lewis XVI. But before the negotiations which led to it were terminated, and the money or supplies were arrived in America, a long time had elapsed; and the evil was grown to such a head, that the remedy had well nigh come too late. The subsidy in itself was by no means adequate to the necessity. But even had it been sufficient to answer the present exigencies, it could not be considered as having accomplished its object, so long as the same disorder continued to reign in the public expenses. The treasury suffered still less from the poverty of revenues than from the prodigalities it had to supply. It had not escaped the congress that this primordial defect in the administration of the finances was the source of those perpetual embarrassments which had beset them since the origin of the revolution. Firmly resolved to introduce into that department a rigorous system of order and economy, they appointed for treasurer Robert Morris, one of the deputies of the state of Pennsylvania ; a man of high reputation, and possessed of extensive knowledge and experience in commercial and financial affairs.   His mind was active, his manners pure, his fortune ample, and his zeal for independence extremely ardent. He was authorized to oversee and direct the receipt and disbursement of the public money, to investigate the state of the public debt, and to digest and report a new plan of administration.   If the charge imposed on Morris was ponderous, the talent and firmness with which he sustained it, were not less astonishing.   He was not slow in substituting regularity for disorder, and good faith in the room of fraud.

The first, the most essential of the qualities of an administrator, being exactness in the fulfillment of his obligations, the new treasurer adhered with rigor to an invariable punctuality.   He soon gathered the fruits of it ; instead of a general distrust, there sprung up, by little and little, a universal confidence. *One of the first operations of the treasurer was to lay before congress an outline of a national bank, for all the United States of America.* He assigned to this bank a capital of four hundred thousand dollars, divided in shares of four hundred dollars each, in money of gold or silver, to be procured by means of subscriptions ; by the same means this capital might be increased, when expedient, and according to certain restrictions. Twelve directors were to manage the bank ; it was recognized by congress under the name of the president, directors and company of the bank of North America.   All its operations were to be subject to the inspection of the treasurer.   Such were the bases and principal features of this establishment.   The utility to be derived from it was, that the bills of the bank, payable on demand, should be declared legal money for the payment of all excises and taxes in each of the United States, and receivable into the chests of the public treasury as gold or silver. The congress adopted this plan by a special decree. Subscribers presented themselves in throngs, and all the shares were soon taken. The states realized an extraordinary benefit from this institution. The treasurer, by means of exchequer notes, was enabled to anticipate the produce of imposts and taxes. Not content with having brought, by means of the bank, the capitals and credit of the stockholders to the support of public credit, he was disposed to operate the same effect in his own name, and with his private credit.   He accordingly threw into circulation no small sum of obligations signed by himself, and payable at different terms out of foreign subsidies, or even out of the revenues of the United States. And although with time these obligations had amounted to upwards of five hundred and eighty-one thousand dollars, they still never depreciated, excepting, perhaps, a little towards the end of the war; so great was the confidence of the public in the good faith and punctuality of the treasurer. Thus, at the very epoch in which the credit of the state was almost entirely annihilated, and its bills nearly without value, that of a single individual was stable and universal. It is impossible to overrate the advantages which resulted to the government from having, in these obligations of the treasurer, the means of anticipating the produce of taxes, at a time when such anticipation was not only necessary, but indispensable. By this aid it was enabled to provide for the wants of the army, no longer by way of requisitions, but by regular contracts. This new mode had the most happy effects; it produced economy in purchases, exactness in supplies, and a cordial satisfaction among the people, who had always manifested an extreme disgust at the compulsory requisitions. It cannot be advanced, assuredly, that this anticipated employment of the produce of taxes is an example to be imitated; nor even can it be denied, on the contrary, that it has dangers. But Robert Morris had the faculty of using this resource with so much discretion, and of introducing so admirable an order and economy into all parts of the public expense, that no manner of inconvenience resulted from it.

But a foundation was necessary to all these new dispositions of the treasurer; and this foundation consisted in taxes. The congress therefore decreed that the states should be required to furnish the treasury, by way of assessments, with the sum of eight millions of dollars; and at the same time determined what should be, in this sum, the contingent of each state. Such was the urgency of the affairs of the republic, and the confidence that all had placed in the treasurer, that the states conformed willingly to this new decree of congress; and thus an efficacious remedy was at length applied to the penury of the treasury. The solicitude of Robert Morris for the prosperity of the state did not end here.

The province of Pennsylvania, as a country abounding in wheat, was that from which was drawn the greater part of the supplies of flour for the use of the army. The want of money had occasioned, towards the beginning of the year, an extreme slowness in the delivery of these supplies. But Morris was no sooner in place, than he employed his private credit in the purchase of flour for the soldiers. He afterwards undertook, with the approbation of government, to furnish the requisitions for similar supplies that might be made upon Pennsylvania during the present year, on condition, now-ever, of being authorized to reimburse himself from the produce of the apportioned contribution of that province. It amounted to upwards of eleven hundred and twenty thousand dollars. In this manner, by the cares of the treasurer, public credit was resuscitated, and the exhausted treasury was sufficiently replenished to meet expenses. To him it was principally owing that the armies of America did not disband ; and that the congress, instead of yielding to an inevitable necessity, recovered the means not only of resisting the efforts of the enemy, but even of resuming the offensive with vigor and success. Certainly, the Americans owed, and still owe, as much acknowledgment to the financial operations of Robert Morris, as to the negotiations of Benjamin Franklin, or even to the arms of George Washington.

Before the salutary effect of this new system had braced the tottering state, a sinister event had given room to fear that the present year would prove the last of the republic. The terror it occasioned was the first cause, or at least the most powerful incitement, of the introduction of a better method. At this time, as we have already remarked, the soldiers experienced the most intolerable destitution, not only of all the parts of military equipment, but even of articles the most necessary to life. Their discontent was extreme. A particular motive still aggravated the ill humor of the regular troops of Pennsylvania. They had enlisted for three years, or during all the war. The ambiguity of the terms of their engagement led them to think it had expired with the year 1780. They claimed, therefore, the right to return to their homes, while the government contended that they were bound to serve to the end of the war. These two causes combined, so heated all heads, that a violent tumult broke out in the night of the first of January. The mutineers declared that they would march under arms, to the very place where congress was in session, in order to obtain the redress of their grievances. Their number amounted to near fifteen hundred men. The officers endeavored to quell the insurrection, but it was in vain ; and in the riot that ensued, several of the seditious and one officer were killed. General Wayne presented himself, a man by his valor of great authority with the soldiers ; he advanced against the mutineers pistol in hand ; but he was told to take care what he was about to do, or that even he would be cut to pieces. Already their bayonets were directed against his breast. Immediately after, collecting the artillery, baggage and wagons, which belonged to their division, they put themselves on the march, in the best order, upon Middlebrook. At night they intrenched themselves with the same caution as if they had been in an enemy's country They had elected for their chief a certain Williams, a British deserter, and had given him a sort of counci. of war, composed of all the sergeants of the companies. From Middlebrook they marched upon Princeton, and encamped there. They would not suffer officers among them. The marquis de la Fayette, general St. Clair, and colonel Laurens, who had hastened to Princeton to endeavor to allay the ferment, were constrained to leave the town.

The news of the insurrection reached Philadelphia. The congress viewed the affair in that serious light which its importance demanded. They immediately dispatched commissioners, among whom were generals Reed and Sullivan, to investigate facts and ordain measures calculated to re-establish tranquillity. Arrived in the vicinity of Princeton, they sent to demand of the mutineers what was the motive of their conduct, and what would content them ? They answered with arrogance, that they were determined to be put off no longer with empty promises ; and their intention was, that all the soldiers who had served three years should have their discharge ; that those who should be discharged, and those who should remain in service, should receive immediately the full arrears of their pay, clothing and provisions : and moreover, that they insisted on being paid punctually for the future, without even the delay of twenty-four hours.

General Clinton, who was at New York, being soon informed of this defection in the American army, resolved to leave no means untried that could turn it to advantage. He hastened to dispatch to the insurgents, three American loyalists, commissioned to make the following proposals to them in his name ; to be taken under the protection of the British government ; to have a free pardon for all past offenses ; to have the pay due to them from congress faithfully paid, without any expectation of military service in return, although it would be received if voluntarily offered ; and the only conditions required on their side, were to lay down their arms, and return to their allegiance. The inability of congress to satisfy their just demands, and the severity with which they would be treated if they returned to their former servitude, were points to be strongly urged by the agents ; and the insurgents were invited to send persons to Amboy, to meet others who would be appointed by Clinton, in order to discuss and settle the treaty, and bring matters to a final conclusion. But the British general thought proper to do yet more ; in order to embolden the insurgents by his proximity, he passed over to Staten Island with no small part of his troops. He would not, however, proceed still farther, and venture to set foot in New Jersey, for fear of exciting a general alarm, and throwing the mutineers directly back into the arms of congress. The insurgents made no positive answer to Clinton : and they detained his emissaries. In the meantime, the committee of congress and the delegates of the rebels had opened a negotiation; but such was the exasperation of minds on both sides, that it seemed next to impossible that the differences should be settled by an amicable adjustment. They first offered to grant discharges to those who had taken arms indeterminately, for three years, or for the term of the war. In cases where the written engagements could not be produced, the soldiers should be admitted to make oath. They were promised certificates in reimbursement of the sums they had lost by the depreciation of paper money; they were assured of the earliest possible payment of arrears; of the immediate delivery of such articles of clothing as they stood in the most urgent need of; and of a total oblivion with respect to their past conduct. These propositions were not fruitless; the mutineers accepted them, and the disturbance was appeased. They afterwards marched to Trenton, where the promises which had been made them were realized. They delivered into the hands of the commissioners the emissaries of Clinton, who were accordingly hanged without ceremony or delay.

Thus terminated a tumult which had occasioned the most anxious apprehensions to the American government, and inspired the British general with the most flattering hopes. It is true that many excellent soldiers solicited their discharge, and abandoned the army to rejoin their families. Washington, during the mutiny, made no movement whatever. He remained tranquil in his head-quarters at New Windsor, on the banks of the Hudson. His conduct is to be attributed to several motives. He apprehended lest his own soldiers might take part in the insurrection, or lest their inconsiderable number might not be capable of overawing the mutineers. In retiring from the borders of the Hudson, he must have left exposed to the enterprises of the British general those passages which already had been so often contested. His principal fear, however, was that of lessening his authority over the troops, if he exerted it without success, and it must be admitted that it might have had the most disastrous consequences. Perhaps also, within his own breast, he was not sorry that the congress, as well as the governments of the several states, should have been roused by such a spur; that being struck with the difficulty of collecting the funds necessary to the support of the army, they might for the future redouble activity in that vital part of the public service. A few days after this event, the regular troops of New Jersey, excited by the example of the insurrection of the Pennsylvanians, and encouraged by the success that attended it, erected in like manner the standard of revolt. But Washington marched against them a strong corps of soldiers whose fidelity has been proved in the late sedition; the mutineers were soon brought to a sense of duty; and their ringleaders chastised with exemplary severity. This act of rigor put an end to all mutinies. They were followed at least by this salutary consequence, that the government, more clear sighted with respect to its interests, made useful efforts to remedy the origin of the evil. It sent to camp a sufficient quantity of money, in gold and silver, to discharge the pay of three months. The soldiers, consoled by this relief, resumed patience to wait till the operations of finance, which we have mentioned above, had produced the happy effects that were to be expected from them.

During the time in which the congress, supported by the opinion of Washington and of the most influential individuals of the confederation, labored to re-establish order in the internal administration, the first source of military successes, the war was carried on with spirit in the provinces of the south. General Greene marched at the head of formidable forces to the deliverance of South Carolina. Lord Cornwallis, considering it as a prey that could not escape him, had left it almost without defense, in order to prosecute his designs against Virginia. After his departure, the command of that province devolved upon lord Rawdon, a young man full of ardor and talents. He had established his head-quarters at Camden, a place fortified with much diligence. Its garrison, however, was feeble, and, if it sufficed for the defense of the town, it was by no means in a condition to keep the field. The same weakness existed in all the other posts of the province, that were still occupied by the English. As the public sentiment was every where hostile to their domination, they were compelled to divide their troops into a great number of petty detachments, in order to maintain themselves in positions necessary to their safety and subsistence. The principal of these points were, the city of Charleston itself, and those of Camden, Ninety-Six, and Augusta.

Upon the first rumor of the retreat of Cornwallis towards Virginia, the Carolinians had conceived hopes of a new order of things. Already, in many places, they had broken out with violence against the British authorities. Sumpter and Marion, both very enterprising men, fanned the fire of insurrection. They organized in regular companies all those of their party who rallied under their banners. They held in check the frontiers of lower Carolina, while Greene, with the main body of his army, marched upon Camden. His approach was already felt in that city by a secret movement in his favor. To animate the minds still more, he had detached colonel Lee, with his light horse, to join Marion and Sumpter. Thus lord Rawdon found himself all of a sudden assailed not only in front by the army of

Greene, but also in jeopardy of having the way intercepted to his retreat upon Charleston.   He was slow, however, in believing the accounts which reached him respecting the movements of the enemy. Lord Cornwallis had not neglected to notify him in an authentic manner, that he evacuated Carolina to march against Virginia ; but the inhabitants were so adverse to the British cause, that none of his couriers had been able to traverse the country without falling into their hands.   And how was Rawdon to conceive that the fruit of the victory of Guildford should be to constrain lord Cornwallis to retire before the enemy he had beaten ?   Rawdon, however, did not allow himself to be intimidated by the peril of his position ; he set himself, on the contrary, to devise means for eluding it by his courage and prudence.   He would have wished to approach Charleston, but seeing the country infested by the light troops of Sumpter and Greene, he soon relinquished the idea.   He was also determined by the consideration that Camden was a strong place, and capable of sustaining the first efforts of the enemy.   He hastened, however, to re-inforce the garrison with all those which he withdrew from posts unsusceptible of defense; only leaving troops in fortified places. Greene, at the head of his army, appeared in view of the ramparts of Camden ; but he found them too well guarded to afford any prospect of success from an attack, which he could only undertake with insufficient forces.   He accordingly merely occupied the heights, and intrenched himself upon an eminence, called Hobkirk Hill, about a mile from the place.   He was not without hopes of being able to entice the British to combat; for, though not in a situation to force them behind their walls, he felt strong enough to fight them in the open field.   His position was formidably strong. His front between the hill and Camden was covered by thick brushwood, and his left by a deep and impracticable swamp.   The Americans guarded themselves with little care in this encampment; they placed too much confidence in the strength of the place, or in the weakness of the enemy, or perhaps they did but abandon themselves to that natural negligence which so many disasters had not yet been able to cure them of.   Lord Rawdon caused them to be watched attentively; he knew that they had sent their artillery to some distance in their rear, and immediately took a daring resolution, but urged by circumstances, that of attacking.   After having armed the musicians, drummers, and every being in his army that was able to carry a firelock, he left the city to the custody of the convalescents, and marched towards Hobkirk.

Not being able to cross the brushwood, nor yet the swamps, which he had before him, he drew off to the right, and by taking an extensive circuit, turned the morass, and came down by surprise upon the left flank of the American line. At the appearance of so pressing a danger, Greene endeavored to repair, by the promptitude of his dispositions, the negligence of which he felt himself culpable. Having observed that the English marched very compact in a single column, he conceived hopes of being able to fall upon their two flanks. He accordingly ordered colonel Ford to attack the enemy's left with a Maryland regiment, while colonel Campbell should assail them on the right. He then directed a charge in front to be led by colonel Gunby, while colonel Washington with his cavalry should turn their right, and assault them in rear. The combat soon became general, and was pushed with equal resolution on both sides. The royal troops began at first to give way ; the ranks of their infantry and cavalry were broken. Their disorder was still increased by a violent fire of grape-shot, with which they were taken in rear by an American battery which had just arrived upon the field of battle. In this critical moment, lord Rawdon pushed forward a battalion of Irish volunteers and some other companies, of which he had formed a reserve. These fresh troops restored the fortune of the day. The action was grown excessively hot, and alternate undulations equalized the success. But at length a Maryland regiment, vigorously charged by the enemy, fell into confusion and took flight. This struck a damp into the whole line, and the rout was shortly general. The Americans attempted several times to rally, but always in vain ; the English pushed them too fiercely. They entered almost at the same time with them into the intrenchments upon the ridge.

Meanwhile, colonel Washington, agreeably to the orders of his general, had arrived with his corps of cavalry upon the rear of the British army, before it had recovered from the disorder into which it had been thrown by the first shock. He took advantage of it to make a great number of prisoners. But when he saw that the position of Greene was forced, he thought proper to retreat. A part of the prisoners escaped ; the remainder he conducted to camp, where he rejoined the main body of the army.

General Greene, after this check, had fallen back upon Gun Swamp, five miles from Hobkirk, where he remained several days, to collect the fugitives and re-organize the army. This affair, which was called the battle of Hobkirk, was fought the twenty-fifth of April. Lord Rawdon, being inferior in cavalry, and enfeebled by a great loss of men, instead of pursuing Greene, had re-entered within the walls of Camden. He was desirous to make that place the center of his operations, and this he was the more inclined to do, since he nad just received a re-inforcement of troops under the con duct of colonel Watson. But he was informed that the inhabitants of the whole interior country at his back, had revolted with one consent, that already fort Watson had capitulated, and that those of Granby, Orangeburgh and Motte, were closely invested. The last, situated near the junction of the Congaree with the Santee, and containing extensive magazines, was of no little importance. Lord Rawdon, reflecting that all these forts were upon his rear, judged his situation imminently hazardous. He therefore resolved to evacuate Camden, and retire lower down towards Charleston ; this resolution he executed the ninth of May. He razed the fortifications, put in safety all the artillery and baggage, and brought off the families of the loyalists, who by their zeal for the royal cause had rendered themselves odious to the republicans. The whole army arrived on the thirteenth at Nelsons Ferry, upon the banks of the Santee river. Here, having received the unwelcome tidings that all the forts mentioned above were fallen into the hands of the Americans, the British general raised his camp, and carried it still farther back to Eutaw Springs.

General Greene, perceiving that Rawdon, by retreating into the lower parts of Carolina, had abandoned all thoughts of maintaining himself in the upper country, formed a design to reduce Ninety-Six and Augusta, the only posts that still held out for the king. These two forts were already invested by the militia headed by colonels Pickens and Clarke. Greene appeared with his army before the walls of Ninety-Six, and proceeded to push the siege by regular approaches. One of the officers who distinguished themselves the most in that operation was colonel Kosciusko, a young Pole, full of enthusiasm for the cause of the Americans. The defense of the place was directed by lieutenant-colonel Cruger. During this time, colonel Pickens vigorously pushed his operations against the town of Augusta, which was defended with equal bravery and ability by colonel Brown. These two places were very strong, and could not be reduced but by a long siege.

Meanwhile, Lord Rawdon saw with extreme solicitude that in losing these posts, whose value he justly appreciated, he must also lose the garrisons which defended them. A re-inforcement of three regiments, newly arrived at Charleston from Ireland, gave him hopes of being able to relieve these fortresses, and principally Ninety-Six. Every course which presented itself to his mind being equally difficult and dangerous, he preferred, without hesitation, that which appeared the most magnanimous. He received intelligence on his march of the loss of Augusta. Pressed with great industry by colo-

nel Pickens, and witnout hope of relief, that place had just surrendered to the arms of congress. This disaster operated with the
British general as a new motive for endeavoring to preserve Ninety-
Six. Upon the rumor of the approach of Rawdon, Greene reflected
that the number and discipline of his soldiers was not such as to
afford a hope that he would be able to resist, at the same time, the
garrison of Ninety-Six, and the fresh and warlike troops that were
advancing against him. On the other hand, to raise the siege before
having attempted some vigorous stroke against the place, appeared
to him too disgraceful a step. Accordingly, however imperfect
were the works of attack, he resolved to hazard an assault. He
had already reached the ditch, it is true, and had pushed a sap to
the foot of a bastion, but the fortifications were yet in a great measure entire. The body of the place was therefore to be considered
as being proof against insult. But general Greene was desirous at
least to save in his retreat the honor of the American arms. A
general assault was therefore given with extreme impetuosity, which
the English sustained with no less valor. Greene, seeing the terrible
carnage which the artillery made among his soldiers, in the ditch
not yet filled up with the ruins of the breach, determined at length
to retire. Soon after this check, lord Rawdon being now but a
small distance from his camp, he raised it all at once, and withdrew
beyond the Tiger and the Broad rivers. The royalists followed
him, but in vain. The British general, having entered into Ninety-
Six, examined the state of the place, and was of opinion that it
could not hold out against a regular attack. He therefore put himself again on the march, directing it towards the lower parts of
Carolina, and proceeded to establish his head-quarters at Orangeburgh. Imboldened by his retreat, Greene soon showed himself
before this last place. But at sight of the British forces, and of
their excellent position, covered by the windings of the river, he
paused, and bent his march towards the heights which border the
Santee.

The hot and sickly season being arrived, it effected that which
could not have been expected from the rage of men; hostilities
ceased. It would seem that during this suspension of arms, civil
hatreds were rekindled with increase of fury. The English especially, as if to revenge their defeats, showed themselves more exasperated
tnan the Americans. It was at this epoch that there passed a lamentable event, which excited to the highest degree the indignation of
all America, and particularly of the Carolinas. Colonel Isaac Hayne
had warmly espoused the cause of American Independence. During the siege of Charleston he had served in a volunteer corps of

light horse. After the surrender of that city, Hayne, who was
tenderly attached to his family, could not find in his heart to part
with it, in order to seek refuge in distant places against the tyranny
of the victors. He knew that other American officers had obtained
permission to return peaceably to their habitations, on giving their
parole not to act against the interests of the king. He repaired
therefore to Charleston, went to the British generals, and constituted
himself their prisoner of war. But knowing all the resources of his
mind, and the authority he possessed among the inhabitants, they
wished to have him entirely in their power, and refused to receive
him in the character he was come to claim. They signified to him
that he must acknowledge himself for a British subject, or submit
to be detained in a rigorous captivity. This idea would not have
intimidated colonel Hayne ; but he could not endure that of being
so long separated from his wife and children. He knew also that
they were under the attack of small-pox ; and soon after, in effect,
the mother and two of the children became the victims of that cruel
malady. Neither could he overlook, that if he did not accede to
what was exacted of him, an unbridled soldiery waited only the
signal to sack and devastate his plantations.

In this distressing alternative, the father, the husband triumphed
in his breast ; he consented to invest himself with the condition of
British subject. The only favor he demanded was, that he might
not be constrained to bear arms against his party. This was solemnly
promised him by the British general Patterson, and by Simcoe, superintendent of police at Charleston. But before taking this perilous resolution, he had waited upon doctor Ramsay, the same who
afterwards wrote the history of the American revolution, praying
him to bear witness to the future that he by no means intended to
abandon the cause of independence. As soon as he had signed the
oath of allegiance, he had permission to return to his residence.

Meanwhile the war re-kindled with new violence ; and the Americans, hitherto beaten and dispersed, resumed the offensive with such
vigor that the British generals were alarmed at their progress. Then,
no longer regarding the promises which they had made to colonel
Hayne, they intimated to him an order to take arms and march with
them against the revolted republicans. He refused. The troops of
congress afterwards penetrated into the country ; the inhabitants of
his district rose and elected him for their chief. No longer considering
himself bound to keep that faith which it appeared that others were
not disposed to keep towards him, he yielded to the wish of his
countrymen, and again took up those arms which he had laid
down through necessity. He scoured the country in the vicinity of

Charleston, at the head of a corps of dragoons. But it was not long before he fell into an ambuscade laid for him by the British commanders. He was immediately conducted to the city, and thrust into a deep dungeon. Without form of trial, lord Rawdon and colonel Balfour, the commandant of Charleston, condemned him to death. This sentence appeared to every one, as it was in reality, an act of barbarity. Even deserters are indulged with a regular trial, and find defenders; spies only are deprived of this privilege by the laws of war. Royalists and republicans all equally pitied the colonel, whose virtues they esteemed; they would fain have saved his life. They did not restrict themselves to mere wishes; a deputation of loyalists, having the governor in behalf of the king at their head, waited upon lord Rawdon, and earnestly solicited him in favor of the condemned. The most distinguished ladies of Charleston united their prayers to the general recommendation that his pardon might be granted. His children, still of tender age, accompanied by their nearest relations, and wearing mourning for their mother, whom they had so recently lost, threw themselves at the feet of Rawdon, demanding with the most touching cries the life of their unhappy father. All the bystanders seconded with floods of tears the petition of these hapless orphans. Rawdon and Balfour obstinately refused to mitigate the rigor of their decision.

When about to be conducted to death, colonel Hayne called into his presence his eldest son, then thirteen years of age. He delivered him papers addressed to the congress, then said to him; 'Thou wilt come to the place of my execution; thou wilt receive my body, and cause it to be deposited in the tomb of our ancestors.' Being arrived at the foot of the gibbet, he took leave in the most affecting manner of the friends who surrounded him, and armed himself to his last moment with the firmness which had honored his life. He was, in the same degree, a man of worth, a tender father, a zealous patriot, and an intrepid soldier. If the tyranny of the prince, or the impatience of the people, render political revolutions sometimes inevitable, it is certainly much to be deplored that the first and principal victims of this scourge, should be, almost always, citizens the most worthy of general esteem and affection. After having taken this cruel vengeance of a man so universally respected, lord Rawdon left the capital of Carolina clouded with melancholy, and brooding terrible reprisals; he made sail for England. To this act of rigor on the part of the English generals, without doubt, may be applied the ancient adage; 'An extreme justice is an extreme injury.' But whatever may be thought of its justice, it must be admitted, that the English, in showing themselves so ruthless at a moment when their affairs were already in such declension, appeared much more eager to satiate the fury of a vanquished enemy than to accomplish an equitable law. The aversion of the Americans for their barbarous foes, acquired a new character of implacable animosity. The officers of the army of general Greene solicited him to use reprisals, declaring that they were ready to run all the risks that might ensue from it He issued, in effect, a proclamation, by which he threatened to retaliate the death of colonel Hayne upon the persons of the British officers that might fall into his hands. Thus to the evils inseparable from war, were joined the excesses produced by hatred and vengeance.

General Greene, during this interval, had not remained idle in his camp upon the heights of the Santee. He had occupied himself without relaxation in strengthening his army, in perfecting the old troops by frequent maneuvers, and in disciplining the new corps. His diligence had not failed of success. Re-inforced by the militia of the neighboring districts, he saw under his banners soldiers no less formidable to the English by their warlike ardor than by their number. The temperature of the season being become less burning, at the commencement of September, he resolved to employ his forces in expelling the British troops from the few towns which they still occupied in South Carolina, besides the city of Charleston. Having taken a circuitous march towards the upper Congaree, he passed it, and descended rapidly along the right bank with all his army, in order to attack the English, who, under the command of colonel Stewart, occupied the post of Macords Ferry, near the confluence of that river with the Santee. The royalists, on seeing the approach of an enemy so superior in force, and especially in cavalry, reflected that they were too remote from Charleston, whence they drew their subsistence. They hastened therefore to quit Macords Ferry, and fell back upon Eutaw Springs, where they labored to intrench themselves. Greene pursued them thither, and the eighth of September witnessed the battle of Eutaw Springs. According to the dispositions of the American general, the vanguard was composed of the militia of the two Carolinas, and the center of the regular troops of those provinces, of Virginia, and of Maryland. Colonel Lee with his legion covered the right flank, and colonel Henderson the left. The rearguard consisted of the dragoons of colonel Washington and the militia of Delaware. It was a corps of reserve destined to support the first lines. The artillery advanced upon their front.

The British commander formed his troops in two lines; the first was defended on the right by the little river Eutaw, and on the left by a thick wood. The second, forming a reserve, crowned the

heights which command the Charleston road. After some skir-
mishing between the marksmen of the one and other army, they fell
back behind the ranks, and the engagement became general. It was
supported for a considerable time with balanced success ; but at
length, the militia of Carolina were broken, and retired in disorder
The British division, which formed the left of the first line, quitted its
position to pursue them. In this movement it lost its distances, and
could no longer combat in company with the other part of the line.
The Americans observed this opening, and profited of it immediately.
Greene pushed forward his second line ; it charged so vigorously,
that the English, in their turn, were shaken, and began to recoil in
confusion. To complete their rout, colonel Lee with his cavalry
turned their left, and fell upon their rear. This maneuver precipitated the flight of all that wing of the British army. The right alone
still held firm. But Greene caused it to be attacked briskly in front
by the regular troops of Maryland and Virginia, while the cavalry of
colonel Washington took it in flank. The trepidation then became
general ; all the corps of the British army tumbled one over another,
through haste to recover their intrenchments. Already the Americans had taken several pieces of artillery and a great number of
prisoners. Victory seemed completely in their hands. But how
often has it been remarked, that the events of war depend upon the
caprices of chance ! Troops accustomed to a rigid discipline are
frequently able to rally in the midst of disorder, and recover, in an
instant, what they appeared to have lost irreparably. The battle we
describe affords a memorable example of it. The English, in their
flight, threw themselves into a large and very strong house, where
they resolved to make a desperate defense. Others took shelter in
a thick and almost impenetrable brushwood ; and others in a garden
fenced with palisades. Here the action re-commenced with more
obstinacy than at first. The republicans did all that was to be expected of valiant soldiers, to dislodge their enemies from these new
posts. The house was battered by four pieces of artillery. Colonel
Washington, on the right, endeavored to penetrate into the wood, and
colonel Lee to force the garden. Their efforts were vain ; the
English defended themselves so strenuously, that they repulsed the
assailants with heavy loss. Colonel Washington himself was wounded
and taken. The conflict was fierce, the carnage dreadful ; but no
where more than about the house. Meanwhile, colonel Stewart,
having rallied his right wing, pushed it forward, by a circuitous
movement, against the left flank of the Americans. This bold maneuver convinced the American general that he would but vainly
waste torrents of blood in further attempts to drive the enemy from

their posts, and he ordered a retreat. He returned to his first en-campment, some miles distant from the field of battle. This retro-grade march was attributed to want of water. He brought off about five hundred prisoners, and all his wounded, with the exception of those who were too near the walls of the house. He lost two pieces of cannon. The English passed the rest of the day in their intrench-ments. At night, they abandoned them, and descended to Monks Corner. The Americans write that the royalists, in their hurry, had staved the casks containing spirituous liquors, and broken, or thrown into the Eutaw, a great quantity of arms. The loss of Greene in this action was estimated at upwards of six hundred men in killed, wounded and prisoners; that of Stewart, inclusive of the missing, was much more considerable. The American soldiers exhibited in this combat an extraordinary valor. Impatient to close with their enemies, they promptly resorted to the bayonet; a weapon which they seemed to dread in the commencement of hostilities, and which was now become so formidable in their war-trained hands. The congress voted public thanks to those who had taken part in the battle of Eutaw Springs. They presented general Greene with a conquered standard and a medal of gold.

A short time after, having received some re-inforcements, he re-solved to make another trial of fortune, and marched against the English in lower Carolina. His appearance in the environs of Monks Corner, and of Dorchester, decided them to evacuate the open country, and shut themselves up entirely within Charleston. They contented themselves with sending out scouts, and foraging parties, who durst not venture far from the place. Greene, from his great superiority in light troops, repulsed them upon all points, and intercepted their convoys. In this manner the American general put an end to the campaign of the south. After a long and sanguinary struggle, his masterly maneuvers recovered to the confederation the two Carolinas and Georgia, excepting only the two capitals of the one and other province, which still obeyed the English, with a slender portion of territory in their immediate vicinity; such were the fruits of the resolution taken by lord Cornwallis, at Wilmington, of carrying his arms against Virginia. But to Greene great eulogies are due for the talents he signalized in this conjuncture. When he came to relieve general Gates in the command of the southern army, the state of things was not only calamitous, but almost desperate. By his genius, activity and boldness, the evil was remedied so promptly, that from vanquished, his soldiers became soon victorious; from despondency, the people passed to a confidence without bounds;

and the English, but now so arrogant, were forced to seek their only safety behind the walls of Charleston.

The social qualities, ingenuousness and affability of manners, set off in Greene the glory of the warrior. His virtues triumphed over envy itself; illustrious for the eminent services which he rendered his country, and uniformly modest and unaffected, he merited that his name should be transmitted immaculate to posterity. Virginia was less fortunate than Carolina; Arnold, as if he had coveted to couple the name of bandit with that of traitor, carried fire and sword into that province. Private property he respected as little as that of the state. This horrible expedition, as we have already remarked, had been ordained by the British generals with no other view but that of seconding the efforts of Cornwallis in the Carolinas, by diverting the attention and dividing the forces of the enemy. In effect, the reduction of Virginia to the power of the king, with means so inadequate, was a thing impossible to be executed, or even to be expected. This was soon demonstrated. The disastrous consequences of the plan adopted by Cornwallis, were equally fatal for Arnold. Already, the rising of the militia of all the adjacent parts had forced him to abandon the open country, and fall back with precipitation upon Portsmouth, where he fortified himself with extreme diligence. On the other hand, Washington, attentive to all his movements, and wishing to gratify the just resentment of the American nation towards its betrayer, formed a design to environ him so effectually, by land and sea, as to render his escape impossible. With this intent, he had detached the marquis de la Fayette towards Virginia, at the head of twelve hundred light infantry ; and had also induced the commander of the French fleet at Rhode Island to dispatch a squadron of eight sail of the line, under the chevalier Destouches, to cut off the retreat of Arnold from the Chesapeake. But the English being early apprised of it, admiral Arbuthnot made sail from New York with a squadron of equal force, and fell in with the French off Cape Henry. A warm engagement ensued, in which the loss of the two fleets was nearly balanced. The French, however, found themselves constrained to relinquish their designs, and returned to Rhode Island. Upon this intelligence, M. de la Fayette, who was already arrived at Annapolis in Maryland, marched thence to the head of Elk. Thus Arnold escaped from, probably, the most imminent danger in which he had ever been involved. The Americans had afterwards occasion to send a flag to his headquarters. It is related, that the traitor general asked the person who bore it, what they would have done with him if they had taken him? The American answered without hesitation ; " If we had taken thee we should have buried, with every mark of honor, that of thy legs, which was wounded when thou wast in our service ; the rest of thy body we should have hanged."

On hearing of the danger which had menaced Arnold, general Clinton doubted the generals of congress might be more happy in a second attempt.　He therefore immediately dispatched a re-inforcement of two thousand men, under the conduct of general Phillips. His junction with Arnold put them in condition to resume the offensive ; and their inroads into Virginia were again signalized by devastation and pillage.　At Osborn, they destroyed a great number of vessels, rich magazines of merchandise, and principally of tobacco. The baron Steuben, who commanded the republicans, found himself too weak to resist.　Fortunately, the marquis de la Fayette arrived in time to save the opulent city of Richmond.　There, however, he was forced to witness the conflagration of Manchester, a town situated opposite to Richmond, upon the right bank of the James river. The English were pleased to burn it without any necessity.　But soon this partisan war was directed towards a single and determinate object.　General Phillips had received intelligence that lord Cornwallis approached, and that he was already on the point of arriving at Petersburgh.　M. de la Fayette was advised of it likewise. Both, accordingly, exerted themselves to reach Petersburgh before the troops that were advancing from Carolina ; the one to join Cornwallis, the other to prevent this junction.　The English outstripped their adversaries, and occupied that little city.　There general Phillips was carried off by a malignant fever; his military talents rendered his loss peculiarly painful to his party.

After a march of three hundred miles, in the midst of difficulties of every sort, lord Cornwallis at length arrived at Petersburgh, where he took the general command of all the British forces.　The establishment of the seat of war in Virginia, coincided perfectly with the designs which the British ministers had formed upon this province.　As soon as they were informed of the victory of Guildford, they had persuaded themselves that the two Carolinas were entirely reduced under the authority of the king, and that little else remained to be done, besides re-organizing in them the accustomed civil administration.　They had not the least doubt that wise regulations would consummate the work, which the arms of Cornwallis had so happily commenced.　They built, with particular confidence, on the support of the loyalists.　Notwithstanding so many fatal experiments, so many abortive hopes, they still eagerly listened to all the illusions, and to all the news spread by the refugees, so unavoidably impelled by their position to cherish the wildest chimeras.　The British —

government therefore expected that the co-operation of the loyalists, a few garrisons left in the most important posts, together with the terror of the arms of Cornwallis, would suffice to curb the patriots, and to confirm the submission of these provinces. As to Virginia, intersected by a great number of broad and deep rivers, whose mouths form upon its coasts several gulfs or bays suitable for anchorage, the naval forces sent thither by Rodney from the West Indies, seemed to guaranty the naval superiority of England in those waters. Accordingly, the ministers never allowed themselves to doubt, that if this province could not be entirely reduced, it would at least be very easy to press it and waste it to such a degree that its utility should cease for the American union. They had therefore decided that the commanders of the land forces should make choice of an advantageous position upon the coasts of Virginia, and that they should secure the possession of it by fortifications capable of repelling all attacks of the enemy. This measure and the presumed superiority of the British marine, appeared to the cabinet of St. James a sure pledge of the entire subjugation of Virginia; and for the reasons already stated, it felt perfectly assured of the possession of the two Carolinas, as also of Georgia. It was deemed the more certain that nothing was to be feared from the French squadrons, as the coasts of these vast provinces are nearly without ports, and since the few they offer were in the power of the royal troops. Finding themselves thus already masters of four rich provinces in the south, as well as of that of New York, inestimable alike for its resources, and for its ports, the ministers persuaded themselves that the moment could not be distant when the Americans would yield through weariness and exhaustion. They felicitated themselves that, at all events, they were able to resume the offensive.

Such were the reasonings at London; but it was not known there that the British fleets, instead of having the advantage in point of force, were decidedly inferior in the American seas; that the Carolinas, instead of being in the power of the king, were returned almost totally under that of the congress; and that although Cornwallis was indeed arrived in Virginia, he had shown himself there, notwithstanding his success at Guildford, rather as vanquished than victor.

Meanwhile, Cornwallis, after having staid a few days at Petersburgh, where he was re-inforced by some hundred soldiers, sent him from New York by Clinton, took a resolution to cross the river James, and penetrate into the interior of Virginia. He had little apprehension of meeting American troops; supposing them both too weak and too much dispersed to attempt resistance. In effect, the baron

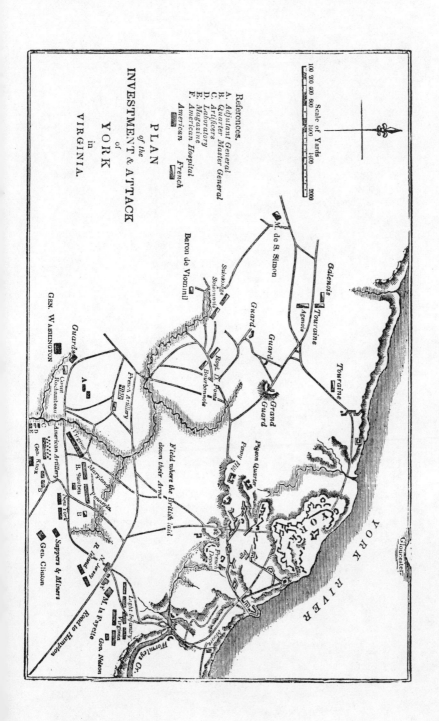

PLAN
of the
INVESTMENT & ATTACK
of
YORK
in
VIRGINIA.

American ___ French

References.
A. Adjutant General
B. Quarter Master General
C. Artificers
D. Laboratory
E. Magazine
F. American Hospital

Scale of Yards
100 200 400 600   1000   1400   2000

M. de S. Simon

Galenois

Touraine

Agenois

Baron de Viomini

Stiesonges
Soisonnis

Guard

Guard

Touraine

GEN. WASHINGTON

Guard

Roy. Ponts

Bourbonnois

French Artillery

Grand
Guard

A

Count
Rochambeau

French

American Artillery

B. Steuben

Maryland

New York

Gen. Knox

Pensarda

Pigeon Quarter

Penny Hill

Field where the British laid
down their Arms

YORK

Sappers & Miners

Gen. Clinton

M. la Fayette

Light Infantry

Virginia

Gen. Nelson

Road to Hampton

Wormleys Cr.

YORK RIVER

Gloucester

Steuben occupied the upper parts of the province, the marquis de la Fayette, the maritime districts, and general Wayne, who was on the march with the regular troops of Pennsylvania, was still at a great distance. The British general therefore crossed the river without opposition at Westover; the marquis de la Fayette had retired behind the Chickahominy. Thence Cornwallis detached a corps which occupied Portsmouth. The loyalists, or those who wished to appear such, repaired to that city in order to give in their paroles and receive protections. The county of Hanover was entirely overrun by the foragers of the British army. Lord Cornwallis was informed, about this time, that many of the most considerable men of the country were assembled in convention at Charlotteville, to regulate the affairs of the province; and that the baron Steuben was posted at the Point of Fork, situated at the junction of the rivers James and Rivana. The Americans had established at this place magazines of arms and munitions of war. These advices, added to the consideration that this part of the territory, not having yet been the theatre of war, was likely to abound in every kind of supplies, determined lord Cornwallis to attempt, first of all, the expeditions of Charlotteville and the Point of Fork. He committed the first to Tarleton, the second to Simcoe. Both were crowned with success. The first, by the rapidity of his march, arrived so unexpectedly upon the city that he seized a great number of deputies, and made himself master of a considerable quantity of warlike stores and provision. But the personage whom he had it most at heart to secure, was one of those who escaped him, and that was Thomas Jefferson, since president of the United States; having had the good fortune to be timely apprised of the approach of the British troops, he put himself out of their reach; not, however, without having first, with extreme pains and the assistance of his neighbors, provided for the safety of no small quantity of arms and ammunition. If Tarleton had sometimes complained of the too great benignity of his comrades, no one, assuredly, could make him the same reproach. His rapacity and imprudence no longer observed any bounds; nothing was sacred in his sight, nothing escaped his barbarous hands. Simcoe, on his part, had moved with equal celerity against the baron Steuben. That general might have made a vigorous resistance; it is not known what motive could have decided him to a precipitate retreat; and yet he was not able to protect his rear guard against the pursuit of the British, who reached it, and cut a part of it in pieces. When the colonels Tarleton and Simcoe were returned to camp, lord Cornwallis, traversing a rich and fertile country, marched upon Richmond, and, a little after, upon Williamsburgh, the capital of Virginia.

His light troops, however, could no longer forage at large; the marquis de la Fayette had joined the baron Steuben, and having been re-inforced by the Pennsylvania regiments of general Wayne, he found himself in a situation to watch all the movements of the British army, and to cut off the parties that ventured to stray from it. Cornwallis received at this same time orders from general Clinton, requiring him to re-embark a part of his troops for New York Not that Clinton meditated any important stroke; but he had been advised of the approach of the allies, and he expected to see the storm burst upon his head. He feared at the same time for New York, Staten Island, and Long Island; his force was not sufficient for their defense. In order to obey, Cornwallis marched his troops towards the banks of the James river. He intended, after having passed it, to repair to Portsmouth, where he would have embarked the corps destined for New York. But as M. de la Fayette followed him extremely close, he found himself constrained to make a halt upon the left bank of the river, and to take possession of a strong position, in order to repress the impetuosity of his adversary, and give time to his troops for passing the artillery, munitions and baggage to the other side. He encamped therefore along the river, having his right covered by a pond, and the centre and left by swamps.

Meanwhile, the American vanguard, commanded by general Wayne, had advanced very near. The English dispatched spies among the Americans, in order to make them believe that the bulk of the royal army had already passed to the right bank, and that only a feeble rear guard remained upon the left, consisting of the British legion and some detachments of infantry. Whether the republicans allowed themselves to be caught in this snare, or that they were hurried away by an inconsiderate valor, they fell with great fury upon the royal troops. Already the regular regiments of Pennsylvania, led by general Wayne, had passed the swamp, and fiercely assailed the left wing of the royalists; and notwithstanding the great superiority of the enemy, the assailants appeared nowise daunted. But the English, having passed the pond, advanced against the left wing, which consisted entirely of militia. Having dispersed it without difficulty, they showed themselves upon the left flank of Wayne. At the same time, extending their own left beyond the swamp, they had turned his right, and manifested an intention of surrounding him on every side. The marquis de la Fayette perceived this maneuver, and immediately directed Wayne to fall back. He was unable to execute this movement without leaving two pieces of cannon in the power of the enemy   M. de la Fayette remained some time at Green Springs, in order to collect the scattered soldiers. Cornwallis re-entered his intrenchments. The approach of night, and the nature of the country, broken with woods and marshes, prevented him from pursuing the Americans. The next morning before sunrise, he detached his cavalry upon the route taken by the marquis de la Fayette, with orders to hang upon his rear, and harass him as much as possible. All the harm it did him, consisted in the taking of a few soldiers who had lagged behind. It is presumable, that if Cornwallis had advanced the following day with all his force, he might have cut off the republicans entirely. But all his views were directed towards Portsmouth, in order to embark the troops there which Clinton expected at New York. When he had passed the river James with his whole army, he accordingly hastened to Portsmouth; but upon a strict examination of places, he was convinced that they did not offer him a position suitable by its strength and other advantages to favor the ulterior designs of Clinton. He proceeded, however, with diligence to embark the troops. In the meantime, he received new instructions from Clinton, directing him to return to Williamsburgh, to retain all the troops he had with him, and instead of Portsmouth, to make his place of arms of Point Comfort, in order to have, in any event, a secure retreat.

Two principal causes had determined general Clinton to embrace this new resolution; he had received from Europe a re-inforcement of three thousand Germans; and he was influenced, besides, by a desire to open himself a passage by way of Hampton and the James river, towards that fertile and populous part of Virginia which lies between the James and York rivers. But Point Comfort, on attentive examination, was found an equally unfavorable and defective position for an intrenched camp, and no less incompetent than Portsmouth for the purposes in view. It was therefore determined to relinquish the design of fortifying it. The plan of future operations requiring, however, the occupation of a fixed point in the country comprehended by the above mentioned rivers, lord Cornwallis resolved to repass the river James with all his army, and take up his head-quarters at Yorktown. The marquis de la Fayette was desirous to oppose his passage; but the Americans that were in his camp would not consent to march lower down towards Portsmouth.

Yorktown is a village situated upon the right bank of the river York, and opposite to another smaller town called Gloucester. The latter is built upon a point of land which projects into the river from the left side, and which considerably diminishes the breadth of its channel. The water is deep there, and capable of receiving the largest ships of war. On the right of Yorktown flows a marshy stream; in front of the place, for the distance of a mile, the ground is open and level. In advance of this plain is a wood, whose left extends to the river, and whose right is bordered by a creek. Beyond the wood the country is champaign and cultivated. Cornwallis applied his attention to intrench himself in the strongest possible manner upon this ground.

After the affair of Jamestown, the marquis de la Fayette had retired between the rivers Mattapony and Pamonky, the waters of which, united, compose the York river. Upon intelligence of the new position taken by Cornwallis, he re-crossed the Pamonky, and took post in the county of New Kent; not that he intended to attack the English; his force did not admit of it; but he was disposed, at least, to harass them, to repress their excursions, and to prevent their foraging in the country. Washington had intrusted M. de la Fayette with the charge of defending Virginia; he acquitted himself of it in the most satisfactory manner; sometimes by his maneuvers holding Cornwallis in check, and sometimes combating him with vigor, he at length conducted him to a place, where he might hope to be seconded by the powerful French fleet that was expected upon the American coast.

Hitherto the campaign of Virginia had presented no inconsiderable vicissitude of events; but all equally destitute of importance. The scene was changed; and the plan which tended, by a decisive stroke, to put an end to the whole American war, drew day by day more near to its accomplishment. The American government was informed that the count de Grasse, with his fleet and a body of land troops, was about to arrive. It therefore neglected no dispositions that were demanded by the occasion, in order to be in a situation to profit of the great superiority which the allies were soon to have, as well by land as by sea. To this end, Washington and Rochambeau had an interview at Wethersfield. The count de Barras, who commanded the French squadron at anchor in Rhode Island, was likewise to have been present at the conference, but was detained by other duties. The siege of New York was resolved upon between the two generals. They agreed, that it was necessary to wrest from the English that shelter, which, from the commencement of hostilities to the present hour, had been so favorable to their enterprises. From that day, all the movements of the French and Americans were directed towards this object. They had calculated them in such a manner as that the appearance of the count de Grasse upon the American coasts, should be the signal for commencing the siege. Clinton so dreaded the blow, that solely on this account he had determined, as we have seen, to recall a part of the troops of Cornwallis, prior to the arrival of the German corps. Washington cherished good hope of success in the expedition of New York; he felt assured that the states of the Union, particularly those of the north, would promptly satisfy the requisitions which had been made them, to furnish each a determinate number of soldiers. But they had accomplished only in part the desires of the commander-in-chief. Instead of twelve or fifteen thousand continental troops that he had hoped to assemble for an operation of this importance, he found himself at the head of only four or five thousand regulars, and about an equal number of militia. It was, however, to be considered, that the conquest of New York would require great efforts, since general Clinton had a garrison there of more than ten thousand men. The enterprise could not reasonably be undertaken with so inadequate a force. Moreover, the count de Grasse had declared that, in consequence of the orders of his sovereign, and of the convention he had made with the Spaniards in the West Indies, it would not be possible for him to remain upon the coast of America later than the middle of October; and assuredly so short a space of time would not have sufficed for the reduction of New York. Finally, it was known that sea officers in general, and especially the French, had no little repugnance to crossing the bar which lies at the entrance of the harbor of that city. All these considerations diverted Washington from his purpose of besieging New York. He reflected, that although his army was too weak for that enterprise, it was nevertheless sufficient to act with great probability of success against Cornwallis in Virginia; and he accordingly decided for the more attainable object. But the movements he had already made, having given jealousy to Clinton for New York, he resolved, notwithstanding that he had changed his plan, to nourish the suspicions of his adversary by a series of the most spirited demonstrations; to the end that he might not penetrate his real design, and throw obstacles in its way. In order to lead him more speciously into the snare, he wrote letters to the southern commanders and to members of the government, informing them of his determination to attack New York. He sent these dispatches by such ways as he knew would expose them to be intercepted by the enemy. The stratagem succeeded perfectly. Clinton, full of apprehension for a city which had become his place of arms, was indefatigable in multiplying its defenses. In the meantime the count de Rochambeau had set out from Rhode Island, at the head of five thousand French, and was already advanced near the borders of the Hudson. Washington broke up his camp at New Windsor, and went to meet him upon the eastern bank. After their junction, the combined armies encamped at Philipsburgh, in a situation to overawe Kingsbridge and the adjoining posts, and even to alarm the island of New York. They afterwards actually took post at Kingsbridge, and continued to insult the British outposts on all sides. Not content with these demonstrations, the principal officers of both armies, attended by the engineers, reconnoitered the island of New York closely on both sides from the opposite shores; and to render appearances the more serious, took plans of all the works under the fire of their batteries. At the same time, a report of the expected daily arrival of the count de Grasse was sedulously propagated; and to give it full confirmation, when they had received advices from that commander of the time at which he hoped to arrive at the Chesapeake, the French troops advanced towards Sandy Hook, and the coasts opposite Staten Island, with an apparent view of seconding the operations of the fleet, in forcing the one and seizing upon the other. This deception was carried so far, as to the establishment of a bakery near the mouth of the Rariton, and just within the Hook.

According to these different movements of the combined army, general Clinton no longer doubted but that New York was menaced with an immediate attack. But the time was now at hand, when this bandage, which had been drawn with so much address over the eyes of the British commander, was ready to fall, and admit him to a clear view of the truth. When Washington had authentic intelligence that the count de Grasse was no longer far from the Chesapeake, he suddenly passed the Croton, then the Hudson; and proceeded by forced marches through New Jersey to Trenton upon the Delaware. He gave out, however, and even persuaded the British general by his demonstrations, that his only object was to draw him out of New York, in order to fight him in the open field with superior forces. Clinton, thinking to defeat one shrewd turn by another, remained behind his walls; but the American generalissimo, having at length received advice that the French fleet was in sight of the coasts, no longer delayed to cross the Delaware. He marched with extreme celerity across Pennsylvania, and appeared all of a sudden at the head of Elk, upon the northern extremity of the Chesapeake bay. An hour after, so admirably had the operations been concerted, or rather by the most fortunate accident, the count de Grasse entered into the bay the twenty-eighth of August, with twenty-five sail of the line; and no sooner was he arrived than he set himself to execute the plan agreed upon. He blocked up the mouths of the two rivers of York and James. By making himself master of the first, he cut off all maritime correspondence between Cornwallis and New York; by the occupation of the second, he opened a communication with the marquis de la Fayette, who had already descended as far as Williamsburgh. His position had occasioned at first some disquietude. It was feared lest Cornwallis, perceiving at length the circle that was traced around him, might profit of the superiority that he still had over the marquis, to fall upon him, overwhelm him, and thus escape into the Carolinas. Not a moment was lost in preventing so fatal a stroke; three thousand French troops embarked in light boats, and, commanded by the marquis de St. Simon, ascended the James river, and made their junction with the marquis de la Fayette; he had established his head-quarters at Williamsburgh. The English had already much increased the fortifications of Yorktown, and were still at work on them with indefatigable industry. The allies had therefore to expect a siege in form; and a powerful train of heavy artillery was indispensably necessary. Three days before the arrival of M. de Grasse in the Chesapeake, the count de Barras had made sail from Rhode Island with four ships of the line and some frigates or corvettes; he had embarked whatever implements of siege he had been able to collect. But he was not ignorant that a numerous British squadron lay in the port of New York, and he was sensible that the succor with which he was charged could not be intercepted without destroying all hope of success. He had therefore stood far out to sea, and, after reaching the waters of the Bahama islands, had shaped his course for the Chesapeake. Admiral Hood had appeared at the entrance of that bay, with fourteen sail of the line, the very day on which the count de Grasse had arrived there; disappointed at not finding admiral Graves, whom he had counted upon meeting in those waters, he immediately dispatched a swift-sailing frigate to apprise him of his arrival, and proceeded, without loss of time, to join him with all his fleet at Sandy Hook. Admiral Graves, as we have already seen, had received no previous notice whatever of the intended approach of Hood. His ships also had suffered extremely by violent gales of wind, during his cruise in the waters of Boston, and were entirely out of condition to put to sea. The chief command having devolved on him, as senior officer, the moment he was informed that the count de Barras had set sail from Rhode Island, he had pushed the reparation of his fleet with so much activity, that by the last day of August it was again fitted for sea. At the head of nineteen sail of the line, he set sail for the Chesapeake, which he hoped to gain before the count de Barras. It appears, that he was still in total ignorance of the arrival of the count de Grasse in that bay. As soon as the British admiral had made Cape Henry, he discovered the French fleet, which consisted at that moment of twenty-four sail of the line. It extended from the cape to the bank called the Middle Ground. Notwithstanding he had five ships less than his adversary, Graves prepared himself instantly for action. On the other hand, the count de Grasse, at sight of the British fleet, slipped his cables with admirable promptitude, and, full of confidence in victory, advanced with press of sail to encounter the enemy. The intention of the English was to engage as close an action as possible. They perceived how fatal an influence the loss of so important an occasion might have upon the success of the British arms, and even upon the issue of the war. A total defeat would scarcely have been more prejudicial to the interests of England than a loose and indecisive battle. It left the French masters of the Chesapeake, and lord Cornwallis still exposed to the same perils. But the count de Grasse, sensible of his advantages, would not commit to the caprices of fortune the decision of events, which he considered himself as already certain of controlling. This prudent course seemed also to be prescribed him by the absence of fifteen hundred of his seamen, who were then employed in conveying M. de St. Simon's troops up the river James; and the British fleet made its appearance so suddenly, that there was no time for recalling them. The count de Grasse wished only to arrest the enemy by partial and distant collisions, long enough to cover the arrival of the count de Barras.

With these opposite intentions the two admirals advanced the one against the other. The engagement soon became extremely warm between their vans; some ships of the center also took part in it. The French, who were not willing that the action should become too general, drew off their vanguard, which had already suffered severely. The approach of night, and the nearness of hostile shores, dissuaded the British admiral from the resolution of renewing the engagement. His own van had likewise been very roughly treated. The ships most damaged were the Shrewsbury, the Montague, the Ajax, the Intrepid, and the Terrible. The latter was so shattered and torn, that the water gained upon all the efforts of her pumps; she was burnt by order of admiral Graves. The English lost in this action, in killed and wounded, three hundred and thirty-six sailors and marines; the French little more than two hundred.

The hostile fleets continued for four successive days, partly repairing their damages, and partly maneuvering in sight of each other; but the French having generally maintained the wind, and their motives for not engaging a general affair remaining always the same, the battle was not renewed. When at length the count de Grasse had advice that the count de Barras was entered sound and safe into the

Chesapeake, with his squadron and convoy, he retired from the open sea and came to anchor in the interior of the bay. Fortune showed herself in every thing adverse to the English. They had endeavored to profit of the absence of the count de Grasse, to transmit dispatches to lord Cornwallis, by the frigates Isis and Richmond; they could not accomplish their mission, and both fell into the power of the French.

Admiral Graves, seeing the disastrous condition of his fleet, the sea becoming daily more tempestuous, and his hopes of intercepting the convoy of M. de Barras entirely foiled, had, a few days after, returned to New York. The French, becoming thus entirely masters of the bay, disembarked, in the first place, the artillery and munitions of war which they had brought from Rhode Island, and then employed the transports, with the frigates and light vessels of the fleet, in conveying the army of Washington from Annapolis to the mouth of James river, and thence to Williamsburgh. At the head of Elk, the combined army had not been able to collect shipping enough for this passage.

Thus Cornwallis found himself restricted to the place he occupied. By an admirable concurrence of well concerted operations, and of circumstances the most auspicious to his adversaries, his troops, still seven thousand strong, were surrounded on every side. An army of twenty thousand combatants, of which only a fifth part were militia, invested Yorktown upon every point on the side of the land, while a fleet of near thirty sail of the line, and a multitude of light vessels, stationed at the mouths of the rivers James and York, rendered the blockade of the place as complete as possible. The head-quarters of the combined army had been established at first in Williamsburgh, a city which is only a few miles distant from Yorktown. Care had been taken, however, to detach a considerable corps, consisting mostly of cavalry, under the conduct of M. de Choisy and general Wieden, to encamp on the left bank of the York, before the village of Gloucester, in order to prevent the English from issuing thence to forage. The French had taken post before Yorktown, on the left of the camp, extending from the river above the town to the morass in the center, where they were met by the Americans, who occupied the right from the river to that spot.

General Clinton had it very much at heart to extricate Cornwallis; and in consequence, while admiral Graves was under sail for the Chesapeake, had meditated a diversion in Connecticut. He hoped, by insulting that province, to draw thither a part of the American forces; knowing but too well that if they were left at liberty to push the siege of Yorktown, the blockaded army must inevitably surrender

The principal object of this expedition was to seize New London, a rich and flourishing town, situated upon the New Thames. The command of it was given to Arnold, who had just returned to New York from his inroad into Virginia.

The access of the port of New London was rendered difficult by two forts erected upon the opposite banks ; one called fort Trumbull, the other Griswold.   The royalists, having disembarked, unexpectedly, at daybreak, carried the first without much effort; but the second made a vigorous resistance.   Colonel Ledyard had promptly thrown himself into it with a body of militia, and the work itself was very strong, consisting in a walled square with flanks.   The royal troops nevertheless attacked with extreme vigor and gallantry ; they were received with no less bravery and resolution.   After a very heavy fire on both sides, the English, with the utmost difficulty and severe loss, effected a lodgment upon the fraizing, and at length made their way good, with fixed bayonets, through the embrasures, notwithstanding the fierce defense made by the garrison, who, now changing their weapons, fought desperately hand to hand with long spears.   The assailants, when finally masters of the place, massacred as well those who surrendered as those who resisted.   The town of New London itself was laid in ashes ; it is not known whether by design or chance.   A great number of vessels, richly laden, fell into the power of Arnold.   This first success obtained, the English, seeing no movement made in their favor, and observing, on the contrary, the most menacing dispositions among the inhabitants, decided for retreat. It was signalized by the most horrible devastations.   This expedition was, on their part, but a piratical inroad, absolutely without utility. In vain did they endeavor to make a great noise with their march, and their bloody executions in Connecticut ; Washington scarcely deigned to notice it.   Unshaken in his prior designs, he knew perfectly that whoever should triumph at Yorktown would have decided the whole of this campaign in his favor.   Instead, therefore, of sending troops into Connecticut, he drew them all into Virginia.

Of the two attempts made to succor Cornwallis, the naval battle, and the diversion against New London, neither had obtained its object.   Clinton assembled all the principal officers of his army in council, in order to take their opinion upon the most prudent course to be pursued in the present circumstances.   Admiral Digby had just arrived from Europe at New York, with three ships of the line, another ship of the same force, and several frigates had also repaired thither from the West Indies.   And although, notwithstanding these different re-inforcements, the British fleet was still inferior to that of France, yet the pressure of the peril, and the importance of the conjuncture, determined the British commanders to put to sea, and hasten to the relief of the besieged army.   They would have wished not to defer an instant the execution of their resolution ; but the refitting of the ships damaged in the late engagement, constrained them to wait.   They hoped, however, that nothing would detain them later than the fifth of October.   This is what Clinton announced to Cornwallis in a dispatch written in ciphers, which, notwithstanding the extreme vigilance of the besiegers, reached him the twenty-ninth of September.   This letter made such an impression upon the mind of Cornwallis, that he abandoned all his outposts and defenses, and withdrew entirely within the works of the place.   This resolution has been much censured by experienced military men ; and some even of the superior officers of the garrison, opposed it openly. Though the general-in-chief wrote that he had every reason to hope his re-inforcements would set sail from New York the fifth of October, should not Cornwallis have reflected that a multitude of unforeseen causes might derange this plan ; in a word, that of all human enterprises, maritime expeditions are the most exposed to the accidents of fortune ?   All his cares, all his efforts, should therefore have tended to prolong his defense ; and the outer works afforded him the means for it.   They were sufficiently strong ; nothing had been neglected in that respect, and the troops were numerous enough to man them suitably.   Is it possible, therefore, not to disapprove the determination taken by Cornwallis to crowd his army into a town, or rather into an intrenched camp, the works of which were still imperfect?   Except, perhaps, upon the declivity of the hill towards the river, the British troops were exposed on all sides to be raked by the artillery of the enemy.

It may be presumed that in contracting his defenses, the British general flattered himself this apparent indication of fear would redouble the temerity of the French, and that by rushing immediately to the assault, they would place in his hands a certain and decisive victory.   But Washington was as prudent as intrepid ; and the French generals, in those distant regions, showed themselves with reason extremely sparing of the blood of their soldiers.   An unanimous sentiment, moreover, repulsed every measure that could render doubtful an enterprise having such fair pretensions to be considered as certain.   It was therefore resolved to open trenches, and to carry on the siege in form, before attempting any attack with open force against the body of the place.

Yorktown, as we have already said, is situated upon the right bank of the river York.   Its narrow circuit now comprised the definitive fate of all the war.   The English had surrounded it with fortifications of different kinds. On the right or upper part, they had walled it with a chain of redoubts, curtained one to another by a parapet and palisade. The redoubts were fraized and palisaded, and were covered besides by abattis and breastworks. A morassy ravine extended along the front of these works. The besieged had erected upon it another large redoubt with palisades and ditch ; · this was the strongest side of the place. In front, that is, in the center of the circuit of the place, before which the morass became inundated, the defenses consisted in a line of strong palisades, and in batteries which commanded the dikes over which it was necessary to cross the ravine. Upon the left flank of this front had been constructed a horn work, in like manner defended by a ditch and palisade ; and although not yet entirely completed, it was in such forwardness as already to have opened several embrasures. As to the left, or lower part, it was likewise fortified with redoubts and batteries interlinked by an earthen parapet. Two other smaller, and not yet finished redoubts, had been erected at a certain distance without towards the country, in order the more effectually to cover this side, against which it was presumed the principal attack would be directed. The adjacent ground was flat, or furrowed by ravines, and consequently favorable to the besiegers. The space comprised within the fortifications was extremely circumscribed, and afforded no safety to the garrison. Upon the opposite side of the river, the village of Gloucester had been surrounded with earthen works, furnished with artillery where the position admitted ; but these works were of little importance. The trenches were opened by the allied armies in the night, between the sixth and seventh of October. Notwithstanding the violent fire of the besieged, they pushed their works with so much perseverance, that soon they had completed their first parallel, erected the batteries, and covered them with little less than a hundred pieces of heavy ordnance. The thickest walls could not have withstood the shock of so heavy a fire, much less those of Yorktown, which were not com pleted. So far were they from that state, that the British troops were not less employed in their construction under the fire of the enemy, than they were in their defense. In a few days most of their guns were silenced, their defenses in many places ruined, and the shells reached even the ships in the harbor, where the Charon of forty-four guns, with some of the transports, were burnt. It was manifest that valor was impotent against so formidable means of attack, and, conse- quently, that the defense could not be of long duration. The artillery of the Americans was commanded by general Knox, who in this siege, as in all the other actions of the war, displayed the talents of a consummate engineer. He had formed his cannoniers with such success, that the French themselves were astonished at the precision of their maneuvers.

In the midst of so many perils, Cornwallis received a dispatch from Clinton, which held out the hope that if the winds and unforeseen accidents did not prevent, the relief would sail from New York the twelfth of October. He reminded him, however, that a plan of this nature was subject to a thousand unlucky casualties; that he wished, therefore, to be informed if it was deemed possible to hold out till the middle of November; his intention, in the contrary case, being to march himself by way of the land, and to fall upon Philadelphia. He could not, doubtless, have undertaken a more efficacious diversion in favor of the besieged. Such were the formal promises of general Clinton to lord Cornwallis. How, it may be asked, could the English have deceived themselves so grossly with respect to the time necessary for the reparation of their ships, that instead of departing from New York the fifth of October, as they had announced, they did not make sail until the nineteenth? This miscalculation seems difficult to be accounted for. It is certain only that the promise of succors, and their unexpected delay, occasioned the loss of the army. In the firm expectation of being soon relieved, Cornwallis persisted in his defense, and thus abstained from resorting to the means of safety that were in his power. If it be just to acknowledge a motive of excuse for his conduct in the first letter, by which Clinton assured him that the fleet would set sail the fifth of October, it will still remain very difficult to justify the resolution to which he adhered, when he had been apprised by a second dispatch, that the squadron could not put to sea until the twelfth, a dispatch which left room for doubts even with respect to that. Among the principal officers of the garrison commanded by lord Cornwallis, there were not wanting those who advised him to evacuate a place so little susceptible of a long defense, and to transport his army suddenly to the left side of the river, where there was still left him a way to escape from the fate that menaced him. They urged him to withdraw in the night to Gloucester with the greater part of his army. This passage might be effected easily with the shipping that lay in the harbor. The superiority of force, and the surprise of an unexpected attack, precluded all doubt of their being able to disperse the corps of M. de Choisy, who invested Gloucester. The British army would thus find itself in that fertile country which is situated between the York and the Rappahanock. Not having yet been made the seat of war, it was sure to afford horses and provision in abundance. By forced marches it would be possible to gain an hundred miles upon the enemy, and to protect the retreat by a rear

guard of three thousand picked men, both infantry and cavalry
Once masters of the country beyond the York, they would be at
liberty to march upon Philadelphia, and there join general Clinton
who would have repaired thither through New Jersey, or to bend
their course towards the Carolinas, keeping the upper route, in order
to pass the rivers above the points where they divide into several
branches.   Either of these ways offered some hope of safety, since
Washington, for want of shipping, would not be able to cross the
river soon enough to follow the British army; and not knowing the
direction it would have taken, he would be obliged to divide his
troops into several detachments.   And even in the supposition that
he was apprised in time of their march, his pursuit would not be
prompt enough to come up with them; since lodgings and subsistence for so numerous an army must necessarily fail him.   'By
remaining here,' added the partisans of this opinion, 'we devote
ourselves to certain destruction; by opening ourselves a passage, we
may yet find safety.   We shall, in any event, have the consolation of
thinking that so magnanimous an attempt will shed new lustre upon
the arms of the king.   If it is fated that so gallant an army cannot
escape captivity, let this not be till after it has exerted its utmost
force to avert it, and after having acquired an honored name and
bright fame among the brave!'
    Lord Cornwallis, whatever might have been his motives, would
never listen to these salutary counsels; he persisted in his determination to defend himself behind walls that were indefensible
Perhaps he persuaded himself that he could prolong his resistance
until the arrival of relief, and thus escape the blame to which he
exposed himself on the part of his sovereign, in hazarding his
army by an attempt to retreat.   Perhaps, also, the uncertainty of
saving it by this resource, appeared to him as great as that of the
arrival of succors.   But whatever was the private opinion of the
British general, it could have no influence upon that fatal issue which
was rapidly approaching.   The besiegers had already commenced
the labors of the second parallel, and their activity seemed to increase
every day.   They were now but three hundred yards from the place.
The English endeavored to arrest them by a deluge of bombs and
balls.   But the artillery of the first parallel kept up so heavy a fire,
that the besieged, far from being able to interrupt the labors of the
second, soon beheld all their batteries upon their left flank dismounted.   This event was the more prejudicial to them, as it was against
that very part that the allies directed their principal attack.   In order
to complete their trenches, it remained for them to dislodge the English from the two advanced redoubts of which we have made mention

above.   Washington gave orders that they should be carried by assault.   With a view of exciting emulation between the two nations, the attack on the redoubt upon the right was committed to the Americans, and of the other to the French.   The American detach-ment was commanded by the marquis de la Fayette and by colonel Hamilton, aid-de-camp of the commander in chief, a young man of the highest expectation.   They were accompanied by colonel Lau-rens, son of the former president of congress, who was at that time confined in the tower of London.   He was also a youth of the fairest hope, and would infallibly have furnished a brilliant career if an un timely death had not snatched him from his family, and from his country.   The baron de Viomesnil, the count Charles de Damas, and the count de Deux Ponts, commanded the French.   The commanders addressed their soldiers a short exhortation to in-flame their courage ; they represented that this last effort would bring them to the term of their glorious toils.   The attack was extremely impetuous.   On its success depended in a great meas-ure that of the siege.   Relying entirely upon their bayonets, the Americans advanced with unloaded arms ; they passed the abattis and palisades without waiting to remove them.   The English, as-tonished at so much audacity, attempted in vain to put themselves upon defense.   The humanity of the conquerors equaled their courage.   They granted life to all those who demanded it, notwith-standing the cruelties recently committed at New London.   Young Laurens gained great credit upon this occasion, and personally took the commanding officer prisoner.   The loss was very moderate on both sides.   The redoubt upon the left cost more efforts ; but at length, the French chasseurs and grenadiers, animated by the exam-ple of their chiefs, carried it with the bayonet.   This double conquest was no less useful to the allies than it was honorable for their arms Washington presented the two regiments of Gatinois and Deux Ponts, who had contributed to it, with the two pieces of cannon which they had taken.   The besieged made no attempt to recover the two redoubts.   The besiegers hastened to include them in the second parallel, which before the next morning was entirely completed. The situation of the garrison was become so critical, that it could no longer hope for safety.   Cornwallis foresaw perfectly, that when the besiegers should have opened the fire of the batteries of their second parallel, all means of resistance would fail him.   The greater part of his artillery was dismounted, broken, or otherwise disabled ; the walls were crumbled into the ditches ; in a word, almost all the de-fenses were rased.   Having lost the use of his heavy artillery, the

British commander gave with difficulty some sign of resistance by firing at intervals with his howitzers and small mortars.

In this state of things Cornwallis, in order to retard as much as was in his power the completion of the batteries upon the second parallel, resolved to reach them by a vigorous sortie. He did not flatter himself, however, that even by this expedient he should be able to extricate himself from the alarming position he was in, nor yet to protract his defense for any considerable space of time. He wrote to general Clinton, that being exposed every moment to an assault in ruined works, and an almost open town, with a garrison weakened by sickness, the distress of Yorktown was such that he could not recommend to the fleet and army to run any great risk in endeavoring to save it.

Meanwhile a detachment sallied from the place, on the night of the sixteenth of October, under the conduct of colonel Abercrombie. They deceived the enemy by answering as Americans; and having penetrated to the second parallel, made themselves masters of two batteries, the one French and the other American. The French, who had the guard of that part of the intrenchment, suffered considerably. The English spiked eleven pieces of cannon, and would have done much more mischief, if the viscount de Noailles had not charged them furiously, and driven them before him into the town. This sortie was not of the least advantage to the besieged. The cannon, which were hastily spiked, were soon again rendered fit for service.

The fire of the place was entirely extinct. Scarcely did it throw from time to time a cohorn shell into the camp of the besiegers; and this last source of defense was nearly expended. The garrison was sensibly enfeebled by disease; fatigue and discouragement overwhelmed even the soldiers who remained for service. All hope was vanished; an assault must prove irremediable. Straitened on all sides, Cornwallis was constrained to resort to new expedients. He had recourse to a measure which he ought to have embraced before it was too late; and that was, to pass the river suddenly with his garrison, and to try fortune upon the opposite bank. He reflected, that even if it was not in his power to escape the enemy entirely, he had at least the hope of retarding the moment of his surrender; and that, in any event, the allies occupied in pursuing him, would not so soon have it in their power to turn their thoughts and arms upon new enterprises. The boats are prepared; the troops embark; they leave behind the baggage, the sick and wounded, and a feeble detachment, in order to capitulate for the town's people, with a letter from Cornwallis to Washington, recommending to the

SURRENDER OF LORD CORNWALLIS. Vol. II.—p. 401.

generosity of the conqueror the persons not in a condition to be removed. Already a part of the troops are landed at Gloucester Point; another embarks; the third division only is waited for; a perfect calm prevails in the air and upon the waters; every thing seemed to favor the design of the British commander. But all of a sudden, at that critical moment of hope, apprehension and danger, arose a violent storm of wind and rain, and all was lost. The boats were all driven down the river, and the army, thus weakened and divided, was involved in a state of the most imminent danger. The day began to appear. The besiegers opened a tremendous fire from all their batteries; the bombs showered copiously even into the river. But the tempest, in the meantime, had abated; the boats were able to return, and the English, finding this last way of safety interdicted them by inexorable fortune, came back, not without new perils, to that shore, where a certain death or an inevitable captivity awaited them. Again in Yorktown, Cornwallis being sensible that his position was now past all remedy, and preferring the life of his brave troops to the honor they might have acquired in a murderous and desperate assault, sent a flag to Washington, proposing a cessation of arms for twenty-four hours, and that commissioners might be appointed on both sides for settling the terms of capitulation. The American general was not disposed to grant so long a time, on account of the possible arrival of British succors. He answered, that he could only grant a truce of two hours; and that during this interval he should expect the propositions of the British commander. Cornwallis was desirous that his troops might obtain the liberty of returning to their respective countries, the English to England, the Germans into Germany, upon giving their parole not to bear arms against France or America until exchanged. He demanded, besides, the regulation of the interests of those Americans, who, having followed the British army, found themselves involved in its fate. Both of these conditions were alike refused; the first, because it was not intended to leave the king of England at liberty to employ his captive regiments in the home garrisons; the second, because it was a civil affair, and not within the competence of the military commanders As to this last article, Cornwallis prosecuted the negotiation of it with so much ardor, that he at length obtained permission to dispatch the sloop Bonetta to New York, with the privilege of passing without search or visit, he being only answerable that the number of persons she conveyed should be accounted for as prisoners of war upon exchange. After various discussions, the two hostile generals having agreed upon the terms of capitulation, the commissioners charged with drawing it up convened in a habitation near the river, called

Moore's house; they were, on the part of the English, the colonels Dundas and Ross; on the part of the allies, the viscount de Noailles and colonel Laurens   The posts of York and Gloucester were surrendered on the nineteenth of October.   The land forces became prisoners to America, and the seamen to France.   The officers retained their arms and baggage.   The soldiers were to be kept together as much as possible in regiments, and to be cantoned in Virginia, Maryland and Pennsylvania; a part of the officers engaged to accompany the corps into the interior of the country; the others were at liberty to go upon parole either to England or New York. The Bonetta, on her return from that city, was to be delivered to the count de Grasse.   All the shipping and naval munitions were put into the hands of the French.   The British flotilla consisted of two frigates, the Guadaloupe and Fowey, besides about twenty transports; twenty others had been burnt during the siege.   The Americans had for their portion the field artillery.   They found in Yorktown and Gloucester a hundred and sixty pieces of cannon, the greater part brass, and eight mortars.   The number of prisoners, exclusive of seamen, amounted to upwards of seven thousand.   Out of this number, more than two thousand were wounded or sick. The besieged had about five hundred and fifty slain; but they lost no officer of note except major Cochrane.   On the side of the besiegers, about four hundred and fifty were killed or wounded.

When the garrison had deposited their arms, they were conducted to the places of their destination.   The talents and bravery displayed in this siege by the allies, won them an immortal glory; and they still enhanced it by the humanity and generosity with which they treated their prisoners.   The French officers, in particular, honored themselves by the most delicate behavior.   They seemed to have no other cares but that of consoling the vanquished by every mark of the most sympathising interest.   Not content with professions, they made the English the most pressing offers of money, both public and private.   Lord Cornwallis in his public letters acknowledged in warm terms the magnanimity of this conduct.

The fate of Yorktown and its defenders was thus decided, when the twenty-fourth of October, the British fleet, consisting of twenty-five sail of the line, with two of fifty guns and several frigates, appeared at the entrance of the Chesapeake.   It had made sail from New York the nineteenth, the day of the capitulation; it brought a corps of seven thousand men to the succor of Cornwallis.   Upon positive intelligence of the catastrophe of Yorktown, the British commanders, filled with grief and consternation, re-conducted their forces to New York.

At the news of so glorious, so important a victory, transports of exultation broke out from one extremity of America to the other. The remembrance of past evils gave place, in all minds, to the most brilliant hopes. Nobody dared longer to doubt of independence If the victory of Saratoga had produced the alliance with France, that of Yorktown was to have the effect of establishing, on an unshaken basis, the liberty of the American people. If the one had been the cause of the successes of the war, the other was about to create the blessings of an honorable peace. In all parts of the United States, solemn festivals and rejoicings celebrated the triumph of American fortune and the downfall of that of the enemy. The names of Washington, of Rochambeau, de Grasse, la Fayette, resounded every where. To the unanimous acclaim of the people, the congress joined the authority of its decrees. It addressed thanks to the generals as well as to the officers and soldiers of the victorious army. It ordained, that there should be erected at Yorktown of Virginia, a marble column, adorned with emblems of the alliance between the United States and the king of France, and inscribed with a succinct narrative of the surrender of the earl Cornwallis. It decreed, that Washington should be presented with two stands of British colors; the count de Rochambeau with two pieces of cannon, and that his most christian majesty should be requested to permit the count de Grasse to accept a like present. The congress repaired in body to the principal church of Philadelphia, to render their joyful thanksgivings to the most high God for the recent victory. By a special decree, the thirteenth of December was appointed to be observed as a day of prayer and acknowledgment for so signal an evidence of the divine protection.

The demonstrations of public gratitude towards the captain-general, were not confined to these honors. The provincial assemblies, the universities, the literary societies, addressed him the sincere homage of their felicitations and admiration. He answered with exemplary modesty, that he had done no more than what his duty required of him; he was eloquent in extolling the valor of the army, and the efficacious assistance of an ally no less generous than powerful.

Washington would have wished so to profit of the conjuncture as to expel the British entirely from the American continent. He meditated in particular the recovery of Charleston. His design might have been put in execution, if the count de Grasse had been at liberty to remain longer upon the American coasts; but the express orders of his government recalled him to the West Indies. He made sail for those islands the fifth of November, taking with him the corps which had served under the marquis de St. Simon. The troops which had reduced Yorktown were marched in part upon the banks of the Hudson, to watch the motions of Clinton, who had still a great force at New York. The rest were sent to the Carolinas to re-inforce general Greene, and confirm the authority of congress in those provinces. The English totally evacuated the open country, and withdrew behind the walls of Charleston and Savannah. The marquis de la Fayette embarked about the same time for Europe, bearing with him the affection and the regrets of the Americans. The congress, while testifying their high satisfaction with his services, prayed him to advocate the interests of the United States with the French ministry, and to recommend them especially to the benevolence of his most christian majesty. Washington repaired to Philadelphia, where he had frequent conferences with the congress upon military operations, and the business of the state. Thanks to his cares and activity, the service of the war department was secured for the following year much earlier than it had ever been before.

Such was the termination of the campaign of Virginia, which was well nigh being that of all the American war. The disaster of Yorktown so prostrated the British power upon that continent, that thenceforth the English, utterly despairing of being able to re-establish it, abandoned all idea of acting offensively, and thought only of defending themselves. With the exception of strong places, or countries accessible to their powerful navy, such as the province of New York, the contiguous islands, and the cities of Charleston and Savannah, all the territory was recovered into the power of congress. Thus, by a sudden reverse of fortune, the victors became vanquished; thus those, who, in the course of a cruel war, had learned from their enemies themselves how to wage it, made such proficiency in the art as in their turn to give lessons to their masters.

The arms of England were not more fortunate in the West Indies than they had been upon the American continent. The marquis de Bouille was informed that the governor of St. Eustatius, relying upon the strength of the island, or upon the absence of the fleet of the count de Grasse, kept a very negligent guard. Without loss of time he embarked, at Martinico, twelve hundred regular troops with some militia in three frigates, one corvette and four smaller armed vessels. He sailed immediately for St. Eustatius. To confirm the enemy in that profound security to which he abandoned himself, he gave out that he was going to meet the French armament on its return from America. He appeared in sight of the island the twenty-fifth of November. But formidable obstacles awaited him there; an unusually rough sea not only prevented him from landing all his troops, but even rendered it impracticable for the frigates to approach the shore, and the boats were dashed in pieces against the rocks. The activity of the marquis de Bouille enabled him, after unprecedented efforts, to put ashore four hundred soldiers of the Irish legion with the chasseurs of two French regiments. This detachment, separated from the rest of the troops by the fury of the sea, was exposed to the most imminent danger ; it was about to encounter a garrison consisting of seven hunared veteran soldiers. But the marquis de Bouille, with the presence of mind that characterized him, immediately took the only determination that could lead him to success ; and that was to push rapidly forward, and seize by surprise what he was in no condition to carry by force. He appeared unexpectedly under the walls of the fortress ; such was his celerity, and such the negligence of the enemy, that he found a part of the garrison exercising in full security upon the esplanade. The day had but just commenced. The rest of the soldiers were dispersed in the barracks and houses. Deceived by the red coats of the Irish, the garrison took them at first for English ; they were first made sensible of their error by a discharge of musketry, at half portice, which killed several, and wounded a great number. They were thrown into confusion ; governor Cockburne, who returned at this moment from a promenade on horseback, came up, on hearing the strange noise, and was made prisoner. Meanwhile, the French chasseurs had pushed rapidly behind the English, and had already reached the gate of the fortress. The English rushed into it tumultuously, and attempted to raise the drawbridge; but the French, still more prompt, threw themselves in pell mell with them. Surprised upon all points, and unable to rally, the garrison laid down arms and surrendered. Thus the island of St. Eustatius fell into the power of the French. The booty they made was immense ; twenty pieces of cannon were the fruit of victory. A million of livres, which had been put in sequestration by the English, was forthwith restored by the generous victor to the Dutch, from whom it had been wrested. Governor Cockburne claimed a sum of two hundred and sixty-four thousand livres as belonging to him personally ; it was assigned him with the same liberality. But the marquis de Bouille thought he had right to distribute among his troops sixteen hundred thousand livres appertaining to admiral Rodney, general Vaughan and other British officers ; as being the produce of the sales they had made at St. Eustatius. Thus M. de la Motte Piquet, at first, then the marquis de Bouille, stripped the plunderers of this island of the riches they had amassed in it ; they had scarcely any thing left of all their spoils. The neighboring islands of Saba and St. Martin came likewise the next day into the power of the French.

1782. In the commencement of the following month of February, a squadron of seven light vessels armed for war, under the command of the count de Kersaint, recovered to Holland the colonies of Demerary, Issequibo and Berbice ; so that all the conquests of admiral Rodney, on which the British nation had founded the most brilliant hopes of mercantile advantage, were wrested from it with as much promptitude and facility as they had been made. As to France, the preservation of the Cape of Good Hope, and the retaking of the Dutch colonies in America, acquired her the reputation of a faithful and disinterested ally, and thus considerably increased the number of her partisans in Holland. After the conquest of St. Eustatius, the return of the count de Grasse decided the French to follow up their victories. Their superiority, both in land and naval forces, authorized them, in effect, to entertain hopes of the most important successes. They directed their views at first towards the opulent island of Barbadoes. Its position, to windward of all the others, renders it very proper for securing the domination of them. Twice they embarked upon this expedition with all the means fitted to ensure its success, and twice they were driven back by contrary winds. It was necessary that the efforts of human valor should yield to the power of the elements. The French commanders then determined to attack the sland of St. Christophers, situated to leeward of Martinico. The count de Grasse arrived there the eleventh of January, with thirty-two sail of the line, and six thousand men, under the marquis de Bouille. The fleet anchored in the road of Basse Terre, and the troops were disembarked. The inhabitants of the island were discontented with the British government; they had always condemned the American war, and they considered themselves, besides, aggrieved by certain acts of parliament. Their indignation was extreme, moreover, that the merchandise which they deposited in the warehouses of St. Eustatius, had been so shamefully pillaged by Rodney and Vaughan. Consequently, instead of taking arms against the French, they remained tranquil spectators of events.

The British retired from Basse Terre upon Brimstone Hill. Their force consisted of seven hundred regulars, who were afterwards joined by about three hundred militia. The governor of the island was general Frazer, a very aged officer. The militia were commanded by general Shirley, governor of Antigua. Brimstone Hill is a steep and almost inaccessible rock. It rises upon the sea shore, not far from the little town of Sandy Hill, which is considered the second of the island, and situated about ten miles from Basse Terre, which is the capital. The fortifications constructed upon the summit of Brimstone Hill, were by no means correspondent to its natural strength.

They were, besides, too extensive to be susceptible of an efficient defense by so feeble a garrison. No sooner were the French disembarked, than they marched in four columns to invest the hill on all its faces at once. As the artillery of the place incommoded them exceedingly, they found themselves necessitated to proceed with much regularity and caution. They opened trenches, and covered themselves by breastworks. They were almost entirely destitute of heavy artillery, the ship that bore it having foundered near Sandy Point. Their industry and patience, however, succeeded in recovering from the bottom of the sea the greater part of the pieces. They hastened also to procure them from the neighboring islands. They likewise made themselves masters of some heavy cannon at the foot of the mountain, which had been sent from England a long time before, and which, through the negligence of the governor, had not been carried into the fortress. Independent of this artillery, a considerable quantity of bombs and cannon-ball fell into the power of the French Thus the arms and ammunition, sent by the British government for the defense of the island, were left to be employed for its reduction. The late surprise of St. Eustatius ought, however, to have put the commandant of St. Christophers upon the alert.

The French, thus finding themselves provided with the apparatus necessary for their operations, established themselves upon the most commanding of the neighboring heights, and began to batter the fortress. The garrison defended themselves valiantly, and with more effect than could have been expected from their small number.

In the meantime, admiral Hood returned from the coasts of America to Carlisle bay, in the island of Barbadoes, with twenty-two sail of the line. Upon intelligence of the peril of St. Christophers, notwithstanding the great inferiority of his force to that of the count de Grasse, he put to sea again immediately for the relief of the island attacked. He first touched at Antigua to take on board general Prescott with a corps of about two thousand men, and then sailed without delay for the road of Basse Terre, in St. Christophers. At the unexpected appearance of the British fleet, the count de Grasse instantly took his resolution ; he weighed anchor, and sailed forthwith to meet the enemy. His intention, in standing out of the harbor, was to put himself in condition to take advantage of the superiority of his force, and to prevent Hood from anchoring off Sandy Point, whence he might easily have thrown succors into the fort on Brimstone Hill. The British admiral, who observed the movements of his adversary, made a feint of intending to await the battle ; then, all at once, fell back, in order to draw the count de Grasse more and more distant from the fort. As soon as he had effected this object, availing himself of the swiftness of his ships and the advantage of the wind, he stood into tne bay of Basse Terre, and came to anchor in the same spot whence the French admiral had departed. This able maneuver was admired by the French themselves. They followed, however, and with their van engaged that of the English, but to little effect. The count de Grasse afterwards presented himself with all his fleet at the entrance of the bay. The attack was extremely vigorous; but the British ships, lying fast at anchor in a line across the mouth of the harbor, afforded no assailable point. The French were unable to make the least effective impression, and lost not a few men in the attempt. It was followed, however, by a second, which had no better success. The count de Grasse then renounced open force, and contented himself with cruising near enough to block up the British fleet in the bay, and protect the convoys of munitions which were on their way to him from Martinico and Guadaloupe.

Admiral Hood, on finding that the French had given up all thoughts of disturbing him in his anchorage, put ashore general Prescott, with a corps of thirteen hundred men; that general, having driven in a French post stationed in that part, encamped in a strong position upon the heights. He hoped to find some favorable occasion to succor the fortress. The strength of the place seemed to promise him that general Frazer would be able to hold out still for a long time. Admiral Hood, moreover, had received positive advice, that Rodney was not far off, and that he had brought from Europe a re-inforcement of twelve sail of the line. It appeared to him impossible that after the junction of all the British forces, the count de Grasse, and still less the marquis de Bouille, should be able to keep the field.

The capture of all the French troops then on shore was in his opinion an infallible event. But, in spite of all calculations, already the marquis de Bouille, having marched two thousand men against general Prescott, had compelled him to evacuate the island and re-embark precipitately. On the other hand, the French artillery kept up so terrible a fire against Brimstone Hill, that a number of breaches began to open in the walls; one of them in the part fronting the French camp was already practicable. A general assault would inevitably carry the place. The governor did not think proper to await this terrible extremity. All hope being now extinct, he demanded to capitulate. The conditions granted him were honorable for the soldiers, and advantageous for the inhabitants of the island. In consideration of their gallant defense, the generals Frazer and Shirley were left in perfect liberty upon their parole. The surrender of Brimstone Hill placed the whole island of St. Christophers in the power of the French. Admiral Hood, therefore, had no longer a motive for maintaining his anchorage in the bay of Basse Terre; and, moreover, his fleet was in some degree exposed there to the fire of the batteries which the French might have established upon the shore. Nor could he overlook the importance of effecting his junc tion with admiral Rodney, who was daily expected, and who perhaps was already arrived at Barbadoes. Retreat, however, was perilous in the presence of so formidable a force as the French fleet. But the conjuncture admitted of no hesitation. Accordingly, in the night that followed the capitulation, the French being four leagues off, the English cut their cables in order to get under way at the same time, and thus keep their ships more collected and together. This maneuver succeeded perfectly; they gained Barbadoes without op- position. Great was their joy at meeting Rodney in that island, who had just arrived there with twelve sail of the line. The count de Grasse incurred, on this head, the most violent reproaches of negli- gence and excessive circumspection. It was maintained, that he should have closely blockaded the British fleet in its anchorage, or attacked it at its departure, or else pursued it in its retreat. His partisans defended him, by alledging that he experienced an extreme scarcity of provisions; that his ships were by no means so good sailers as those of the enemy, and finally, that he was under an absolute necessity of returning promptly to Martinico, in order to cover the arrival of convoys which were expected there from Eu- rope. However these things might be, it remains demonstrated that the junction of the two British admirals produced, in the issue, an incalculable prejudice to the interests of France; as the sequel of this history will sufficiently evince. About the same time, the island of Montserrat surrendered to the arms of the counts de Barras and de Flechin. A few days after, the count de Grasse came to anchor at Martinico.

We have just seen the fortune of Great Britain depressed alike upon the American continent and in the West Indies. The arms of king George were not more successful in Europe than in the New World. His enemies had there also the gratification of witnessing the declension of his power. It was especially agreeable to Spain, who first gathered its fruits. The duke de Crillon, knowing with what ardor the Catholic king desired to have in his power the island of Minorca, applied himself with the utmost zeal to the siege of fort St. Philip. All the resources of the art of war had been employed to reduce it; a more formidable artillery had never been leveled against a place. But its natural strength, the immense works which covered it, and the perseverance of the besieged, creating apprehensions that the defense might be protracted still for a long time, the Spanish general had recourse to an expedient too little worthy of him.   He attempted to seduce governor Murray, and to obtain by corruption what he despaired of carrying by force.   He had, it is true, for this degrading step, the positive instructions of his .government.   General Murray repulsed the offers of his adversary with as much dignity as disdain.   He reminded the duke de Crillon, that when one of his valiant ancestors had been requested by his king to assassinate the duke de Guise, he had made him the answer that his descendant should also have made to those who had presumed to commission him to attempt the honor of a man sprung from a blood as illustrious as his own, or that of the Guises.   He ended his letter with praying him to cease to write or offer parley, his resolution being to communicate with him no more, except at the point of the sword.*

The duke de Crillon gave general Murray to understand, that he could not but honor him for his conduct; that he rejoiced it had placed them both in that position which befitted them alike; and that it had greatly increased the high esteem in which he had always held the governor.   Meanwhile the situation of the besieged was become painful in the extreme.   Notwithstanding the success of a vigorous sortie, in which they had dislodged the duke de Crillon from Cape Mola, where he had established his head-quarters, their weakness rendered this transitory triumph more hurtful to them than beneficial.   The garrison would by no means have sufficed for the defense of so extensive fortifications, even if they had been free from sickness.   But very far from that was their condition.   The seeds of the scurvy, with which they were infected, even before the opening of the siege, had developed themselves with a fury which increased from day to day.   All who were seized with it either died, or became totally useless for the defense of the place.   The causes of this mortal disease were principally the scarcity, or rather absolute want of vegetables, the amassment of soldiers in the casemates, the horrible fetor which resulted from it, and the excessive fatigues of a

---

* Henry III., despairing of being able to reduce the Duke of Guise, consulted the mareschals d'Aumont, de Rambouilet and de Beauvais Nangis, who decided that con sidering the impossibility of bringing that illustrious rebel to trial, it was necessary to take him off by surprise.   The king proposed to the celebrated Crillon to undertake the execution of this murder; ' I will not assassinate him, answered *the bravest of the brave*, but I will fight him.   When a man is ready to give his life, he is master of that of another.'

The affectation of general Murray in vaunting in his answer the nobility of his origin, grew out of his pretending to have descended from the earl of Murray, natural son of James V. and brother of Mary Stuart.

service almost without remission.   To the scurvy, as if not sufficient of itself to exterminate the unhappy garrison, putrid fevers and the dysentery united their destructive rage.   Overwhelmed by so many evils, these intrepid warriors piqued themselves upon braving them. Those who were already attacked with pestilential maladies, dissembled their sufferings, for fear of not being admitted to share the perils of their comrades.   Their ardor had survived their bodily strength ; some of them were seen to expire under arms.

Nature at length triumphed over the firmness of these generous spirits.   In the beginning of February, the garrison found itself so diminished, that there remained only six hundred and sixty men capable of any sort of service ; and, even of this number, the most part were tainted with the scurvy.   It was to be feared lest the enemy, apprised of this disastrous state of things, might precipitate his attacks, and carry the place by storm.   There was the more foundation for such an apprehension, as the artillery had already ruined the greater part of the upper defenses.   Scarcely did there remain a few pieces of cannon in a serviceable state, and the fire of the enemy was still unremitting.

In a situation so utterly hopeless, to resist any longer would have been rather the delirium of a senseless obstinacy, than the effect of a generous constancy.   Murray accepted a capitulation, the tenor of which was honorable for his garrison.   He was allowed all the nonors of war ; the British troops were to be sent to England as prisoners upon parole ; all the foreigners had permission to return to their countries with their effects ; the Minorcans, who had adhered to the British party, were left at liberty to remain in the island in the undisturbed enjoyment of their possessions.   When the remains of this valiant garrison evacuated fort St. Philip, they had more the appearance of specters than of men.

They marched through the French and Spanish armies, which were drawn up fronting each other, and formed a lane for their passage.   They consisted of no more than six hundred old decrepit soldiers, one hundred and twenty of the royal artillery, two hundred seamen, and about fifty Corsicans, Greeks, Turks and Moors.   The victors manifested compassion for the fate of their prisoners ; they could not refuse them even a tribute of admiration, when, arrived at the place where they laid down their arms, they heard them declare, while lifting up to heaven their eyes bathed in tears, that they had surrendered them to God alone.   The humanity of the French and Spaniards was highly conspicuous, and worthy of lasting praise.   Yielding to the most generous emotions, the common soldiers of the two nations were forward to administer refreshments and consolations to their unfortunate enemies. The duke and count de Crillon, as well as the baron de Falkenhayn, commander of the French troops, signalized themselves by the most feeling and delicate attentions. Such actions and conduct cast abroad a pleasing shade, which serves to soften the horrors of war, and to hide and alleviate its calamities ; should they not also mitigate the fury of national rivalships and animosities ?

Thus did the island of Minorca return to the dominion of Spain, after it had been in the possession of Great Britain for upwards of seventy years.

The news of so many and so grievous disasters, and especially that of Yorktown, produced in England a general consternation, accompanied by an earnest desire of a new order of things. The length of the war was already become wearisome to all ; the enormous expenses it had occasioned, and which it still exacted, were viewed with disquietude and alarm. The late reverses still increased this universal discontent ; and with the diminution of the hope of victory was strengthened in all the impatience for the return of peace. The possibility of resuming the offensive upon the American continent, and of re-establishing there, by dint of arms, the sovereignty of Great Britain, was now considered as a chimera. The secret machinations in order to divide the people of America, the terror and barbarity of the Indians, the attempts of treason, the destruction of commerce, the falsification of bills of credit, odious means to which the British ministers had resorted, and even the victories of their generals, all had failed of wresting from the Americans the smallest indication of a disposition to resume their ancient yoke. If such had been their constancy, when their ship, battered by the tempests, seemed hastening to the bottom, how could it be hoped to see them bend, while the most propitious gales were conducting them into the wished-for port ? It was self-evident that henceforth the war of America could have no other object but that of obtaining the most honorable conditions possible, after having acknowledged independence. On the other hand, the immense losses sustained in the West Indies, gave occasion for fear lest they might be followed by others still more afflicting. The most anxious apprehensions were entertained for Jamaica, against which the house of Bourbon seemed ready to display the entire apparatus of its power. The fall of a place of such importance as fort St. Philip, and the loss of the whole island of Minorca, inspired doubts for Gibraltar itself.

The people, always the same every where, imputed these disasters, not to the contrariety of fortune, but to the incapacity of ministers. Their adversaries, both within parliament and without, raised the most violent clamors.　They exclaimed, that such were the fore-seen results of ministerial infatuation and obstinacy.　They demanded with vociferation the immediate dismission of these perverse and imbecile servants of the crown; they affirmed, that it was urgent to prevent those who had brought the country to the brink of a preci-pice, from plunging it headlong down it by the last frantic shock; that there was no chance of safety but in removing instantly those senseless instigators of a fatal war.　These cries of hatred coincided with the prevailing spirit; they were echoed with unanimity by the discontented multitude.　Besides, it escaped no one that since the course of things had created the necessity of entering into negotia-tion with the Americans, and of acknowledging their independence, it was not suitable that those who had at first so highly exasperated them by their laws, and afterwards had imbittered them to the utmost by a barbarous war, should undertake to treat with them.　The work of a durable pacification appeared little proper to be confided to hands which had fanned the fire of war.　Already general Conway, by a very eloquent speech, pronounced the twenty-second of Febru-ary, in the house of commons, had moved and obtained that his majesty should be entreated to command his ministers not to persist any longer in the attempt to reduce the colonies to obedience by means of force, and by continuing the war upon the American con-tinent.　He did more; in the sitting of the fourth of March, he proposed and carried a resolution, purporting that those who should advise the king to continue the war upon the continent of North America, should be declared enemies of the sovereign and of the country.　From this moment, the leading members of the privy council, the center and source of all great deliberations, perceived that it was full time to resort to the usual remedy of a change of ministry.　The general attention was excited to the highest degree.　At length, the twentieth of March, the earl of Surrey having moved in the house of commons that the king should be supplicated to change his ministers, lord North rose, and declared with dignity that it was superfluous to spend any more time upon this subject, since it had already occupied the attention of his majesty, who would shortly make known his new choice.　'Before I take leave of this house,' added lord North, 'I feel it a duty to return it thanks for the support and favor it has afforded me during so long a course of years, and in so many trying situations.　It will be easy to give me a successor, endowed with a greater capacity, of better judgment, and more qual-ified for his situation; but it will not be equally so to find a man more zealous for the interests of his country, more loyal to the sov-ereign, and more attached to the constitution.　I hope the new servants of the crown, whoever they may be, will take such measures as shall effectually extricate the country from its present difficulties, and retrieve its fortune at home and abroad.   I should declare, in retiring, that I am ready to answer to my country for all the acts of my administration.   If it is wished to undertake the investigation of my conduct, I offer myself to undergo it.'

The new ministers were selected from among those members of the two houses of parliament, who had shown themselves the most favorable to the pretensions of the Americans.   The marquis of Rockingham was appointed first lord of the treasury; the earl of Shelburne and Mr. Fox secretaries of state; lord John Cavendish chancellor of the exchequer.   Admiral Keppel was at the same time created viscount and first lord of the admiralty.   So great was the exultation caused by this event, particularly in the city of London, that it was feared the people of that capital, would, according to their custom, break out into some blamable excesses.   Every body felt assured that the end of the war was at hand, and that of all the calamities it had caused.   All that was desired was, that the conditions of peace might be honorable.   Accordingly the partisans of the new ministers were earnest in their prayers that some favorable event might gloriously repair the checks which the British arms had received towards the close of the past, and in the commencement of the present year.

END OF BOOK FOURTEENTH.

BOOK FIFTEENTH.

1782. THE belligerent powers, in order to execute the plans they had formed in the beginning of the present year, only waited the completion of their preparations, the return of spring, and the fitness of occasion. Alike weary of a long war, all had the same persuasion that this campaign was to be decisive. Nor were they ignorant that it is at the moment of peace that reverses have the most fatal consequences, as there no longer remains either time or hope for retrieving them. Under these considerations, each of the powers at war redoubled vigilance and efforts, in order to secure the definite triumph of its arms. The allied courts directed their views especially upon the domination of the European seas, the reduction of Gibraltar, and the conquest of Jamaica. The French were in the highest degree solicitous to transmit succors to their establishments in the East Indies, where, notwithstanding the valor and distinguished ability displayed by M. de Suffren, in several hard fought engagements with admiral Hughes, their affairs were in a state of declension; and already two Dutch places of great importance, Trincomale and Negapatam, were fallen into the power of the English. The attention of the allies had therefore two principal objects; to defend their own possessions, and to seize those of the enemy.

It was agreed that the Dutch and Spanish fleets should effect their junction with the French in the port of Brest. This mighty armada was afterwards to scour the open sea, and clear it of all hostile force from the straits of Gibraltar to the coasts of Norway. It was intended that the ships of the line should blockade the squadrons of the enemy in all the channels and ports, while the frigates and other light vessels should intercept the convoys, and utterly ruin the commerce of the English. The views of the allies extended yet farther; they hoped by incessantly spreading new alarms upon the coasts of Great Britain, that some opportunity might present itself for making descents, ravaging the country, and even for striking still more important blows, according to circumstances. They proceeded with the greatest zeal to the execution of their designs; the junction of their armaments was to present a powerful mass of sixty sail of the line, besides a prodigious number of frigates and sloops of war. The English were very far from possessing means sufficient to withstand so formidable a display of forces. Accordingly, the allied courts entertained not the least doubt but that their arms would be as successful in the West Indies and Europe, in this year's campaign, as they had been in the last upon the American continent. A glorious peace must, they felt assured, inevitably result from these decisive successes.

On the other hand, the new members of the British cabinet neglected nothing that could tend to remedy the calamitous state of affairs, and enable them to resist with effect the storm that rumbled over their heads. They hoped to compensate the inequality of force by the skill of commanders, the courage of troops, and the success of projected expeditions. Their cares were directed to the equipment of the fleet and the lading of the convoy destined to re-victual Gibraltar. After the security of the kingdom, there was nothing which they had so much at heart as the safety of that place. But they were sensible that, first of all, it was necessary to prevent the junction of the Spanish and Dutch squadrons with the French fleet; thus interrupting also, at the same time, the commerce of the Dutch in the Baltic, and protecting that of England against their insults.

Admiral Howe was therefore ordered to put to sea from Portsmouth with twelve sail of the line, and to establish his cruise upon the coasts of Holland. This measure had the desired effect. The Dutch squadron, which had already set sail from the Texel, abandoned the sea to the English, and made the best of its way back into port. After having cruised off the Dutch coasts for the term of a month, admiral Howe, finding that the enemy made no movement demonstrative of a disposition to put to sea again, and the unhealthiness of the season having occasioned much sickness on board his fleet, took the determination to return to Portsmouth. Admiral Milbanke relieved him almost immediately. If he was not able to annoy the Dutch trade in the Baltic, he at least effectually protected that of the English; and, moreover, he constantly interdicted to the enemy's squadron the entrance of the channel. Thus, with the exception of the brilliant action of Doggers Bank, the republic of Holland, formerly so famous, did nothing in all this war that was worthy of her, and of her ancient renown. Such was the decay of her glory and of her power, the deplorable result of excessive riches, of insatiable avidity, and perhaps still more of the party spirit which rent those provinces. If in a republic the counterpoise of parties, in matters relating to internal administration, may sometimes turn to the advantage of liberty, and maintain more energy in the people, those factions which have foreign powers for object, produce an entirely opposite effect. They divert the public spirit upon that which is abroad, and paralize all its activity at home. The most evident symptom of the decay of the strength of a state, and of the loss of its independence, is, doubtless, a division between citizens in favor of foreigners ; and such was the situation of the Dutch at this epoch. If, at the conclusion of the present war, their republic was not reduced to the last degree of depression, if it even repaired a great part of its losses, this it owed, not to its own force, but entirely to the arms and protection of France.

We resume the course of events ; undoubted intelligence had been received in England that a considerable convoy of troops and military stores, destined for India, was on the point of sailing from the port of Brest. Fearing, on the one hand, for Jamaica, and on the other, for the establishments of the coast of Malabar, the ministers, without any delay, dispatched admiral Barrington, at the head of twelve sail of the line, with orders to watch this convoy, and to capture it, if the opportunity should offer itself. He shaped his course for the bay of Biscay, and soon discovered the convoy, which consisted of eighteen transports, under the guard of two ships of the line, the Pegase and the Protecteur. The wind was violent and the sea tempestuous. The English nevertheless continued to crowd sail. The ship Foudroyant, an excellent sailer, commanded by captain Jarvis, at length came up with and engaged the Pegase, under the chevalier de Sillan. The forces of the two ships being about equal, the action lasted with extreme violence for a full hour. The Frenchman did not strike till after having seen the greater part of his men either killed or disabled. The sea was so rough that captain Jarvis was scarcely able to shift a small part of the crew of the prize. It was to be feared that the small number of men he sent aboard of it might be risen upon, and the ship rescued. But captain Maitland, who commanded the Queen, came up at this moment, and assisted his companion to secure his prize. Immediately after, they were again separated by a gust of wind. Captain Maitland afterwards fell in with another French ship called the Actionnaire, and captured her, after a feeble resistance. In the meantime, the frigates had given chase to the transports, which, at the first appearance of the English, had obeyed a signal for dispersing with all celerity. Twelve fell into the power of the enemy. This was a sensible loss to France ; for independent of the artillery, munitions of war, and provision, there were on board these vessels upwards of eleven hundred regular troops. Admiral Barrington brought his prizes safely into the ports of England.

The British admiralty, having realized the utility of cruises in the seas of Europe, resolved to multiply them. It adopted this determination the more willing'y, as it had not yet received any intimation of the approaching ppearance of the grand combined fleet

Notwithstanding the ardent desire which animated alike the French and the Spaniards, to depress the power of their implacable enemy, their operations suffered too often from that slowness which seems inseparable from all coalitions. The English, on the contrary, enjoyed the advantages attached to the unity of powers, and to the concert of movements. As soon as Barrington was returned, Kempenfeldt had orders to put to sea, and stand in like manner towards the bay of Biscay. His instructions were, to do the French commerce all the harm possible, to protect that of the British, and especially to cover the arrival of two rich convoys shortly expected, the one from Jamaica, the other from Canada.

After having wasted much precious time, the allies had set themselves at length to carry into effect the plans they had meditated. The count de Guichen, commanding the French squadron, and don Lewis de Cordova, admiral in chief of the combined fleet, set sail from the port of Cadiz, in the beginning of June, with twenty-five sail of the line, between Spanish and French. They stood to the north, towards the shores of England, animated with a desire and with a hope to wrest from those audacious islanders the empire of the ocean. As they sailed along the coasts of France, they were joined by several ships of war, which lay in the ports of that part, and even by a squadron that came from Brest to meet them. These different re-inforcements carried the combined fleet to forty sail of the line. Fortune smiled upon these first operations. The two convoys of Newfoundland and Quebec, escorted by admiral Campbell with one ship of fifty guns, and some frigates, fell into the midst of this immense line. A part were taken, the rest dispersed. Eighteen transports came into the power of the victors; this capture was valued at considerable sums. The ships of war made good their escape, and gained the ports of England in safety. This advantage indemnified the French, in some measure, for the loss of their convoy destined to the East Indies.

After this, if not difficult, at least useful success, become entirely masters of the sea, they repaired towards the entrance of the channel. As they had done in their preceding campaigns, they stretched their line across it, from the Scilly islands to that of Ushant. While observing the coasts of England, two objects especially occupied their attention; the protection of their own convoys, and the seizure of those of the enemy. Meanwhile, the British ministers were not reckless of the danger. Admiral Howe put to sea with twenty-two sail of the line. His instructions enjoined him to avoid a general action, and to use every possible endeavor to protect the arrival of the Jamaica convoy, become still more precious since the loss of that of Canada. This able commander displayed the rarest talents in the execution of his orders. He put himself out of the reach of the hostile fleet, by steering to the west, upon the route likely to be taken by the convoy. This maneuver was crowned with full success. Admiral Howe rallied to himself the whole convoy, with its escort, commanded by Peter Parker, and, towards the last of July, entered with them sound and safe into the ports of Ireland. The allies then returned to their own coasts, after demonstrations as vain and fruitless as those of their two preceding campaigns.

But of all the enterprises of the belligerent powers in Europe, none appeared to them more worthy to absorb all their attention than the siege of Gibraltar. The English were all intent upon succoring that fortress; the French and Spaniards upon preventing it. These two opposite aims were become the object of their reciprocal emulation. Independent of the glory of their arms, and the honor of crowns, there was nothing less at stake than the empire of the Medi- terranean, which seemed to depend on the possession of this celebrated rock. Never did any military operation attract, to the same degree, the gaze of the entire world; this siege was compared to the most famous recorded in history, whether ancient or modern. To preserve Gibraltar, was in England the first wish of all minds; it was known there that a scarcity began to prevail, within that place, of munitions of war, and especially of provisions. It was equally known that the besiegers intended to convert the blockade into an open attack. Already they were preparing machines of a new construction, in order to carry, by dint of force, what they had failed of attaining by famine. Accordingly, since Gibraltar, notwithstanding all that art and nature had done for its defense, was menaced with perils of a new species, the British government assembled at Portsmouth all the naval forces of the kingdom. The squadrons that were cruising upon the coasts of Holland and of the bay of Biscay, had orders to repair thither. An immense number of transports were there laden with munitions and necessaries of every denomination. At length, all preparations being terminated, towards the beginning of September, admiral Howe, commander-in-chief, accompanied by the admirals Milbank, Robert Hughes, and Hotham, set sail from Portsmouth. His force consisted of thirty-four sail of the line, and a proportionate number of frigates and fire-ships. Upon the fortune of this armament hung that of the besieged fortress.

Arms were not, however, the only means which the British ministers resolved to employ in order to attain the object they had in view; namely, a glorious war and an honorable peace. It was not permitted them to hope to be able to reduce their enemies entirely, so long as they persisted in their strict union; they, therefore, formed a design to throw division among them, by making to each of them separate proposals of peace. The dissolution of the coalition appeared to them the certain pledge of definitive triumph. They calculated also, that even in case they should not succeed in their attempt, they would nevertheless obtain a real advantage; that of contenting the minds of the people of Great Britain, and of rendering the war less odious to them, by demonstrating the necessity of continuing it. Another no less powerful consideration had influence upon their determination; they felt, that in order to preserve the partisans they had made themselves both in and out of parliament, it was necessary that they should hold out at least an appearance of inclining towards peace. Under these considerations, the British cabinet made application to the empress of Russia. She accepted the character of mediatress with the States-General of Holland; she offered them, in the name of king George, a suspension of arms, and conditions of peace upon the footing of the treaty of 1674. The ambassador of France, who was then at the Hague, watched these secret maneuvers, and labored with all his power to prevent the effects of them, and to maintain the States-General in their fidelity to the alliance. He reminded them that they were pledged not to make peace with England until that power should have acknowledged the unrestricted freedom of the seas. While recapitulating the plans of naval operations concerted between the two states against the common enemy, he intimated that Holland could not renounce them all of a sudden, without as much prejudice to her own honor, as to the interests of her faithful ally, the king of France. He glanced also at the gratitude by which the Dutch were bound to his most christian majesty for the preservation of the Cape of Good Hope, and the recovery of St. Eustatius, as well as the colonies of Guiana, owing entirely to his arms. In support of the representations of the French ambassador, the States-General could not but add a tacit reflection. The colonies above mentioned were still in the hands of the French, as guarantee of treaties; was it not to be feared that they would refuse to restore them, if their allies departed from their engagements? These considerations were backed also by the efforts of the partisans of France. They at length prevailed totally. The States-General rejected the propositions of the court of London, declaring that they would not disparage the incorruptible faith of which their ancestors had left them the example. The overtures that were made at the same time to the governments of France and of Spain were not attended with any better success. The first entertained hopes of expelling the British altogether from the West Indies, and thereby of acquiring more efficacious rights to stipulate for the liberty of the seas. The second, swayed by the same motives, had, besides, the prospect of recovering possession of Jamaica and Gibraltar. Intimately united also by the family compact, the two monarchs would have thought it derogatory to the dignity of their crowns, not to have fulfilled the obligations it imposed.

But the British ministers hoped for more fruit from their intrigues with the United States of America. With a view to this object, they had recalled general Clinton, and replaced him by general Carleton, who, by his moderation and humanity during the war of Canada, had conciliated the esteem and confidence of the Americans He was invested, as well as admiral Digby, with power to negotiate peace with the United States, upon the basis of independence, and to conclude with them a treaty of amity and commerce.

But the Americans took into consideration, that no act of the parliament had as yet authorized the king to conclude peace or truce with America ; and consequently it was to be apprehended that proposals and promises, made at the mere motion of ministers, might afterwards be disavowed by the two houses. They were aware also of the extreme repugnance which the king personally had to acknowledge their independence. They began therefore to suspect the existence of a hidden snare. These conjectures acquired new force with them, on hearing that the British cabinet had made separate overtures to each of the belligerent powers. They no longer doubted but that its drift was, by means of these overtures, to sow division among them, and to amuse them by vain words. The proposition of peace appeared to them a mere stratagem of the English to divert their attention from the preparations requisite to the prosecution of the war, and thereby secure for themselves easy advantages. The French minister at Philadelphia exerted himself to the utmost to interrupt all negotiations. He placed in the strongest light the grounds which the Americans had for apprehending bad faith on the part of England, and for confiding, on the contrary, in the sincerity and generosity of the king of France. The most influential members of the American government were little disposed of themselves to commence their career in the political world by a violation of treaties, and to exchange an approved alliance for a suspicious friendship ; their opinion prevailed. The congress declared formally, that they would enter into no negotiation wherein their ally should not participate.

Moreover, that not the slightest doubt should remain respecting the good faith of the United States, in order to bar all hope to England, and all suspicion to France, the provincial assemblies decreed, that peace should never be concluded with Great Britain without the consent of his most christian majesty; declaring enemies to the country all those who should attempt to negotiate without authority from congress. Thus the first days of the year witnessed the failure of all hope of pacification. The cause for which the belligerent powers had taken arms, appeared still undecided. In the midst of that reciprocal distrust which imbittered minds, no form of conciliation was admissible, till ushered by the last necessity. While such was the posture of affairs upon the American continent, they were about to be decided, in the islands, by one of those events which triumph over all the measures of prudence. The war of the West Indies was destined to have an issue similar to that which the catastrophe of Cornwallis had operated in Virginia. The allied courts had made formidable preparations for executing at last their long meditated projects against Jamaica. The Spaniards had, in the islands of St. Domingo and Cuba, a numerous fleet, and a considerable body of troops, both perfectly equipped, and in readiness to move wherever the good of the service might require. On the other hand, the count de Grasse was at Fort Royal in Martinico, with thirty-four sail of the line, and a great number of frigates. The French admiral was occupied with the care of refitting his fleet, while awaiting a second convoy, which departed from Brest early in February, and which brought him an immense quantity of arms and military stores, of which he stood in great need. After having terminated his preparations, his intention was, to effect his junction with the Spaniards at St. Domingo, in order to act in concert against Jamaica. Their combined forces were to consist of sixty sail of the line, and near twenty thousand land troops; a prodigious armament, and such as had never before been seen in those seas. The English were very far from having the means of resistance adequate to those of attack. When Rodney, who was then anchored at Barbadoes, had been joined by admiral Hood, and three ships of the line from England, he found himself at the head of no more than thirty-six sail of the line. The garrisons of the British islands were all very weak; and even in Jamaica there were only six battalions of troops, inclusive of militia. The terror was so great there, that the governor of the island proclaimed martial law, the effect of which was to suspend all civil authority, and to confer it entire upon the military commanders.

Admiral Rodney was perfectly aware that the success of the West Indian war, and the fate of all the British possessions in those seas, depended on two decisive events. It was necessary to intercept the Brest convoy before it should arrive at Martinico, and to prevent the French fleet from uniting with that of Spain at St. Domingo. In order to accomplish the first of these objects, he had put to sea, and so stationed his fleet to windward of the French islands, that it extended from the island of Desirade to that of St. Vincents; thus occupying the route usually followed by vessels coming from Europe bound to Martinico. He had also taken the precaution to detach his frigates still more to windward, that they might observe and promptly report to him all the movements of the enemy. But the French presaged the snare that was laid for them. Instead of taking the ordinary track, they stood with their convoy to the north of Desirade, and then keeping close under the lee of Guadaloupe and Dominica, brought it in safety to the bay of Port Royal in Martinico. This re-inforcement was most opportune for the French. It was, on the contrary, extremely fatal for the English, who had now no other means of averting their total ruin in those parts, but by preventing the junction of the fleets of France and Spain at St. Domingo. With this object in view, Rodney came to anchor in Gros Islet bay at St. Lucia, in order to be able to watch continually all that passed at Fort Royal. His frigates kept up a very active cruise; and in the meantime he took care to recruit his water and provisions, in order to be in a situation to keep the sea as long as possible. Meanwhile, the count de Grasse felt himself pressed to act. His instructions required it of him; and their object was of the last importance to the glory and prosperity of the French realm. On the safety of his convoy depended the success of the expedition of Jamaica. He sent it forward under the escort of two ships of the line, the Sagittaire and Experiment, and followed it shortly after with all his fleet. He would have wished to avail himself of the trade winds to sail directly towards St. Domingo; but he reflected that in so doing, incumbered as he was with upwards of a hundred transports, and the wind always blowing from the same point, it was almost impossible for him to keep out of the reach of the British fleet. It was evidently in the interests of his designs to avoid a battle; he therefore took a different route. He shaped his course to the northward, standing along near the shores of the islands with all his vast armament. Prudence could not but applaud this measure, and every thing promised its success. The pilots of the count de Grasse had the advantage over those of the enemy of being better acquainted with the bearings of these coasts, for the most part French or Spanish; and they might of course approach them as near as they should think proper. Besides, the different channels formed between these islands, offered both secure retreats and favorable winds for escaping the pursuit of the enemy. The French admiral might thus pass his convoy along the coasts, while his ships of war should form in order of battle to cover it against the attempts of his adversary. It was easy for the French by this means to keep to windward of the British, and consequently to preserve a free passage to St. Domingo. The count de Grasse had therefore sufficient grounds for hoping that all the vessels under his command would, by little and little, make their way good to the point of general rendezvous. The British frigates, which kept a diligent watch, soon apprised Rodney of the sailing of the French fleet. Immediately, with his accustomed promptitude, he put to sea in quest of the enemy. It was the ninth of April. Already the French had begun to pass Dominica, and were to leeward of that island when they descried the whole British fleet. The count de Grasse ordered the captains of the transports to crowd all sail and take shelter in the port of Guadaloupe. The two admirals prepared themselves for battle with equal skill and bravery. The Frenchman, however, chose to keep his enemy at a distance in order to give his convoy time to retire, and not to commit to the caprice of fortune a certain operation. The Englishman, on the contrary, felt that he could not engage his adversary too close, since there was no remedy for the critical situation of affairs except in a complete and decisive victory. The count de Grasse had thirty-three sail of the line; among which, one of one hundred and ten guns, the Ville de Paris, five of eighty, twenty-one of seventy-four, and the rest of sixty-four. The crews were complete, and there were on board the French fleet five or six thousand land troops, forming the garrison of the ships. The center was under the immediate orders of the count de Grasse; the marquis de Vaudreuil commanded the van, and M. de Bougainville the rear. The fleet of admiral Rodney consisted of thirty-six sail of the line, of which one of ninety-eight guns, five of ninety, twenty of seventy-four, and the others of sixty-four. The British van was commanded by vice-admiral Hood, and the rear-guard by rear-admiral Drake. The English were desirous to engage a general action, but they had not yet been able to get abreast of the island of Dominica, and their advance was retarded by calms. They endeavored nevertheless to profit of the puffs of wind which sprung up from time to time, in order to fetch the French. But the latter, favored by a breeze, made for Guadaloupe. The van of the British fleet receiving the wind soon after, admiral Hood seized the occasion to come up with the French within cannon-shot reach, and the action commenced towards nine o'clock in the morning. The count de Grasse was full of confidence at seeing that he could bring all his force to bear upon a part only of the enemy's.

The engagement was extremely fierce ; but however impetuous was the attack of the French, the British withstood it without losing their order.   The headmost ships of their center having at length a sufficiency of wind to carry them to the support of their van, which suffered excessively, they renewed the action with inexpressible fury. The French received their shock with a valor no less worthy of admiration.   Rodney's own ship, the Formidable, of ninety-eight guns, and his two seconds, the Namur and the Duke, both of ninety, made a tremendous fire.   The captain of a French seventy-four, so far from being dismayed at it, ordered his mainsail to be furled, that his crew might abandon all idea of retreat, and fight with the more desperation.   He waited the approach of the three British ships, and engaged them with admirable intrepidity.   His conduct inspired the English themselves with so much enthusiasm, that one of them, in a letter which was made public, did not hesitate to call him the *godlike Frenchman.*   The other ships of the British center came up successively, and the rear, under admiral Drake, was not far behind them.   But the French admiral, who had accomplished his purpose, thought proper to draw his ships out of action, and accordingly gave the signal for retreat.   Such was the issue of this first combat ; it would be difficult to decide on which part the most ability and gallantry were signalized.   The English made no attempt to follow their enemies, whether because the wind was less in their favor, or because their van, and especially the Royal Oak and the Montague, had been grievously damaged.   On observing this, the French admiral ordered the convoy, which had taken refuge at Guadaloupe, to put to sea again immediately, and continue its voyage.   This order was executed with as much precision as promptitude by M. de Langle, who commanded the convoy ; which a few days after arrived safe and entire at St. Domingo.   Some French ships had suffered considerably in the action.   Among others the Cato was so damaged, that it became necessary to send her to Guadaloupe to be repaired.   The Jason also had been so shattered in her engagement with the Zealous, that she was also obliged to make the best of her way to the same island.   These accidents prevented the count de Grasse from gaining so soon as he could have wished to windward of the group of islands called the Saints, in order afterwards to stand to windward of Desirade, and repair to St. Domingo by the north of the islands.   The English, after having hastily refitted their ships, had again set themselves to pursue the French.   The count de Grasse continued to beat to windward, in order to weather the Saints, and he was already arrived, on the eleventh, off Guadaloupe.   He had gained so much distance upon the British fleet, that its topsails only could be descried, and that with difficulty, by the French. Rodney had pushed his pursuit with all the diligence exacted by the urgency of the conjuncture; but he began to despair of overtaking the enemy. It was agitated in a council of war, whether it would not be better for the interests of their affairs to give over the direct pursuit of the enemy, and stand to leeward, in order to arrive, if possible, before them in the waters of St. Domingo. While this important point was under deliberation, and while an anxious lookout was kept at the mastheads, in painful expectation of the moment which was to decide the fate of Jamaica, and whether the empire of the West Indies was to remain with the French or with the English, a signal announced, about noon, the appearance of two French ships. They had fallen to the leeward, and were drifting continually nearer to the English. They were the Zélé, of seventy-four guns, a ship which seemed destined to bring disaster to the French fleet, and the frigate Astree, which the count de Grasse had detached to take her in tow. A little before, the Zélé had got foul of the Ville de Paris, and lost her foremast and mizzenmast in the shock. In consequence of this accident she was unable to keep up with the rest of the fleet. The English now conceived new hopes of engaging the battle for which they so ardently panted. They calculated that by bearing down rapidly to cut off the drifted ships, they should constrain the French admiral to come to their succor, and thereby place himself under the necessity of fighting. They accordingly maneuvered with so much promptitude and sagacity, that the two ships could no longer escape them, unless the French admiral bore down with his whole fleet for their preservation. It is thought, and not without reason, that if the count de Grasse, content with the glory acquired upon the coasts of Virginia, had known how to yield in time to fortune, and had abandoned the two fatal ships to the destiny that menaced them, he might easily have made his way good to St. Domingo. Once arrived in that island, where the forces of Spain would have joined his own, he might have given the final blow to the British power in the West Indies. He had already gained so far to windward, that if he had continued his voyage, it was become impossible for the English to come up with him. But deeming it contrary to the dignity and reputation of the mighty armament which he commanded, to suffer two ships to be taken almost under the fire of its guns, he took the brave but no less adventurous resolution of going to their succor; thus, for the sake of protecting an inconsiderable part of his fleet, exposing himself to the hazard of losing the whole. He formed his line of battle, bore down upon the English, and rescued the Zélé. But this movement had brought him so near to the enemy, that it was no longer in his power to avoid an engagement. The two admirals prepared for it with equal ardor. The same high spirit was shared by all their crews; there was not a sailor of the two nations who did not feel that he was about to contend for the honor of his sovereign, and the dominion of the West Indies. But the night was already come; it was employed on either side in making every preparation for the great day of the morrow.

The space of sea which was to serve as the field of battle, is contained between the islands of Guadaloupe, Dominica, the Saints, and Maria Galante. Both to windward and leeward, the waters abound in shoals and very dangerous reefs. The twelfth of April, at six in the morning, the two fleets found themselves drawn up in presence of each other, but on opposite tacks. The wind at this moment, having veered from east to southeast, became more favorable to the English. They profited of it without loss of time; their van and the greater part of their center ranged up to within half cannon-shot of the enemy, and commenced the attack with unexampled fury. The action lasted from seven in the morning till seven at night. The other ships of the center, and the greater part of those of the rear, edged up successively, and took part in the battle. Among them was distinguished the Barfleur, of ninety guns, the ship of admiral Hood. During this time the Zélé, towed by the Astree, was endeavoring to gain Guadaloupe.

Never did warriors the most inflamed with desire of victory, display more desperate valor or determined resolution, than the French and English in this memorable day. The broadsides, from their rapid succession, appeared continual, through the thick smoke that covered the two fleets, nothing was seen but the blaze of their guns, nothing was heard but the thunder of artillery, and the crash of the spars that were shivered into splinters. The Formidable, admiral Rodney's ship, discharged, in the course of this terrible conflict, no less than eighty broadsides; the Ville de Paris an equal number. The fight continued for several hours without any apparent superiority of success; almost all the ships were excessively shattered; the crews were exhausted with fatigue. From the very commencement of the action, the English, according to their custom, had endeavored to break the enemy's line of battle. But the wind was not strong enough; and the French, perceiving their design, held firm and repulsed them with vigor. Meanwhile the van and center of the count de Grasse had suffered extremely in their rigging, which occasioned a sensible retardment in the movements of these two divisions. The third commanded by M. de Bougainville, not having regulated its maneuvers by those of the rest of the line, had fallen into extreme disorder. To this fatal event, which could only be imputed to men, there soon succeeded another, originating in the contrariety of fortune. The wind became all at once so unfavorable to the French, that their sails filled aback; it was for the same reason extremely propitious to the English. Rodney took advantage of it instantly. He bore rapidly down with the Formidable, the Namur, the Duke and the Canada, and penetrated through the French line at the post occupied by the Glorieux, which was completely dismasted, at the distance of three ships from the Ville de Paris. His other ships were directed by signal to follow him. This order having been executed with great promptitude, the whole British fleet found itself to windward of the enemy's. From this moment the fate of the day could no longer be doubtful. The English wore round close upon their adversaries, who, broken and in total confusion, could ill withstand an enemy fighting in compact line, and animated by the prospect of infallible victory. The French protracted their resistance only by detached groups, or partial engagements of ship with ship. Their desperate situation, however, had not yet abated their courage. They endeavored to re-establish the line to leeward, but all their efforts were vain, though they signally honored their misfortune. The English of preference closed with those ships which they judged unable to escape them. The Canada engaged the Hector, which did not surrender till after having exhausted all its means of defense. The Centaur attacked the Cesar; they both remained entire. A furious action ensued. The French captain would not surrender. Three other ships of war assailed him; but after his ship had been battered to pieces, and his ensign-staff shot away, M. de Marigny, who commanded the Cesar, ordered his colors to be nailed to the mast, and redoubled the fire of all his batteries. He was slain; his successor defended himself with the same courage. At length his mainmast being fallen, and all his tackling destroyed, he yielded to number. The captain of the Glorieux did not surrender till after the most honorable resistance. The Ardent, after a no less gallant defense, fell also into the power of the English. The Diademe, torn all to pieces, went to the bottom. If all the French captains, whom fortune betrayed on this day, displayed an heroic bravery, none of them deserved more lasting praises than the unfortunate count de Grasse. He seemed inflexibly resolved rather to sink with his ship, than to surrender her to the enemy. Totally dismasted, and admitting the water on all parts, the Ville de Paris, after a combat of ten hours, continued to keep up a terrible fire with starboard and larboard guns. Captain Cornwallis, in the Canada, appeared to rest his glory upon reducing her; but by her very mass she repulsed all his efforts; six other British ships joined the Canada, to give the final blows to the French admiral, but still in vain. Several of his ships had attempted to succor him; at first his two seconds, the Languedoc and Couronne, then the Pluton and the Triumphant. But, overwhelmed by number, the captains of these ships had been constrained to abandon their captain-general to all the dangers of his position. The count de Grasse found his last hope extinct; his fleet, lately so flourishing, were either dispersed or fallen into the power of the enemy, but his invincible courage refused to bend. He persisted in this manner, facing with the most admirable intrepidity the repeated attempts that were made upon him from every quarter, till past six o'clock in the afternoon. Admiral Hood's approach in the Barfleur, of ninety guns, did not alter his determination. He bore a heavy fire from him during some time, without any appearance of yielding; and it was not till after a dreadful destruction of his people that he consented at last to strike. He and two more were the only men left standing upon the upper deck. Thus fell into the hands of the English the Ville de Paris, justly considered as one of the fairest ornaments of the French marine. This magnificent ship had been presented to Louis XV. by his capital, at the epoch of the disasters occasioned by the war of Canada. It had cost four millions of livres. Thirty-six chests of money, and the whole train of artillery, intended for the attack on Jamaica, became the prey of the victors. The English lost in this battle, and in that of the ninth, upwards of a thousand men. The loss of the French was much more considerable, without reckoning prisoners. The first had in particular to regret the captains Bayne and Blair of the Alfred and Anson. Lord Robert Manners, son of the marquis of Granby, a young man of the greatest promise, survived his wounds but a short time. This day cost life to six captains of French ships; among whom were the viscount d'Escars and M. de la Clocheterie; the first of the Glorieux, the second of the Hercule.

To reap the fruits of his victory, admiral Rodney would have wished to pursue the enemy after the battle. But as it grew dark, he thought it necessary, in order to secure his prizes, and to afford time for inquiring into the condition of the ships that had suffered in the action, to bring to for the night. The following morning he was still detained upon the coasts of Guadaloupe by a calm, which lasted three days. Having at length examined the bays and harbors of the neighboring French islands, and being satisfied that the enemy had sailed to leeward, Rodney dispatched sir Samuel Hood, whose division being in the rear, and coming up late, had suffered but little in the battle, to the west end of St. Domingo, in the hope that he might be able to pick up some of their disabled ships. Hood was afterwards to repair to Cape Tiberon, where admiral Rodney had appointed to meet him with the rest of his fleet.

With the exception of some French ships, which M. de Bougainville conducted to St. Eustatius to be repaired, all the others under the marquis de Vaudreuil, keeping together in a body, made the best of their way to Cape Francois. In the meantime, admiral Hood had arrived in the waters of St. Domingo, and while cruising in the Mora passage, which separates that island from Porto Rico, he descried four sail of French vessels, two of the line, and two of less force. These were the Jason and Caton, which were returning from the anchorage of Guadaloupe, with the frigate Aimable and the sloop of war Ceres. Their captains were not informed of the action of the twelfth of April, and were pursuing their voyage in full security. They fell into the midst of the squadron of sir Samuel Hood, who had little difficulty in forcing them to surrender. A fifth sail, which was discovered in the distance, had the fortune to escape the pursuit of the English by an unexpected shift of wind in her favor. Thus the French loss amounted to eight ships of the line; but the Diademe having been sunk, and the Cesar having blown up, there remained but six in the possession of the English, as trophies of their victory.

Admiral Hood rejoined sir George Rodney off Cape Tiberon; the latter then proceeded with the disabled ships and the prizes to Jamaica. The former remained, with twenty-five ships that had suffered the least, in the waters of St. Domingo, to watch the enemy, and prevent him from attempting any expedition of importance against the British possessions. Though discouraged by the check which they had just received, the allies were still formidable. They had at Cape Francois twenty-three sail of the line, under the marquis de Vaudreuil, and sixteen Spanish, commanded by don Solano. Their land forces amounted to near twenty thousand men. They relinquished, however, the enterprise of Jamaica, and indeed every sort of attempt in the West Indies. The Spaniards returned to the Havanna. Some French ships took under their guard a convoy of merchantmen, and arrived in Europe without accident. The marquis de Vaudreuil repaired with the rest of his fleet to the ports of North America. Thus ended the projects against Jamaica, and all this campaign in the West Indies. It produced afterwards one only event; the Bahama islands, which had hitherto served as a shelter for British privateers, surrendered the sixth of May to the Spanish arms. The French obtained also another success in the most northern regions of America; a feeble compensation of their late losses.

The marquis de Vaudreuil, a little before his departure for the United States, had detached M. de la Peyrouse, with the ship of war Sceptre, and the frigates Astree and Engageante. His instructions were, to repair to Hudson's bay, and do all the harm possible to the establishments of the British northwest company. The expedition succeeded completely ; the English estimated the damage he caused them at seven millions of livres. It was much more remarkable for the almost insurmountable obstacles which the nature of the places and climate presented to the French, than for the resistance of their enemies, whom they surprised in full security and without defense. The coasts were difficult and little known, and the shoals very dangerous. Though it was only the last of July when the ships of the expedition arrived in Hudson's bay, yet the cold was already so rigorous there, and the masses of floating ice so numerous, that they were very near being shut up for the winter in those bleak and dismal regions.

In the meantime, admiral Rodney had repaired to Jamaica; he had made a triumphal entry into the port of Kingston. The inhabitants of the island crowded with eagerness to behold their deliverer, and to enjoy the spectacle of the victorious and of the captured ships. But no object more excited their curiosity, than the French admiral himself, who, already become illustrious by great success in America, and ready but now to fall upon their island at the head of the most formidable armament, appeared there at present as a memorable example of the caprices of fortune. The victory of Rodney and the exultation of the colonists did not, however, cause them to forget what generosity exacted of them towards an unfortunate enemy. They loaded him with all the attentions which they judged suitable to console him.

Meanwhile, before the news of the victory of the twelfth of April had reached England, admiral Pigot had been appointed to the command of the West India fleet, in the room of Rodney. The latter obeyed without delay, and departed for Europe after having embarked the count de Grasse in the homeward bound Jamaica convoy. The odious pillage committed at St. Eustatius, had brought Rodney into great discredit with the public. His conduct had been censured with extreme asperity even in parliament. The complaints which arose on all parts against this admiral, might have contributed no less to his recall than his attachment to the party in opposition to ministers. But when arrived in England, he answered his accusers only by showing them the count de Grasse prisoner. Immediately, the infamous spoiler of St. Eustatius became the idol of the nation. Those same individuals, who had inveighed against him with the most vehemence, showed themselves the most forward to load him with panegyric in the same measure.

The count de Grasse encountered in England the most honorable reception ; he owed it perhaps as much to ostentation as to politeness. As soon as he was arrived at London, he was presented to the king, and waited on by all the great. The people assembled in throngs before the hotel where he lodged ; forced to appear at the balcony, the multitude greeted him with loud acclamations, and applauses without end. They called him the brave, the valiant Frenchman. Such is the fascination of courage even in an enemy ! In the public places where the count made his appearance, numerous crowds gathered about him, not to insult him, but, on the contrary, to pay him homage. The enthusiasm of the people of London seemed to redouble, when it was generally agreed to find him an English physiognomy. He was obliged to consent to have his portrait painted ; copies of it were profusely distributed throughout the country ; and whoever was without it, exposed himself to be accounted a bad patriot. Admiral Rodney was created an English peer, by the title of lord Rodney. Hood was honored with an Irish peerage ; Drake and Affleck with baronetages.

The grief which the news of the disaster of the twelfth of April produced in France, was the more profound, as it immediately succeeded the most sanguine hope. But the French, constant in their gayety, and intrepid by their nature, rapidly lose impressions of sadness ; they soon resumed courage. The king was the first to give the example of firmness ; it was imitated by all France. In order to repair the losses of his marine, the monarch ordered the immediate construction of twelve ships of the line of one hundred and ten, eighty, and seventy-four guns. The counts de Provence and d'Artois, his brothers, offered him each one of eighty ; the prince of Conde one of one hundred and ten, in the name of the states of Burgundy. The chamber of commerce, with the six corps of retailers of the city of Paris, the merchants of Marseilles, of Bordeaux, of Lyons, resolved with the same zeal to furnish to the state each a ship of one hundred and ten guns. The receivers-general of the revenue, the farmers-general, and other financial companies, offered to advance considerable sums. All these offers were accepted, but not those which patriotism had dictated to private citizens ; the king, not willing to increase the burdens that already weighed upon his people, ordered the sums which had been subscribed or advanced by particulars, to be placed again at their disposal. Thus the ardent zeal which manifested itself in all parts towards the country and the sovereign, raised the French above the malice of adverse fortune, and cheered them with new hopes of a brilliant future.

We have seen the war brought to an end upon the American continent, by the irreparable check which the arms of England sustained at Yorktown; and we have also seen it suspended in the West Indies, by the disaster of the French marine. We shall now return from those distant regions, to consider the issue of this long and bloody war in that part of the globe which we inhabit, and in those countries whence it drew its principal aliment. The attention of all the informed part of mankind was turned upon the siege of Gibraltar. For many ages, Europe had not witnessed an enterprise of this sort which presented more formidable difficulties, or more important results.

Admiral Howe had sailed for the relief of that fortress. Various were the conjectures of men respecting the success of his efforts. Some, full of confidence in the dexterity and audacity of the English, inferred from the event of their preceding expeditions, the most favorable issue to this; others, reflecting upon the naval superiority of the allied courts, and impressed with esteem for the talents and valor of the count de Guichen and don Lewis de Cordova, formed a contrary opinion. In one place, the extraordinary preparations that had been made and were still making by the besiegers, appeared to answer for the approaching fall of Gibraltar. In another, on the contrary, the strength of its position, the perfection of its works, and the intrepidity of its defenders, seemed to place it beyond the reach of danger. Every where but one opinion prevailed upon this point; that the obstacles were numerous, and that blood must stream copiously before they were all surmounted. But the very hazards of this great enterprise so inflamed the valor of all warlike men, that even those who were not called to take an active part in it, wished at least to be spectators of the glorious scenes that were about to be represented at the foot of this formidable rock. Hence it was, that not only from France and Spain, but also from Germany, and the remoter regions of the north, the most distinguished personages were seen hastening to arrive at the camp of St. Roch, and in the port of Algesiras. Even those nations which are accounted barbarous, and who have communicated that appellation to so large and so fine a portion of Africa, were seized with an irresistible curiosity; they repaired to the nearest shores in order to contemplate a spectacle so new for them. All was in movement in the camp, in the arsenals, and aboard the fleets of the allies. From the summit of his rock, Elliot awaited with an heroic constancy the attack with which he was menaced. But before relating the memorable events that ensued, it appears to us necessary to enter into a description of the places, and of the works within and without the citadel ; and to trace an outline of the plans and preparations of the besiegers.

The fortress of Gibraltar is seated upon a rock which projects in the form of a tongue for the space of a league, from north to south, out of the continent of Spain, and which is terminated by a promontory called the point of Europe. The top of this rock is elevated a thousand feet above the level of the sea. Its eastern flank, or that which looks towards the Mediterranean, is entirely composed of a living rock, and so perpendicularly steep as to be absolutely inaccessible. The point of Europe, which is also of solid rock, slopes and terminates in an esplanade, which rises twenty feet above the sea ; here the English had planted a battery of twenty pieces of heavy artillery. Behind this point the promontory dilates, and there is formed a second esplanade, which overlooks the first, and affords space enough for the troops of the garrison to parade in without difficulty. As the declivity is gentle, and of easy access, the English have made cuts in the rock in front, and surrounded the platform with a wall fifteen feet in height and as many in thickness, copiously furnished with artillery. Within this platform they have constructed, besides, an intrenched camp, which offers them a secure retreat in case they should be driven from their outer works. From this post they communicate with another still more elevated, and situated among steep and irregular masses ; here the besieged had established their camp. Upon the western flank of the promontory, and upon the seashore, the town of Gibraltar itself occupied a long and narrow space. It had been almost totally destroyed by the artillery, in one of the preceding attacks. It is closed on the south by a wall, on the north by an ancient fortification called the castle of the Moors, and in front, next the sea, by a parapet sixteen feet thick, and furnished from distance to distance with batteries, which fire level with the water. Behind the town, the mountain rises abruptly quite to its summit. The English, for the greater security of this part, have constructed two other works, which project considerably into the sea. Both are armed with formidable batteries. The first, which looks to the north, is called the Old Mole ; the second the New Mole. Not content with these defenses, they have erected in front of the castle of the Moors, and of Old Mole, another work consisting in two bastions, connected by a curtain, of which the scarp and covered way, being well countermined throughout, are very difficult to mine. The object of this construction is to sweep, by a raking fire, that narrow strip of land which runs between the rock and the sea, and which forms the only communication of the Spanish continent with the fortress. In the front of this work, the water of the sea had been introduced by means of dikes and sluices, which, forming a pool or fen, adds much to the strength of this part.   The north side, or that which faces Spain, is by far the loftiest flank of the rock.   It fronts the camp of St. Roch, and presents upon all its surface a prodigious quantity of batteries which descend in tiers towards the Spanish camp.   Thus art had combined with nature to make of this immense rock an impregnable citadel.   Between the promontory of Gibraltar and the coast of Spain, lies, towards the west, a deep gap filled by the waters of the sea ; it is the bay of Gibraltar or of Algesiras.   The port and city of this name are situated upon the western shore of the bay. The garrison of Algesiras amounted to little over seven thousand men, with about two hundred and fifty officers.   Such was the nature of that rock, against which the Spanish monarchy displayed the greatest part of its forces, and invoked besides the powerful assistance of France.   This enterprise was the object of the most ardent wishes of Charles III. ; he considered the honor of his crown as deeply interested in its success.   The king of France likewise saw in the reduction of Gibraltar the termination of the war.   In order to push the operations of the siege and secure its success, the conduct of it was committed to the duke de Crillon ; the public opinion designated the victor of Minorca as the conqueror of Gibraltar.

The preparations directed against this place exceeded every thing that had ever been heard of in like circumstances.   Upwards of twelve hundred pieces of heavy cannon, eighty-three thousand barrels of powder, a proportionable quantity of bombs and balls, were destined to batter the works of the English.   Forty gunboats, with as many bomb ketches, were to open their fire on the side of the bay, under cover of a formidable fleet of fifty sail of the line, twelve French, the others Spanish.   Frigates and light vessels hovered in front of this line, in waiting to carry succor wherever it might be wanted.   Upwards of three hundred large boats had been assembled from all parts of Spain, which came to join the immense number already in the bay of Algesiras.   It was intended to employ them, during the attack, in carrying munitions and necessaries to the ships of war, and in landing the troops as soon as the works should be ruined.   Nor were the preparations by land inferior to those that were made by sea.   The Spaniards had already advanced by sap ; and their lines, as soon as they were terminated, presented an astonishing number of batteries of heavy artillery.   Twelve thousand French troops were brought to diffuse their peculiar vivacity and animation through the Spanish army, as well as for tl e benefit to be derived from the example and exertions of their supe rior discipline and experience. At sight of the immense warlike apparatus assembled against the place, and of the ardor manifested by the soldiers, the generals who directed the siege considered themselves as so sure of success, that they were upon the point of ordering, without further delay, a general assault. They had resolved, that while the land forces should assail the fortress on the side of the isthmus, the fleet should batter it upon all the points contiguous to the sea. They hoped that the garrison, already little numerous, experiencing besides a great diminution in dead and wounded, would be totally incapable of sufficing for the defense of so extensive works. The loss of some thousands of men, and several ships of the line, would have seemed to the besiegers but a slender price for so inestimable a conquest. Meanwhile, the project of an attack by main force was not adopted by all the members of the council. Those who blamed its temerity, observed, that until the defenses of the place on the land side were entirely prostrated, to attempt the assault would be sending the troops to a certain death, without any hope of success. On the part of the sea, they showed that an attack would be attended with the inevitable destruction of the ships, without producing the smallest effect upon the fortress. ' Nevertheless,' they added, ' as a simple attack by land must necessarily be fruitless, it is highly desirable that a kind of ships could be procured more capable of resisting artillery than those of an ordinary construction.' It could not be expected to carry Gibraltar by an attack of short duration ; but was it possible to prolong it without hazarding the ruin of the fleet ? This consideration occupied the thought of several men of talents. They presented plans of various inventions, all having for object to facilitate the battering of the fortress on the part of the sea. These schemes were examined with extreme attention. Several were rejected as incompetent to the purpose in view, none as too expensive. At length, after long deliberation, it was agreed to adopt the plan of the chevalier d'Arcon, a French engineer of high note ; it was thought ingenious and infallible. His project went to the construction of floating batteries, or ships, upon such a principle, that they could neither be sunk nor fired. The first of these properties was to be acquired by the extraordinary thickness of timber, with which their keels and bottoms were to be fortified ; the second, by securing the sides of the ships, wherever they were exposed to shot, with a strong wall, composed of timber and cork, a long time soaked in water, and including between a large body of wet sand. But the ingenious projector, not being yet satisfied with his work, and wishing to render it more proof against the redhot shot from the fortress, executed a contrivance for communicating water in every direction to restrain its effect.   In imitation of the circulation of the blood in a living body, a great variety of pipes and canals perforated all the solid workmanship, in such a manner, that a continued succession of water was to be conveyed to every part of the vessels; a number of pumps being adapted to the purpose of an unlimited supply.   By this means, it was expected that the redhot shot would operate to the remedy of its own mischief; as the very action of cutting through those pipes would procure its immediate extinction.

To protect his floating batteries from bombs, and the men at the batteries from grape or descending shot, the chevalier d'Arcon had contrived a hanging roof, which was to be worked up and down with ease, and at pleasure.   The roof was composed of a strong rope-work netting, laid over with a thick covering of wet hides; while its sloping position was calculated to prevent the shells from lodging, and to throw them off into the sea before they could take effect.   All this scaffolding was constructed upon the hulks of great ships, from six hundred to fourteen hundred tons burthen, cut down to the state required by the plan.   There were ten of these floating batteries; they were armed in all with a hundred and fifty-four pieces of heavy brass cannon, that were mounted; and something about half the number of spare guns were kept ready to supply the place of those which might be overheated, or otherwise disabled in action.   The Pastora alone, which was the largest, carried twenty-four in battery, and twelve in reserve.   The Talla Piedra, commanded by the prince of Nassau, and the Paula, which was also one of the stoutest, mounted a no less numerous artillery.   That its fire might not be slackened by losses in dead or wounded, thirty-six men, as well Spaniards as French, were allotted to the service of each piece. The command of this flotilla had been confided to admiral don Moreno, a seaman of equal valor and ability, who had served with distinction at the siege of Port Mahon.   The vast bulk of the battering ships, the materials employed in their construction, and the weight of their artillery, seemed likely to render them extremely heavy and unmanageable.   They were, however, rigged with so much skill and ingenuity, that they executed their various evolutions with all the ease and dexterity of frigates.

When all these preparations were completed, there were few persons in the camp of the besiegers who did not consider the fall of a place so vigorously attacked as inevitable.   It was at this epoch, towards the middle of August, that two French princes arrived at the army before Gibraltar; the count d'Artois, and the duke de Bourbon.   The object of their mission was to animate the troops by their presence, and that they might themselves come in for a share of the glory of so signal and illustrious an enterprise. The army were impatient to receive the signal of attack ; their ardor had more need of restraint than incitement. So sanguine was the general hope, that the duke de Crillon was thought extremely cautious of hazarding an opinion, when he allowed so long a term as fourteen days to the certainty of being in possession of Gibraltar. Twenty-four hours appeared more than sufficient.

The arrival of the French princes afforded an opportunity for the display of that politeness, and the exercise of those humanized attentions and civilities, by which the refined manners of modern Europe have tended so much to divest war of many parts of its ancient savage barbarity. The Spaniards had intercepted some packets, containing a number of letters directed to the officers in Gibraltar, and had transmitted them to the court of Madrid, where they lay at the time that the count d'Artois arrived at that capital. The French prince obtained the packets from the king, and on his arrival at the camp, had them forwarded to their address. The duke de Crillon sent with them a letter to general Elliot, in which, besides informing him of this particular mark of attention shown by the count d'Artois, he farther acquainted him that he was charged by the French princes, respectively, to convey to the general the strongest expressions of their regard and esteem for his person and character. He requested, in the most obliging terms, that he would accept of a present of fruit and vegetables, for his own use, which accompanied the letter, and of some ice and partridges for the gentlemen of his household ; farther entreating, that as he knew the general lived entirely upon vegetables, he would acquaint him with the particular kinds which he liked best, with a view to his regular supply. General Elliot answered with the same politeness; he returned many thanks to the princes and the duke de Crillon, for the flattering attentions they were pleased to show him. But he informed the duke that in accepting the present, he had broken through a resolution which he had invariably adhered to from the commencement of the war, which was, never to receive, or to procure by any means whatever, any provisions or other commodity for his own private use ; and that he made it a point of honor, to partake of both plenty and scarcity, in common with the lowest of his brave fellow-soldiers. He therefore entreated the duke not to heap any more favors of the same kind upon him, as he could not in future apply them to his own use. This exchange of courtesies was deemed worthy of their authors, and of the sovereigns they represented.

But while these civilities were passing, as in the midst of profound peace, the dispositions were in process for redoubling the horrors of

war. Elliot had hitherto observed in a sort of inaction the prepara
tions of the besiegers, when all of a sudden he saw issuing from the
port of Algesiras the enormous masses of the floating batteries. If
his courage was not shaken, he could not, however, but feel at least a
strong emotion of surprise. In this uncertainty as to what might be
the effect of those new invented machines, prudence urged him to
make every defensive preparation that was calculated to elude and
defeat it. Confiding, moreover, in the strength of the place, and
the valor of his garrison, he was under no apprehension for the issue
of the approaching attack. He did more ; he resolved to anticipate
it, by attacking himself. The besiegers had pushed their works with
so much diligence that some of them were already far advanced
towards the fortress. The governor determined to try how far a
vigorous cannonade and bombardment with redhot balls, carcasses,
and shells, might operate to their destruction. A powerful and
admirably directed firing accordingly commenced from the garrison,
at seven o'clock in the morning of the eighth of September. By
ten o'clock, the Mahon battery, with another adjoining to it, were in
flames ; and by five in the evening were entirely consumed, togethei
with their gun-carriages, platforms and magazines, although the latter
were bomb proof. A great part of the communications to the eastern parallel, and of the trenches and parapet for musketry, were
likewise destroyed ; and a large battery near the bay suffered excessively ; the works were on fire in fifty places at the same instant. It
was not without extreme exertions and considerable loss that the
besiegers at length succeeded in extinguishing the flames, and preserving their works from total destruction.

This affront was so much resented by the duke de Crillon, that
having pressed the reparation of his works during the night, he
unmasked all his batteries by break of day on the following morning ; they mounted one hundred and ninety-three pieces of cannon
and mortars, and continued to pour their fire of shot and shells, without intermission, upon the garrison, through the whole course of the
day. At the same time, a part of the fleet, taking the advantage of
a favorable wind, dropped down from the Orange Grove at the head
of the bay, and passing slowly along the works, discharged their shot
at the Old Mole and the adjoining bastions, continuing their cannonade until they had passed Europa Point and got into the Mediterranean. They then formed a line to the eastward of the rock, and
the admiral leading, came to the attack of the batteries on the point,
and under a very slow sail, commenced a heavy fire with all their
guns. But these combined efforts did very little harm to the besieg-

ed. There prevailed for some days a calm, which was soon to be interrupted by a most sanguinary combat.

The thirteenth of September was destined to witness an ever memorable conflict. History, in effect, presents nothing more terrible for the desperate fierceness and resolution of the two parties, nor more singular for the species of arms, nor more glorious for the humanity manifested by the conquerors. The season beginning to be late, and admiral Howe approaching with intent to re-victual Gibraltar, the allied commanders felt the necessity of precipitating the attack they meditated. According to the plan agreed upon, the artillery of the lines, the floating batteries, the ships of war and gunboats were to attack the place upon all points at once. While the cannon, mortars and howitzers of the isthmus kept up a heavy fire on the land side, it was intended that the floating batteries should direct their fire against the works which commanded the bay, taking their station in front of the Old Mole. At the same time, the gun and mortar boats, with the bomb-ketches, taking post on the two flanks of the line of battering ships, were to enfilade the British artillery which defended the fortifications constructed upon the margin of the sea. As to the fleet, it was destined to concur no less effectually to the attack, according to the wind or the necessity of the service. In this manner, the fortress would be battered simultaneously by four hundred pieces of ordnance, without including the artillery afloat.

General Elliot, on his part, had neglected nothing that could enable him to make a vigorous defense. The soldiers were at their posts, the artillerists at their places with lighted matches ; numerous furnaces were prepared for heating the shot. At seven in the morning, the ten battering ships, under the conduct of admiral don Moreno, put themselves in motion. Between nine and ten they came to an anchor, being moored in a line, at moderate distances, from the Old to the New Mole, lying parallel to the rock, and at about nine hundred yards distance. The admiral's ship was stationed opposite the king's bastion ; and the others took their appointed places successively, and with great regularity, on his right and left. The cannonade and bombardment, on all sides, and in all directions, from the isthmus, the sea, and the various works of the fortress, was not only tremendous, but beyond example. The prodigious showers of redhot balls, of bombs, and of carcasses, which filled the air, and were without intermission thrown to every point of the various attacks, both by sea and by land, from the garrison, astonished even the commanders of the allied forces. The battering ships, however, appeared to be the principal objects of vengeance, as they were of apprehension, to the garrison ; but such was the excellence of their construction that they not only resisted this terrible fire, but answered it with equal fury ; and already they had operated a breach in the works of the Old Mole.   The result of so many mutual efforts seemed for a long time uncertain.   At length, however, some smoke began to issue from the upper part of the battering ships Pastora and Talla Piedra.   It was caused by some redhot balls, which had penetrated so far into their sides, that they could not be extinguished by the water of the internal canals.   They had set fire to the contiguous parts, which, after smouldering for some time, suddenly broke out in flames.   The men were seen, at the hazard of life, using fire engines, and pouring water into the shot-holes.   This fire, though kept under during the continuance of daylight, could never be thoroughly subdued.   The disorder in these two commanding ships in the center, affected the whole line of attack ; and by the evening the fire from the fortress had gained a decided superiority.   The fire was continued from the batteries in the fortress with equal vigor through the night, and by one o'clock in the morning the first two batteries were in flames, and the others visibly on fire, whether by the effect of the redhot shot, or, as the Spaniards pretended, that they were purposely set on fire, when it appeared no longer possible to save them.   The confusion was now extreme.   Rockets were continually thrown up by each of the ships, as signals to the fleet of their distress and danger.   These signals were immediately answered, and all means used by the fleet to afford the assistance they required ; but as it was deemed impossible to remove the battering ships, their endeavors were only directed to bringing off the men.   A great number of boats were accordingly employed, and great intrepidity displayed, in the attempts for this purpose ; the danger from the burning vessels, filled as they were with instruments of destruction, appearing no less dreadful than the fire from the garrison, terrible as that was, since the light thrown out on all sides by the flames afforded the utmost precision in its direction.   Never, perhaps, has a more deplorable spectacle passed before the eyes of men.   The thick darkness which covered the land and waters in the distance contrasted with the frightful glare of the flames which devoured so many victims ; in the midst of the roar of artillery their dolorous cries were audible.   A new incident occurred to interrupt the attempts that were made for their rescue, and to complete the general confusion and destruction.   Captain Curtis, a seaman as able as he was adventurous, advanced at this moment with twelve gunboats, each carrying one eighteen or twenty-four pounder.   They had been constructed to oppose those of the Spaniards, and their low fire and fixed aim rendered them extremely formidable. Captain Curtis drew them up in such a manner as to flank the line of battering ships. The scene was wrought up by this fierce and unexpected attack to the highest point of calamity. The Spanish boats dared no longer to approach, and were compelled to the hard necessity of abandoning their ships and friends to the flames, or to the mercy of a heated and irritated enemy. Several of their boats and launches had been sunk before they submitted to this necessity; and one in particular, with fourscore men on board, who were all drowned, excepting an officer and twelve men, who, having the fortune to float on the wreck under the walls, were taken up by the garrison. Some feluccas had taken shelter upon the coast during the night, but as soon as the day appeared, the English soon compelled them to surrender. It seemed that nothing could have exceeded the horrors of the night; but the opening of daylight disclosed a spectacle still more dreadful. Numbers of men were seen in the midst of the flames, crying out for pity and help; others floating upon pieces of timber, exposed to an equal though less dreadful danger from the opposite element. Even those in the ships, where the fire had yet made a less progress, expressed in their looks, gestures, and words, the deepest distress and despair, and were no less urgent in imploring assistance. Moved with compassion at this dismal scene, the English discontinued their fire, and thought only of saving the enemy they had vanquished; a conduct the more generous, as it was attended with manifest peril. Captain Curtis in particular acquired an imperishable glory, by showing himself regardless of his own existence in his endeavors to preserve that of his enemies. He advanced intrepidly with his boats towards the burning ships, in order to rescue those who were about to become the prey of the one or other element. He was himself the first to rush on board the blazing batteries, and to set the example of dragging with his own hands the terrified victims from the jaws of destruction. Meanwhile death hovered incessantly round him. He was equally exposed to the peril arising from the blowing up of the ships as the fire reached their magazines, and to the continual discharge on all sides of the artillery, as the guns became to a certain degree heated. Several of his people were killed or severely wounded in this honorable enterprise. He was near sharing the fate of one of the largest ships, which blew up only a few moments after he left her. Near four hundred men were thus saved, by the noble exertions of Curtis, from inevitable death. The French and Spaniards, however, lost no less than fifteen hundred men, including the prisoners and wounded, in the attack by sea. The wounded that fell into the power of the conqueror were carried to the hospitals of the fortress, and treated with the greatest humanity. Nine floating batteries were burnt by the redhot shot, or by the Spaniards themselves. The tenth was burnt by the English when they found she could not be brought off. Their loss was inconsiderable; it amounted, according to their account, since the ninth of August, to no more than sixty-five killed, and three hundred and eighty-eight wounded. The fortifications received but slight damage; or at least not so considerable as to afford any room for future apprehension.

In this manner was victory obtained with lasting glory to general Elliot, and the whole garrison of Gibraltar. The treasures which the king of Spain had expended for the construction of these enormous machines, the bravery and perseverance of his troops, the valor and spirit of the French, were all in vain.

It cannot indeed be positively affirmed, that if such formidable means of attack had even been employed in all their efficacy, and according to the intention of the generals, they would have sufficed to carry the place; but neither can it be denied that the allies committed several faults of no little importance. The first was undoubtedly that of having hurried on the attack before M. d'Arcon had been able to bring his floating batteries to that degree of perfection which he could have wished. By working the pumps, he had perceived that the water of the pipes leaked upon the inward parts, and that the powder was exposed to be wet by it, and rendered unfit for use. He would have found a remedy for this inconvenience; but he was not allowed time to seek it. The inner pipes were therefore stopped up, and only the outer ones filled with water, which were found an insufficient defense against the effect of the redhot shot. It is, besides, to be considered that don Moreno was ordered so abruptly to repair to the attack from the point of Majorca, that he found it impossible to form the line of his floating batteries in front of the Old Mole, as contemplated in the plan of attack. From that point his fire would assuredly have been more efficacious, and he might also have retired thence without difficulty if he had thought it necessary; but he was constrained to take post between the Old and the New Mole. Nor did the Spanish gunboats answer the general expectation, whether they were in effect opposed by the wind, as was pretended, or that their spirit of adventure sunk under the dreadful fire from the garrison Only two of them took any considerable share in the attack. The great fleet itself remained in a state of almost total inaction. It is uncertain whether this failure should be attributed to an unfavorable wind, or to secret jealousies between the land and sea commanders. The batteries on shore, whatever was the cause of it, were equally far from performing the services which were expected from them. Their fire was neither so well supported, nor so well directed as it should have been. It resulted from these several causes, that the garrison, instead of being disquieted upon all points at the same instant, found themselves at liberty to direct the whole weight and force of their fire against the floating batteries. In this manner was disconcerted the most ingenious design which for a long time had been framed by the wisdom of man. The most sanguine hopes suddenly gave place to the opinion, that Gibraltar was not only the strongest place known, but that it was absolutely inexpugnable.

Convinced by this attack, that a regular siege could not have the desired issue, the allied commanders resolved to convert it into a blockade, and to await from famine what they despaired of obtaining by dint of arms. It was therefore of the highest importance to prevent admiral Howe from throwing into the place the intended relief.

The combined fleet had accordingly taken its anchorage in the bay of Algesiras, to the number of about fifty sail of the line; among which were five of one hundred and ten guns, and the Trinidad, of one hundred and twelve. The design of don Lewis de Cordova, the commander of these forces, was to engage the British fleet as soon as it should appear, while his light squadron should give chase to the transports, and capture them, one after another. It is not easy to explain why this admiral, instead of advancing to meet the enemy off Cape St. Mary, where he would have been able to display his whole line, took the determination to await him in a narrow bay, where the number of his ships, so far from being an advantage, could only tend to embarrass him. It appears that this disposition emanated immediately from the king of Spain, whose thoughts were all absorbed in the conquest of Gibraltar.

In the meantime, admiral Howe met with much delay through contrary winds and unfavorable weather, on his way to Gibraltar. His anxiety was therefore extreme, lest the place should find itself necessitated to surrender before the arrival of succors. It was not till the fleet had arrived near the scene of action that his apprehensions were removed, by intelligence received from the coast of Portugal, of the total discomfiture of the combined forces. This news increased his hope of succeeding in his enterprise; he calculated that the enemy, discouraged by so severe a check, would show himself less eager to encounter him. Near the mouth of the straits he met with a furious gale of wind, which damaged several of his ships. The combined fleet suffered much more in the bay of Algesiras. One ship of the line was driven ashore near the city of that name;

another fine Spanish ship, of seventy-two guns, was driven across the bay, under the works of Gibraltar, and was taken by the boats of the garrison. Two more were driven to the eastward into the Mediterranean; others lost masts or bowsprits; and many suffered more or less damage.

On the morning that succeeded the storm, the British fleet entered the straits' mouth in a close line of battle ahead, and in the evening of the same day it was opposite the port of Gibraltar; but the wind failing, only four victualing ships could enter the harbor. The rest of the transports, with the squadron, were drifted by the currents into the Mediterranean. The combined fleet took the same direction. A general action seemed inevitable; a calm and fog which came up, prevented it; or perhaps the admirals themselves were not disposed to engage, without all probabilities of success. However it was, admiral Howe, profiting dexterously of an east wind which sprung up in the strait, passed his whole convoy to Gibraltar harbor. To cover this operation, the British fleet had formed in order of battle at the mouth of the straits, fronting the Mediterranean, between the opposite points of Europa and Ceuta.

The combined fleets then made their appearance, bearing directly down upon the enemy; but the British admiral considering that the re-victualing of Gibraltar, the principal object of his mission, was accomplished, he saw that it would be the highest imprudence and rashness to hazard an action in the strait. He knew the superiority of force that he would have to encounter; and he could not but perceive that the vicinity of the enemy's coasts would exceedingly aggravate, for him, the consequences of a defeat. He chose, if he was obliged to come to action, to have sea room enough, in order, by his evolutions, to prevent its being decisive, as it must necessarily be in a confined space. Under these considerations, he took the advantage of a favorable wind, and re-passed the straits into the Atlantic.

The allies followed him with only a part of their fleet. Twelve of their largest ships of the line, being heavy sailers, were left behind. Meanwhile their van came within reach of the British rear, and there immediately ensued between them a brisk, though distant cannonade, the only effect of which was to damage some vessels on both sides. Profiting of their superiority of sailing, the English drew off to such a distance, that the allies lost all hope of coming up with them. They then took the resolution of repairing to Cadiz. Admiral Howe detached eight of his ships for the West Indies, six others to the coasts of Ireland, and returned with the rest to Portsmouth. The destruction of the floating batteries and the re-victualing of Gibraltar, relieved England from all disquietude respecting the fate of that place. This double success was no less glorious for her arms, than afflicting for the enemies she combated. The allies are reproached with having shown upon land too much precipitancy and too little concord ; upon sea, too much indecision and too little spirit. In this occurrence, as in those which had preceded it, the display of their great naval forces had resulted in little more than a vain parade. It is, however, to be considered, that if, during the course of all this war, the fleets of the allied courts gained no brilliant advantages, or rather sustained reverses, in general actions, their seamen more often than once acquired signal renown in particular engagements of ship with ship. The French, especially, manifested in these rencounters a valor and ability alike worthy of admiration, and often crowned with victory. We leave those to account for this difference who are more versed than ourselves in naval tactics.

The events which we have related, as well in this as in the foregoing book, had occasioned among the belligerent powers an ardent desire, or rather an avowed will, to put an end to the war. On all sides, a hope was cherished that an honorable adjustment would soon be brought about. Several successive campaigns, without any important advantage, and the loss of the army taken at Yorktown, with lord Cornwallis, had at length convinced the British ministry of the impossibility of subjugating the Americans by force of arms. The maneuvers employed to divide them among themselves, or to detach them from their allies, had not been attended with any better success than military operations. On the other hand, the victories of Rodney and Elliot had not only dissipated all fears for the West Indies and Gibraltar, but also put in safety the honor of Great Britain. With the exception of the independence of the United States, which she could no longer refuse to acknowledge, she found herself in a situation to treat upon a footing of equality with her enemies relative to all other articles. Victorious at Gibraltar, holding the scale of fortune even in the seas of Europe, she had caused it to incline in her favor in the West Indies. If she had sustained sensible losses in that quarter, she had, however, acquired the island of St. Lucia, so important from its strength, the excellence of its ports, and the advantages of its position. Although it could not be considered as a sufficient indemnification on the part of Great Britain for the loss of Dominica, Grenada, Tobago, and St. Christophers, yet England had made so considerable conquests in the East Indies that she brought into a negotiation more objects of exchange than France could offer. But all these considerations yielded to another of far greater moment; the public debt of Great Britain, already enormous, experienced every day an alarming augmentation. The people did not conceal their desire for the return of peace, and the protraction of the war excited public murmurs. The ministers themselves, who had so severely censured the obstinacy of their predecessors in continuing the war, openly inclined for peace ; whether because they thought it really necessary, or that they were afraid of incurring similar reproaches. An untimely death had carried off the marquis of Rockingham, who, in the general direction of affairs, had conciliated universal esteem, and Fox had resigned. The first had been replaced by the earl of Shelburne, and the second by William Pitt, son of the earl of Chatham ; both known for consenting rather from necessity than choice to the independence of America. The majority of the ministry, however, was composed of those who had obtained the repeal of the rigorous laws against the Americans, and who had afterwards distinguished themselves in parliament by advocating with singular warmth and eloquence an early acknowledgment of their independence. It was therefore determined to send Thomas Grenville to Paris, in order to sound the intentions of the French government, and to prepare the ways for the plenipotentiaries that were to follow him. A short time after, in effect, M. Fitz Herbert and M. Oswald repaired to the French capital in that character; they had little difficulty in penetrating the dispositions of the court of Versailles. The United States had taken care that their plenipotentiaries should assemble at Paris in this conjuncture; they were John Adams, Benjamin Franklin, John Jay, and Henry Laurens, who had recently been released from his detention in the tower of London.

If great was the desire of peace in England, it was not less ardently wished for in France, as well by the government as by the people. The court of Versailles had attained the object it had most at heart, that is, the separation of the British colonies from the mother country. The first of the proposals of the court of London was, in effect, to acknowledge the independence of the United States ; and this was the principal, and indeed the only avowed motive of France for taking up arms. As to the situation of affairs in the West Indies, the operations that were in contemplation against those islands, interested Spain much more than France. And, besides, the discomfiture of the twelfth of April had deranged all plans, and extinguished all hopes. Nor was there any room to expect better fortune in the seas of Europe, since their empire had already been disputed for several years, without the occurrence of any decisive event.

The losses which France had sustained in the East Indies, might counterbalance the conquests she had made in the West. Upon the whole, therefore, she found herself in a condition to treat for herself on equal terms with respect to the chances of war, and upon a footing of decided superiority in regard to its principal cause ; the independence of the United States.   Independent of the foregoing considerations, there existed others which powerfully urged a speedy re-establishment of peace.   The finances were exhausted ; and notwithstanding the judicious regulations and economy which the government had endeavored to introduce into all the departments, the resources were no longer in proportion to the exorbitant charges of the war.   The expenditure exceeded the receipt, and every day beheld the increase of the public debt.   The re-establishment of the marine, expeditions in distant countries, the capture of several convoys which it had been necessary to replace, such were at first the charges which consumed the royal treasure.   The Americans afterwards, deprived in a great measure of all revenue by the slowness with which taxes were paid in their country, authorized themselves, from the insufficiency of their means, to present incessantly new demands to the court of Versailles.   After having permitted the farmers-general to lend them a million of livres, after having guaranteed the loans which they had negotiated in Holland, Louis XVI. had advanced them himself eighteen millions, and they still solicited six others.   The French, at this epoch, had applied themselves with singular ardor to the extension of their commerce.   The war had proved extremely prejudicial to it, and the merchants who had been the greatest sufferers could no longer hope to retrieve their losses, but by the cessation of hostilities.   All these considerations led to a general opinion, that to the possibility of concluding an honorable peace, was added the expediency and even the necessity of so doing.

As to Spain, the hope of conquering Gibraltar and Jamaica had been annihilated by the fatal days of the twelfth of April and the thirteenth of September.   The continuation of the war, with a view to these two objects, would therefore have been rather the effect of obstinacy than of constancy.   On the other hand, the court of Madrid had acquired by its arms the province of West Florida and the island of Minorca.   As England had no compensation to offer it for these two acquisitions, it was natural to think that a treaty of peace would confirm the possession of them to Spain.   Though her views had been aimed much higher, these advantages were at least sufficient to prevent the Spaniards from complaining that they had taken part in the war without any personal interest, and through mere complaisance. It had never ceased to excite general surprise that the court of Madrid should have furnished fuel to a conflagration which might become so fatal to itself, in taking part in a war whose professed object was that of establishing an independent republic in the immediate vicinity of her Mexican possessions. The contagion of example, the seduction of novelty, the natural proclivity of men to shake off the yoke, afforded, without doubt, reasonable grounds of apprehension and alarm. But if Spain had interfered in this great quarrel against her particular interests, she would have been doubly blamable in lavishing so much blood and treasure to prolong it, especially since the possession of Minorca and West Florida secured her honorable conditions. This power therefore inclined also towards the general pacification.

It remains for us to cast a glance upon the Dutch. Following their allies at a distance, rather than marching at their side, they were constrained by their position to will whatever France willed. It was only from that power, and not from their own forces, that they could expect the termination of their disquietudes. If they had recovered St. Eustatius and Demerary, were they not indebted for it entirely to the arms of the king of France? They wished therefore for peace, since experience had taught them that war could yield them no advantage, and that it is never more detrimental than to a people whose existence is founded upon commerce.

To this inclination for peace, manifested at the same time by all the belligerent powers, was added the mediation of the two most powerful princes of Europe; the empress of Russia and the emperor of Germany. Their intervention was accepted with unanimous consent; every thing verged towards a general peace.

Thus, towards the close of the present year, the negotiations at Paris were pushed with mutual ardor. The English and Americans were the first to come to an accommodation. They signed, the thirtieth of November, a provisional treaty, which was to be definitive, and made public, as soon as France and Great Britain should have adjusted their differences. The most important conditions of this treaty were, that the king of England acknowledged the liberty, sovereignty, and independence of the thirteen United States of America, which were all named successively; that his Britannic majesty renounced, as well for himself as for his heirs and successors, all rights whatever over the government, property or territory, of the said states. In order to prevent any occasion for complaints on either side upon the subject of limits, imaginary lines of boundary were agreed upon, which brought within the territory of the United States immense countries, lakes and rivers, to which, up to that time, they had never pretended any sort of claim. For, besides the vast and fertile countries situated upon the banks of the Ohio and Mississippi, the limits of the United States embraced a part of Canada and Nova Scotia; an acquisition which permitted the Americans to participate in the fur trade. Some Indian nations, which had hitherto existed under the domination of the English, and especially the Six Tribes, who had always adhered to their party and alliance, were now included in the new territory of the United States. The English were to evacuate and restore all the parts which they still occupied, such as New York, Long Island, Staten Island, Charleston, Penobscot, and all their dependencies. There was no mention made of Savannah, as the evacuation of that place and of all Georgia, by the English, had already left it entirely in the power of congress.

The Americans were also secured by the treaty of peace in the right of fishing on the banks of Newfoundland, in the gulf of St. Lawrence, and all other places where the two nations had been accustomed to carry on fishery before the rupture. It was expressly stipulated, that the congress should recommend to the different states that they should decree the restitution of all confiscated effects, estates, and property whatsoever, as well to British subjects as to those among the Americans who had adhered to the party of England. It was agreed, besides, that such individuals could not be questioned or prosecuted for any thing which they had said or done in favor of Great Britain. These last articles displeased certain zealous republicans, and became the object of vehement declamations on their part. They little reflected how vengeance, at first so sweet, may prove bitter in the result. The loyalists were not any more satisfied; galled at seeing their fate depend on a mere recommendation, which might have effect or not, according to the good pleasure of the several states, they complained of the ingratitude of England, who unworthily abandoned them to chance. Animated discussions also arose in parliament relative to this point. The party in opposition represented in glowing colors the infamy with which the ministers were about to cover the name of England, in suffering those who had served her to become the prey of their persecutors. It seemed to have been forgotten that in these political convulsions it is necessary to have regard rather to what is possible or advantageous, than to that which is merely just and honorable. Every man who takes part in a civil conflict, must expect, sooner or later, to submit to this common law. Exclusively occupied with its great interests, the state deigns not even to perceive those of individuals. Its own preservation is the sole object of its cares; for it the public good is every thing, private utility nothing. Upon the adoption of these bases, it was agreed that hostilities, whether by land or sea, should cease immediately between Great Britain and America

1783. The preliminaries of peace between France and England were signed at Versailles on the twentieth of January, 1783, by the count de Vergennes, minister of foreign affairs, and M. Fitz Herbert, minister plenipotentiary of his Britannic majesty. England acquired thereby an extension of her right of fishery upon the banks of Newfoundland. But she restored to France in full property the islands of St. Pierre and Miquelon. She likewise restored her the island of St. Lucia, and ceded her that of Tobago. On the other hand, France restored to England the island of Grenada, with the Grenadines, Dominica, St. Vincent, St. Christopher, Nevis, and Montserrat. In the East Indies, France recovered possession of Pondicherry, and Karical, and all her other establishments in Bengal, and upon the coast of Orixa. Still other concessions of no little importance were made her, relating to trade and the right of fortifying different places. But an article singularly honorable for France, was that by which England consented to consider as entirely annulled all stipulations which had been made in regard to the port of Dunkirk, since the peace of Utrecht, in 1713.

The court of London ceded to that of Madrid the island of Minorca and the two Floridas. It obtained, at the same time, the restitution of the Bahama islands; a restitution which was afterwards found superfluous, since colonel Deveaux had just re-conquered those islands with a handful of men, equipped at his own expense. These preliminaries were converted into a definitive treaty of peace the third of September, 1783. It was signed on the part of France by the count de Vergennes, and on that of Spain, by the count d'Aranda, and in behalf of England, by the duke of Manchester. The definitive treaty between Great Britain and the United States was signed the same day at Paris, by David Hartley, on one part, and by John Adams, Benjamin Franklin, and John Jay, on the other. On the preceding day had likewise been concluded, at Paris, the separate treaty between Great Britain and the States-General of Holland; the duke of Manchester stipulating in the name of his Britannic majesty, and M. Van Berkenroode and M. Bransten, in behalf of their high mightinesses. The court of London restored to the Dutch their establishment of Trincomale; but they ceded to the English the city of Negapatam with its dependencies.

Notwithstanding all the pomp with which the allied courts had affected to assert the maritime rights of neutrals, no mention whatever was made in these different treaties of so important a point of public law.

Such was the issue of the long struggle undertaken for the cause of America. If it may be supposed, that the colonists had for a long time sought an opportunity to throw off the yoke, it must be admitted also, that the English were themselves the first to excite them to it. Their rigorous laws irritated, instead of restraining; the insufficiency of their military force and the versality of their measures did but the more imbolden the resistance of the Americans.   The war which ensued was carried on, as civil wars have usually been, often with valor, always with desperation, and sometimes with barbarity. Between the English, on the contrary, and the other European nations which they had to combat, the reciprocal demonstrations of prowess received new luster from that humanity and courtesy which eminently characterize the age in which we live.   The congress, and the Americans in general, displayed the most extraordinary constancy ; the British ministers perhaps merited the reproach of obstinacy, and the cabinet of France distinguished itself by the singular sagacity of its policy.

From these different causes resulted the foundation in the New World of a Republic, happy within by its constitution, pacific by its character, respected and courted abroad for the abundance of its resources.   So far as it is possible to judge of sublunary things, from the extent and fertility of its territory, and the rapid increase of its population, it is destined, at no distant day, to become a vast and exceedingly powerful state.   To consolidate their work, and render its duration eternal, the Americans have only two things to avoid. The one is, that moral depravation which too commonly results from an excessive love of gain ; the other is, the losing sight of the principles upon which the edifice is founded. May they at least return to them promptly, if the ordinary course of human events should introduce disorder and decay into that admirable system of government which they have established !

With the exception of an affair of little importance, in which colonel Laurens was slain, and the evacuation of Charleston, nothing had passed upon the American continent, deserving of particular attention.   As soon as the preliminaries of peace were known there, the public joy manifested itself, but with much less enthusiasm, however, than might naturally be supposed.   Peace had for a long time been looked upon as certain ; and man enjoys more calmly the possession of happiness itself, than the hopes which precede it.   New apprehensions, besides, soon arose to cloud the horizon ; a secret fire menaced a conflagration, and at the very moment in which peace disarmed external enemies, an intestine war appeared ready to rend the republic.   The pay of the army was excessively in arrear ; the greater part of the officers had spent in the service of the state, not only all they were possessed of, but also the fortunes of their friends. They were very apprehensive that the resolutions of October, 1780, by which congress had granted them half pay for a certain term of years, would not be carried into effect.   They had therefore deputed a committee of officers, to solicit the attention of congress to this subject. Their instructions were, to press the immediate payment of the money actually due, the commutation of the half pay above mentioned for a sum in gross, and the indemnification of the officers for the sums which they had been compelled to advance in consequence of the failure of their rations. Some security that the engagements of the government would be complied with, was also to be requested. But whether because a part of the members of congress were little disposed to favor the army, or that others were desirous that the particular states, and not the federal treasury, should support the burthen of these gratifications, nothing was decided. Discouraged at this slowness, the deputies wrote to the army. The other public creditors manifested no less disquietude than the officers. They foresaw plainly that the ordinary revenue would be altogether inadequate to the payment of the sums that were due to them ; and they were equally convinced of the repugnance which the states would have to impose new taxes for the purpose of raising the means to satisfy their demands. The discontent of the first and of the second was extreme ; they already anticipated their total ruin.

The American government, at this epoch, was divided in two parties ; one was sincerely disposed to do ample justice to the public creditors generally, and to this end they desired the establishment of a general tax ; they labored to fund the public debts on solid continental securities ; they wished also to create a revenue to answer the necessities of the republic, and to be subject to the disposal of congress. The opposite party considered this revenue as dangerous to liberty. They contended that the particular states alone, not the congress, should have authority to impose taxes or duties. Already, at the recommendation of congress, twelve states had subjected to a duty of five per cent. all foreign produce or manufactures that should be imported into the United States. One state, however, out of the thirteen, had refused to comply with the wishes of congress, and this refusal paralyzed the action of the twelve others.

It was at this epoch that intelligence was received of the signature of the preliminary and eventual articles of peace ; the disbanding of the army must be its necessary consequence. The partisans of the tax then became apprehensive that their adversaries, when relieved from the maintenance of the troops, and from the fear which they inspired, would show themselves still more adverse to the creation of a national revenue   They saw not only that the creditors of the state would thus be cut off from all hope, but that the republic itself would be exposed for the future to incessant and inextricab e embarrassments, for want of a general authority invested with the power of imposing taxes. They resolved, therefore, to profit of an occasion which would never again present itself, to procure the adoption of a plan whose utility appeared to them incontestable. They were un-decided, however, as to the means to be employed in this conjunc-ture; several contradictory opinions were advanced. The more resolute, not reflecting upon the danger of an irregular appeal to the multitude, in affairs of state, were inclined to resort to force, and to make of the army itself the instrument of their designs. At the head of these were Alexander Hamilton, then member of congress, the treasurer, Robert Morris, with another Morris, his assistant in office. But the more circumspect thought it advisable to pursue a middle course, and to permit the army to threaten, but not to act ; as if the hand which has excited a popular movement could also appease it at pleasure ! In the secret councils that were held upon this affair, the latter opinion prevailed. Colonel Stewart, of the regular troops of Pennsylvania, was sent to camp under pretext of entering upon the exercise of his office of inspector-general. He had instructions to sound the dispositions of Washington, and to endeavor to ascertain how far he would consent to give into the plan agreed upon. It was especially recommended to him to foment the agitation which pre-vailed in the army, and to persuade it not to disband until it had obtained full assurance that the arrears of pay should be liquidated, together with an indemnification for the supplies which it ought to have had, but which had been withheld up to that time. Whether the commander-in-chief was not disinclined towards this scheme, or that he thought it prudent not to declare himself too ostensibly, colo-nel Stewart believed, or at least made others believe, that Washington approved it entirely. Meanwhile, the members of the opposite party were soon apprised of what was passing, and set themselves to coun-teract it. Convinced of the importance of obtaining the countenance of Washington, they put forward a certain Harvey, who had mani-fested an extreme ardor in these discussions. This man wrote to the commander-in-chief, that, under the pretense of wishing to satisfy the public creditors, the most pernicious designs were meditated against the republic ; that nothing less was in agitation than a plot to demolish the fabric of freedom, and introduce tyranny. To these insinuations he joined others relating to Washington personally ; he intimated to him that it was wished to deprive him of his rank, to put down his friends, and, in a word, to destroy the work which they had accomplished with so much glory, and at the expense of so much toil and blood. Washington could not but entertain certain apprehen-sions. He doubted there were machinations in agitation which por-tended no good to the state. He circulated the letter of Harvey, that its contents might be known even to the soldiers. He exerted all his authority to prevent an insurrection. The commander-in-chief thus declared himself publicly against a design, which perhaps within his own breast he did not altogether disapprove, though he blamed, and not without reason, the means by which it was to have been carried into execution. The most alarming rumors were propagated on all parts. It was loudly exclaimed that the troops, before they disbanded, ought to obtain justice ; that they had a right to claim the fruit of victories which their valor had won ; that the other creditors of the state, and many members of the congress itself, invoked the interference of the army, prepared to follow the example which they expected from it. Minds became highly inflamed ; assemblages were formed in the camp, and it was openly proposed in them to make law for the congress. In the midst of this effervescence, circulated anonymous invitations to the officers to convene in general assembly. On the eleventh of March, was passed from hand to hand an address, the author of which did not name himself, but who was known afterwards to be major John Armstrong. This writing, composed with great ingenuity, and with greater passion, was singularly calculated to aggravate the exasperation of the soldiers, and to conduct them to the most desperate resolutions. Blamable in a time of calm, it became really criminal at a moment when all heads were in a state of the most vehement irritation. Among other incendiary passages, it contained the following : ' After a pursuit of seven years, the object for which we set out is at length brought within our reach ; yes, my friends, that suffering courage of yours was active once ; it has conducted the United States of America through a doubtful and a bloody war. It has placed her in the chair of independency, and peace returns again to bless—Whom ? A country willing to redress your wrongs, cherish your worth, and reward your services ? A country courting your return to private life, with tears of gratitude and smiles of admiration, longing to divide with you that independence which your gallantry has given, and those riches which your wounds have preserved ? Is this the case ? or is it rather a country that tramples upon your rights, disdains your cries, and insults your distresses ? Have you not more than once suggested your wishes, and made known your wants to congress ? wants and wishes which gratitude and policy should have anticipated rather than evaded. And have you not lately, in the meek language of entreating memorials, begged from their justice what you could no longer expect from their favor ? How have you been answered ? Let the letter of your delegates to Philadelphia reply.

' If this, then, be your treatment while the swords you wear are necessary for the defense of America, what have you to expect when your voice shall sink, and your strength dissipate by division? when those very swords, the instruments and companions of your glory, shall be taken from your sides, and no remaining mark of military distinction left but your wants, infirmities and scars? Can you then consent·to be the only sufferers by this revolution, and retiring from the field, grow old in poverty, wretchedness and contempt? Can you consent to wade through the vile mire of dependency, and owe the miserable remnant of that life to charity, which has hitherto been spent in honor? If you can, go—and carry with you the jest of tories and the scorn of whigs—the ridicule, and what is worse, the pity of the world. Go, starve, and be forgotten! But if your spirit should revolt at this; if you have sense enough to discover, and spirit enough to oppose tyranny, under whatever garb it may assume; whether it be the plain coat of republicanism, or the splendid robe of royalty; if you have yet learned to discriminate between a people and a cause, between men and principles, awake; attend to your situation and redress yourselves. If the present moment be lost, every future effort is in vain; and your threats then will be as empty as your entreaties now.'

These words, more worthy of a raving tribune of the people, than of a discreet American, chafed minds already exasperated into a delirium of fury. The general fermentation announced the most sinister events; and war between the civil and military powers appeared inevitable. But Washington, whose constancy no crisis could shake, strong in the love and veneration of the people, contemplated the danger of his country, and instantly formed the generous design of extinguishing the kindling conflagration. He was not ignorant how much better it is, in such circumstances, to lead misguided minds than to resist them; how much easier it is to obviate intemperate measures than to correct them. He resolved, therefore, to prevent the meeting of the officers. With this view, in his orders addressed to the officers, he expressed the conviction he felt that their own good sense would secure them from paying any attention to an anonymous invitation; but his own duty, he added, as well as the reputation and true interest of the army, required his disapprobation of such disorderly proceedings. At the same time he requested the general and field officers, with one officer from each company, and a proper representation from the staff of the army, to assemble in order to deliberate upon the measures to be adopted for obtaining the redress of their grievances.

By this conduct, the prudence of which is undeniable, Washington succeeded in impressing the army with a belief that he did not disapprove their remonstrances, and the leaders of the insurrection, in particular, that he secretly favored their designs. By this means he gained time for disposing minds and things in such a manner, that the military committee should take only those resolutions which entered into his plan. The following day, Armstrong circulated a second anonymous paper, in which he congratulated the officers upon the prospect that their measures were about to receive the sanction of public authority; he exhorted them to act with energy in the assembly convoked for the fifteenth of March.

In the meantime, Washington exerted the whole weight of his influence to bring the agitations of the moment to a happy termination; he endeavored to impress on those officers individually, who possessed the greatest share of the general confidence, a just sense of what the exigency required; to some, he represented the dangers of the country; to others, the constancy they had hitherto manifested; to all, the glory they had acquired, and the interest they had in transmitting it entire and unsullied to their posterity. He reminded them also of the exhausture of the public treasury, and of the infamy with which they would brand themselves in giving birth to civil war, at the very moment in which the public happiness was about to revive in the midst of peace. On the day appointed by Washington, the convention of officers assembled. The commander-in-chief addressed them a speech, as judicious as it was eloquent, in which he endeavored to destroy the effect of the anonymous papers. He demonstrated all the horror of the alternative proposed by the author, that in case of peace the army should turn their arms against the state, unless it instantly complied with their demands, and if war continued, that they should abandon its defense by removing into some wild and unsettled country.

'My God!' he exclaimed, 'what can this writer have in view, by recommending such measures? Can he be a friend to the army? Can he be a friend to this country? Rather is he not an insidious foe; some emissary, perhaps from New York, plotting the ruin of both, by sowing the seeds of discord and separation between the civil and military authorities of the continent?' 'Let me entreat you, gentlemen,' he added, 'not to take any measures, which, viewed in the calm light of reason, will lessen the dignity, and sully the glory you have hitherto maintained; let me request you to rely on the plighted faith of your country, and place a full confidence in the purity of the intentions of congress, that, previous to your dissolution as an army, they will cause all your accounts to be fairly liquidated; and that they will adopt the most effectual measures in their power to render ample justice to you for your faithful and meritorious services. And let me conjure you in the name of our common country, as you value your own sacred honor, as you respect the rights of humanity, and as you regard the military and national honor of America, to express your utmost horror and detestation of the man who wishes, under any specious pretenses, to overturn the liberties of our country; and who wickedly attempts to open the flood-gates of civil discord, and deluge our rising empire in blood.

'By thus determining, and thus acting, you will pursue the plain and direct road to the attainment of your wishes; you will defeat the insidious designs of our enemies, who are compelled to resort from open force to secret artifice. You will give one more distinguished proof of unexampled patriotism and patient virtue, rising superior to the pressure of the most complicated sufferings; and you will, by the dignity of your conduct, afford occasion for posterity to say, when speaking of the glorious example you have exhibited to mankind; " Had this day been wanting, the world had never seen the last stage of perfection to which human nature is capable of attaining." '

When Washington had concluded his discourse, a profound silence ensued in the assembly : soon those who composed it communicated to each other, in a low voice, the sentiments with which they were impressed. The authority of such a personage, the weight of his words, the sincere affection which he bore to the army, operated irresistibly upon all minds. The effervescence gave place to a calm. No voice was heard in opposition to that of the chief. The deputies of the army declared unanimously that no circumstances of distress or danger should induce them to sully the glory which they had acquired; that the army continued to have an unshaken confidence in the justice of congress and their country; that they entreated the commander-in-chief to recommend to the government the subject of their memorials; and, finally, that they abhorred the infamous propositions contained in the anonymous writing addressed to the officers of the army. Thus Washington, by his prudence and firmness, was instrumental in preserving his country from the new danger that menaced it, at the very moment when its safety seemed to have been established forever. Who knows what might have happened, if civil war had ensanguined the very cradle of this republic ! The captain-general kept his word, and was himself the advocate of his officers with the congress. He obtained of them a decree, commuting the half pay into a sum in gross equal to five years' full pay, and that either in money, or securities bearing an interest of six per cent. According to the orders of congress, three months' pay was advanced to the officers and soldiers in the notes of the treasurer. But this measure was not taken till late, and not until the Pennsylvania militia had broken out into so violent an insurrection, at Philadelphia, that they blockaded, with arms in hands, the very hall of congress for some hours. The reduction of the continental army became then the principal object of attention, and discharges were granted successively to those soldiers, who, during seven campaigns of a most obstinate war, had struggled with an heroic constancy, not only against sword and fire, but also against hunger, nakedness, and even the fury of the elements. Their work completed, their country acknowledged independent, they peaceably returned to their families. The congress voted them public thanks, in the name of a grateful country. The English were not slow to evacuate New York and its dependencies, in which they had made so long a stay. A little after, the French departed from Rhode Island for their possessions, carrying with them the benedictions of all the Americans.

The congress, in order to celebrate worthily the establishment of peace and independence, appointed the eleventh of December, to be observed as a day of solemn thanksgiving to the Dispenser of all good. By another decree they ordained, that an equestrian statue of bronze should be erected to general Washington, in the city where the congress should hold its sessions. The general was to be represented by it in the Roman costume, with the staff of command in the right hand, and the head encircled with a crown of laurel. The pedestal of marble was to be invested with *bassi relievi* commemorative of the principal events of the war, which had taken place under the immediate command of Washington; such as the deliverance of Boston, the taking of the Hessians at Trenton, the affair of Princeton, the battle of Monmouth, and the surrender of Yorktown. The anterior face of the pedestal was to bear the folowing inscription: *The United States, assembled in Congress, voted this statue, in the year of our Lord* 1783, *in honor of George Washington, captain-general of the armies of the United States of America, during the war which vindicated and secured their liberty, sovereignty, and independence.*

Such was the issue of a contest, which, during the course of eight consecutive years, chained the attention of the universe, and drew the most powerful nations of Europe to take a share in it. It is worthy of the observer to investigate the causes which have concurred to the triumph of the Americans, and baffled the efforts of their enemies. In the first place, they had the good fortune not to encounter opposition from foreign nations, and even to find among them benevolence, countenance, and succors. These favorable dispositions, while they inspired them with more confidence in the justice of their cause, redoubled also their spirit and energy. The coalition of several powerful nations, leagued against a single one, on account of some reform it wishes to establish in the frame of its government, and which threatens not only to defeat its object, but to deprive it of liberty and independence, usually causes its rulers to divest themselves of all moderation and prudence, and to have recourse to the most violent and extraordinary measures, which soon exhaust the resources of the country, and excite discontent among its inhabitants; till, oppressed and harassed in every form by the officers of government, they are driven at last into civil convulsions, in which the strength of the community is consumed. And besides, these violent measures so disgust the people with the whole enterprise, that, confounding the abuse of a thing with the use of it, they choose rather to retreat to the point from which they set out, or even further back, than to continue their progress towards the object originally proposed. Hence it is, that, if that object were liberty, they afterwards rush into despotism, preferring the tyranny of one to that of many. But to these fatal extremities the Americans were not reduced, as well for the reason at first stated, the general favor of foreign states, as on account of the geographical position of their country, separated by vast seas from nations which keep on foot great standing armies, and defended on all other points by impenetrable forests, immense deserts and inaccessible mountains, and having in all this part no other enemy to fear except the Indian tribes, more capable of investing and ravaging the frontiers, than of making any permanent encroachments. One of the most powerful causes of the success of the American revolution, should, doubtless, be sought in the little difference which existed between the form of government which they abandoned, and that which they wished to establish. It was not from absolute, but from limited monarchy, that they passed to the freedom of an elective government. Moral things, with men, are subject to the same laws as physical; *the laws of all nature.* Total and sudden changes cannot take place without causing disasters or death.

The royal authority, tempered by the very nature of the government, and still enfeebled by distance, scarcely made itself perceptible in the British colonies. When the Americans had shaken it off entirely, they experienced no considerable change. Royalty alone was effaced; the administration remained the same, and the republic found itself established without shock. Such was the advantage enjoyed by the American insurgents, whereas the people of other countries, who should undertake to pass all at once from absolute monarchy to the republican scheme, would find themselves constrained to overturn, not only monarchical institutions, but all others, in order to substitute new ones in their stead. But such a subversion cannot take place without doing violence to the opinions, usages, manners, and customs of the greater number, nor even without grievously wounding their interests. Discontent propagates itself; democratic forms serve as the mere mask of royalty; the people discover that they have complained of imaginary evils; they eagerly embrace the first opportunity to measure back their steps, even to the very point which they started from.

Another material cause of the happy issue of this grand enterprise, will be seen in the circumspect and moderate conduct invariably pursued by that considerate and persevering people by whom it was achieved. Satisfied with having abolished royalty, they paused there, and discreetly continued to respect the ancient laws, which had survived the change. Thus they escaped the chagrin of having made their condition worse in attempting to improve it. They had the good sense to reflect, that versatility in counsels degrades the noblest cause, chills its partisans, and multiplies its opponents. There will always be more alacrity in a career whose goal is fixed and apparent, than in that where it is concealed in obscurity. The Americans reared the tree, because they suffered it to grow; they gathered its fruit, because they allowed it to ripen. They were not seen to plume themselves on giving every day a new face to the state. Supporting evil with constancy, they never thought of imputing it to the defects of their institutions, nor to the incapacity or treason of those who governed them, but to the empire of circumstances. They were especially indebted for this moderation of character to the simplicity of their hereditary manners; few among them aspired to dignity and power.

They presented not the afflicting spectacle of friends dissolving their ancient intimacies, and even declaring a sudden war upon each other, because one was arrived at the helm of state without calling the other to it. With them patriotism triumphed over ambition. There existed royalists and republicans; but not republicans of different sects, rending with their dissensions the bosom of their country. There might be among them a diversity of opinions, but never did they abandon themselves to sanguinary feuds, proscriptions, and confiscations. From their union resulted their victory; they immolated their enmities to the public weal, their ambition to the safety of the state, and they reaped the fruit of it; an ever memorable proof that if precipitate resolutions cause the failure of political enterprises, temper and perseverance conduct them to a glorious issue.

The army was disbanded ; but the supreme command still remained in the nands of Washington : the public mind was intent upon what he was about to do. His prudence reminded him that it was time to put a term to the desire of military glory ; his thoughts were now turned exclusively upon leaving to his country a great example of moderation. The congress was then in session at the city of Annapolis in Maryland. Washington communicated to that body his resolution to resign the command, and requested to know whether it would be their pleasure that he should offer his resignation in writing, or at an audience. The congress answered, that they appointed the twenty-third of December for that ceremony. When this day arrived, the hall of congress was crowded with spectators ; the legislative and executive characters of the state, several general officers, and the consul-general of France, were present. The members of congress remained seated and covered. The spectators were standing and uncovered. The general was introduced by the secretary, and conducted to a seat near the president. After a decent interval, silence was commanded, and a short pause ensued. The president, general Mifflin, then informed him, that the United States in congress assembled were prepared to receive his communications. Washington rose, and with an air of inexpressible dignity, delivered the following address :—

' Mr. President ; The great events on which my resignation depended having at length taken place, I have now the honor of offering my sincere congratulations to congress, and of presenting myself before them to surrender into their hands the trust committed to me, and to claim the indulgence of retiring from the service of my country. Happy in the confirmation of our independence and sovereignty, and pleased with the opportunity afforded the United States of becoming a respectable nation, I resign with satisfaction the appointment I accepted with diffidence, a diffidence in my abilities to accomplish so arduous a task, which, however, was superseded by a confidence in the rectitude of our cause, the support of the supreme power of the Union, and the patronage of Heaven. The successful termination of the war has verified the most sanguine expectations ; and my gratitude for the interposition of Providence, and the assistance I have received from my countrymen, increases with every review of the momentous contest. While I repeat my obligations to the army in general, I should do injustice to my own feelings not to acknowledge, in this place, the peculiar services and distinguished merits of the gentlemen who have been attached to my person during the war. It was impossible the choice of confidential officers to compose my family should have been more fortunate. Permit me, sir, to recommend, in particular, those who have continued in the service to the present moment, as worthy of the favorable notice and patronage of congress.

'I consider it as an indispensable duty to close this last act of my official life by commending the interests of our dearest country to the protection of Almighty God, and those who have the superintendence of them to his holy keeping. Having now finished the work assigned me, I retire from the great theater of action, and bidding an affectionate farewell to this august body, under whose orders I have so long acted, I here offer my commission, and take my leave of all the employments of public life.'

Having spoken thus, he advanced to the chair of the president, and deposited the commission in his hands. The president made him, in the name of congress, the following answer :—

'Sir; The United States, in congress assembled, receive with emotions too affecting for utterance, the solemn resignation of the authorities under which you have led their troops with success through a perilous and a doubtful war. Called upon by your country to defend its invaded rights, you accepted the sacred charge, before it had formed alliances, and while it was without funds or a government to support you. You have conducted the great military contest with wisdom and fortitude, invariably regarding the rights of the civil power, through all disasters and changes. You have, by the love and confidence of your fellow-citizens, enabled them to display their martial genius, and transmit their fame to posterity. You have persevered, until the United States, aided by a magnanimous king and nation, have been enabled, under a just Providence, to close the war in freedom, safety, and independence; on which happy event, we sincerely join you in congratulations. Having defended the standard of liberty in this new world, having taught a lesson useful to those who inflict, and to those who feel oppression, you retire from the great theater of action, with the blessing of your fellow-citizens ; but the glory of your virtues will not terminate with your military command ; it will continue to animate the remotest ages. We feel, with you, our obligations to the army in general, and will particularly charge ourselves with the interests of those confidential officers who have attended your person to this affecting moment. We join you in commending the interests of our dearest country to the protection of Almighty God, beseeching him to dispose the hearts and minds of its citizens to improve the opportunity afforded them of becoming a happy and respectable nation. And for you, we address to Him our earnest prayers that a life so beloved may be fostered with all his care ; that your days may be happy as they have been illustrious ; and that he will finally give you that reward which this world can-.not give.'

When the president had terminated his discourse, a long and pro-found silence pervaded the whole assembly.   All minds appeared impressed with the grandeur of the scene, the recollections of the past, the felicity of the present, and the hopes of the future.   The captain-general and congress were the objects of universal eulogium.

A short time after this ceremony, Washington retired to enjoy the long desired repose of his seat of Mount Vernon, in Virginia.

BIOGRAPHY OF THE AUTHOR.

CHARLES JOSEPH WILLIAM BOTTA was born at St. George, province of Vercelli, in Piedmont, in 1766. He studied medicine at the university of Turin, and was employed as physician to the army of the Alps; afterwards to that of Italy. About this time he composed an extensive work, containing a plan of government for Lombardy. Towards the close of 1798, he was sent to the islands of the Levant with the division detached thither by general Buonaparte.

On his return to Italy, he published a description of the island of Corfu, and of the maladies prevalent there during his stay; 2 vols. 8vo.

In the year seven of the French Republic, (1799,) general Joubert appointed him member of the provisional government of Piedmont. This provisional government having been dissolved at the arrival of the commissioner Musset, Botta was appointed member of the administration of the department of the Po. At the epoch of the Austro-Russian invasion, he again took refuge in France. The minister of war, Bernadotte, re-appointed him physician of the Alps; and after the battle of Marengo, the commander-in-chief of the army of reserve appointed him member of the *Consulta* of Piedmont.

At the commencement of 1801, he was member of the executive commission, and afterwards of the council of general administration of the twenty-seventh military division. Botta likewise made part of the deputation which came to Paris in 1803 to present thanks to the government upon the definitive adjunction of Piedmont, and there published an historical sketch of the history of Savoy and Piedmont. Immediately after the union, he was elected member of the legislative body by the department of the Doura, the tenth of August, 1804. The twenty-eighth of October, 1808, he was created vice-president, and on the expiration of his term, was re-elected in 1809, and proposed the ninth of December, as candidate for the questorship.

The emperor granted him soon after the decoration of the order of the Union.

The third of January, 1810, he presented to Buonaparte, in the name of the academy of sciences of Turin, the last two volumes of its memoirs. He adhered, the third of April, 1814, to the deposition of Napoleon and his family. The eighth he accepted the constitutional act which recalled the Bourbons to the throne of France, but ne ceased to make part of the legislative body on the separation of Piedmont. At the return of Buonaparte in 1815, he was appointed rector of the academy of Nanci, but lost this place after the second restoration of the king.

Besides the works already named, he has published,

1. At Turin, 1801, an Italian translation of the work of Born, of which Broussonet had given to the public a French version, in 1784.

2. A memoir upon the doctrine of Brown, 1800, in 8vo.

3. Memoir upon the nature of tones and sounds, read before the academy of Turin, and inserted (by extract) in the Bibliotheque Italienne, tome I., Turin; 1803, 8vo.

4. The history of the war of the independence of America, 1809. 4 vols. 8vo.

5. Il Camillo, O Vejo conquistato, (Camillus, or Veii conquered,) an epic poem in twelve cantos. Paris, 1816. This work has received high encomiums in the European journals. Botta has contributed some articles to the Biographie Universelle, among others, that of John Adams.

6. The history of Italy.

The Translator is indebted for the preceding notice of Botta, to the complaisance of an estimable countryman and acquaintance of the Historian.

LIST OF WORKS

CONSULTED BY THE AUTHOR FOR WRITING THE HISTORY OF THE AMERICAN WAR.

ENGLISH.

Journals of the House of Lords ; Journals of the House of Commons, in folio ; printed by order of the two houses, from 1764 to 1783.

Authentic Account of the Proceedings of Congress, held at New York in 1765. Almon, 1767.

Journals of the Proceedings of the Congress, in 8vo. Dilly, 1775.

Journals of Congress held at Philadelphia, for Almon, 1786.

The Parliamentary Register, &c. ; all the volumes from 1766 to 1783

The Annual Register ; all the volumes from 1764 to 1783.

Historical Anecdotes relative to the American Rebellion, 1 vol. 8vo. 1779.

The Remembrancer, or impartial repository of public events; the second edition, London, for I. Almon, with the prior documents.

Letters on the American Troubles, translated from the French of M. Pinto, 1776.

An impartial History of the War in America between Great Britain and her colonies, from its commencement to the end of the year 1779, in 8vo. for Faulders, 1780.

The History of the Civil War in America, comprehending the campaigns of 1775, 1776, 1777 ; by an officer of the army, in 8vo. for Sewall, 1781.

A genuine detail of the several engagements, positions and movements of the royal and American armies, during the years 1775 and 1776, with an accurate account of the blockade of Boston, &c. ; by William Carter, in 4to. for Kearsley, 1785.

An impartial and authentic narrative of the battle fought on the 17th June, on Bunker's Hill; by John Clarke, 1775.

A History of the Campaigns of 1780 and 1781, in the southern provinces of North America; by lieutenant-colonel Tarleton, Dublin, 1 vol. 8vo. 1787.

Strictures on lieutenant-colonel Tarleton's History of the Campaigns of 1780 and 1781, by Roderick Mackenzie, in 8vo. 1787.

The History of the American Revolution, by David Ramsay, 2 vols. 8vo. Philadelphia, 1789.

History of the War with America, France, Spain and Holland, commencing in 1775, and ending in 1783, by John Andrews, 4 vols. in 8vo. London, for J. Fielding, 1785.

The History of the Rise, Progress, and Establishment of the Independence of the United States of America, by William Gordon, London, printed for the author, and sold by Charles Dilly, 1788, 4 vols. 8vo

An Historical, Geographical, Commercial, and Philosophical View of the American United States, and of the European settlements in America, and the West Indies ; by W. Winterbotham, 4 vols. in 8vo. London, 1795.

The Life of George Washington, by John Marshall, chief justice of the United States, 5 vols. in 8vo. London, for Richard Philips, 1804, 1805, 1807.

The Life of Washington, by David Ramsay, 1 vol. 8vo. New York, 1807, printed by Hopkins and Seymour.

Letters addressed to the army of the United States, in the year 1783, with a brief exposition ; by Buel, Kingston, state of New York, 1803.

FRENCH.

Revolution d'Amerique, par l'abbé Raynal, Londres, 1781.

Lettre adresée à l'abbé Raynal, sur les affaires de l'Amerique Septentrionale, traduite de l'Anglais de Thomas Payne, 1783.

Essais historiques et politiques sur les Anglo-Americains, par M. Hilliard d'Auberteuil, 4 vols. in 8vo. Bruxelles, 1781.

Histoire de l'administration de Lord North, et de la guerre de l'Amerique Septentrionale, jusqu' à la paix de 1783, 2 vols. in 8vo. Londres et Paris, 1784.

Histoire impartiale des evenemens militaire et politiques de la dernière guerre dans les quatre parties du monde, 3 vols. Amsterdam et Paris, chez la veuve Duchesne, 1785.

Constitution des treize Etats Unis d'Amerique, Philadelphie et Paris, 1783.

Affairs de l'Angletere et de l'Amerique, 17 vols. in 8vo. Anvers.

Voyages de M. le Marquis de Chastelux dans l'Amerique Septentrionale, pendant les années 1780, 1781, et 1782, 2 vols. in 8vo. Paris, chez Prault, 1786.

Histoire des troubles de l'Amerique Anglaise, &c. par François Soules, 4 vols. in 8vo. Paris, chez Buisson, 1787.

Histoire de laclernière guerre entre la Grande Britagne et les Etats Unis d'Amerique, la France, l'Espagne et la Hollande, depuis son commencement en 1775, jusqu'à sa fin en 1783, 1 vol. 4to. Paris, chez Brocas, 1787.

Histoire de la Revolution de l'Amerique, par rapport à la Caroline Meridionale, par David Ramsay, membre du Congrès Americain ; traduit de l'Anglais, 2 vols. 8vo. Londres et Paris, chez Frouille, 1787.

Recherches historiques et politiques sur les Etats Unis de l'Amerique Septentrionale, par un citoyn de Virginie, 4 vols. in 8vo. Paris, chez Frouille, 1788.

Discussiones importantes, debattues au parlement Britannique, 4 vols. in 8vo. Paris, chez Maradan et Perlet, 1790.

Mémoires historiques et pièces authentiques sur M. de la Fayette, 1 vol. in 8vo. Paris, l'an 2, (1793.)

To the foregoing works should be added, a great number of pamphlets, which, during the American revolution, were published daily, as well in England as in America and France. Lastly, even among the actors of the great events which he has related, the author has had the good fortune to find individuals as polite as well informed, who have deigned to furnish him with important manuscripts. He prays them to accept here the public expression of his acknowledgment.